Whose Pharaohs?

Whose Pharaohs?

Archaeology, Museums,
and Egyptian National Identity
from Napoleon to World War I

Donald Malcolm Reid

UNIVERSITY OF CALIFORNIA PRESS
Berkeley · *Los Angeles* · *London*

Portions of this book have appeared previously in different form as "Archeology, Social Reform, and Modern Identity among the Copts, 1854–1952," pp. 311–35 in *Entre Réforme sociale et mouvement national: Identité et modernisation en Égypte (1882–1962)*, edited by Alain Roussillon (Cairo: Centre d'études et de documentation économiques, juridiques et sociales, 1995); "Cromer and the Classics: Imperialism, Nationalism, and the Greek and Roman Past in Modern Egypt," *Middle Eastern Studies* 18 (1996): 73–90, Frank Cass Publishers, London; "Cultural Imperialism and Nationalism: The Struggle to Define and Control the Heritage of Arab Art in Egypt," *International Journal of Middle East Studies* 24 (1992): 57–76, Cambridge University Press; "French Egyptology and the Architecture of Orientalism: Deciphering the Facade of Cairo's Egyptian Museum," pp. 35–69 in *Franco-Arab Encounters: Studies in Memory of David C. Gordon*, edited by L. Carl Brown and Matthew Gordon (Beirut: The American University in Beirut, 1996); "Indigenous Egyptology: The Decolonization of a Profession?" *Journal of the American Oriental Society* 105 (1985): 233–46; and "Nationalizing the Pharaonic Past: Egyptology, Imperialism, and Egyptian Nationalism, 1922–1952," pp. 35–69 in *Rethinking Nationalism in the Arab Middle East*, edited by Israel Gershoni and James Jankowski (New York: Columbia University Press, 1997), © 1997 Columbia University Press. Reprinted by permission of the publisher.

University of California Press
Berkeley and Los Angeles, California

University of California Press, Ltd.
London, England

© 2002 by The Regents of the University of California

Library of Congress Cataloging-in-Publication Data

Reid, Donald M. (Donald Malcolm).
    Whose pharaohs? : archaeology, museums, and Egyptian national identity from Napoleon to World War I / Donald Malcolm Reid.
        p.   cm.
    Includes bibliographical references and index.
    ISBN 0-520-22197-4 (cloth : alk. paper)
     1. Egypt—Antiquities. 2. Archaeology—Egypt—History. 3. Archaeological museums and collections—Egypt—History.
    4. Egyptology—History. 5. Nationalism—Egypt—History. I. Title.

DT56.9 .R45 2002
932—dc21   00-047518
                                          CIP

Manufactured in the United States of America

11 10 09 08 07 06 05 04 03 02

10 9 8 7 6 5 4 3 2 1

The paper used in this publication meets the minimum requirements of ANSI/NISO Z39 0.48-1992 (R 1997) *(Permanence of Paper)*. ⊗

For Barbie

Contents

List of Illustrations   ix

Acknowledgments   xiii

Note on Transliteration, Translation, and Dates   xv

Introduction   1

PART ONE: IMPERIAL AND NATIONAL PRELUDES, 1798–1882

1. Rediscovering Ancient Egypt: Champollion
   and al-Tahtawi   21
2. From Explorer to Cook's Tourist   64
3. Egyptology under Ismail: Mariette, al-Tahtawi,
   and Brugsch, 1850–1882   93

PART TWO: IMPERIAL HIGH NOON, NATIONALIST DAWN, 1882–1914

4. Cromer and the Classics: Ideological Uses of the
   Greco-Roman Past   139

5. Egyptology in the Age of Maspero
   and Ahmad Kamal   172
6. Islamic Art, Archaeology, and Orientalism:
   The Comité and Ali Bahgat   213
7. Modern Sons of the Pharaohs? Marcus Simaika
   and the Coptic Past   258

   Conclusion   287

   Appendix: Supplementary Tables   299

   Notes   309

   Select Bibliography   365

   Index   385

Illustrations

FIGURES

1. Framing and claiming Egyptian antiquity: Cécile's
   frontispiece to *Description de l'Égypte,* 1809   3
2. A monument to Western Egyptology: the Egyptian
   Museum, Cairo   4
3. Enshrining Auguste Mariette: Mariette's sarcophagus
   and statue   4
4. Western founding fathers of Egyptology: plaque on the
   Egyptian Museum, Cairo   5
5. The "wet drapery" look: Nekhbet personifying Upper
   Egypt   6
6. Imperial Latin: inscription on the Egyptian Museum,
   Cairo   7
7. Reframing and reclaiming Egyptian antiquity: Arabic
   magazine cover, 1899   8
8. Egypt through classical lenses: Athanasius Kircher
   deciphers the riddle of the Sphinx, 1652   26
9. Egypt through biblical lenses: *Egypt Saved by Joseph,*
   Abel du Pujol, 1827   28
10. Classical or pharaonic trophy: which should go to
    France? Obelisk and pillar, Alexandria   29
11. French savants besieged atop Pompey's Pillar,
    by J. Gillray, 1799   35

12.   Staking a Prussian imperial claim: the Lepsius
      expedition atop the Great Pyramid, 1842   45
13.   Napoleonic plunder, Napoleonic scholarship:
      *Dominique-Vivant Denon travaillant dans la salle
      de Diane au Louvre,* by Benjamin Zix, ca. 1809–1811   47
14.   Rifaa al-Tahtawi, author of the first history of ancient
      Egypt in Arabic   51
15.   Muhammad Ali's choice? A pyramid as a symbol of
      Egypt: masthead of Egypt's official journal, 1829   55
16.   Tourists on the porch of Shepheard's Hotel, Cairo   74
17.   Beset by "lesser breeds"? *Donkey Boys and Foreigners,*
      by C. Rudolf Huber   77
18.   *A Trip to the Pyramids, Old Style,* Reverend Samuel
      Manning   78
19.   Gender and tourism at the Pyramids   79
20.   Aesthetic arrangement in Mariette's Bulaq Museum   107
21.   *Court of the Museum of Antiquities at Boolak,*
      by W. Gentz, 1878   108
22.   Pyramid-and-sphinx postage stamp   119
23.   World's fair fantasies of Pharaoh: entrance to the
      Egyptian Court, Crystal Palace, London, 1854   126
24.   Reproductions of the Abu Simbel colossi of Rameses II,
      Crystal Palace, London, 1854   127
25.   Unchanging Egypt? An Orientalist whimsy: mummies,
      Félix Bonfils, 1878   132
26.   An "Oriental" at the International Congress of
      Orientalists, London, 1874   134
27.   Classical / Oriental fantasy: *Study and the Muse of the
      Arts Reveal Ancient Egypt to Athens,* by
      François-Edouard Picot, 1827   142
28.   Victorious Gaul rediscovers ancient Egypt: medal by
      Barre, 1826   143
29.   Britannia in classical garb, *Punch* cartoon, 1898   155
30.   "Cleopatra before Caesar; or, the Egyptian Difficulty,"
      Punch cartoon, 1882   156
31.   The Greco-Roman Museum, Alexandria   162
32.   Prime Minister Sharif Pasha with a Roman bust   168
33.   Scottish soldiers occupy the Sphinx, 1880s   176
34.   "Fair Iconoclasts in Egypt," the *Graphic,* 1890   184
35.   Ahmad Kamal and the coffin of Queen Ahmose
      Nefertari   187

36. Khedive Ismail's Giza palace, home of the Egyptian
Museum, 1890–1902   194
37. Khedive Tawfiq: guardian of the national patrimony or
Cook's tourist?   207
38. An Orientalist enframes Cairo: Pascal Coste panorama,
1839   221
39. Ali Mubarak, engineer, reformer, and scholar   231
40. The Museum of Arab Art and Khedivial Library   239
41. (Ancient) Egypt welcomes the Holy Family: *Rest on the
Flight into Egypt,* by Luc Olivier-Merson, 1879   262
42. Remains of a Coptic church inside the temple of
Rameses II at Medinat Habu   270
43. The Coptic Museum   277
44. Marcus Simaika, founder of the Coptic Museum   278
45. Honor at last: bust of Ahmad Kamal at the Mariette
Monument, Cairo   295
46. The Pyramids and the Nile as symbols of Egypt   296

MAPS

1. Egypt ca. 1914   xvii
2. Cairo ca. 1914   105

TABLES

1. European and Egyptian scholars, collectors, and rulers   23
2. Egyptologists active 1850–1882   94
3. Archaeologists in the age of Maspero and Ahmad Kamal,
1881–1914   174
4. Promoters of Islamic art, archaeology, and Orientalism   225
5. Coptic scholars and communal leaders   269
6. Egyptian guidebook editions, by language   299
7. Nationalities of Western authors of Egyptian travel
books   300
8. Foreign residents of Egypt (and protégés), by nationality   301
9. Ranking by nationality of number of residents and
indicators of tourism   302
10. Membership in the Institut égyptien and the Khedivial
Geographical Society   303

11. World's fairs and International Congresses, 1851–1882   304
12. Heads of the Egyptian Antiquities Service, 1858–1952   305
13. World's fairs and International Congresses, 1883–1914   306
14. Founding dates of Western archaeological institutes in
     the Mediterranean   307

Acknowledgments

Research in Egypt for this book was made possible by grants from the National Endowment for the Humanities (through the American Research Center in Egypt), the Binational Fulbright Commission, the Fulbright-Hays Faculty Research Abroad program, and Georgia State University. During two academic years in Egypt (1987–1988, 1998–1999), I was variously sponsored by Dr. Gaballah Ali Gaballah, secretary-general of the Supreme Council of Antiquities, Dr. Hassenein Rabie, vice president of Cairo University, Dr. Rafat El-Nabarawi, dean of the Faculty of Archeology at Cairo University, Dr. Raouf Abbas Hamed, vice dean of the Faculty of Arts at Cairo University, and the American Research Center in Egypt. Dr. Mukhtar El Kasibani of the Faculty of Archeology at Cairo University was also most helpful. At Georgia State University, Dean Ahmed Abdelal and history department chairs Timothy Crimmins and Diane Willen enthusiastically supported my research, the Copen Faculty Grant paid indexing expenses, and Dr. James Heitzman and Blake Ussery helped with the maps.

Professors L. Carl Brown and Farhat J. Ziadeh stand out as mentors who have long encouraged my work. Over thirty years of friendship and discussion with William L. Cleveland and F. Robert Hunter have left their mark on all my work. Other friends and colleagues who have greatly assisted me include Ahmed Abdalla, Jere Bacharach, Edmund Burke III, Bruce Craig, Abdel Moneim El Gameiy (Jamii), Israel Gershoni, Arthur Goldschmidt Jr., Alaa El-Habachi, Fayza Haikal, Kenneth

Perkins, Michael J. Reimer, John Rodenbeck, Jason Thompson, May Trad, George Scanlon, Dr. Samir Simaika, Donald Whitcomb, and Caroline Williams. Dr. Abdel Moneim El Gameiy and Mr. Makram Naguib have long provided me with hospitality and assistance in Egypt. My recent correspondence with Éric Gady unfortunately came too late for me to incorporate more than a few of his excellent suggestions and bibliographical references in this work.

As always, my wife, Barbara Gibbs Reid, assisted with encouragement and constructive criticism.

Professor Neil Asher Silberman and an anonymous reader for the University of California Press offered insightful critiques of my manuscript. At the University of California Press, I am particularly indebted to Ms. Lynne Withey, Ms. Laura Harger, and Ms. Robin Whitaker.

Several publishers have kindly permitted me to reuse revised portions of my publications. I thank the Centre d'études et de documentation économiques, juridiques et sociales; Frank Cass Publishers, London; Cambridge University Press; the American University, Beirut; and Columbia University Press.

Responsibility for the views presented is, of course, my own.

Note on Transliteration, Translation, and Dates

Transliteration here generally follows the Library of Congress system but omits diacritical marks. "Sa'd Zaghlul," however, reads better in English than "Sad Zaghlul." Accepted English spelling has been used for place names like "Cairo," and familiar English spellings are preferred for famous individuals such as Nasser, for those who published extensively in English or French, and for living Egyptians who chose to give me their preferred English spelling of their names. Consistency is all but impossible, and apologies are offered to those whose names are not spelled as they prefer. "Husayn" has been preferred to "Hussein," however, and King "Fuad" to "Fouad."

Quotations translated from their original languages into English are my own unless otherwise noted.

C.E. and B.C.E. (and occasionally, depending on the context, A.D. and B.C.) dates have been preferred. When an Islamic A.H. *(anno Hegirae)* date is also needed, a slash (/) separates it from the C.E. date.

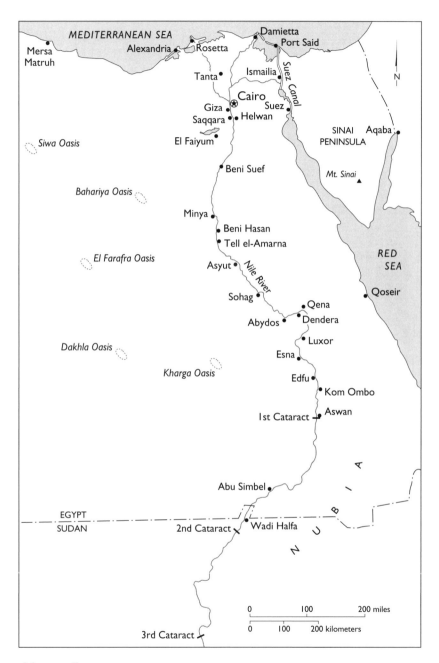

Map 1.   Egypt ca. 1914.

Introduction

France, snatching an obelisk from the ever heightening mud of the Nile, or the savage ignorance of the Turks...earns a right to the thanks of the learned of Europe, to whom belong all the monuments of antiquity, because they alone know how to appreciate them. Antiquity is a garden that belongs by natural right to those who cultivate and harvest its fruits.

Captain E. de Verninac Saint-Maur,
Voyage de Luxor (1835)

It is indeed a matter of deep regret that the monuments should be ours and the history should be ours, but that those who write books on the history of ancient Egypt should not be Egyptians.... Nevertheless we cannot avoid expressing admiration for Professor Selim Hassan on his archaeological skill and his continuous finds, the last of which was the fourth pyramid.

The Arabic newspaper *Al-Balagh*,
26 February 1932

This book examines the evolving uses that Egyptians—mostly nationalists—and Europeans—mostly imperialists—made of various eras of the long Egyptian past between Bonaparte's conquest in 1798 and the outbreak of World War I. European archaeology in Egypt began in earnest during the French expedition. French soldiers uncovered the Rosetta Stone by accident in 1799, and twenty-three years later Jean-François Champollion's decipherment of its hieroglyphic text opened the door to modern Egyptology. In the half-century between 1858 and 1908, Europeans played key roles in the founding of the Egyptian Antiquities Service and four historical museums—the Egyptian Museum (for the pharaonic period), the Greco-Roman Museum, the Coptic Museum, and the Museum of Arab (now Islamic) Art. During those same fifty years, Western imperialism—fueled back home by the industrial revolution, the demand for imported cotton and other raw materials, the quest for overseas markets and investment opportunities, the exigencies of emerging mass politics, and intra-European rivalries—firmly fastened its grip on Egypt. Archaeology and imperialism seemed to walk hand in hand.[1]

Learning about archaeology primarily from the Europeans, Egyptians gradually came to realize that it could be turned to their own ends. Once persuaded of the vital role archaeology could play in shaping their modern national identity, Egyptians began searching for ways to train their own archaeologists. This set the stage for nationalist challenges both to European control of Egypt's archaeological institutions and to Western imperialists' interpretations of its history.

Geopolitical considerations alone would have impelled nineteenth-century Westerners to try to control Egypt, but fantastic visions of its long past powerfully reinforced the impetus. Westerners stepping ashore variously imagined themselves entering the world of the pharaohs, the Bible, the Greeks and Romans, and the Quran and the *Arabian Nights*. Florence Nightingale evoked all four worlds in a single sentence: "Here Osiris and his worshipers lived; here Abraham and Moses walked; here Aristotle came; here, later, Mahomet learnt the best of his religion and studied Christianity; here, perhaps our Saviour's Mother brought her little son to open his eyes to the light."[2]

These were not the only prisms through which Westerners viewed Egyptian encounters. Heirs of Hermeticism saw Egypt as the fountainhead of occult wisdom; belief in mystical "pyramid power" persists today. Others imagined themselves returning crusaders, though this was more usual in Syria-Palestine—General Allenby entering Jerusalem in 1917 or General Gouraud, Damascus in 1920. Romantics grieving for a lost preindustrial world at home looked for noble savages or "natural aristocrats" in the Bedouin. Anglo-Indians saw in Egyptians generic Orientals who could be ruled with techniques honed in India. Since no one arrived a tabula rasa, the only question was which preconceived filters one used and how these affected encounters with Egyptian realities.

Two French visions aptly symbolize Western engagement with Egyptian antiquity across the long nineteenth century—the frontispiece of the Napoleonic expedition's *Description de l'Égypte* and the building of the Egyptian Museum, inaugurated in Cairo in 1902 and still in use today. In the frontispiece, a richly decorated frame invites the viewer into a nostalgic Nile landscape stretching from Alexandria to Aswan (see figure 1).[3]

Figure 1.   Framing and claiming Egyptian antiquity: Cécile's
engraved frontispiece to *Description de l'Égypte,* vol. 1:
Antiquités: Planches (Paris, 1809). The landscape shows no
sign of Cairo, Islamic monuments, or modern inhabitants.

This is an antique land, abounding in pharaonic ruins. There is no sign
of Islamic monuments, Cairo, or modern inhabitants. Atop the frame, a
nude Bonaparte in the guise of Apollo or Alexander brandishes a spear
from his chariot as Mamluks go down before him. Twelve Muses in the
hero's train return the arts to Egypt, their legendary land of origin.

   A century later, in 1902, the facade of Cairo's Egyptian Museum and
the garden monument to its founder, Auguste Mariette, honored heroes
of European Egyptology since Napoleon (see figures 2 and 3). The list
of founding fathers on the facade celebrated six French Egyptologists,
five Britons, four Germans, three Italians, a Dutchman, a Dane, and a

Figure 2. A monument to Western Egyptology: the Egyptian Museum, Cairo, inaugurated in 1902. Photograph by Donald Reid.

Figure 3. Enshrining Auguste Mariette: Mariette's sarcophagus and statue, inaugurated in 1904, in the garden of the Egyptian Museum, Cairo. Photograph by Donald Reid.

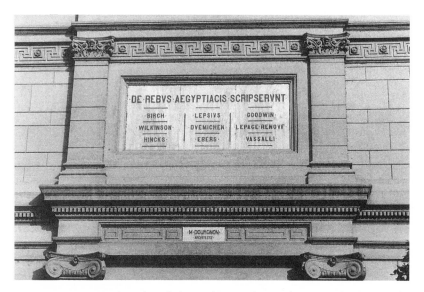

Figure 4. Western founding fathers of Egyptology: plaque on the facade of the Egyptian Museum, Cairo. Architect: M. Dourgnon. Photograph by Donald Reid.

Swede (see figure 4). There were no Egyptians. Another plaque affirmed the classical gateway through which the West had long viewed ancient Egypt, interposing Herodotus, Eratosthenes, Manetho, and Horapollo between plaques commemorating ancient rulers and those honoring the modern scholars.

Goddesses personifying Upper and Lower Egypt flanked the portal (see figure 5). The "wet drapery" look of late classical Greek female sculpture revealed their bodies at a time when upper-class Egyptian women lived in seclusion and wore face veils when they ventured out. Putting the name of the hapless khedive Abbas Hilmi [II] in the inscription over the portal was normal but not much of a concession to local sensibility (see figure 6). The text was in Latin, which not one Egyptian in a thousand could read. No Egyptian government school of the day taught the language. Adding the Islamic (Hijri) date alongside the A.D. one hardly counted as a concession either, for it was doubly disguised in the Latin language and Roman numerals: *anno Hegirae* MCCCXVII. To Egyptians, the facade may well have said: "Egyptology is a European science which has rediscovered the greatness of ancient Egypt, a forerunner of Western civilization. Modern Egyptians are unworthy heirs of ancient ones and incapable of either national greatness or serious Egyptology."[4]

Figure 5. The "wet drapery" look: Nekhbet,
the vulture goddess, personifying Upper
Egypt, flanking the portal of the Egyptian
Museum, Cairo. Photograph by Donald Reid.

In both politics and archaeology, Egyptians had different visions. The
front-page scene of an 1899 issue of a short-lived Arabic magazine for
schoolchildren put ancient Egypt at the center of a modern national renaissance (see figure 7).[5] The sun beams down "The Light of Knowledge" on a traditionally dressed woman who directs her children's attention to the Pyramids and Sphinx. Abbas II—not Napoleon—presides
over this scene, and four additional inset portraits honor reformist officials, scholars, and educators, three of whom (Rifaa al-Tahtawi, Mahmud al-Falaki, and Ali Mubarak) figure prominently in this book. Thus
by the turn of the twentieth century, seeds were already being sown for
the flowering in the 1920s of national pride in both the pharaohs and
Egyptian Egyptology.

It was not only to the pharaonic era that Western scholars and their
publics implicitly laid claim. Europeans took the lead in founding two

Figure 6. Imperial Latin: inscription in the name of Abbas Hilmi (II), the Egyptian Museum, Cairo. The Hijri date, in Latin with Roman numerals, is also well disguised from Egyptians. Photograph by Donald Reid.

other museums in Egypt—the Greco-Roman Museum in Alexandria and the Museum of Arab (now Islamic) Art—and they inspired the Egyptian who founded the Coptic Museum. Like the Egyptian Museum, which displayed the fruits of Egyptology, each of these three museums represented both an emerging scholarly discipline and an era or aspect of Egypt's long past. With these museums and their fields of study too, Egyptians felt the need to train experts who could lend credibility to nationalist insistence that they must manage and interpret the remains of all eras of their national past.

The three museums with European founding directors remained largely European-dominated until the 1950s. The separate origin, institutional affiliation, and evolution of each of the three fragmented what nationalists came to insist was a unified Egyptian past.

The sequence in which the museums came into being also reflected European more than Egyptian priorities. The Egyptian Museum (for pharaonic antiquities) came first because Europeans were rediscovering ancient Egypt and following the ancient Greek example in appropriating it as a forerunner of their own Western civilization. The very words "Egyptian Museum" and "Egyptology" still echo the primacy that Westerners accorded to the pharaonic era. Logically, Egyptology should include the study of any era of Egypt's past, but the term crystallized in the mid–nineteenth century to mean only the study of ancient Egypt,

Figure 7.   Reframing and reclaiming Egyptian antiquity:
Arabic magazine cover, 1899. Ancient Egypt serves here as
an inspiration for a modern Egyptian renaissance. Abbas II
presides, with reformist scholar-officials (clockwise) Ali
Mubarak, Rifaa al-Tahtawi, Abdallah Fikri, and Mahmud al-
Falaki framing the scene. In Bertrand Millet, *Samir, Mickey,
Sindbad, et les autres: Histoire de la presse enfantine en
Égypte,* Dossiers du CEDEJ 1–1987 (Cairo, 1987), 31.
Courtesy of the Centre d'études et de documentation
économiques, juridiques et sociales, Cairo.

with the Greco-Roman and Coptic eras often tacked on as a postscript.
This usage slights Islamic and modern Egypt and seems to imply that
somehow "Egypt ceases to be Egypt when it ceases to be ancient."[6]

Cairo's Museum of Arab Art was founded next, a byproduct of the
Committee of Conservation of Monuments of Arab Art (hereafter simply "the Comité," from the French name by which it is generally known:
Comité de conservation des monuments de l'arte arabe), founded in
1881. The Comité and this museum, which opened to the public in
1884, reflected not the West's search for its roots but the fascination of
some Westerners with an exotic "Oriental other."

The Greco-Roman Museum followed in 1892, situated, appropriately, not in Cairo but in the former Ptolemaic and Roman capital of

Alexandria. Europeans identified far more easily with Greece and Rome than with ancient Egypt or Islam. Many denied any Greco-Roman debt to ancient Egypt or saw it as merely a stepping stone to the greater glories of Greece and Rome. With classical museums flourishing all over Europe, another one in Egypt did not seem urgent at first. By 1892, however, with many of the British elite who were ruling Egypt having been classically trained, and with large European colonies planted there, it was time for a Greco-Roman museum. In Italy, the upper classes had been mining the ancient Roman heritage for legitimacy since the Renaissance, and nationalists proud of the reunification of Italy during the nineteenth century renewed the impulse. Three successive Italian directors of Alexandria's Greco-Roman Museum staked out the cultural claims of their homeland on this former province of Rome.

The Coptic Museum of 1908 was the last of the four museums to be founded. The Protestants and Catholics of the West had long denounced the Coptic Church for heresy and for reflecting the presumed defects of its "Oriental" environment. But Western Christians—and later Jews—eager to "prove the Bible" in the face of secularism, scientism, and the higher criticism also turned to archaeology to bolster their case. They probed Palestine and the rest of the Fertile Crescent for supporting archaeological evidence, and could hardly ignore the land of the Nile, with its associations with Joseph, Moses, Jesus and Mary, and Saint Mark. Copts traced their church back to Mark and had practically invented Christian monasticism. By the 1890s, a few Europeans were turning their attention to Coptic art and architecture, and it was their enthusiasm that inspired Marcus Simaika to found the Coptic Museum. The museum was unusual, having an Egyptian founding director and being under communal Coptic rather than state control.

The primary purpose of this book is to write modern Egyptians into the histories of these four museums and the institutions and disciplines associated with them—Egyptology, classical studies, Coptic studies, and Islamic art and archaeology. Western histories of these disciplines usually downplay the imperial ethos of the day, and even those that highlight it relegate Egyptians to the margins. This book also examines more popular perceptions of the Egyptian past, in both Egypt and the West, tying them to issues of imperialism, nationalism, and Egyptian identity.

These developments in Egyptian archaeology and museology were part of a global process in which states and peoples, over the course of the nineteenth century, struggled to define themselves as modern nations. It made a vast difference whether or not one was a citizen of the

Western great powers—Britain, France, Germany, and eventually the United States—which were caught up in the worldwide contest for political, economic, and cultural influence. In colonized lands such as Egypt and India, museums and archaeology became significant arenas in the struggle for national independence. In independent but semiperipheral countries such as Greece, Italy, imperial Russia, and Mexico, efforts to harness the study and display of the past to national purposes variously reflected features of archaeology in both the dominant and the colonized countries.

This book attempts synthesis on five levels. First, it juxtaposes the relatively familiar history of Western archaeologists with that of their neglected Egyptian counterparts. Even after Michel Foucault, Edward Said, and the revival of Antonio Gramsci, positivist assumptions about progressive, objective, "scientific" knowledge still underlie much writing about Egyptian archaeology. Champollion, Richard Lepsius, Auguste Mariette, Gaston-Camille-Charles Maspero, Adolf Erman, Flinders Petrie, Howard Carter, James Breasted, and George Reisner strut heroically across the stage. Egyptians flicker in the shadows as trusty foremen, loyal servants, laborers, tomb robbers, antiquities dealers, obstructionist officials, and benighted nationalists. Unconventional juxtapositions—Champollion and Rifaa al-Tahtawi, E. W. Lane and al-Tahtawi, Maspero and Ahmad Kamal, Max Herz and Ali Bahgat—are used in this book to challenge such narratives. The point is not to belittle Western achievements or to exaggerate similarities between Egyptians and Europeans but to point up the inequalities of power, challenge assumptions that "never the twain shall meet," and show that disciplinary histories should be more than Western monologues into Egyptian silence.

The first edition of the indispensable reference work *Who Was Who in Egyptology* (1951) omitted the pioneering Egyptian Egyptologist Ahmad Kamal altogether. The second and third editions of this British work made good the slight, but the third edition (1995) accorded Kamal a scant 20 lines to Maspero's 82 and Petrie's 134. Maspero and Petrie were indeed giants, but Kamal's low profile cries out for contextual explanation. Works such as *Who Was Who* tend to abstract science from its sociopolitical context and downplay national and personal rivalries. This makes it impossible to understand Egyptology as these scholars lived it.[7] The reign of English, French, and German as the international languages of Egyptology was just one of many factors that gave Europeans an overwhelming advantage.

A second strand of synthesis is the insertion of the history of archaeology and museums into the mainstream history of modern Egypt.
After the nationalist excesses of World War II, many Western archaeologists reasserted earlier positivist claims of their discipline to be an objective, value-free science. In the past twenty years, this claim has, however, come under increasing fire. Probing the politics of archaeology is
back in fashion in the West,[8] but in the case of Egypt the necessary
reevaluation has only begun. Mariette and Maspero are justly remembered as great Egyptologists, but they should also be remembered as influential actors in the imperialism of their day. Titles such as *The Rape
of the Nile, The Rape of Egypt,* and *The Rape of Tutankhamun* do convey recent Western recognition of the imperialist side of nineteenth-
century Egyptology but leave Westerners center stage and cast Egyptians mainly in the role of victims.[9]
   Meanwhile, modern Egyptian historians have concentrated their re-
visionist efforts elsewhere, paying little attention to archaeology. Few
Egyptians and fewer Westerners have heard of Ahmad Kamal, Ali Bahgat, or Marcus Simaika. Other Egyptians in this book are better known—
al-Jabarti, al-Tahtawi, Ali Mubarak, Ahmad Lutfi al-Sayyid, Taha
Husayn, and King Fuad—but not for their relationship to archaeology,
museums, and ancient history. Who recalls that in his first university
post, Taha Husayn was a professor not of Arabic literature but of Greco-
Roman history?[10]
   At a third level of synthesis, the histories of Egyptology, Greco-Roman
studies, Coptology, and Islamic art and archaeology are considered together. In all four disciplines, the subject of study is Egypt's past, but
specialists in one discipline rarely venture much beyond their own, and
sometimes the next nearest, compartment. Differences in the languages,
writing systems, and religions of different eras make specialization essential, but disciplinary boundaries and periodizations can become blind-
ers. Historians of modern Egypt are usually content to leave the history
of archaeology to archaeologists (and to popular writers), but something is thereby lost. Insider histories of disciplines by their practitioners are indispensable, but modern historian outsiders to these special-
ties may well be better suited to setting them in the wider contexts of
modern Egyptian history.
   The fourth strand is the synthesis of scholarly and popular interest
in the Egyptian past, both in Egypt and the West. Scholarly histories of
Egyptology and the other disciplines frequently sidestep popular ideas—
some of which are fantastic—about the objects of their study. The bur-

geoning literature on "Egyptomania" has, however, examined pharaonic themes in Western painting, photography, clothing styles, travel literature, novels, popular songs, classical music, world's fairs, guidebooks, postcards, and postage stamps. Beginning with London's Great (or Crystal Palace) Exhibition of 1851, a world's fair without an Egyptian exhibit hardly seemed worthy of the name. On the Egyptian side, "pharaonist" or "pharaonicist" motifs in the nationalist symbolism of the 1920s and early 1930s have lately received scholarly attention.[11] In tracing the little-known earlier background of the phenomenon, I have preferred, although they are somewhat awkward, such phrases as "Egyptian Egyptomania" or "popular Egyptian enthusiasm for ancient Egypt" to "pharaonism" or "pharaonicism," which for many Muslims evoke unpalatable images of the idolatrous Quranic (and biblical) tyrant who oppressed Moses and the Israelites.

Where Egyptology leaves off and Egyptomania begins is not always clear. Promoters enlisted Mariette, his German colleague Heinrich Brugsch, and the Comité architect Max Herz to guarantee authenticity in the Egyptian displays at the great exhibitions. Karl Baedeker, Thomas Cook, and John Murray recruited expert scholars to write sections of the guidebooks that tourists carried up the Nile. Western painters and photographers ranged from casual tourists to professional archaeologists. Georg Ebers wrote Egyptological monographs with one hand and novels with pharaonic settings with the other. Mariette the Egyptologist ran the Antiquities Service and museum, while Mariette the Egyptomaniac dreamed up the fantasy that became Verdi's *Aida*. Mariette insisted on meticulous authenticity in the sets and costumes for the opera, but what does authenticity mean in a European musical extravaganza that no ancient Egyptian and few Egyptians of his own day could have understood?

The fifth strand of attempted synthesis in this book relates the interplay between nationalism and imperialism on the one hand to the ideal of objective, universal science on the other. Neither Westerners nor Egyptians had much success in resolving the dilemma of being good citizens simultaneously of two imagined communities—one political and particularist (either Western imperialist or Egyptian nationalist) and the other internationalist. In this book's opening quotation, Saint-Maur justified carrying off an obelisk from Luxor to Paris by mixing an internationalist appeal to "the learned of Europe" with one to French patriotism and French imperialism.[12] A century later, an anonymous Egyptian writer in *Al-Balagh* similarly mixed internationalist and nationalist rhetoric: "Science neither has nor should have a country, for it is the fruit of efforts made by human thought for the welfare of humanity. It must have no geographical boundaries and must be free from local or national prejudices. Nevertheless we cannot avoid expressing admiration for Professor Selim Hassan on his archaeological skill and his continuous finds, the last of which was the fourth pyramid."[13]

Western imperialism versus Egyptian nationalism thus provides a necessary—but neither a simple nor a sufficient—framework for this account. British, French, German, Italian, Austro-Hungarian, and American archaeologists all showed imperialist tendencies in their approach to archaeology in pre-1914 Egypt. Some scholars were more consciously political than others, and individual rivalries between compatriots could be fierce. Individual Egyptian archaeologists also differed in the degree of their commitment to nationalism and their means of expressing it. Sometimes Westerners closed ranks, donned the pious mantle of progressive science, and denounced Egyptians as mere chauvinists. "For the native," remarked Frantz Fanon, "objectivity is always directed against him."[14]

The creative tension between Edward Said and anti-Orientalist critics on the one hand[15] and empirically minded historians critical of Said on the other is never far beneath the surface of this book. Said emphasizes the complicity of Orientalists in imposing Western imperialism on the Islamic world. Historians among his critics often concede Said's insights while finding his indictment of Orientalism too doctrinaire and inadequately grounded in historical specifics.

John MacKenzie's *Orientalism: History, Theory, and the Arts* argues that despite the inequalities of power, the encounter between Westerners and "Orientals" was a two-way street and led to varied, unpredictable results. Limiting himself to the arts, the English-speaking world, and Western views of the encounter, he argues that many Orientalist painters, architects, designers, dramatists, and musicians were neither hostile to their subject nor promoters of imperialism.[16] Edmund Burke III points out that Said's concentration on J. B. Fourier's highly ideological preface to the *Description de l'Égypte* made him miss other implications of the work. "Said's Orientalism," says Burke, "endlessly recycles the same essentialisms, tropes and stereotypes, forever tainted by the colonial auspices under which it operates. It has a genealogy, but it has no history."[17] Carter Findley ("An Ottoman Occidentalist in Europe") acknowledges Said's insights while opening other fruitful lines of interpretation.[18]

This book also occasionally suggests spaces within which supplementary or alternative narratives might be developed. From a subalternist perspective, Prasenjit Duara urges the necessity of "rescuing history from the nation."[19] Some might try to do so on behalf of objectivity—"that noble dream"—but Peter Novick doubts that this is a viable option.[20] To subalternists, nationalist discourse is a tool for perpetuating elite dominance—ruling elites over subalterns, the metropolis over the province, males over females. One might develop narratives of the history of Egyptian archaeology as seen from "below" or from the viewpoints of "fragments of the nation"[21]—women, Copts, Upper Egyptians, tourist guides, archaeological laborers, antiquities dealers, Nile boat crews, villagers from the Giza pyramids or Qurna (across the river from Luxor), or Islamists, including the splinter groups who have attacked tourists.[22] Despite the cogency of Duara's postcolonialist prescription, an account of the early stages of the Egyptian attempt to enlist archaeology in "rescuing the nation from the empire" is a central thread in this discussion.

What follows is not a comprehensive history of Egyptology, Coptology, Greco-Roman studies, or Islamic art and archaeology. Because this book focuses on developments in Egypt itself, Egyptologists like Samuel Birch of the British Museum and Adolf Erman of the University of Berlin, who preferred their studies or museum halls at home to working in the field, are marginalized. Mariette and Maspero, in contrast, loom large here because of their long and influential activities in Egypt.

As for periodization, a "long nineteenth century" from 1798 to 1914 works reasonably well for the purposes of this book. Revisionists have successfully challenged the function of Bonaparte's expedition of 1798 or the accession of Muhammad Ali in 1805 as clear-cut divides between "medieval" and "modern" Egypt.[23] The assumption that a dynamic West imparted motion to a stagnant East is untenable, and many continuities bridged the presumed chronological divide. Nevertheless, 1798 works as a starting point for this book: Without the French expedition, there would have been no Rosetta Stone or *Description de l'Égypte*. Without the stone, the decipherment of hieroglyphics would have been delayed and, until the decipherment, most pharaonic history would have remained missing. Modern Egypt and Egyptology would have emerged in any case, but at a different pace and in unknowably different ways.

The terminal point is 1914, the year both Maspero and Ahmad Kamal retired, World War I halted German and Austro-Hungarian archaeology in Egypt, and fieldwork by the British, French, and others slowed to a crawl. The departure of the Austro-Hungarian Max Herz from the Comité and the Museum of Arab Art suddenly opened the door to the Egyptianization of the museum under Ali Bahgat. In the wake of World War I, the uprising of 1919 and the British concession of limited independence in 1922 ushered in a new, semicolonial era for national politics, museums, and archaeology. For thirty years thereafter, Egyptianization of archaeology and the government progressed fitfully, and rearguard actions enabled Europeans to keep a tenuous grip on the levers of power until the 1952 revolution.

This book draws on archival and published sources in Arabic and Western languages, which are supplemented with interviews. It uses unpublished documents from the Egyptian National Archives (Dar al-Wathaiq al-Qawmiyya), the archives of the Egyptian Ministry of Finance (Dar al-Mahfuzat), the Cairo University archives, the foreign affairs archives of Britain and France, and the archives of the British Library and the University of Pennsylvania's University Museum. The most remarkable find was the hitherto unexploited manuscript memoirs of Marcus Simaika, the founder of the Coptic Museum.

Part 1, "Imperial and National Preludes," narrates the period before the British occupation of 1882. Chapter 1 examines Western and Muslim images of ancient Egypt before the nineteenth century, the French expedition and the *Description de l'Égypte,* and the evolution of Anglo-French Egyptological rivalry until mid-century. It inserts al-Jabarti, Rifaa al-Tahtawi, Muhammad Ali, and Joseph Hekekyan into the usually Eurocentric history of Egyptology.

Chapter 2 shows how the steamship, railroad, modern guidebook, and tourist hotel came together in the invention of mass tourism, with Egypt and Thomas Cook playing leading parts. Economic, political, and social transformations in the West made this new age of tourism possible. The travel accounts, painting, and photography of Egypt have received considerable scholarly attention, but the roles Egyptians played in these processes still await serious examination.

Chapter 3 treats Egyptology in the three decades—centered on Ismail's reign—that culminated in the British occupation of 1882. As the shadow of Western imperialism lengthened after mid-century, viceroys Said and Ismail supported Mariette in establishing the Egyptian Antiquities Service and Egyptian Museum. Mariette also fed the European appetite for Egyptomania in his arrangements for the Suez Canal ceremonies, the plot for *Aida,* and two universal expositions in Paris. Al-Tahtawi wrote the first Arabic history of ancient Egypt, and Minister of

Education Ali Mubarak brought Heinrich Brugsch in from Germany to direct an Egyptian School of Egyptology. A few Egyptians began to participate—albeit on unequal terms—in the Khedivial Geographical Society, Institut égyptien, and International Congresses of Orientalists.

Part 2 covers the heyday of the British occupation (1882–1914), with a chapter on each of the four museums and their associated disciplines. The terms of the consuls general Lord Cromer and Lord Kitchener bracketed the era politically, while Maspero and Petrie dominated the Egyptological scene. The aging Ali Mubarak discussed Egyptian monuments of all eras in his topographical encyclopedia *Al-Khitat al-tawfiqiyya*, and Ahmad Kamal, Ali Bahgat, and Marcus Simaika led a new generation in promoting, respectively, Egyptology, Islamic archaeology, and Coptology.

Chapter 4 takes up the Greco-Roman Museum and classical studies. British and French imperialists in Egypt from Napoleon to Cromer and Kitchener donned the mantles of Alexander and Caesar. The Greco-Roman Museum flourished under Italian directors Guiseppe Botti and Evaristo Breccia, with the cosmopolitan Archaeological Society of Alexandria and the municipality providing key support. No Egyptian classicist or classical archaeologist of the stature of Kamal, Bahgat, or Simaika had emerged by 1914, but a few Egyptians had experimented with the classical discourse that Western imperialists found so congenial.

Chapter 5 examines Egyptology between 1882 and 1914. Maspero, Petrie, and the Egyptian Exploration Fund stand out on the European side; Ahmad Kamal, on the Egyptian. Anglo-French archaeological skirmishes foreshadowed the two powers' showdown at Fashoda in the Sudan in 1898, and the 1904 *entente cordiale* had an archaeological as well as a geopolitical aspect. The government moved the Egyptian Museum from Bulaq to Giza, then back across the Nile to its present building in Midan al-Tahrir. Around the turn of the century, Germans resumed fieldwork in Egypt and American Egyptologists began to make their mark. Ahmad Kamal plugged away at his dual causes of contributing to Egyptological scholarship and popularizing ancient Egypt among his countrymen. He helped persuade writers and politicians such as Ahmad Lutfi al-Sayyid to embrace the pharaonic patrimony.

Chapter 6 turns to the Comité de conservation des monuments de l'art arabe, the Museum of Arab Art, and the neo-Islamic architectural revival. Julius Franz, a German, and Max Herz, a Hungarian Jew, successively guided the Comité and museum from 1881 to 1914. Yaqub Artin, an Armenian Catholic, tried to mediate European scholarly culture to Egyptians.

Ali Bahgat served restlessly under Herz for a decade before beginning his pioneering excavations at the early Arab-Islamic provincial capital of al-Fustat in 1912. Two years later, Herz's sudden departure opened the way for Bahgat to become curator of the Museum of Arab Art.

Chapter 7 examines Coptic studies and the Coptic Museum, drawing especially on Marcus Simaika's hitherto unexploited memoirs. The chapter situates archaeology and Coptic history both in intra-Coptic debates over social reform and in Egyptian national politics. The "Modern Sons of the Pharaohs?" in the title of this chapter highlights the affinity for ancient Egypt that some educated Copts began to assert around the turn of the century.

After summing up developments in the four fields over the course of the nineteenth century, the conclusion points toward the changes in store after World War I. In 1922, Britain's declaration of qualified Egyptian independence and the discovery of Tutankhamun's tomb linked Egyptology and nationalism more explicitly than ever before. Egyptians used their new autonomy to open a state university in 1925. It included departments of Egyptology and classics, and a graduate program in Islamic archaeology followed a few years later. Nationalists trumpeted pride in pharaonic forefathers, and writers, painters, architects, sculptors, textbook authors, and postage-stamp designers expressed this through the adoption of pharaonic symbolism.

The deaths of Ahmad Kamal, in 1923, and Ali Bahgat, in 1924, deprived archaeology of experienced Egyptian leaders at a critical moment, however, and in 1924 the fall of Sa'd Zaghlul's government dashed hopes for full and immediate independence. Over the next quarter century, Pierre Lacau and Étienne Drioton in turn kept a tenuous French grip on the Antiquities Service and Egyptian Museum, Achille Adriani followed Breccia at the Greco-Roman Museum, and the Museum of Arab Art reverted to a European director, Gaston Wiet. Europeans headed the Egyptian University's Egyptology department, and in 1933 Captain Keppel Archibald Cameron Creswell founded the university's Islamic archaeology program. That Drioton, Wiet, and Creswell were great scholars did not lessen the frustration of nationalists. It would take Nasser's 1952 revolution to achieve two goals that eluded the generation of 1919—full independence and national control of museums and archaeology.

PART ONE

Imperial and National Preludes, 1798-1882

Rediscovering Ancient Egypt

Champollion and al-Tahtawi

Foreigners are destroying ancient edifices, extracting stones
and other worked objects and exporting them to foreign
countries. If this continues, it is clear that soon no more
ancient monuments will remain in Egypt. . . . It is also
known that the Europeans have buildings dedicated to the
care of antiquities; painted and inscribed stones, and other
such objects are carefully conserved there and shown to the
inhabitants of the country as well as to travelers who want
to see them. . . . Having considered these facts, the
government has judged it appropriate to forbid the export
abroad of antiquities found in the ancient edifices of
Egypt . . . and to designate in the capital a place to serve as a
depot. . . . It has decided to display them for travelers who
visit the country, to forbid the destruction of ancient edifices
in Upper Egypt, and to spend the greatest possible care on
their safekeeping.

Decree of Muhammad Ali, 15 August 1835,
quoted in Gaston Wiet, *Mohamed Ali
et les Beaux-Arts*

Westerners may find it strange that the title of this chapter juxtaposes
the French genius who deciphered hieroglyphics and the less-renowned
Egyptian scholar Rifaa al-Tahtawi. What the two had in common was
that each revolutionized his audience's understanding of ancient Egypt
by putting back into circulation knowledge derived from the long-
silent hieroglyphs. Champollion wrote in French for Westerners, al-
Tahtawi in Arabic for Egyptians. Champollion opened the door to a
lost world. Al-Tahtawi, although unable to read hieroglyphics him-

self, was the first to urge his countrymen to look inside the doorway. This chapter reviews what Westerners and Muslims thought they knew about ancient Egypt before 1800, examines the French expedition's archaeological work, discusses Anglo-French rivalry in early Egyptology, and notes the German arrival on the scene with Richard Lepsius. It integrates the archaeological interests of al-Jabarti, al-Tahtawi, Muhammad Ali, and Joseph Hekekyan with the usually Eurocentric narrative of Egyptology during the first half of the century. Because Hekekyan's education and archaeological activities drew him more toward European than Egyptian circles, the central figure on the Egyptian side is al-Tahtawi. He was central to Muhammad Ali's abortive attempt to create an antiquities service and museum in 1835, and in 1868 he published in Arabic the history of ancient Egypt that will be examined in chapter 3. Table 1 sets Egyptians involved in Egyptology in the first half of the century alongside their European contemporaries.

EUROPEAN IMAGES OF ANCIENT EGYPT
BEFORE CHAMPOLLION

Before Champollion, Europeans knew ancient Egypt only dimly, through Greco-Roman accounts, the Bible, and reports on surviving ruins. A panel on the facade of Cairo's Egyptian Museum honors Herodotus, Eratosthenes, Manetho, and Horapollo—Greeks and Hellenized Egyptians who wrote on ancient Egypt. When Herodotus visited Egypt about 450 B.C.E. he could question priests who still served the old gods and knew hieroglyphics. He wrote with some authority on the contemporary Persian Twenty-seventh Dynasty, the preceding Saite Twenty-sixth Dynasty (664–525 B.C.E.), and the "Ethiopian" Twenty-fifth Dynasty (745–664), but further back the historicity of his account became as uncertain as Homer's. Two thousand years already separated the "father of history" from the age of the pyramid builders. The Egyptian priest Manetho and Eratosthenes, the polymath Greek librarian of Alexandria, wrote in Greek after Alexander had formally incorporated Egypt into the Greek world. Only a king list survives of Manetho's history,[1] but Egyptologists still use its convenient dynastic framework.

Emphasizing the secular side of Western ideas about Egypt, the museum facade ignored Abraham, Joseph, Moses, and Jesus. Nevertheless, these biblical (and Quranic) personalities had long been crucial to what

TABLE I
EUROPEAN AND EGYPTIAN SCHOLARS, COLLECTORS, AND RULERS

European Scholars and Collectors	Egyptian Scholars	Rulers
Denon 1747–1825	al-Jabarti 1754–1822	Napoleon r. 1799–1814
Young 1773–1829	Hasan al-Attar 1766–1835	M. Ali r. 1805–1848
Drovetti 1776–1852		
Jomard 1777–1862		
Belzoni 1778–1823		
Burckhardt 1784–1817		
Champollion 1790–1832		
Wilkinson 1797–1875		
Rosellini 1800–1843		
Lane 1801–1876	Rifaa al-Tahtawi 1801–1873	Ibrahim r. 1848
Lepsius 1810–1884	J. Hekekyan 1807–1875	Abbas I r. 1848–1854

Europeans thought they knew about ancient Egypt. Christianity's triumph over paganism in the fourth and fifth centuries brought a break with the old gods, divine kings, and knowledge of hieroglyphics. Christians defaced or plastered up idolatrous images and turned pagan temples into churches. Knowledge of hieroglyphics and demotic Egyptian died out along with the old priesthoods.

The pharaonic legacy lived on, but mostly beneath the surface of consciousness. Images of Isis nursing Horus elided into Mary and the infant Jesus, the resurrection of Osiris blurred into that of Christ, Osiris's enemy Seth blended into the dragon that Saint George slew, and the hieroglyphic *ankh* (the "key of life") became an early form of the Christian cross. The ancient Egyptian language lived on as Coptic, which was written in the Greek alphabet with seven additional demotic signs. Coptic continued to be spoken for centuries after the Islamic conquest but survives today only as a scriptural and liturgical language of the Coptic Church.

During the West's Middle Ages, pilgrimage, crusade, and commerce drew Europeans to Egypt. Jerusalem-bound pilgrims stopped off in search of Egyptian sites associated with Joseph, Moses, Jesus, Saint Mark, and Saint Antony. The Pyramids were biblicized in pilgrim itineraries as the granaries of Joseph, built with Hebrew labor. On the commercial side, in the 1580s John Sanderson shipped home to England six hundred pounds of "mummy," believed efficacious for treating cuts and bruises.[2]

Renaissance humanists added education or self-improvement to medieval justifications for travel and made squaring classical accounts with first-hand observations in Egypt a new method of research. Printed editions of the Egyptian reports of Herodotus, Strabo, and Diodorus Siculus came off the presses within twenty years of Gutenberg's Bible, facilitating classical as well as religious pilgrimages. In 1610, twenty-two-year-old George Sandys visited Giza on a grand tour. He endorsed the Greco-Roman belief that the Pyramids were royal tombs and denied them any connection to Joseph or the Hebrews. But classical learning had its limitations. No one yet knew if most of Manetho's kings were fact or fiction, and Sandys reported that the quarries of Tura were named for Trojans imprisoned there.[3]

Classical lenses distorted the very shape of the Pyramids. Until the nineteenth century, many Europeans took the steep (ca. seventy-five-degree) pyramid of Caius Cestius in Rome rather than the less accessible pyramids of Giza (fifty-two degrees) as the archetypal pyramid. The article "Pyramid" in *Encyclopaedia Britannica*'s first edition (1771) mentions Cestius's pyramid before those of Giza. Sandys had seen the Giza pyramids with his own eyes, but his sketch showed them rising at far too steep an angle. The angle of Cestius's pyramid still influences perceptions today through the pyramid on the great seal of the United States, which appears on every dollar bill. Freemasons among the founding fathers designed the great seal.[4]

Oxford mathematician, astronomer, and Orientalist John Greaves took an empirical approach, arriving with instruments to measure the Pyramids. His *Pyramidographia, or a Discourse of the Pyramids in Aegypt* (1646) gave more accurate dimensions, showed the Great Pyramid's inner passages, and affirmed that the Pyramids were tombs.[5] But he too got the angle of the Great Pyramid wrong. Even 125 years later, the *Encyclopaedia Britannica* was content to pass along uncritical estimates of the Great Pyramid's height ranging from nearly seven hundred feet to little more than five hundred.

The recognition of fifth-century C.E. author Horapollo on the facade of the Cairo Museum is surprising. Many of the sound values in his *Hieroglyphica* eventually did prove to be correct, but the mystical symbolism he read into hieroglyphics misled scholars for centuries. In the fifteenth century, Florentine Neoplatonists rediscovered both Horapollo and the *Corpus Hermeticum* and put them back into circulation. The ostensible author of the *Corpus* was Hermes Trismegistus — a conflation of Hermes and the Egyptian god Thoth — who was believed to have antedated Moses and prefigured the truths of Christianity. In 1600 Giordano Bruno died at the stake for teaching that hermetic wisdom was purer than Christianity. Although Isaac Casaubon proved in 1614 that the *Corpus* actually postdated Christ, mystical visions of ancient Egypt as the fount of occult wisdom passed underground to the Rosicrucians and Freemasons and thrive in New Age circles today.[6]

Jesuit polymath Athanasius Kircher (1601–1680), who read Hebrew, Syriac, Arabic, and Coptic, kept to the mystical path. He wrote three thousand pages claiming that hieroglyphics prefigured Christianity. The frontispiece of his *Oedipus aegyptiacus* shows him seeking the riddle of the Egyptian sphinx, whose female form and wings draw on Greek more than Egyptian tradition (see figure 8). Although Kircher proved to be wrong about hieroglyphics — and believed in mermaids, gryphons, and geocentricity — he laid the foundation for Coptic studies in Europe.[7]

Figure 8. Egypt through classical lenses: Athanasius Kircher as Oedipus deciphering the riddle of the Egyptian sphinx. Frontispiece, by J. A. Canixus, engraved by C. Biolmaert, to Kircher, *Oedipus aegyptiacus*, 4 vols. (Rome, 1652–1654), vol. 1.

THE EUROPEAN REDISCOVERY
OF UPPER EGYPTIAN ANTIQUITIES

In the century and a half before Bonaparte, Frenchmen published at least twenty-seven travel accounts of Egypt, well ahead of the sixteen by Britons. The Germans, Dutch, Italians, and Swiss trailed far behind at six, four, two, and two, respectively.[8] Europeans entered Egypt through its Mediterranean ports or overland from Palestine and, until the 1660s, rarely ventured much south of Cairo. Then monks began making daring trips upriver on missions to convert Copts to Roman Catholicism. En route to Esna's Monastery of the Martyrs in 1668, two Capuchins stumbled onto Karnak. Later, Father Vansleb and Claude Sicard added to their missionary duties commissions from the king of France to buy early Christian manuscripts. Sicard, who traveled between 1714 and 1726, was the first modern traveler to identify Luxor's ruins as Thebes. He also visited the temples of Kom Ombo and Elephantine. Reading ancient Egypt through biblical lenses is still widespread in Western Christian and Jewish circles to this day (see figure 9).

Secular motives counted for more with Benoît de Maillet, French consul in Cairo around the turn of the eighteenth century. He did not visit Upper Egypt himself but encouraged others to do so. His published *Description de l'Égypte* is not a travelogue but a thematic compendium of information.[9] One illustration shows "Pompey's Pillar" and the standing obelisk of Alexandria side by side. His classical education made him feel at home with the Roman pillar, not the mysterious pharaonic obelisk. He rendered the pillar with careful precision but made no attempt at accuracy in his crude sketch of the obelisk's unreadable hieroglyphs. Unlike his compatriots a century later, it was the pillar, not the obelisk, that he suggested as an appropriate trophy to take to France (see figure 10).[10]

In 1737 two Protestants from northern Europe—F. L. Norden, a naval officer exploring for the king of Denmark, and Anglican priest Richard Pococke—joined in the exploration of Upper Egypt. After passing each other on the Nile without realizing it, Norden and Pococke went home, wrote travel accounts, and joined the ephemeral Egyptian Society, which John Montagu, earl of Sandwich, organized in London in 1741. The society followed the model of the Society of the Dilettanti (1732), a gathering of classical enthusiasts who had been to Italy. Pococke's romanticized view of the Sphinx showed it with its nose intact; Norden was the first to draw it realistically, with the nose missing.[11]

Figure 9.   Egypt through biblical lenses: *Egypt Saved by Joseph*, by Abel du
Pujol, 1827. On a ceiling in the Egyptian section of the Louvre. Photograph
by Donald Reid.

Disturbances in Upper Egypt kept most Europeans out for half a century after 1750, although Scottish lord James Bruce blustered through
en route to Ethiopia. He stopped at Karnak and the Valley of the Kings.
Neither the Orientalist Claude Savary nor the *philosophe* Comte de Volney went beyond Cairo. Volney's picture of Egypt and Syria languish-
ing under Oriental despotism unintentionally helped prepare the way for
Bonaparte's conquest.[12]

Far from starting from scratch, as is often assumed, Bonaparte's savants built on a cumulative, if still severely limited, body of Western
knowledge of ancient Egypt. Before 1798 Western travelers had noted
all the great Upper Egyptian temples as far as Aswan, although Edfu and
Abydos had only been sighted from a distance.[13]

MUSLIM IMAGES OF ANCIENT EGYPT
BEFORE AL-TAHTAWI

Pre-nineteenth-century European ideas about ancient Egypt are far better known than those of Muslims. Standard Western accounts stress

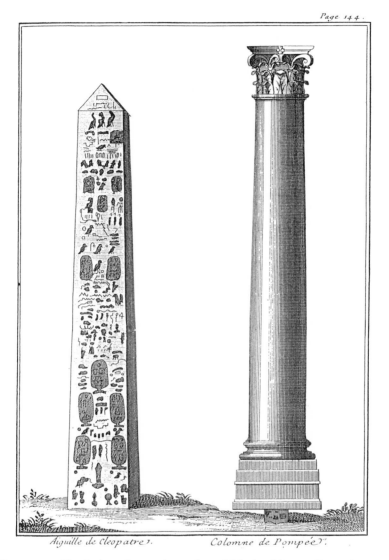

Page 144.

Aiguille de Cleopatre.   *Colomne de Pompée.*

Figure 10.   Classical or pharaonic trophy: which should go to France? "Cleopatra's Needle" and "Pompey's Pillar," Alexandria. In Benoît de Maillet, *Description de l'Égypte*, ed. L'abbé le Mascrier (Paris, 1735), 144.

Muslim hostility toward ancient Egyptians as polytheistic idolaters from the age of pre-Islamic ignorance and sin (the *jahiliyya*). Doubly distanced from the pharaohs by breaks in both language and religion, Islamic Egypt produced no equivalent of the *Shahnameh*, the medieval Persian epic celebrating the Sassanids and legendary earlier kings of Iran. The

Arabic hermetic tradition in Egypt, which associated the pharaohs with magical wisdom, may have been imported from Iraq in the eleventh century rather than springing directly from local roots. Only a single premodern Arabic source takes note of the great temple of Karnak, and the fourteenth-century traveler Ibn Battuta mentions the mosque-shrine of Muslim saint Abu al-Hajjaj without noting its perch atop the ruined Temple of Luxor.[14] In the thirteenth and fourteenth centuries, war, pestilence, and famine fostered an atmosphere of crisis in Egypt that encouraged religious dogmatism and iconoclasm. Muslim zealots destroyed a statue of Isis at al-Fustat, used inscribed blocks from a "green chapel" at Memphis for the threshold of a Sufi lodge, and demolished the temple of Akhmim. An iconoclastic Sufi also attacked the Giza sphinx.[15]

Al-Tabari's (d. 923) classic history drew on Judeo-Christian, Iranian, and Arabian pre-Islamic sources but mentioned ancient Egypt only in passing, in connection with Joseph, Moses, and Jesus. Al-Tabari's pharaoh of the Exodus has an Arab name and epitomizes pagan tyranny. With little more than a king list, al-Tabari passes over Egypt's Greco-Roman millennium.[16]

Ulrich Haarmann has shown, however, that medieval Arabic literature had a positive countertradition about ancient Egypt. Al-Masudi (d. 956) sailed up the Nile as far as Aswan, quizzing Muslims and Copts for his literary compendium *Muruj al-Dhahab* (Prairies of gold). It reviews Greek history beginning with Philip of Macedon, Roman-Byzantine history, and fantastic legends of the pharaohs. Al-Masudi admired pharaonic skill in medicine, astronomy, and stone and metal work.[17]

Many Muslim writers transmitted lore depicting ancient Egypt as a land of magic and mystery. A Yemeni king who conquered Egypt (Shaddad ibn Ad), legendary Egyptian king Surid ibn Shluq, and Hermes Trismegistos (identified with the Quranic Idris and the biblical Enoch) were variously said to have built the Pyramids to preserve wisdom during the Flood. Abd al-Latif al-Baghdadi (d. 1231/2) described pharaonic remains in fascinating detail. Al-Maqrizi (d. 1422) thought hieroglyphs encoded lost knowledge about chemistry and boasted that Egypt held twenty of the world's thirty marvels, among them the Pyramids and the temples of Akhmim and Dendera.[18]

Jamal al-Din al-Idrisi (ca. 1238) wrote a book on the Pyramids, hailing them as divine warnings to humanity. He Islamized them by pointing out that Companions of the Prophet had been content to live in their shadow, and he told of a Moroccan shaykh who sent a pilgrim just returned from Mecca all the way back to Egypt because he had failed to visit the Pyramids. Al-Idrisi segregated fantastic lore in a separate chapter, cited measurements for the Pyramids, and described the Great Pyramid's interior.[19] It would be four centuries before John Greaves gave the West a comparably sober account.

Westerners did have an advantage over Muslims in knowledge of ancient Egypt, because they had the accounts of Herodotus, Diodorus Siculus, and Strabo. Greek works of history, drama, mythology, and travel had not been included among the numerous books earlier translated into Arabic. The Western advantage was limited, however, because the Greco-Roman classics transmitted neither a verifiable chronology or history of ancient Egypt nor a correct account of how to read its writing. In the later eighteenth century the great *Encyclopédie* of the French *philosophes* still had to admit that "the history of Egypt is in general a chaos in which the chronology, the religion, and the philosophy are replete with obscurity and confusion."[20]

THE FRENCH EXPEDITION
AND THE INSTITUT D'ÉGYPTE

Egyptology was born amid violence, imperialism, and Anglo-French rivalry. Realizing a colonial project that Leibniz had proposed as far back as 1672, the French expedition seized Egypt as a way of attacking British interests in the Mediterranean and India. French soldiers stumbled onto the Rosetta Stone while digging fortifications. The British seized the stone as spoils of war in 1801, touching off a century and more of Anglo-French Egyptological rivalry. Without the French military conquest, there would have been no *Description de l'Égypte*.[21]

Revisionists have shown that 1798 was less of a watershed for Egypt than often assumed. Ali Bey's (r. 1760–1772) reforms anticipated those of Muhammad Ali, Egypt was not sealed off from the world market before 1798, and the French occupation left few immediate cultural traces behind.[22] Even the impact of the *Description* on Europe may also have been overestimated. Freemasonic mysteries, Mozart's *Magic Flute,* and Piranesi's architectural designs evidence a lively Egyptomania before 1798. Europeans could already read Coptic, had visited the main Egyptian churches and monasteries, identified sites mentioned by classical authors, and reached all the great Upper Egyptian temples but Abydos and Edfu. Only the Islamic monuments were poorly known.[23] There had even been an earlier *Description de l'Égypte* (1735), which declared: "The Nile is as familiar to many people as the Seine."[24]

Nevertheless, the French expedition was a turning point in confirm-
ing Egypt as a cockpit of Anglo-French geopolitical rivalry, fatally weakening the Mamluks, and paving the way for Muhammad Ali. There had
been harbingers, but Muhammad Ali's reign drove home major economic, fiscal, military, political, and cultural changes.[25]

In archaeology, the French expedition and Muhammad Ali's reign
ushered in a new era. The Rosetta Stone paved the way to the decipherment of hieroglyphics and the birth of modern Egyptology, and the
Description advanced the documentation of pharaonic art, architecture,
and topography.

Realizing that the *Description* could repackage the disastrous military expedition as a cultural triumph, Napoleon endorsed the work as
a state project in 1802. The massive undertaking proved to be a worthy heir of the famous *Encyclopédie*. Some 170 members of the Commission des sciences et arts had accompanied Bonaparte to Egypt. The
commission's leading savants belonged to the Institut d'Égypte (hereafter, simply the Institut), which was closely modeled on the newly
founded Institut de France. Gaspard Monge, the founder of descriptive
geometry, presided over the Institut, and "Citizen Bonaparte" was vice
president. In addition to Jean-Baptiste Fourier, Monge stood out in the
mathematics section, Vivant Denon in literature and beaux arts, Déodat Dolomieu and Geoffroy Saint-Hilaire in natural history, and Claude
Louis Berthollet in physics.[26]

The commission boasted forty-five engineers (including geographers),
a dozen mechanics and balloonists, a dozen doctors and pharmacists, and
thirty geometers, astronomers, chemists, zoologists, botanists, and min-
eralogists. There were some fifteen draughtsmen, painters, and architects
and a sprinkling of men of letters, antiquarians, musicians, and political
economists. Ten Orientalists served as translators, and in 1799 "orientaliste" first appeared in its modern French meaning of one who studies
or paints the Orient. Eighteen printers manned two presses, one of which
had been seized from the Vatican and had Arabic and Greek as well as
Latin fonts. There were a library, botanical and zoological garden, chem-
ical laboratory, observatory, workshop, and collections of minerals and
antiquities. Could Francis Bacon or Denis Diderot have asked for more?

Bonaparte's six questions at the Institut's inaugural meeting brought
any dreamers down to earth: How could the army make beer without
hops, improve its bread ovens, purify water, and manufacture gunpow-
der locally? Should it build windmills or watermills? What reforms in
local law and education might be feasible and popular?[27]

Of all the expedition's savants, it was Vivant Denon (1747–1825) who subsequently caught the European public's eye. He returned to Paris early with Bonaparte, and his lively *Voyage dans la basse et l'haute Égypte* (1802) had a long head start on the ponderous *Description*. English and German editions of the *Voyage* quickly followed the French. Denon was already fifty-one when he signed on for the expedition, with a career behind him as an artist, writer, and courtier. He had also served as a diplomat in Saint Petersburg, Sweden, and Naples. Denon had lost property in the French Revolution but survived the Terror through the protection of the painter David.[28]

Denon joined General Desaix's chase of the Mamluks through Upper Egypt, sketching antiquities all the way. The soldiers mocked the savants, but the army burst into applause at the sight of Thebes, "as though the occupation of the ruins of this capital had been the aim of their glorious deeds, had completed the conquest of Egypt." Not surprisingly, Denon's pharaonic sketches betrayed a classical warp. He described Egyptian temples as monotonous and sad but also said of Dendera: "The Greeks have invented nothing and done nothing greater"—a challenge to Quatremère de Quincy's reigning dogma that Egyptian architecture paled before its Greek counterpart.[29]

Two young engineers, Edouard de Villiers du Terrage (often referred to as Devilliers) and Jean-Baptiste Prosper Jollois, followed up on Denon's Upper Egyptian foray, bringing back drawings and plans of the temples, and the expedition sent two later scientific commissions upriver to study antiquities. Devilliers juxtaposed the common tropes of ancient splendor and present squalor, Oriental barbarism and European enlightenment:

> An Arab village, made up of miserable mud huts, dominates the most magnificent monument of Egyptian architecture and seems placed there to attest to the triumph of ignorance and barbarism over centuries of light which in Egypt raised the arts to the highest degree of splendour.
>
> We were pleased to think that we were going to take back to our country the products of the ancient science and industry of the Egyptians; it was a veritable conquest we were going to attempt in the name of the arts.[30]

THE *DESCRIPTION DE L'ÉGYPTE*

The man who eventually shepherded the *Description* through to completion was Edmé-François Jomard (1777–1862), a geographer who had helped map Cairo, Alexandria, and the countryside for the expedition. The *Description* consisted of four folio volumes of text on antiquities, two (in three parts) on the *état moderne,* and two (in five parts) on natural history. Five grand folio volumes of plates covered antiquities; two, the *état moderne;* and two volumes (in three), natural history. Since the Islamic era came after the end of classical antiquity, the *Description* consigned it to the *état moderne.* In this case, the framework of an ancient-modern dichotomy had not yet given way, as it soon would, to a tripartite periodization with an intervening "medieval" era.[31] Nearly four hundred engravers worked on the 974 plates. The first installment did not come off the imperial press, which Egyptian veteran Jean-Joseph Marcel directed, until 1810 (despite its title-page date of 1809), and the last (not counting the separate atlas of 1829) was published in 1828. Meanwhile C. L. F. Pankoucke undertook an abridged second edition (1820–1830) as a commercial venture.

Edward Said and others have dissected J. B. Fourier's preface, which Napoleon himself approved. Fourier hailed Egypt, strategically located at the juncture of three continents, as the home of the arts even before the Trojan War. Homer, Lycurgus, Solon, Pythagoras, and Plato had studied there, he declared, and Alexander, Pompey, Caesar, Mark Antony, and Augustus had come seeking worldly power. The great Napoleon followed in their steps. But "this country, which has transmitted its knowledge to so many nations, is today plunged into barbarism."[32] Hence the need for the French conquest, which would restore the benefits of civilization.

The frontispiece (figure 1), already discussed, suggested a similar message.[33] Cartouches with a star and a bee—which a note explained only as "symbols of the emperor"—flanked Napoleon's crowned monogram in the frame. Even Napoleon dared not admit openly that initiates read the star and bee to mean "divine king."[34]

A decade earlier, while the French army and savants were still trapped in Egypt, British cartoonist James Gillray had ridiculed the savants, portraying them trapped atop Pompey's Pillar while Bedouin gave siege below (see figure 11). The text beneath the cartoon explained that a captured letter from General Kléber recounted that when the approach of an Ottoman army forced the French to retreat to secure positions in Alexandria, "a party of the Scavans, who had ascended Pompey's Pillar for Scientific Purposes, was cut off by a Band of Bedouin Arabs, who, having made a large Pile of Straw and dry Reeds at the foot of the Pillar, set Fire to it, and rendered unavailing the gallant Defence of the learned Garrison, of whose Catastrophe the above Design is intended to convey an Idea."

Figure 11.   French savants besieged atop Pompey's Pillar: *Siège de la Colonne de Pompée: Science in the Pillory*, engraving by J. Gillray, 6 March 1799, as reproduced in *Napoleon in Egypt* (Brookville, N.Y.: Hillwood Art Museum, Long Island University—C. W. Post Campus, 1990), 12. From the collection of Patricia Remler (p. 43, object no. 16). Courtesy of Hillwood Art Museum, Long Island University.

The *Description* followed the *Encyclopédie* in sidestepping a pharaonic history and largely missed the mark on pharaonic society, politics, and religion.[35] The work's strength with regard to antiquity was in classical scholarship and in comparing classical accounts with visible remains. The *Description* quoted sources in parallel Greek and Latin texts.

Its hieroglyphics were obsolete long before the last volume came out in 1828. The savants had made little effort to transcribe most of the unreadable hieroglyphs accurately, and Jomard himself never accepted Champollion's system.

Despairing of chronology and history, the editors arranged the antiquities plates topographically from Philae in the south to Alexandria in the north. Plates of antiquities that perished after the French left retain particular value today. Muslim writings on pharaonic relics lacked a comparable tradition of visual documentation.

AL-JABARTI AND THE FRENCH EXPEDITION

Abd al-Rahman al-Jabarti (1754–1822) was the Azhari professor whose great *Ajaib al-Athar* chronicled Egyptian history from the late seventeenth century until the author's death. His account of the French occupation passes over the Egyptological side of the expedition. Probably he never saw the *Description,* which was coming out in installments in Paris when he died. Al-Jabarti ridiculed the form and substance of Bonaparte's initial Arabic proclamation. He mercilessly catalogued the grammatical errors and dismissed French claims of being friends of Islam and the sultan, enemies of the pope, and deliverers of Egyptians from Mamluk tyranny. His chronicle for the year the French arrived opens: "This is the beginning of a period marked by great battles; serious results were suddenly produced in a frightening manner; miseries multiplied without end, the course of things was troubled, the common meaning of life was corrupted and destruction overtook it and the devastation was general."[36]

Al-Jabarti reported that the French were antireligious materialists, behaved licentiously with European and Egyptian women, and desecrated the beloved al-Azhar mosque. Yet al-Jabarti loved learning too much not to recognize and admire it in the savants. He visited the Institut's library and laboratory:

> The administrators, astronomers, and some of the physicians lived in this house in which they placed a great number of their books and with a keeper taking care of them and arranging them. And the students among them would gather two hours before noon every day in an open space opposite the shelves of books, sitting on chairs arranged in parallel rows before a wide long board. Whoever wishes to look up something in a book asks for whatever volumes he wants and the librarian brings them to him. Then he thumbs through the pages, looking through the books, and writes. All the while they are quiet and no one disturbs his neighbour. When some Muslims would come to look around they would not prevent them from entering. Indeed they would bring

them all kinds of printed books in which there were all sorts of illustrations. . . .

I have gone to them many times and they have shown me all these various things and among the things I saw there was a large book containing the
Biography of the Prophet, upon whom be mercy and peace. . . .

The glorious Qur'an is translated into their language! Also many other
Islamic books. . . . I saw some of them who know chapters of the Qur'an by
heart. They have a great interest in the sciences, mainly in mathematics and
knowledge of languages and make great efforts to learn the Arabic language
and the colloquial. In this they strive day and night. And they have books
especially devoted to all types of languages, their declensions and conjuga-
tions as well as their etymologies. They possess extraordinary astronomical
instruments of perfect construction. . . .

[They have] neat and well-designed stoves and ovens, and instruments for
distilling, vaporizing, and extracting liquids and ointments. . . . [37]

Al-Jabarti does not mention the Institut's antiquities collection, but
he did see books with pictures of countries, seacoasts, and seas, and of
Upper Egyptian temples, including their scenes, figures, and inscriptions.
Thus an Egyptian had reported favorably on Western library and laboratory research, knowledge of Islam and Arabic, and pictorial representations of temples and hieroglyphs.

THE CONSUL-COLLECTORS:
SALT, DROVETTI, AND ANGLO-FRENCH RIVALRY

Britain's seizure of the Rosetta Stone touched off a century and more of
Anglo-French Egyptological rivalry. William Hamilton, secretary to Lord
Elgin, British ambassador to the Porte, landed in Egypt in 1801 to help
oversee the French evacuation. He foiled a French attempt to smuggle
the stone out of Egypt and later made a reconnaissance up the Nile.
Hamilton's *Aegyptiaca* (1809) included a transcript and translation of
the Greek text of the Rosetta Stone. Later Hamilton helped Elgin out-
maneuver the French in acquiring the marbles of the Parthenon, which
Elgin finally sold to the British Museum at a loss to both his reputation
and his purse.[38]

Consul-general Henry Salt and his French rival Bernardino Drovetti
continued the archaeological contest in Egypt, racing to snatch up the
best antiquities. Salt arrived in 1815 and died in harness a dozen years
later. He had welcomed the suggestion of Sir Joseph Banks, the botanist
and trustee of the British Museum who long dominated the Royal Society, that he collect antiquities for the museum. Salt's private income

and £1,500 a year from the Foreign Office barely supported his consulate-household in Egypt, and he hoped to turn a profit in antiquities. But the quarrel over the British Museum's purchase of the Elgin marbles had soured the air. Salt first presented the museum a colossal head of Rameses II as a gift, then offered to sell his whole collection. Banks turned his back, and "poor Salt"—in the words of his friend and biographer—"was accused unheard of being a dealer, a Jew, and a *second Lord Elgin.*"[39]

Salt's field agents included Giovanni Caviglia, a Malta-based sea captain who dug at Giza, and Giovanni Belzoni, an ex–circus strongman and the hero of half a dozen biographies. Belzoni brought Salt's head of Rameses II downriver and opened the temple of Abu Simbel, Seti I's tomb, and the second pyramid at Giza. Breaking with Salt, Belzoni organized an exhibit in Egyptian Hall, Picadilly, in 1821, and published a boastful account of his own exploits.[40]

Drovetti was a Tuscan who served in the French army in Italy, came to Egypt as French vice-consul in 1802, and moved up to consul general. The restored Bourbons dismissed him in 1814, but he stayed on to collect antiquities in hopes of selling them to the Louvre. Unlike his rival Salt, Drovetti made no pretense of being a scholar. He regained his consular post in 1821 and kept on collecting. Salt's and Drovetti's agents came to blows at Karnak, leading the rivals to agree to partition Egypt, with Salt working the antiquities on the west bank of the Nile, and Drovetti those on the east. Jean Jacques Rifaud dug at Karnak from 1817 to 1823 as one of Drovetti's half dozen agents.[41]

Salt's and Drovetti's successors carried the Anglo-French consul-collector rivalry into the 1850s—John Barker, Patrick Campbell, and Charles Murray for the British, and Jean François Mimaut and Raymond Sabatier for the French. Adrien Louis Cochelet, the consul who served between Mimaut and Sabatier, attracted comment by *not* being a collector.[42]

Other states fielded consul-collectors as well. Guiseppe di Nizzoli, chancellor at the Austrian consulate, collected during the 1820s. Giovanni Anastasi, the son of an Armenian provisioner to the French expedition, bridged the three decades between the Salt-Drovetti era and that of Mariette. He collected antiquities while serving as consul general of Sweden-Norway from 1828 to 1857. Keeping purchasing agents at Saqqara and Luxor, Anastasi amassed collections that ended up in the Netherlands, London, and Paris. Belgian consul general Stephan Zizinia, a Chios-born naturalized Frenchman, also collected antiquities.[43]

Political fragmentation deprived Italy of the full fruits of Italian collecting in Egypt. In the tradition of Columbus and Vespucci, Italian adventurers sought opportunity under other flags. Belzoni, Caviglia, and Alessandro Ricci worked for the British, and Drovetti, Piedmontese by birth, became a French citizen. "The great Corsican"—as a chronicler of Italian activities in Egypt pointedly called Bonaparte[44]—had started out more Italian than French. In the 1820s, Prussia bought Heinrich von Minutoli's and Giuseppe Passalacqua's Egyptian collections for the Berlin museum. Minutoli was an Italian-born Prussian general; Passalacqua, an Italian from Trieste who followed his collection to Berlin and became Egyptian curator there. Citizens of other small states who worked for foreign powers included Giovanni d'Athanasi, who dug for Salt at a time when the Ottomans still ruled his native Greece, and the Swiss explorer Johann Ludwig (anglicized as John Lewis) Burckhardt, who explored for the British.[45]

The nationalist dimensions of these intra-European rivalries would have embarrassed eighteenth-century aristocrats, who crossed national lines more easily than ones of class. But twenty years of revolutionary warfare took their toll on cosmopolitanism in science and culture. France adopted the metric system in 1793; Britain delayed an international treaty standardizing it for science until 1875.[46]

The mix of patriotism, profit, and antiquarian zeal varied with the collector, and museums back home often brought patriotic collectors up short. The Louvre rejected Drovetti's first Egyptian offering, which ended up in his native Piedmont instead of his adopted France. The British Museum paid a paltry £2,000 for Salt's first collection, but the Louvre snatched his second collection up at five times the price. Mimaut's table of kings from Abydos also ended up on the wrong side of the Channel—in the British Museum.

AL-JABARTI AND THE FRANKISH ARCHAEOLOGISTS

The frenetic activity of the consul-collectors did not go unnoticed among Egyptian scholars. In 1817, al-Jabarti's chronicle finally took the measure of European Egyptology, reporting on

> . . . the activities of a group of English Europeans who wanted to investigate the famous Pyramids at Giza, west of Fustat. By nature and desire they like to study curious objects and inquire into trivial details, especially ancient ruins and wonders of the land, paintings and statues found in caves and ancient temples in Upper Egypt and elsewhere. Some of these Englishmen rove

all over the world for such purposes, spending great sums of money for their supplies and hired attendants. They even went to the southern border of Upper Egypt and brought back pieces of stone bearing carvings, writing, and pictures; they also found white marble sarcophagi containing corpses still in their shrouds. . . .

These English Europeans also brought back the head of a large idol. This they transported in a ship they hired for 16 purses, or 320,000 silver paras. They sent the objects to their homeland to sell at double the amount they had spent on them. . . . When I heard about these figures I went with our son . . . and Sidi Ibrahim al-Mahdi al-Inklizi [Johann Ludwig Burckhardt] to see them in the consul's [Henry Salt's] house. . . . We admired their craftsmanship and uniformity and the sheen of their surfaces that have endured through centuries unnumbered save by the Knower of the invisible. After securing the pasha's permission to explore the Pyramids, they pitched a tent and took workers with spades and palm baskets to the site. They penetrated into the interior and after removing large quantities of dirt, bat excrement, etc., they descended the ramp. There too they removed a great deal of dirt and dung and finally reached what they said was an undiscovered square chamber made of dressed stone. In addition they excavated around the huge head near the Pyramids popularly called the head of Abu 'l-Hawl [the Sphinx]. They exposed an enormous complete body, apparently made of a single stone, stretched out as if resting on its body with its head in the air. It is this head which people see, the rest of its body being hidden under the sand heaped upon it. . . . The Englishmen continued their work for approximately four months.[47]

Thus al-Jabarti admired pharaonic craftsmanship and noted the European passion for archaeology, finding it strange but not condemning it. But this passage, buried in the hundreds of pages of his chronicle, probably passed unnoticed by most of his readers.

Al-Jabarti died in 1822, the year of Champollion's breakthrough in hieroglyphics. It would be a dozen years until another Azhari shaykh, al-Tahtawi, would begin conveying some of the fruits of Champollion's labor to Egyptians.

THE DECIPHERERS: YOUNG, CHAMPOLLION, AND ANGLO-FRENCH RIVALRY

In contrast with the prehistoric archaeologies of the Americas, Europe, and sub-Saharan Africa, Egyptology and Near Eastern archaeology developed as text-aided archaeologies, with written records playing a critical role in the interpretation of material remains. Archaeology in the Middle East put a high priority on deciphering Egyptian, Akkadian, Sumerian, Old Persian, and Hittite. As each of these codes was cracked, excavators added texts to art objects as prime objects of search. Although Greek and Latin never had to await decipherment, Egyptology developed roughly along lines marked out since the eighteenth century in Greco-Roman archaeology. Assyriology (the study of ancient Mesopotamia) and biblical archaeology grew up alongside and somewhat behind Egyptology.[48]

British hopes in the race to decipher hieroglyphics rested on Thomas Young (1773–1829), a physician and linguist, who also made original contributions to optics. Young recognized Coptic as the language of ancient Egypt and deduced that some demotic signs derived from hieroglyphs and that hieroglyphics mixed alphabetic and nonalphabetic signs. He deciphered the cartouches of Ptolemy and Queen Berenike and made a partly correct list of alphabetic signs but still fell short of a decisive breakthrough.[49]

Jean-François Champollion (1790–1832) took up the challenge for France. His older brother Jacques-Joseph, who had hoped to accompany Bonaparte to Egypt, steered the brilliant youngster toward Egyptology. At sixteen Champollion "the younger" read a paper to the Grenoble Academy affirming Coptic as the language of ancient Egypt. He studied in Paris with Sylvestre de Sacy and Louis Langlès at the Collège de France and Ecole spéciale des langues orientales vivantes. In 1822 Champollion's *Lettre à M. Dacier, relative à l'alphabet des hiéroglyphes phonétiques* announced his decipherment to the French academy.[50]

The British boasted of holding the Rosetta Stone, but it took a Frenchman to read it! Revealing book titles pressed British counterclaims: Young's *Account of Some Recent Discoveries in Hieroglyphical Literature and Egyptian Antiquities, including the author's original alphabet as extended by M. Champollion* (1823) and Salt's *Essay on Dr. Young's and M. Champollion's Phonetic System of Hieroglyphics* (1825). Champollion's refusal to acknowledge any debt to Young still rankles in the stone's label in the British Museum.

The debate over Champollion's system also cut across national lines. In Germany, naturalist Alexander von Humboldt and his linguist brother Wilhelm championed Champollion, while Heinrich Klaproth and Gustavus Seyfarth rejected him. Only Lepsius's endorsement in 1837 and Champollion's posthumous *Grammaire* (1836–1841) and *Dictionnaire* (1841–1844) finally proved the decipherment right beyond a reasonable doubt.[51]

Frenchmen were also divided. S. de Sacy threw his weight behind Champollion in 1822, but Edmé-François Jomard's implacable opposition helped keep the decipherer out of the Académie des inscriptions until 1830. The patronage of the duc de Blacas, a royalist and former émigré, was critical in enabling Champollion to live down his family's Jacobin reputation and beat out Jomard for the Egyptian curatorship at the Louvre in 1826. Jomard busied himself with the last volumes of the *Description,* helping run the Geographical Society, supervising a student mission Muhammad Ali sent to Paris, and curating maps at the Bibliothèque nationale. But sadly, his rejection of Champollion ultimately deprived Jomard *"le Égyptien"* of a label he would have cherished. *Who Was Who in Egyptology* lists him as an engineer, geographer, and antiquarian but not as an Egyptologist.[52]

THE COPYISTS, BRITISH AND FRENCH

In the 1820s an eager young group of copyists joined the consul-collectors in the field. Britons led the way, characteristically without official sponsorship or public funds. The Swiss J. L. Burckhardt had explored Nubia, Syria, and Mecca on behalf of London's African Association. The Britons who followed him to Egypt in the 1820s were determined to capture the antiquities, landscape, and modern society with brush and pen. Gardner Wilkinson (1797–1875) became the leading British Egyptologist and Edward William Lane (1801–1876) the leading British Orientalist of their generation. The inherited fortune of painter Robert Hay (1799–1863) supported a whole team of draughtsmen, but the Hay team's study of Egyptian architecture was never published. Lane, Wilkinson, and Hay all donated antiquities to the British Museum, but recording, not collecting, was their passion.[53]

Wilkinson spent much of his time in Egypt (1821–1833) at Qurna (opposite Luxor), copying tomb scenes for *Manners and Customs of the Ancient Egyptians.* Unbelievable as it would be by today's standards, he lived in an inscribed tomb and burned mummy cases for fuel. With hieroglyphics still only half deciphered, Wilkinson's main sources were not inscriptions but the Bible, the classics, and scenes from tombs. Wilkinson fretted that if Hay failed to publish, some German or Frenchman might steal the credit Britons deserved for their intensive fieldwork of the 1820s and 1830s.[54]

Trained as an engraver, Lane arrived in Egypt in 1825. His long unpublished *Description of Egypt* was partly a counterpoint to the great French work. The famous *Manners and Customs of the Modern Egyptians* was a reworked portion of Lane's longer *Description.* Lane's *De-*

scription evidences a deep knowledge of Egyptology, but thereafter he specialized as an Orientalist, translating *The Arabian Nights* and compiling his *Arabic Lexicon* under aristocratic patronage. Universities had yet to move to the center of modern British learning; Wilkinson and Lane, like their contemporaries Charles Lyell and Charles Darwin, subsisted on private patronage or inherited wealth.

Britons published at least 114 travel accounts of Egypt between 1798 and 1850, well outpacing the French total of 54. (From a late start in the 1820s, Americans edged out the Germans for third place).[55] Reports of British archaeological activity on the Nile helped spur Champollion to mount his expedition of 1828–1829. Champollion's Tuscan disciple, Ippolito Rosellini, became second in command on this joint Franco-Tuscan venture.

The text-hungry scholars threw themselves into copying, but collecting for the Louvre was also central to their mission. Joseph Bonomi, a copyist working for Robert Hay, heard that Champollion intended to cut out reliefs from the tomb of Seti I and wrote him:

> Sir, I have been informed that certain people have arrived here at Gourneh by your orders to cut certain pictures from the tomb in the Valley of Biban el Molook [the Valley of the Kings] opened by Belzoni at the expense of the late English consul Mr Salt. If it be true that such is your intention I feel it is my duty as an Englishman and a lover of antiquity to use every argument to dissuade you from so Gothic a purpose.

Champollion shot back:

> Rest assured, Sir, that one day you will have the pleasure of seeing some of the beautiful bas-reliefs of the tomb of Osirei [Seti I] in the French Museum. That will be the only way of saving them from imminent destruction and in carrying out this project I shall be acting as a real lover of antiquity, since I shall be taking them away only to preserve and not to sell.[56]

The Franco-Tuscan expedition resulted in two great sets of plates: Champollion's posthumous *Monuments de l'Égypte et de la Nubie* (4 vols., 1835–1847) and Rosellini's *I Monumenti dell' Egitto e della Nubia* (9 vols. plus 3 vols. of atlases, 1832–1844).[57]

In the 1840s, the cockpit of Franco-British archaeological rivalry temporarily shifted from the Nile to the Tigris. Breakthroughs in copying, collecting, and decipherment were laying the foundations for Assyriology, the study of the ancient civilizations of Mesopotamia. Back in the 1810s, Claudius Rich, Baghdad agent of the East India Company and a consul-collector like Salt and Drovetti, had explored Babylon and collected cuneiform tablets, which ended up in the British Museum. In the 1840s, Paul Émile Botta, the French vice-consul at Mosul and an Italian-born Frenchman like Drovetti, astonished the world by digging out colossal human-headed winged bulls and other Assyrian sculptures at Khorsabad and shipping them home to the Louvre. Botta's friendly rival Austen Henry Layard, later British ambassador to Istanbul, unearthed similar statues, reliefs, and cuneiform inscriptions at Nimrud and Kuyunjik for the British Museum. The outbreak of the Crimean War brought this heroic phase of Mesopotamian field archaeology to an end in 1855.[58]

Meanwhile, breakthroughs in deciphering cuneiform narrowed Egyptology's lead over the nascent field of Assyriology. In 1802, German schoolteacher Georg Grotefend had discovered the values of twelve signs in Old Persian by comparing the names of Darius and Xerxes, but like Young in hieroglyphics he fell short of an effective decipherment. In 1846–1847 Henry Rawlinson published a transcription and translation of the whole Old Persian text of the trilingual cuneiform inscription of Darius I at Behistun, Persia. A decade later Rawlinson and two other scholars triumphantly confirmed the decipherment of Akkadian, the language of ancient Babylon and Assyria, by independently translating the same cuneiform text.

THE GERMAN DEBUT: THE LEPSIUS EXPEDITION

While French and British attention was fixed on the Tigris, Richard Lepsius's Prussian expedition of 1842–1845 triumphantly worked its way through Egypt and Nubia. Even more than with Champollion's Franco-Tuscan expedition, state support made possible this large-scale campaign in both copying and collecting. Berlin and other German universities were emerging as centers of research in the early 1830s when Lepsius was studying philology at Leipzig, Göttingen, and Berlin. The year after Champollion died, Lepsius arrived in Paris to complete his studies. He methodically prepared himself in allied fields before plunging into Egyptian philology, where his intervention in 1837 proved decisive. His *Lettre à M. le Prof. H. Rosellini sur l'alphabet hiéroglyph* reduced Champollion's detractors to the status of cranks.

When Friedrich Wilhelm IV (r. 1840–1861) ascended the Prussian throne, Alexander von Humboldt and diplomat-scholar Christian Karl von Bunsen quickly persuaded him to sponsor Lepsius on an expedition to Egypt. As early as 1820–1821, his father, Friedrich Wilhelm III (r. 1797–1840), had supported Heinrich von Minutoli on a modest Prus-

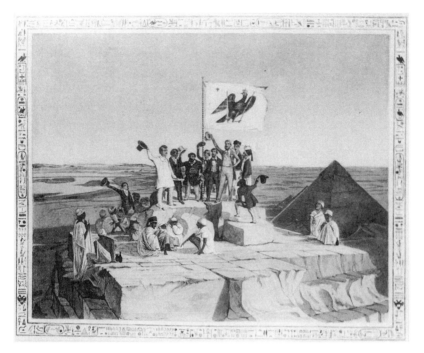

Figure 12.   Staking a Prussian imperial claim: the Lepsius expedition celebrating the birthday of King Friedrich Wilhelm IV atop the Great Pyramid in 1842. Engraving by Georg Frey, reproduced in Bernhard Lepsius, *Das Haus Lepsius* (Berlin, 1933), facing p. 80.

sian expedition that visited Upper Egypt and reached the oasis of Siwa.[59] Minutoli fueled the Egyptian interests of the crown prince, who arranged for the purchase of G. Passalacqua's Egyptian collection and installed him in Berlin as its curator. The Lepsius expedition was so well supported that it even took along a Lutheran pastor as chaplain. The party celebrated their king's birthday atop the Great Pyramid by unfurling the Prussian flag and lighting a bonfire (see figure 12).

Muhammad Ali welcomed the Prussians by providing corvée labor and free river transport. Lepsius collected and copied his way up the Nile and returned with fifteen thousand antiquities and plaster casts. He took up the chair of Egyptology created especially for him at the University of Berlin and methodically brought out his *Denkmäler aus Aegypten und Aethiopien* (12 vols., 1849–1859). Passalacqua nominally directed Berlin's Egyptian museum until his death in 1865, but Lepsius was the moving spirit behind its overhaul and expansion. Lepsius had lost one skirmish to French adventurer Prisse d'Avennes (1807–1879). Hearing that Lepsius intended to remove the Karnak table of kings to Berlin, Prisse rushed there first and, working furtively at night, sawed loose the table, loaded it, and started down the Nile. Passing Lepsius on the river, he could not resist inviting him aboard and seating him unaware on one of the crates containing the treasure! A copyist as well as a collector, Prisse published plates on both pharaonic art and the Arab art of Cairo.[60]

INSTITUTIONAL CONTEXTS:
MUSEUMS AND LEARNED SOCIETIES IN EUROPE

Until the later nineteenth century, museums and learned societies, more than universities, provided the main institutional support for Egyptology. Champollion announced his decipherment to the Académie des belles lettres et inscriptions, served as curator at the Louvre, and only won a chair at the Collège de France two years before his death. England's Samuel Birch was a museum man, not a professor, and Conradus Leemans (1809–1893) pioneered Egyptology in the Netherlands while directing the Leiden Museum.[61]

Britain's confiscation of the French expedition's antiquities, including the Rosetta Stone, got the Louvre's Egyptian collection off to a slow start. Becoming director of the Central Museum of Arts a decade after the Revolution had thrown the royal art collection open to the public, Denon soon moved up to director general of national museums. He gathered confiscated masterpieces from Napoleon's vanquished European foes. Denon lost his post in 1815 in the Bourbon purge of Napoleon's appointees, and much of the plunder had to be repatriated after Waterloo. Nevertheless, the Louvre emerged as a model for national museums throughout Europe and as far afield as the United States, Mexico, Egypt, and Istanbul. (See figure 13.)

In 1824 the Louvre missed an excellent opportunity when Jomard persuaded it to reject Drovetti's first collection. Drovetti's native Piedmont bought it instead, and Champollion had to follow the collection to Turin in search of texts for his philological research. There he advised on the organization of the world's first major Egyptian museum.[62] The Louvre soon made up for lost time, snatching up both Salt's and Drovetti's second collections and appointing Champollion curator of a new Egyptian section in 1826. The following year, just short of three decades after Bonaparte's expedition, Champollion opened the Egyptian collection at the Louvre, officially the Musée Charles X. He broke sharply with the custom of organizing collections along aesthetic lines,

Figure 13. Napoleonic plunder, Napoleonic scholarship: *Dominique-Vivant Denon travaillant dans la salle de Diane au Louvre*, allegorical portrait by Benjamin Zix, ca. 1809–1811. Courtesy of the Musée du Louvre, Département des arts graphiques.

displaying instead three series of chronologically ordered objects — religious, civil, and funerary. The fruits of his own Egyptian expedition helped fill in some of the gaps.

Characteristically, the British Museum began not with a royal collection but with a bequest in 1753 of the private collection of physician and naturalist Sir Hans Sloane. The library and collections were to be "for public use" and free to "all students and curious persons." The separate antiquities department, created in 1807, got off to an uneven start, as Elgin's and Salt's difficulties with the institution suggest. Samuel Birch, who shares a place of honor on the Cairo Museum facade alongside Champollion, Lepsius, and Rosellini, began his half century of labor at the British Museum in 1836.

In Berlin, the Monbijou Palace could no longer contain the Egyptian collection after the return of Lepsius. The Neues Museum opened in 1850 on Museum Island, with Passalacqua still nominally heading the Egyptian section and Lepsius at his elbow. A stunning neopharaonic interior court almost upstaged the antiquities displayed.[63]

As for learned societies, Paris was the first to establish a geographical society in 1821. Berlin followed in 1828, London in 1830, and New York in 1851. The Champollion brothers were founding members of the Société de géographie of Paris, but it was Jomard who made it his turf for forty years, often steering its *Bulletin* toward Egyptian subjects.[64]

London's Royal Geographical Society (RGS) fell heir to the Association for the Promotion of the Discovery of the Interior Parts of Africa (1788), the Palestine Association (1804), and the Raleigh Travellers' Club (1826). Spurred on first by informal imperialism and later by the "new imperialism," the RGS outstripped its foreign rivals in promoting exploration and scholarship.

Paris founded its Société asiatique (1822) and London its Royal Asiatic Society of Great Britain and Ireland (1823) in the same critical decade as their geographical societies. In Britain's case, the colonies had inspired the metropolis rather than the other way around; William Jones's Asiatic Society of Bengal went back to 1784, its Bombay counterpart to 1804. The German and American Oriental societies did not appear until the 1840s, so it was primarily the geographical and Asiatic societies of London and Paris, the defunct Institut d'Égypte, the Institut de France, and Britain's Royal Society that offered possible models when Europeans in Cairo founded the Egyptian Society in 1836.

TRANSPLANTING A EUROPEAN MODEL: CAIRO'S EGYPTIAN SOCIETY

Bonaparte's expedition and Champollion's and Lepsius's Egyptological expeditions were self-contained forays mounted from Europe. They collected data and objects in the field, then returned home to analyze, display, and publish.

The memory of the Institut d'Égypte lingered among European residents after the French left. An obscure English Reading Society opened in Alexandria about 1828, and in Cairo in 1836 Europeans founded the Egyptian Society—"a rendezvous for Travellers, with the view of associating literary and scientific men, who may from time to time visit Egypt."[65] Briefly known as the Société orientale, the Egyptian Society intended to provide a reference library and to "collect and record information" on Egypt and adjacent countries. "Any Gentleman or Lady travelling in Egypt" and introduced by a member could use the reading room, and "Gentlemen of all nations" were eligible for membership at a guinea a year.[66] Excluding women from membership was in tune with the practice back home.

Anthony Harris (1790–1869), the society's first president, was a merchant and antiquities dealer whose papyrus collection eventually enriched the British Museum. The society listed only twenty members in 1839, when its library made "the larger works of the new Archaeological School available in Egypt for the first time."[67] Four years later regular membership had shot up to 110. Over two-thirds were Britons; the French came next (including Antoine Clot Bey, Linant de Bellefonds, and Ferdinand de Lesseps), and there was a sprinkling of Italians, Germans, and Americans. Like President Harris, Clot Bey and British doctors Henry Abbott and Alfred Walne were passionate antiquities collectors. The sixteen honorary members included Birch, von Bunsen, Hamilton, Jomard, Lane, Lepsius, Rosellini, and Wilkinson. Jomard filled the society's book orders in Paris, Lane in London.[68] Sulayman Pasha, the French convert to Islam who commanded the Egyptian army, and Armenians Hekekyan and Anastasi were the closest the society came to having Egyptian members.

In 1842 a quarrel over an overdue book charged to Prisse d'Avennes[69] precipitated a secession and the founding of the rival Egyptian Literary Association. The schism was personal, not national. British doctors Walne and Abbott led the opposing factions, and a majority in both camps were Britons. Wilkinson and Prisse d'Avennes contributed to the single volume of *Miscellanea Aegyptiaca*, which the association brought out before fading from view. As late as 1867, Wilkinson's *Handbook* still recommended the society's library to travelers, but the organization was no longer very active. In 1873–1874 Hekekyan, Linant de Bellefonds, and another survivor presented the society's remaining books to the new Khedivial Library.[70]

AL-TAHTAWI REDISCOVERS THE PHARAOHS

When there is a fourth edition of *Who Was Who in Egyptology,* it should include Rifaa al-Tahtawi. He did not excavate or read hieroglyphics, but he was as important in spreading interest in ancient Egypt among his fellow Egyptians as many of the Western travelers, collectors, and authors included in the first three editions were in fostering interest among Europeans.[71] Al-Tahtawi, an Azhari shaykh who topped off his education in Paris, pursued an official career in translation, education, and journalism, becoming the most famous Egyptian thinker of his generation. (See figure 14.)

The title of this chapter juxtaposes al-Tahtawi with Champollion to emphasize that both scholars provided their respective audiences with new information derived from hieroglyphic texts. In other ways, however, al-Tahtawi's career more closely resembles that of British Orientalist E. W. Lane. Al-Tahtawi and Lane were both born in 1801. In the mid-1820s, one went east and one went west, crossing the Mediterranean in search of knowledge that would change their lives. Each lived in a great capital of the other's civilization, learned its language, and returned home to publish in the mid-1830s a landmark book introducing his compatriots to the manners and customs of the other. (Al-Tahtawi lived in Paris rather than Lane's London and learned French rather than English.) Both books highlighted a single metropolis—Paris and Cairo— to the near exclusion of the provinces. Lane's *Modern Egyptians* included well-executed illustrations, but al-Tahtawi's text-centered Azhari education had not prepared him for visual illustration of his text.

Both scholars followed up their initial books with translations and other studies to familiarize their audiences with the civilization of the other. Although their stays in Cairo overlapped and Lane bought a copy of al-Tahtawi's *Takhlis* when it came out, there is no evidence that they ever met. The two were unusual in being deeply interested in both ancient and modern Egypt. After lifetimes spent mediating between their two cultures, al-Tahtawi died in 1873 and Lane in 1876.

Al-Tahtawi and Lane of course differed in personality, in ideas, and in their relationships to national and global power. Over the course of their lifetimes, the balance of power shifted decisively against Egypt and in favor of the West. Lane deplored many Western-inspired changes in

Figure 14. Rifaa al-Tahtawi, reformist scholar-official, head of the Translation Bureau, the School of Languages, and the abortive antiquities service and museum (1835). Author of the first history of ancient Egypt in Arabic (1868). This postage stamp is evidence of his current recognition.

Egypt, perhaps partly because of his unease with the rapid socioeconomic and political changes back in England. Although his work depended on aristocratic patronage, Lane was reclusive and kept his distance from the British establishment. Al-Tahtawi, in contrast, served rulers eager to enhance their power by borrowing Western technology and administrative techniques.

Al-Tahtawi was born in Tahta, south of Asyut, in the year of the French evacuation—1801. Some of his forebears had been *ulama* (religious leaders), but Muhammad Ali's abolition of tax farming had ruined al-Tahtawi's father. The boy nevertheless obtained an elementary religious education and was able to move on to Cairo to study at the great mosque-university of al-Azhar in 1817. His broad-minded mentor there, Hasan al-Attar, had conversed with Bonaparte's savants and would later head the institution as shaykh al-Azhar. Al-Attar recommended al-Tahtawi as chaplain *(imam)* to a group ("mission," in Egyptian English usage) of forty-four students Muhammad Ali sent to Paris in 1826. Hitherto a number of the Egyptians in France had been collaborators who fled with the French evacuation of Egypt in 1801. Now a new type appeared—the student sent to France to learn a modern skill, bring it back, and apply it in Egypt.[72] Al-Tahtawi justified his quest in the land of the infidel with the prophet Muhammad's saying "Seek knowledge, even in China."

In Paris, the chaplain turned out to be the most ardent student of all. As director of the Egyptian mission, Jomard introduced al-Tahtawi to Sylvestre de Sacy, the dean of French Orientalists,[73] and a wide range of French learning. In 1830, al-Tahtawi witnessed first-hand the July revolution, which sent Charles X into exile and put Louis-Philippe on the throne. That same year al-Tahtawi showed de Sacy a draft of *Takhlis al-ibriz fi talkhis Baris* (The distillation of pure gold in summing up Paris),[74] which described his journey and observations on Parisian life. In 1831 he went home to the career in education, translation, and journalism, which made him a star of the nineteenth-century Arabic *nahda* (renaissance).

In 1834 the government press at Bulaq published *Takhlis,* the first of three landmark books of the decade in which Egypt and the West took each other's measure. Lane's *Account of the Manners and Customs of the Modern Egyptians* followed in 1836 and Wilkinson's *Manners and Customs of the Ancient Egyptians* in 1837. Lane's and al-Tahtawi's books made an obvious pair; al-Tahtawi might even have called his work *The Manners and Customs of Modern Frenchmen.* Lane and Wilkinson made a natural pair in the suitcases of Western travelers until late in the century, when Wilkinson was superseded. Lane remains a classic.

Al-Tahtawi's observations on Paris have been fully discussed in other studies; his awakening interest in ancient Egypt is the main concern here. *Saidi*s (Upper Egyptians) are sometimes assumed to have a special affinity for ancient Egypt, a proposition that is difficult to pin down. Al-Tahtawi did not grow up in the shadow of Karnak or Edfu, although in his youth temple columns still stood at Qaw al-Kabir (Antaeopolis) seven miles south of his native Tahta.

The first evidence of al-Tahtawi's interest in ancient Egypt comes from Paris in 1827, when he published an Arabic translation of Joseph Agoub's (1795–1832) *Dithyrambe sur l'Égypte.* Agoub's family had cast their lot with the Napoleonic expedition and fled when the French evacuated, taking the six-year-old boy with them. Starting in Marseilles and

moving on to Paris, he studied languages, taught Arabic, frequented literary salons, assisted Jomard with the *Description,* and tutored al-
Tahtawi and the Egyptian students in Paris. Agoub's *Dithyrambe* was
an exile's romantic lament for his lost homeland, "mother of the gods,
heroes, and sages" amid whose ruins "forty centuries assembled."[75]

Champollion personally delivered a progress report on al-Tahtawi's
Parisian studies to Muhammad Ali in 1828,[76] but the shaykh and the
decipherer may never have met. Despite his friendship with Jomard, al-
Tahtawi's book on Paris shows no awareness of the *Description de l'É-
gypte,* which loomed so large in European consciousness. *Takhlis* notes
that an "organization for the preservation of antiquities"—presumably
the Louvre—contains "historical wonders of the ancients, such as their
buildings, mummies, and clothing," including such antiquities from
Egypt as the Dendera zodiac, "from which French scholars have been
able to learn the ancient Egyptians' understanding of the stars."[77]

Takhlis mentions ancient Egypt again toward the end, obliquely and
with an almost postmodern twist on monuments and memories. Heading home to Egypt in 1831, al-Tahtawi stopped at Fontainbleau, where
he noticed an obelisk commemorating the Bourbon restoration. He explained to his readers that Europeans, like the Egyptians and other ancients, commended themselves to posterity by inscribing monuments. In
this case, however, the recent revolutionaries of 1830 had hacked out
the royal names.[78]

The monument made him think of the Pyramids, on which he presents a mix of old lore and recent European findings. Some Franks say
a king named Quf (Khufu) built the Giza pyramids three thousand years
ago, he reports. Others attribute them to Khamis or Khiyups (Cheops).
(Cheops, however, is merely the Greek form of Khufu.) Some say it took
twenty-three years and 360,000 workers to build the Great Pyramid;
Pliny reported twenty million Egyptian piastres spent on leeks and
onions for the workers. The open entrance to the Great Pyramid indicates the king was not buried there, he misinforms his readers, while the
sealed second and third pyramids contain the remains of his wife and
daughter.

Al-Tahtawi recalls al-Suyuti's (d. 1505) surprise at the attention lav-
ished on the Pyramids, since the obelisks of Upper Egypt seemed more
remarkable. Al-Tahtawi adds that Europeans had taken an obelisk to
Rome, and "in our own days" to Paris. Continuing, he editorializes on
Muhammad Ali's gift of an obelisk to the French: "In my opinion, since
Egypt has undertaken to adopt civilization and instruction on the model

of European countries, it would be better to preserve the ornaments and works which their ancestors have left them."

Printed on the government's Bulaq Press, *Takhlis* was distributed free of charge to schools and officials. A Turkish translation in 1839 may have influenced Young Ottoman thinking on constitutionalism. In 1835 al-Tahtawi became founding director of Muhammad Ali's School of Languages. Later he also directed the translation bureau and edited Egypt's official journal.

Shaykh al-Azhar Hasan al-Attar's preface endorsing *Takhlis* may have deflected some criticism, but Lane overheard the book described as a tale of how Frankish vices had corrupted the author in the land of the infidel.[79] The second Bulaq edition of 1849 may have precipitated al-Tahtawi's fall from favor at a time when Abbas Hilmi I was pruning European influence, especially French, and replacing Muhammad Ali's men with his own. Abbas closed the School of Languages, translation bureau, and official gazette; sold the Bulaq Press; and exiled al-Tahtawi to Khartoum. Al-Tahtawi feared the post might be his death warrant; he reported that half the Egyptians who accompanied him to Khartoum died.[80] Salvation finally came in 1854, when Said succeeded Abbas, who was murdered in a private quarrel. Said pardoned the remaining exiles, and al-Tahtawi returned home, eager for a new assignment.

MUHAMMAD ALI'S ARCHAEOLOGICAL DIPLOMACY

To Muhammad Ali, antiquities were primarily bargaining chips to be exchanged for European diplomatic and technical support. Yet there are hints of a less utilitarian attitude—his dismay at the exhumation of mummies he saw at Qurna and the choice of a pyramid as the masthead symbol of his official journal in 1829 (see figure 15).[81] Conventional wisdom has it that in the early nineteenth century, only Europeans thought of the Pyramids as symbols of Egypt. The neopharaonic lotus capitals in Muhammad Ali's Citadel mosque may reflect European influence rather than direct local inspiration.[82] Muhammad Ali's praise of Champollion's drawings of antiquities may have been mere diplomacy, but the pasha's requests that the French scholar furnish a translation of the text on an Alexandrian obelisk and a sketch of pharaonic history suggest real intellectual curiosity.[83]

In 1830, Champollion made a plea to Muhammad Ali to protect endangered antiquities, pointing out that thirteen temples had vanished in the thirty years since Napoleon's expedition. Champollion spread the

Figure 15. Muhammad Ali's choice? A pyramid as a symbol of Egypt.
Masthead of *Al-Waqai al-Misriyya*, Egypt's official journal, 1829. In Amin
Sami, *Taqwim al-Nil*, vol. 2 (Cairo, 1928), 346.

blame among the fellahin, antiquities dealers, and European collectors.
Donning the mantle of "science," he assured the pasha that "all of Europe will take notice of the active measures which His Highness would
want to take to assure the conservation of temples, palaces, tombs, and
all kinds of monuments which still attest to the power and grandeur of
ancient Egypt, and which are at the same time the most beautiful ornaments of Modern Egypt."[84]

The destruction continued, however. Consul General Mimaut
warned Muhammad Ali that the temple of Dendera was being quarried for a cotton cloth factory at Qena. Mimaut hoped that the ensuing exemplary punishment would ensure that "none of these savages"
would again use temples to build "wretched factories."[85] Informed once
more that the despoliation of antiquities continued, Muhammad Ali
declared that Europeans, who were beyond his reach, were the chief
offenders.

Muhammad Ali's decree of 15 August 1835 put the main blame for
the despoliation on Europeans, but it also cited European precedents to
justify banning the export of antiquities and ordering that they be collected for display in Cairo: "It is also well known that the Europeans

have buildings for keeping antiquities; stones covered with paintings and inscriptions, and other similar objects are carefully conserved there and shown to the inhabitants of the country as well as to travelers . . . such establishments bring great renown to the countries which have them."[86]

The decree specified that antiquities were to be sent to al-Tahtawi, director of the School of Languages, in Ezbekiyeh. Al-Tahtawi and Hekekyan were to inspect the proposed site for a museum next to the school, and Hekekyan, an engineer, was to design the building. A certain Yusuf Diya Effendi was to supervise the museum and make a yearly inspection of Upper Egyptian sites. Diya began his inspections and appointed deputies to forward any antiquities uncovered to Cairo. Although Muhammad Ali's decree had noted that in Europe both locals and foreign visitors visited museums, it mentioned only "travelers who visit the country" as the projected audience of the museum at Cairo.

Had the plan taken hold, Egypt would have been neck and neck with Greece—whose national museum dates from 1829, archaeological service from 1833, first antiquities law from 1834, and archaeological society from 1837—in asserting national control over antiquities and putting them on display. Indeed, Egypt would have barely trailed France and would have led Britain by half a century in extending official protection to historic monuments. In France, the sacking of royal and religious monuments during the Revolution had provoked the founding of a museum of lapidary relics at the monastery of the Grands Augustins in the 1790s. Romanticism and the restoration of the Bourbons further promoted nostalgia for the Middle Ages. In 1830, François Guizot, a historian and perennial minister of Louis-Philippe, arranged for the appointment of an inspector of historic monuments. Four years later the French government established the Commission des monuments historiques. In Britain, concern for individual property rights delayed the naming of an inspector of ancient monuments until 1882.[87]

Egyptians sometimes look back to the 1835 decree as the founding of Egypt's Antiquities Service and the Egyptian Museum.[88] French sources, however, dismiss the decree as a vengeful attempt to disrupt Consul General Mimaut's collecting. In any case, it was unfortunate that Muhammad Ali's order for the construction of eighteen saltpeter factories came at about the same time. Karnak's ninth pylon was dynamited for blocks for one of the factories.[89] American consul George R. Gliddon actually cheered Muhammad Ali's defeat in the "Eastern question" showdown of 1840–1841, because the ensuing halt in factory construction slowed the plundering of antiquities sites for building materials.[90]

The West's appetite for antiquities encouraged Europeans from the consuls on down to make a mockery of the export ban. Champollion himself had cut a bas-relief out of the exquisite tomb of Seti I, and Mimaut made off with the Abydos table of kings. Even without consular support, Prisse d'Avennes bribed his way through customs at Alexandria with the Karnak table of kings.

Obelisks were the most spectacular prizes of all. The Romans had carried them off as trophies to Rome and Constantinople, and General Desaix suggested that Bonaparte take one home to Paris.[91] After defeating the French in 1801, British officers talked of taking one of the Alexandrian obelisks to celebrate their victory. Tastes had changed since the early eighteenth century, when Benoît de Maillet had recommended taking Pompey's Pillar, not an obelisk, to Paris. Trying to curry favor with Louis XVIII, Drovetti persuaded Muhammad Ali to present one of the Alexandrian obelisks to France. Champollion promoted a swap for a better-preserved obelisk from the Temple of Luxor, and the shaft finally went up in Paris in the place de la Concorde in 1836. The British government refused to pay for shipping the obelisk that Muhammad Ali had promised them, but in 1877 philanthropist Erasmus Wilson finally put up the money to transport it and erect it by the Thames at the Embankment.[92]

In 1841, American consul Gliddon, a member of Cairo's Egyptian Society, published *An Appeal to the Antiquaries of Europe on the Destruction of the Monuments of Egypt*. Why not erect a limestone wall at each site, he asked sarcastically, "especially for the accommodation of Anglo-Indian passengers, whereon each traveller may be able to cut his Name"? Or perhaps tourists bored by the antiquities they visited could pass their time noting for publication the names of vandals who had chiseled their names on decorated walls.[93]

Gliddon charged Mimaut with taking the tablet of Abydos, not out of antiquarian interest, but for "solid cash." He blamed Drovetti and Salt for quarreling "over a granite Sphinx, not as to which Pharaoh it had belonged, but as to what *price* its sale would bring in Europe."[94] Gliddon had second thoughts about the acerbity of his attacks, however, and he praised Champollion for delivering antiquities "out of the house of bondage" to the safety of European museums and added a footnote calling Salt "a gentleman and a scholar." Gliddon denounced the antiquities decree of 1835 as insincere, a "new act of Monopoly" that interfered with free trade under the pretense of civilization and establishing a museum in Egypt! He urged that an Ottoman *firman* (special decree) make the consuls "Conservators of Monuments" and order Egyptians to obey them with regard to preserving antiquities.[95] Gliddon popularized ancient Egypt in the United States in the 1840s, propagating pernicious views that ancient Egyptians owed their creativity to being Caucasians rather than African blacks.[96]

In 1842 Muhammad Ali told Lepsius that the museum in Cairo had failed, pleading that modern Egypt had only the rudiments of "civilization." Wilkinson's appraisal was bleak:

> The formation of a museum in Egypt is purely Utopian; and while the impediments raised against the removal of antiquities from Egypt does an injury to the world, Egypt is not a gainer. The excavations are made without knowledge or energy, the Pasha is cheated by those who work, and no one there takes any interest in a museum. . . . after all the vexatious impediments thrown in the way of Europeans, no such institution will ever be formed by the Pasha of Egypt.[97]

A few years later, in A.H. 1265 / 1848–1849, Linant de Bellefonds received an Egyptian government order to inventory the country's antiquities sites and to ship to the Cairo museum pieces in danger of being carried off by tourists or dealers. His efforts, however, came to nothing.

The viceroy's son Ibrahim Pasha engaged a Turk to dig at Luxor and drive off other excavators. Wilkinson dismissed the resulting collection in a palace of Ibrahim's: "a confused mass of broken mummies and cases, some imperfect tablets, and various fragments."

After Muhammad Ali, Abbas I paid sporadic attention to antiquities, ordering two engineers to inspect Upper Egypt and the director of education to report on sites near Cairo.[98] According to Gaston Maspero, Abbas moved the Ezbekiyeh collection to the citadel in 1851,[99] but another source asserts that in October 1849 Abbas ordered the School of Languages transferred to Nasriyya (Sayyida Zaynab). For want of space there, the antiquities were moved to the School of Engineering in Bulaq. In any case, Abbas drew on the collection for a gift to Sultan Abdulaziz, and Said presented the remainder to Archduke Maximilian of Austria in 1855. That the Ottoman governor of Egypt would judge Egyptian antiquities an appropriate gift for the sultan in Istanbul was new indeed. In Istanbul too, authorities were beginning to pay attention to antiquities, museums, and the heritage they represented. Maximilian's share of the collection rests today in Vienna's Kunsthistorischen Museum.

ARMENIAN MEDIATIONS:
YUSUF OR JOSEPH HEKEKYAN?

Like al-Tahtawi, Yusuf (Joseph) Hekekyan (1807–1875) studied in Europe, came to appreciate antiquities, and learned languages essential for mediating between Europe and Egypt. Among other things, al-Tahtawi, an Egyptian-born Muslim, used his intermediary position to interest his countrymen in ancient Egypt. In contrast, Hekekyan was an Istanbul-born Armenian Catholic whose education in England alienated him from his adopted Egyptian homeland. After Abbas I forced him out of government service, Hekekyan excavated under British auspices, assisted European visitors to Egypt, and wrote extensively on the problem—pressing to Westerners—of reconciling biblical and pharaonic chronologies. "Joseph" won out over "Yusuf" in Hekekyan's identity, and his papers fittingly rest not in Cairo but in the British Library.

Hekekyan was one of a small group of Armenian intermediaries who held high posts in nineteenth-century Egypt. Numbering something over two thousand in 1840, Armenians were split into adherents of the Gregorian and the Armenian Catholic Church. Muhammad Ali brought Hekekyan's father, an Armenian Catholic, from Istanbul as a translator early in his reign. Another Armenian immigrant translator from Istanbul, Bughus Yusufyan, acted as Muhammad Ali's minister of commerce and foreign affairs, and two more Armenians followed him as such in the 1840s. Shallow Egyptian roots and mastery of Turkish and European languages commended these Armenians to the ruler. Bughus Yusufyan chose four Armenians for inclusion in the educational mission al-Tahtawi escorted to Paris in 1826. Future prime minister Nubar Pasha was one of six Armenians in the 1844 educational mission to France.[100]

When his father left for Cairo, Yusuf Hekekyan stayed behind in Istanbul until Muhammad Ali agreed to sponsor his schooling in England. Ten-year-old Yusuf arrived in England in 1817 to the news that his father was dead. Samuel Briggs, formerly a merchant and acting consul in Alexandria, oversaw the boy's seven years of formal schooling (English, Greek, and Latin) and five-year apprenticeship in civil engineering. Imbibing the utilitarian gospel of industrial progress and free trade, Hekekyan inspected canals and locks, visited cotton mills in Manchester and Glasgow, and witnessed the birth of the railroad age.[101] In his journal, he poured out prescriptions for an Egypt he had yet to see:

> I think the establishment of small steamers on the Nile and open carriages on the roads between Cairo and Alexandria would be a good speculation.

Railroads must be established for the quick conveyance of troops and stores. . . . Telegraphs or contrivances similar to those which are used between London and Portsmouth should be erected between Alexandria and Cairo. The towns should be supplied with water by means of pipes. The prisons should be looked to. . . . [102]

By the time Muhammad Ali finally ordered him to Egypt in 1830, the young man had become more Joseph than Yusuf. He had forgotten his native Turkish and had to speak through an interpreter. He was taken aback at his "disgrace in Egypt for having presumed to wear gloves and stockings."[103] Hekekyan found it hard to conceal his English schoolboy prejudices: "Prosperity to the Greeks, confusion to the Turks; sound thrashings to the Monsieur frog-eaters—such were the toasts I brought to Egypt with me."[104]

He was a quick study, however, and soon acquired a courtier's touch. Muhammad Ali's drive to industrialize put a premium on expertise in engineering, and Hekekyan plunged into inspecting factories, prospecting for minerals, designing buildings, and directing the School of Engineering. He added Turkish, Arabic, and Persian to his English, French, Latin, and Greek, and went on to Italian, Armenian, and German. He kept his diaries mainly in English or French but sometimes switched to another language for practice. He wrote his wife in Italian. It was his English that made him most valuable at the Turkish-speaking court,[105] for Muhammad Ali's interpreter and effective foreign minister Bughus Bey Yusufyan (d. 1844) and his understudy, Artin Bey Chrakian, knew French and Turkish but not English.[106] Hekekyan translated English correspondence into French, which Yusufyan or Artin put into Turkish for Muhammad Ali.

Hekekyan's engineering training had not taught him reverence for antiquities. Before reaching Egypt, he had proposed:

If the Pyramids in the neighbourhood of Cairo are composed of an entire mass of squared granite and other stones, it would be well to pull down some of them and use the [blocks?] in the construction of Bridges and other public buildings. One or two should be preserved for ever. . . . The sides of the Pyramids being inclined planes, the largest stones, beginning from the summit might be easily let down by chains and pullies. A rail road or a stone tram way might be laid from the foot of the Pyramid to [the] Nile at Cairo with an inclination of a quarter of an inch in a yard. . . . As to anything being said against pulling down a pyramid, it ought to be treated with contempt. I could spare statues, columns, temples, and the "marbles.". . . [107]

In 1836, when Muhammad Ali did consider quarrying the Pyramids to build the Nile barrage, Mimaut went public with an appeal:

You have made a glorious name for yourself by your works and the great things you have undertaken. . . . public opinion, which has great power in civilized countries, would rise up against this act of vandalism.

The Pyramids are regarded in Europe as the most venerable monument of the ancient human race. They were in antiquity one of the seven wonders of the world. . . . These monuments are interesting for all peoples. They are above all such for the French since the immortal words of Napoleon, before the battle which bears their name: Remember that from the heights of the Pyramids, forty centuries are looking down on you. . . . The great Pyramids are a trust which the ancient world has left on the soil of Egypt. The masters of the country must succeed in transmitting it intact to posterity, after their brief moments of passage on the earth.[108]

Influenced by Europeans after arriving in Egypt, Hekekyan reversed himself and became an ardent advocate of conserving antiquities. He was a founding member of the Egyptian Society. Traveling throughout the land on business, he tirelessly sketched temples, reliefs, and hieroglyphics. Egyptologists still consult his papers. At Kom Ombo he waxed romantic:

As our boat glided past these proud walls I could not but give free vent to my feelings in beholding the standing witness of our being unworthy strangers in possession of the soil in which they stand. If we were solicitous to preserve Egypt we should not neglect the monuments raised by our predecessors. . . . The only interest we take in the ruins of antiquity is in their capacity of production in saltpeter.[109]

At Edfu, he lamented the "accumulated dust and filth of its modern inhabitants. They have been suffered to build their miserable huts on its spacious roofs. An European government would clear the mountain of dust away—restore the building. . . . "[110]

As the 1840s wore on, Hekekyan's diary reflected his mounting alienation from Egypt and his embrace of European stereotypes of Muslim fanaticism.[111] European-style freedom of worship, the abolition of slavery, and antiquities converged in his mind: "Would to God every temple could be transported to England and France by some fairy enchanter and some stringent measures taken to preserve them in Egypt. The granting of liberty of worship, [the ending of] slavery and [the conservation of] antiquities will be agitated by the three powers."[112]

His growing insecurity compounded Hekekyan's alienation from Egyptian society. Appreciating that only an Armenian could read another's correspondence in that language, Muhammad Ali fostered rivalries among the Armenians at court.[113] Hekekyan's marriage to Artin Bey Chrakian's sister Banuma Nekava was an asset at first, but after the

accession of Abbas, Hekekyan began to fear that future prime minister
Nubar, the nephew of Bughus Yusufyan, was intriguing against him.[114]
Artin warned his brother-in-law Hekekyan to exercise extreme caution.
Artin and his brother Khusrev, wrote Hekekyan, could rely on French
and Ottoman protection. But in 1850 Artin fled to Istanbul amid charges
of corruption, leaving behind Hekekyan, unprotected and terrified.
Under Abbas, Hekekyan wrote in panic, people of both sexes simply dis-
appeared.[115]

Hekekyan begged Consul General Murray and Anthony Harris—
colleagues in the Egyptian Society—and his old mentor Briggs for British
protection. It was arranged for Leonard Horner of London's Royal Geological Society to hire Hekekyan to excavate at Heliopolis, thus turning him into a British protégé. Murray had leverage with Abbas, who
authorized the British project for an Alexandria-Cairo railway as a partial alternative to the French scheme for a Suez Canal. Abbas went so
far as to subsidize Hekekyan's archaeological excavations, supplying
him with an engineer, corvée labor, and tools. But Hekekyan was too
shrewd to let down his guard. He reported that a palace official "did
not hide from me that there reigned a general impression that the researches at Heliopolis were for gold, and asked me what I would do with
the treasures I might find. I replied that I would send them all to the
Viceroy's treasury."[116]

Hekekyan began digging at Heliopolis in June 1851[117] and later dug
for Horner at Memphis in 1852–1854. Hekekyan's geological training
enabled him to conduct the first recorded stratigraphical excavations in
Egypt. This was far in advance of Mariette, who merely kept a list of
finds.[118] Horner believed that the annual rate of accumulation of Nile
silt on Egyptian monuments could settle disputes between biblical literalists and proponents of the higher criticism over chronology. The
Twelfth Dynasty Heliopolis obelisk of Senusret I and the Nineteenth
Dynasty Memphis colossus of Rameses II seemed good places to start.
Horner's published results outraged biblical literalists, who fixed creation at 4004 B.C.E. He dated prehistoric artifacts in Hekekyan's Memphis borings at 11,500 B.C.E.

Hekekyan quit digging in 1854, went into gentlemanly retirement,
and introduced a stream of European visitors to Egypt. He made voluminous chronological calculations on Nile flood data, the Bible, and
Manetho, succumbing to fantastic theories of mystical wisdom encoded
in the monuments. His magnum opus on the subject was privately

printed in London in 1863 as *A Treatise on the Chronology of Siriadic Monuments.*

Hekekyan's reputation suffered posthumously, partly because he did not fit into later nationalist and archaeological pigeonholes. He began life as an Ottoman at a time when Egypt was distancing itself from Istanbul. His British formation alienated him from his adopted Egyptian home, excluding him from later Egyptian nationalist historiography. He was a British protégé but not a citizen, a Catholic rather than a member of the Armenian Gregorian Church. In Egyptology, his drawings of monuments and his stratigraphical excavations retain value, but, like Piazzi Smith, his mystical bent put him beyond the pale of the emerging discipline. His papers in the British Library remain underexplored.

By the time Hekekyan began digging at mid-century, the French, British, and Germans had made archaeological reconnaissances, founded great Egyptian collections, deepened knowledge of hieroglyphics, and vindicated Manetho's dynastic framework. Muhammad Ali viewed antiquities primarily as bargaining chips, but al-Tahtawi helped him to take the first hesitant steps toward protecting the pharaonic heritage. The stage was set for Mariette, who would refound the Antiquities Service and museum on solid foundations, and for al-Tahtawi to renew his campaign to persuade Egyptians to embrace their pharaonic heritage. Between 1850 and 1882, these developments unfolded against the darkening storm clouds of Western imperialism. In 1849, Hekekyan, who had succumbed to European stereotypes, warned:

> Egypt is destined not to remain much longer immersed in the shadows of ignorance, overwhelmed by the weight of relative barbarism. The country which in ancient times passed to Europe the sacred fire of science and civilization will without disgrace be able to come to re-ignite its torch in Europe. European civilization and power press upon us from all sides; sooner or later it will be necessary to open our barriers to them, or they will force the barriers open.[119]

CHAPTER 2

From Explorer
to Cook's Tourist

At the turn of the twentieth century, an Egyptian in Muhammad al-Muwaylihi's fictional *Period of Time* comments on Europeans encountered in a Cairo nightclub:

> They're tourists from Western countries. . . . They're used to civilized living and regard Oriental people with utter contempt. . . . They posture and show off, and keep bringing in innovations. Their activities are evil and their knowledge is pernicious. They're the people who rob others of their wages. . . .
>
> When they travel to the East, they can be divided into two categories. The first consists of the leisure classes with modern ideas who are besotted by their own wealth and amused by novelties of civilization. As far as they're concerned, there's nothing left to do. . . . They're beset by the twin diseases of listlessness and boredom. They wander around on their own from one area and country to another. . . .
>
> The second group consists of scholars, politicians, imperialists and spies, who use their knowledge and ideas to occupy and control countries . . . and crowd folk out of their land and homes. They're the precursors of destruction, even more deadly to people at peace than the vanguards of armies in wartime.[1]

Al-Muwaylihi's Western tourists with nothing left to do but wander around are the subject of this chapter. Unlike the rest of the book, the chapter tells only half the story of this Western-Egyptian encounter, seeing it mainly through Western eyes. The quotation suggests that a history of Western tourism through Egyptian eyes may be possible, but it is beyond the reach of this book. Exploratory studies are largely lacking,

64

and primary sources for nineteenth-century Egyptian views are likely to be thin. Many Egyptians involved in the growing tourist industry were illiterate, and most Egyptian authors of the day wrote of other things.

In contrast, Western sources on travel and tourism in Egypt abound. The industrial revolution accorded a burgeoning proportion of Westerners the means and leisure to travel, and the steamship and railroad shrank the globe. Egypt, imagined as antique and exotic, the land of the pharaohs, the Bible, Herodotus, and the *Arabian Nights,* lured more and more tourists east. In recent years, nostalgia for a belle époque of Egyptian travel before 1914 has called forth a rush of books ranging from coffee-table picture books to serious studies. This chapter draws on these and the primary sources behind them to show how modern tourism, museums, and archaeology grew up together in Egypt.[2] Archaeologists wrote guidebooks and chapters in guidebooks, founded museums at home and in Egypt with tourists in mind, organized Egyptian displays at international exhibitions, and regaled readers with tales of adventure and discovery. Many of the Western consumers of these products of archaeology became tourists, and a few tourists even went on to become archaeologists.

EXPLORER, TRAVELER, AND TOURIST

You see the back of a native turban, long blue gown,
red girdle, bare brown legs; "How truly oriental!" you
say. Then he turns around, and you see "Cook's Porter"
emblazoned across his breast. "You travel Cook, sir,"
he grins; "all right." And it is all right. . . . Cook's representative is the first person you meet in Egypt, and you
go on meeting him. He sees you in; he sees you
through; he sees you out. . . .

> G. W. Steevens, as quoted in John Pudney,
> *The Thomas Cook Story*

The steamship and the railroad took off in the 1830s, underpinning a revolution in travel that shifted Egypt, the Levant, and much of the world beyond Europe out of the realm of the explorer or adventurous traveler and into that of the ordinary tourist.

In the 1700s, Dr. Samuel Johnson had confessed that "a man who has not been to Italy is always conscious of an inferiority, from his not having seen what it is expected that a man should see."[3] In the following century, Thomas Cook and his son, John, did more than anyone else to add the Pyramids to the list of "what it is expected" that a man (and, increasingly, a woman) should see. To the dismay of old elites, Thomas Cook and Son also extended the range of such expectations considerably down the social scale.

James Buzard argues that modern tourism and the impulse to disown it belong to a single field of discourse that emerged in northern Europe and the United States with the industrial and democratic revolutions. Travelers bent over backward to set themselves apart from tourists—to be more sensitive, leisurely, and contemplative. The traveler / tourist divide is steeped in assumptions of class distinction, aesthetic sensibility, and sometimes intellectual superiority. "The tourist is the other fellow," said Evelyn Waugh, and Paul Fussell lamented, "We are all tourists now and there is no escape."[4]

To eighteenth-century Europeans, Cairo and Alexandria already belonged not to the explorer—who reveals unknown lands—but to the adventurous traveler. Accounts of Alexandria, Cairo, and the Pyramids were plentiful. In the wake of Bonaparte's Egyptian expedition, Muhammad Ali's establishment of a strong central government added Upper Egypt as far as Aswan to the realm of the traveler and, before long, of the ordinary tourist.

South of Aswan, John Lewis Burckhardt, who had already discovered (from a Western viewpoint) the Nabataean city of Petra, explored Nubia nearly to the Third Cataract in 1813. He was the first Westerner to report on Rameses II's rock-hewn temple at Abu Simbel. In 1820, Muhammad Ali's conquest of the northern Sudan made Nubia below the Second Cataract—the present-day Egyptian-Sudanese border—more accessible to travelers. Rifaud's pioneering Egyptian guidebook of 1830 included lower Nubia,[5] and Wadi Halfa near the foot of the Second Cataract soon became the accepted "boundary where travelers not animated by a passion for rugged exploration and dangerous discoveries ordinarily stop."[6]

STEAMSHIP, RAILROAD, AND TRAVEL TIME

The term "tourist" first appeared in English in 1780. By the time "tourism" joined it in 1811, the Napoleonic Wars had bottled most Britons up on their islands. An adventuresome few, like Lord Byron, took advantage of Britain's naval preeminence to substitute Greece and the Balkans for the traditional grand tour in France and Italy.[7] "Touriste" cropped up in

French in 1816, just as a post-Napoleonic wave of British tourists was washing over the Continent. *"Tourisme"* followed in 1841, the year that Thomas Cook organized his first excursion in the English Midlands.

Regular passenger steamer service began on the Dover-Calais run in 1821, the Rhine in 1828, and the Rhône and Danube in the 1830s.[8] Railroad mania swept western Europe and the United States in the 1830s, the decade that also saw the birth of the railway timetable, the modern guidebook, and the electric telegraph. A steadily expanding group of middle-class travelers began transforming elite travel into mass tourism. "Wherever the steamboat touches the shore adventure retreats into the interior, and what is called romance vanishes," remarked Thackeray, "but this is a small price to pay for the spread of civilisation."[9]

In 1802–1803, it took Henry Salt six months to reach Calcutta from London around the Cape of Good Hope. No wonder the British East India Company wanted to develop overland passenger and mail transit through Egypt, cutting 41 percent off the 10,700-mile London-Bombay trip around the Cape. Even in the Mediterranean, it took al-Tahtawi a month to reach Marseilles by sail from Alexandria in 1825, after which he had to endure another eighteen days in quarantine. Bad weather stretched Wilkinson's Alexandria-Malta transit to over a month in 1833.[10]

The steamer changed all that. In 1837 the Peninsular and Oriental Company (P&O) won a contract to carry British mail via Gibraltar and Malta to Alexandria, and in 1842 it obtained a royal charter to carry official mail through to India on its Suez-Bombay steamer. The P&O's luxurious ships added "posh" (*p*ort *o*utbound, *s*tarboard *h*ome—i.e., cabins on the shady side of the ship) to the language. In 1843, P&O steamers out of Southampton reached Alexandria in fifteen days. A shortcut across France to the Marseilles-Alexandria steamer of the Messageries Maritimes shaved three or four days off that.[11]

Thomas Waghorn organized a five-day overland transit from Alexandria to Suez, making it possible to reach Bombay forty-one or forty-two days out from London. The number of transit customers through Egypt leaped from 275 in 1844 to 3,000 in 1847.

What was the wonder of Napoleon, demanded Thackeray from his Cairo hotel,

> compared to Waghorn? Nap massacred the Mamelukes at the Pyramids: Wag has conquered the Pyramids themselves; dragged the unwieldy structures a month nearer England than they were, and brought the country along with them.

Lt. Waghorn is bouncing in and out of the court-yard, full of business. He left Bombay yesterday morning, was seen in the Red Sea on Tuesday, is engaged to dinner this afternoon in Regent's Park and (as it is about two minutes since I saw him in the court-yard) I make no doubt he is by this time in Alexandria or Malta, say, perhaps, both.[12]

A bust in the city of Suez later honored this wizard of speed.[13]

In 1834, Britons proposed a Cairo-Suez railway to speed overland transit. Muhammad Ali said no, but his son Abbas I (r. 1848–1854) awarded George Stephenson, son of railway pioneer Robert Stephenson, a concession for an Alexandria-Cairo line. The Cairo-Suez rail link followed in 1858. By 1873, express trains had cut the four-day Alexandria-Cairo journey to four and a half hours.[14] Additional railways unrelated to Indian transit fanned out through the delta and upriver to extract cotton for export. The electric telegraph network accompanied the railroads.[15]

Ferdinand de Lesseps had befriended Prince Said as a boy, and the latter's accession to the throne opened the door to the concession to build the Suez Canal. Overcoming British and Ottoman resistance, de Lesseps's Suez Canal Company began digging in 1859. Ten years later, the opening of the canal put Egypt at the choke point of European-Asian trade. Railroad transit of Egypt instantly became obsolete, and guidebooks grew more specialized, no longer lumping Egypt and India together as a single excursion.[16]

Wilkinson's guidebook of 1847 prescribed a minimum of three months for an Egyptian excursion. A Cairo-Luxor round trip on the river averaged twenty days, with fourteen more to include the Second Cataract. Three months in Egypt cost the single traveler £80, or £60 apiece for two. By 1880, one could rush from London to the Second Cataract and back in six weeks, although Murray's guide recommended two and a half to five months.[17]

MONEY, LEISURE, AND SOCIAL CLASS

The grand tour had bound together eighteenth-century English gentlemen—who fancied themselves in an Augustan age—with a shared adventure in French manners, Italian painting, and Roman antiquities.[18] Over the course of the nineteenth century, a growing segment of middle-class beneficiaries of the industrial revolution joined the upper class in traveling for pleasure or cultural improvement. Thomas Cook, the apostle of industrialized tourism, fittingly sprang from the mine, factory, and railroad country of the Midlands and worked tirelessly to extend the benefits of travel down the social scale. American clergymen, teachers, writers, and artists joined Britons in touring the Continent. After the Civil War, Americans found it easier to embrace travel as pleasure-seeking consumption. Study, writing, or painting could help exorcise Puritan fears of self-indulgence.[19]

P&O fares encoded gender, class, and racial / national hierarchies. In 1847 the England-to-Aden fare for a gentleman was £77; a lady, £82; a European maidservant, £37; a European manservant, £35; a "native" maidservant, £30; and a "native" manservant, £26. Women must have seemed more expensive, delicate, or deserving of luxury than men, and even among servants, fare distinctions kept "natives" in their place. By 1858, second-class Southampton-Alexandria fares accommodated frugal travelers, who paid more than servants. By 1880, second-class and servant fares were the same, and the 1895 Baedeker no longer mentioned fares for servants.[20] Fare distinctions between the sexes had also disappeared.

Overcoming upper-class fears of rowdiness, Thomas Cook transported frugal, self-improving parties of the working class to London's Great Exhibition in 1851. Two years after the 1867 Reform Bill had enlarged manhood suffrage, Cook led his first group of middle-class tourists as far as Egypt. Not even Cook, however, could bring overseas travel within the means of the lower and lower-middle classes, except for their members who traveled as servants, soldiers, or sailors.[21]

THE BIRTH OF THE MODERN GUIDEBOOK: MURRAY, BAEDEKER, AND JOANNE

With speedy, dependable, and cheaper land and sea transport facilitating travel, three young entrepreneurs married practical advice to concise factual coverage in the 1830s and 1840s to invent the modern guidebook. John Murray III (1808–1892) and Karl Baedeker (1801– 1859) inherited publishing-bookselling firms, and Adolphe Joanne (1813–1881) began as a lawyer and journalist. The venerable genre of the travelogue had often played up the author's courage, physical prowess, knowledge, and sensitivity, inviting readers to vicarious adventure from the safety of home. Some travelogues reflected their authors' inward journeys; others reported factually on such matters as climate, terrain, flora, fauna, peoples, languages, foods, architecture, and monuments.[22]

In contrast with travelogues, modern guidebooks usually subordinated the author's voice to that of an impersonal editor. Actually intending to travel, readers of guidebooks craved reassuring tips on prices, exchange rates, routes, transport, lodging, food, health, useful phrases, and souvenirs. Guidebooks ranked sights in order of priority and provided a welter of objective-sounding facts. Compact enough to carry in the hand (handbooks) or pocket *(livres de poche),* guidebooks were meant for on-the-spot consultation.

As table 6 shows (see the appendix), the first modern guidebooks to Egypt came out in the 1830s—the first in 1830, the second in 1835. Five more guidebook editions followed in the 1840s and six in the 1850s. Only one guidebook was published in 1882, the disturbed year of the Urabi revolution and the British conquest. Appropriately a product of a ministry of war, it was ironically a French, not an English, production. Only four guidebook editions came out in the remainder of the 1880s, a reflection of the uncertainties of the early British occupation and the Mahdist challenge in the Sudan. The ensuing late-Victorian and Edwardian golden age overflowed with eighty-two editions of Egyptian guidebooks between 1890 and 1914.

J. J. Rifaud (1786–1852) was first in the field with his *Tableau de l'Égypte, de la Nubie et des lieux circonvoisin* (Paris, 1830). Born in Marseilles, he studied sculpture and served with Napoleon's army in Spain before coming to Egypt in 1812 for fourteen years and assisting Drovetti in collecting antiquities. Eschewing scientific and literary pretensions, Rifaud's *Tableau* guided travelers from Alexandria to Cairo, to the pyramids ranging between Giza and the Fayum, and upriver to Thebes, Aswan, and the Second Cataract. Optional side trips brought in the Delta, Red Sea, and Sinai, and special chapters covered geography, the people, and their customs.[23] The appendixes included a forty-page vocabulary of Upper Egyptian Arabic and a seven-page one of Nubian. Rifaud's guide was a rough first attempt in a genre not yet perfected. The *Tableau* lacked maps, gave only superficial information on antiquities, and did not mention Champollion's decipherment of hieroglyphics. And what was the ordinary tourist to make of the list of the names of 353 islands of the Second Cataract?

Gardner Wilkinson met the French challenge with his far more scholarly *Topography of Thebes, and General View of Egypt* (1835). Wilkinson had signed its preface at Thebes in 1831; one wonders how potential tourists reacted to his apology that cholera and the death of his intended publisher at Alexandria had long delayed the publication of the work!

The delay proved to be a boon, enabling Wilkinson to find the ideal publisher in John Murray. John Murray II was still in charge, but John

Murray III (1808–1892) was already busy developing the famous Murray guides. Perceiving that Britons flocking to the Continent after Waterloo craved practical guidance, the younger Murray wrote the *Handbook for Travellers in Holland, Belgium, Prussia, and Northern Germany, & on the Rhine from Holland to Switzerland* (1836). This volume introduced the cognate of the German *"handbuch"* into English. Murray's organization by itinerary rather than by alphabetical order proved popular.[24] Other Murray handbooks followed. Wilkinson was one of three fellow members of the Royal Geographical Society whom Murray recruited as authors for the series.

Wilkinson's *Topography of Thebes, and General View of Egypt* preceded Murray's first European handbook. *Topography* plunged straight into nearly two hundred pages on ancient Thebes before pausing for sixty pages entitled "The Manners and Customs of the Ancient Egyptians" and twenty-five entitled "Productions of Modern Egypt." Only then did Wilkinson jump to Alexandria, the normal point of entry from Europe, and work his way up the Nile to Aswan, skipping already-treated Thebes. Alexandria received a mere five pages, Cairo only eighteen, and the pyramids of Giza twelve.

Wilkinson's first edition already had features that would become standbys of Egyptian guidebooks: an English-Arabic vocabulary, a section on hieroglyphics, a list of pharaohs' cartouches, and a chronology of rulers down to the Ottoman conquest. His next edition added Ottoman governors and the Muhammad Ali family to the present.

Wilkinson's second edition (1843), though not yet part of the Murray handbook series, moved closer to the emerging Murray format. The title became *Modern Egypt and Thebes,* the itinerary began with 85 pages on Alexandria, and greater Cairo received 185 pages. The 1847 edition, the first in the Murray handbook series, was called *Hand-book for Travellers in Egypt.* In the third edition in the handbook series (1867), Murray's name replaced Wilkinson's on the title page. Wilkinson / Murray was already in its fourth edition (the second in the handbook series) in 1858, when Murray's first guide to Syria and Palestine came out. Thomas Cook spoke of pilgrims touring the Holy Land "with the Bible in one hand and Murray in the other."[25]

In France, Joanne's first guidebook of 1841 covered the Alps. It followed Murray in arranging by itineraries.[26] Joanne's guides to other regions of France followed, and in the 1850s Joanne branched out with French-language guides to Britain, Germany, and Spain. The Orient, including Egypt, came next, in 1861,[27] and Greece followed in 1888–1891.

Like W. H. Smith in England, Joanne's publisher, Louis Hachette, developed a new market with newsstand-bookstores in railway stations. Distinctive red covers marked out Murray and Baedeker tourists from afar, and Joanne tourists could be spotted by the covers that later marked out the famous "blue guides."

Joanne's first guide to the Orient (1861) roamed Egypt and Sinai, Malta, Greece, "Turkey in Europe," "Turkey in Asia," Syria, Palestine, and "Arabia Pétrée." Egypt received two hundred pages out of eleven hundred. After preliminary essays, Joanne took the beaten path from Alexandria to Cairo and up the Nile to the Second Cataract, interspersing side trips along the way. Catering to French readers, he gave a full page each to the battle of Abu Qir (Nelson over the French fleet) and the battle of the pyramids (Bonaparte over the Mamluks). He noted the site of the house where Bonaparte had lodged in Ezbekiyeh and the spot of Kléber's assassination and described at length Mariette's recent discovery of the Serapeum.[28]

In Germany, Karl Baedeker established his publishing firm in 1827 on the Rhine at Koblenz, a stop on the Köln-Mainz passenger steamer inaugurated that year.[29] Inspired like Joanne by Murray, Baedeker brought out his first guide, on Germany and Austria, in 1842. The first Egyptian Baedeker, in German, came out in 1877 and an English edition in 1878.

Being a travel, not a publishing, firm, Cook at first sold its clients guides by Murray or Murray's short-lived rival Henry Gaze. In 1876, however, the company published its own *Cook's Tourist Handbook for Egypt, the Nile and the Desert*. Ten years later Cook commissioned a guide from British Museum Egyptologist Ernest A. W. Budge,[30] which by 1912 had reached its twelfth edition.

Rifaud's amateurish guide had reflected the heyday of the consul-collectors, whereas Wilkinson's came from the hand of a premier Egyptologist. Other Egyptologists followed Wilkinson's example; Mariette wrote a guide for guests at the Suez Canal festivities, and Budge wrote for Cook. In an age of triumphant science, Baedeker obtained chapters from first-rate specialists: naturalist Georg Schweinfurth, Capt. H. G. Lyons of the Geological and Cadastral surveys of Egypt, Islamic architecture expert Julius Franz, Orientalist Carl Becker, and Egyptologists Samuel Birch, Georg Ebers, and Georg Steindorff.

Given Western preponderance in power and new knowledge, the absence of nineteenth-century Arabic guidebooks to Europe is not surprising. There were travelogues, such as al-Tahtawi's, which reported on society and customs, but these were not guidebooks. Egyptians became dependent on Western guidebooks, not only for Europe, but even for their own country. Marcus Simaika, the founder of the Coptic Museum, learned about the antiquities of Egypt from Murray and Baedeker, and it was a Cook's tour of Upper Egypt that introduced Coptic writer Salama Musa to the pharaonic history of his own land.[31]

HOTELS IN CAIRO AND ALEXANDRIA

Until the 1830s, European travelers unable to lodge with their consul or a resident merchant compatriot had had to resort to a hostel or an indifferent inn. Thereafter, substantial European-run hotels sprang up to provide comfortable public accommodations. Britons arriving in Alexandria in 1843 took room and board at Hill's (later Rey's) Hôtel de l'Europe at forty piastres a day; and Frenchmen patronized Coulomb's Hôtel de l'Orient. The Hôtel de l'Europe was still Murray's first choice in 1880, with the Hotel Abbat in second place.[32]

In Cairo in 1830, Rifaud's guide steered travelers to the Frankish quarter along al-Muski Street, where the hostels of the Catholic Fathers of the Propaganda and Fathers of the Terre Sainte offered room and board at seven to eight piastres a day. A European-run inn nearby charged twelve piastres. By 1843 the new Hôtel de l'Orient in spacious Ezbekiyeh had succeeded Hill's in the Frankish quarter for overland Indian transit; room and board cost fifty piastres. By 1846 patrons were calling the hotel Shepheard's after the English entrepreneur who took it over.[33]

Frenchmen and Italians frequented Doumergue's more basic Giardino (or Giardano) Hotel in the Frankish quarter at thirty piastres.[34] In 1858 and again in 1880, Murray praised Shepheard's, Williams's, and the Hôtel de l'Orient—all in Ezbekiyeh (see figure 16). Britons and Americans flocked to Shepheard's; the French, to Coulomb's Hôtel de l'Orient. Expanded to 350 rooms, Shepheard's still topped the list in the 1908 Baedeker. Those indifferent to the Ezbekiyeh social whirl could try the Gezira Palace Hotel, on an island in the Nile, or the Mena House, at the Pyramids, which first appeared in a guide of 1889. The 1908 Baedeker also listed the new three-hundred-room Semiramis, on the Nile near the British Residency.[35]

Figure 16.   Tourists on the porch of Shepheard's Hotel, Cairo. Photographer
unknown, n.d. In Deborah Bull and Donald Lorimer, *Up the Nile: A
Photographic Excursion: Egypt 1839–1898* (New York, 1979), 17. Courtesy
of the Department of Egyptian and Classical Art, Brooklyn Museum of Art.

FIRMANS AND DRESS, FLAGS AND FIREARMS

The guidebooks document radical changes between the 1820s and the
1850s with regard to *firman*s (official permits) and the dress, flags,
and firearms of Western travelers. In 1830 Rifaud prescribed, upon
arrival, an immediate meeting with one's consul. The consul would
arrange an audience with Muhammad Ali to obtain a *firman* authorizing travel and perhaps excavation. By 1847, the audience and the *firman* had been discontinued. As late as 1908, Baedeker reported: "Pass-
ports are not absolutely necessary; and one's visiting-card practically
serves all its functions in the interior."[36] World War I soon put an end
to that.

Well into the 1800s, Europeans routinely donned local dress to min-
imize unwanted attention, suspicion, and possible hostility. Previously,
Franks had ventured out of their compounds in Western garb only in
Alexandria. Dressing as Turks elicited deference, and being taken for
Turkish provided a ready excuse for halting Arabic. Burckhardt, Belzoni,
Lane, Wilkinson, Champollion, Rosellini, and Prisse d'Avennes all

sported the turbans, loose garments, and full beards of Turks. Several of them took Arabic names as well.

Rifaud still advised local dress in 1830, but already a few years earlier Salt had rebuked Wilkinson for expecting consular protection while dressed as a Turk.[37] In 1835 Wilkinson recommended local dress in Cairo, the western oases, and Bernike on the Red Sea but judged it no longer necessary in Upper Egypt or on the overland transit. In the late 1830s, Lord Lindsay's dress proudly proclaimed the enhanced status of Europeans:

> The insults Christians were formerly subject to are now unknown. . . . travellers . . . may travel in the Frank dress with perfect safety. What would old Sandys or Lithgow have said, had any one prophesied in their days that two Britons would, in 1836, walk openly through Cairo, preceded by a native servant clearing the road before them by gentle hints indiscriminately administered to donkeys and Moslemin, to get out of the Gaiours' way?[38]

In 1847 Wilkinson declared that a person in Eastern dress "who is ignorant of the language, becomes ridiculous."[39]

In 1835 Wilkinson recommended another badge of Western status—raising one's national flag on his *dahabiyya* (houseboat) to deter harassment from soldiers on gunboats. Mendes Cohen boasted that in 1832 he was the first to fly the American flag on the Nile. The British consulate encouraged citizens to register their personal pennants so that one could spot friends' boats without the trouble of hailing.[40]

In Muhammad Ali's early years, Europeans armed themselves and hired a "Janissary" or two as bodyguards. Rifaud's advice never to travel unarmed was already obsolescent when published in 1830, for Muhammad Ali had imposed his stern order as far as Nubia. In 1843 Wilkinson made no mention of firearms for protection. In Syria and Palestine, in contrast, much later Murrays insisted that although travelers could dispense with a compass and sextant, they should go armed and escorted. In 1895 Baedeker pronounced travel in Egypt "as safe as in Europe," advising that "weapons for self-defence are an unnecessary encumbrance." Only sportsmen need carry them.[41]

"INTERCOURSE WITH ORIENTALS"

The guidebooks were full of paternalistic and often racist advice on what Baedeker called "intercourse with Orientals." Dragomen, or interpreter-guides, had peddled their services at least since Herodotus, who warned that they were devious and ignorant. In 1835 Wilkinson restricted the term "dragoman" to middlemen who could converse with the Turkish-speaking ruling elite. He judged their services unnecessary and recommended instead hiring a European servant at Malta or an Egyptian from the Frankish quarter of Cairo who could speak Italian and perhaps French. By 1873 Murray saw no need for Turkish and re-ported that for a fixed sum an English-, French-, or Italian-speaking dragoman would hire a boat and servants and arrange provisions for a Nile excursion.[42]

Several early dragomen were French or British veterans who had de-serted or been captured during the Napoleonic Wars. François-Auguste-René de Chateaubriand met "French mamluks" in Muhammad Ali's service. One was Ismayl Rechouan, formerly Pierre Gary, who showed the Comte de Forbin around in 1817. The best known such Briton was Osman Effendi, a Scottish drummer boy or medical aide captured dur-ing the British invasion of 1807, enslaved, and converted to Islam. Con-sul General Salt arranged for his manumission, but Osman had no wish to return to Scotland. He assisted Burckhardt, worked as an interpreter and guard at the British consulate, rented out houses in Cairo, and of-fered his services to Robert Hay and others.[43]

Murray warned of the clamor awaiting the tourist at the Pyramids of Giza:

> Strangers justly complain of the torment of the people of the village, who collect around them like a swarm of flies, forcing their troublesome services upon them to their great discomfort and inconvenience. It is the duty of the traveller's dragoman to prevent this; to fix upon a suitable number of guides; and to allow no others to come near him. . . . Nothing, on any account, should be given to them when in the pyramid, and all attempts at exaction should be firmly resisted.[44]

An 1870s cartoon, *Donkey Boys and Foreigners,* captures Europeans' usual perception of such encounters (see figure 17).

These interactions often carried overtones of gender. One illustration shows two tourists, a woman and a man, being carried across flooded terrain before the raised road to the Giza pyramids opened in 1869 (see figure 18). A remarkable photograph shows Victorian women in long skirts being pulled up the Great Pyramid backward by sashes tied round their waists! (See figure 19.) Western male fantasies of "Oriental" women have been much analyzed of late. The highlight of Gustave Flaubert's tour was not Karnak or the Pyramids but spending the night with dancer Kuchuk Hanum at Esna.[45]

Figure 17.   Beset by "lesser breeds"? *Donkey Boys and Foreigners,* by
C. Rudolf Huber, in G. Ebers, *Egypt: Descriptive, Historical, and Picturesque,*
vol. 2, trans. Clara Bell (London, 1878). Note the hostile portrayal of the
Egyptians.

Baedeker sternly warned against unearned *"bakshish"* while conceding childlike virtues to some "natives":

> The average Oriental regards the European traveller as a Croesus, and sometimes too as a madman,—so unintelligible to him are the objects and pleasures of travelling. Travellers are often tempted to give for the sake of affording temporary pleasure at a trifling cost, forgetting that the seeds of insatiable cupidity are thereby sown, to the infinite annoyance of their successors and the demoralisation of the recipients themselves. Bakshish should never be given except for services rendered. . . .
>
> The Egyptians, it must be remembered, occupy a much lower grade in the scale of civilisation than most of the western nations, and cupidity is one of their chief failings; but if the traveller makes due allowance for their shortcomings, and treats the natives with consistent firmness, he will find that they are by no means destitute of fidelity, honesty, and kindliness.[46]

Already in 1830 Rifaud warned against forged antiquities, blaming them on Upper Egyptian fellahin and Cairene Jews. Five years later Wilkinson reported that the price of antiquities at Qurna, opposite Luxor, had risen steeply because of the increase of foreign visitors since 1816.[47]

Figure 18. *A Trip to the Pyramids, Old Style,* in Reverend Samuel Manning,
The Land of the Pharaohs: Egypt and Sinai (London, n.d.), 48.

As the century wore on, guidebooks increasingly condemned slavery
and the *doseh,* in which a Sufi shaykh rode horseback over prone dis-
ciples. Rifaud had reported without censure that a ten-year-old "pretty
little negress" cost six hundred to eight hundred piastres in Cairo, and
a Georgian girl six thousand piastres or more. Wilkinson and Lane purchased female slaves, presenting this—unconvincingly—as a simple act
of charity. Lane eventually married the slave girl he had purchased.[48] In
1858 Murray reported that since Said had abolished the slave trade, the
Cairo slave market was no longer one of the sights.[49]

Murray declared in 1858 and again in 1880 that

> no European can witness the ceremony of the Doseh . . . without feelings of
> horror and disgust. On this occasion the shekh of the Saadeeh, mounted on
> horseback . . . goes in procession to the Uzbekeeh, where between 200 and
> 300 fanatics, having thrown themselves prostrate on the ground, closely
> wedged together, the shekh rides over their bodies . . . giving proofs of wild
> fanaticism which those who have not witnessed it cannot easily imagine.

In 1895 Baedeker noted the *doseh* as a "barbarous custom" suppressed
by Khedive Tawfiq but reported that 'Ilwaniyah Dervishes still "sometimes go through their hideous performance of chewing and swallow-
ing burning charcoal and broken glass, and their wild dances."[50]

Figure 19.   Gender and tourism at the Pyramids: "Few people visit the Pyramids without climbing up them as their energy permits. Just look at those American women on their way up, falling into the clutches of the Bedouin before your very eyes." (Character in Muhammad Muwaylihi's *A Period of Time*, trans. Roger Allen [Reading, England, 1992], 358.) Photograph courtesy of the National Anthropological Archives, Smithsonian Institution (photograph no. 94–9104). Photographer unknown.

TOURISTS AND EUROPEAN RESIDENTS:
NATIONALITY AND QUANTITY

In 1830 Rifaud lamented that Cairo offered no journals, stock ex-
changes, academies, or spectacles, and that Europeans congregated only
in two gardens, one at the French consulate and the other at the Coptic convent, where the Catholics held services. Murray agreed in 1858
that "Cairo offers scarcely any places of public resort for travellers,"[51]
but the influx of Europeans seeking their fortunes in the "Klondike on
the Nile" soon changed that. Europeans and their protégés in Alexandria increased nearly tenfold, from 4,824 in 1848 (5 percent of the population) to 42,884 in 1878 (nearly 25 percent).[52] In 1873 Murray
listed—for Cairo and Alexandria—consulates, foreign and Egyptian
post offices, telegraph offices, banks, cafes, restaurants, booksellers,
photographers, pharmacists, physicians, dentists, "general outfitters,"
"provision merchants," jewelers, and hairdressers. He also listed religious services for Roman Catholics, Anglicans, Scottish and American
Presbyterians, Lutherans, French Protestants, Greek Orthodox, Greek
Catholics, Maronites, Armenians, and Jews. In the 1840s, Wilkinson's
list of "things useful for a journey to Egypt" had included many items
unobtainable in Egypt. By 1873 everything was available in Cairo and
Alexandria, though not necessarily at a reasonable price, and by 1895
Baedeker saw no need for such a list.[53]

In 1873, Amelia Edwards estimated that of every twenty-five *dahabiyya*s
at Luxor, Englishmen occupied twelve, Americans nine, Germans two, and
Frenchmen and Belgians one each.[54] In the appendix to this book, table 7
shows a breakdown of the nationalities of authors of Egyptian travel
books, table 8 gives statistics on European nationals and protégés resident
in Egypt, and table 9 summarizes the data from tables 6 through 8. There
was almost an inverse correlation between the size of a country's resident
community in Egypt and its prominence in the tourist scene. Greeks were
invisible as tourists but had the most European residents, and Italians registered only a single guidebook but had the second largest colony. Britons,
with only the third largest number of residents, outnumbered others in
guidebooks and, until passed by Americans, in travel books.

The inverse correlation, in so far as it holds, came about because, in
rapidly industrializing Britain and then the United States, the expanding middle classes obtained the means and leisure for travel. Greece and
Italy (particularly in the south) had little modern industry; they imported
tourists and exported emigrants in search of work.

"The English are everywhere except in London," wrote Théophile Gautier in 1840, "where there are only Italians and Poles."[55] During the winter, some of his missing Englishmen were in Egypt, where British tourists long outnumbered all others. The number of American visitors may have passed the British as early as the 1880s, when the United States took a commanding lead in the number of Egyptian travel accounts published. In 1907, however, the resident American population in Egypt was still a negligible 521.

Despite the durability of Franco-Egyptian ties, Britons published far more Egyptian travel accounts and guides than the French. French travel accounts only topped British ones in the 1860s, the heyday of Napoleon III, de Lesseps, and the francophile Khedive Ismail.

After being held in check by the Civil War, Americans poured across the Atlantic as eagerly as Britons had crossed the Channel after Waterloo.[56] The number of American travel accounts of Egypt shot up, but there were hardly any pre–World War I American guidebooks to Egypt.[57] Americans must have been content with their Murrays, Cooks, and Baedekers.

Germans, like the Americans, began publishing significant numbers of Egyptian travel accounts in the 1840s. Although Germans could not keep up with the rush of post–Civil War American travel accounts, German guidebooks to Egypt reflected Germany's enhanced global stature after unification in 1871. George Steevens reported in 1898: "British and American predominate, but perhaps what strikes you most is the swarm of Germans. Ten years ago you would have said they had neither the money nor the enterprise to take them farther than Naples. Today you meet them everywhere. We had a sing-song on one of the tourist steamers coming up, and a German . . . gave up forty-five minutes of the 'Nibeleing's Ring.' "[58] Baedeker's popular English-language editions were another channel of German influence.

RECOMMENDED READING
AND "POINTS REQUIRING EXAMINATION"

Wilkinson may have overestimated most of his readers in recommending a substantial traveling library of Herodotus and other classical authors, Champollion, eighteenth- and nineteenth-century travel accounts, Lane's *Modern Egyptians,* and his own *Ancient Egyptians.* Such lists became standard in later Murrays and Baedekers.

Wilkinson also recommended taking a sextant and artificial horizon, chronometer, telescopes, siphon, barometer, thermometers, and measuring tape!⁵⁹ His prescriptions are a reminder that gentlemen amateurs outside the universities—like Lyell, Darwin, Lane, and Wilkinson himself—still conducted most research in mid-Victorian Britain. From the 1840s to the 1870s, Wilkinson / Murray listed "Certain Points Requiring Examination," a vestige of the dying genre of *ars apodemica,* or the art of travel. Its devotees had traveled more to compile facts than for prestige, profit, amusement, education, collecting, or preparing for a profession. Leopold Berchtold's *Essay to Direct and Extend the Inquiries of Patriotic Travellers* (1789), nearly the last of the genre, had posed 2,443 questions for investigation.⁶⁰

Wilkinson / Murray suggested that readers excavate Heliopolis, the Sphinx at Giza, and the Delta town of Sais and that they copy astronomical ceilings in the Valley of the Kings, all reliefs and hieroglyphs in a single tomb, a seventy-nine-column inscription at Edfu, and the kingly names and sculptures of "Upper Ethiopia." Readers were also urged to search for trilingual inscriptions on reused stones in Cairo mosques, early "Saracenic" pointed arches at Aswan, the site of the Greek colony of Naucratis, and the sites of ancient Alexandria's landmarks. These suggestions ring strangely now, because tourists and archeologists have gone their separate ways. By 1873 Murray implicitly conceded that even his pared-down list was an anachronism. He noted that "Mariette and others had already answered many of the listed questions and that all old Egyptian remains have been placed by the Khedive under the charge of M. Mariette, no private individual is allowed to dig or excavate anywhere without his permission, and the exportation of objects of antiquity from the country is strictly forbidden."⁶¹ The list had disappeared by the 1880 edition.

FROM LAND OF PESTILENCE TO HEALTH RESORT

Ailing Britons were already fleeing dank winters in hope of Mediterranean cures when Keats died in Rome in 1821. Four years later, Lane abandoned his intended career as an engraver for reasons of health and set out for Egypt. But Europeans also remembered Egypt as the land of biblical plagues. Burckhardt died in Cairo of dysentery in 1817, and Salt's wife and Wilkinson's intended publisher died of the plague. Kinglake reported in *Eothen* that nearly everyone he met in Cairo in 1835 died of the plague.⁶² Cholera carried off Samuel Shepheard's infant son and Mariette's wife.

After the plague had receded from western Europe around 1670 (for unknown reasons), lazarettos at Marseilles, Leghorn, Genoa, and Venice and land cordons on the Hapsburgs' eastern frontier were erected to block entry of a scourge still endemic in the Middle East. The transmission of the plague bacillus by the rat flea remained unknown until 1898. In 1843 Wilkinson devoted nine pages to procedures for the nineteen- to twenty-four-day quarantine at Malta for Europe-bound travelers.[63] The all-sea route from Alexandria to England had the advantage of using up most of the quarantine time in transit.

Quarantines reflected European belief, prevalent in the seventeenth century, that the plague was contagious. During the eighteenth and nineteenth centuries, anticontagionists challenged this view. Clot Bey, the French director of Muhammad Ali's medical school, injected himself with the blood of plague victims three times to prove that the disease was not contagious. In northern Europe, the commercial and industrial revolutions helped tip the balance toward the anticontagionists. Dr. John Bowring's report on Egypt and Crete in 1840 emphasized the huge costs quarantines imposed on trade and travel. Manchester-school free traders, who won repeal of the protectionist Corn and Navigation Laws in Britain in the 1840s, backed the anticontagionists, whose prescriptions included sanitary waste disposal, fresh air, adequate housing, and temperate habits.

Italians, however, knew from experience that epidemics arrived by sea and spread inland from the ports. They also had considerable capital and human investment in lazarettos. Italian doctors set up new lazarettos in Alexandria and the Levant in the 1830s. France, with both Atlantic and Mediterranean coasts, was divided over the issue. De Lesseps's grandiose dream of canals and world trade predisposed him to Clot's anticontagionist views.

In any case, the plague mysteriously vanished from Egypt after 1844. The 1847 Wilkinson / Murray still detailed the quarantine regime at Malta, but the lazarettos in Malta, Marseilles, and Italy closed soon thereafter. In 1858 Murray mentioned the plague only as a former scourge.[64]

Shortly before the plague receded, however, steamship and railroad connections catapulted cholera far beyond its home in Bengal. The expansion of irrigation in Egypt also facilitated the spread of this water-borne scourge. Pilgrims returning from Mecca in 1831 brought the pandemic of 1829–1837 to Egypt, whence it leaped on to Europe and America. Cholera struck Egypt eleven times between 1831 and 1902. Indian pilgrims brought the disease to Mecca in 1865, and pilgrims returning on the Suez-Cairo-Alexandria railroad quickly spread it through Egypt. German bacteriologist Robert Koch pursued the cholera bacillus in Egypt during the epidemic of 1883 and pinned it down in India a year later.[65]

The cholera epidemic of 1831–1832 led Muhammad Ali to have the European consuls organize a health board and a lazaretto in Alexandria under an Italian doctor. Spurred on by the epidemic of 1846–1850, European, Ottoman, and Egyptian delegates met in the first international sanitary conference in Paris in 1851. The second sanitary conference at Istanbul in 1866 followed another cholera pandemic and led to the establishment of an international quarantine regime on Egypt's Red Sea coast.[66]

Despite the periodic return of cholera, the disappearance of the plague paved the way for Egypt to project itself as a European health resort. In 1859, W. Reil published *Ägypten als Winteraufenthalt für Kranke* (Egypt as a winter resort for the sick). Lucie Duff Gordon, who arrived with tuberculosis in 1862, spread the word of Egypt's salubrious winter climate before succumbing to the disease seven years later.[67]

The 1873 Murray's recommended Egypt for "phthisical and bronchial affections, chronic diseases of the mucous membranes, congestive diseases of the abdominal viscera, nervous exhaustion, debilitated circulation from progressive disease of the heart . . . scrofulous diseases of every kind, and struma." Murray distanced Europeans from cholera, which "found a favourable nidus for propagation in the pestiferous houses of the towns and in the personal dirtiness of the fellaheen." High mortality was due to "the ignorance, superstition, and filthiness of the natives," poor medical care, and the "privations, hard work, and exposure they have to endure."[68]

By 1858 the sulfur springs of Helwan, south of Cairo, were drawing Turks and Europeans seeking cures. By the turn of the century, the Mena House at the Pyramids and hotels at Luxor and Aswan were also established health resorts with seasonally resident European physicians and nurses.[69]

UP THE NILE: *DAHABIYYA*, STEAMER, AND RAILROAD

Upper Egyptian tourism progressed through three stages in the nineteenth century, each tied to a mode of transport—the *dahabiyya,* the steamer, and the railroad. *Dahabiyya* travel was slow, expensive, and limited to the well-to-do. In 1858 a large furnished *dahabiyya* for three or four, with two or three cabins and a bath, cost £50–79 a month. A moderately large one with a crew of ten (including cook and dragoman) could take two passengers to the Second Cataract and back, all expenses included, in two months for £200. A forty-day round trip from Cairo to Luxor cost about £110; a fifty-day trip to Aswan and back, about £150. The Luxor schedule allowed ten days' stoppage for sightseeing, but contrary winds could greatly prolong the trip.[70]

Wilkinson's 1843 guide recommended a preliminary sinking of one's hired boat to rid it of "rats and other noxious inhabitants" and advised bringing an iron rat-trap. He prescribed a chicken coop and supply of biscuit, bread often being unavailable in the villages. He gave a sample contract to be drawn up at one's consulate for a *dahabiyya* tour.[71]

By 1858, the steamer was emerging as an alternative to the *dahabiyya,* but it made the twenty-day Cairo-Aswan round trip only upon sufficient demand. The total cost was £20 per person, £10 for an accompanying servant. By 1873 the steamer tour ran regularly during tourist season. Steamers had cut the time required for Upper Egyptian tours by one-half to two-thirds, freed tourism from the vagaries of the wind, and produced the precise schedules the industrial age demanded.[72]

By 1900, the railroad had sharply cut Upper Egyptian travel time and cost once more. After reaching Minya in 1867 and Asyut in 1874, the railroad stalled for nearly two decades. Its main purpose in Upper Egypt was to get sugar cane to market, but tourists could use it to board a steamer or *dahabiyya* at Asyut and disembark there for a quick return to Cairo. Horatio Herbert Kitchener's Sudanese campaign finally spurred the extension of the railroad to Aswan in 1898. From Aswan, one took the steamer to Wadi Halfa, whence Kitchener's military railroad struck out across the desert to the Nile at Abu Hammad on the way to Khartoum.[73] In 1908, the Cairo-Luxor sleeper took fourteen hours, with another six and a half to Aswan, and a Cairo-Luxor trip could be squeezed into a few days.[74] The railroad had cut Upper Egyptian steamer time by one-half to two-thirds, just as the steamers had earlier done to the *dahabiyya. Dahabiyya* tourism dwindled, and the steamer, which had catered to those hard-pressed for time and money, became a symbol of luxury and leisure compared with rail.

Meanwhile, the electric telegraph had accompanied the railroad around the world and sometimes outrun it. The first international telegraph line linked Britain to France in 1851 just in time for the Great Exhibition. The Calcutta-Bombay telegraph, opened in 1854, helped the British crush the "Mutiny" three years later, but it took forty days for news of the upheaval to reach London. A patchwork of cables tenuously linked India to London through the Ottoman Empire and Russia in 1865, a year before the laying of the first successful transatlantic cable. In the showdown at Fashoda in 1898, Kitchener's Omdurman-Cairo telegraph kept him in touch with London while Jean Baptiste Marchand was hopelessly cut off from Paris.[75]

In 1880 the standard steamer tour with a party of twenty-five to thirty, with doctor and dragoman aboard, stopped three days at Luxor and a day and a half at Aswan. In 1873 Murray weighed the luxury of a leisurely *dahabiyya* voyage against the cheaper steamer tour:

> Those who merely propose to do the country in the shortest possible time . . . may go from London to the Second Cataract and back in six weeks. . . .
>
> On a boat of your own you are your own master, and can stop or go on as you feel inclined; but on a steamer, in addition to being amongst a number of people you never saw before, you are obliged to do everything at a fixed time, and are only allowed a certain number of minutes or hours at each place of interest. The advantages of a steamer are economy of time and money. . . . But to all those who have the time to spare and the money to spend, we would say, choose the dahabeeah and avoid the steamer.

Being "jammed on a boat with a hundred Englishmen and English-women, to disembark all together at the same stops, to admire for a set number of minutes the same monuments, to always feel packed together," wrote Gabriel Charmes, "didn't tempt me for an instant."[76]

Murray's guidebooks outgrew their condescension toward the steamer. The 1908 Baedeker assumed "the ordinary traveller" would take steamboat or rail and even made the *dahabiyya* set—those travelers to whom economy of time and money is no object—seem frivolous. By then Cook had expanded into the luxury market with seven steam and thirteen sailing *dahabiyyas*. Its top-of-the-line *Nitocris* cost £400 a month for four people, double the £50 individual fare for a twenty-day Cairo-Aswan steamer round trip.[77]

Dahabiyya and steamer accommodations long delayed the demand for tourist hotels in Luxor and Aswan. Early editions of Wilkinson recommended taking bedding, a "fly-flap," and a broom to sweep out a tomb for accommodations at Giza and in the first pylon at Karnak. But already in 1836–1837 Lord Lindsay observed, "What is there to prevent our English ladies and their beaux from wintering at Thebes, as they have hitherto done at Paris and Rome? A hotel in the city of Sesostris would in that case prove a most profitable speculation."[78] In 1877 Cook made an exception to its policy of providing clients with vouchers for existing hotels and opened its own Luxor Hotel. Later the company sold it off to its manager, Pagnon, whose empire came to include the Grand Hotel and Cataract Hotel at Aswan as well as the Winter Palace at Luxor.[79]

REPORTING HOME: PAINTINGS AND TRAVELERS' TALES, PHOTOGRAPHS AND POSTCARDS

Sightseeing loses half the fun unless folks back home follow one's progress with admiration and envy. Victorian Britons reported home with letters, papers read at the Royal Geographical Society, travelogues, scholarly books, paintings, photographs, and postcards.

Romantic Orientalist dreams drew many travelers eastward. Many were fleeing industrial urban ugliness back home, but it was the very wealth and power of the industrial revolution that gave a widening segment of the middle classes the means to travel. Aristocrats searching for Bedouin "noble savages" could imagine they were traveling back in time to a society where the lower orders naturally deferred to their "betters."

Consumers of the Eastern tour retraced the real or imagined paths of literary heroes. John Murray II was the publisher of both Byron and Walter Scott, and John Murray III's guidebooks freely quoted these stirring romantics. (As Tories, however, the Murrays carefully filtered Byron's radical politics out of their guides.)[80] "Every Englishman carries a Murray for information, and a Byron for sentiment, and finds out by them what he is to know and feel at every step."[81] Shelley never got past Italy, but who could forget his Egyptian lines: "I met a traveller from an antique land" and " 'My name is Ozymandias, king of kings; / Look on my works, ye Mighty, and despair' "? Visits by Alexander Kinglake, William Thackeray, and Anthony Trollope added to the literary lore of Egyptian tours, as did those of French writers Chateaubriand, Alphonse-Marie-Louis de Lamartine, Gérard de Nerval, Flaubert, and Théophile Gautier. Herman Melville, Mark Twain, and Ralph Waldo Emerson stood out among the American writers who stretched their European tours to take in Egypt.

As the guidebook and the specialist's monograph increasingly divided between them the travelogue's former function of describing antiquities, travel literature was freed—or impelled—to reach out in new directions. Alexander Kinglake's *Eothen* (1844) broke with the tradition of descriptive travelogue: " 'I take no antiquarian interest in ruins' he stated, and no ruins appear."[82] Gérard de Nerval pioneered the hedonistic Oriental tour, lingering in Cairo and dismissing Upper Egyptian antiquities with "The customs of living towns are more absorbing to observe than the remains of dead cities."[83] Flaubert voiced the pangs of the belated traveler to his friend Gautier: "It is time to hurry. Before very long the Orient will no longer exist. We are perhaps the last of its contemplators."[84]

William Thackeray and Mark Twain skewered the prescribed awe of too-earnest pilgrims at obligatory sights. Thackeray's party caught a glimpse of the Pyramids from the river steamer: "Several of us tried to be impressed; but breakfast supervening, a rush was made at the coffee and cold pies. . . . Then I wanted (naturally) to see whether my neighbors were any more enthusiastic than myself—Trinity College, Oxford, was busy with the cold ham; Downing Street was particularly attentive to a bunch of grapes. . . . But the truth is nobody was seriously moved."[85] Thackeray's and Twain's accounts of the Pyramids emphasized abrasive encounters with the locals more than the monuments themselves.

Those more talented with the brush than with the pen reported home with the Orientalist paintings so much studied of late. Subject matter, not style, defined the genre, as neoclassicists, romantics, realists, impressionists, postimpressionists, and others all tried their hand at painting "the Orient." Some never visited it, and others—like Eugène Delacroix—traveled elsewhere than in Egypt. David Roberts and John Frederick Lewis stand out among the British and Gérôme and Eugène Fromentin among the French Orientalist painters inspired by Egypt. Linda Nochlin uses Edward Said's approach for analyzing Orientalist painting, but John MacKenzie warns against wholesale ahistorical condemnation of Orientalist artists.[86]

After mid-century, photography began to challenge painting as a way of reporting home. In Paris in 1839, when Louis Daguerre announced his daguerreotype, which caught images on silver-plated copper sheets, scholars immediately thought of Egypt:

> Had we had this process in 1798 we would possess today faithful pictorial records of that which the learned world is forever deprived of by the greed of the Arabs and the vandalism of certain travelers. . . . To copy the millions and millions of hieroglyphics covering only the exterior of the great monuments of Thebes, Memphis, Karnak, twenty years and scores of draughtsmen would be required. With the daguerreotype, a single man could execute this immense task . . . and the new images would surpass in fidelity and local color the work of our most skilled artists.[87]

Frédéric Groupil-Fesquet was off to Egypt that very fall of 1839 with his mentor, the painter Horace Venet. Groupil-Fesquet joined the Swiss Pierre Joly de Lotbinière in daguerreotyping there and in Palestine. Reproducing daguerreotypes' single positives by engraving, Nicolas Lerebour published *Excursions daguerriennes* (1840–1844), and Hector Horeau based his aquatint *Panorama d'Égypte et de Nubie* (1841) on Joly's daguerreotypes.

The calotype, which produced multiple positives from a wet paper negative, was also announced in 1839, to London's Royal Society. Later the French government dispatched Maxime du Camp, who traveled with his friend Gustave Flaubert, to take the calotypes he published in 1852 as *Égypte, Nubie, Palestine, et Syrie.* Calotypist Félix Teynard conceived his *Égypte et Nubie* (1854–1858) as a photographic complement to the *Description de l'Égypte.*

The wet collodion-on-glass process (1851) enabled professionals to produce photographs that the middle classes could afford. Francis Frith used the process on three trips up the Nile in the late 1850s. In 1862, the Prince of Wales took photographer Francis Bedford along on his Nile excursion, and Antonio Beato opened a studio in Luxor to sell photographs to tourists. The Bonfils family began selling Egyptian photos in 1870. The 1858 Murray mentioned no photographers or booksellers in Egypt, but the 1873 edition lists Cairo photographers Otto Schoefft and Hippolyte Délile and recommends Pascal Sebah's firm and two bookshops as distributors for Frith's prints.

The 1890s brought the breakthroughs of the penny picture postcard, which replaced "the shilling view," and Eastman's hand-held Kodak camera and its cellulose film. Any amateur with a Kodak could now take on-the-spot photos for later development back home.[88]

Photography of course found many uses outside the tourist industry. Well before the end of the century, Egyptologists and other archaeologists began putting it to work, and early in the twentieth century photography became a fundamental tool of scientific excavation.

THE INDUSTRIALIZATION OF TRAVEL: THOMAS COOK AND SON

The nominal suzerain of Egypt is the Sultan; its real suzerain is Lord Cromer. Its nominal Governor is the Khedive; its real governor, for a final touch of comic opera, is Thomas Cook & Son.

> G. W. Steevens, as quoted in John Pudney, *The Thomas Cook Story*

The births of both John Murray III and Thomas Cook (1808–1892) made 1808 an auspicious year for the future of tourism.[89] Cook had a hard-scrabble childhood and little formal education. In 1841 he opened a press in Leicester to publish temperance tracts and conducted his first tour—a railroad excursion of temperance enthusiasts to a rally eleven miles away. The same year saw the first publication of *Bradshaw's* railway timetable and the founding of the companies that would grow into the Cunard Line and the American Express Company (Wells Fargo Co.).[90]

Cook carried his Baptist evangelism over into the tour business. Trying to offer morally uplifting tours to customers as far down the social scale as possible, he brought working men from the Midlands to London for the Great Exhibition in 1851. Four years later his tours crossed the Channel to the Paris Exposition. In 1864, he led his first party over the Alps to Italy and moved his headquarters to Fleet Street in London. In the 1860s Cook's Swiss tours included clergymen, physicians, bankers, civil servants, merchants, and manufacturers with respectable but modest incomes of £300–600 a year. The cannons of the American Civil War had scarcely cooled when Cook disembarked to scout out the transatlantic market. In 1869 he included the Suez Canal opening ceremonies on his first tour of Egypt and the Holy Land, following the Prince of Wales's party up the Nile in two chartered steamboats. The completion of the American transcontinental railroad the same year and the Bombay-Calcutta railroad shortly thereafter set the stage for Cook's 222-day around-the-world tour in 1872–1873. The journey may have inspired Jules Verne, whose *Around the World in Eighty Days* was running serially in *Le Temps*.

The eighteenth-century grand tour had been a male affair, but Cook took on families and—proclaiming himself "the travelling chaperone"— "unprotected females." (The party in Anthony Trollope's short story "An Unprotected Female at the Pyramids" arrived a few years too early to avail themselves of Cook's services).[91] Wilkinson warned in 1843: "When Ladies are of the party, on the Nile, the boatmen should be supplied with drawers, and an order given that they never go into the water without them." Naked monks swimming out to the steamer from a monastery shocked Cook's first Nile party; thereafter ladies were warned to remain in the lounge until past the offending spot.[92]

John Mason Cook (1834–1899) began assisting his father, Thomas, as a child and never got beyond the elementary stage in his formal education. John came to believe that business should be business, not evangelism. He clashed fiercely with his father and finally forced him into unofficial retirement in 1878. This freed the company to court the wealthy, aristocratic, and royal travelers who sneered at the earnest, penny-pinching "Cookite" hordes. In 1885 Cook branched out in yet another profitable direction, opening a hajj branch to carry Indian Muslims on pilgrimage to Mecca.

In British Mediterranean tourism, as measured by the number of guidebook editions, Egypt was a distant third to France and Italy but stood well ahead of Greece, Palestine, Spain, and Algeria. Wilkinson / Murray's Egyptian guide was already in its fourth edition in 1858, when Murray published its first Syria-Palestine handbook. By World War I, Murray and Baedeker together had issued only eleven English editions on Greece and twelve on Spain; Cook published none. The three firms together published only 16 editions on Palestine before the war, well behind their 25 on Egypt and 106 on Italy.[93]

East Mediterranean winter tourism balanced Cook's summer tours in Europe. In 1872 John Mason Cook began furnishing his clients the company's own Mediterranean guidebook, including Egypt.[94] As already noted, Cook later commissioned Egyptologist E. A. W. Budge to write an Egyptian guidebook. Cook opened offices in Shepheard's Hotel in Cairo and in Jaffa in 1873, but Palestine-Syria tourism, still tied to tent camps and horses, lagged far behind Egypt. In 1870, the year Khedive Ismail awarded Cook a concession for passenger traffic on the Nile, he ran one steamer and 136 *dahbiyyas* up the Nile. Twenty years later the proportion had shifted to fifteen Cook's steamers and only thirty *dahabiyyas*.

In 1880 Minister of Works Ali Mubarak signed over to Cook an exclusive concession for Cairo–Aswan–Wadi Halfa steamer passenger service during the November-March tourist season. The government would furnish seven steamers with crews and maintenance, while Cook would provide 150 Cairo-Aswan and 60 Aswan–Wadi Halfa passengers a season or pay an indemnity if it fell short.[95]

Cook's concession proved to be a harbinger of British occupation two years later. Seven weeks after the British defeated Urabi at Tall al-Kabir, John Mason Cook was touring the battlefield, feting British officers, and treating convalescent soldiers to Nile excursions. From 1885 on, he spent part of almost every winter in Egypt. Shifting from leasing to owning his Nile fleet, he commissioned four new first-class steamers in 1886–1887, and the following year opened a maintenance yard at Bulaq. Henry Gaze's rival Nile steamer service went bankrupt under his sons shortly after he died in 1890. For the tourist season ending in March 1895, Cook toted up 742 bookings on his Nile steamers.[96]

Cook named only one of his four new steamers for a pharaoh—the *Ramses*. The names of the other three flattered his royal patron—the *Tewfik, Prince Abbas,* and *Prince Mohammed Ali*.[97] In 1891 Cook conducted Khedive Tawfiq from Asyut to the Second Cataract and back. Stopping at Luxor, Tawfiq inaugurated the charitable Luxor Hospital for Natives, which the company had organized.[98] A Cook's crew marched in Tawfiq's funeral in 1892, and the company's *Excursionist* praised the deceased's "freedom from intrigue" and "loyalty to his best friend—England." The paper noted hopefully that Tawfiq's son Abbas II had spent five years in Europe and published a photograph of him and his brother with Thomas Cook during their 1886 trip to England.[99]

Cook's steamers carried Charles Gordon from the Asyut railhead on his fateful journey to Khartoum, transported Wolseley's futile Gordon relief expedition, and handled all river transport for Kitchener's reconquest of the Sudan. In 1898, John Mason Cook outdid himself in conducting Queen Victoria's grandson Kaiser Wilhelm II on his tour of the Holy Land. The overworked master of tourism died upon returning to England. John Mason's sons, Frank and Ernest Cook, took the helm, keeping the firm in family hands for another generation before handing it over in 1928 to the Wagon Lits Company of Belgium.

One historian effused that "the influence of the Cooks in Egypt was wholly good. They brought trade and they found employment for large numbers of Egyptians." That was hardly the view of al-Muwaylihi's fictional Egyptian quoted at the beginning of this chapter. Pemble concluded of Victorian and Edwardian Mediterranean tourism: "It is sad to have to admit that the level of international goodwill and understanding would not have been reduced, and may have been enhanced, if the British had stayed at home to cultivate their gardens."[100] Benign, malignant, or both, the industry that Thomas Cook and Son pioneered had come to stay and would play an even larger role in Egyptian life as the twentieth century unfolded. Even a patriarch of the Coptic Church, Kirullus VI, began his career as a clerk at Cook's.[101]

Auguste Mariette saw the European tourists and scholars who were flocking to Egypt in ever-increasing numbers as his primary audience. Chapter 3 takes up Mariette's life work in establishing the Antiquities Service and Egyptian Museum. Egyptians too began expressing more interest in the pharaonic civilization that so fascinated Europeans, and the chapter also analyzes the attempts of al-Tahtawi, Ali Mubarak, and German Egyptologist Heinrich Brugsch to make Egyptology and ancient Egyptian history accessible to Egyptians.

CHAPTER 3

Egyptology under Ismail

Mariette, al-Tahtawi, and Brugsch,
1850–1882

> And on those stones is writing in the ancient temple script
> which no Egyptian knows how to read, although some
> Europeans in this thirteenth [nineteenth] century have
> deciphered its riddles to a certain extent.
>
> <div style="text-align:right">al-Tahtawi, <i>Anwar tawfiq al-jalil fi akhbar
Misr wa-tawthiq Bani Ismail</i></div>

Less than two years after writing these lines, al-Tahtawi had the satisfaction of seeing a school opened in Cairo to teach Egyptians how to read ancient Egyptian. The distinguished German Egyptologist Heinrich Brugsch became its director. Mariette's hostility was a major factor in forcing the school to close five years later, but not before it had started Ahmad Kamal and one or two others of the younger generation down the road to Egyptology.

During these same years under Said and Ismail, Mariette was setting up the Antiquities Service and Egyptian Museum. The usual celebration of him as the founder of these institutions ignores the abortive earlier attempt associated with Muhammad Ali and Rifaa al-Tahtawi in 1835.[1] In any case, Mariette had to start over in 1858. Mariette's career frames the era covered in this chapter: He first set foot in Egypt in 1850 and died there in January 1881, a year and a half before the British occupation. Table 2 juxtaposes the European Egyptologists active during this era with the Egyptians relevant to this narrative.

During these years, the old and new nations of Greece and Italy were also bringing excavation under national control and building up national museums. Unlike them, however, Egypt—on the wrong side of the Mediterranean and Muslim—was marked out for European

TABLE 2
EGYPTOLOGISTS ACTIVE 1850–1882

European Egyptologists		Egyptian Egyptologists and Other Scholars		Rulers	
Wilkinson	1797–1875	Rifaa al-Tahtawi	1801–1873	Abbas I	r. 1848–1854
Leemans	1809–1893	Joseph Hekekyan	1807–1875	Said	r. 1854–1863
de Rougé	1811–1872	Mahmud al-Falaki	1815–1885		
Mariette	1821–1881	Ali Mubarak	1823–1893		
H. Brugsch	1827–1894			Ismail	r. 1863–1879
Amelia Edwards	1831–1892				
Duemichen	1833–1894				
Ebers	1837–1898				
Naville	1844–1926				
Grébaut	1846–1915	Ahmad Najib	1847–1910		
Maspero	1846–1916	Ahmad Kamal	1851–1923	Tawfiq	r. 1879–1892

imperial domination. Like scores of other officials, Mariette was both an employee of the khedivial government and a patriotic citizen of a European imperial power that was steadily undermining Egyptian autonomy.

Meanwhile, in Paris, London, Berlin, and New York, national museums were emerging as both expressions and shapers of industrial capitalism, nationalism, and democracy. In Egypt as in other colonies, the Egyptian Museum and Antiquities Service served as instruments of European penetration and domination. More obvious instruments of imperial intrusion included railroads and steamships, the Suez Canal, and the telegraph; the cotton trade, international loans, tourism, missionary work, the Capitulations, the Mixed Courts, and Western military power. Museums in semicolonial and colonial lands like Egypt, however, were not simply or exclusively "tools of empire." Europeans promoted and visited them out of varied motives, and so did Egyptians.

World's fairs, which offered more ephemeral exhibits than museums, also came of age in the decades after London's Great Exhibition of 1851. The fairs developed in tandem with the mass tourism epitomized by Thomas Cook. Ancient, Islamic, and modern Egypt figured in almost every great world's fair of the next sixty years. But who represented Egypt at these Western celebrations of nationalism, imperialism, industrial capitalism, and consumerism, and with what intentions and what results? Mariette organized Egypt's displays for two *expositions universelles* in Paris; dispatched displays to exhibitions in London, Vienna, and Philadelphia; and helped orchestrate the extravaganza celebrating the opening of the Suez Canal. After the British occupation of 1882, representations of Egypt at world's fairs were mostly a case of Western and Levantine entrepreneurs marketing "the Orient" to Western consumers.

Until mid-century, learned societies and academies, museums, and leisured circles of wealth and privilege had provided the prime patronage for Egyptology in Europe. Now, Egyptology began changing into an academic discipline, with German universities leading the way. In Egypt, with a Western-style university still half a century in the future, Khedive Ismail and Minister of Education Ali Mubarak set up a specialized school of Egyptology. Al-Tahtawi wrote his history of ancient Egypt in Arabic, and Mubarak's topographical encyclopedia *Al-Khitat al-tawfiqiyya* paid careful attention to pharaonic sites. *Al-Ahram,* which survives today as the leading daily newspaper, seized on "the Pyramids" for its name, and every postage stamp used from 1867 to 1914 projected a pyramid and the Sphinx as symbols of Egypt.

Two European-dominated learned societies emerged in Egypt as forums of archaeological discussion. The Institut égyptien, founded in Alexandria in 1859, and—to a lesser extent—the Khedivial Geographical Society, established in 1875 in Cairo to foster Ismail's African empire, supplemented the museum and Antiquities Service in disseminating the fruits of Egyptology. Members of these societies joined the international congresses of Orientalists and geographers, which began meeting in Europe in the 1870s. Many Egyptians were still preoccupied with their own circles of Arabic-Islamic learning, but al-Tahtawi, Ali Mubarak, and astronomer Mahmud al-Falaki encouraged their countrymen to participate in these Western-dominated—but potentially universal—institutions of expanding knowledge.

ISMAIL'S PRECARIOUS RENAISSANCE

Official patronage of the Arabic renaissance *(nahda)* peaked under Khedive Ismail (r. 1863–1879). The financial, political, and socioeconomic catastrophe that engulfed Egypt toward the end of his reign led to his deposition, the Urabi revolution, and the British conquest, events that overshadowed the cultural advances of a small elite. Ismail made mistakes, but given that European empires would on the average annex an area the size of France each year from 1871 to 1914,[2] blaming him personally for the disaster is superficial.

Like his contemporaries in Istanbul and Tunis, Ismail's predecessor, Said, started down the treacherous path of European loans in the 1850s. The North's blockade of Southern ports during the American Civil War had sent the prices for Egyptian cotton soaring by the start of Ismail's reign, encouraging a euphoric sense of prosperity. Eager to project himself as an enlightened, European-style ruler, Ismail tried to do everything at once—expand his African empire, finish the Suez Canal, remake Cairo *à la parisienne,* erect Abdin and other palaces, dig irrigation canals, build railroads, elaborate a state school system, and overhaul the courts. European officials hired for their presumed expertise in the customs department, police, post office, railroads, telegraphs, Mixed Courts, and army proved to be entering wedges of imperialism. When the bill came due, Ismail's desperate sale of Egypt's dearly bought Suez Canal shares to Britain barely slowed the plunge into bankruptcy.

Searching for roots of the nineteenth-century *nahda* in the works of Azhari scholars such as Hasan al-Attar[3] and perhaps al-Jabarti provides a salutary corrective to stereotypes of a dynamic West awakening a stagnant East. But as the century wore on, the renaissance flourished not at al-Azhar but in such new or reformed milieus as the press, state and missionary schools, study missions to Europe, telegraph offices, translation bureaus, and the offices of judges, lawyers, and import-export merchants. Al-Tahtawi, Ali Mubarak, and Mahmud al-Falaki were both products of Muhammad Ali's educational reforms and proponents of further change.

In 1840–1841, the British-led rollback of Muhammad Ali's dominance in the Levant ushered in an era of retrenchment, which continued under Abbas I. Then Said reversed course and flung wide the door to European fortune-seekers. De Lesseps was first in the door with his Suez Canal proposal. The Institut égyptien, Antiquities Service, and Egyptian Museum were all products of this intensified European influx. Ismail decreed one new cultural institution after another—the Khedivial Library, the Khedivial Geographical Society, the opera house, a state theater, the Dar al-Ulum teachers college, and other schools at all levels. A half-hearted attempt to reform al-Azhar met resistance, so Ismail and Ali Mubarak bypassed it in 1867 with a decree for a state school system, which became the cultural centerpiece of the reign. Arabic replaced Turkish as the official language of administration, and both the Arabic and Western press in Egypt came of age.

By the end of the reign, the press and the Majlis al-Nuwwab (Chamber of Deputies) were developing minds of their own. The charismatic reformer Jamal al-Din al-Afghani had taught on the fringes of al-Azhar, attracting not only young Muslims like Muhammad Abduh and Sa'd Zaghlul but also Syrian Christian journalists. Ahmad Faris al-Shidyaq's Istanbul-based Arabic paper, *Al-Jawaib,* brought in news of the ferment in Istanbul, which culminated in the Ottoman constitution of 1876 and the parliamentary experiment of 1876–1878.

Al-Tahtawi, Ali Mubarak, and Ahmad Kamal—each representing a different generation—were critically involved with Egyptology under Ismail. Beneficiaries of the educational reforms set in motion under Muhammad Ali, each learned at least one European language—increasingly a prime key to bureaucratic advancement. They began thinking not only in terms of Islamic loyalties but also of an Egyptian nation rooted in the pharaonic past.

Al-Tahtawi was sixty-two when Ismail ascended the throne, Ali Mubarak forty, and Ahmad Kamal a schoolboy of twelve. In al-Tahtawi's

youth, Quran schools and al-Azhar were almost the only formal schooling available, but as already seen, his appointment as chaplain to a student mission to Paris in 1826 enabled him to add on a liberal education
in France. Mubarak's al-Azhar-educated father hoped his son would follow in his footsteps, but the rebellious boy ran away to a new state
school. Chancing to see an official as dark-skinned as himself in an influential post, Mubarak had jumped to the conclusion that high state
service need not be restricted to Turks. His educational path to the top
led through a provincial primary school, the Cairo Preparatory
(Tajhiziyya) School and School of Engineering, the Egyptian school in
Paris, the French military academy at Metz, and a year's service in the
French army.[4]

For some years, al-Tahtawi's and Mubarak's careers proceeded on
nearly opposite trajectories. Abbas I exiled al-Tahtawi to Khartoum and
rewarded Mubarak for drastically pruning the school system that al-
Tahtawi had helped to build. Mubarak fell from favor under Said, who
shipped him off to the Crimean War and then alternated minor appointments with abrupt dismissals. Said rescued al-Tahtawi from Khartoum
and made him director of a military school, but later al-Tahtawi also suffered from Said's capriciousness. Under Ismail, al-Tahtawi and Mubarak
flourished in tandem, although not at the same level. Friends with Ismail
since their student days in Paris, Mubarak became a pasha and cabinet
minister, variously in charge of public works, education, *awqaf* (charitable endowments), communications, and railways; al-Tahtawi never rose
above bey, but he had a productive final decade directing a revived translation bureau, writing textbooks, overseeing Arabic instruction in the
schools, and editing *Rawdat al-madaris* (Garden of the schools).

Al-Tahtawi and Mubarak were renaissance men, with Egyptology
merely one interest among many. Benefiting from the schools Mubarak
and al-Tahtawi had helped to build, the younger generation of Ahmad
Kamal had the possibility of specialization. Kamal would have come
across al-Tahtawi's textbooks in school, and he owed his vocation to the
School of Egyptology, which Ismail and Mubarak founded. Unlike these
two elders, Kamal long knew the West only indirectly through books
and resident Europeans; he traveled in Europe only briefly and rather
late in life. If al-Tahtawi ever met Kamal, it would provide a personal
link across the century between al-Tahtawi's awakening to antiquity in
the 1820s and the refounding of Cairo's School of Egyptology in 1923,
the year Kamal died. Kamal's career coincided with the heyday of the
British occupation and is treated in chapter 5.[5]

(RE-)FOUNDING THE ANTIQUITIES SERVICE

Born two years after Mubarak in Boulogne-sur-Mer, Mariette (1821–1881) turned eleven the year that Champollion died. Jacques-Joseph Champollion-Figeac published his brilliant younger brother's uncompleted works but could not advance Egyptian philology. Nestor l'Hôte and I. Rosellini followed their mentor Champollion to early graves. Champollion's successor at the Louvre, Léon Dubois, cut colored pictures of the gods out of papyri for framing and discarded the texts as unreadable scraps. Only at mid-century did Emmanuel de Rougé, who took over as curator of Egyptian antiquities in 1849, and Mariette put French Egyptology back on track.[6]

Mariette earned a *baccalauréat ès-lettres* at Douai and tried teaching and journalism. Inheriting his relative Nestor l'Hôte's papers turned him toward Egyptology, but he struggled with Coptic and hieroglyphics for seven years in provincial isolation before winning a minor temporary post at the Louvre in 1849. Envious of the manuscripts Robert Curzon and Henry Tattam had obtained from Coptic monasteries for the British Museum in the 1830s, the Louvre sent Mariette to Cairo in 1850 for early Christian manuscripts. The Coptic patriarch remembered Curzon and Tattam only too well and refused to cooperate.[7]

Mariette gambled his funds and future instead on finding the Serapeum described by the Greek traveler Strabo. He traced to Saqqara sphinxes he saw in European gardens in Alexandria and Cairo and hit on the avenue of sphinxes leading to the sepulchre of the Apis bulls. In its enthusiasm the French Chamber back in Paris voted credits for transporting the finds to the Louvre before Abbas had agreed to their export. The angry pasha dispatched guards to stop Mariette from digging. British consul general Charles Murray, Prussian-born Anglican missionary Reverend Rudolf Lieder, and Austrian consul general Baron de Huber—all antiquities collectors themselves—lobbied Abbas against Mariette. Mariette had an assistant manufacture fake votary tablets to fob off on Abbas and kept on digging, secretly, at night. French consul general Arnaud Lemoyne finally brokered a compromise. Mariette could send 515 pieces to the Louvre and keep on digging, but future finds would stay in Egypt.[8] Just before his funds ran out and he headed home, Mariette discovered Khafra's valley temple near the Giza sphinx.

The Louvre rewarded Mariette with an assistant curatorship, but with his superior de Rougé only in his early forties, further promotion was blocked. Mariette found himself daydreaming of his adventures at

Saqqara and decided he preferred art to philology. In 1857, he leapt at the chance to excavate antiquities for Said, who had succeeded Abbas I, to present to Prince Napoleon on a projected visit. Said had given away the remnants of the state collection to Archduke Maximilian of Austria in 1855. (These objects are now in the Kunsthistorischen Museum in Vienna).[9] De Lesseps and Consul General Raymond Sabatier persuaded the impressionable Said that he could not afford to be less generous to France. Said furnished Mariette a steamer and corvée labor, and the delighted archaeologist set gangs digging simultaneously at Giza, Saqqara, Abydos, Thebes, and Elephantine. Prince Napoleon's visit fell through, but Said went ahead and presented the discovered objects to the Louvre.

With Napoleon III's backing, de Lesseps, Sabatier, and Nubar Pasha (Said's Armenian secretary and director of communications and railways) persuaded the viceroy to have Mariette refound the Egyptian Antiquities Service. Said's Alsatian secretary and former tutor König Bey worked out the details, and on 1 June 1858—a year before Alexander Cunningham founded the Archaeological Survey of India[10]—Mariette became *mamur al-antiqat* or *directeur des monuments historiques de l'Égypte et du musée* at 18,000 francs (£720) a year.[11] His Service des antiquités was variously called Maslahat Antiqat, Maslahat Antikhana, and Maslahat al-Athar in Arabic. Mariette became a bey second class, with exclusive excavation rights throughout the country, a steamboat, and authorization to levy corvée labor. Maspero's imperialist simile on the appointment says it all: "This was like taking possession of Egypt for the cause of science."[12]

Bonnefoy and Gabet, two obscure Frenchmen whose first names remain unknown, assisted Mariette early on, and the Louvre seconded Théodule Devéria to copy inscriptions. Luigi Vassalli long worked under Mariette, and Heinrich Brugsch's younger brother Émile began his long Antiquities Service career at this time.[13] Mariette set gangs to work at six sites from Giza to Aswan. The first entry in the museum's *journal d'entrée* dates from June 1858.[14] Mariette at first suggested a force of 2,380, including 200 at Karnak, 500 to 1,000 at Edfu, 750 at Esna, and 400 at Giza but cautioned that the estimate was provisional—archaeology was not like digging a canal.[15] At one time he had authorization for seven thousand laborers.[16]

The victims of Mariette's forced labor may also have associated archaeology with the ongoing digging of the Suez Canal. Both were miseries inflicted by Europeans, Said, and Ismail without tangible benefit to the workers. The *reises* (foremen) who recruited the corvée gangs did well, however. Mariette's foremen would levy the richest men in a village, accept bribes to exempt them, and move on down until the poorest had to serve.[17]

Like Paul Émile Botta and Austen Henry Layard in Mesopotamia a few years before, Mariette employed huge gangs to dig for art objects and inscriptions. Attention to stratigraphy, field notes, and detailed scientific publication were not yet the order of the day. Heinrich Schliemann's treasure hunts at Troy and Mycenae in the 1870s were no better. In 1864, Mariette had a thousand men clearing temple walls to give de Rougé access to inscriptions on an upcoming visit.[18] Flinders Petrie later complained that, except at nearby Giza and Saqqara, Mariette left European assistants or Egyptian *reises* digging on their own for months on end. Antiquities from Mariette's digs leaked onto the market, because he would not pay individual *bakhshish* for finds. *Reises* even kept up Mariette's interest in unpromising sites by salting it with antiquities bought on the market.[19] By the 1860s in Italy, Giuseppe Fiorelli and Pietro Rosa were pioneering more scientific digging at Pompeii and Rome, and in the 1870s in Greece, Alexander Conze of Austria and Ernst Curtius of Germany were elaborating techniques which left Mariette far behind.

In Egypt, excavation by other Europeans ceased when Mariette enforced his monopoly and the ban on export without a permit. Periodic orders to officials to enforce the ban on digging and report any finds confirm, however, that Egyptians kept on digging fertilizer *(sabakh)*, selling antiquities, and burning temple stones to produce lime. No, Mariette told a village petitioner in 1880, he could not quarry the Giza pyramids to build a house.[20]

In 1861, Said's foreign debt reached £8 million and he fled to his yacht to escape European creditors. He had already mortgaged revenues far in advance, laid off officials, slashed the army to twenty-five hundred, and sold off military equipment. Mariette implored Paris to beat out London in advancing a new loan: "Whoever makes the loan to viceroy will have put the cord around the neck (the words of the viceroy himself), and in other words will be master of Egypt."[21] Napoleon III seized the chance to press Mariette to obtain Said's help in finding new sources for a biography he was writing on Julius Caesar and in obtaining manuscripts from Coptic monasteries. Mariette ignored Napoleon's remark that the antiquities Mariette was assembling in Bulaq would be better off in the Louvre. Although British and German, rather than French, financiers eventually made the new loan, Said was so relieved that he made Mariette bey first class, promised more publication and museum subsidies, awarded him a pension, and made him commissioner-general to the London International Exhibition of 1862.

Despite Mariette's success in stanching the flow of antiquities from Egypt, he could not prevent the loss of two more obelisks. In the 1820s Muhammad Ali had offered both Britain and France one of Alexandria's two obelisks. The French traded theirs for a better one from the Temple of Luxor, which they took in 1831–1832 for reerection in the Place de la Concorde. Wilkinson warned of national disgrace if the French got their obelisk first, but his friend Robert Hay said it would be a disgrace to *take* the proffered obelisk, since France had gotten a finer one. Wilkinson later opposed bringing the obelisk to London on the vaguely sinister grounds that its original purpose was unknown. Thackeray mocked the whole project:

> Then we went to see the famous obelisk presented by Mehemet Ali to the British Government, who have not shown a particular alacrity to accept this ponderous present. . . . If our country takes the compliment so coolly, surely it would be disloyal upon our parts to be more enthusiastic. I wish they would offer the Trafalgar Square Pillar to the Egyptians; and that both of the huge, ugly monsters were lying in the dirt there, side by side.[22]

Only in 1877 did the physician Sir Erasmus Wilson finally finance the obelisk's transportation to London and its erection at the Embankment on the Thames the following year.

This spurred on the Americans, to whom Ismail offered the remaining Alexandria obelisk in appreciation for the Civil War veterans serving in his army. This was too much for Mariette, who protested that only five obelisks still stood in Egypt, which now had

> two Museums. One is the Museum of Boulaq. The other is all of Egypt. . . . It is moreover a principle universally adopted in all Museums. Namely that if a Museum can receive, it cannot ever give away. That Egypt requests of the Louvre Museum the Venus de Milo, of the Museum of London the Rosetta Stone, of the Museum of New York a monument from the Abbott Collection, for nothing in the world would they make it this gift. Why treat Egypt differently? . . . The time when Lord Elgin carried off the bas reliefs of the Parthenon is passed. Egypt has the oldest extant archives in human history. These are the deeds of her ancient nobility, and she intends to keep them.[23]

The Egyptian cabinet reluctantly honored Ismail's promise, even though he lost his throne a few months before the Americans loaded the monolith late in 1879. It went up in Central Park, New York, in January 1881, the month that Mariette died. At least Mariette had extracted a cabinet resolution that "hereafter no Egyptian monument shall be given to any Power or to any city whatever not forming a part of the Egyptian territory."[24]

THE EGYPTIAN MUSEUM: MARIETTE AT BULAQ

Over the course of the century, three very different east Mediterranean states—Greece, the Ottoman Empire, and Egypt—developed antiquities departments and national archaeological museums. An impetus from northwest Europe was critical in each case, but the museums were also arenas in which local citizens began forging their modern identities.

Greece was first, with the Aigina National Museum of 1829, even before the European powers had finished forcing the Ottomans to concede Greek independence. The powers imposed Otto I of Bavaria on the fractious little state. He arrived from Munich, where neoclassicism was in full swing. The founders of the Greek Antiquities Service (1833) and National Archaeological Museum (1834) were also German. The National Archaeological Museum, in Athens, was housed in the Hephaisteion until 1874, when it began moving into its new German-designed neoclassical edifice. Most Greeks identified more easily with Byzantium and Greek Orthodoxy than with the distant classical past extolled by western Europeans and Americans. Reconciling these two legacies became a central issue in the negotiation of a modern Greek national identity.[25]

The antiquities museums of Istanbul and Cairo began in makeshift quarters, as in Athens, but had more fitful starts. Neither the Cairo collection, begun in 1835, nor the Istanbul one, started in the former Byzantine church of Saint Irene in 1845, was open to the public. The Imperial Ottoman Museum, decreed in 1869 under a British director named Goold, was quickly abolished but reemerged three years later under a German, Dethier. He transferred the collection to the Çinili Kiosk in the Topkapi Palace, drafted an antiquities law, and in 1875 opened the museum daily to the public, with Wednesdays reserved for women.

The Cairo and Istanbul museums survived national bankruptcies in the late 1870s and, in 1881, the deaths of their European directors. Thereafter, their paths diverged. The Ottomans under Sultan Abdulhamid II retained enough independence to have an indigenous antiquities director, the Turkish painter Osman Hamdi. In British-occupied

Egypt, however, the French maintained their grip on the museum and Antiquities Service.[26]

Mariette assembled his Bulaq collection in the former quarters of the overland transit company, which the railroad had just put out of business. The riverside location—near the present-day Television Building and the Ministry of Foreign Affairs—was convenient for off-loading heavy antiquities floated down the Nile.

Mariette initially envisioned building his promised permanent museum in Alexandria.[27] But the railroad cut Alexandria-Cairo travel time to a few hours, making it easy for arrivals by sea to move inland to the capital. Mariette now set his sights on the Ezbekiyeh quarter of Cairo, where Shepheard's, other hotels, and shops and cafes drew crowds of Europeans.

Said's death in January 1863 at forty-one took Mariette aback, but Ismail hastened to reassure him. As Maspero put it, Mariette was delighted to meet in Ismail "someone with an imagination even more fantastic than his own."[28] "Improvising ever grander projects as he became intoxicated with his own words," Ismail spoke of a huge complex at Ezbekiyeh with museums for Greek, Arab, and pharaonic antiquities. Inclusion of the Institut égyptien, with a full-time director, librarian, and library, would make the complex "the true scientific center of Egypt." The new Ismailiyya quarter, laid out on the eve of the Suez Canal ceremonies, began drawing the fashionable residents westward toward the Nile, and Mariette changed his ideal site to the southern tip of Gezira,[29] the undeveloped island facing Bulaq and the Qasr al-Nil barracks. (See map 2.)

Meanwhile, Mariette remodeled the Bulaq premises for a modest temporary museum. By the summer of 1860, the foundations had been laid, and he expected an Italian construction firm to finish within a year. The decorative ironwork for a *"belle façade mauresque"* had already arrived in Alexandria from Paris. Later he wrote:

> You would no longer recognize our old court at Boulak. At the center now is a vast monument, in ancient Egyptian style, consisting of a dozen rooms built to my plans. This is our provisional museum. I don't say we will be lodged there like kings, but at least we will have an ensemble of galleries while we await the definitive museum. On the interior as on the exterior, all is decorated *à l'égyptienne*, and the monuments will soon begin to take their places. . . . The inauguration of these new constructions will take place Oct. 1.[30]

Mariette's detractors charged that the structure had cost hundreds of thousands of francs. Maspero put the sum at under sixty thousand, with Mariette paying part out of his own pocket.[31]

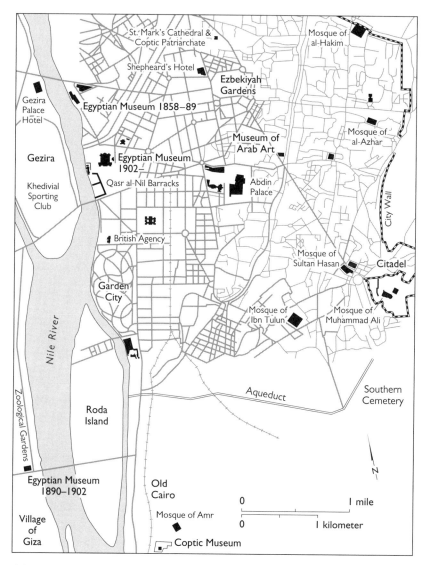

Map 2.   Cairo ca. 1914.

Ismail opened the Bulaq Museum on 16 October 1863, in the presence of a French museum curator and a senator close to Napoleon III. This may have been Egypt's first building in neopharaonic style. It had a court for the museum and one for Mariette's residence and the garden where his pet gazelle sported. Mariette later convinced Ismail that two additional display halls would impress the Europeans attending the Suez festivities.[32]

Mariette organized displays along the lines of de Rougé's Egyptian materials in the upper level of the Louvre, with divisions for religious, funereal, civil, and historical monuments. (He later displayed Greek, Roman, and Christian objects in a fifth section). Lepsius's rather similar arrangement in Berlin had historical, civil, and mythological series. Mariette was proud that in contrast with Egyptian collections in Europe, he had recorded the provenance of every object.

Mariette admitted that he sometimes fell back on aesthetic rather than "scientific" arrangements, defending this as an attempt to attract Egyptians (see figure 20):

> Certainly as an archaeologist, I would be disposed to deplore these useless arrangements of no use to science; but if the Museum thus arranged pleases those for whom it is intended, if they come back often and in so doing are inoculated without knowing it with a taste for the study and, I would almost say, the love of the antiquities of Egypt, my intention will have been accomplished.[33]

Mariette explained that

> the Museum of Cairo is not only intended for European travelers; the viceroy intends that it should above all be accessible to the natives *(indigènes)* whom it is charged to instruct in the history of their country. I would not be maligning the civilization introduced to the banks of the Nile by the dynasty of Mehemet-Ali in saying that Egypt is still too young in the new life which she has just received to have a public easily impressed in matters of archaeology and art. Some time ago, Egypt destroyed its monuments; she respects them today; tomorrow she should love them.[34]

Abdallah Abu al-Suud, a pupil and younger colleague of al-Tahtawi's, translated Mariette's museum guidebook into Arabic. It opens with a *bismillah* invocation, evokes the Prophet, and declares its purpose: to explain the contents of the museum Mariette created to Egyptians so that they will know about their ancestors.[35] Little is yet known of what the Egyptian public made of the museum. An intriguing picture by a German artist shows veiled Egyptian women and a Western woman tourist and girl looking at the sphinxes in the forecourt (see figure 21).

Mariette had European as well as Egyptian audiences in mind when he emphasized that ancient Egyptians were not idolatrous polytheists but believers in "a sole God, immortal, uncreated, invisible and hidden in the inaccessible depths of his being; he created all that exists. . . . "[36] The perplexing variety of lesser gods merely personified attributes of this creator.

Figure 20.   Aesthetic arrangement in Mariette's Bulaq Museum. Although dismissing such arrangements as "useless to science," Mariette said he used them to catch the attention of Egyptians. In Auguste Mariette-Bey, *Album de Musée de Boulaq* (Cairo, 1871), plate 37. Photograph by Hippolyte Délile and Émile Béchard.

Said's and Ismail's personal attitudes toward antiquities remain elusive. Once Said took Mariette aboard the royal steamboat and asked where he might dig for antiquities. To the viceroy's annoyance, nothing was found. Said visited the embryonic museum only once, when escorting the comte de Chambord, the legitimist claimant to the French throne. Said and the French consul passed the forty-five-minute visit in the courtyard on silk divans, talking and smoking, and never followed the *comte* in to see the collection.[37]

According to Maspero, Ismail would not enter the museum with his French guests on inauguration day: "Like the true Oriental he was, the horror and fright which he had for death kept him from entering an edifice containing mummies. While the ceremony took place inside, he remained in the garden, amusing himself with the grimaces of the apes and the gamboling of Finette, the archaeologist's gazelle."[38] The Orientalist wrap of such anecdotes may reveal as much about Mariette, Maspero, and their Western audiences as it does about Said and Ismail.

Figure 21. *Court of the Museum of Antiquities at Boolak,*
by W. Gentz, in G. Ebers, *Egypt* (London, 1878), vol. 2.
Mingling of veiled Egyptian women and Western tourists.

AL-TAHTAWI'S HISTORY OF PRE-ISLAMIC EGYPT

In his campaign to interest his compatriots in ancient Egypt, al-Tahtawi
drew heavily on Mariette's works. Shortly after his accession, Ismail made
al-Tahtawi head of a revived translation bureau and member of an advisory board on education. Later, he also oversaw Arabic instruction in
the schools and edited the educational magazine *Rawdat al-madaris.*

In 1838–1839, Abdallah Abu al-Suud and two of al-Tahtawi's other
students had translated a French history of ancient Egypt into Arabic
as *Bidayat al-qudama* (Primer of the ancients). Al-Tahtawi revised it and
added a preface.[39] Abu al-Suud returned to the subject in 1864–1865
with his translation of Mariette's *Aperçu de l'histoire d'Égypte depuis
les temps les plus reculés jusqu'à la conquête musulmane (Kitab
Qudama al-Misriyyin)*. Ismail had commissioned this textbook sketch,

Abu al-Suud explained, because "the Khedive wants to waken us from this torpor by the study of the history of our ancestors so that we can revive their glorious virtues and follow their example in working together as true Egyptians and true patriots, for the renaissance of Egypt."[40]

Love of country, Abu al-Suud explained, meant working together for the good of fellow citizens regardless of origin or race. Abu al-Suud legitimated Ismail's empire by rejecting the First Cataract at Aswan as Egypt's southern boundary and endorsing a civilizing mission to the "pagan savages" to the southernmost reaches of the Nile basin.[41] The title of the journal Abu al-Suud launched in 1867 with a subsidy from Ismail— *Wadi al-Nil* (The valley of the Nile)—reflects an Egyptian consciousness that comfortably embraced both pride in the pharaohs and the renewed Sudanese empire. Abu al-Suud, who taught history at Dar al-Ulum and wrote for *Rawdat al-madaris,* also translated Mariette's museum guide into Arabic.

Al-Tahtawi conceived his history of ancient Egypt, *Anwar tawfiq al-jalil fi akhbar Misr wa-tawthiq Bani Ismail* (Glorious light on the story of Egypt and authentication of the sons of Ishmael, 1868), as the first volume of a longer survey. The volume covered the pharaonic, Greco-Roman, and Byzantine eras up to the Islamic conquest. The year after al-Tahtawi's death in 1873, his son Ali Fahmi Rifaa brought out the unfinished sequel, *Nihayat al-Ijaz fi Sirat Sakin al-Hijaz,* which held the life of the Prophet Muhammad up for emulation.[42]

As he had done three decades earlier in writing of Paris, al-Tahtawi prefaced *Anwar* with endorsements in hopes of warding off conservative attacks. Shaykh al-Azhar Mustafa al-Arusi noncommittally praised al-Tahtawi's grace in the historical arts, but Azhari professor Muhammad al-Damanhuri praised the book for holding up models of virtuous men who had served the Egyptian fatherland across the millennia. Khedive Ismail's private secretary Ahmad Khayri noted that European hieroglyphic scholarship enabled al-Tahtawi to dispense with uncritical lore from Arabic sources pertaining to the Jews (Israiliyyat). Ali Mubarak also praised the book's use of evidence from European archaeology and philology rather than merely repeating old legends. Al-Tahtawi opened with a Quranic quotation validating human reason and flattered Ismail as "the guardian of the Egyptian land, the restorer of its former splendour and the renewer of the Islamic community."[43]

Setting aside divine history "written in the books of heaven," al-Tahtawi divided human histories into universal ones that treat all nations *(umam)* and particular ones that focus on a single *umma,* such as Egypt, "the ancient Iraqis and the Kurds," Phoenicia, Persia, India, or Greece. He boasted that Egypt, unlike other nations, had not just shone in a single era and then gone into eclipse but had kept its luster across seventy centuries. "At the time of the pharaohs it was the mother of all the nations of the world," and under Alexander, the Ptolemies, and the Romans, it won fame for its learning and philosophy. Egypt then became a pole of Islamic culture, defeating the kingdoms of the Franks, delivering Jerusalem from the crusaders, and even capturing the king of France. Egypt played a leading role in spreading civilization to the West, defeated the French invaders at the beginning of the present century, and was now flourishing under the beneficent Muhammad Ali dynasty.[44]

A dozen preliminary chapters treated the geography and sources of the Nile, the annual flood, Nilometers, ancient Egyptian agriculture, canals and lakes, flora, fauna, minerals, and geopolitics. A three-page chapter on antiquities, emphasized the uniqueness of pyramids, obelisks, sphinxes, hieroglyphic inscriptions, and the monumental column in Alexandria.[45] Al-Tahtawi mentioned France's taking of an obelisk to Paris. Although from the region himself, he disposed of the wondrous ruins of the Said (Upper Egypt) in a mere three lines. He cited Muhammad Ali's order of 1835 to collect antiquities, again with a Quranic justification.

Identifying Noah's grandson Misrayim, the son of Shem, with the legendary founding pharaoh Menes carried al-Tahtawi from Quranic and biblical tradition to the dynastic framework Manetho had elaborated for his Greek-speaking Ptolemaic overlords. Al-Tahtawi followed Mariette's long chronology in placing Menes at 5626 before the Hijra (5004 B.C.E), although he noted that some European scholars would lower this by two or three millennia.[46]

Al-Tahtawi marched reign-by-reign through Manetho's thirty dynasties, with thematic summaries at the end of each era. He noted that the Europeans' decipherment of hieroglyphics had revealed the correct names of the three pyramid builders of Giza, though whether they came before or after Abraham was still in dispute.[47] *Anwar*'s references to Herodotus, Strabo, and Diodorus Siculus were presumably filtered through Champollion, Mariette, and other modern Europeans. Al-Tahtawi followed Mariette in pointing out where evidence from the monuments confirmed, augmented, or contradicted Greek literary sources. He departed from Mariette in his literary flourishes and moral lessons from the Quran and such Arabic writers as al-Masudi, al-Maqrizi, Ibn Abd al-Hakam, and al-Suyuti.

Anwar necessarily reflected the limitations of European scholarship at the time. It lacked evidence from the monuments for the first two dynasties, the Fifth Dynasty, and the First Intermediate Period following the Old Kingdom. Al-Tahtawi considered the Hyksos "Shepherd Kings" Arabs. He knew little of Hatshepsut or Amenhotep IV's (a modern editor's note points out that this was Ikhnaton) religious revolution and the move of the capital to Tell el-Amarna. He followed Mariette in identifying Rameses II as the Sesostris of the Greeks and accepting Herodotus's inflated account of his conquests. Al-Tahtawi noted that some equated Rameses-Sesostris with Hermes Trismegistus, the Quranic Idris. He reviewed arguments over the pharaoh of the Exodus, favoring Merenptah of the Nineteenth Dynasty.[48]

Al-Tahtawi felt no need to give Gregorian equivalents for his "before the Hijra" dates. Not until around 1900 did including both Gregorian and Islamic dates become common in Arabic publications in Egypt. Like Mariette in his *Aperçu,* al-Tahtawi gave pre-Hijra rather than B.C. and early A.D. dates, but pointed out that these were counted in solar years. Thus "2314 before the Hijra" means 2,314 *solar* years before the Hijra, even though the Hijri calendar is lunar. The editor of a twentieth-century edition of *Anwar* adds B.C. and A.D. equivalents and points out that by not allowing for the overlap of Manetho's dynasties, long chronologies overestimated the length of the pharaonic period by two millennia.[49]

Citing inscriptions on the pyramids of Saqqara, al-Tahtawi identified the ancient Egyptians religiously as Sabi'a, or Sabians. *Anwar*'s modern editor identifies the Sabians as practitioners of a pre-Islamic religion from Harran in northern Iraq, who revered the stars and planets. "Sabians" is also applied to two little-known gnostic groups in early Islamic times, one Christian and one pagan.[50] Since the Quran mentions Sabians along with Christians and Jews as monotheistic "people of the Book," assimilating ancient Egyptians to the Sabians made it easier for modern Egyptian Muslims—and perhaps Copts as well—to identify with the pharaonic heritage.

Ending the volume with the Islamic conquest of Egypt in 640 C.E. / A.H. 18 reflected the Muslim vision of the mission of the Prophet Muhammad as the great historical divide. But then, without acknowledging any discrepancy, al-Tahtawi followed Mariette in speaking of two main eras of

pre-Islamic Egyptian history, the "heathen" *(jahili)* period up to Theodosius's decree of A.D. 391—241 solar years before the Hijra—banning
pagan cults and closing the temples, and the "Christian" period of 259
years until the Islamic conquest. This was fine for Mariette, but for a
Muslim it seems to imply that Egypt's 259 years of Christian rule were
not part of the *jahiliyya*. In speaking of Egypt's "middle centuries" as beginning with the Islamic conquest, he also imported, perhaps uncon-
sciously, the West's tripartite ancient-medieval-modern model without appreciating its problems when applied to Islamic history.[51]

The publication of *Anwar* put a solid survey of pharaonic history at
the disposal of Arabic readers, but this takes up less than a fifth of the
volume. Al-Tahtawi devoted nearly as many pages to each of four subsequent eras—Alexander and the Ptolemies, the Romans up to Theodosius, the Byzantines from Theodosius to the Islamic conquest, and—
shifting the geographical focus to Arabia—the pre-Islamic Arabs.
Egypt's Greco-Roman-Byzantine millennium thus received nearly three
times as much space as the whole pharaonic era.

In 1865, the Bulaq Press received orders to print five hundred copies of
al-Tahtawi's *Tarikh Misr* for the schools. Since *Anwar* came out only in
1868, this may refer to a reprinting of *Bidayat al-qudama*. Muhammad
Abduh recommended *Anwar* as a text for young Egyptians, but further
information about its reception is lacking.[52] It was not reprinted until 1971.

With al-Tahtawi as editor, contributors to the magazine *Rawdat al-
madaris* included at least four scholars firmly committed to promoting
the pharaonic legacy among modern Egyptians—al-Tahtawi, Ali Mubarak,
Abdallah Abu al-Suud, and Heinrich Brugsch. Half a dozen Egyptians
and Brugsch sat on the board,[53] Mubarak and Abu al-Suud were among
the contributors, and al-Tahtawi's son, Ali Fahmi Rifaa, assisted his father. Al-Tahtawi had had previous journalistic experience as chief editor of the government's *Al-Waqai al-Misriyya*. Taking *La Revue ency-
clopédique* and *Le Journal asiatique* loosely as models,[54] *Rawdat* ranged
through the humanities and the social and natural sciences. Its initial
press run was 350, later rising to 700.

Having opened the School of Egyptology several months earlier,
H. Brugsch was on hand for *Rawdat*'s birth. He published in it, in Arabic translation, a study on the history of coinage and the text of lectures
he delivered at the fledgling Dar al-Ulum.[55] One of his students, a
Muhammad Ali, contributed Arabic translations of hieroglyphic texts,
and Coptic journalist Mikhail Abd al-Sayyid offered the study "Customs
of the Ancient Egyptians."[56]

EGYPTOLOGICAL RIVALRIES IN CAIRO:
FRANCE, GERMANY, AND THE REST

Said's and Ismail's affinity for French culture, de Lesseps's canal, Mariette's triumphs, and Napoleon III's prestige converged to make the 1860s France's decade in the Egyptian sun. The word "imperialism" caught on in English in the 1850s, often in connection with the Second French Empire.[57] Napoleon's assertiveness in the Crimea, Mexico, Indochina, and Egypt fostered its association with overseas expansion. The 1860s were the only decade when more Egyptian guidebook editions came out in French than in English.[58] Empress Eugénie starred at the Suez ceremonies in November 1869, an apogee of French prestige on the Nile.

Ten months later, Prussia shattered the French army and Second Empire at Sedan, clearing the way for Bismarck to unify Germany under Prussia as the Second Reich. The German siege trapped Mariette in Paris for months, and when freed at last he hurried back to Bulaq to head off any German challenge to France's archaeological preeminence there.[59]

Mariette had little to fear from British Egyptology. French had been the first language to coin words for the new field. *Égyptologue* (Egyptologist) cropped up in 1827, the year Champollion opened the Egyptian section at the Louvre, and *égyptologie* followed around 1850. Not until 1856 did an English writer try out "Egyptologue" as a loan word from the French. "Egyptology" followed in 1859 and began to catch on in the 1860s. Even without a word for their new field, however, Salt, Wilkinson, Hay, and Lane had forcefully represented it on the Nile in the 1820s and 1830s. By Mariette's day, Samuel Birch was the leading British Egyptologist. He would share the founding-father honors on the facade of the Cairo Museum of 1902 with Champollion, Lepsius, and Rosellini, yet he never set foot in Egypt. British diplomats, merchants, and financiers were hardly so passive. It augured ill for France—and for Egypt—that 66 percent of the tonnage passing through the French-built Suez Canal the year after it opened was British. By 1880 the figure had risen to 79 percent, and the British were taking 80 percent of Egyptian exports and supplying 44 percent of its imports.[60]

"The German problem" preoccupied French patriots after 1870, but they could not agree on how to meet the challenge. Georges Clemenceau deplored overseas imperialism as a distraction from the German frontier and rebuilding at home. In contrast, Jules Ferry's fragile Opportunist republican cabinets of the early 1880s and the *parti colonial*—a coalition of seaport, military, *colon*, missionary, and geographical society interests—seized on overseas empire as the very tonic needed to spark regeneration at home.[61]

France's *mission civilisatrice* took on new urgency after 1870, with Mariette in the forefront. It must have been difficult for him to hear his old comrade H. Brugsch often mentioned in rumors of a German bid to take over the Antiquities Service and museum. Brugsch's experience at Cairo's Prussian consulate, his presence now at the School of Egyptology, and his scholarly stature briefly gave German Egyptology a prestige in Cairo unknown since Lepsius's day.

Back in Europe after Lepsius's return to Berlin in 1846, Germans were soon in a position to challenge French leadership in Egyptology. With a dual base in Berlin's Egyptian Museum and the University of Berlin, Lepsius trained most of the next generation of German Egyptologists. Kaiser Wilhelm I had him over for tea, and the scholar's dazzling circle included Orientalist Max Müller, the Grimm brothers, geographer Karl Ritter, historian Leopold von Ranke, classical archaeologist E. Curtius, naturalist Alexander von Humboldt, philosopher Friedrich Schelling, and Roman historian Theodor Mommsen.[62] Even Maspero hailed Lepsius as "the master of us all."[63]

While Bismarck was unifying Germany under Prussia and German research seminars and laboratories were becoming the envy of the world, Egyptology was establishing itself as an academic discipline. Chairs of Egyptology proliferated across Germany: Göttingen (1868, H. Brugsch); Strasbourg (1872, Johannes Dümichen); Heidelburg (1872, August Eisenlohr); and Leipzig (1875, Georg Ebers). The names of Brugsch, Dümichen, and Ebers joined that of Lepsius on the Cairo Museum facade.[64] Brugsch carried this German Egyptological florescence to Cairo. He was seventeen years younger than Lepsius, who treated him not as a protégé but as an upstart rival. Brugsch took his doctorate from Berlin but considered his Egyptian more self-taught than learned from Lepsius. After further studies in Paris, Brugsch won a Prussian fellowship to Egypt, where he worked at Saqqara alongside Mariette for eight months. After undertaking a diplomatic mission to Persia and founding the first lasting journal of Egyptology *(Zeitschrift für Ägyptische Sprache und Altertumskunde)* in 1863, he returned to Cairo as Prussian consul. An Egyptology chair finally opened up for him at Göttingen in 1867, but two years later he was back in Cairo to direct the new School of Egyptology.[65]

In 1864, an incident aggravated Mariette's relations with the Germans. Dümichen had copied a king list Mariette's workmen had uncovered at Abydos and sent a copy to Lepsius. Lepsius published it with-

out acknowledging Mariette. National honor seemed at stake in the ensuing uproar, and Dümichen was on the point of challenging Mariette
to a duel.[66]

Mariette and Brugsch's friendship weathered the storm, and late in
June 1870 they shared an Alexandria-Marseilles steamer on their way
home for the summer. When Mariette reached Paris on 6 July, Louis-
Adolphe Thiers was making a last futile effort to prevent the French assembly from declaring war on Prussia. In a later distant echo of the
Franco-Prussian War, an old Sudanese shaykh "knew well that the King
of the Germans had only acquired the resources to vanquish the French,
through the treasures which the Howadji Lepsius had found at Meroe
and sent back to his native land."[67] Mariette's enemies deplored his long
absence from Bulaq during the siege of Paris, urging Ismail to replace
him with Brugsch. Brugsch dissociated himself from the intrigue, and
Mariette replied:

> For me you are not a German, you are Brugsch; and you have no need to
> explain yourself with regard to such events. They have been able to affect
> my heart as a Frenchman; they have not been able to modify my heart as a
> man, especially vis-à-vis you. I love you as a true friend and have always
> loved you deeply with a natural sympathy that nothing has destroyed and
> that nothing will destroy.[68]

Two years later Mariette took on Brugsch's younger brother Émile as
a photographer for what proved to be a long career in the Antiquities
Service.

De Rougé's death in 1873 opened vacancies at the Collège de France
and the Louvre, but Mariette was not interested. Maspero and François
Chabas could carry the ball in Paris, he said; his duty was to hold on
"in Egypt against German influence which is being pushed by all
means."[69]

When George Bancroft, "the illustrious author of the History of the
United States, the Thucydides of America," toured Egypt, Mariette
found him too pro-German even to concede France's help in winning
American independence.[70] Later, as ambassador to Berlin, Bancroft
joined the Lepsius circle. Such "Anglo-Saxon" ties to Germanic cousins
were not unusual. Two Britons—sculptor Joseph Bonomi and architect
James Wild—had joined the Lepsius expedition. Prussian diplomat
Baron von Bunsen, an ardent promoter of Egyptology and an anglophile,
had an English wife and served as Prussian ambassador in London.[71]

An Italian bid to take over the Antiquities Service in Cairo was out of
the question. Italian was still the lingua franca of the eastern Mediter-

ranean in the first half of the nineteenth century, and in 1845 *Lo Spet-tatore egiziano* became the first Egyptian journal of note after the short-lived journals of the French expedition and the official *Al-Waqai al-Mis-riyya*. Three more Egyptian-based Italian journals joined *Lo Spettatore* in the 1850s, when three French journals also sprang up.[72] As late as the 1860s, the French still considered Italian the main language of merchants and missionaries in the eastern Mediterranean.[73] An Italian company ran the postal service in Egypt, and Italians headed the sanitary and statistical services. But in 1867 French replaced Italian as the second language on Egyptian stamps, and in the 1870s French won out as the working language of the Mixed Courts, the Anglo-French "Dual Control" over the Egyptian government, and cosmopolitan high society.

Rosellini, Luigi Vassalli, and Amadeo Peyron made up the rather spotty Italian contingent honored on the facade of the Egyptian Museum in 1902. Peyron had published a Coptic dictionary in 1835 before concentrating on Greek studies, and Rosellini's early death had cut short his promising work. Vassalli (1812–1887) assisted Mariette at the museum but was older than he and an unlikely successor.[74] The real plum for Italian archaeology was Guiseppe Botti's appointment in 1892 to direct Alexandria's Greco-Roman Museum, which became an Italian cultural enclave.

EGYPTOLOGY FOR THE EGYPTIANS:
BRUGSCH AND THE SCHOOL OF EGYPTOLOGY

Ismail and Ali Mubarak wanted to produce Egyptologists to work along-side Europeans in the Egyptian Museum and Antiquities Service. Mariette opposed this, fearing for his own position. Franco-German rivalry, however, opened a crack in European solidarity, enabling Egyptians to try for a toehold in Egyptology. In the fall of 1869, Mubarak offered Heinrich Brugsch a five-year contract to direct a "School of the Ancient Language" (Madrasat al-Lisan al-Qadim) or School of Egyptology at five hundred francs a month.[75] The 1871–1872 budget earmarked £E1,009 for three professors and £E112 for student scholarships.[76]

Ismail and Ali Mubarak personally welcomed Brugsch back to Cairo, Ismail reminiscing about student days in Paris and Mubarak reporting on the progress of his encyclopedia, *Al-Khitat al-tawfiqiyya*. As a board member and contributor to *Rawdat al-madaris,* Brugsch would have known al-Tahtawi, its editor, and their paths probably also crossed at the Institut égyptien.

Brugsch opened the school in a rat- and bat-infested villa near the Bulaq Museum, with ten students selected from other state schools for their high marks in French.[77] Instructions to recruit them from among pupils as dark-skinned as the southernmost Upper Egyptians and Sudanese are puzzling,[78] recalling Muhammad Ali's failed attempt to fill his new army with Sudanese. Brugsch commented on the light skins of some students, suggesting that they must have had Turkish mothers. Though French was the language of instruction, Brugsch hired his younger brother Émile to teach German. Brugsch taught Egyptian, the patriarchate sent a Copt to teach Coptic,[79] and a shaykh taught Arabic. Brugsch occasionally took his students on field trips to Upper Egypt. Once, while on medical leave, he took two students to Europe to widen their horizons, leaving lesson plans for the rest. Humidity in the Bulaq building was a problem, so the school moved into a wing of the educational complex in Darb al-Jamamiz.

Like Mariette and al-Tahtawi, Brugsch tried to make the Egyptian pantheon palatable to Muslims. Finding that some epithets of Amon of Thebes, Ptah of Memphis, and other divinities were identical to Islam's ninety-nine "names" or attributes of God, he emphasized that a single divine being underlay the surface pluralism of the ancient religion.[80]

Meanwhile, Ismail and Ali Mubarak also turned to a German to direct the Khedivial Library they founded in 1870, a few months before the Franco-Prussian War reversed the relative prestige of France and Germany in Cairo. In 1872, Brugsch's former student Ludwig Stern became director of the library. Stern had studied Egyptology at Göttingen while also taking Hebrew, Arabic, and Ethiopic and would end his career as a Celtic specialist and keeper of manuscripts in the Berlin Royal Library.[81] Four more German Orientalist directors followed Stern at the library, turning it into a sphere of German influence until 1914.

Brugsch's appointment as Egyptian commissioner for the 1873 Vienna Exposition diverted some of his energy from the School of Egyptology; in 1876 he served as commissioner again, to the Philadelphia world's fair. The Egyptian government's decision, in the wake of the Franco-Prussian War, to introduce German into the schools also undercut the School of Egyptology. Brugsch's students were among the few Egyptians who had made a start on German, and it was suggested that he take five of them to Prussia or Austria for preparation to teach it. They did not go, but in 1872 Ahmad Kamal and six other Egyptology students were appointed translators and assistants in the Ministry of Education. Brugsch was abroad late in 1874 when the School of Egyptology closed, its five remaining students being transferred to posts in the railroad administration and Ministry of War.[82]

Brugsch's absence due to the Vienna Exposition was the ostensible reason for the closure,[83] but Mariette's hostility probably doomed the school from the start. Brugsch's report calls into question Mariette's commitment to interesting Egyptians in their ancient past:

> The Viceroy was highly satisfied with my work, the minister of education [Ali Mubarak] was delighted, and the director of government schools almost burst with envy. . . . my old friend Mariette worried that it might lead the Viceroy to have it up his sleeve to appoint officials who had studied hieroglyphics to his museum. No matter how much I tried to set his mind at ease, he remained so suspicious that he gave the order to museum officials that no native be allowed to copy hieroglyphic inscriptions. The persons in question were thus simply expelled from the Temple.[84]

A Swiss inspector rated most of the School of Egyptology's students deficient in language, history, and "scientific adaptability" and at best suitable for only minor museum and antiquities posts.[85] Mariette's refusal to consider them at all undercut the school's raison d'être. Years later, Petrie met an alumnus in Benha who "spoke very fair English." The fellow had been a secretary to a British engineer and administrator of the district where Memphis was situated but was currently unemployed.[86] Kamal and Ahmad Najib did make it back to Egyptology, but for a time Mariette seemed to have derailed Egypt's first try at training its own Egyptologists.

ANCIENT EGYPT AND THE EGYPTIAN PUBLIC

Outside the Antiquities Service, museum, and School of Egyptology, scattered indicators show a modest but growing interest in ancient Egypt among the Egyptian public. In August 1876, the newspaper *Al-Ahram* appeared, with two pyramids and the Sphinx on its masthead. Its editors, Salim and Bishara Taqla, were Syrian Christian immigrants with francophile leanings. The first issues gave a rather garbled history of the pyramids of Giza, mentioning speculations that the pyramids were built to preserve knowledge before the Flood, to store grain, or to observe the stars. Chephren, the son of Cheops I was said to have laid the cornerstone of the Great Pyramid, which was completed in the reign of a Cheops II.[87]

In 1867, a pyramid-and-sphinx design replaced the calligraphy and arabesques that had decorated Egypt's first postage stamps the year before. At least at first, the pyramid and sphinx probably reflected Euro-

Figure 22. Pyramid-and-sphinx postage
stamp. From 1867 to 1914, all regular
Egyptian postage stamps projected the
pyramid and sphinx as symbols of Egypt.

pean ideas of appropriate Egyptian national symbols, but Khedive Ismail
would have had to ratify the choice. Italians had run Egypt's private
postal system until the state post office opened in 1865 under G. Muzzi,
the director of the old private company. The ubiquitous pyramid-and-
sphinx stamp design on every letter mailed from 1867 to 1914 ham-
mered home the idea of these as national symbols (see figure 22). Coins
did not share in the new symbolism. Being one of the traditional symbols of Islamic sovereignty and inherently more conservative, they bore
the name of the Ottoman sultan down to 1914, when Britain severed
Egypt's nominal link to Istanbul and declared it a British protectorate.[88]

Even Persian-born Jamal al-Din al-Afghani, famous for his pan-
Islamic activism, occasionally appealed to local patriotic pride in ancient Egypt: "Look at the pyramids of Egypt, the temples of Memphis,
the remains of Thebes, the shrines of Siwa, and the fortresses of Dimyat,
all testifying to the invincibility of your fathers and the might of your
grandfathers!"[89] Less surprising was a series of articles that Afghani's
Egyptian disciple Muhammad Abduh published in 1876 linking the
glory of ancient Egypt with the renaissance under Ismail.[90]

In 1862 an Egyptianized landowner of central Asian background
wrote his son a manual of advice in Arabic. He grumbled about the
intrusion of European clothes, manners, medicine, and ideas. He
backed traditional dress unless state service required Westernized effendi garb, preferred the Islamic calendar, and advised studying Islamic
before European languages. Yet his table of Egyptian rulers and gov-

ernors went back not just to the Islamic conquest but all the way to
the pharaohs.[91] Even such a conservative member of the landed elite
was already assimilating ancient Egypt as an integral part of the national heritage.

EGYPTOLOGY AT THE INSTITUT ÉGYPTIEN
AND KHEDIVIAL GEOGRAPHICAL SOCIETY

In 1859, with the founding of the Institut égyptien, European residents
transplanted a Western-style learned society to Egyptian soil. For its first
four decades and less intensely thereafter, the Institut was a significant
forum for discourse on ancient Egypt.

In Europe, such academies and learned societies were often nationalist and internationalist at the same time. Eighteenth-century *philosophes* had taken for granted a pan-European "republic of letters"—
Voltaire's "Grande Republique."[92] In the nineteenth century, Western
socialist, religious, and learned communities had to struggle to keep international bridges open across moats of competing nationalism. Even
dedicated internationalists often imagined their communities as only
Western.

Egypt's semicolonial status complicated the picture at the Institut
égyptien. The viceroy officially sponsored the Institut, but Europeans
dominated it just as they were increasingly dominating the state. Here
Europeans had to interact with other European nationals far more than
did their counterparts in nationally framed learned societies at home.
Members extolled "pure science" but never lost sight of where each individual fit into the Anglo-French, Franco-German, and other European
rivalries pervading the scene.

Behind intra-European rivalries loomed issues of imperialism and
racism. Was the ideal of international "science" really meant for Westerners alone, or was it universal? Could an "Oriental" join the privileged club of Orientalists or an Egyptian that of Egyptologists?

Fittingly, the Institut came into being in 1859, the year work on the
Suez Canal began. The canal accelerated the influx of Europeans and
the resulting proliferation of their churches, schools, hospitals, period-
icals, clubs, and benevolent societies. At the Institut égyptien, Antiquities Service, Egyptian Museum, Khedivial Library, Khedivial Geographical Society, and government offices, the less tribally inclined tested
the limits of their internationalism, but national and European-Egyptian
fault lines were never far beneath the surface.

The founders of 1859 looked back to Bonaparte's Institut d'Égypte (patterned on the Institut de France back in Paris) and less explicitly to the Egyptian Society of 1836. The Institut de France had several state academies, each with a fixed number of seats. Entry was by election, usually upon the death of a member. A majority of the Egyptian Society's members had been Britons, but its membership was more open, at least to Western men. Eighty-three-year-old Jomard was a living link between the Institut d'Égypte, which disappeared from Cairo in 1801, and the Institut égyptien.[93] He wrote from Paris accepting an honorary membership in the latter and in 1861 became honorary president. Linant de Bellefonds may have been the only veteran of the Egyptian Society to join the new Institut.[94]

Despite this second Institut's Egyptian-state sponsorship and avowed internationalism, membership lists document the enduring predominance of Frenchmen and the marginality of Egyptians for decades. Prince Napoleon topped the list of honorary members in 1859. Four Frenchmen and a gallicized Egyptian Armenian (Yaqub Artin) followed each other as honorary presidents from 1861 to 1917. The French also had the edge in the regular presidency and vice presidency for the first thirty years. English, Italian, and German were acceptable languages at the Institut, but the lingua franca was French.

As table 10 indicates (see the appendix), in 1859 60 percent of the Institut's honorary members were French, as were 43 percent of resident members and 38 percent of corresponding members outside the Middle East. Italians—on the eve of Italian unification—were a distant second. Antonio Colucci, physician to the khedivial family, was vice president for five years and president for ten. Mariette stood out among the European founders of the Institut. Naming König Bey, Said's Alsatian secretary and former tutor, the first president assured royal patronage. Said visited the Institut and, in a familiar cliché, praised it for "reviving on the banks of the Nile the knowledge which was the glory of our ancient Egypt, the cradle of letters, sciences, and arts."[95] Mariette was one of two founding vice presidents, a Briton being the other.

The Institut's first seat was Alexandria, the main port of entry and location of the largest European colony. Muhammad Ali had revived the port, and the Suez Canal put the Mediterranean back in the mainstream of world trade. The new Cairo-Alexandria railroad made it feasible for Cairenes like Mariette to join the Institut égyptien as resident members. Of course, the requisite rhetoric invoked the memory of ancient Alexandria's museum and library.

With a Comtean summons to "Union and Progress," the Institut declared itself open regardless of race or caste—gender had not crossed
its horizon—and to all fields of knowledge. Like the first Institut égyptien and the Saint-Simonians, who had tried to colonize Egypt in the
1830s, the second Institut proposed to give practical advice to the government on crops, animals, and human diseases.[96] The Institut met
monthly from fall to spring, when wealthy residents often left to summer in Europe.

The Institut survived the financial and political upheavals of 1875–
1882 with difficulty. In 1880, it revised its statutes and moved to Cairo
to its current building at the north end of Qasr al-Ayni Street, across
from the American University. There were to be fifty resident members,
up to one hundred honorary members, and an unlimited number of corresponding members. President Mariette, who had less than a year to
live, complained that the bankrupt state had not paid the Institut's fifteen hundred–franc annual subvention since 1875. Once Britain was
installed in Egypt, Vice President Edward Rogers, an official in the Egyptian government, persuaded financial advisor Auckland Colvin to double the annual subvention.[97]

What of Egyptian members? Seven founding resident members (14
percent) were Egyptians, including future prime minister Nubar, astronomer Mahmud al-Falaki, and al-Tahtawi.[98] Al-Falaki was the sole
Egyptian on the original eighteen-man board. Al-Tahtawi served two
years alongside two Europeans on the publications committee, where
al-Falaki later took a turn. Ali Mubarak joined the Institut later but did
not play an active role.[99]

Surprisingly, an "Armenian gentleman resident in Cairo, whose name
is mentioned in almost every book or letter written about that city" in
the 1860s, did not belong.[100] Joseph Hekekyan had relished Western company in the Egyptian Society, and his alienation from his adopted country of Egypt and his eagerness to lay bare its secrets to Europeans have
already been noted. After the Indian "Mutiny" of 1859, he wrote a British
friend: "You must disarm India. Compel the people to make railways and
electric telegraphs and canals of navigation in every direction. Stock the
rivers with steamers. I would not have a native in the army. You must
maintain 100,000 Englishmen in the mountains—ready—by rail—to de-
scend into the valley like mountain torrents. . . ."[101] Hekekyan made
friends with Mariette while digging at Memphis and wrote Edouard Naville and H. Brugsch introductions to de Lesseps. He corresponded with
Sir Charles Lyell on geology, sent Lucie Duff Gordon an Arabic diction-

ary, and met the Prince of Wales on his Egyptian tour. Explorer Henry Stanley even asked Hekekyan for a character reference to the family of a Greek woman he hoped to marry! Hekekyan's nephew Yaqub Artin later relished a similar mediating role, as did Marcus Simaika.

The Institut égyptien's emphasis on ancient Egypt began with Vice President Mariette's reading of several reports at the very first session. Mariette was president for seven of the Institut's first twenty-one years and honorary president for eleven more. He and his successors at the Antiquities Service used the Institut regularly to announce their discoveries. H. Brugsch read a paper there; and Lepsius, three. A non-Egyptologist briefly followed as president after Mariette's death, then Maspero assumed the mantle until his return to France in 1886.

Two of Mahmud al-Falaki's five papers at the Institut égyptien involved Egyptology, one on an ancient branch of the Nile and one on classical Alexandria. Al-Falaki served as vice president for a dozen years. An astronomer—the meaning of "al-Falaki"—he had won a belated chance to study in France when his former engineering student Ali Mubarak commended him to Abbas I. Al-Falaki stayed in Europe nine years, returning home the same year the Institut was founded. Al-Falaki's publications in French in scattered European journals included articles on the calendar of the pre-Islamic Arabs, weights and measures in Islamic Egypt, excavating and mapping ancient Alexandria, and pyramid chronology in relation to the star Sirius. He was minister of education in the same cabinet as Urabi during the 1882 crisis but survived the British occupation politically, making his way back to the same post in Nubar's 1884–1885 cabinet before dying in office. President Artin praised al-Falaki alongside Mariette, Maspero, and Georg Schweinfurth as Institut members who were worthy successors of Monge, Jacques Lepère, and Claude Berthollet of Bonaparte's Institut d'Égypte.[102] After al-Falaki, Egyptians dropped out of the Institut's Egyptological discourse until Ahmad Kamal's election in 1904.

Egyptology was more marginal in the other main learned society of the day—the Khedivial Geographical Society. Nevertheless the society deserves mention as a prominent feature of the cultural scene and a minor forum for Egyptology. Ismail founded it in 1875 to promote and legitimize his expanding empire in Africa. The German explorer and naturalist Georg Schweinfurth was its first president. He also served as president of the Institut égyptien and wrote the "Origin and Present Condition of the Egyptians" for Baedeker.[103]

Early Geographical Society membership differed from that of the Institut égyptien in two ways: the prominence of Italians and the presence, at first, of Americans. As table 10 shows, Italians outnumbered the second-place French among the founders. Two Italians long monopolized the leadership of the society—Dr. Onofrio Abbate as president (1890–1915) and Federico Bonola as salaried secretary-general (1881–1912). Italian advisers were close to the ruling dynasty for most of its history; Abbate was personal physician to the family from Said on. He also was one of the Institut égyptien's two vice presidents from 1882 to 1910.[104]

The Institut included no Americans, but the American advisers in Ismail's army were prominent in the Geographical Society for its first eight years. Americans helped explore and map the Sudan, and General Charles Stone became chief of staff of the Egyptian army. Ismail's bankruptcy forced him to dismiss most American officers, but Stone stayed on and presided over the Geographical Society from 1879 to 1883. He did not return home until the British occupation made it clear that there was no longer a place for him in the Egyptian army.[105]

Twenty-five of the society's 140 founders were Egyptians. An index of the *Bulletin de l'Institut égyptien* for 1881–1887 shows that Egyptians read four papers out of thirty-two. Mahmud al-Falaki attended the International Geographical Congress at Venice in 1881, was twice vice president of the Geographical Society, and succeeded Stone as president.

Like early geographical societies in the West, the Khedivial Geographical Society began as a collection of amateurs with a sprinkling of professionals from other disciplines. There were occasional Egyptological papers. H. Brugsch spoke on the Nubian language and pharaonic quarrying in Wadi Hammamat. A few months before his death, Mariette was made an honorary member alongside de Lesseps and others.[106] The 1888–1893 index of the *Bulletin de la Société khédivial géographique* lists five papers on pharaonic and Ptolemaic Egypt out of a total of thirty-two.[107]

Unlike the European-driven Institut d'Égypte and Geographical Society, the Jamiyyat al-Maarif (Society of Knowledge), which was founded with Ismail's blessing in 1868, sprang from local initiative and was not concerned with Egyptology. The *jamiyya* collected subscriptions, bought its own press, and published Arabic and Islamic classics. It fell apart, however, when Ismail won a change in the succession law in favor of his own sons, and several members of the losing court faction had to flee to Istanbul.[108]

REPRESENTING EGYPT: WORLD'S FAIR
FANTASIES OF PHARAOH

In the second half of the nineteenth century, many Westerners got their most vivid impressions of Egypt at world's fairs. Mariette and H. Brugsch played central roles in organizing Egyptian exhibits at several of these celebrations of industrial progress, capitalism, and consumerism. In 1851, London's Great Exhibition of the World's Industry inaugurated these extravaganzas, which the British call universal exhibitions; the French, *expositions universelles;* and Americans, world's fairs. Reaching a far wider public than scholarly societies or museums, these events were part museum, part market, and eventually part amusement park. They also served as either a substitute for or a prelude to foreign travel.

Britain's Royal Society of Arts had displayed manufactured goods at national fairs since 1756, and French national expositions went back to 1797. Prince Albert, president of the Royal Society of Arts, and civil servant and writer Henry Cole moved to an international stage with the Great Exhibition of 1851. Manchester-school free enterprise was riding high, and public subscriptions, private companies, and entry fees paid most of the cost. Conservatives feared popular rowdiness, but working-class "shilling people" attended quietly in droves. At the opening and closing ceremonies in Joseph Paxton's Crystal Palace of glass and steel, Queen Victoria proceeded to her private lounge down the main axis, receiving the symbolic imperial homage of the strategically situated Indian exhibit at the transept. British displays were spread throughout the building, and other Western nations had their own national courts. The exhibition took in six million visitors in 140 days before closing and moving to Sydenham, where the Crystal Palace exhibits remained until the building burned in 1936. Historicism ran riot in the decorations at Sydenham, with Greek, Roman, Pompeian, Byzantine, Romanesque, Gothic, Renaissance, Chinese, Moorish, and Egyptian courts.[109]

Tunisia and "Turkey"—as Europeans insisted on calling the Ottoman Empire—sent commissioners to the Great Exhibition,[110] and the shah of Persia came in person. Egyptian exhibits were unofficial. The Ottomans may have discouraged separate Egyptian participation, and Abbas I presumably felt little compulsion to impress the West with antiquities, art, and proofs of progress. The official catalogue began a display on taxidermy and ethnological models with "Egyptian embalmers." There were printed books from the Bulaq Press, cloth, saddles, food

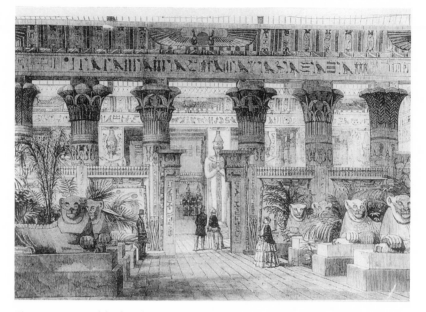

Figure 23. World's fair fantasies of Pharaoh: entrance to the Egyptian Court, Crystal Palace, Sydenham, London, 1854. *Illustrated London News,* 5 August 1854, as reproduced in Nicholas Warner, ed., *Egyptian Panorama: Reports from the 19th Century British Press* (Cairo, 1994), 19. Courtesy of Nicholas Warner.

crops, and slabs of "Oriental alabaster." "It is agriculture and commerce, not manufactures, that nature has assigned to Egypt in the territorial division of labor," intoned the catalogue.[111] Pharaonic antiquity came into its own only with the move to Sydenham. An avenue of lions preceded a Ptolemaic-style temple facade that proclaimed in hieroglyphics that "in the seventeenth year of the reign of Victoria, the ruler of the waves, this Palace was erected and furnished with a thousand statues, a thousand plants, etc., like as a book for the use of men of all countries."[112] Joseph Bonomi's stunning replica of two colossal statues from Abu Simbel dominated the Egyptian court (see figures 23 and 24).

France's riposte to the Great Exhibition was Napoleon III's Exposition Universelle on the Champ de Mars in 1855. Saint-Simonian Frederic Le Play elaborated a complex sociological scheme for arranging the products of human industry. The death of Prince Albert overshadowed London's second international exhibition in 1862, when Egypt and Japan sent official exhibits for the first time. As Said's commissioner-general for the fair, Mariette sent objects from the collection he was

Figure 24.   Reproductions of the Abu Simbel colossi of Rameses II,
Crystal Palace, Sydenham, London, 1854. Replicas by J. Bonomi.
Illustrated London News, 22 July 1854, as reproduced in Nicholas
Warner, ed., *Egyptian Panorama: Reports from the 19th Century
British Press* (Cairo, 1994), 18. Courtesy of Nicholas Warner.

assembling in Bulaq for his as yet unopened museum. Mariette escorted Said to Paris and stayed with him in the Tuilleries, then took him on to London to see the exhibition.[113]

The Paris Exposition universelle of 1867 was a triumph for Napoleon III, urban renewal maestro Baron Haussmann, Khedive Ismail, and Mariette. This time Le Play had an outer ring of machinery in the main building and an inner ring parading evolutionary progress of civilization from the Stone Age to the present. The Egyptian pavilions, the serail of the bey of Tunis, Turkish baths, an Ottoman kiosk, and a Chinese tea house clustered together in an Oriental section of the park.[114]

Ismail, eager to flaunt his new khedivial title and greater autonomy from Istanbul, enlisted Mariette to organize a striking display. Ancient, medieval, and modern Egypt each had a pavilion, as did de Lesseps's rapidly progressing Suez Canal. Mariette modeled the pharaonic pavilion on Emperor Trajan's kiosk at Philae, with eclectic Old and New Kingdom and Ptolemaic touches thrown in. An avenue of sphinxes led into the pavilion, which boasted the famous diorite statue of Chephren and the wooden "sheikh al-balad" from the Bulaq Museum.

The ornate Islamic *selamlik,* or men's reception room, was decorated with mosque lamps, a gold crescent at the top, and busts of Ismail. Mahmud al-Falaki had furnished relief maps of ancient and modern Alexandria, and other maps highlighted geology, industry, commerce, and hydrology. A collection of Arabic and Turkish books, mostly printed on the Bulaq Press, represented enlightenment and revival under the reigning dynasty. The third pavilion was a *wikala,* or caravansary, with *mashrabiyya* screens stripped from Cairene houses. Ten painted scenes showed men and women engaged in agriculture and industry. The neopharaonic Suez pavilion had a diorama of the isthmus and relief maps of the canal towns.

What was real and what was showmanship? Egyptian craftsmen, two camels, and two donkeys populated the *wikala.* Khedive Ismail and de Lesseps played themselves in the drama. De Lesseps held court in the Suez pavilion, and Ismail received Napoleon III and Empress Eugénie in the *selamlik.* The empress declined Ismail's present of a luxury *dahabiyya, Daughter of the Nile,* which ended up with Prince Napoleon instead. Although he later attended the Suez Canal ceremonies in Egypt, romantic writer Théophile Gautier declared that his visit to the exposition was his real Egyptian trip. In Paris, Gautier watched the opening of a mummy and saw five hundred skulls that had been removed from mummies and arranged chronologically according to current anthropological theory!

When Empress Eugénie coveted the jewelry of Queen Iahotep and some pharaonic statues, Ismail referred her to Mariette. She offered him directorship of the French imperial press or the Bibliothèque national, a senatorial seat, a conservatorship at the Louvre, or a role in writing her husband's biography of Caesar. At the cost of temporarily forfeiting her favor, Mariette flatly refused to give her any treasures from the Bulaq Museum. Mariette, Ismail, de Lesseps, and Ali Mubarak went back to Egypt with ideas for staging the opening celebration for the Suez Canal two years later.

The festivities Khedive Ismail, de Lesseps, Mariette, and Ali Mubarak staged for the inauguration of the Suez Canal in the fall of 1869 were something of an Egyptian answer to the great exhibitions. Like the fairs, the festivities mobilized state and private resources to impress the world, entailed breakneck construction of ephemeral pavilions, and drew an international cast of stars. Mariette wrote a special guidebook and personally escorted the European royalty on an Upper Egyptian tour. He also proposed the plot for what became Verdi's *Aida*. Drawing on events from Rameses III's reign and patterning costumes after scenes from the pharaoh's tomb, Mariette also personally painted watercolor backdrops for the December 1871 world premier at the Cairo Opera House.[115]

In 1873 Vienna staged the Germanic-speaking world's only major international exposition. Ismail named H. Brugsch, who had helped Mariette at Paris in 1867, Egypt's commissioner-general. Having taken the precaution of sending only reproductions and originals of minor value to the exposition this time, Mariette relaxed as he escorted Habsburg empress Augusta through the Egyptian exhibit. A cholera epidemic turned this world's fair into something of a failure.

Exhibition mania crossed the Atlantic with Philadelphia's Centennial Exhibition of 1876. Smithsonian Institution anthropologists arranged the main building's exhibits on racial lines, with American and British "Anglo-Saxons," Latins (especially France), and Teutons in prime locations. Denied their own exhibits, American blacks figured in demeaning roles in depictions of the South. Crowds of white ruffians harassed Turkish, Egyptian, Spanish, Japanese, and Chinese visitors.[116] Egypt, Tunisia, and the Ottoman Empire had all scraped up resources for their exhibits despite looming bankruptcy. Brugsch organized the Egyptian exhibit under the slogan "The Oldest People to the Youngest." The pavilion had the facade of an ancient temple, and books from the Bulaq Press again suggested modern progress.

The Paris Exposition Universelle of 1878 continued an eleven-year cycle of French fairs that culminated in 1900. Eager to forget for the moment nightmares of the Franco-Prussian War, the Paris Commune, and President MacMahon's attempted coup of 1877, France went all out with a building in the Champ de Mars that covered fifty-four acres. Pavilions in varied styles lined the Avenue des Nations for nearly half a mile. Thirteen million visitors came.[117]

With the Turco-Russian War straining his already exhausted treasury, Ismail almost withdrew from the fair. Mariette's dream of ancient, medieval, and modern pavilions remained only a dream. De Lesseps's Suez Canal Company came through with a neopharaonic pavilion, and Egypt obtained space for modest displays in the Palais Trocadéro. There were copies of tomb scenes from Beni Hasan, a head of Chephren, and a model of ancient artisans' houses. A house facade with *mashrabiyya* balconies, illuminated Qurans, pottery, and swords and armor were classified as medieval. Jewels, rugs, and brocade work were presented as modern—"the country has no industry at all, properly speaking," explained the guidebook.[118] Artifacts and maps boasted of Egypt's annexation of Sudanese Equatoria even as Egypt itself teetered on the brink of Western conquest.

REPRESENTING EGYPTOLOGY: INTERNATIONAL CONGRESSES OF ORIENTALISTS

The transportation and communication revolutions that made world's fairs and Cook's tourism possible also underpinned the international congress movement, which reached its stride in the 1870s. The other prerequisite was networks of national organizations—in this case, Asiatic, Oriental, and geographical societies—that had sprung up since the 1820s. By 1870, national geographical societies, the Asiatic Societies of Paris (1822) and Great Britain and Ireland (1823), and the American (1842) and German (1845) Oriental Societies were all well-established. With its Antiquities Service, Egyptian Museum, Institut égyptien, and Geographical Society, Ismail's Egypt was ready—or at least its European residents were—for the international congress movement.

The idea for an International Congress of Orientalists (ICO) crystallized in the Société d'ethnographie de Paris,[119] and it was in that city that the First ICO assembled in 1873. Egyptology constituted an important section of the meetings for a century after ICO's founding. Twentieth-century usage usually separates "Egyptology" from "Orientalism," al-

though institutions like the American Oriental Society, the Institut
français d'archéologie orientale du Caire (IFAO), and the University of
Chicago's Oriental Institute keep the older overlapping terminology alive.
In 1973, Egyptologists seceded from the International Congress of Orientalists, which itself bowed to changing times by renaming itself the International Congress of Asian and North African Studies.

"Orientalist," in the sense of one versed in Oriental languages and
literatures, first appeared in English in 1781. "Egyptologist" did not appear until 1859 and only became common in the 1870s, when the field
began to set itself apart as a distinct discipline.[120]

Around the middle of the nineteenth century, European Egyptologists
working in Egypt began to change their habits of dress. Pioneer Orien-
talists-Egyptologists Champollion, Rosellini, Wilkinson, Lane, and Prisse
d'Avennes wore beards and Turkish garb. This was useful, protective col-
oration in their day, although when they displayed themselves in such
garb back home, other questions about identity, disguise, and claims of
expertise on foreign cultures came into play. As Egyptology became a
distinct discipline, and Western ascendancy in Egypt grew, Egyptologists like Maspero and Petrie no longer presented themselves in "Oriental" dress. Egyptologists did not need fluent Arabic to establish their
credentials. Orientalists, however, who sometimes tested themselves by
trying to disappear temporarily into a still-living "other" society, kept
the urge to disguise longer.

A disquieting note on definitions: Egyptology was, and still is, the study
of ancient Egypt. This definition implicitly slights Islamic and modern
Egypt. Another Western trope that emphasizes continuity rather than dis-
continuity in Egypt is also unsettling—the assumption that quintessen-
tial fellahin have not changed since ancient times. This assumes an unchanging Orient juxtaposed to an evolving, dynamic West. This seems to
be the implication of an Orientalist photograph posing a fellah with his
head tilted to resemble a just-excavated mummy at Thebes (see figure 25).

The First International Congress of Orientalists in Paris in 1873 included seven papers on Egyptology and one on Coptic studies. Seven of
the eight presenters were French, including Maspero and Chabas; the
eighth was Samuel Birch. German troops still occupied French soil until
16 September 1873, so the hosts were in no mood for papers by Germans. Thirty-five Germans nevertheless subscribed to the congress (not
all of the 1,064 "subscribers" attended), and Lepsius spoke up from the
floor. Khedive Ismail, Mahmud al-Falaki, Yaqub Artin, and six other
Egyptians were among the twenty subscribers listed from Egypt. Three

Figure 25.   Unchanging Egypt? An Orientalist whimsy. "Momies
trouvées dans un tombeau à Thebes," photograph by Félix Bonfils,
1878. Courtesy of the Bibliothèque nationale, Paris. Jean-Claude
Simoën, in *Égypte éternelle: Les Voyageurs photographes au siècle
dernier* (Paris, 1993), 104, gives the photograph's date as 1860.

of the eleven others were Egyptologists—Mariette, H. Brugsch, and Albert Daninos. Curiously, Schweinfurth was listed as representing the
Khedivial Geographical Society, which had not yet been founded.[121]

Scholars disagree on Egyptian reactions to representations of their
country at world's fairs and International Orientalist Congresses. Timothy Mitchell, using a Saidian or postmodern approach, emphasizes
Egyptian dismay and embarrassment, while Carter Findley finds Egyptian and Ottoman reactions more positive and nuanced. Mitchell and

Findley draw their main evidence from the ICO held jointly in Stockholm and Christiania (now Oslo) and the Paris Exposition universelle of 1889, which falls in the period taken up in chapter 6.[122]

Already at the first ICO, an energetic Japanese scholar blurred the categories for anyone who presumed that only Western Orientalists were qualified to discuss "Orientals." The Persian ambassador, General Nazar Aga, lauded Orientalists for discovering that the language of Firdawsi, Cyrus, Darius, and Xerxes was kin to those of Europe. "Thanks to the progress of comparative philology," he effused, "Persians can today say—what they had not suspected—that they belong to the same race as the Europeans, that they are brothers to the noble nation which inaugurated this year the grand and magnificent international work of the Congress of Orientalists."[123]

Egyptologist Samuel Birch took the chair at the Second International Congress of Orientalists in London in 1874. (See table 11, in the appendix, and figure 26.) Mixing imperial pride and scholarly internationalism, he pronounced London

> distinguished for its extent as well as for its devotion to the study of the East, and connected by a thousand ties, the interests of commerce, the spread of civilization, missionary labors, and the duties of governing Oriental Dependencies of various tongues and sites in the East. . . .
>
> Orientalists, too, are all, so to say, men born of the same family. . . . as students, all the distinctions of race, creed, and nationality disappear or are forgotten. Even criticism ought neither to be nor become personal, in as much as Science places for its object the highest scope of the mind—truth, which is in most cases difficult to find, and no reproach to miss.[124]

Alongside the Archaeological and Ethnological sections, Semitic, Hamitic, Turanian, and Aryan sections reflected prevailing linguistic-racial categories. Birch announced: "The Hamitic Section will represent the progress made in Egyptology since the first discovery of the mode of deciphering and reading this pictorial language of Ancient Egypt in 1817."[125] The date implied recognition of Thomas Young and a swipe at Champollion, but no Frenchmen were present to protest. Lepsius and five other Germans dominated the Egyptology section as thoroughly as the French had in Paris the year before. H. Brugsch officially represented Egypt. Birch, still the lone British Egyptologist presenting, invited his seven colleagues to a workshop at his home.[126]

The Third International Congress of Orientalists moved east in 1876 to Saint Petersburg. Mariette represented Egypt as a corresponding member of the organizing committee. At the Fourth International Congress

Figure 26. An "Oriental" at the International Congress of Orientalists,
London, 1874. Samuel Birch explains the Rosetta Stone to Western scholars
as a beturbaned man looks on. *Illustrated London News*, 26 September 1874,
as reproduced in Nicholas Warner, ed., *Egyptian Panorama: Reports from the
19th Century British Press* (Cairo, 1994), 23. Courtesy of Nicholas Warner.

of Orientalists in Florence in 1878, Franco-German rivalry was muted.
Maspero chaired the "Egyptology and African Languages section,"
which in practice included only Egypt. A German, a Swiss (Naville), and
two Italians (one was Ernesto Schiaparelli) read papers, but no Egyptian or foreign resident of Egypt did so.[127]

Thus, down to the British occupation in 1882, international congresses of Orientalists provided the emerging discipline of Egyptology
an important forum. With specialists of the caliber of Maspero, Birch,
Lepsius, and Brugsch setting the tone, few amateurs ventured papers.
Franco-German rivalry was pervasive, on stage and off. Egyptians lacked
a voice in the ICO's Egyptology section; there were as yet no Egyptian
Egyptologists.

THE GATHERING STORM:
ISMAIL AND MARIETTE IN THE 1870s

Mariette and Ismail both celebrated triumphs early and later endured
many tribulations. How could one top discovering the Serapeum, found-

ing the Antiquities Service and Egyptian Museum, orchestrating the sensational Egyptian display at the Paris Exposition universelle of 1867, or opening the Suez Canal? The tragedies in the archaeologist's private life were appalling. Cholera carried off his wife in 1865, six of their ten children died before him, and he fought diabetes for years before it killed him.[128]

Mariette's job was never secure. "For better or worse," as one Frenchman put it, "Mariette Bey is part of the viceregal household, on a level with the head of the stables and the chief black eunuque. One has an Egyptologist in the way that one's forebears had an astrologist, a master of parades, awkwardly placed between the fool and the physician."[129] Not until 1883, after Mariette's death and the beginning of the British occupation, did inclusion of the Antiquities Service in the Ministry of Public Works end its precarious dependence on khedivial goodwill.

Mariette's rivals whispered that he was merely an agent of French control, secretly sold antiquities, and was assembling the Bulaq collection only to advance his personal fortunes. Briefly heeding the slander, Ismail took back Mariette's steamboat and revoked his right to corvée.[130] Mariette soon got the steamboat back, but with a leaner budget and without the right of corvée. By 1867 he had funds only to pay several hundred laborers.

By 1873 there was almost no money for excavation, and none for publications or museum expansion. Mariette's salary was in arrears, and he again temporarily lost his steamboat He wrote a popular book, *Itinéraire de la haute Égypte* (2 vols., 1878–1880), to pay the bills. In 1878, the French minister of public works in Nubar's cabinet squeezed out £E1,000 for Mariette's most pressing excavation and surveillance needs, and the French Ministry of Public Instruction contributed an emergency subvention of 10,000 francs.[131]

Mariette's publication dreams were as gargantuan as his initial Antiquities Service excavations, but most fell through for want of funds and time. Excavation, museum work, travel, planning world's fairs, escorting famous visitors, and ventures into diplomacy left little time for scholarship. Devéria's early death deprived him of much-needed assistance with the publication of inscriptions.

Ignoring looming bankruptcy, the government let bids in March 1873 for the foundations of a great new museum on Gezira. The work was to be finished by 1 October at the cost of 186,000 francs. In Paris, the Académie des inscriptions et belles lettres set a prize of twenty thousand francs for a design of the facade. After news of the true state of Egyptian finances broke that summer during the Vienna Exposition, the proposed new museum—like the School of Egyptology—disappeared from view.[132]

According to Cromer, "The nadir both of financial chaos and of popular misery was reached in the summer and autumn of 1878."[133] France and Britain stripped Ismail of his family estates and forced him to install Nubar as prime minister, with a Briton at finance and a Frenchman at public works. The Nile flood that reduced some peasants to starvation rampaged through the Bulaq Museum and Mariette's living quarters in October 1878, destroying or damaging books, manuscripts, squeezes, and antiquities. A proposal to move the museum to the unfinished Girls School building in the compound of the Ministry of Public Works—apparently the quarters the Institut égyptien obtained in 1880—remained a dead letter.

In the summer of 1879, Britain and France forced Sultan Abdulhamid II to depose Ismail in favor of his son Tawfiq. Mariette doggedly cleaned and repaired the Bulaq premises and in 1880 reopened the museum. He was not quite sixty when he died of diabetes in January 1881, a year and a half before the Urabi revolution precipitated the British occupation. His last years did have a few bright spots, such as election in 1878 to the Académie des inscriptions et belles lettres and becoming a pasha on 5 June 1879, just weeks before Ismail's deposition. On Mariette's deathbed, the Brugsch brothers told him of the wonderful pyramid texts in the pyramid of Unas at Saqqara.

The flamboyant age of Ismail and Mariette was over. After the turbulent ensuing year of the Urabi revolution and the British conquest, Cromer and Maspero, with the independent-minded Petrie in the wings, would work out new parameters for Egyptian archaeology under colonial rule. Anglo-French rivalry in Egypt entered a new stage, with France on the defensive in archaeology and elsewhere. With al-Tahtawi dead, Ahmad Kamal and several colleagues took up the uphill battle to establish an Egyptian Egyptology.

PART TWO

Imperial High Noon, Nationalist Dawn, 1882-1914

Cromer and the Classics

Ideological Uses of the
Greco-Roman Past

This book opens with Bonaparte seizing Egypt in self-conscious emulation of Alexander and Caesar, and it closes with Lord Cromer in retirement, musing about his rule in Egypt compared with that of the pro-
consuls of Rome. In between, Consul Henry Salt divided his leisure time
between Greek manuscripts and Egyptian antiquities, Flaubert read the
Odyssey in Greek while floating down the Nile, and British officials
fresh from Oxford and Cambridge stepped ashore reciting Herodotus.[1]
Europeans founded the Greco-Roman Museum and the Archaeological
Society of Alexandria in 1892 and brought the Second International
Congress of Classical Archaeology to Cairo in 1909.

The title of this chapter is lopsidedly Western, because by 1914 no
Egyptian had yet tried to make the Greco-Roman heritage central to
Egyptian national identity. The Egyptians of 1800 had been as deaf to
European classical discourse as Europeans were to evocations of Amr
ibn al-As as a war hero or Abu Nuwas as a timeless poet. Pious Muslims modeled themselves on the Prophet Muhammad and the Rightly-
Guided Caliphs while the worldly sighed for the splendors of Harun al-
Rashid's Baghdad or Mamluk Cairo. Bonaparte's classical masquerade
would have meant nothing to al-Jabarti. In the 1880s, in two monologues that never met, Cromer played the Roman proconsul in Cairo
while the Mahdi Muhammad Ahmad reenacted the life of the Prophet
in Khartoum. Perhaps Charles Gordon, who preferred biblical to classical metaphors,[2] understood the Mahdi better than Cromer.

By 1914, classical studies had produced no Egyptian who aspired to succeed the Italian curators at the Greco-Roman Museum—no counterpart to Ahmad Kamal, Ali Bahgat, or Marcus Simaika. Nevertheless, officials, writers, and politicians as prominent and diverse as al-Tahtawi, Mahmud al-Falaki, Ali Mubarak, Jurji Zaydan, Qasim Amin, Ahmad Lutfi al-Sayyid, Mustafa Kamil, and Muhammad Farid had made tentative forays into Greco-Roman discourse. This paved the way for the 1920s, when Taha Husayn and Lutfi al-Sayyid would promote Greek and Latin classics as vital ingredients of Egyptian national identity.

With the partial exception of the Maghrib (northwest Africa), the classical metaphor through which nineteenth-century Europeans related to the Middle East has been little noticed. General histories of Egypt scarcely mention modern Egyptian ideas on the Greco-Roman legacy, which admittedly had far less attraction than Islamic, Arab, or pharaonic discourse.

CLASSICAL DISCOURSE IN WESTERN IDENTITY

From Petrarch to Sartre, the classics rivaled even the Bible as a widespread, flexible vehicle of Western thought.[3] Greeks were read as conservative and liberal, radical and reactionary, religious and atheistic, rational and romantic. The Roman republic was played off against the empire, Greece against Rome, Athens against Sparta, Plato against Aristotle, and even one Aristotle against another.[4] The American and French revolutions were steeped in Roman symbolism, and Marx so relished Prometheus's defiance of the gods that he reread Aeschylus every year in Greek.[5]

Yet the survival of classics at the core of Western liberal education in the 1800s owed more to conservative than to radical impulses. In response to democratic and meritocratic challenges from the middle classes, British public schools and Oxbridge raised standards, and the Home Office and Indian Civil Service instituted examinations.[6] With patronage and privilege under siege, Greek and Latin became a key means of perpetuating upper-class status.

Not all literary Britons revered the classics. Churchill regretted the new rigor; his lack of Greek kept him out of Oxford. Thackeray's classical schooling reminded him of castor oil. Anticipating Mark Twain's irreverent tourism, he sneered at Athens: "I would rather have two hundred a year in Fleet Street, than be King of the Greeks, with Basileus written before my name round their beggarly coin. . . . The shabbiness of this place actually beats Ireland, and that is a strong word."[7]

From Europe's Middle Ages through the French Revolution, most Westerners identified with Rome more than Greece. Prussian antiquarian Johann Winckelmann, however, inaugurated an aesthetic and intellectual movement that hailed classical Greek society as vigorous and youthful in contrast with ponderous and tired Rome. Winckelmann's *History of the Art of Antiquity* (1764) made him a founding father of both modern art history and classical archaeology. Idealizing Greece often worked well for promoters of bourgeois and liberal causes.

Goethe and Prussia's reformist minister of education Alexander von Humboldt did much to spread this philhellenism in Germany.[8] Frenchmen also awakened to the tug of ancient Greece, but speaking a Latin language and feeling themselves heirs of Roman history and law kept most of them from traveling as far as Germans down the philhellenic road.[9]

Britons caught Hellenic fever too, flocking to the Elgin marbles at the British Museum, erecting Greek Revival buildings, and cheering Byron's philhellenism. "The battle of Marathon," wrote John Stuart Mill, "even as an event in English history, is more important than the battle of Hastings."[10] No longer priding themselves in living in an "Augustan age," Britons dismissed Augustus as a scheming despot and Virgil as a mere courtier. Homer and Plato came into vogue, and the reform-minded elevated democratic Athens over authoritarian Sparta. A recent study, however, has emphasized the persistence of Rome in many spheres of British culture right through the nineteenth century.[11] In any case, imperial Rome regained its luster for many Britons with the "new imperialism" of the 1880s and 1890s.

EGYPT THROUGH EUROPEAN CLASSICAL LENSES

The frontispiece of the Napoleonic expedition's *Description de l'Égypte* deploys powerful classical images—Napoleon in his chariot like Apollo and Alexander, the muses of the arts and sciences returning to Egypt, the eagle battle standards. In a similarly rich symbolic vein, a ceiling in the Louvre's Egyptology section displays François Picot's *Study and the Muse of the Arts Reveal Ancient Egypt to Athens* (see figure 27).[12] Athens is a regal, classically robed woman; Egypt, a voluptuous semireclining one, languorously sniffing a lotus blossom.

On his Egyptian campaign Bonaparte carried the *Iliad* (so had Alexander), Xenophon's *Anabasis* (the tale of heroic Greeks fighting their way home through Asiatic hordes), and Plutarch's *Parallel Lives*.[13]

Figure 27.   Classical / Oriental fantasy: *Study and the Muse of the Arts Reveal Ancient Egypt to Athens,* by François-Edouard Picot, 1827. Painting on the ceiling of one of the Egyptian rooms, the Louvre. Photograph by Donald Reid.

Bonaparte harangued his soldiers: "The first city we shall see was built by Alexander. At every step we shall find traces of deeds worthy of being emulated by the French."[14] With hieroglyphics still a riddle, his savants viewed Egypt through the eyes of Herodotus, Strabo, Diodorus Siculus, and Pliny the Elder, quoting them in parallel Greek and Latin texts in the *Description.* Even the artists' renderings of pharaonic antiquities had a classical warp. A medal struck in 1826 to promote the second edition of the *Description* shows a Gaulish-Roman conqueror unveiling a voluptuous female Egypt (see figure 28).

Two years after the completion of the *Description* in 1828, France invaded Algeria. After a destructive "Arab interval," it was said, the heirs of ancient Rome had returned to civilize North Africa. Let the *indigènes* know, French officers were later told in Morocco, that "we Romans were here before the Arabs."[15] For over a century in Algeria, statues, architecture, museums, street names, literature, postage stamps, and postcards did just that.[16]

Long after Champollion opened direct access to the pharaohs through hieroglyphic texts, European Egyptologists still cut their teeth on the

Figure 28.   Victorious Gaul rediscovers
ancient Egypt: medal by Barre, 1826,
commemorating the French expedition.
In Peter A. Clayton, *The Rediscovery of
Ancient Egypt* (London, 1982), 7.
Courtesy of Peter Clayton.

classics. Lepsius's circle in Berlin read Greek masterpieces in the original on Friday nights; Latinist Theodor Mommsen, English ambassador
Lord Russell, and Ambassador Rangabe of Greece were among the reg-
ulars. In 1903, Alexandre Moret earned his Egyptology doctorate with
the last thesis in France written in Latin.[17]

Sometimes one cannot tell whether the classics framed and distorted
European views of modern Egypt or the other way around:

> Just as in the Cairo of to-day the whole circle of Mohammedan science is
> taught in the University of El-Azhar on the basis of the Qoran, so in the He-
> liopolis which Herodotos visited all the circle of Egyptian knowledge was still
> taught. . . . The feelings with which the Greek traveller viewed the professors
> and their pupils . . . must have been similar to those with which an English
> tourist now passes through the Azhar mosque.[18]

Mirrors within mirrors, with Orientalist and classical discourse inex-
tricably intertwined.

Not all Egyptologists were so classically minded. Mariette took little
interest in Greco-Roman sites and denounced Herodotus:

> I detest this traveller who came to Egypt at a time when the Egyptian lan-
> guage was spoken, who with his own eyes saw all the temples still standing;
> who only had to ask the first comer the name of the reigning king, the name

of the king who preceded him, who only had to refer to the first temple for the history, religion—for everything of interest concerning the most fascinating country in the world. And who, instead of all that, tells us gravely that Cheops built a pyramid with the fruit of prostitution.[19]

Petrie never mastered the classics. His mother had thought it "quite natural to stuff me with English, French, Latin and Greek grammars all together at the age of eight." Ten starts on Latin and five or six on Greek by the age of ten produced a breakdown, and he was left alone to educate himself.[20]

Maspero was quite the opposite. A century after Bonaparte, a Latin stela uncovered on Philae gave him a patriotic thrill. The text recounted how Augustus's governor Cornelius had subdued the Nile Valley to the Philae frontier. Noting that Cornelius had been born on "Gallic soil," Maspero was

> reminded immediately of the other, more recent inscription, which is prominently displayed on the inner jamb of the great gate at Philae. Eighteen centuries after the Gaul Cornelius, other Gauls, brought to Nubia by chance and wanting to leave a souvenir of their presence, recorded in stone how in Year VI of the Republic, the 12th of Messidor, a French army, commanded by Bonaparte, disembarked at Alexandria. Twenty days later, the army, having put the Mamluks to flight at the Pyramids, Desaix, commandant of the first division, pursued them beyond the cataracts, where he arrived the 18th of Nivôse of the Year VII.
>
> . . . one must see, in the *Voyage* of Denon or in the volumes of the *Description,* how greatly they were nourished by reminders of classical antiquity, and what a thrill they felt to fly their banners over the rocks where the Legions had carried out, in a few weeks, an enterprise which had seemed almost impossible. . . . [21]

MUSLIM VIEWS ON CLASSICAL GREECE AND ROME BEFORE AL-TAHTAWI

Greek and Latin literature was not "the classics" to medieval Muslims, and Bonaparte knew better than to masquerade as Alexander or Caesar before Egyptian audiences. Instead his Arabic propaganda cast him, albeit unsuccessfully, as almost a Muslim—an anticlerical who had attacked Islam's enemy the pope, and a friend of the Ottoman sultan bent only on liberating Egypt from Mamluk tyranny.

It was not that al-Jabarti and his fellow Azharis knew nothing of Greco-Roman civilization. Early Arabic translations from Greek philosophy, science, medicine, and mathematics had been fundamental to

Islamic advances in these fields, and Aristotelian logic became an essential tool of Islamic theology.[22] Islamic literature even spun its own Alexander legends. But medieval Muslims did not inherit the drama, poetry, mythology, or early history of Greece. Before the Islamic conquests, Christian schools had already purged these subjects as too pagan, and in any case the Arabs brought their own folklore, poetry, and new religion out of Arabia with them. Thus the first Arabic translation of the *Iliad* came out not in Harun al-Rashid's Baghdad in 804 but in Cromer's Cairo in 1904.[23]

Early Muslims felt no threat from a Greco-Roman paganism dead before their time. In the eleventh century, al-Biruni's *India* discussed Greek as well as Hindu gods. Muslims so inclined could rationalize borrowing from pagan Greece by dismissing its polytheism as the inability of the masses to think abstractly, by assimilating the Greeks to the Quranic Sabian believers in Allah, or by depicting Neoplatonists as monotheists in the Jewish tradition.[24]

Medieval Muslim historians wove their histories of the pre-Islamic era from Judeo-Christian, pagan Arabian, and Persian lore. Al-Tabari knew nothing of Greek history before Philip of Macedon and dismissed the Ptolemies with a bare list. Roman history entered his ken when Julius Caesar brought Rome to Egypt. Only an occasional tidbit interrupted al-Tabari's bare list of emperors through Heraclius—Jesus was born under Augustus, Nero slew Peter and Paul, and Titus crushed a Jewish rebellion and destroyed Jerusalem.[25]

Latin never took root in the east Mediterranean lands Muslims wrested from Byzantium, and with one exception Latin texts were not translated into Arabic in medieval times.[26] For most Muslims, *"Rum"* and "Caesar" conjured up Byzantium, not the vanished Romans of the West.

AL-TAHTAWI'S CLASSICAL GREECE AND ROME

Al-Jabarti admired the library at the Institut d'Égypte, but a generation passed before another Azhari was in a position to give his countrymen their first glimpse of what Greece and Rome meant to Europeans. Poring over the books his French mentors prescribed in Paris in the 1820s, al-Tahtawi encountered Greece and Rome at every turn. He read a book on the lives of the Greek philosophers, a history with sections on Greek mythology "during their *jahiliyya*," Montesquieu's *Considerations on the Causes of the Greatness of the Romans and of Their Decline,* and

Fénelon's *Adventures of Telemachus*. The selections al-Tahtawi read from Racine, Montesquieu's *Spirit of the Laws,* Voltaire's *Philosophic Dictionary,* and Rousseau's *Social Contract* were also saturated with classical allusions.[27]

As a gift for their star pupil, the French savants presented al-Tahtawi the *abbé* Jean-Jacques Barthélemy's *Travels of Anacharsis the Younger in Greece during the Middle of the Fourth Century before the Christian Era* (5 vols., Paris, 1788). This forgotten philhellenic bestseller told of a fictional Scythian's travel through Greece, where he converses with Plato, Aristotle, Demosthenes, and Xenophon. Al-Tahtawi later divided *Anacharsis* among his pupils for translation into Arabic, but the project was never carried through.[28]

As head of the translation bureau under Muhammad Ali and again under Ismail, al-Tahtawi selected for translation to Arabic a history of Greek philosophy, Montesquieu's *Considerations on the Causes of the Greatness of the Romans and of Their Decline,* and a history of the ancient Near East, Greece, and Rome.[29]

Al-Tahtawi's *Anwar,* published in 1868, has rightly attracted notice for its innovative coverage of pharaonic Egypt,[30] but it devotes twice as many pages to the Greco-Roman-Byzantine era. Al-Tahtawi took a favorable view of Greeks as far back as the Twenty-sixth Dynasty, when they were coming to Egypt as mercenaries. For him, Greece outshone every ancient civilization—Babylon, Assyria, Phoenicia, Persia, and India—except Egypt. Taking his cue from nineteenth-century Europeans, he took literally Herodotus's tale of Sesostris's (Rameses II) vast conquests in Europe and Asia as well as Greek legends of Egyptian colonies in prehistoric Greece. "Greece," declared al-Tahtawi simply, "is the daughter of Egypt."[31]

Al-Tahtawi also followed the Greeks in excoriating the Persians of the Twenty-seventh Dynasty as oppressors who attacked Egyptian priests and temples. The Twenty-eighth through the Thirtieth dynasties briefly regained the Egyptian fatherland's *(watan)* independence, only to fall again to Persia. This set the stage for Alexander and the Ptolemies as liberators. The priests at Siwa hailed Alexander as the son of Amon-Re. Al-Tahtawi praised Alexander and the Ptolemies for building temples to Egyptian as well as Greek gods and founding Alexandria as a great entrepôt linking Africa, Asia, and Europe:

> At [the] time of Alexander the Great, the Ptolemies and during the dark days
> of Roman domination, Egypt was as much respected for its cultural and

moral influence as it was feared under the Pharaos [*sic*] for her material strength. Alexandria was the seat of many scientists, men of letters and philosophers who excelled in many sciences, especially in the study of customs and manners, and its culture spread to all the other nations. Her specialized knowledge was a great benefit to everybody whether living in it or coming from outside.[32]

According to al-Tahtawi, Egypt flourished especially under the first two Ptolemies. Manetho wrote his history of ancient Egypt in Greek, Jews translated their Torah into Greek, the Nile–Red Sea canal was reopened, and the lighthouse, museum *(madrasa),* and library of Alexandria were founded. Mention of the Rosetta Stone (bearing a decree of Ptolemy V) brings al-Tahtawi to Champollion's decipherment. In treating Claudius Ptolemy's geocentric cosmology, al-Tahtawi attributes heliocentrism to Pythagoras, Copernicus, and modern Europeans but warns that it contradicts the Quran.[33] He says that the internecine quarrels of the later Ptolemies hurt Egypt and that, after all, a Greek elite was ruling over Egyptians.

Al-Tahtawi sweeps through Roman history from Romulus and Remus to Julius Caesar in a single page, barely mentioning the Punic Wars. Unlike Ahmad Shawqi, whose 1928 play *The Death of Cleopatra* depicted her as an Egyptian nationalist fending off Roman imperialism, al-Tahtawi felt no affection for the last of the Ptolemies. He takes pains to clear the caliph Umar of the charge of burning the library of Alexandria, saying it had already burned during Julius Caesar's siege.[34] Despite Rome's initial religious toleration and temple building as far as Nubia, al-Tahtawi sees the Romans as exploiters bent on extracting Egypt's wealth. Not entirely consistently, however, he follows Western stereotypes of good and bad emperors. Hadrian was good, for example, and Egypt prospered under his rule.[35]

Al-Tahtawi mentions the birth of "Jesus the Son of Mary" under Augustus, the flight into Egypt, and the Quran's denial of the Christian belief in Jesus' death and resurrection. He describes how Christianity gradually displaced Egypt's old "Sabian" religion. He discusses Roman persecutions of Christians and the conversion of Constantine, and begins his Thirty-fifth Dynasty, which ruled from Constantinople until the Islamic conquest, with the accession of Theodosius, who banned the old gods.[36]

Al-Tahtawi's *Anwar* and its sequel, *Nihayat,* could have carried students into the third year of the history curriculum in effect in the 1870s in the two state preparatory schools—Ras al-Tin in Alexandria and Darb al-Jamamiz in Cairo. The first-year curriculum covered ancient Egypt and the Near East; and the second, ancient Greece, the Hellenistic period, the Roman Republic and the early Roman Empire. The third year included the empire to the accession of Theodosius, the era of the barbarian invasions, pre-Islamic and early Islamic history, and Islamic Spain and Sicily; the fourth covered medieval Arab history—the Crusades, Ayyubids, and Mamluks to the Ottoman conquest.[37] Although it omitted post-1517 Egypt and much of Asian, African, and American history, this curriculum opened vast new historical vistas to modern Egyptians.

The four-year history sequence at Dar al-Ulum from at least 1875 paid less attention to the pre-Islamic era and more to post-1517 Ottoman history and modern Europe. A 1911 report deplored Dar al-Ulum's stress on European history at the expense of Islamic.[38]

Al-Tahtawi treated Greece and Rome in other works besides *Anwar*. An article in *Rawdat al-madaris* on Greek and Roman customs proposed the treatment of women as a gauge of a society's progress.[39] In 1869 Khedive Ismail had al-Tahtawi oversee an Arabic translation of Offenbach's *La Belle Hélène* (as *Hilana al-Jamila*) for the inaugural performance at the Théâtre Comédie in Cairo.[40]

In *Paths of Egyptian Hearts in the Joys of the Contemporary Arts (Manahij)*, al-Tahtawi mixed Greco-Roman and pharaonic maxims with ones from the Quran, Hadiths, and other Islamic sources. He cited Solon, Alexander, and the Ptolemies and praised the patriotism of pharaonic, Roman, and Muslim heroes. He enlisted the hadith "Love of one's country is an article of faith" to reconcile his Egyptian patriotism with Islam, and he quoted the proverb hailing Egypt as "Mother of the World."[41]

Although al-Tahtawi justified Muhammad Ali's attempt to crush the Greek war for independence on the grounds that Greeks had attacked Muslims and mosques, he believed that as in ancient times, immigrant Greeks would help contemporary Egypt prosper. He likened Muhammad Ali to Alexander: Both were foreign-born monarchs who ruled Egypt tolerantly and well.[42] After treating Alexander's brief Thirty-second, or "First Macedonian," Dynasty, he emphasized that "God blessed it [Egypt] with another Macedonian conqueror of the region . . . Muhammad Pasha Ali."[43] He might have added that Alexander's home in Pella was only a hundred miles from Muhammad Ali's native Kavala.

GREEKS, ITALIANS, AND ALEXANDRIA'S
NINETEENTH-CENTURY RENAISSANCE

Muhammad Ali's youthful Macedonian-Ottoman experience made him at home in the world of Mediterranean commerce and geopolitics. The Ptolemies and Romans had moved the Egyptian capital seaward to Alexandria, but Muslim rulers had returned it inland to al-Fustat / Cairo, between ancient Memphis and Heliopolis. By the time that Bonaparte arrived, Alexandria had shrunk to only eight thousand people. Without abandoning Cairo, Muhammad Ali revived the city as his prime gateway to the European-dominated world economy. The "second Macedonian" built a palace on the sea at Ras al-Tin and spent a good deal of time there. He conscripted peasants to dig the Mahmudiyya Canal, which provided Alexandria with fresh water and transport to the Nile. He built up a Mediterranean fleet, established an arsenal in the port, dispatched troops to put down the revolt in Ottoman Greece, and began developing cotton as a cash crop to pay for European imports.

In 1821 Alexandria was still a small town of only 12,000–13,000, but by the end of the reign in 1848 it had swelled to 104,000. This grew to 231,000 in 1882 and to 403,000 by Cromer's retirement in 1907. The proportion of Europeans and their protégés also shifted sharply, from fewer than 5 percent of Alexandria's population in 1848 to 25 percent in 1882.[44] In Alexandria, as in Renaissance Italy, a merchant elite riding a booming economy drew inspiration and legitimacy from the Greco-Roman past. In modern Alexandria, however, nearly all the merchant princes were foreign, and it was they rather than Egyptians who imagined themselves continuing the classical past.

The very name of Alexandria kept alive memories of its founder, and with Greco-Roman antiquities crunching under foot, the classical legacy loomed larger than in Cairo. Both al-Fustat and Fatimid Cairo were Islamic foundations, after all, and Europeans made up a far smaller proportion of its population (about 5 percent in 1897).[45] Cairo's Islamic monuments and the nearby pharaonic wonders at Giza and Saqqara overshadowed the remnants of Roman Babylon at "Old Cairo."

Greeks, with 33 percent of Alexandria's Europeans in 1897 and 41 percent in 1907,[46] were the largest foreign colony. Here and in other Egyptian cities, Greeks became stereotypical grocers, liquor store owners, moneylenders, and intermediaries in the provincial cotton markets. Greeks flourished under the protective umbrellas of the Muhammad Ali family, the European consuls, and—eventually—British rule. Independent Greece was too weak, divided, and preoccupied with Balkan, Aegean, and Anatolian irredentism to revive imperial claims on Egypt. Greece did obtain capitulatory rights in Egypt in 1854 and a seat on the Mixed Court of Appeals in 1889.

Like their counterparts in independent Greece into the twentieth century, Egyptian Greeks found it difficult to sort out their national heritage from their Orthodox religious one, and classical from Byzantine nostalgia.[47] In the eighteenth century, Greeks living in Egypt had simply seen themselves as members of the Greek Orthodox *millet,* whose communal institutions in Alexandria included the patriarchate, a church, and a monastery that ran a hospice and a hostel for travelers.

Greek identity became more complicated with the establishment of independent Greece in 1830. Greece opened a consulate in Alexandria in 1833. Ten years later the Greco-Egyptian Orthodox Community of Alexandria was formally constituted, with elected officers, a school, and a hospital. The Greek patriarch protested, fearing erosion of his authority, but in vain. The choice of neo-Gothic rather than neo-Byzantine style for the Church of Evangelismos, begun in 1844 in Alexandria and dedicated in 1856, indicates a westward-looking gaze. In 1887, the community changed its name to the Hellenic Community of Alexandria, implicitly excluding Arabic-speaking Orthodox Christians. Greeks in Cairo followed a similar but slower trajectory toward Hellenism, constituting the Greek Orthodox Community in 1856 and renaming it the Hellenic Community in 1904.

Until the Turks drove the Greeks from Anatolia in 1923, Alexandrian Greeks, like their Aegean fellows, might have dreamed of the *Megali Idhea* (Great Idea) of reconstituting the Byzantine Empire in the east Mediterranean and Balkans. Mainland Greeks were torn between nostalgia for Byzantium and for the fifth-century B.C.E. golden age so dear to Western philhellenes, but Alexandrians, like the poet Constantine Cavafy,[48] were drawn to the Hellenistic age of the Ptolemies.

The physician Tassos Démétrios Néroutsos (1826–1892) and merchant notables Count Stephan Zizinia (1794–1868) and Sir John Antoniadis (1818–1895) were among the Alexandrian Greeks with antiquarian interests. Néroutsos had a medical degree from Munich, where he had also done a thesis on the names of Roman divinities. He read papers on ancient Alexandria at the Institut égyptien and donated his antiquities collection to it. But the Institut left for Cairo, and Greeks were less active in it after Néroutsos's death.[49] Zizinia epitomized the confusingly nebulous national identities of some cosmopolitan Alexandrians. Born in Chios, he obtained French citizenship while conducting business in Marseilles but served as president of the Greek Community in Alexandria and consul general of Belgium. Queen Victoria knighted Antoniadis, a major patron of the Greco-Roman Museum who left his palace and garden to the municipality of Alexandria.[50]

Alexandria lost some fine collections of Greco-Roman antiquities to Athens and elsewhere, but in 1907 E. Glymenopoulo declared of his collection: "These ancient objects belong by right to the Museum of Alexandria, having been found in Egypt, and acquired exclusively for science and with money earned in the same country, as hospitable as celebrated. That is why, in sending them to their destination, I consider that I am not making a gift properly speaking, but simply a restitution."[51]

The name of L'Association des hommes de science hellénes à Alexandria, Ptolémée Ier (1909), most of whose members were Greek medical doctors, kept alive the memory of the founder of the Ptolemaic dynasty. In Cairo, the short-lived Hellénion Society took its name from an ancient temple in the Delta city of Naucratis, where colonists from nine Greek cities had supported a common cult.[52]

Like Cardinal Lavigerie's White Fathers in Tunisia, Greek tobacco magnate Nestor Gianaclis set out to reconstitute the North African viticulture he had read about in classical texts. Gianaclis's estates near Alexandria, nationalized by Nasser but recently privatized, still produce Crue des Ptolémés and Reine Cléopatre wines. The absence of rainfall agriculture spared Egypt a costly failure like the French attempt, based on classical allusions to North Africa as "the granary of Rome," to establish Morocco as a major grain exporter.[53]

Italians made a strong second behind the Greeks among Alexandria's foreign residents (the Italians constituted 25 percent of the European residents in 1897).[54] Italian builders, craftsmen, and mechanics were as ubiquitous as Greek grocers, and the royal family from Ismail through Fuad had close Italian advisers in their entourage. A weak sixth among the powers of Europe, Italy had no hope of satisfying its neoimperial longings in Egypt. Outmaneuvered by France in Tunisia and humiliated by Ethiopia at the battle of Adua in 1896, Italy's new Roman Empire had to make do with Libya and Eritrea—whose classical names it revived—and part of Somalia. Only Mussolini, who steeped his Fascist regime in Roman symbolism, would later pursue the mirage of conquering Egypt.[55]

The directorship of the Greco-Roman Museum, in Italian hands for over half a century, nevertheless asserted modern Italy's claim on the legacy of classical Alexandria. Dreaming of Julius Caesar, Marc Antony, Augustus, and Hadrian, a number of Italian notables of Alexandria collected Greco-Roman and pharaonic antiquities. Pietro Pugioli (1831–1902), for example, assembled a collection that was later scattered among museums in Cairo, Bologna, Vienna, and New York.[56]

Britain and France were a distant third and fourth behind Greece and Italy among foreigners in Alexandria, and Egypt, around the turn of the century.[57] (Many of the "English" of the census were actually Maltese; and the "French," Tunisians and Algerians). Nevertheless, Britain's occupation and France's cultural prestige and control of the Antiquities Service lent weight to their nationals' opinions in Alexandrian archaeology.

MAHMUD AL-FALAKI: EXCAVATING AND MAPPING ANCIENT ALEXANDRIA

Although not a specialist in Greek and Latin, Mahmud al-Falaki (1815–1885) was the only Egyptian before World War I to win recognition from Europeans who were. Like al-Tahtawi and Ali Mubarak, he was a scholar-official of wide-ranging interests. Al-Falaki applied his scientific training as an engineer and astronomer to research problems in three of the four fields treated in this book—Greco-Roman, ancient Egyptian, and Islamic studies.

Like Mubarak, Mahmud Ahmad Hamdi al-Falaki was an indigenous Egyptian who climbed from rural origins through the new state schools to the cabinet at a time when Turco-Circassians still dominated the ruling elite. He left his village in the Delta province of Daqhaliyya to attend Muhammad Ali's naval school at Alexandria and engineering school in Cairo. He began teaching in the latter in 1839, the year Ali Mubarak entered. Mubarak studied under Mahmud (he had not yet added "al-Falaki" to his name), went on to advanced studies in France, and upon returning won the favor of Abbas I. Mubarak persuaded the viceroy to send Mahmud, already thirty-five, to Paris to study astronomy. One of the two men who accompanied him was Ismail Mustafa, who, like Mahmud, would add "al-Falaki"—literally, "the astronomer"—to his name. Mahmud al-Falaki spent four years at the Paris Observatory and five more visiting observatories in Edinburgh, Berlin, Vienna, Dublin, and Brussels before returning in his mid-forties to become royal astronomer at the Abbasiyya Observatory.[58]

Mahmud al-Falaki was unique among Egyptians of his day in publishing in a variety of European scholarly journals. He represented Egypt at international geographical congresses in Paris in 1875 and Venice in 1881. Al-Falaki seems to have accepted the implicit European consensus that Europe was now the global center for "pure science" and that scientists in the periphery should concentrate on secondary tasks like gathering data and working on applied problems. His scholarly contributions were not in astronomy proper but in related practical fields—meteorology, geodesy, terrestrial magnetism, chronology, cartography, and archaeology. He discussed pyramid triangulation with Flinders Petrie and published on the subject. He excavated in Alexandria and drew up a map of the city in ancient times, and his work on the Islamic calendar interested Orientalists.

None of al-Falaki's Egyptian contemporaries rivaled his activities in the European-dominated Institut égyptien, the Khedivial Geographical Society, and the Comité de conservation des monuments de l'art arabe. He was vice president of the Institut and president of the Geographical Society and, unlike some notables there, presented scholarly papers himself. For over ten years al-Falaki labored on a map of Lower Egypt, which the Bulaq Press published in 1871. In 1865–1866, he dug in Alexandria in an effort to clarify points for a map of the city in ancient times and published his results in the *Bulletin de l'Institut égyptien* (1868–1869) and in Copenhagen.[59] Few Egyptians paid attention, but classical archaeologists have used his research ever since as a baseline for the city's ancient topography.[60]

GLADSTONE, CROMER, AND ANCIENT AND MODERN IMPERIALISM

The British prime minister who ordered the army into Egypt in 1882 and the consul general who ran the country for a quarter of a century would have been half mute without the classics. William Gladstone wrote seven volumes on Homer and lectured on him whenever he could.[61] In 1892 in London, the Ninth International Congress of Orientalists elected him chair of their section on relations between the Orient and archaic Greece.[62] Seven ministers in Gladstone's first cabinet had firsts in classics from Oxford or Cambridge, and in his day Latin quotations were staples in the House of Commons. Gladstone, Salisbury, and Foreign Secretary Granville first read classics at Eton, then at Christ Church College, Oxford. In the next generation, Prime Minister Asquith, South African proconsul Alfred Milner, and viceroy of India George Curzon—all Balliol men—sealed Oxford's reputation as the cradle of empire.[63]

For all his anti-imperialist rhetoric, Gladstone now comes across as a believer in informal empire. He was typically mid-Victorian in exalting Homer and denigrating Virgil, the poet of empire, and Virgil's master, Augustus. But Virgil, Augustus, and formal empire made a comeback with the "new imperialism" late in the century, and the aged Gladstone seemed out of touch. Anchises' prophesy in the *Aeneid* of cultural glory for Greece and an imperial destiny for Rome now struck a ready chord: "When an Englishman of the last century read these central words of all Latin poetry, how could he fail to think of his own country? To the English fortune, or, as the later Victorians increasingly believed, Destiny had assigned the splendours and burdens of empire."[64]

"There was a time no doubt," wrote Cambridge professor John Seeley, "when the Roman Empire, because it was despotic and in some periods unhappy and half-barbarous, was thought uninteresting. . . . [But] there are many good things in politics besides liberty; for instance there is nationality, there is civilisation."[65] "Colony," "colonialism," "dominion," "empire," and "imperialism" all derive from Latin roots.[66]

A classically draped Britannia, attended by Knowledge and Power, surveyed her empire from atop the Colonial Office in Whitehall.[67] Foucault could not have expressed it better. In *Punch* cartoons, Athena with a trident became a standard image of Britannia,[68] as in the cartoon hailing Kitchener as conqueror of Khartoum in 1898 (see figure 29).

War hawks in and out of Gladstone's cabinet wore him down in the Egyptian crisis of 1882. Perhaps he deluded himself that a temporary occupation was possible, but he was reading Thomas B. Macaulay's *Lays of Ancient Rome* (1842) as he sent in the troops.[69] Cromer recalled Scipio's and Cato's opposition to imperial conquests lest they corrupt society at home: "The Romans, therefore—or, at all events, some of the wisest among them—struggled honestly and manfully to check the appetite for self-aggrandizement as ever Mr. Gladstone and Lord Granville strove to shake off the Egyptian burthen in 1882."[70]

A year earlier, a British journalist had accused France of waging the "last Punic War" in occupying Tunisia.[71] Now, a British garrison on the Nile challenged France's claim to be sole heir of imperial Rome's lost North African provinces. A *Punch* parody of Gérôme's painting of Cleopatra before Caesar has toga-clad Gladstone puzzling what to do when General Wolseley presents him with a bare-breasted Egypt (see figure 30).

Cecil Rhodes's favorite quotation, "Remember always that you are a Roman,"[72] could well have been Cromer's. Born into the banking fam-

PUNCH, OR THE LONDON CHARIVARI.—November 5, 1898.

WELCOME!

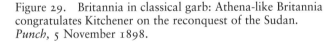

BRITANNIA. "SIRDAR! I THANK YOU! I AM PROUD OF YOU!"

"It was not merely a great victory for Egypt and Great Britain, but it was a great victory for civilisation."
(*Lord Rosebery at Perth, October 24.* "*Times*" *report.*)

Figure 29. Britannia in classical garb: Athena-like Britannia congratulates Kitchener on the reconquest of the Sudan. *Punch,* 5 November 1898.

ily of Baring as Evelyn Baring, the future Lord Cromer had a military education at Woolwich. Among Cromer's successors in Egypt, Lord Kitchener and Reginald Wingate were also Woolwich men (so was Charles Gordon "of Khartoum"), while Henry McMahon and Field Marshall Edmund Allenby attended Sandhurst. Always regretful of missing a classical education, Cromer taught himself Greek and Latin. Untranslated Greek and Latin quotations in his *Modern Egypt* asserted his arrival among the classical cognoscenti. He skewered Islamic slavery with a quotation in Greek, denounced Islam's treatment of women with one in Latin, and dismissed Egyptian foreign minister Tigrane Pasha

PUNCH, OR THE LONDON CHARIVARI.—October 7, 1882.

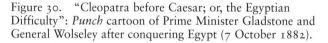

CLEOPATRA BEFORE CÆSAR;

OR, THE EGYPTIAN DIFFICULTY.

[*Slightly* (!) *altered from* GÉRÔME's *celebrated Picture.*

Figure 30. "Cleopatra before Caesar; or, the Egyptian Difficulty": *Punch* cartoon of Prime Minister Gladstone and General Wolseley after conquering Egypt (7 October 1882).

(Dikran d'Abro) as having a "Franco-Byzantine" mind and being "prey to intellectual oversubtlety—*Graecorum ille morbus,* as it was termed by Seneca."[73] What gentleman would dare request a translation?

Cromer had served his imperial apprenticeship in India, the outer fringe of the classical world. Even here, Britons scoured the classics for tidbits to help them understand—and rule—India.[74] Years later, "in the hot and brooding nights of the Egyptian summer, when all who were at liberty to do so had fled to cooler climes, Cromer and [Oriental secretary] Harry Boyle might often have been seen seated after dinner on the verandah of the Agency in Cairo, reading aloud alternatively passages from the Iliad."[75]

Flattered as "one in whom the Greek lucidity of intelligence is combined with the Roman faculty of constructive administration,"[76] Cromer
presided over London's Classical Association after his retirement. His
little book *Ancient and Modern Imperialism* was his presidential address. Two of Cromer's contemporaries also wrote books comparing the
British and Roman empires, and his parliamentary critic John M.
Robertson insisted that empire was corrupting Britain as it had Rome.[77]

Cromer rejected any unsettling parallels between Greek and British
imperialism. He dismissed Alexander as "not a true Greek" and "a conqueror rather than an empire-builder" and opined that "British imperialists may derive some consolation from the reflection that the experience of Athens cannot be used as an argument to prove that democratic
institutions must necessarily be incompatible with the execution of a sane
Imperial policy, but rather as one to show the fatal effects produced by
democracy run mad."[78] He enlisted the classics to confirm a stereotypi-
cally timeless Orient and pointed up universal moral lessons: "The Romans . . . assure us that the Egyptians were proud of the scourge-marks
for perpetrating frauds in taxation. As it was in the days of Augustus,
so it was in the days of Ismail." Ismail "fell victim to hubris [printed in
Greek letters], the insolent abuse of power. A great Nemesis fell upon
the Egyptian Croesus."[79]

Alfred Milner, who served under Cromer, played with the classical
trope of Egyptian paradox: "Egypt is still, like the Egypt of Herodotus,
the chosen home of what is strange and unexampled and paradoxical."
A few pages later he asks us to "imagine a people the most docile and
good-tempered in the world in the grip of a religion the most intolerant
and fanatical."[80]

Cromer noted that Britain and Rome had both expanded in search
of natural frontiers, won battles against long odds, recruited auxiliaries
from the vanquished, and conferred a famous pax on their subjects. Like
Thomas Arnold, he faulted the Romans for not being Christians—
Byzantium was beyond his horizon—and therefore inferior to modern
Britons on issues of slavery and humanitarianism. Cromer shared none
of Edward Gibbon's fascination with the uncomfortable subject of
Rome's decline.

Cromer conceded that Rome had assimilated European subjects east
of Greece, whereas England was failing to assimilate its Asian and
African subjects. But Rome had faced only tribes, not self-conscious nations; Roman religion could accommodate deities of the vanquished,
and Christianity could not; and the Romans and the Greeks had not had

the problem of color prejudice. He consoled himself that no other Europeans had succeeded where England had failed; even the modern Greeks rarely intermarried with Egyptians.[81]

He reflected that "the world has not so very much changed in 2,000 years": "When I read in Dr. Adolf Holm's monumental history that the Greeks in Alexandria, under the Ptolemaic rule, had the privilege of being beaten with a stick instead of a whip, I am reminded that their descendants, in common with other foreign subjects, possess privileges of substantially greater importance."[82]

When Ronald Storrs, who rose at 6:30 to read Homer before breakfast, started work in the British Residency near the end of Cromer's long reign,

> Lady Cromer handed me a Latin invitation which the Lord had received from the University of Aberdeen ... and bade me answer it in the same tongue. I ... undertook to do it most cheerfully: I had no books of any kind, but furbished up a good Roman roll, which I gave to her when she came to tea. She hadn't been gone an hour when I got a note, asking me to luncheon and telling me the Lord had called it "devilish" good. I found the old man very much pleased about it: he said he felt an infernal hypocrite signing it, and was quite sure he'd be found out, etc. Gave me a copy of his translation from the Greek Anthology, and hoped that the Varsities would retain Greek.[83]

Retiring under fire from Egypt and back home, Cromer reproached his critics with Euripides: "Dost see how thy country, when reproached for wanting in deliberation, looks sternly at those who assail her? For she grows great in the midst of toils." Lest anyone miss the point, he condescended to add an English translation to the Greek original.[84]

As proud as any Roman that he could toss off a Greek epigram, Cromer's classical outlook cramped his vision. Except for Greek, the Romans rarely learned their subjects' tongues, and the latter-day proconsul, who prided himself on his intimate knowledge of Egypt, never stooped to learn Arabic.

Like many a philhellene, Cromer found it hard to tolerate living Greeks. After insisting too much that "many influential and highly respectable Greeks" brought "an unmixed benefit" to Egypt, he unleashed a tirade against

> low-class Greeks exercising the professions of usurer, drink-seller, etc. The Greek of this class ... will risk his life in pursuit of petty gain. It is not only that a Greek usurer or a *bakal* (general dealer) is established in almost every village in Egypt; the Greek pushes his way into the most remote parts of the Soudan and of Abyssinia.... In 1889, I visited Sarras, some thirty miles

south of Wadi Halfa. It was at that time the farthest outpost of the Egyptian army, and is situated in the midst of a howling wilderness. The posts had only been established for a few days. Nevertheless, there I found a Greek already selling sardines, biscuits, etc. . . . out of a hole in a rock in which he had set up a temporary shop.[85]

"The low-class Greek" usurer, he declared,

tempts the Egyptian peasant to borrow at some exorbitant rate of interest, and then, by a sharp turn of the legal screw, reduces him from the position of an allodial proprietor to that of a serf. . . . Under Greek action and influence, the Egyptian villagers are taking to drink. Mr. Gladstone . . . once said that it would be a good thing if the Turks were turned "bag and baggage" out of Europe . . . [but] it would be an excellent thing for Turkey and its dependencies if some of the low-class Greeks . . . could be turned bag and baggage out of Turkey.

THE GRECO-ROMAN MUSEUM AND THE SOCIÉTÉ D'ARCHÉOLOGIE D'ALEXANDRIE

"Founded upon cotton with the concurrence of onions and eggs," wrote E. M. Forster, "modern Alexandria is scarcely a city of the soul."[86] Alexandria lacked a mosque-university of the stature of al-Azhar and had no modern university until the 1940s. Arabic-speaking intellectuals gravitated to Cairo, whence the newspaper *Al-Ahram* migrated in 1898.

From 1859 until 1880, the Institut égyptien provided Alexandrians, particularly Europeans, a ready forum for classical discourse. Speakers often presented papers on Greco-Roman topics, and the Institut published them in its bulletin. In the 1860s, the Institut pointed out the need for a museum in Alexandria and set up the Permanent Committee of Archaeology to protect fast-perishing antiquities from the vandalism of travelers. (The "Permanent Committee," however, quickly proved itself less than permanent.) The Institut acquired a modest collection of antiquities. Although the Institut touched the lives of only a small segment of Europeans and even fewer Egyptians, its transfer to Cairo in 1880, along with its library and antiquities, left a void in Alexandrian cultural life.[87]

While a guest of British consul Sir Charles Cookson in 1889, Rev. Archibald Sayce met Guiseppe Botti, the director of Alexandria's Italian school. Arriving from Italy five years earlier, Botti had devoted his leisure to trying to square classical accounts with the scanty remains of the ancient city. The three talked of the need for a museum. Two years later in 1891, Cookson and a few others formed the Athenaeum Society, which successfully lobbied the municipality for a Greco-Roman museum.[88]

In 1892, European notables and professionals worked through the new Alexandria municipality to found the Greco-Roman Museum and the Municipal Library. The government—probably Eugène Grébaut of the Antiquities Service—initially opposed the idea of a museum run by "amateurs." Then, in an implicit compensation for the damage the Ismailia–Port Said railway was expected to do to Alexandrian commerce, the government reversed itself and authorized the museum.[89] The Antiquities Service would oversee the Greco-Roman Museum, but the municipality of Alexandria would pay for it. Botti became the first director.

A European commercial elite dominated the municipality, founded in 1890. Half the municipality's twenty-eight-man board held ex officio seats or were Egyptian government appointees. An exclusive college of merchants, property owners, and well-to-do tenants elected the other half. Three-fourths of the electors turned out to be Europeans. The municipality levied taxes and spent the money on urban infrastructure.[90]

The founders of the Municipal Library and Greco-Roman Museum naturally played on nostalgia for the city's legendary ancient Museum and library. The modern museum and the Archaeological Society built up their own scholarly library, freeing the Municipal Library to serve general readers in several European languages and Arabic. Successive Swiss directors (Victor Nourrisson and Étienne Combes) ran the library's European section—which of course had priority over the Arabic section—for fifty years (1892–1943).[91]

Members of the Athenaeum were prominent among the dozen enthusiasts who formed the Société d'archéologie d'Alexandrie in 1893 to support the new museum. With the glaring exception that its founding members included no Muslims or Copts, the society was as cosmopolitan and polyglot as the city itself. Britons made up the largest contingent: Cookson, Admiral R. Blomfield (comptroller of the port), two other British officers, and banker John Reeves. Botti and architect A. Manusardi were Italian; Nourrisson, Swiss; and banker Georges Goussio, Greek. Baron Jacques de Menasce was an Egyptian Jew with Austro-Hungarian citizenship, and Egyptologist Albert Daninos was variously reported to be of Greek and Algerian-French background.[92] In 1897, the Archaeological Society mourned the loss of its Greek presi-

dent, Goussio, in the Ottoman-Greek War but consoled itself that he had
lived to see "a dream realized, and the new Alexandria of the Khedives
linked up to the ancient one of the Lagides [Ptolemies]. Out of this dream
he achieved happiness."[93]

The Greco-Roman Museum was unique among Egypt's archaeological museums in enjoying the support of an organized community group.
The Archaeological Society sponsored lectures and tours and in 1898
began publishing a bulletin with articles in French, Italian, English, and
German. Greek and Arabic did not meet the Europeans' test of inter-
nationally accessible scholarly languages. Prince Umar Tusun long served
as the society's honorary president. Otherwise the society had had
British, French, Italian, Greek, Spanish, and American presidents by
1952, but not an Egyptian one.

The Greco-Roman Museum went up around the corner from its par-
ent municipality's building, in the modern section east of the center of
town. Khedive Abbas II inaugurated the museum on 17 October 1892
and returned three years later to open its new building. The Doric neoclassical facade fit Western ideas of proper museum architecture, the
Alexandrian milieu, and the contents of the collection inside (see figure
31).[94] The museum's own excavations in greater Alexandria, donations
from civic-minded citizens, and transfers of Greco-Roman antiquities
from the Egyptian Museum gradually filled the new building.

Botti ran the museum until his death in 1903, conducting small excavations around greater Alexandria and turning out a stream of publications. The choice of Evaristo Breccia (1876–1967) as his successor
confirmed the museum as an Italian cultural enclave in colonized Egypt.
Breccia had studied ancient history at the University of Rome and excavated with Egyptologist Ernesto Schiaparelli at Ashmunein (Her-
mopolis Magna). Directing the museum from 1904 until 1931, he followed Botti's example of intermittent excavations and frequent
publication. When Breccia moved on to a chair of classical antiquity at
Pisa in 1931, Achille Adriani (1905–1982) kept the post in Italian
hands.[95]

The Greco-Roman Museum had no monopoly on classical expertise
in Egypt. The Egyptian Museum and the Institut français d'archéologie
orientale du Caire usually had classicists on hand. In 1894, Hellenist
Pierre Jouguet began working on the Greek papyri of the Antiquities Service; he would be active in the field for more than half a century.[96]

The Egypt Exploration Fund (EEF) took the lead in retrieving the
treasure trove of Greek papyri preserved in Egypt's dry sands. The EEF's

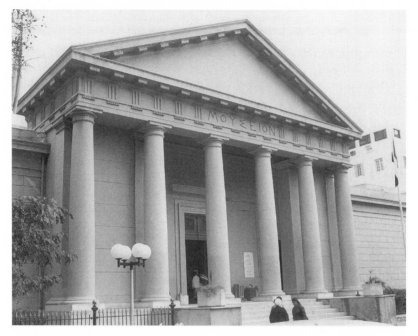

Figure 31.   The Greco-Roman Museum, Alexandria. Inaugurated 1895.
Photograph by Donald Reid.

founding statement had ranked the Greeks second only to the Hebrews
as objects for investigation. The Land of Goshen in the eastern Delta
came first because of the Bible, but finding the Greek city of Naucratis,
which might shed light on an obscure period of Greek art, was the second priority.[97] Petrie found Naucratis for the EEF in 1884–1885. Digging on his own later in the decade he turned up a roll of Homer at
Hawara and Ptolemaic mummy cases made of inscribed papyrus scraps
at Gurob. Ernest Budge entered the papyrus race for the British Museum,
purchasing scrolls that included Aristotle's lost Constitution of Athens.[98]

Bernard Grenfell and Arthur Hunt, who had read classics at Queens
College, Oxford, became the EEF's champion hunters of Greek papyri.
In 1895–1896 they found at Al-Bahnasa (Oxyrhynchus) in the Fayum
some three thousand, mostly fragmentary Greek papyri and a few in
Latin, Coptic, and Arabic. The EEF responded by setting up the Graeco-
Roman Research Account (now the Graeco-Roman Branch), which
backed their excavations for over a dozen years and organized publi-
cation of the finds. By the time World War I intervened, Grenfell and
Hunt had already turned from excavation to publishing their rich finds.

The Oxyrhynchus publishing project, in which Edgar Lobel was a leader for sixty years, continues to this day.

Grenfell and Hunt have been accused of treasure hunting papyri at the expense of everything else. They published no site plans. Defenders point out that their Oxyrhynchus excavations were in trash heaps in which few or no stone blocks or bricks remained in situ. They had their own priorities at a time when illicit digging was rapidly devouring these sites.

SYRIAN CHRISTIAN IMMIGRANTS
AND THE GRECO-ROMAN CLASSICS

In 1902, only 4 of 102 members of the Archaeological Society of Alexandria were Egyptians, and several of these (including future prime minister Ismail Sidqi) belonged only because of their official posts. Prince Umar Tousoun was the only Egyptian among nineteen honorary members.[99] No state school in Egypt taught Latin or Greek,[100] and Egyptians found it harder to identify with the Greco-Roman than with other eras of their past.

For a time, Syrian Christians helped introduce Egyptians to the Greco-Roman heritage that the Europeans so cherished. From the 1870s until World War I, Syrian Christian immigrants stood out in translation, theater, journalism, and commerce. Opportunity in Egypt beckoned, and political repression and press censorship in greater Syria under Sultan Abdulhamid II also propelled some of those who left for Egypt. First Ismail and then the British welcomed the Syrians, who flourished whether defending the occupation like Faris Nimr in his newspaper *Al-Muqattam,* opposing it like the francophile Taqla brothers of *Al-Ahram,* or carefully staying neutral like Jurji Zaydan of *Al-Hilal.* Syrian Christian prominence in Egypt had already peaked by 1900, as more Egyptians entered the fields in which the Syrians flourished.[101]

Syrian Christians translated, adapted, and produced French plays featuring Greco-Roman themes. Salim al-Naqqash and Adib Ishaq came from Lebanon in the mid-1870s, established a theatrical troupe with Ismail's support, joined Jamal al-Din al-Afghani's circle, and went on to publish Arabic newspapers. Al-Naqqash's adaptation of Corneille's *Les Trois Horaces et les trois Curices* as *Mayy wa Huras* (May and Horace) retained polytheistic allusions to Roman gods. In translating Antonio Ghislanzoni's libretto for Verdi's *Aida* into Arabic, however, al-Naqqash took the precaution of excising references to Isis and Osiris. Al-Naqqash's dedication declared that Khedive Ismail's deeds outshone those of

Alexander, Chosroes, and Caesar and also thanked Greek notable Antoniadis for his patronage.[102]

Before leaving Beirut for Cairo, Adib Ishaq had translated Jean
Racine's *Andromaque* into Arabic rhymed prose for the French consul.
Widowed when her husband, Hector, died defending Troy, Andromache
fell into the hands of Pyrrhus as spoils of war. Orestes later slew Pyrrhus.
Racine's *La Thébaïde ou les frères enemies,* in which the sons of Orestes
die contesting the throne of the Greek Thebes, was adapted for production in Arabic in Alexandria and Cairo in 1878.

Members of the Bustani family of Beirut undertook two ambitious
projects involving the Greco-Roman heritage—the encyclopaedia *Dairat
al-Maarif* (11 vols., 1876–1900) and the translation of the *Iliad* into Arabic. Egypt figured in both enterprises.[103] Butrus al-Bustani (1819–1883)
belonged to Ali Mubarak's generation and, as he did, displayed wide-
ranging learning by compiling an encyclopaedia. Al-Bustani was born
a Maronite in Lebanon and studied in the Maronite seminary at Ayn
Waraqa, getting a leg up on his Egyptian contemporaries in learning
Latin. He worked at the British and American consulates in Beirut, converted to Protestantism, taught in American missionary schools, and
helped the missionaries translate the Bible into Arabic. He also edited
Arabic magazines, founded his own National School in Beirut, and compiled an Arabic dictionary.

Al-Bustani lived all his life in Lebanon, but the encyclopedia he started
began and ended with Egyptian involvement. Two high Ottoman notables declined to support the project in advance, but Khedive Ismail characteristically promised to buy a thousand copies. Crown Prince Tawfiq
and Egyptian minister Mustafa Riyad (usually known as Riyad Pasha
or Riad Pasha) added their support. The French title *Encyclopédie arabe*
beneath the Arabic *Dairat al-Maarif* on the title page underlines the
Western sources of the editor's inspiration. Al-Bustani brought out six
volumes in Beirut but died in 1883. His son Salim edited two more but
died himself the following year. Two of Salim's brothers, Najib and Amin
al-Bustani, stepped into the breach, with assistance from their kinsman
Sulayman al-Bustani. Volume nine appeared in 1887, and after a long
interruption, volumes ten (1898) and eleven (1900) appeared. Jurji Zaydan printed the last two in Cairo on his *Al-Hilal* press. There the project broke off, two thirds of the way through the Arabic alphabet.

The encyclopedia emphasized modern science, technology, and European and Arab history. The article "Tarikh" (History) starts with
Herodotus and the Greeks, thereby removing Arab and Islamic history

from its privileged center and reducing it to one strand in world history. Al-Bustani succumbed to Eurocentrism, describing Europe as "the smallest continent but one, but the most important in the history of civilization."[104] As Albert Hourani pointed out, a medieval Muslim would have recognized only Theodosius among six closely grouped entries from the classical world in one volume; the other entries were for Themistocles, Thucydides, Theseus, Theophrastus, and Theocritus.

Butrus al-Bustani urged the translation of Homer and Virgil into Arabic as early as 1859. His encyclopedia's long entry on Homer detailed the European debate on the poet's authenticity and historicity. Butrus's kinsman Sulayman al-Bustani (1856–1925) took up the challenge in 1886, and over the next eighteen years rendered the *Iliad* into Arabic verse.

In wanderings worthy of Odysseus, Sulayman began at Butrus al-Bustani's National School in Beirut, worked as a dragoman at the U.S. consulate, and roamed Iraq, Iran, and India on commercial ventures. The 1890s found him in Istanbul, and in 1893 he was the Ottoman commissioner to the 1893 Columbian Exposition in Chicago. He spent the decade before the 1908 Ottoman revolution in Cairo, then went home to win election from Beirut to the Ottoman parliament. In Istanbul, he became vice president of the Chamber of Deputies, senator, and minister of commerce and forests before resigning to protest the fateful coup that took the Ottomans into World War I on the German side. Sulayman sat out the war in Switzerland, returned to Egypt, and finally went to the United States.

In addition to publishing the last two volumes of *Dairat al-Maarif,* Jurji Zaydan's press published the Arabic *Iliad.* Zaydan was another Syrian Christian with encyclopedic interests who founded the versatile literary magazine *Al-Hilal* in Cairo. In 1899 he published his Arabic *History of the Greeks and Romans.*[105]

The 200-page introduction to the 1,260-page volume of al-Bustani's *Iliad* reviewed European debates on "the Homeric question" and came down in favor of Homer's being a single poet. Al-Bustani explained that the *Iliad* was to the Greeks what pre-Islamic poetry was to the Arabs. He related that he had started translating from French and English versions before deciding to go back to the Greek original.

Egyptian Muslims joined Syrians at Shepheard's Hotel to celebrate the Arabic *Iliad.* Zaydan, Faris Nimr, Yaqub Sarruf (editor of *Al-Muqtataf*), *Al-Ahram*'s Jibrail Taqla, the poet Khalil Mutran, and Ibrahim al-Yaziji were among the Syrian Christian celebrants. Egyptian Muslims included neoclassical poets Ahmad Shawqi and Hafiz Ibrahim and future prime ministers Sa'd Zaghlul and Abd al-Khaliq Tharwat. Muhammad

Abduh sent his regrets, but his disciple Rashid Rida, a Muslim from Syria, delivered a long celebratory speech.

EGYPTIAN EXPERIMENTATION
WITH THE GRECO-ROMAN CLASSICS

Al-Tahtawi and his associates had already encountered Europe's emphasis on the classics independently of the Syrians, and Egyptians would have continued these explorations—perhaps at a slower pace—even without Syrian mediation. In addition to the aforementioned works of al-Tahtawi's school, his former pupil and colleague Uthman Jalal included Arabic translations of Racine's *Iphigénie* and *Alexandre le grand* in a book he edited in 1893–1894.[106]

Ali Mubarak scattered information about Greco-Roman times through *Al-Khitat*. Under the entry for Akhmim, for example, he identifies the town as the Panopolis of the Greeks and follows Taqi al-Din al-Maqrizi on the Greco-Roman-era temple that stood there until the fourteenth century. Here he inserts the legend of Cadmus, an Egyptian or Phoenician who brought civilization to prehistoric Greece. Mubarak mentions visits to Egypt by Homer, Herodotus, Plato, and Lycurgus. This leads him into a discussion of Socrates, Plato and his Academy, Pythagoras, and Anaxagoras.[107]

Mubarak presented his most detailed information on the Greco-Roman era in *Al-Khitat*'s volume seven, on Alexandria. Ten densely packed pages sketch Egypt's history from Alexander to the Arab conquest—the reigns of each Ptolemy down through Cleopatra, the Roman conquest, and the early history of Christianity. In the topographically arranged section that follows, Mubarak draws on al-Maqrizi, French sources, and Mahmud al-Falaki in treating the ancient layout of the city and such landmarks as the harbors, lighthouse, obelisks, Alexander's tomb, the Museum, and the libraries.[108]

Egyptians also encountered the West's classical heritage through Roman law, which was mediated through the Napoleonic Code, taught in the Egyptian state law school and the private French École de droit in Cairo, and practiced in the Mixed and National courts. Judge Qasim Amin, the discipline of Muhammad Abduh who won fame for two turn-of-the-century books advocating the emancipation of women, had earlier included classical references in his defense of Islam against a French detractor. Like al-Tahtawi, Qasim Amin pointedly rejected the story that the caliph Umar had ordered the burning of the Library of Alexandria.[109]

Like Europeans since the Renaissance, Egyptian political leaders also toyed with Greco-Roman allusions as a means of claiming heritage and conveying legitimacy. Although it was only a standard photographer's prop, a classical bust was displayed in the background in a portrait of Prime Minister Muhammad Sharif (see figure 32).

The lawyers who successively led the National (Watani) Party experimented with turning classical discourse against the West. Mustafa Kamil, the nationalist hero who founded the newspaper *Al-Liwa* in 1900 and the National Party in 1908, compared Islamic slavery favorably with its Roman counterpart. In 1912, Kamil's successor Muhammad Farid wrote an Arabic *History of the Romans,* which turned the West's classics against Egypt's British occupiers. Significantly, Farid covered the republic only to the end of the Punic Wars, omitting the late republic and the imperial periods (during which Egypt came under the Roman yoke), which Cromer found so congenial. Farid urged Egyptians to emulate the patriotism *(hubb al-watan)* of the Romans and their unity against outside aggressors.[110]

Faris Nimr's sarcastic review of Farid's *Romans* in the pro-British newspaper *Al-Muqattam* shows why Egyptian nationalists often attacked Syrian Christian immigrants as "intruders." Exactly who were the contemporary foreign aggressors Farid had in mind? demanded Nimr. The khedivial family? The Ottomans? The "Arab umma," which "had attacked the land of the Copts?" Or simply any foreigner who made Egypt his home?

As noted earlier, an event in 1902 captures the difference between European and Egyptian relationships to the Greco-Roman legacy. Khedive Abbas II, with Cromer and Maspero in attendance, inaugurated the new Egyptian Museum. Cromer and Maspero did not think twice about the inscriptions on the facade. They felt at home in the Latin with which Westerners often embellished monumental architecture. Abbas Hilmi II may have been able to read the inscription in his name. He had studied at the Theresianum in Vienna, where students not only read and wrote but also had to speak Latin (see figure 6).[111] But few other educated Egyptians could read the inscription; no Egyptian state school taught Latin.

AN INTERNATIONAL CONGRESS
OF CLASSICAL ARCHAEOLOGY IN CAIRO

By convening the Second International Congress of Classical Archaeology in Cairo in 1909, Europeans underlined the salience of Egypt in

Figure 32.   Prime Minister Sharif Pasha with a bust of a Roman
emperor: an appropriation of a Western symbol of statesmanship. In
Muhammad Khalil Subhi, *Tarikh al-Hayat al-Niyabiyya fi Misr,* vol. 4
(Cairo, 1947), unnumbered plate following p. 112.

Western classical discourse. Egypt symbolically took a place of honor
between Greece and Rome as a classical land; the first congress met in
Athens in 1905 and the third in Rome in 1911. But the shape of the
Cairo congress merely confirms the marginality of Egyptians to the
West's Greco-Roman classics.

At the first congress, the German, Austrian, English, French, and American archaeological "schools" in Athens had assisted the University of Athens and Greek government in hosting the event. Maspero presided over a section on prehistoric and oriental archaeology. Other Egyptologists attending included Petrie and Ludwig Borchardt. Pierre Jouguet and young Alan Wace, classicists who would long work in Egypt, were there. Institutions from sixteen European countries, the United States, and "Turkey" were represented. The Ottoman ambassador to Greece and his wife were the only Turks, and there were no Egyptians.[112]

Maspero headed the Executive Committee, which then planned the Cairo congress. His committee included Pierre Lacau of the Antiquities Service, the directors of the IFAO (Émile Chassinat) and the new German Archaeological Institute (Borchardt), Evaristo Breccia of the Greco-Roman Museum, and a British official—in all, three Frenchmen, a Briton, a German, and an Italian. The Municipality of Alexandria and the Archaeological Society of Alexandria lent a hand. The schedule consisted of three days of papers and touring in Alexandria and six in Cairo, then four days of tourism in Luxor. The Egyptian government promised a £E1,000–2,000 subsidy, and Cook offered steamer and hotel discounts.[113]

The preclassical archaeology section made a bow to pharaonic antiquity, and the Byzantine archaeology one added a postclassical coda. The other sections were classical archaeology, papyrology and epigraphy, religious archaeology, numismatics, and geography. Papers were in French, German, English, and Italian but not Greek or Arabic.

Abbas II headed the ceremonial Organizing Committee and gave a welcoming speech at the Opera House. Prime Minister Butrus Ghali and ex–prime minister Mustafa Fahmi, cabinet ministers Sa'd Zaghlul and Ismail Sirri, Ahmad Zaki (secretary to the Council of Ministers), and Yaqub Artin also sat on the Organizing Committee. Yaqub Artin welcomed the delegates in his capacity as vice president of the Institut égyptien. Four British advisers to Egyptian ministries, Max Herz of the Comité and the Museum of Arab Art, and Bernhard Moritz of the Khedivial Library also served on the Organizing Committee.[114]

Egypt had no classicists of its own, and only one Egyptian read a paper. Atiya Wahby gave a nationalist interpretation of Coptic art, asserting its affinity to pharaonic rather than Byzantine art.[115] Only 21 registrants out of 906 were Egyptians. These included Ali Bahgat of the Museum of Arab Art and five Egyptologists, among them Ahmad Kamal and Muhammad Chaban. Armenian notable Boghos Nubar (son of the former prime minister) was there, as were at least three Copts—Wahby, Claudius Labib, and nationalist lawyer and future minister Murqus Hanna. The new Egyptian University hosted several panels, and its rector, future king Fuad, presided at closing ceremonies.[116] After World War I, he would enhance his image as an enlightened ruler by bringing many international congresses to Egypt.

THE GRECO-ROMAN LEGACY
ON THE EVE OF WORLD WAR I

The year after the Second International Congress of Classical Archaeology, Mahmud Fahmi, a graduate of the Tawfiqiyya Teachers College who taught at the School for Qadis, published *Tarikh al-Yunan* (History of Greece). He would also teach the History of the Ancient East course at the Egyptian University from 1913 until his death in 1916. Fahmi intended to provide Arabic readers a history of the land where Western civilization and literature had begun. We borrowed from the Greeks under Harun al-Rashid and al-Mamun, he explained, yet know little of Greek history. Fahmi drew on textbooks written by a principal and teacher at the Greek community school in Cairo. He began with geography, discussed Homer, moved through the age of Herodotus, "the father of history," and Socrates, "the *sayyid* of philosophy," and ended with the division of Alexander's empire among his generals.[117]

Other Egyptian University courses gave students like Taha Husayn glimpses of the classical world. Percy White taught Shakespeare's *Antony and Cleopatra* in his English literature class, and French literature presumably conveyed its share of classical lore.[118]

Ahmad Lutfi al-Sayyid, the influential editor of *Al-Jarida* who would join the university's governing council in 1915 and guide the state-run Egyptian University as rector beginning in 1925, was also pondering the Greek legacy. In *Al-Jarida* in 1913, he held the Greeks up for emulation. Through centuries of "Turkish" rule, they had not forgotten that they were the Hellenes of antiquity, and their enduring sense of identity had finally carried them through to national independence. His observation was noteworthy at a time when Egypt was still nominally Ottoman. Most Ottomans and Egyptians had seen the Greek war for independence during the 1820s as a blow to Ottoman, Egyptian, and Islamic power.[119] In the 1920s, Lutfi would make translation of Aristotle his main scholarly project.

In 1912, Muhammad Lutfi Juma published an Arabic translation of Machiavelli's *The Prince,* which is saturated with classical references. Long before, Muhammad Ali had halted its translation into Turkish on the grounds that the Florentine had nothing to teach him.[120]

With a classicist of the caliber of Oriental secretary Ronald Storrs holding the fort at the British Residency in 1914, the Greco-Roman legacy that Westerners from Bonaparte to Cromer had deployed to legitimate their domination of Egypt remained in trusty hands. Who could have foreseen that in the wake of World War I, Oxford and Cambridge would drop Greek as a matriculation requirement or that classicists like E. M. Forster and Robert Graves would favor slackening Britain's imperial grip overseas? Who could have guessed that future star of Arabic letters Taha Husayn would return from Paris in 1919 bent on inserting Greco-Roman classics into the core of Egyptian education or that the new Egyptian University of 1925 would open with a department of classics?[121]

CHAPTER 5

Egyptology in the Age of Maspero and Ahmad Kamal

In 1923 Ahmad Kamal proposed that Egyptians be trained to understand, work in, and ultimately administer the archeology of their own land. The Director-general of the Service of Antiquities caustically remarked that with the exception of Ahmad Bey himself, few Egyptians had shown any interest in antiquity. Ahmad Kamal responded: "Ah, M. Lacau, in the sixty-five years you French have directed the Service, what opportunities have you given us?"

John A. Wilson, *Signs and Wonders upon Pharaoh*

Forty-two years before this conversation, the death of Mariette in January 1881 and the accession of the more flexible Maspero had given Kamal a chance for a toehold in Egyptology. This generational change in the early 1880s was unusually sharp, as shown in table 3. Maspero remarked that with Mariette gone, Chabas was now the "last living [French Egyptologist] of our heroic age."[1] Chabas died within the year; Lepsius followed in Germany in 1884, and Birch in Britain in 1885.

In addition to Maspero and Kamal, the new generation included Flinders Petrie, who began work at the pyramids of Giza in December 1880; Adolf Erman, who started teaching at Berlin in 1881; and Ernest Budge, who followed Birch at the British Museum. In 1882, the year Britain occupied Egypt and the Egyptian Exploration Fund was founded, Maspero turned thirty-six, Kamal thirty-one, Petrie twenty-seven, Erman twenty-eight, and Budge twenty-five. On the political and military side, Lord Cromer (then still Evelyn Baring) and Ahmad Urabi both turned forty-one, Kitchener thirty-two, and Khedive Tawfiq thirty.

From the perspective of this study, Erman was largely offstage in Berlin, and Budge's swashbuckling Egyptian forays were brief. Petrie dug in Egypt almost every winter for forty years, revolutionized excavation technique, and trained many Egyptologists and archaeological laborers. But he is less central to this narrative than Maspero, who ran the Antiquities Service for nearly twenty years, and Ahmad Kamal, who struggled tirelessly to establish Egyptian Egyptology and persuade his countrymen of its importance.

The era ended abruptly in 1914, when Maspero and Kamal retired and Kitchener hurried home to direct Britain's war effort. The British replaced Abbas II with his pliable uncle Husayn Kamil, severed Egypt's nominal Ottoman tie, and declared a protectorate. Kitchener and Maspero died in 1916, Cromer in 1917, and Kamal in 1923. Petrie lived on until 1942, but was no longer in the vanguard of Egyptology and dug mostly in Palestine.

MASPERO, IFAO, AND THE ANTIQUITIES SERVICE TO 1886

The privileged and brilliant Maspero was only twenty-eight when he reached the pinnacle of professor of Egyptian philology and archaeology at the Collège de France. Born in Paris, he had climbed straight up its elite educational ladders—the Lycée Louis-le-Grand, École normale supérieur, the Sorbonne, and the École des hautes études. At twenty-eight his predecessor Mariette, who had had only a provincial education, had only just become a temporary Egyptological assistant at the Louvre, and Ahmad Kamal had yet to find any post related to Egyptology.

Fearing for his own primacy, Mariette had shelved an early proposal of Maspero's for a French archaeological "school" located in Cairo. But as Mariette lay dying of diabetes late in 1880, education officials in Paris revived the proposal. Maspero pointed to France's École d'Athens (1846) and École de Rome (1875) as models and warned that foreign rivals were outdistancing French field archaeology in the Middle East. In the 1840s, Botta had enriched the Louvre with Assyrian sculptures and reliefs. French work in Mesopotamia had then tapered off, but the British Museum had continued to enrich its Mesopotamian holdings. In Palestine, English and German scholars of Hebrew and Phoenician were forging ahead, and in Cairo, Germany might try to put in Heinrich Brugsch as Mariette's successor. By stationing a French

TABLE 3

ARCHAEOLOGISTS IN THE AGE OF MASPERO AND AHMAD KAMAL, 1881–1914

Western Egyptologists	Egyptian Egyptologists	Other Archaeologists	Other Scholars and Political Figures
H. Brugsch 1827–1894		J. Franz 1831–1915	A. Mubarak 1823–1893
A. Edwards 1831–1892			Nubar 1825–1899
É. Brugsch 1842–1930		G. Botti ?–1903	A. Urabi 1841–1911
Naville 1844–1926			J. Artin 1842–1914
Maspero 1846–1916	A. Najib 1847–1910		M. Abduh 1849–1905
Petrie 1853–1942	A. Kamal 1851–1923		Tawfiq r. 1879–1892
Erman 1854–1937		M. Herz 1856–1919	Cromer, con. gen. 1883–1907
Schiaparelli 1856–1928			Abbas II r. 1892–1914
Budge 1857–1934			
de Morgan 1857–1924		A. Bahgat 1858–1924	Kitchener, con. gen. 1911–1914
Loret 1859–1946			
Borchardt 1863–1938		Berchem 1863–1921	Zaghlul 1860?–1927
Daressy 1864–1938		Simaika 1864–1944	
Breasted 1865–1935			
Reisner 1867–1942			
Lacau 1873–1963			
Carter 1874–1939		E. Breccia 1876–1944	
Junker 1877–1962			

heir apparent on the spot, the Cairo *école* could "confirm and assure French superiority."[2]

On 28 December 1880, Prime Minister Jules Ferry decreed the founding of "a Permanent Mission, under the name of the École française du Caire." The École biblique et archéologique française would stake out a similar claim in Jerusalem a decade later. In 1898 the Cairo *école*, also known as the Mission archéologique, became the Institut français d'archéologie orientale du Caire and launched its first excavations.

Maspero reached Cairo as the *école*'s first director just weeks before Mariette died, bringing with him two Egyptology students, an architect inspired by Arab art, and an Arabist. When Maspero smoothly succeeded Mariette as the Antiquities Service director, one of the students (Urbain Bouriant) took over direction of the *école*. From 1881 to 1936, IFAO would furnish all but one (de Morgan) of the directors of the Antiquities Service.[3] IFAO's printing press, established in 1898, greatly enhanced the institution's scholarly stature. By 1910, IFAO directors and fellows had totaled twenty Egyptologists, eight Arabists, six Hellenists or Byzantinists, a geologist, and eight auxiliary artists.[4]

During his five-year first term, Maspero thoroughly reorganized the Antiquities Service and continued opening Fifth and Sixth dynasty pyramids at Saqqara and publishing their pyramid texts. He also resumed the clearance of Upper Egyptian temples.

The 1883 antiquities law declared all antiquities and museum objects property of the state and anchored the Antiquities Service in the Ministry of Public Works. In independent Istanbul, in contrast, the Ottoman antiquities law of 1884 put the antiquities service and archaeological museum under the Ministry of Education,[5] implicitly claiming the antiquities as part of the national patrimony. The Egyptian Antiquities Service remained under public works until the achievement of limited independence permitted its transfer to the Ministry of Education in 1929, where it remained until its transfer to the Ministry of Culture and National Guidance in 1958.[6]

THE RETURN OF BRITISH EGYPTOLOGY: PETRIE AND THE EGYPT EXPLORATION FUND

British troops settled into the Qasr al-Nil barracks south of the Bulaq Museum in 1882 and, like Bonaparte's troops before them, took symbolic possession of Egypt's monuments (see figure 33). Maspero had to deploy all his diplomatic skill to preserve France's "archaeological pro-

Figure 33.   Scottish soldiers occupy the Sphinx. Photograph by J. Pascal Sebah, 1880s. In *Excursions along the Nile: The Photographic Discovery of Ancient Egypt* (Santa Barbara: Santa Barbara Museum of Art, 1993), 134. Courtesy of the Santa Barbara Museum of Art. Collection of Michael and Jane Wilson.

tectorate."[7] He courted the British by ending Mariette's monopoly on excavation and encouraging the Egypt Exploration Fund, Petrie, and others to dig. He arranged for them to keep a generous share of their finds. With the minor exceptions of Alexander Rhind at Thebes and Piazzi Smyth and Waynman Dixon at Giza, British Egyptologists had not worked in the field since Wilkinson, Richard Vyse, and John Perring in the 1830s. Ali Gabri, whom Petrie hailed as an "excellent companion in all my work,"[8] provided a personal link across half a century. He had started as a basket boy for Vyse and assisted Smyth and Dixon.

In their own unique ways, Petrie and Maspero both flourished under the British occupation. They shared a migratory rhythm of long winters in Egypt and long summers back home but were otherwise a study in contrasts. Petrie lived rough in tents and tombs and ate out of cans; Maspero worked out of his museum office and an official steamer. Maspero had had an elite classical education in the best schools of Paris. Petrie had made ten failed starts on Latin and five or six on Greek before he was left alone to educate himself through collecting coins, studying antiquities, and surveying ancient English sites.

On the northern shore of the Mediterranean, excavation had become more scientific during Mariette's later years, a revolution that passed him by. In the 1860s, G. Fiorelli at Pompeii and P. Rosa in Rome put the excavations on a scientific basis. In the Aegean in the 1870s, the Austrians at Samothrace (A. Conze) and the Germans at Olympia (E. Curtius) recorded careful stratigraphy as they dug. Curtius agreed to leave all finds in Greece, subordinating the hunt for objets d'art to the recovery of information. Even Schliemann, who at Troy and Mycenae had moved dirt as heedlessly as Mariette, improved his standards in the 1880s with the assistance of Wilhelm Dörpfeld, an architect and veteran of Olympia.[9]

The practical Petrie did not borrow directly from such models but worked out scientific digging largely on his own. He drew plans of a site, recorded the loci of objects found, emphasized the importance of small, everyday objects, developed pottery-sequence dating, and hurried a selective report on each season's results into print. He put the first two dynasties and (along with Jacques de Morgan) Egyptian prehistory on the archaeological map. The richness of Egypt's historic remains probably explains why the revolutionary advances in European prehistoric archaeology in the middle decades of the century were so slow to reach Egypt. Petrie trained workers from the village of Quft, who later dug with him and others all over Egypt. Dispensing with a foreman *(reis)*, he worked closely with his men, minimizing leakage to dealers by paying *bakhshish* for individual finds. Except at Tell El-Hesy in Palestine in 1890, however, he took little account of stratigraphy.[10]

As a technician, antiquarian, and surveyor, not a classically trained humanist, Petrie appreciated the value of pedestrian objects such as potsherds. "The aristocratic Naville was willing to spend time on raising historical questions by copying and interpreting inscriptions, but to him the less said about the base work of digging the better, and as to collecting observations on pottery and the like, it might be fitting for the mere scientist, but it was no work for a man trained in the humanities."[11]

Petrie savaged the methods of Mariette, who had resorted to dynamite, and his own contemporary Émile Amélineau, who mangled early dynastic royal tombs at Abydos. He was little happier with the fieldwork of Maspero, Edouard Naville, and É. Brugsch. Maspero nevertheless remained cordial, warning Petrie not to bring precious finds to the museum where É. Brugsch might seize them and suggesting that he smuggle small items past customs in his pockets.[12]

Like many of his contemporaries, Petrie rejected earlier optimistic assumptions of unilinear cultural evolution. Instead he shackled cultural to biological change, attributing progress to the immigration of cultural innovators. Such beliefs were in keeping with and fueled the pessimistic militarism and racism of many European nationalists of his day.[13]

Petrie preferred the independence of working through his own organizations—the Egyptian Research Account and then the British School of Archeology in Egypt—but he dug for the Egypt Exploration Fund (EEF) on and off for a dozen years. The EEF's moving founders in 1882 were the philanthropist surgeon Sir Erasmus Wilson, Reginald Stuart Poole—a nephew of Edward W. Lane's and a numismatist at the British Museum—and woman of letters Amelia Edwards.

Although fascinated since childhood by the *Arabian Nights* and Wilkinson's *Ancient Egyptians*, Edwards first made her name as a journalist and novelist. At forty-two, she made the journey—described in *A Thousand Miles up the Nile* (1877)—that led her to study hieroglyphics and devote all her energy to Egyptology. Hitherto the field had been overwhelmingly male. Edwards excelled as a popularizer, and without her persistence as an administrator, the EEF might not have remained a going concern.[14]

Egypt's bankruptcy by 1879 had finally cut off all funds for Mariette's excavations. Naville pointed out that the Germans were digging at Olympia and Maccan without any promise of taking museum pieces home. Perhaps British donors could also be persuaded to support digging for information instead of objects, especially if this cast light on the Bible. The biblical Land of Goshen—the eastern fringe of the Delta—held out the best prospects.[15] The Society for the Promotion of Excavation in the Delta of the Nile, soon renamed the Egypt Exploration Fund, came into being in April 1882, with the declared primary goal of documenting the four centuries of Hebrew sojourn in Egypt leading up to the Exodus. In 1919 the EEF became the Egypt Exploration Society (EES).

The British Museum's Samuel Birch deplored the EEF's approach as "emotional archaeology." He did not object to the EEF's biblicist goals; he himself had been founding president of the Society of Biblical Archaeology in 1870. His complaint was that the EEF's finds would enrich not the British Museum but the French-run museum in Bulaq.[16] As it turned out, Birch underestimated Maspero's generosity with Egypt's antiquities. Maspero instructed the EEF to apply to dig for strictly "scientific" goals, without mentioning any desire to take objects home. He in turn "persuaded" the now captive Egyptian government to return a generous share of excavators' finds to them as a gift.

In 1883 Naville began digging for the EEF at Tell el-Maskhuta. He reported: "The *entente cordiale* with Maspero is perfect and could not be better. In fact I am allowed to dig wherever I choose to do so in Lower Egypt."[17] At the end of the season, the khedive and the cabinet balked at the proposed "gift" to the EEF, but Maspero maneuvered it through. Naville's *Store-City of Pithom and the Route of the Exodus* (1885) set an example for the EEF of rapid-fire publication of excavation reports. The book delighted supporters by pronouncing Tell el-Maskhuta the biblical city of Pithom (an identification no longer accepted) and part of Wadi Tumilat the Land of Goshen. With Naville, Petrie, or others in charge, EEF expeditions became a regular feature of the Egyptian winter scene.

Petrie's friendship with Amelia Edwards survived his secession from the EEF to dig on his own. At her death in 1892, she endowed a chair of Egyptian archaeology for him at University College, London—the first chair of Egyptology in Britain. Thus, in marked contrast with continental Europe, both British excavations in Egypt and the first British chair of Egyptology were products of private initiative.

PYRAMIDS AND PROGRESS: ALI MUBARAK'S ANCIENT EGYPT

In 1886–1887, as Maspero was settling back into Paris after his first term in Cairo and Petrie and the EEF were establishing themselves in Egypt, Ali Mubarak published *Al-Khitat al-tawfiqiyya al-jadida*. The twenty-volume topographical encyclopaedia ran to over two thousand closely packed pages. Historians usually refer to it for the Islamic era or the nineteenth century, but it also treated ancient Egypt.[18]

Mubarak took fifteenth-century compendiums by al-Maqrizi and al-Suyuti as models; the *khitat* (a lot or district) of his title echoes al-Maqrizi's title. Mubarak's work was also a response to the French *Description de l'Égypte* (which he calls "the French *Khitat*"), an attempt to reclaim Egypt's past and present for his compatriots.[19] Cairo, he explained,

> is no longer the way it once was . . . due to the change of dynasties and the upheavals of time. . . . We have found no one among the sons of Egypt who

can interpret for us these changes or instruct us in the causes thereof, or guide us aright in understanding the country's notable monuments. We look upon these works but do not know the circumstances of their creation, we wander through them but do not know who made them. . . . How many the mosques which are ascribed to men who did not build them, and temples to persons who had not even seen them. . . . But it is our duty to know these things, for it is not fitting for us to remain in ignorance of our country or neglect the monuments of our ancestors. They are a moral lesson to the reflective mind, a memorial to the thoughtful soul. . . . For what our ancestors have left behind stirs in us the desire to follow in their footsteps, and to produce for our times what they produced for theirs; to strive to be useful even as they strove.[20]

Mubarak's fictional *Alam al-Din,* published in 1882, has the son of an Azhari shaykh complain of embarrassment in Europe because he cannot answer questions on ancient Egypt.[21] Drawing on both Islamic and European sources, *Al-Khitat* began to remedy the problem. It devoted long sections to Thebes and Memphis and treated many other ancient sites—Heliopolis, under the entry "al-Matariyya," is one example—more briefly.[22]

The Memphis article, which includes discussion of the Pyramids, legitimizes Mubarak as a Muslim scholar with lengthy quotations from al-Maqrizi's and al-Suyuti's compilation of medieval Arabic pyramid lore. Europeans too had long speculated that the Pyramids might be granaries, hiding places for treasures, or bulwarks to preserve knowledge during the Flood. Mubarak reported that Jomard, Mariette, and other modern European researchers maintained that the Pyramids were royal tombs. Mubarak himself inclines slightly toward the latter theory, but he does not simply dismiss al-Maqrizi's and al-Suyuti's lore as unworthy of attention.

As an engineer, Mubarak was fascinated with the measurement system of the pyramid builders. He believed that this system had been the basis for all other ancient standards of measurement. He mentioned John Taylor's and Piazzi Smyth's mathematical calculations on the Pyramids but, unlike his fellow engineer Hekekyan, did not follow them into mystical affirmation of divinely inspired wisdom encoded in the proportions of ancient monuments. Like his older contemporary al-Tahtawi, Mubarak left no doubt of his conviction that ancient Egypt had once been *the* source of human civilization, and that Egypt had remained a beacon to the world under the Ptolemies and again under Islam. Both scholars perceived a troubling decline under the Ottomans but praised Muhammad Ali and his successors for putting Egypt back on the path to greatness. Both believed that pride in ancient Egypt was an essential ingredient of their modern national identity. Mubarak's and al-Tahtawi's heirs, however, would have to confront more directly the extent to which British and French imperialism hindered Egyptians' attempts to rediscover and repossess their own past.

EGYPTOLOGICAL SKIRMISHES
ON THE ROAD TO FASHODA, 1886–1899

Maspero resigned from the Antiquities Service in 1886, returning to Paris for the sake of his wife's health. Three Frenchmen succeeded him in the thirteen years before he returned for a second stint at his old post: Eugène Grébaut (1886–1892), Jacques de Morgan (1892–1897), and Victor Loret (1897–1899). (See table 12, in the appendix.) During these intervening years, Anglo-French imperial rivalry ran rampant, culminating in the showdown at Fashoda in the Sudan in 1898.

Grébaut (1846–1915) happened to be directing the Cairo Mission archéologique in 1886 when Maspero, his former professor, went home. Grébaut stepped into his mentor's post grimly determined to defend French archaeological hegemony in Egypt at all costs. He immediately clashed with the British Museum's Ernest Budge, the protégé of the late Samuel Birch. Budge arrived in 1886 to buy antiquities and dig out rock tombs at Aswan for Col. Sir Francis W. Grenfell, commander (sirdar) of the Egyptian army. Grenfell, like Sirdar Kitchener after him, was an amateur of antiquities.[23]

Sir Evelyn Baring, who would become Lord Cromer in 1892, favored deferring to France in Egyptology in return for concessions elsewhere. He objected vehemently to Budge's intentions and methods. Once Baring burst out, "I wish there were no more antiquities in this country; they are more trouble than anything else."[24] He peremptorily summoned Budge to warn him against

> any scheme of excavation by any agent of the trustees of the British Museum. . . . He thought that excavations made in Egypt by a British official were likely to "complicate political relationships," and that the occupation of Egypt by the British ought not to be made an excuse for filching antiquities from the country, whether to England or anywhere else.[25]

Few men stood up to Baring, but Budge

> pointed out to him that every great Power (and many Little Powers) in Europe already had an agent in the country buying for its Central Museum, and

that Great Britain had at least an equal right to have an agent collecting antiquities for it. . . . I felt obliged to remind him that I was not a member of
his staff, and that I intended to carry out the instructions of the Trustees, and
to do my utmost to increase the collections in the British Museum. Here the
interview ended abruptly.[26]

Budge ran gleeful circles around Grébaut and Baring. Grébaut's
agents sequestered a Luxor storeroom of relics Budge had collected. But
that night Budge had his workmen tunnel through the back wall of the
guarded storeroom from the adjoining compound of the Luxor Hotel
and whisk the treasures away. Sympathetic Britons in the army, police,
and a shipping company helped him smuggle them out of Egypt.[27] Budge
had a ready justification: "The objects would have been smuggled out
of Egypt all the same; the only difference would have been that instead
of being in the British Museum they would be in some museum or private collection on the Continent or in America."[28]

Maspero had welcomed the EEF and Petrie, but Grébaut trumpeted
his refusal "to abandon ancient Egypt to the English societies, and become the humble servant of English tourists."[29] He vetoed Baring's suggestion that private expeditions be allowed to sell part of their finds to
help finance their work. He dismissed a proposal for an English antiquities inspector for Upper Egypt and a French one for Lower Egypt as
an English ploy to get the richest sites.[30] To a suggestion that since most
tourists were English, an English society might help pay the salary of an
English assistant director of antiquities, he retorted that more Egyptians
than Westerners visited the Egyptian Museum. Besides, American
tourists perhaps outnumbered the English, and if the latter had their
own assistant director, wouldn't the Americans demand one too?[31]

In 1888, the Society for Preservation of the Monuments of Ancient
Egypt (SPMAE) was formed in London to put pressure on Baring and
the French.[32] Baring had already forced the Consultative Archaeological Committee (or "Egyptology Committee") on Grébaut. In 1889, it
included Colonel Francis Grenfell, three other Britons, Grébaut and another Frenchman, Armenian-Egyptians Yaqub Artin and Tigrane, and
Prime Minister Mustafa Fahmi. Petrie grumbled that the Armenians
joined Grébaut in nit-picking obstructionism. That was not all. In 1890,
Tigrane orally assured Paris, in return for approval of a loan, that Egypt
would not name Britons to the Antiquities Service.[33]

The SPMAE lobbied for better protection of antiquities sites and new
housing for the Bulaq Museum. Tourists were indeed carrying out shock-

ing acts of vandalism. In 1890, the *Graphic* published an illustration of tourists attacking temple columns with chisels (see figure 34). In a case of double displacement, the chauvinist piece blamed such vandalism mostly on "certain types of ladies," generally American.[34]

The Bulaq Museum had flooded in 1878, and even in normal times. "In early winter mornings the building was full of white, clinging, drenching mist . . . and it was no rare thing to see water trickling down inside the glass cases which held the mummies of the great kings of Egypt."[35] Fire was as worrisome as flood. With display space so cramped, flammable resin-soaked mummies and their cases were stacked to the ceiling in makeshift storage around the grounds.

The SPMAE opposed the Egyptian government's decision in 1887 to transfer the museum temporarily to a palace in Giza. But Baring declared flatly that there was no money for a new museum, and to Giza the museum went. *Cook's Handbook* could not resist an aside that Ismail had built the palace at extravagant cost "to accommodate his harim."[36] At least the palace was safe from flooding, had less danger of fire, and had far more display space.[37] On 12 January 1890, Khedive Tawfiq inaugurated the Giza Museum. (See map 2.)[38]

Even the French consul general finally conceded in private that the undiplomatic Grébaut would have to go, but he bristled when Baring and Naville suggested A. Daninos, a former assistant of Mariette's, as a possible successor. Daninos was an Algerian, came the reply, who had become "almost oriental. His name is not French and his loyalty to France hasn't been proven to me."[39] Caught without a suitable heir on tap at the Mission archéologique, the French brought in Jacques de Morgan, a protégé of Xavier Charmes, a high official in the French Ministry of Education. It took the coordinated maneuvering of Charmes, de Morgan, and the French representative in Cairo to force the stubborn Grébaut, who refused to resign, out of his post and out of the country. De Morgan had graduated from France's École des mines and had traveled, prospected, and dug in India, Malaya, the Caucasus, and Persia. Although not an Egyptologist, he quickly "proved that it was possible to safeguard the interests of the Egyptian Museum in Cairo, and of Egyptian Archaeology in general, without robbing or persecuting the natives, or causing his own name to be cursed everywhere from Alexandria to Wadi Halfah." De Morgan abandoned Grébaut's night raids on dealers and drew on "previous experience in dealing with Orientals in Persia and other oriental countries" to reach a " 'give and take' arrangement with the native diggers for antiquities and dealers. He paid natives

Figure 34. "Fair Iconoclasts in Egypt," from the *Graphic,* 26 July 1890, as reproduced in Nicholas Warner, ed., *Egyptian Panorama: Reports from the 19th Century British Press* (Cairo, 1994), 13. In a double displacement, the misogynist British editor makes American women the worst such vandals. Courtesy of Nicholas Warner.

well when they supplied him with the information that led him to a site which yielded good results."[40]

De Morgan quickly opened many more rooms in the new Giza museum to visitors, but the mining engineer preferred excavation to museum work and built a house for himself at Dahshur. He uncovered the *mastaba* of Meruruka at Saqqara, discovered Middle Kingdom royal jewelry at Dahshur, dug out the temple of Kom Ombo, and set Georges Legrain to excavating the Temple of Karnak. He and Petrie opened up Egyptian prehistory with excavations at several sites in Upper Egypt. De Morgan also made enemies, however. Maspero criticized his scientific methods, deploring de Morgan's pulverizing of sixty ancient, though uninscribed, blocks at Kom Ombo for a dike to protect the temple from Nile floods. De Morgan also fell out with Georges Foucart, an Antiquities Service inspector whom he accused of spying for the British and taking liberties with Muslim women. The affair reverberated as far as Athens and Paris; Georges's well-connected father, Paul Foucart, directed the French archaeological *école* in Athens and held a seat in the Institut de France. Someone persuaded the Egyptian minister of public works to pronounce de Morgan's prehistoric researches geology, not archaeology, and order him to stop spending ministry money on them.[41]

Cromer and the Caisse de la dette publique had meanwhile won their race against bankruptcy and began planning to fund a new museum. But some Frenchmen accused de Morgan of being too friendly with the British,[42] and he had had enough. He left in 1897 to head a French expedition to Persia, where he spent fifteen years excavating at Susa.

French fears that Germany might promote assistant curator Émile Brugsch as de Morgan's successor proved unfounded,[43] and Victor Loret, a former pupil of Maspero's and veteran of the Mission archéologique, took over. Petrie reported that Loret "was entirely under the direction of a young effendi, Aref, who wore a great cloak turned back to show a brilliant scarlet lining, by which he would strike an effect half a mile away."[44] "Loret is already out of touch and disliked by everyone—Museum people, officials and natives," Petrie wrote. "He was a man of limited vision; when I told him of a place being pillaged he remarked: 'That's impossible! There's a law against it.'"[45] Frenchmen joined Americans, Britons, and even Russians in pressing for his removal.[46]

French consul general Cogordon stressed the urgency "of retaking here the Egyptological terrain, the rightful place to which we are entitled by the French origin of this science, the work of Mariette, and the sacrifices France has always made for knowledge of Ancient Egypt, from the expedition of General Bonaparte to the creation of the Institut d'archéologie orientale du Caire."[47]

Cromer asked Sayce to sound out Maspero,[48] who returned, to general relief, in 1899.

A TOEHOLD IN EGYPTOLOGY:
AHMAD KAMAL AND HIS GENERATION

Even during the heyday of Western dominance, intra-European rivalries occasionally opened opportunities to Egyptians. A German presence in Cairo, H. Brugsch, had enabled Ahmad Kamal and a few others to study Egyptology despite Mariette's objection. In the 1890s, Grébaut tried a different tack—promoting Kamal from museum secretary to assistant curator to thwart demands for hiring a Briton. Grébaut claimed that ten times as many *"indigènes"* as Britons visited the museum, praised Kamal's knowledge, and noted that he would be able to escort Egyptian as well as European visitors around the museum.[49]

Kamal was born in Cairo in 1851.[50] His father was of Cretan background and presumably in Muhammad Ali's service. The boy attended Cairo's elite Primary School (Mubtadiyan) and Preparatory School (Tajhiziyya), acquiring the French that gave him his entree to the School of Egyptology. Kamal took to Egyptology with a passion, but Mariette's refusal to hire the school's alumni forced Kamal to fall back on teaching German in the schools and translating for the Ministry of Education, postal service, and customs.

Kamal was thirty by the time he landed a professional post related to Egyptology. Enlisting the support of Prime Minister Riyad himself,[51] Kamal won the post of secretary-translator at the Bulaq Museum. A few months later, while Maspero was summering in Paris, Kamal assisted É. Brugsch in clearing the spectacular cache of royal mummies that the Abd al-Rasul family had discovered some years before in the cliff above Deir al-Bahri. Brugsch later photographed Kamal beside the huge outer coffin of Queen Ahmose Nefertari (see figure 35).

Maspero earmarked £E500 for Kamal to conduct a tiny school of Egyptology at the museum. It opened as a boarding school with only five pupils in February 1882. Kamal directed the school and taught Egyptian, French, and history for a salary of £E8 a month. Other Egyptians came in to teach Arabic, arithmetic, and geography.[52] In April of 1882 the minister of public works proposed adding ten more students, including four Copts, "from among the children of notables of the

Figure 35. Ahmad Kamal and the coffin of Queen Ahmose
Nefertari from the Dayr al-Bahri Cache of Royal Mummies.
Original photograph by É. Brugsch. In Edward Wilson,
"Finding Pharaoh," *Century Magazine*, May 1887, as
reproduced in John Romer, *Valley of the Kings* (New York,
1994), 139. Courtesy of Michael O'Mara Books Ltd.

Coptic sect, whom the hieroglyphic language interests all the more since it was the language of their ancestors and they still retain some expressions which will facilitate their study."[53] Chapter 7 returns to the question of a special Coptic affinity for Egyptology.

Kamal's little school survived the Urabi revolution and the British conquest and graduated its only class in 1885. The only way for Maspero to hire the graduates was to close the school and reallocate its funds as inspectors' salaries. Before returning to Paris in 1886, Maspero arranged a £E38 bonus for Kamal to buy books for his personal library.[54]

A salary scale at the end of 1885 shows what a small agency the Antiquities Service was. Maspero earned £E1,000 a year; assistant curators É. Brugsch and Urbain Bouriant received £E420 and £E300, respectively; five Egyptian inspectors second-class got £E90 each; and five inspectors third-class—the new graduates—£E60. In addition, Muhammad Khurshid was a supervisor (nazir) at £E240; Ahmad Kamal, the secretary at £E240; and two storeroom men (magasiniers) earned £E72 and £E45.[55]

When Bouriant resigned from the service in 1885 to resume direction of the Mission archéologique, Grébaut demanded qualifications for a successor that ruled out all Egyptians: knowledge of hieroglyphics, hieratic and demotic Egyptian, Coptic, Greek, and Latin. (Petrie would not have qualified either.) Students at Brugsch's and Kamal's schools of Egyptology had all the languages they could handle without Greek and Latin. Not surprisingly, a student of Grébaut's, Georges Daressy, won the post.[56]

By 1891, however, Grébaut had changed his mind and made Kamal assistant curator in order to keep out the British.[57] Shortly after, Kamal, now forty, heard that É. Brugsch was going to retire from his more senior assistant curatorship and that foreigners were eyeing the post. Kamal petitioned Prime Minister Mustafa Fahmi that he be named instead:

> The sole indigenous Egyptologist and former student of Brugsch Pasha ... I have been waiting during twenty-two years of government service to be promoted and rewarded for my sincere and beneficial services to the country.... Being assistant curator and in view of my seniority, merit, and Egyptian law, I respectfully take the liberty of confidentially asking you to help me obtain this post despite all foreign demands.[58]

Kamal added, in an Arabic note, that although a French assistant curator (Daressy) and he had similar knowledge and educational credentials, he himself knew Arabic and had twenty-one years of service to the

Frenchman's six. He closed with a patriotic plea for an Egyptian instead
of a Frenchman or Englishman. Nothing came of it, for Brugsch stayed
on until 1914. Under Grébaut's successor, de Morgan, Kamal was lucky
even to retain the post he had. De Morgan reportedly wanted to dismiss him and refused to speak to him for a whole year.[59] After Maspero's
return in 1899, he entrusted Kamal with significant, if not very glamorous, archaeological and publication duties but did not promote him.
Daressy passed Kamal by, moving up to secretary-general of the service
in 1913. Kamal was more than a dozen years older than Daressy and
James Quibell, who became curator in January 1914.[60]

Only one other alumnus of Brugsch's school stands out as more than
a name—Ahmad Najib (1847–1910). His translation of Brugsch's
grammar was the first hieroglyphic textbook in Arabic. Mariette's boycott forced Najib to teach history in the state schools, a post he held in
1882 when he wrote a preface to Kamal's history of ancient Egypt. In
1892, Anglo-French rivalry opened the way to Najib's appointment as
one of two provincial inspectors general of antiquities (the other being
G. Foucart). Najib became a bey, retired early in 1905 because of ill
health, and briefly published a magazine, *Al-Manzum*.[61]

A list of antiquities inspectors for 1899 includes two alumni of
Kamal's 1881–1885 school: Muhammad Chaban (Sha'ban), who would
briefly serve as assistant curator after Kamal retired, and Hasan Husni.
Ali Habib, inspector for the Delta, was the most senior and best of Mariette's old inspectors, who were mostly military veterans. He retired in
1907. Other inspectors had been noncommissioned officers in the post-
1882 army or minor officials, and one had even been a servant.[62]

EGYPTOLOGY AND EGYPTIAN REPRESENTATION
IN THE INSTITUT ÉGYPTIEN

Maspero and his three Antiquities Service successors carried on Mariette's tradition of using the Institut égyptien and its bulletin as forums
for Egyptology. From 1885 to 1899, the bulletin devoted much of its
space to an inventory of Egyptian Museum collections. The Institut's
separate Mémoires series included pharaonic topics. The Institut made
Maspero honorary president upon his return in 1899, but the launching of the Antiquities Service's *Annales* decreased Egyptology's dependence on the Institut and its bulletin.[63]

In 1890, 31 percent of Institut members were Egyptians, double the
14 percent at its founding thirty years before.[64] Egyptians were also

more prominent in the leadership, particularly if one counts Yaqub Artin (1842–1914) as Egyptian. Like his uncle Joseph Hekekyan before him, Artin relished mediating between Europeans and Egyptians. A French-educated Armenian Catholic, Artin claimed French protection in Egypt. His father, Artin Sikyas, had studied in Paris on the same mission as al-Tahtawi and served as Muhammad Ali's effective minister of foreign affairs and commerce. A lifelong Egyptian government official, Yaqub Artin presided over the Institut égyptien for twenty of the years between 1889 and 1916 and read nine papers there. He put his large personal library at the disposal of visiting Orientalists.[65]

Artin made an interesting pair with Husayn Fakhri, who served a dozen years under him as one of the Institut's two vice presidents. In 1905–1906 and 1909 they briefly traded posts, with Fakhri taking turns in the presidency. In the world of work, Fakhri, as long-serving minister of public works and education under Cromer, was Undersecretary Artin's superior, and Artin his right-hand man in education. Fakhri and Armenian notables Prime Minister Nubar and Foreign Minister Tigrane, unlike Artin, took Institut membership as their aristocratic due, feeling no compulsion to prove themselves with scholarly papers. Like so many European notables, Tigrane collected Egyptian antiquities.[66]

The election of Ali Bahgat to the Institut égyptien in 1900 and Ahmad Kamal in 1904 recognized their emerging reputations. In 1903, the Institut elected its first Copt—Kyrillos Makarius, who presented historical studies on Christian calendars.[67] In addition to the Institut, Kamal also joined the Geographical Society and published in its bulletin.

Europeans still set the tone at the Institut. Its secretary-general, assistant secretary, and treasurer-librarian were Europeans throughout the era, and between 1883 and 1914, Egyptians averaged only a single paper a year at the Institut. The Egyptian share of the membership fell off slightly from 31 percent in 1891 to 27 percent in 1909.

REPRESENTING ANCIENT EGYPT: WORLD'S FAIRS AND INTERNATIONAL CONGRESSES OF ORIENTALISTS

Mariette, de Lesseps, and Brugsch largely shaped the images of Egypt at world's fairs of the 1860s and 1870s, but Khedive Ismail was in charge. Under the British, Egypt no longer controlled even indirectly the images of it projected at world's fairs. Since the British-dominated Egyptian government was unwilling to fund world's fair exhibits, Tawfiq and Maspero and their successors could not compete with Ismail's and Mariette's showmanship. At Paris's Exposition universelle of 1889, the representation of Egypt went by default to a French entrepreneur whose "rue du Caire" catered to Western Orientalist fantasies and will be discussed in chapter 6. Thomas Cook displayed a painstakingly exact replica of the Temple of Edfu.[68] This exposition, which left Paris the Eiffel Tower, unsettled monarchies because it celebrated the centennial of the French Revolution. The German and Ottoman empires stayed away, and Great-Britain, Austria-Hungary, Russia, Italy, and China had only unofficial representation.

The Columbian Exhibition in Chicago—staged a year late, in 1893— incongruously sported a pylon and an obelisk before the Arab-Islamic "Street of Cairo," which a Belgian and a Greek entrepreneur assembled.[69] In 1900, the Egyptian government again declined official participation in a Parisian *exposition universelle*. Lebanese-Egyptian entrepreneur Philippe Boulad stepped in, engaging Marcel Dourgnon, the architect of the Egyptian Museum then going up in Cairo, to design an Egyptian pavilion. Dourgnon mixed three sections in a single structure, one in pharaonic style (a mixture of Theban and Memphite) and the other two in neo-Arab or Islamic style.[70] Egyptians who visited these late nineteenth-century fairs reacted primarily to representations of modern, not ancient, Egypt, as chapter 6 will show.

Egypt, along with Turkey, Persia, and Morocco, did name a commissioner-general (a foreigner) and a delegate (an Egyptian) to the Louisiana Purchase Exposition in Saint Louis in 1904. Anthropology ran riot at Saint Louis, with such living specimens as Filipinos from the United States' recent colonial acquisition and "Mysterious Little Japanese Primitives," the "St. Louis Ainu," who were judged "polite and clean." Egypt's mailing address at the fair was in care of the anthropology department. The display in the section "Egypt and Prehistoric Man" included Stone Age flints from Egypt, and there was, "befitting the Land of the Lotus, in which civilization found its earliest germ, an entire tomb, mummies and mummy cases of royal personages and of the deified cat, with scarabs and other sacramental symbols of an early cult. . . . "[71]

On the scholarly front, International Congresses of Orientalists continued making the rounds of great imperial European cities—Vienna, London, Paris, and Rome, with forays also to lesser European centers—Leiden, Genoa, Hamburg, Copenhagen, and Athens. The Sixth ICO met in the Dutch city of Leiden the year after the British seized Egypt. Once the congress ventured into the object of its studies by convening in Algiers.[72]

Egyptology continued to dominate the African studies sections of the ICO. Jacques de Morgan mentioned Ahmad Kamal favorably in his report to the Tenth ICO at Geneva in 1894, but not until the Eighteenth Congress in Leiden in 1931 would an Egyptian Egyptologist (Sami Gabra) address the body. In Arabic and Islamic studies, in contrast, Egyptians began presenting at the ICOs in the 1880s, as chapter 6 will show.

MARCEL DOURGNON'S EGYPTIAN MUSEUM, CAIRO

The jury that in 1895 selected the design for Cairo's new Egyptian Museum settled on Beaux Arts neoclassicism. An Egyptian architect and indigenous design were out of the question. Cromer was at the peak of his power, museums were imported institutions, European architects were dominant in Cairo, Italians dominated the skilled construction and decorative trades, traditional Islamic architecture was in eclipse, and the neo-Islamic Revival was still in its early stages. Not least, the jury consisted of a Frenchman, a Briton, and an Italian. Even among these three nationalities, the deck was stacked. Twenty-six Italians, sixteen Frenchmen, sixteen Englishmen, and fifteen of other nationalities entered the design contest, but the five projects in the final running were all French.[73]

The jury could look back on a century of revival styles in the West—including classical, Gothic, and—more feebly—pharaonic and Islamic.[74] European museums built as such during the first half of the nineteenth century looked to Rome and Greece for inspiration. Karl Friedrich Schinkel's Altes Museum and Friedrich Stüler's Neues Museum in Berlin, Leo von Klenze's Glypothek of Munich, and Sir Robert Smirke's British Museum all linked museums and neoclassicism in Western minds. How better could one approach the Elgin marbles than through the British Museum's Ionic facade, in which pedimental sculptures trumpeted "the Progress of Civilization"?[75]

Romanticism, however, challenged neoclassical hegemony, including its Beaux Arts incarnation, with Victorian "national" Gothic and Eugène-Emmanuel Viollet-le-Duc's idealized Gothic restorations. Gothic Revival style flourished for churches and, particularly in the United States, colleges and showed up in the New Science Museum at Oxford (1855–1859) and the Ruskinesque original Museum of Fine Arts in Boston (1876).

Romantics who found Gothic too tame could try pharaonic and Islamic Revival styles, which ironically reached Egypt at first more as European imports than directly from local roots. William Bullock's neopharaonic Egyptian Hall (1812), in Piccadilly, had seemed tailor-made for London's first major show of Egyptian antiquities—by Belzoni—in 1821.[76] Champollion protested plans for Greek or Roman instead of pharaonic decor in his Egyptian rooms at the Louvre,[77] but so powerful was the grip of classicism (cum Orientalism) that François-Edouard Picot's *Study and the Muse of the Arts Reveal Ancient Egypt to Athens* decorated one ceiling (see figure 27).[78]

The classical exterior of Berlin's Neues Museum (1850) concealed a stunning pharaonic court,[79] and pharaonic and Islamic motifs mingled indiscriminately in world's fair pavilions. Mariette oversaw the replication of pharaonic temples for Egyptian exhibits in the Paris expositions of 1867 and 1878 and introduced neopharaonic style to Cairo in the exterior of his Bulaq Museum. Even as Marcel Dourgnon's neoclassical Egyptian Museum was going up in Cairo, the architect displayed his versatility with the pharaonic-Islamic pavilion at the 1900 Paris Exposition universelle.

Cairo's Egyptian Museum had a brush with ornate "half French, half Oriental" style when temporarily housed in Ismail's Giza palace in the 1890s (see figure 36). To Budge, "a more incongruous place for them [pharaonic antiquities] could hardly have been found. The massive mummies of Rameses II and other great kings looked sadly out of place in rooms with walls painted blue, and moldings of salmon-pink picked out in gold, and ceilings decorated with panels, on which were painted Cupids, Venuses, etc."[80]

Beaux Arts neoclassicism reasserted itself in the West and its colonies toward the end of the century. This was in keeping with the imperial apogee associated with Curzon and Milner, Frederick Lugard and Rhodes, Cromer and Kitchener. The overpowering Victoria Memorial in Calcutta, the first major classical monument in India in fifty years, commemorated British heroes of India in classical garb.[81] New York's Metropolitan Museum of Art acquired its classical facade in 1902, and in 1907–1909 Boston's Museum of Fine Arts traded in its Ruskinesque Gothic for a neoclassical look. In Istanbul, Antoine Valaury's neoclassical Antiquities Museum (1891–1907) sat incongruously beside the ornate Çinili Kiosk in the grounds of Topkapi Palace.[82]

The "veiled protectorate" in Cairo ruled out imperial pomp like that of Calcutta or New Delhi. The British Residency occupied a prime site on the Nile but was relatively modest. The Egyptian Museum, on a commanding site in what is now Tahrir Square, came as close as any pub-

Figure 36.   Khedive Ismail's Giza palace, home of the Egyptian Museum,
1890–1902. Photograph No. 99 by Félix Bonfils. In the photo album entitled
"Egypt and Palestine." Courtesy of Rare Books and Special Collections
Library, The American University in Cairo.

lic building to an imperial statement, but that statement could not be
exclusively British.

Marcel-Lazare Dourgnon (1858–1911) was born the same year Said
and Mariette founded the Egyptian Antiquities Service. He graduated
from the École des Beaux-Arts in Paris and spent a dozen years in Chile
as official architect. In his Egyptian phase, he designed the Egyptian
Museum, IFAO's building, and a French hospital, as well as the Egyptian pavilion for the Paris Exposition universelle of 1900.[83]

At the turn of the century, the British-occupied Qasr al-Nil barracks—
another symbol of the colonial age, although erected slightly earlier
under Said—were the Egyptian Museum's main visual competition in
the square. The museum anchored the district's archaeological aspect:
Mariette Pasha Street ran alongside the museum to Midan Mariette
Pasha, and Egyptian Museum Street (Sharia al-Antikhana al-Misriyya)
ran eastward behind the building. Behind the museum and across An-
tikhanah Street, Dourgnon's IFAO building served its archaeological
clientele (see map 2).

The museum's central arch, dome, Ionic columns and pilasters, balanced wings, dentils, and halls centered around a skylighted court, situated it firmly in Beaux Arts tradition (see figures 2, 5, and 6). Two urn-shaped designs with the dates of construction provided a baroque touch above the portal. Pharaonic accents rescued the exterior from being totally alien to the museum's contents. The Roman arch and Ionic columns of the portal were set in the outline of a pylon, a cow-horned Hathor or Isis protected the keystone, and goddesses symbolizing Upper and Lower Egypt flanked the portal.

Khedive Abbas laid the cornerstone on 1 April 1897,[84] but difficulties delayed the inauguration until 1902. The cost was £E251,000. Dourgnon and the French consul blamed the delays on British gallophobia. De Morgan claimed the British used his absence on an expedition in Sinai as an excuse to drag their feet. Dourgnon complained that the Ministry of Public Works shouldered aside the Italian construction firm that won the contract. When Dourgnon's name turned up over a secondary door instead of at the center of the facade (figure 4), he sued for £E300 above his £E1,000 fee.[85] Thus the museum that so encoded Europe's appropriation of the pharaonic past to the exclusion of modern Egyptians also reflected the long Anglo-French political and Egyptological rivalry on the Nile.

MASPERO AND THE *ENTENTE CORDIALE*

Egyptologists and diplomats, both British and French, sighed with relief at Maspero's return in 1899. He abandoned his predecessors' fight to exclude Britons from the Antiquities Service, conceding them generous representation, and finally won formal British recognition of French archaeological preeminence in Egypt. Taking stock in 1899, Maspero seems not to have worried that three Britons sat on the "Egyptology Committee" along with himself, another Frenchman, a German, and three Egyptians.[86] To what extent the gallicized Egyptians—Armenians Artin and Tigrane and the pliant prime minister Mustafa Fahmi—really represented Egypt is open to question.

Maspero's survey of the troubled service found two Cairo-based inspectors-in-chief, Georges Legrain and Ahmad Najib, and eight Egyptians, mostly demoralized, who rarely left Cairo to inspect their districts. Maspero named two British chief inspectors instead—J. Quibell in the north and Howard Carter in the south. By 1911, Maspero had five inspectorates, manned by three Britons, a Frenchman, and an Italian. Breccia of the Greco-Roman Museum oversaw greater Alexandria; and Campbell Edgar, the Delta. Quibell was based at Saqqara, Gustave Lefebvre in Asyut, and A. Weigall at Luxor.[87] Anglo-French tensions still flared occasionally, as when French tourists clashed with Egyptian guards under Carter at Saqqara. Maspero scurried to patch together a compromise, but Carter, proud and stubborn, resigned rather than make a pro forma apology.[88]

The dedication ceremonies for the Mariette monument in the museum's garden in March 1904 overflowed with international bonhomie.[89] Back in Europe, Britain and France were only weeks away from their famous *entente cordiale*. One of its clauses affirmed that the director of the Egyptian Antiquities Service should be French. The love feast continued under Cromer's successor, Sir Eldon Gorst (1907– 1911). Maspero won a British knighthood (KCMG) in 1909, and Cromer, retired and presiding over the EEF, flattered France as "the mother of Egyptology."[90] France renounced any claim to the Temple of Luxor's remaining obelisk and Britain relinquished claims on the Mitrahina colossus of Rameses II, which Muhammad Ali had offered Caviglia and Sloane in 1818.[91] From his retirement, Cromer advised against a proposed British archaeological institute in Egypt, because it might stir up hostility with the French as well as the Egypt Exploration Fund.[92]

The collapse of a huge column at Karnak a few days after Maspero's return in 1899 confirmed his decision to concentrate on conservation and publication and leave most excavation to foreign expeditions.[93] De Morgan had assigned G. Legrain to work at Karnak in 1895, and this *"direction des travaux de Karnak"* continues today as the Centre franco-égyptien d'étude et restauration des temples de Karnak.[94] Maspero forged ahead with the service's *Annales*, which Loret had begun to prepare, and implemented Borchardt's plan for international collaboration on the *Catalogue générale* of the Egyptian Museum.[95]

Consul General Kitchener (1911–1914) closed out the era with harder-edged maneuvering vis-à-vis French archaeologists. Unlike Cromer, Kitchener himself collected antiquities, bringing full circle the tradition of consul-collectors Henry Salt had inaugurated a century earlier. In 1913 he backed the creation of a secretary-generalship of antiquities in hopes of maneuvering Quibell into the post.[96] By the spring of 1914, Maspero felt worn out and presented his choice for a French successor to Kitchener.[97]

THE RETURN OF THE GERMANS AND THE ITALIANS

Britons and Frenchmen almost monopolized Egyptian excavation in the 1880s and 1890s, but then Germans, Americans, and Italians came in. The turning point came in 1905–1907 with a rush of American expeditions and the founding of the German Archaeological Institute. Germany's global ambitions after unification, the preeminence of its universities, and its leadership in Egyptian philology did not translate into a sustained Egyptological presence in Cairo until sixty years after the Lepsius expedition. Ebers, Dümichen, and H. Brugsch, honored along with Lepsius on the facade of Cairo's Egyptian Museum, did not organize major expeditions.[98] In Istanbul and its Fertile Crescent provinces, German activity in the army and railroad building spilled over into archaeology. The director of Istanbul's antiquities service and museum in the 1870s had been German. German excavations at Pergamon in 1878 and later at Babylon and later at the Hittite capital of Boghazkoi fanned Frenchmen's uneasiness.[99]

Erman himself worked out of Berlin, but the great Egyptian dictionary project he launched in 1895 required epigraphic fieldwork and increased the demand for a German archaeological institute in Cairo like those in Rome and Athens. The Deutsche Orient-Gesellschaft (German Oriental Society), founded in 1898, sponsored Middle Eastern excavation.[100] Ludwig Borchardt and Friedrich Bissing began excavating Nyuserre's Fifth Dynasty sun temple at Abu Gurob that same year. Borchardt later dug for the society at Abu Sir and Tell el-Amarna. His ambitious project for a scientific catalogue of the holdings of the Egyptian Museum brought together German, French, British, and American Egyptologists.[101] Borchardt was also cultural attaché at the German consulate and sat on the Egyptian government's Egyptology Committee. The German House opened on the Theban west bank in 1904, and three years later Borchardt became first director of the German Archaeological Institute's (Kaiserlich Deutsche Institut für Ägyptische Altertumskunde) Egyptian activities.[102]

World War I aborted this promising beginning. German property in Egypt was sequestered. After the war, the dispute over Borchardt's quiet export of the bust of Nefertiti to Berlin flared up. The Egyptians refused to allow German excavation or reopening of the German Archaeological Institute until 1929, when Hermann Junker replaced the embittered Borchardt. Junker was German and had taken his doctorate at Berlin, but since 1907 he had taught at the University of Vienna. The Prussian Academy sponsored his early excavations in Nubia, but the Vienna Academy sponsored him at Giza in 1912–1914 and again in 1925–1929. Professor of Egyptology at the Egyptian University in the 1930s, he clung to his post until 1939 despite British accusations that he worked for the Nazis.[103]

Italy was the remaining pre–World War I power with possible designs on Egypt. Botti's obtaining the directorship of the Greco-Roman Museum in Alexandria in 1892 was a cultural coup, and in 1904 Breccia's succession to the post confirmed it as an Italian cultural enclave. While Botti and Breccia dug in greater Alexandria and emphasized the Greco-Roman era, Egyptologist Ernesto Schiaparelli (1856–1928) excavated throughout the country in twelve seasons between 1903 and 1920. His most famous find was the tomb of Nefertari in the Valley of the Queens. After studying at Turin and with Maspero, he directed first the Egyptian section of the museum at Florence and then the Turin Museum.[104]

Maspero and the French consulate worried about the Italians whom Prince Ahmad Fuad hired to teach at the Egyptian University. In 1909, Italy followed other powers with an archaeological institute in Athens, and there was talk of an Italian institute of Oriental studies in Cairo. Italy's invasion of Libya in 1911 doomed the latter project, and irate Egyptians ousted the Italians from their Egyptian University posts.[105]

THE AMERICAN DEBUT

No American names adorn the facade of Cairo's Egyptian Museum. Edward Robinson had pioneered biblical archaeology as far back as the 1830s, and the American Oriental Society dated from 1842, but the drive to develop major universities and museums that could support archaeology only came together after the Civil War. In the 1870s, newly rich industrialists hungry for cultural legitimacy joined older elites worried about mass democracy in founding major art museums in Boston, New York, and Philadelphia. Americans returning with German doctorates grafted research seminars and laboratories onto undergraduate colleges to create the modern American university.

Toward the close of the century, several American museums and universities became interested in the ancient Near East and Egyptology. After an exploratory Mesopotamian survey the year before, the University of Pennsylvania inaugurated excavations at Nippur (now in Iraq) in 1888. In 1907, Pennsylvania's University Museum of Archaeology and Anthropology, founded in 1890, extended operations to Egypt. The Society of Biblical Literature and Exegesis, founded in 1895, and the American Schools of Oriental Research[106] pooled resources from many colleges and universities, and in 1900 the latter began sponsoring research in Palestine.

As in France and Germany, American Egyptology roughly followed a path pioneered by classical archaeology. Harvard art professor Charles Eliot Norton presided for eleven years over the classically oriented Archaeological Institute of America, founded in 1879. Its *American Journal of Archaeology* was founded in 1882, the year the American School of Classical Studies opened in Athens. Rome followed, with the American School of Architecture (1894) and the American School of Classical Studies (1895). These merged in 1913 to become the American Academy in Rome.[107] American Egyptology owed more to German and British than to French inspiration. Two of three promising Americans who studied with Maspero died young,[108] and the wealthy amateur Charles Wilbour's (1833–1896) failure to publish left him on the margins despite his expertise and regular winters in his luxurious *dahabiyya* on the Nile. Wilbour studied in Berlin as well as Paris, and German scholarship shaped America's first generation of professional Egyptologists—James Henry Breasted, George Reisner, and Albert Lythgoe.[109] The three were born in the 1860s, studied Egyptology in Germany in the 1890s, and then began fieldwork in Egypt.

Egyptology got a slow start in British universities, so it was the EEF and Petrie who left a British mark on early American Egyptology. The EEF's many enthusiastic American members made Amelia Edward's speaking tour of the United States in 1889 a rousing success. Until they were ready to launch their own expeditions, the Boston Museum of Fine Arts, the Metropolitan Museum of Art, the University of Pennsylvania's University Museum, and the Brooklyn Museum built their collections through subscriptions to the EEF.[110]

As the first curator (1890–1905) of the Egyptian and Mediterranean section of the University of Pennsylvania's University Museum of Archaeology and Anthropology, Sara Yorke Stevenson obtained Egyptian objects through Petrie and the EEF. In 1898 she visited Egypt to see about a University Museum expedition. She reported that the British were "our natural allies" in Egyptology and forwarded a proposal from Yaqub Artin for "a scientific station of American and English Egyptologists and Orientalists." Another option was an "American School at Cairo for Egyptology and Arabic and Christian antiquity," which could "give American Science a representation on the ground. . . . Other nations are keen and actively struggling for a share of the rich scientific plunder and America is absolutely nowhere here."[111] Not until 1924 did the University of Chicago's Oriental Institute establish a permanent American Egyptological base in Egypt—the Chicago House, at Luxor. And not until 1951 did the American Research Center in Egypt establish itself in Cairo.

Millionaire philanthropists stand out as sponsors of American expeditions to Egypt—Phoebe Hearst, Theodore Davis, Eckley Brinton Coxe Jr., John D. Rockefeller Jr., and the Rockefeller Foundation. Phoebe Hearst, wife of mining magnate George Hearst and mother of newspaper baron William Randolph Hearst, sponsored Reisner's University of California expedition (1899–1905). Theodore Davis financed his own dig in the Valley of the Kings (1903–1912), with Englishman Percy Newberry, among others, providing the expertise. Coxe underwrote the University Museum's Egyptian excavations until his death in 1916. John D. Rockefeller Jr. and the Rockefeller Foundation supported Breasted and the Oriental Institute he organized at the University of Chicago.

Reisner began digging in Egypt in 1899 and Davis in 1903, but 1905–1907 marked the takeoff of American fieldwork, with expeditions from Harvard-Boston (Reisner), the Metropolitan Museum of Art (MMA; Lythgoe, soon joined by Herbert Winlock), the Brooklyn Museum (J. de Morgan's brother Henri de Morgan), and Pennsylvania's University Museum (David Randall-MacIver, then Clarence Fisher). Breasted was also in the field from 1905 to 1907 for the University of Chicago's photographic survey of Nubia. He insisted that recording rapidly perishing inscriptions was more urgent than excavation. It was in 1907, too, that Norman and Anna de Garis Davies began recording Theban tombs for the Graphic Section of the MMA.

Brooklyn's expedition and Chicago's Nubian Survey ended in 1907 after two seasons, but Harvard-Boston, the MMA, and the University Museum kept digging, with intervals, into the 1930s. Reisner's Harvard camp at Giza and the Metropolitan Museum House and the Chicago House at Luxor became familiar interwar landmarks.

Lythgoe, Breasted, and Reisner each excelled in a different niche of Egyptology. Lythgoe stood out as the first curator of Egyptian Art at the Boston Museum of Fine Arts (BMFA; 1902) and founding curator of the Egyptian art department of the MMA (1906–1929). Breasted excelled as a scholar, teacher, and administrator. His Chicago chair of Egyptology in 1905 was the first in the country, and the Oriental Institute, which he opened in 1919 with Rockefeller money, became a hub for Egyptology and ancient Near Eastern studies. Reisner combined his Harvard professorship with the curatorship of Egyptian art at the BMFA, but he won his fame as a master excavator who surpassed Petrie's once innovative standards. He denounced mere hunts for museum objects and emphasized excavating entire cemeteries, digging layer by layer in inverse chronological order, documenting every step with drawings, notes, and photographs, and publishing definitive scholarly reports.[112]

On a popular note, American consul general Frederic Penfield offered in 1909 to pay for moving the remaining obelisk of the Temple of Luxor to central Cairo. London, Paris, New York, Rome, and Istanbul all had Egyptian obelisks; shouldn't Cairo? In Luxor, only a few hundred tourists could see it each winter. In Cairo "not only visitors from all countries, but the enormous native population as well, may see it daily in their goings and comings." The Egyptian cabinet declined the offer, citing objections from archaeologists.[113]

THE WORK OF AHMAD KAMAL

The Egyptians are as yet [not] civilized enough to care
about the preservation of their ancient monuments....
No moral guilt of any kind is attached to the offence,
which is considered as absolutely venial.... We say to
the Egyptians: we civilized governments care about
their ancient monuments. If you pretend to be a civilized nation you ought to care about them too.

> Lord Cromer, as quoted in William
> Welch Jr., *No Country for a Gentleman*

Cromer's condescending remarks ignored the struggle of Ahmad Kamal to establish Egyptology for Egyptians in a hostile colonial environment. Kamal had a two-part task—to establish himself as a serious Egyptologist and to persuade his countrymen to identify with ancient Egypt. His French publications primarily addressed the first goal; his Arabic publications, the second. Maspero showed his respect for Ahmad Kamal by including him in the international team compiling the *Catalogue général* of the Cairo Museum. Kamal produced volumes on Ptolemaic and Roman stelae and on offering tables. The Antiquities Service paid him the standard bonus of a month's salary (£E33.33 in his case) when the first came out.[114]

Kamal contributed twenty-nine items in French to the Antiquities Service's *Annales du Service des antiquités de l'Égypte* (hereafter, *ASAE*) in its first ten years, over twice as many as all his Egyptian contemporaries together. His old classmate Ahmad Najib had four items in the few years between the *ASAE*'s founding and his retirement. Two of Kamal's former pupils from the 1881–1885 school also contributed; Muhammad Chaban had five items in the first ten years and several more in the next ten.[115]

Many of these items were short, often inspector's notices on sites rescued by authorities from illicit digging. Sometimes Kamal conducted brief follow-up excavations. This was the best he could hope for at a time when Westerners were opening pyramids and digging at glamorous sites like Giza, Saqqara, Karnak, and the Valley of the Kings. In principle, Maspero denied excavation permits to non-Egyptologists and those who lacked sponsorship by a museum or academic institution. He admitted that this excluded Egyptians but opined that thus far they had only wanted to dig for treasure, not out of "scientific passion."[116]

Kamal's numerous Arabic works were invisible to his Western colleagues. He seems to have imagined an audience of Arabic-reading fellow specialists, students, and the general public, but the first category scarcely existed as yet.

Part of Kamal's Arabic work was translation from French in the tradition of al-Tahtawi and his school. Moving the museum to Giza made Abu al-Suud's Arabic translation of Mariette's guide obsolete, and it was Kamal who translated de Morgan's new guide into Arabic in 1892–1893. A decade later, when the museum moved to its present site, Kamal did the job over again with Maspero's new guidebook. This was no mean task; the Arabic text of the translation, admittedly with many illustrations, ran to 788 pages. Kamal also rendered Botti's guide to the Greco-Roman Museum into a 639-page Arabic version.[117]

By 1915 Maspero's guide was in its fourth French and fifth English edition but had not gone beyond the first in Arabic.[118] Was this a gauge of the relative interest of Europeans and Egyptians in antiquities or more a measure of the priorities of the European-run Antiquities Service? Grébaut's testimony that Egyptians flocked to the museum has been noted. Baedeker advised avoiding Tuesdays, when the waiver of the five-piastre entry fee brought a crowd of "Arab visitors of the lower classes." Maspero experimented with free admission during the summer, the tourist off-season. When this produced crowds eager to rub against antiquities as a cure for various ills, he instituted a one-piastre off-season fee.[119]

Kamal wrote a book in Arabic on ancient Heliopolis before landing his first museum post. While teaching at the museum's modest School of Egyptology in the early 1880s, he wrote two more Arabic books—a history of ancient Egypt (244 pages) and a hieroglyphic grammar. Unfortunately the school closed the year the grammar came out. He also wrote books in Arabic on Memphis, a voluminous study on crafts and other aspects of ancient Egypt, and a long manual on ancient Egyptian plants. Kamal inserted illustrations of tomb scenes and hieroglyphics into his texts and supplied both transliterations and translations. Perhaps he imagined an Arabic-reading audience comparable to the Anglo-American one that Wilkinson's *Manners and Customs of the Ancient Egyptians* had tapped during the decades before writing on Egypt bifurcated into specialist and popular works.[120]

One of Ahmad Najib's books described a tour of Upper Egypt with students from the Dar al-Ulum teachers college. To counteract the failure of the "sons of our fatherland" *(watan)* to value antiquities, Najib wrote a book of essays on ancient Egypt for the Ministry of Education. It included the hieroglyphic text of a story, with transliteration and translation running underneath. Najib also reported on de Morgan's recent excavations.[121]

After 1900, Ahmad Kamal began achieving a little hard-won recognition. His *ASAE* items and work on the *Catalogue général* raised his visibility to Europeans, and his election to the Institut égyptien in 1904 broadened his contacts and provided another outlet for his work.

Kamal's well-attended lectures at the Higher Schools Club sometime between 1906 and 1908 enabled him to preach his agenda to an influential elite of students and higher-school alumni. Founded in 1905 with 240 members, the club jumped to 774 by 1909. These were the crowded years of ferment, which included protests against British repression in the Dinshaway trial, Cromer's departure, the emergence of political parties, the death of national hero Mustafa Kamil, and the founding of the private Egyptian University.[122]

In 1908–1909, Kamal leapt at the chance to teach a course on ancient Egypt at the new Egyptian University. Maspero was on the board and no doubt recommended him. The university published Kamal's lectures covering up to the Fifteenth Dynasty.[123] Kamal opened with the invocation "In the Name of God," a prayer for the prophet Muhammad, and a religious justification for his work. He then took up prehistory, noting European disputes about whether humans were created with Adam and Eve or evolved from an animal state and whether all civilizations came from a single source.

The university solicited his lectures because "advanced nations"—
the Arabs under the Abbasids, Europeans since the Renaissance, and
now America and Japan—had benefited from the wisdom of the Egyptians of the *jahiliyya* (pre-Islamic age), a topic still "unknown among
us."[124] With foreigners flocking to see pharaonic antiquities, Egyptians
too must appreciate their "beloved fatherland's heritage." He was proud
that Egyptian priests had dismissed the Greeks as mere children and that
the Greeks had hailed Egypt as the source of writing, philosophy, law,
arts, and civilization.[125]

Kamal's secondary sources ranged from Brugsch, Lepsius, Mariette,
Chabas, and Maspero to Herodotus, Manetho, and Diodorus Siculus.
He cited Ali Mubarak on the Nile but ignored the medieval Arabic pyra-
mid lore that Mubarak had passed along.

Like Mariette and al-Tahtawi, Kamal followed a long chronology, putting Manetho's Menes at 5,626 (solar) years before the Hijra (5004 B.C.).
In his 1882–1883 history, Kamal had dated events in (solar) years before the Hijra, as in al-Tahtawi's and Mariette's Arabic textbooks. But
by now B.C. dates were common enough that he no longer bothered with
"before the Hijra" dates.

Thematically organized chapters from his university lectures discussed
the Nile, the ecology along its banks and in the Delta, religion, geographical division into nomes, the sociopolitical order, language and
writing systems, and Champollion's decipherment. Chronologically organized chapters followed, dynasty-by-dynasty and reign-by-reign,
bringing in the evidence from the monuments and showing the relevant
cartouches. Thematic sections such as "Commerce in the Memphite
Age" and "Ancient Egyptian Art" interrupted the chronological sections
from time to time.

Kamal's next breakthrough was to persuade the Ministry of Education to form an Egyptology section in the Higher Teachers College in
1910. He lectured twice a week to seven students, took them to the
Egyptian Museum, and even led a tour of Upper Egypt. The first class
graduated in 1912, and a second cohort entered the program.[126]

On another front, Kamal and Maspero encouraged provincial authorities to establish small regional museums. Maspero and the Egyptology Committee permitted a local notable, Ahmad Khashaba Pasha,
to dig near Asyut. Parts of his finds went to the Cairo museum, and he
was encouraged to preserve the rest in a local museum. The municipality of Tanta founded a museum in 1913 with the help of the Antiquities Service, and Minya considered doing so.[127]

ANCIENT EGYPT IN TURN-OF-THE-CENTURY
NATIONAL CONSCIOUSNESS

As already noted, an 1899 magazine masthead shows a peasant woman pointing her children toward "the light of knowledge," which shines on a pyramid and the Sphinx while the khedive and four educator-officials frame the scene (see figure 7). Though hardly typical of Egyptian world views at the time, it shows that Kamal was not alone in laying the foundations for identification with ancient Egypt that would flourish in the 1920s.

The exclusive use of the pyramid-and-sphinx design on letters mailed in Egypt from 1867 to 1914 drummed home the association of the postal service, and presumably the country, with these antiquities (see figure 22). In January 1914, when the British-dominated government finally introduced some variety, six out of the ten designs in the new set featured pre-Islamic antiquities. Similarly, the Sphinx, the Pyramids, and the temple of Philae were among the scenes the National Bank of Egypt circulated on the country's first set of paper currency between 1899 and World War I.[128] Coins, traditionally symbols of sovereignty in the Islamic world, were more conservative. Down to 1914, they bore the name of the Ottoman sultan, other inscriptions in Arabic calligraphy, and supplemental floral or abstract designs.

Probably Europeans rather than Egyptians made the original choices for the visual propaganda on the stamps and paper currency. Italians had first organized the Egyptian postal service, British shareholders predominated in the National Bank of Egypt, and the British monopolized critical decisions in Egypt between 1882 and 1922. Nevertheless, the long-term drumbeat of these symbols did not go unheard. The paper currency and postage stamps of fully independent Egypt make prominent use of pharaonic symbolism to this day.

Egyptian heads of state have presented themselves as protectors of pharaonic antiquities at least since Muhammad Ali's 1835 decree, and for over a century they have incorporated visits to antiquities sites into their ceremonial agendas. Early in 1880, the newly enthroned khedive Tawfiq set off with three large steamers and a supply boat to show himself to his subjects in Upper Egypt. He stopped for the homage of provincial governors and local notables along the way, but he also visited the temples of Dendera, Esna, Elephantine Island, Philae, Luxor, and Karnak.[129] In 1886, he attended the ceremony at the Bulaq Museum for the first unwrapping of the mummy of a New Kingdom pharaoh.[130]

Tawfiq's progression through Upper Egypt in 1890 was on a Cook's steamer with American tourists aboard. The first stop was Badrashin, for a visit to Memphis and Sakkara. Later antiquities stops included Dendera, Karnak, the Valley of the Kings, the Ramesseum, Esna, Edfu, Kom Ombo, Aswan, and Philae. He and his entourage discussed the potential for developing tourism further through Cook's.[131] The next year, Tawfiq took the Antiquities Service director Grébaut along on a cruise from the First Cataract to Wadi Halfa (see figure 37).[132]

Hopeful that Abbas II would continue to favor his company, John Cook arranged for fifty Egyptian students from the Dar al-Ulum to tour Upper Egypt free of charge on the steamer Abbas. Boarding the students' steamer when it passed his, John Cook addressed them:

> I met the late Khedive and found him very sorry for the Egyptians who thru their good education and knowledge have been appointed in high positions and on account of time the[y] could not voyage in upper-Egypt to visit the monuments and he informed me that very few from the Egyptians has [sic] voyaged in the country, while we see that tourists come from America and Europe to visit these monuments. . . . you must therefore know the history of your ancestors so that you can manage your work after what you have picked up of their good example. . . .

Cook had given the students the company's best dragoman, Hajj Muhammad Abu Elewa.[133]

Abbas II's ceremonial laying of the foundation stones and later the inauguration of new buildings for the Greco-Roman and Egyptian museums have been noted above, and he did the same for the Museum of Arab Art. No Egyptian head of state since has failed to present himself as chief protector of the pharaonic as well as the Islamic heritage.

Two aristocrats in exile—neoclassical Arabic poet Mahmud Sami al-Barudi and Prince Ibrahim Hilmy—incorporated ancient Egypt into their longing for their homeland. Despite being a "Turco-Circassian," like Khedive Tawfiq, al-Barudi as prime minister had cast his lot with Urabi and paid with seventeen years' exile in Ceylon. He wrote:

> Ask the spacious Giza about two pyramids of Egypt, so that
>   you may know the secret of that unknown to you before.
> Two structures repelling the assault of ages. What a
>   wonder is their overcoming of this assault!
> . . . . .
> They stood despite the calamities of ages to prove the glory
>   of their builders in the world.
> How many nations have perished and ages lapsed while they
>   remain the wonder of the eye and the mind.[134]

Figure 37. Guardian of the national patrimony or Cook's tourist? Khedive Tawfiq (with the furled white umbrella) and entourage at the Temple of Philae. In the photo album entitled "Voyage de Son Altesse le Khédive dans la Haute-Egypte, 1891," by Abdullah Frères, 28. Courtesy of Rare Books and Special Collections Library, The American University in Cairo.

In 1886, Prince Ibrahim Hilmy, a Royal Military Academy (Woolwich) graduate dedicated his *Literature of Egypt and the Soudan from the Earliest Times* to ex-khedive Ismail, whose Italian exile he shared. This bibliography, alphabetical by subject and author, included Arabic and Western-language sources on all periods. Hilmy explained:

> Egyptian lore in all its branches has always proved to be a magic attraction to the most celebrated authors of every age; and whether there be occasion to consult some occult treatise on the hieroglyphic teachings of THE BOOK OF THE DEAD, or a modern statement of a contemporary question of social economy, some fruitful fount of knowledge is sure to be at hand if the seeker only knows where to find it.[135]

Exile for supporting the Urabi revolution also sharpened Muhammad al-Muwaylihi's sense of Egyptian identity. After returning, he wrote the serial *Fatra min al-Zaman* (published in English translation as *A Period of Time*) for the newspaper *Misbah al-Sharq*, which he and his father, Ibrahim al-Muwaylihi, founded in 1898. The fictional narrator escorts a pasha resurrected from Muhammad Ali's day through Europe and Egypt, commenting on changing aspects of life and society, including attitudes toward antiquities.[136] The author collected the installments in a book, *Hadith Isa ibn Hisham,* which came out in 1905 and later revised editions.

Al-Muwaylihi's own views are elusive in this fictional work. A visit to the pyramids of Giza elicits a range of opinions: They are marvelous evidence of ancient Egypt's high civilization, symbols of slavery and tyranny, a good place to frolic with a "lewd dancer," and "a source of income for a group of Bedouin who have been using it [the Great Pyramid] as a means of avoiding the need to earn a living by fleecing tourists." A visit to the museum, then housed in Giza, produces an argument for antiquities as priceless evidence of the glory of pharaonic Egypt and regret at the absence of works in Arabic to convey this message. Another character dismisses the relics as worn-out junk that should be sold to foreigners, accepts only "noble Arabs" as forebears, and deplores the millions spent on excavation and the successive museum buildings at Bulaq, Giza, and the new one under construction.

Ahmad Shawqi's exile came later, with the deposition of Abbas II, whom he served as court poet. He had recited "Great Events in the Nile Valley," at the International Congress of Orientalists in Geneva in 1894, celebrating pharaonic and Ptolemaic glories alongside Islamic glories. Shawqi emphasizes the monotheistic achievements of Moses, Jesus, and Muhammad but also mentions Isis favorably. The Hyksos, Achaemenid Persians, and Romans join the Crusaders as oppressors who were endured and eventually overthrown.[137]

For history, Arabic readers had recourse not only to Kamal and Ahmad Najib but also to surveys by nonspecialists. Ahmad Hasan wrote a general history of Egypt to the Islamic conquest (1888), and Husayn Zaki's *Tarikh al-Sharq al-Qadim* (History of the ancient East) (1892) had a volume each on ancient Egypt, Iraq and Babylon, the Persians and Medes, and the Kingdom of Tyre.[138] Ismail Sarhank's *Haqaiq al-Akhbar an Duwal al-Bihar* (True relations of the maritime nations),[139] a world history emphasizing naval affairs, devoted its second volume to Egypt but only eighteen pages to pharaonic history from Menes to Alexander and nineteen more up to the Islamic conquest. Sarhank's mix of Western and Arabic sources included not only such standards as Manetho, Abd al-Latif al-Baghdadi, and Mariette but also Ahmad Najib's *Al-Athar al-Jalil.*

Mikhail Sharubim's (1853–1920)[140] *Al-Kafi fi tarikh Misr al-qadim wa al-hadith* (Basic history of ancient and modern Egypt) offered far more detail than Sarhank on ancient Egypt—178 closely packed pages on the thirty dynasties up to Alexander. A Cairo-born Copt, Sharubim entered the Ministry of Finance's Department of Foreign-Language Publications at fourteen, worked as a judge in the national courts, and retired in 1903. His first volume surveyed ancient Egypt from Noah to the Arab conquest, the second from the Arab to the Ottoman conquest, the third from 1517 to the advent of Muhammad Ali, and the last from Muhammad Ali to the death of Tawfiq.

Sharubim's first volume resembles al-Tahtawi's *Anwar* in organization, scope, and content. Both cover Egypt up to the Islamic conquest. Sharubim's first two pages sketch in biblical lore—Adam, Noah and the Flood, Noah's son Ham settling in Africa, and Ham's son Misrayim giving Egypt the name by which it was known in Semitic languages, Misr. Like al-Tahtawi, Sharubim deftly links biblical tradition to Manetho's Menes— "whom they say was the Misrayim of the Torah."[141] Sharubim cites Lepsius, H. Brugsch, and Mahmud al-Falaki's "The Age of the Pyramids and Their Purpose."[142] His use of al-Falaki indicates a nascent strand of cumulative modern Egyptian scholarship on ancient Egypt. Sharubim gives "before the Hijra" dates (counted in solar years) but, unlike al-Tahtawi, adds B.C. equivalents. Like al-Tahtawi, he marches through Manetho's thirty dynasties, Alexander, the Ptolemies, and the Romans-Byzantines to the Islamic conquest, interrupting the flow occasionally for a thematic essay.

Sharubim quoted Josephus to the effect that Greek historians do not mention "what is in the Heavenly Books" on the Exodus, then devoted several pages to Moses, placing the Exodus in the reign of Merenptah (whom he mislabels "the Second"), son of Rameses II. He equated Rameses II with the Greeks' Sesostris, noting that "some historians" identify "Danaus the Egyptian," who founded colonies in Greece, as Rameses II's brother.[143]

He went beyond al-Tahtawi in trying to reconcile the legendary pharaohs of Islamic lore with Manetho's list and the monuments. The invading Asian founder of the Fifteenth Dynasty, Salatis, was "known to the Arabs as al-Walid ibn Ruqa'," and Ababi or Abufis of the Sixteenth Dynasty was the Arabs' al-Riyan ibn al-Walid, whom Joseph served as vizier. Sharubim tapped modern Egyptology for the text of Rameses II's treaty with the Hittites and Piankhi's Jabal Barqa inscription in the Bulaq Museum describing his conquest of Egypt.[144]

Sharubim shares al-Tahtawi's pride in the Greeks' acknowledgement of Egypt's early leadership in civilization. He follows al-Tahtawi and

Western historians in ascribing tyranny to the Persian conquerors and welcoming Alexander as a liberator. Sharubim devotes as many pages to the millennium from Alexander to the Islamic conquest as he had given the pharaohs. His dense four volumes could have reached only a very limited audience.

By the early twentieth century, nationalists were criticizing the British-controlled schools for neglecting ancient Egypt. When Salama Musa, a Coptic writer and journalist, visited Europe after graduating from secondary school in 1907, he was embarrassed at being unable to answer questions on ancient Egypt. On his return, he took a two-month Cook's tour of Upper Egyptian antiquities. Musa accused the British of keeping ancient Egypt out of the curriculum of the schools for fear of fanning national pride and demands for independence.[145] Mustafa Kamil, founder of the nationalist paper *Al-Liwa* and the National Party, saw Egypt as the first great civilized state in history, the progenitor of all others.[146] After his premature death in 1908, Kamil's partisans commemorated him with the bronze statue, supported by a sphinx's head, which still decorates Midan Mustafa Kamil.

Lutfi al-Sayid of the rival Umma Party, who focused on gradual reform rather than immediate independence, rooted his national vision firmly in ancient Egypt. He promoted visits to museums and both pharaonic and Islamic sites, "For the truth of the matter is that we do not know as much about the stature of our fatherland and its glory as tourists do!"[147]

> I don't ask that each Egyptian show proof of capacity of observation of a Champollion, encyclopedic knowledge of Egyptian antiquities of a Maspero or the archeological competence of a Kamal Bey. What we need are regular lectures and permanent teaching, at the Egyptian University or in other scientific establishments, of a sort that the sons of Egypt can have access to familiarity with their past, not in a scientific and precise manner, but in the manner in which the European tourists who visit our country know our history and that of our ancestors.[148]

A rough count of Arabic books published on ancient Egypt yields two for the 1870s, three for the 1880s, six for the 1890s, and twenty-four for 1900–1914. The last figure suggests a growing, though still modest, interest that would have heartened Ahmad Kamal.

Like independence, "Egyptology for the Egyptians" nevertheless seemed elusive on the eve of the Great War. The Antiquities Service's refusal to hire the Egyptology graduates from the Higher Teachers School forced the program to close in 1913. The Asyut museum project was an embarrassing failure, with antiquities leaking onto the market and the Antiquities Service revoking Ahmad Khashaba Pasha's excavation license. At the Egyptian University, the course on the ancient East drifted away from emphasis on the pharaonic era. In the early 1920s, Taha Husayn taught it as Greco-Roman history with attention to Ptolemaic and Roman Egypt.[149]

At Kamal's retirement in 1914, no Egyptian successor was in sight. His son Hasan had gone to Oxford in 1912 to study Egyptology but ended up in medicine. Kamal's former students Selim Hassan and Mahmud Hamza (who married Kamal's daughter) had fallen back on secondary school teaching, trying to keep up their Egyptology by visiting the museum and their old professor. Shafiq Ghorbal, later a famous modern historian, also taught secondary school. It looked as though another generation would be lost to Egyptology.[150]

Another blow came in 1916, when the secretary-general of the Antiquities Service, Georges Daressy, attacked an article by Kamal, his retired colleague. The prolific Daressy was personally writing much of the *ASAE* at the time. He challenged not only Kamal's specific points but also his very competence in Egyptian philology. Personal animosity gave an edge to the clash. It was Daressy, thirteen years his junior, whom Kamal had tried to beat out for promotion a quarter of a century earlier. Daressy had reached the Institut égyptien a decade before Kamal and passed him by in the Antiquities Service.

Daressy attacked a study that Kamal had presented at the Institut égyptien and published in its bulletin. Analyzing the origins of hieroglyphic signs, Kamal derived the Greek "Aiguptos," from which "Egypt" derives, from the name of the Upper Egyptian town of Coptos, not—as H. Brugsch had suggested—from the name of a shrine in Memphis. Kamal's patriotism presumably inclined him to derive "Misr," the Arabic name for Egypt, from an indigenous hieroglyphic root rather than seeing it as a term originated by external Semitic neighbors.[151]

Daressy warned that Kamal had made "a number of assertions which cannot be accepted by Egyptologists" and opined that "the author sins gravely from a philological and historical point of view," giving hieroglyphic signs several different Arabic equivalent letters and switching their order as needed. He charged that Kamal had ignored historical contexts of hieroglyphic words and exaggerated the influence of Semites, including the Arabs, on ancient Egypt.[152]

Kamal fought back in print and on the floor of the Institut. Ancient Egyptian dialects differed on the phonetic values of certain signs, he noted, and he had followed philological rules on metathesis. He defended the long list of Arabic words he derived from Egyptian and declared, "Egyptian is the mother language of Arabic and therefore of Hebrew."[153] If Kamal's nationalism colored his scholarship, Western Egyptologists like Petrie were not without sin in this regard. The attempt of the second-highest official in the Antiquities Service to read Kamal out of the profession should be viewed in the imperialist context of its day.

That same year, in 1916, Kamal reported finishing sixteen volumes of his twenty-two-volume dictionary of Egyptian, with Arabic and French equivalents. Kamal's son Hasan contrasted his father's valiant one-man enterprise with the vast dictionary Erman's team was compiling in Berlin. Plans for publishing Kamal's dictionary fell through upon his death, and its potential contribution to scholarship and Egyptian national pride remains unknown. Thus, by the time World War I interrupted normal activities, the generation of Maspero, Petrie, Erman, and Ahmad Kamal had carried Egyptology far beyond the frontier where Mariette, Lepsius, and Birch had left it. The advances were across the board—in museology, philology, epigraphy, art history, history, and excavation technique. From an Egyptian nationalist perspective, however, the picture was discouraging. Interest in ancient Egypt was percolating into the educated elite, but Kamal's struggle to establish Egyptology as a profession for Egyptians seemed to have failed. He plugged away at his dictionary in retirement, not knowing that after World War I his efforts would suddenly bear fruit in a national commitment to reasserting Egyptian control over antiquities and to training Egyptian Egyptologists and in a broader public pride in the achievements of the ancient Egyptians.

In the far less developed field of Islamic archaeology, by 1914 the Comité de conservation des monuments de l'art arabe had put into effect a conservation program for Islamic and Coptic monuments and created the Museum of Arab Art. When World War I suddenly deprived the Comité of the leadership of Max Herz, Ali Bahgat came into his own both as a pioneer of Islamic archaeology and as the first Egyptian curator of the Museum of Arab Art. Chapter 6 turns to these developments.

CHAPTER 6

Islamic Art, Archaeology, and Orientalism

The Comité and Ali Bahgat

No race has the genius for stonework to as high a degree as the Arab race; its rage to build is matched only by its lack of concern for keeping up what has been built.... As soon as a mosque, as soon as a palace is finished, they let it fall apart....

The Turks are the least artistic race that ever existed. Mehmed Ali, Abbas Pasha, Said Pasha, Ismail Pasha have built more walls than almost all their predecessors together, but what walls, good God! If only one of them had had the inspired idea to build an Arab palace!...He would have found all around finely carved woodwork, ceilings of an exquisite color and design, mushrabiyyas more delicately worked than the most delicate lace. But they allowed these treasures which could have been collected with so little trouble to be dispersed....

But the Turks....May the curse of the god of arts be on them!

Gabriel Charmes, *Cinq Mois au Caire
et dans la Basse-Égypte*

Writing in 1880 on the eve of both the founding of the Comité de conservation des monuments de l'art arabe and the British occupation, French journalist Gabriel Charmes voiced views that seem tailor-made for Edward Said. Charmes extolled "Arab" art while attributing serious flaws to the race he assumed had produced it, lambasted the Turkish "race" for wretched taste, and attacked the reigning "Turkish"

Muhammad Ali dynasty for neglecting historic preservation.[1] Only Western control could save the day. For Charmes, Orientalism, imperialism, and historic preservation all marched hand in hand.

This chapter's study of the European-Egyptian encounter in the Comité and Museum of Arab Art at times seems to support Said's thesis, but sometimes the evidence seems closer to the views of historians like John MacKenzie and Marc Crinson, who argue for more open-ended and historically grounded treatment of the Orientalist-Oriental encounter.[2] Western imperialism in Egypt was never monolithic, and Europeans on the Comité were not simply tools of their countries' imperialisms. The main Comité leaders between 1881 and 1914 came from countries with only modest imperial leverage in Cairo; Julius Franz was German, and Max Herz Austro-Hungarian.

On the Egyptian side, Ali Bahgat was the Ahmad Kamal of Islamic archaeology and the Museum of Arab Art. Like Kamal, he had to fight an uphill battle to establish himself as an archaeologist during the heyday of Western imperialism. As a young man Bahgat joined a secret nationalist society and nearly lost his job in a clash with British education adviser Douglas Dunlop. Yet like Kamal, Bahgat owed his very calling to European mentors and worked hard to win recognition from their international scholarly community.

Bahgat's relationship with Yaqub Artin illustrates the complexities of ethnic, religious, and national consciousness in the modern Middle East. An Egyptian Muslim of Turkish extraction, Bahgat entered his career at the Museum of Arab Art through the patronage of Artin, a gallicized Armenian Catholic, and Artin's friend and superior, cabinet minister Husayn Fakhri. Nationalists might dismiss Artin and Fakhri as collaborators with imperialism, but those two rescued Bahgat from Dunlop and steered him toward his life's work in Islamic art and archaeology.

Bahgat's service under Max Herz, the Comité's Austro-Hungarian chief architect and the curator of the Museum of Arab Art, ended abruptly when World War I made Herz an enemy alien in British eyes. Bahgat had already begun the excavation of al-Fustat, the first Arab-Islamic capital of Egypt, which would make him a pioneer of Islamic archaeology; now he was about to become the first Egyptian to direct the Museum of Arab Art.

The published proceedings of the Comité, until recently largely overlooked for Egyptian cultural history, are the prime source for this chapter. Europeans kept the Comité's minutes for much of its history, but one can occasionally read against the grain to recover Egyptian points of view.

The choice of terminology for this chapter is problematic. Is it better to follow earlier usage and speak of "Arab art" or use today's "Islamic art"? In the late nineteenth century, Stanley Lane-Poole opted for "Saracenic" over "Arabian," "Mohammedan," and "Moorish" art—all obsolete terms today. Since Marshall Hodgson's distinction between "Islamic" and "Islamicate" has not prevailed, one is left with a choice between "Islamic" or "Arab" art. "Arab art" runs the danger of association with discredited belief in Arab, Turkish, Persian, Berber, and Negro races as discrete entities that expressed their essences through art. The usage also does violence to the polyglot, multiethnic character of the Ottoman Empire, its Egyptian province, and earlier Islamic states. Today's "Islamic art," however, raises the sort of questions that troubled Hodgson: Could Christian architects and craftsmen, for example, produce Islamic art? The choice in this book has been for occasional inconsistency rather than a surface consistency that papers over the problem. "Arab art" will occasionally be used when speaking of earlier European perceptions, and "Islamic art" will usually be used to reflect more recent perspectives.[3]

PRELUDE TO PRESERVATION: HAUSSMANNIZING CAIRO

Had Edmé-François Jomard revisited Cairo sixty years after mapping it for Bonaparte, he could still have recognized the city. As late as Ismail's accession in 1863, wrote Arthur Rhoné, "the city of Cairo was still intact, at least in the sense that its monuments continued to fall quietly into ruin following the eternal way of the Orient; at least nothing was attempted in the way of works called 'improvement' and 'restoration.' "[4]

For all the far-reaching changes in Egypt during Muhammad Ali's reign, and in contrast with the booming port of Alexandria, both the physical face of Cairo and its population remained remarkably stable. Muhammad Ali did fill in the seasonal Ezbekiyeh lake, remove *mastaba* benches as hindrances to traffic, arrange for street sweeping and garbage removal, widen and extend al-Muski Street, and begin Muhammad Ali Street to link Ezbekiyeh to the citadel. Abbas I abandoned radical street building, added the military suburb of Abbasiyya, and allowed a British company to build an Alexandria-Cairo railway. Work on the Suez Canal begun under Said— "Port Said" bears his name—still did not radically alter Cairo.[5]

Ismail changed all that. His urban renewal transformed the landscape and triggered the founding of both the Comité and the Museum of Arab Art. Looking back from 1882, Amelia Edwards sighed: "Twenty years ago, Cairo—the Cairo of the Kaliphs—was intact, save for the ravages of time. Its fairy minarets, its traceried mosques and street-fountains, its noble gates, though crumbling slowly away in a land where nothing is ever done to arrest the progress of decay, were more lovely in the pathos of their gradual dissolution than they could have been even in their prime."[6]

City planner Baron Georges Haussmann himself showed Ismail and his minister Ali Mubarak the new Paris during the *exposition universelle* of 1867.[7] Dazzled, Ismail pressed Mubarak into playing Haussmann in Cairo to his own Napoleon III. Mubarak and Ismail, who had known each other since their student days in Paris in the 1840s, drew in another French-educated technician—the astronomer Mahmud al-Falaki—to draft a renewal plan for Cairo. The plan included traffic hubs radiating boulevards, formal gardens, gas streetlights, a water system, a bridge across the Nile, a tourist road to the Pyramids, and even an opera house modeled on La Scala in Milan. By the time Ismail hosted European dignitaries at the Suez Canal opening in 1869, he could display at least a preview of a Cairo remade in the image of Paris.[8]

The new quarter of Ismailiyya between Ezbekiyeh and the Nile contained boulevards radiating from traffic hubs. The neoclassical Abdin Palace was one such hub. The overcrowded old city, where Ismail had been born—which has since been reconceived as "medieval," "Islamic," or "Fatimid"—deteriorated when the upper classes followed the khedive's migration to fashionable new quarters. Narrow, irregular lanes had worked for pack animals and pedestrians, but in the nineteenth century wheeled vehicles returned to Egypt for the first time since the Roman era. Muhammad Ali at first had the only European-style carriage in town, but by 1875 there were nine hundred passenger carriages and twice as many goods carts.[9] New boulevards were cut to open up old quarters to vehicular traffic:

> One of the great "embellishments" of Cairo, one in which there was the most pride, is the Boulevard of Muhammad Ali. It took off like a shot one fine day from Ezbekiyah, without knowing where it was going, and found itself two kilometers later bumping into the formidable corner of the mosque of Sultan Hasan, which it couldn't avoid. In leaving, it had carried away a hill full of houses and mosques.... To conclude on the high spirits of this boulevard, it still had the force, after this escapade, to carry off an enormous corner of the mosque of Emir Koussoun (1329), one of the largest and most beautiful.[10]

Gabriel Charmes condemned the reigning dynasty on aesthetic grounds: "That which Ismail Pasha, in particular, took for the most refined art was a disgraceful compound of the most vulgar European style and of the most grotesque Turkish style."[11] Europeans came to Cairo looking not for Paris but for the *Arabian Nights* of their imagination. Lane-Poole linked nostalgia for a lost England to his quest for a still medieval Cairo but added:

> It is all very well for artists and antiquaries—who, like myself, care more about the past than the future—to groan over the changes which are taking place in Egypt under European influences; but...these changes are...inevitable. It is as much a waste of time to lament the passing away of the old order in Cairo as to deprecate the triumph of incompetent democracy in England.[12]

Even when Ismail tried to please Europeans by restoring monuments, he could not win. Amelia Edwards wrote:

> In works of "restoration," two methods are employed. The first and simplest is to entirely demolish the ancient structure and then to rebuild it in a base imitation-Italian-Gothic style. The second is to pull it partly down; to strip the ceiling of its carved wood-work, and the walls of their precious tiles and panellings; then to replace the former with cement and stucco, and the latter with slabs of polished granite or alabaster. In either case, the tiles are sold to tourists and *bric-à-brac* dealers, and the carved wood-work comes in usefully to light the workmen's fires.... The mosques of Sitteh Zeyneb and El Hassaneyn...have been restored according to the first method; the mosques of Keyssoon, El Moaiyud, and El Yousefee, or Ezbek, are cited as specimens of the second.[13]

Charmes was even more vehement:

> Destruction pure and simple would be a hundred times better! One can see at the mosque of Sultan Hasan marbles of rare fineness covered with crude painting representing false marbles.... It was to receive the guests at the fêtes of the Suez Canal that the ministers of Ismail Pasha had this abominable painting carried out on the principal monuments of Arab art. My God, forgive them; they know not what they do![14]

HISTORIC PRESERVATION IN EUROPE AND APPRECIATION OF ARAB ART

Two trends back in Europe prepared the way for Cairo's Comité and Museum of Arab Art—the historic preservation movement and growing appreciation of "Arab" art. The changes wrought by the French and industrial revolutions unleashed powerful nostalgia for lost pasts, fostering the urge to historic preservation. Louis-Philippe's minister François Guizot sought legitimacy for the July Monarchy by fostering a mix of revolutionary, Napoleonic, and old-regime memories. The government named an inspector of historic monuments in 1830 and in 1837 established the Commission of Historic Monuments. Victor Hugo had lobbied for the commission, and fellow romantic novelist Prosper Mérimée long served as its chief inspector. Eugène-Emmanuel Viollet-le-Duc, the commission's chief architect, fought a running battle for Gothic Revival architecture against neoclassicists entrenched in the École des Beaux-Arts and state building council. Viollet-le-Duc's philosophy was to strip away later accretions from a monument and, if necessary, rebuild portions in idealized original style.

By the 1850s, even Haussmann—Napoleon III's "Attila of the straight line"[15]—had to make some concession to existing monuments in remaking Paris. In 1887 a rather feeble French law first authorized expropriation of historic properties.

Laissez-faire Britain lacked a counterpart to France's Commission of Historic Monuments, but in 1877 William Morris and other followers of John Ruskin formed the Society for the Protection of Ancient Monuments. Appalled at Viollet-le-Duc, Ruskin shunned reconstructions and emphasized stabilizing historic buildings in their existing state. In 1882, half a century after France, Britain established an inspectorate of ancient monuments under Lieutenant General Pitt-Rivers.[16] A weak historic preservation law followed in 1883. The stricter Ancient Monuments Act had to wait until 1931. As with many institutions in Egypt, Cairo's Comité imported a French model; a British alternative did not yet exist.[17]

Biblical, classical, and pharaonic allusions in Western art were part of the West's quest for its own imagined past. Arab, Turkish, and Persian—or Islamic—motifs, in contrast, evoked an "Oriental other," variously hostile or alluringly exotic. Catholic missionary travelers of the seventeenth and eighteenth centuries had added classical and pharaonic ruins to their religious itineraries but still shunned mosques as bizarre bastions of fanaticism and heresy. Even had they been interested, Cairo's mosques were then usually off-limits to non-Muslims. French consul Benoît de Maillet and artist Louis François Cassas were unusual in the eighteenth century in their appreciation of Cairene mosques. De Maillet wrote: "One cannot admire enough the beauty of these domes, their grace, their proportion, their boldness, and above all the astonishing grandeur of some. The interior ornaments which embellish them are no less worthy of consideration. Some are worked with dentils, others in compartments of flowers, others in the form of parquet...."[18] De Maillet's plates omitted Islamic buildings, however, and he showed conventional classical taste in suggesting the removal from Alexandria to Paris of Pompey's Pillar—

not the hieroglyph-covered "Cleopatra's Needle," which he also drew. It was the latter that would captivate his nineteenth-century successors.

Denon's *Voyage en Égypte* (1802) showed mosques only as distant silhouettes.[19] The *Description de l'Égypte* had detailed plates on Sultan Hasan and several other mosques, but its text had little to say on Islamic architecture. Charmes complained that "the companions of Bonaparte" had thrilled to classical and pharaonic ruins but "took so little account of the value of the monuments of Cairo that in the plate...where they reproduced the mosque of Sultan Hasan they only forgot one thing, the splendid cornice which crowns the edifice!"[20] The absence of Islamic Cairo in the *Description*'s frontispiece reinforces his point.

As the century wore on, at least two types of Orientalism sought to capture Islamic essences. One, of which Edward W. Lane was a master, seized upon Arabic texts such as the Quran and the *Thousand and One Nights* as keys to understanding Islamic society. The other enlisted drawing, painting, and photography to portray architecture, street scenes, landscapes, and portraits (often illustrating racial or ethnic "types"). To the French, *"orientaliste"* was as likely to conjure up a painter as a scholar. Although he ultimately emphasized literary texts in his search for Islamic and Egyptian essences, Lane did extensive drawing as well. His *Manners and Customs of the Modern Egyptians* also drew on a third Orientalist medium—oral inquiry and ethnographic observation.[21]

Antoine Galland's *Mille et une nuits* (1704–1717) and later translations from French to English popularized the *Arabian Nights*. E. W. Lane and Richard Burton went back to the Arabic original for their rival translations (published in 1838–1841 and 1885, respectively). Lane censored sexually explicit passages, but Burton played them up. Stanley Lane-Poole later separated his great uncle Lane's voluminous notes from the text and rearranged them for republication as *Arabian Society in the Middle Ages: Studies from the Thousand and One Nights* (1883). In drawing on personal experiences in Cairo, Lane-Poole declared, Lane

> was guilty of no anachronism: for the Arabian Society in which a Saladin, a Beybars, a Barkook, and a Kait-Bey moved...survived almost unchanged to the time of Mohammad 'Alee, when Mr. Lane spent many years of intimate acquaintance among the people of Cairo....The continuity of Arabian social tradition was practically unbroken from almost the beginning of the Khalifate to the present century....[22]

With scholars propagating the idea of an Orient frozen in time, it was a rare tourist who could write home of contemporary Cairo without invoking the *Arabian Nights*.

Perhaps Europeans' appreciation of Islamic art and architecture could not flourish until they had historicized it and reconceived it as "medieval." The *Description* had classified Islamic monuments as "modern," placing them under *"état moderne,"* not *"antiquités."* The nineteenth-century's invention of "medieval Europe" implied by analogy a "medieval Islam," and "Arab (or Islamic) antiquities" manufactured after the "end of [classical Greco-Roman] antiquity" no longer seemed oxymoronic.[23]

Such Orientalist artists as Eugène Delacroix, Jean-Léon Gérôme, and Henri Matisse have received much attention of late, but more relevant here are artists whose rendering of Cairo's Islamic architecture had a strong documentary bent. Beginning in the 1830s, lavishly illustrated books provided the detailed documentation of "Arab art" that the *Description* had not. Pascal Coste's *Architecture arabe ou monumens [sic] du Caire* (Paris, 1839) led off. A graduate of Paris's École des Beaux-Arts, Coste entered Muhammad Ali's service in 1817 on the recommendation of Jomard. Later the pasha's chief architect, he obtained a special decree authorizing him to enter, measure, and draw unhindered the mosques of Cairo.[24] The ornately framed frontispiece to his study planted the city of Cairo firmly in the Nile landscape from which the *Description* frontispiece had expunged it. (See figures 1 and 38.)

Robert Hay's *Illustrations of Cairo* (1840) soon followed, and then David Roberts's famous *Egypt and Nubia* (3 vols., 1846–1849). John Frederick Lewis's Cairo years in the 1840s furnished him a lifetime repertoire for painting street scenes and domestic interiors of Cairo. The French responded with Prisse d'Avennes's *L'Art arabe d'après les monuments du Kaire* (3 vols., 1877). On Islamic architecture outside Egypt, Owen Jones's study of the Alhambra (1842–1845) was especially influential. The expense and bulk of all these works limited their ownership to libraries and the wealthy. At mid-century, photography joined painting and drawing as ways of taking home images of Islamic art and architecture, and by the 1890s the "shilling view" and penny postcard were carrying Cairo's sights to wider audiences.[25]

Even lovers of Islamic art such as Charmes, Lane-Poole, and Julius Franz revealed their prejudice that Islamic civilization was fatally flawed. Franz confessed:

> Our admiration of the harmonious and tasteful ornamentation, unsurpassed by any school of architecture, is counterbalanced by a certain feeling of aesthetic dissatisfaction.... The main reason why Arabian art failed to reach a

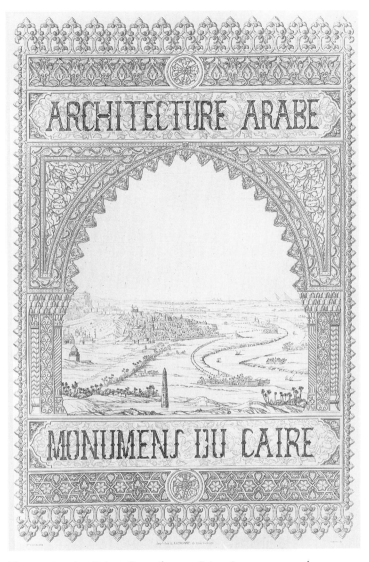

Figure 38. An Orientalist enframes Cairo: in contrast to the
frontispiece of the *Description de l'Égypte*, Pascal Coste's panorama
of 1839 centers on Cairo and reduces pharaonic antiquities (the
Heliopolis obelisk and several pyramid groups) to framing devices. In
Pascal Coste, *Architecture arabe ou monumens [sic] du Caire mesuré
et dessinées, de 1818 à 1825* (Paris, 1839).

high level in technical ability as well as in ornamentation must be looked for in the early collapse of the great empire of the Caliphs; in the uncertain and vacillating political circumstances of the period that followed; in climatic and geological conditions; in the influence of superstition; and in the characteristic Oriental tendency to adhere with obstinate fidelity to ancient forms and to leave unaltered anything that has once been accomplished. However much the arabesque may excite, however great an influence it may exert on industrial art, we still miss in it the reproduction of living beings, the contemplation of anything which invites, as it were, an intelligent and active sympathy.[26]

With Islamic as with pharaonic monuments, European admiration accelerated their destruction. Charmes complained that "overly enthusiastic amateurs of Arab art" were stripping Cairo mosques of glass lamps and ivory pulpit inlays. Lane-Poole denounced "travellers, Vandals by instinct and profession, who will spare nothing and ruin everything to take home a 'souvenir' of their travels to other barbarians at home."[27]

IMPERIALISM, PRESERVATION, AND THE BIRTH OF THE COMITÉ

Two years before the British occupation, Charmes hailed Ismail's bankruptcy—a catastrophe for Egyptians—for interrupting the urban renewal projects that were destroying artistic masterpieces. Charmes decided that only European control could preserve Cairo's monuments and that a country that neglects its antiquities does not deserve independence:

> It is clear that if Egypt wants to escape the shocks with which the Orient is menaced, his [Tawfiq's] first duty is to link up the new power of the Muhammad Ali dynasty to a long and glorious national tradition.... The Greeks spare nothing to make one believe they are the descendants of Pericles and Phidias; why don't the Egyptians try to persuade the world that they are the descendants of Saladin, of Qait Bey, and of Sultan Hasan? The Acropolis has done more for the independence of Greece than all the exploits... of Canaris and Lord Byron; it is the best title of the small hellenic kingdom to the protection and the favors of Europe; why shouldn't the mosques of Cairo render the same kind of service for Egypt? The day when they are restored... it will be impossible to deny the right to independence to a country capable of understanding and conserving such works.[28]

As a French patriot, of course, the occupation of Egypt by Britain alone was not what Charmes had in mind. A few months after the French took Tunisia in 1881 and before the British invaded Egypt,

Gabriel Charmes's brother Xavier, a high French official, spelled out an Orientalist-imperialist vision of France as both conqueror and heir of "Arab" civilization:

> It was we who saved Europe from the Arab invasion.... Now we have in turn invaded the Arab countries and...destroyed those states, so appropriately called *barbaresque*, where Arab civilization expired in the most savage anarchy. But our military work ought to be followed by political, administrative, and scientific construction. Heirs of the Arabs, it is up to us to search in their history what they have done that is great and deserves to last; it is up to us to rejuvenate their forgotten art, to probe their language, and bring to light their poetry, their literature, their moral and scientific discoveries.[29]

The roots of the Comité and the Museum of Arab Art go back to a decree issued in the midst of Ismail's urban renewal frenzy of 1869. An Austro-Hungarian architect working for the Awqaf (charitable endowments) Department, Auguste Salzmann, suggested the idea, and Julius Franz, a German in the same department, was to have assembled objects for a museum in the ruined mosque of al-Zahir Baybars.[30] Nothing came of the decree, so in 1874 British consul Edward T. Rogers urged the International Congress of Orientalists to appoint a committee to preserve, restore, and record Oriental monuments and art. Lane-Poole had practical reservations: Only a government could muster the resources for such a task, and a recent bill for a similar program in Britain had failed. Besides, Ismail, "the principal sinner in the matter of art-demolition...would perhaps ask whether Parisian boulevards and Italian villas planted in the historical soil of Egypt were not more artistic than tumble down mosques and ruined houses? And would it be possible, even with the temper of an angel, to answer such a question?"[31]

The timing of the 18 December 1881 decree establishing the Comité was no accident. Khedive Tawfiq was under siege from the Urabists, who were challenging both European intrusion and the Turco-Circassian monopoly on high military rank. Tawfiq was desperate to rally European support to save his throne; perhaps even the tiny lobby of European amateurs of Islamic art might help tip the balance in his favor. "How curious!" wrote Charmes, "the idea of control and surveillance by Europe, applied directly to finances, has extended indirectly to everything else, even to art."[32]

Lane-Poole's *Cairo* interspersed descriptions of old-city architecture with a tribute to "the admirable results of British influence, exerted by Lord Cromer" and declared, "It may be mere patriotic conceit, but I am convinced that no other nation is fit to teach Egypt the way she should walk but the race which has planted its colonies over all the broad face of the globe, and has shown in its matchless government of India what splendid results the rule of Englishmen may achieve among alien creeds and nationalities."[33]

Tawfiq's initial appointments to the Comité included three European connoisseurs of Islamic art: Edward T. Rogers, now an advisor in the Egyptian government; French architect Ambroise Baudry, whose "Arab" villa Charmes hailed as one of the sights of Cairo; and German architect Julius Franz of the Ministry of Awqaf. (See table 4.) Britain, France, and Germany all had their own Orientalists, both textual and visual, and these countries also happened to be critical in the approaching showdown with Urabi. In January 1882, Jules Bourgoin joined the Comité, and the following November the addition of Pierre Grand, chief engineer of the *tanzim* department (which oversaw streets and public buildings), brought French representation up to three. French, the lingua franca of diplomacy and Westernized high society in Egypt, became the working language of the Comité.[34]

Bourgoin, who had taught in Paris at the École des Beaux-Arts and written two books on Arab design, was a fellow of the new École française. He saw Islamic art as the product of *"races sémitiques"* or *"semitisées,"* including a *"race arabe."* His Orient had a static quality: "One should not expect to recover in the history of the art of the Orient the equivalent of that rigorous chain of different phases characteristic of the art of the Occident." Introducing Bourgoin's *Les Arts arabes,* Viollet-le-Duc himself explained how religious and racial factors in a mixed population accounted for the geometric abstraction of Arab art.[35]

The lone Briton on the Comité, Edward T. Rogers (d. 1884), had pursued a consular career in the Levant and Egypt before becoming an educational and financial official in the Egyptian government. He collected Islamic antiquities and coins. Julius Franz (1831–1915), although partly educated in Austria and eventually buried there, grew up in a north German Protestant family and kept his German citizenship all his life. As chief architect of the Awqaf Department and the Comité, he oversaw preservation and repair work on monuments and started collecting for the Museum of Arab Art. For a dozen years after his retirement in 1888, Franz wintered in Egypt and attended meetings of the Comité.[36]

The Comité managed only a single organizing meeting, on 1 February 1882, three days before the Urabists swept away Sharif's cabinet and installed Mahmud Sami al-Barudi as prime minister, with Ahmad Urabi

TABLE 4
PROMOTERS OF ISLAMIC ART, ARCHAEOLOGY, AND ORIENTALISM

Europeans Active on the Comité		Other Orientalists (Scholars and Artists)		Egyptians Active on the Comité	
E. Rogers	d. 1884	P. Coste	1787–1879	Ali Mubarak	1823–1893
		David Roberts	1796–1864		
J. Franz	1831–1915	Robert Hay	1799–1863		
A. Baudry	1838–1906	E. W. Lane	1801–1876		
J. Bourgoin	1838–1907	Prisse d'Avennes	1807–1879		
				Yaqub Artin	1842–1914
				Husayn Fakhri	1843–1910
Harry Farnall	1852–1929				
S. Lane-Poole	1854–1931			M. Fahmi	1856–1925
Max Herz	1856–1919			Ali Bahgat	1858–1924
				Ahmad Zaki	1860–1934
Max van Berchem	1863–1921			Marcus Simaika	1864–1944

as minister of war.[37] Even at such a critical moment, historic preservation received the highest attention: Two of the seven cabinet ministers sat on the Comité and participated in the meeting. Minister of Foreign Affairs Mustafa Fahmi presided, and Minister of War Barudi—soon to be prime minister—attended. One source, unconfirmed by the minutes, reported that recommendations on building repairs would go to Barudi, since he took "an enlightened interest" in preservation.

The Comité elected Rogers secretary; Awqaf official Yaqub Sabri, second secretary; and Franz, archivist. Not surprisingly, the Comité did not meet again until December 1882, after the dust from the Urabi revolution and the British conquest had settled. Riots in Alexandria in June 1882 triggered European flight, and war hawks maneuvered Prime Minister Gladstone into bombarding the city. British troops landed in the wake of the ensuing conflagration. The main British force later struck through the Suez Canal, landing at Ismailia, routing Urabi at Tel el-Kabir, and seizing Cairo. That fall, European residents trickled back into Egypt in the shocked silence that followed.

THE COMITÉ UNDER THE BRITISH OCCUPATION

On 18 December 1882, a week before Urabi and his entourage were deported to Ceylon, the Comité met for a second time. Although hemmed in by financial austerity until the late 1890s, European preservationists found the British occupation a congenial milieu in which to work. The Comité being affiliated with his Ministry of Awqaf, Minister Muhammad Zaki presided at the December meeting. Zaki had fallen from the cabinet along with Sharif in February and returned to power with him in August in Alexandria, under the protection of British guns. Ex–prime minister Barudi, in prison with Urabi awaiting deportation, took no further part in the Comité. Former ministers Mustafa Fahmi and Mahmud al-Falaki were also absent. Perhaps they were temporarily under a cloud, but they kept their Comité seats and were back in the cabinet in little more than a year. Minister of Public Works Ali Mubarak had abandoned Urabi in Cairo that summer, casting his lot with Khedive Tawfiq in Alexandria just in time to win a seat in Sharif's August cabinet. A November decree added him, Pierre Grand, and Yaqub Artin to the Comité.[38]

Although Egyptians outnumbered foreigners on the Comité except for a brief interval around 1890, Europeans dominated it as clearly as the British "veiled protectorate" controlled Egypt. Rogers took the lead in the Comité's First Commission, which listed monuments worthy of preservation. In selecting buildings for the list, Westerners aestheticized and "monumentalized" them as antiquities. Although Orientalist beliefs in timeless essences undercut theories of evolutionary development, ideal types of Tulunid, Fatimid, Ayyubid, Bahri and Burji Mamluk, and Ottoman styles were carefully elaborated. Franz, with Bourgoin's support, effectively ran the Second Commission (later the Technical Section), which oversaw repairs and salvaged relics for the Museum of Arab Art. The Second Commission became the active heart of the Comité, carrying out on a day-to-day basis the repairs voted by the full body.

Baring clamped Egypt into a fiscal straitjacket, with top priority to servicing the debt to European creditors and paying for the occupation. In 1885, the Comité spent £E3,651 of its austere budget of £E3,889 for repairs on forty-odd monuments, the small balance going for salaries, museum purchases, and office furniture. At first the Awqaf Department provided the Comité's entire budget. By 1896, however, the government's financial situation had turned the corner, and Baring—now Lord Cromer—was ready to consider other expenditures. Stanley Lane-Poole, author of *The Art of the Saracens in Egypt* (1886) and honorary member of the Comité since 1890, recommended that the Caisse de la dette publique, the watchdog for Egypt's European creditors, allocate £E20,000 to the Comité. Cromer agreed and appended Lane-Poole's report to his own annual report.[39]

By the Comité's twenty-fifth anniversary in 1906, it had spent a total of £E205,500—£E166,000 from the Awqaf Department, £E39,000 from the regular state budget, and £E500 from the Coptic patriarchate (whose historic buildings were now under Comité surveillance). £E29,000 had gone for salaries, and £E205,500 for repairs on monuments.[40] The budget continued at a respectable level until World War I reimposed austerity.

As for the Comité's philosophy of preservation, in 1882 an anonymous Briton recommended that, in dealing with Cairo's monuments, "all that can now be done is to preserve them in their present condition as long as possible with the help of every resource of science; to repair such portions as admit of being repaired, while allowing no rash restoration; and to copy, cast, squeeze, photograph, and survey them while they yet stand, and thus preserve their plans and decorations. . . . "[41]

In 1895 the Comité was treating monuments differently according to period. "Early and unique" monuments, such as the mosques of Ibn Tulun and the Fatimids, were stabilized in their current state—a bow perhaps to Ruskin—whereas major reconstructions were done on the more numerous Mamluk and Ottoman buildings[42]—a page from Viollet-le-Duc. The remains of the Fatimid mosque of Salih Talai, however, were later disassembled, its Ottoman-era minaret removed, and the whole reconstructed according to a Fatimid ideal type.[43]

Whether preserved in their current state under the first policy or reconstructed under the second, the monuments were isolated in lonely splendor, with the shops and dwellings that had engulfed their exteriors for centuries stripped away. To Europeans, such add-ons were clutter that blocked vistas of the main structures. Thus, preservationists turned demolitionist in dealing with structures not privileged as "monuments." The Comité of course vetoed projects for new buildings that would encroach on the now isolated monuments. Tourists won easy access and grand vistas for photographing monuments, but at the price of stripping them from the living fabric into which they had been woven. Preserving entire historic districts or giving neighborhoods a stake in preservation was not yet on the horizon, either in Egypt or in the West.

The Comité's emphasis on mosques and mausolea left most houses and other structures unprotected. Sometimes the Comité lost out to the demolition-minded *tanzim* department's plans for streets and public buildings, but adding *tanzim* director general Pierre Grand to the Comité assured the preservationists at least a hearing there.

Entrepreneur George Pangalo drove home the limitations of the Comité's mandate and its vision. Belzoni, the buccaneer-collector of pharaonic antiquities for the British Museum early in the century, had nothing on Pangalo. Cromer's piastre-pinching regime's refusal to fund an exhibit at the Columbian Exposition of 1893 in Chicago opened the door to Pangalo to develop the "Streets of Cairo" as a business venture. He signed on 250 Egyptians—from belly dancers and donkey boys to a muezzin—to populate his "Streets" and combed the real Cairo for architectural relics to lend authenticity to his imagined one:

> For the past thirty years merchants in antiquities have been despoiling old Cairo of its treasures for the benefit of tourists, artists and museums.
>
> It was now my turn to join the ranks of the despoilers...and although I blush in saying it, I went to work with a vim that would have done credit to a vandal....
>
> In many instances it was necessary to agree to pay a certain sum in cash and to replace the old lattice windows, balconies and doors bought by new ones of modern design; in others, a whole building would have to be bought, stripped of its mousharabieh and then resold.

Thus, in about nine months, over fifteen residences had been despoiled of their entire old woodwork, and over fifty others had contributed their share of carved panels, doors, etc.[44]

Max Herz, the watchdog of Egypt's Islamic architectural heritage, actually signed on as a consultant to the self-confessed vandal. The Comité had no objection, provided Herz consulted after hours. Herz would probably have pointed out that the Comité had no jurisdiction over unlisted structures, that the destruction was racing ahead in any case, and that at least the woodwork reassembled in the exhibit was spared immediate destruction.

THE FORMATION OF ALI BAHGAT

In 1881, the year of the Comité's founding, Ali Bahgat turned twenty-three and began working as a French teacher. He came from the Middle Egyptian village of Baha al-Ajuz, several miles from the provincial capital Beni Suef. Like Ali Mubarak, Muhammad Abduh, and Ahmad Lutfi al-Sayyid, he sprang from a family of rural notables, but unlike them, he was of Turkish stock. His paternal grandfather, Ali Agha, had held posts in Sharqiyya Province under Muhammad Ali and received an estate in Baha al-Ajuz as his pension. Bahgat's father, Mahmud Bey Ali, was born in Baha al-Ajuz, pursued a career in the Domains d'état, and married the daughter of a Turkish official from a nearby village. Bahgat's obituarist commented that such Turkish families in the provinces kept aloof from their indigenous neighbors and that Bahgat loved solitude, rarely mixed socially, and had an irritable streak.[45]

By Ismail's day, Cairo's state schools were becoming a prime way to get ahead and to pass elite status on to the next generation. Bahgat climbed surely up through these select schools—the Nasriyya primary school, the Tajhiziyya (Preparatory School), the School of Engineering, and the reopened School of Languages. For Bahgat, as for his friend Lutfi al-Sayyid, Arabic studies under Shaykh Hasuna al-Nawawi, who later became Shaykh al-Azhar, left an indelible impression.[46] Bahgat's performance in school was unremarkable, but he acquired European language skills that would serve him well. He emerged from three years at the School of Languages with Arabic, French, German, and Turkish. Later he would pick up enough English for research purposes. Like a growing number of Muslim and Coptic Egyptians, his languages prepared him for competition with the Syrian Christian translators and middlemen who had become so prominent under Ismail and the early British occupation.

Bahgat began teaching French at the Preparatory School on 9 October 1881, a month after the Urabists forced Khedive Tawfiq to replace Riyad with Sharif as prime minister and ten weeks before the founding of the Comité. His salary began at £E5 a month. Five years later he became inspector of French teaching in elementary schools funded by the Awqaf Department. Then he taught French at the Khudaywiyya Secondary School, and by the turn of the century he was earning £E28 a month as chief translator at the Ministry of Education. In December 1901, he left education with twenty years credit toward a pension and went to work for the Comité.[47]

Nearly two years before, in January 1900, Bahgat had joined the nine Europeans and twelve Egyptians on the Comité. The Egyptians included eight Muslims, two Copts, and two Armenians. Four of the Muslims came from the Awqaf Department, two were cabinet ministers (Prime Minister Mustafa Fahmi, who rarely came, and Husayn Fakhri), and one each from the Railways Administration and the Ministry of Interior. One Copt was retired from the Ministry of Finance, and the other worked in the Ministry of Justice. The Armenians were Tigrane, ex-minister of foreign affairs, and Yaqub Artin, undersecretary of education. The Europeans included Maspero of the Antiquities Service, Paul Casanova (an Orientalist from IFAO), at least one other Frenchman, two Germans, a Briton, an Italian, and Herz, an Austro-Hungarian. An examination of Egyptian-European relations in the Comité and the Museum of Arab Art provides the essential context for Bahgat's subsequent career.

ALI MUBARAK AND THE
EUROPEAN PRESERVATIONISTS

The ubiquitous Ali Mubarak had been the first to clash with the Comité's European preservationists. Although Mubarak sided with Khedive Tawfiq (and thereby the British) against the Urabi revolution, Egyptians glorify him today as a national hero of cultural reform. Whether out of national pride or an engineer's impatience with preservationists who obstructed his vision of progress, Mubarak broke with the Comité's dominant Europeans in December 1882, at his very first meeting. It was he, after all, who had implemented Ismail's urban renewal plan, driving Muhammad Ali Street through the hundreds of densely packed buildings in its path. With the Comité, however, he could not simply have his way. (See figure 39.)

Figure 39. Ali Mubarak, cabinet
minister and engineer who planned
modern Cairo, elaborated a state
school system, and wrote the
classic geographical encyclopedia
Al-Khitat al-tawfiqiyya al-jadida.
The commemorative postage stamp
suggests his contemporary place of
honor.

Certain Europeans dominated the Comité through a combination of
political clout, expertise, and hard work. Most Egyptian members were
less involved, whether out of having other priorities, resentment of European domination, weakness in French, or lack of technical expertise.
This reinforced the Europeans' assertion that Egypt was unfit to care for
its own monuments. On the popular level, community resentment of
and resistance to the Comité's demolition of shops clustered around
monuments would reward further research.[48]

Egyptians were not as indifferent to monuments as Charmes, Lane-
Poole, and Franz suggested. Al-Jabarti deplored the French expedition's
destruction in the Cairo citadel:

> They built on the foundations of Bab al 'Azab in al Rumayla and changed
> its features and disfigured its beauties and wiped out the monuments of schol-

ars and the assembly rooms of sultans and great men and took what works
of art were left on its great gates and in its magnificent sitting-rooms *(iywan)*
such as arms, shields, axes.... They demolished the palace of Yusuf Salah al-
Din [Saladin] and the council halls of kings and sultans which had high sup-
ports and pillars, as well as the mosques and chapels *(zawaya)* of religious
orders and shrines. They disfigured the Great Mosque, the lofty distinguished
one which was built by the man of glorious deeds, Muhammad ibn Qalawun
al-Malik al-Nasir.... Thus they behaved as the enemies of the Religion would
behave....[49]

Most Egyptians were more attached to the religious associations of
holy sites than to the artistic or historical value of particular structures.
People from many walks of life poured out their devotion at the shrines
of al-Azhar, Sayyidna Husayn, Sayyida Zaynab, Imam al-Shafii, and (in
Tanta) Sayyid Ahmad al-Badawi. Devotion to the text and message of
the Quran and lesser religious classics outshone attachment to the specific architecture or decoration of a building, however old or beautiful
Westerners might pronounce it. Most Egyptians valued mosques as living centers of worship and study and resented preservationist pressure
to aestheticize, historicize, and monumentalize them for the enjoyment
of Western tourists and scholars.

In mosques, as in European cathedrals, demolition, addition, and reconstruction had been going on for centuries. Why freeze a structure in
time after it had outgrown the historical moment, purpose, and style it
had originally expressed? The water jugs, textiles, *mashrabiyya* lattice-
work, and jewelry now enframed in the cases of the Museum of Arab
Art were once the stuff of everyday life for rich or poor. Now, at the
very moment when Western fashions in architecture, furniture, and dress
were sweeping the Egyptian upper classes, Europeans—both empow-
ered and unsettled by industrial and political transformations back
home—were intervening to preserve "Arab art" they thought beautiful, exotic, or "traditional." Perhaps preservationism, not its converse,
cried out for explanation.

Mubarak agreed with Orientalists' belief that Cairo had decayed
under the Ottomans. He cited crumbling buildings and rubbish heaps
that endangered public health—"until God sent the late Muhammad Ali
Pasha."[50] But Mubarak parted company with the Orientalists when he
hailed the Westernized building styles of the reigning dynasty as signs
of civilization and progress.

Mubarak's *Al-Khitat* "did not use representational evidence, what
has been called optical memories.... His was a city of 'sites' (places)

where social interaction took place, where collective memory was at work, not a city of 'sights' or a city of spectacles."[51]

Reading between the lines of the Comité's minutes, one can tease out resistance, first by Mubarak and later by other Egyptians against the dominant Europeans. At the December 1882 meeting, Mubarak proposed that a fountain near Bab Zuwayla be moved because it obstructed carriage and pack-animal traffic. Europeans shot back that their mandate was preservation, not demolition. The minutes record only that Mubarak attended another meeting or two—no further comments by him are recorded—and then resigned, ostensibly under the pressure of ministerial work. Years later as minister of education, he refused the Comité's request to move the Museum of Arab Art into vacant rooms in his building. Perhaps he was settling old scores.[52]

Ali Mubarak was no philistine, indifferent to the Islamic past. *Al-Khitat al-tawfiqiyya* had catalogued its monuments and history in painstaking detail. Mubarak felt a rush of nostalgia for vanished Islamic greatness as he gazed out over the mounds of al-Fustat from the minaret of the mosque of Amr.[53]

Al-Khitat owed debts not only to Arabic sources but also to the *Description de l'Égypte* and many other nineteenth-century European works. Mubarak had studied in Paris, after all. He translated Louis A. Sédillot's *Histoire des arabes* into Arabic, concurring with the French medievalist's finding of Arab decline under the Ottomans and praising the Muhammad Ali dynasty for ushering in a new age of civilization and progress.[54] Mubarak also portrayed a British Orientalist positively in his sprawling fictional *Alam al-Din*.

There were, or came to be, Egyptians who cared for preserving Islamic art. But they had to fight on several fronts at once. If they were to be professionals, they often had to study or apprentice themselves under European masters. Insufficient deference to European professionalism and political hegemony, whether springing from nationalist resistance or personal assertiveness, could be disastrous for one's career. Nor was it easy to convince fellow Egyptians that preserving what Europeans extolled as masterpieces of Islamic art and architecture should take priority over Egypt's other pressing needs.

Europeans might wax eloquent on masterpieces of Islamic art and architecture in a land they had colonized, but they owed their dominance in large part to power based on the industrial ugliness they were fleeing back home. No one yet knew how to make preservation and modernization work hand in hand. In their rush to modernize on European lines, Ismail and Mubarak refused to let nostalgia stand in their way. The engineer won out over the antiquarian in Mubarak: "Does one need so many monuments? When one preserves a sample, isn't that enough?" Bab Zuwayla had once been used for hanging criminals: "We don't want to keep those memories; we ought to destroy them as the French destroyed the Bastille."[55]

Comité minutes are silent on what Husayn Fahmi, undersecretary of the Awqaf Department, thought as he listened to Mubarak clash with the preservationists. Fahmi had been in Paris along with Mubarak and Ismail, studying civil administration and engineering. Back home, he became the original architect of the al-Rifai Mosque, an eclectic jumble of Western and Islamic styles commissioned by Ismail's mother. He also designed other government buildings. Fahmi showed his love of Islamic art in 1903, when the new Khedivial Library decked out old manuscripts with modern bindings. He purchased the discarded bindings for display in his house, "which was more like an Arab Museum."[56]

EUROPEAN NATIONAL REPRESENTATION ON THE COMITÉ

A cosmopolitan bond knit together the small circle of Cairo's Europeans who loved Islamic art. Yet they never forgot their nationalities or the ranking of their mother tongues in the elaborate political, social, and cultural hierarchies in Egypt.

French was the lingua franca of the Comité, Antiquities Service, Egyptian Museum, Mixed Courts, and cosmopolitan high society. Nevertheless, it was native speakers of German who took the lead at the Comité and Khedivial Library until 1914. Austro-Hungarian and German representation at the Awqaf Department went back to Ismail's day, when an Austro-Hungarian had lobbied for the stillborn decree of 1869 protecting Arab monuments and providing for a museum of Arab art. When the Comité finally came into being a dozen years later, Franz was still on the spot to take charge. He and Max Herz successively guided the Comité and the Museum of Arab Art for thirty-three years. In 1903, bringing the Museum of Arab Art and Khedivial Library together in the same building effectively consolidated a Germanic cultural enclave there.

Max Herz was a Hungarian Jew who went to Egypt in 1881 to tutor the children of a European hotel owner. (Austria-Hungary, incidentally, had extended capitulatory protection to some Alexandrian Jews several decades earlier.) Franz soon took Herz on as an architectural assistant at the Awqaf Department and the Comité. Herz inherited both functions upon Franz's retirement in 1888. The Museum of Arab Art drifted for four years until Herz formally added it to his responsibilities in 1892. Franz's and Herz's daily work with Islamic architecture, art, and the museum enabled them to develop an expertise that most Comité members lacked. Meeting only five or six times a year, the full Comité usually deferred to their professional judgment.[57]

Two of the five German Orientalists who directed the Khedivial Library between 1870 and 1914, Karl Vollers and Bernhard Moritz, sat on the Comité, as did O. de Mohl, the German representative on the Caisse de la dette publique. Austro-Hungarians on the Comité included Herz and Comte Charles Zaluski, who lived in one of Baudry's Arab villas.

The prominence of German as a medium of Orientalist scholarship, including Islamic art, gave this German–Austro-Hungarian presence at the Comité and Khedivial Library cultural, but only limited political, significance. Even so, the Germans jockeyed hard to maintain their position at the Khedivial Library and Egyptian Museum in the years leading up to World War I. In 1904, when the British at last agreed that Frenchmen should continue to head the Antiquities Service, they also promised that future Khedivial Library directors should be German. Such deals made over their heads by foreign governments angered Egyptians, who were not yet in a position to overturn such colonial arrangements. When Bernhard Moritz had to resign the library directorship in 1911, Kaiser Wilhelm II personally intervened on behalf of German representation in Egyptian cultural institutions. The British rejected Germany's chosen successor to Moritz, Dr. Kurt Prüfer. Prüfer was Oriental secretary at the German Agency, and Britons worried that the new post would put him "in close and daily contact with the Intelligentsia of Young Egypt." Egyptian backing for Ahmad Zaki, secretary to the Council of Ministers, as library director came to nothing, and in 1913 another German Orientalist, Dr. Arthur Schaade, stepped into the post. World War I soon forced him out of Egypt, and he and Prüfer put their linguistic skills to use in German military intelligence advising Ottoman forces in Palestine.[58]

Unlike the Turks of the Ottoman heartland, few Egyptians learned German. Bahgat, Abbas II, and Ahmad Kamal were among the few who did. Abbas had studied at the Theresianum in Vienna and chose Antonio Lasciac, an Austro-Hungarian by birth although an Italian patriot, as his palace architect. Austria-Hungary's Balkan expansion at Ottoman expense did not endear it to Muslims, but Germany's military, political, and cultural ties in Istanbul, Anatolia, and the Fertile Crescent reinforced each other. The Berlin to Baghdad railroad was a striking symbol of this alliance. The antiquities that Kaiser Wilhelm II took home as a result of his visit in 1898 to Sultan Abdulhamid II's Istanbul and Jerusalem filled a good portion of the new Imperial Museum building in Berlin.[59]

The Anglo-French rivalry evident in the Antiquities Service and schools sometimes cropped up in Comité circles. Charmes had pleaded the case for establishing the Comité: "France rightly prides itself with having discovered modern Egypt, recovered ancient Egypt and paved the way for future Egypt; will she leave to others the task of reconstituting Arab Egypt and making it known to the world?"[60]

Lane-Poole did not hesitate to parade his gallophobia in print:

> Our French friends, who are so fond of twitting us with our supposed trick of whittling our names on the monuments of Egypt (where the biggest and most glaring names are always French), are the chief spoilers of Cairo. Where are all the missing bronze doors of the mosques, and the other treasures of Arab art...which are now seen no more? At Paris. And if we ask who was the Goth who cut a great square piece out of the mosaics of the mosque of Bars Bey in the Eastern Cemetery, the doorkeeper will amaze us by answering that it was the enlightened Mariette, the denouncer of English tourists, who ruined the mosaics in order to send an *objet* to the Paris Exposition![61]

Cromer seems not to have worried about French influence on the Comité, which successive Antiquities Service directors (Grébaut, de Morgan, Maspero, and Lacau) and IFAO scholars (Bourgoin, Casanova, and Chassinat) anchored. Not until the 1930s, when Egyptianization was well under way, did Britons on the Comité outnumber the French.

Rogers's death in 1885 removed the Comité's sole Briton, but advisers at public works (Scott Moncrief, later William Garstin) and finance (Edgar Vincent) soon filled the gap. Although not as devoted to Islamic art as Rogers was, they provided crucial links to the British Residency. Architect Somers Clarke was an obvious addition when the Comité extended its responsibilities to include Coptic monuments in the 1890s. Harry Farnall, from the Caisse de la dette publique, joined in 1910 and was soon the leading British voice on the Comité.[62]

Despite having the second largest European colony and dominating the construction and decoration trades, Italy had no voice on the Comité until architect Alfonso Manescalo joined in 1897 and Botti, of the Greco-Roman Museum, became a corresponding member.[63] Greece, where the Westward-looking political elites evinced interest in neither Egyptology nor Oriental studies, went unrepresented.

THE MUSEUM OF ARAB ART

For two decades the Museum of Arab Art got by in makeshift housing in the al-Hakim Mosque, adjacent to one of the northern gates of the Fatimids' city. The mosque was in ruins in the early 1880s, when the Ministry of Awqaf and the Comité removed rubbish, leveled the courtyard, and restored the central section of the sanctuary to house the museum. A school of art was planned for the courtyard.[64]

Franz assembled salvaged Islamic relics, and Rogers and Yaqub Artin advised on ordering the collection. In 1883 the Comité added a temporary building in the courtyard for the overflowing relics. The museum opened in 1884 with only a *bawwab* (doorkeeper) as permanent staff. Since he proved to have neither "suitable dress nor manners for showing visitors around," the Comité went looking for "an effendi of good education, with the necessary qualifications and speaking French."[65] Until 1895 two manuscript catalogues in French provided the only written guide. Herz then published a French guide to the collection, which Stanley Lane-Poole put into English.[66] Organized by materials—glass, metal, ceramics, wood, and so forth—the museum filled eight rooms, a passageway, and two annexes.

The makeshift museum was nearly invisible to tourists at a time when Islamic collections in the West were scarcely more developed. In arranging the Bulaq Museum, Mariette could look for ideas at the pharaonic collections of Paris, London, Berlin, and Turin. But in Islamic art, both Egypt and Europe were still feeling their way a generation later.

Islamic objects from the Crystal Palace exhibition of 1851 went to the new Museum of Ornamental Art, which later became the South Kensington, then the Victoria and Albert Museum. Objects from the Paris Exposition universelle of 1867 also enriched its holdings. In the wake of the British occupation of Egypt, the South Kensington dispatched Lane-Poole to Cairo in search of objects brought onto the market by the upheaval. In 1891, Istanbul's Royal Museum of Antiquities' new building in the Topkapi Palace garden included an Islamic section.[67]

Friedrich Sarre founded an Islamic section at Berlin's Staatliche Museum in 1904.

By 1898, with the new Egyptian Museum in the works, Cromer got the Caisse de la dette publique to allot £E45,000 for a building to house jointly the Museum of Arab Art and the Khedivial Library. A Doric temple facade signaled the contents of the Greco-Roman Museum; why not neo-Islamic decor for the Museum of Arab Art and Khedivial Library, which had one of the finest collections of Arabic and other Islamic manuscripts in the world? Alfonso Manescalo, the Italian architect who joined the Comité in 1897, designed the building (see figure 40). Its massive entrance portals, pointed arches, stalactites, ornate crenellations, and alternating dark and light *ablaq* stripes drew on Mamluk inspiration, and the slightly horseshoe-shaped arches added a hint of Andalusia. Despite the Islamic decor, the building conformed to Western functional ideas of museum and library. The museum occupied the ground floor; the Khedivial Library, with a separate entrance, was upstairs.[68]

The site seemed appropriate too—on Muhammad Ali Street in Bab al-Khalq, at the juncture of modern Cairo and what was coming to be seen as "medieval" Cairo (see map 2). A few blocks to the east, al-Muayyad Mosque and Bab Zuwayla guarded the entrance to the Fatimids' city; to the west stood Abdin Palace and the modern city. The filled-in canal (al-Khalij) and another thoroughfare intersected with Muhammad Ali Street, and the museum-library stood out on one of the resulting wedges. In contrast with the Egyptian Museum's Latin, the dedicatory corner plaque here in Abbas II's name was only in Arabic.

On 28 December 1903, Khedive Abbas opened this "handsome new building in the Arabic style" in the presence of Cromer, other consuls, cabinet ministers, former shaykh al-Azhar Hasuna al-Nawawi, Grand Mufti Muhammad Abduh, and Sufi shaykhs al-Bakri and al-Sadat.[69] A new guide book was necessary; Herz brought it out in 1906.

Not long after the opening, it became clear that an attempt to finance the museum's annual budget out of revenues from earmarked *waqf* lands had failed. A revenue of £E2,053 from these lands had been projected, but from 1900 through 1904 the average reached only £E1,160. The government canceled the experiment and authorized £E2,053 annually from the treasury instead, with a one-time addition to compensate for the accumulated shortfall.[70]

While the Museum of Arab Art was still in its old quarters in the 1890s, Lane-Poole doubted whether one European visitor in a hundred had heard of it. Those who thought they had had usually confused it

Figure 40.   The Museum of Arab Art and Khedivial Library, in neo-Islamic style. Opened in 1903. Architect: A. Manescalo. Photograph by Donald Reid.

with the Egyptian Museum.[71] Even in its striking new premises, the Museum of Arab Art never rivaled the Egyptian Museum as a cultural landmark in either Western or Egyptian eyes. The Egyptian Museum's building of 1902 cost over four times as much as the building of the combined Museum of Arab Art and Khedivial Library. Today the Egyptian Museum remains a landmark in Cairo's central square—despite being overshadowed by the Nile Hilton, Arab League, Mugamma (a government office complex), and commercial high-rises—while the Museum of Arab Art lies off the beaten tourist track. The 1908 Baedeker suggests the relative value of the two museums in the eyes of the travel industry. The Egyptian Museum receives twenty-four pages and a fold-out floor plan; the Museum of Arab Art, a mere two and a half pages.[72] In 1913 the Egyptian Museum drew 29,879 visitors, six times as many as the 5,166 who visited the Museum of Arab Art.[73]

NEO-ISLAMIC ARCHITECTURE

Manescalo's Museum of Arab Art–National Library, Herz's revised design for completing the al-Rifai Mosque, and the new Awqaf Department building put the Comité's personnel near the center of Cairo's revival of "Arab," or Islamic, architecture. A revival presumes a previous decline, and by the mid-nineteenth century Egypt had largely broken with both Mamluk and Ottoman traditions for major buildings. Muhammad Ali's great Citadel mosque had appropriated the architectural vocabulary of Istanbul's great imperial mosques, symbolically challenging the sultan against whom he was rebelling. But even as the mosque was going up in the 1830s, al-Tahtawi was lauding "civilized" Parisian architecture as a model.[74] Lane confirmed—but deplored—the inroads European architecture was making in Cairo. Under Said and Ismail, well-to-do Egyptians and the burgeoning European communities overwhelmingly embraced European styles, and Italians increasingly came to dominate skilled work in construction and decoration.[75]

The Islamic architectural revival began less as a locally inspired renaissance than as another fashionable European import. In the nineteenth-century West, the central battle was between Gothic Revival and Roman-, Greek-, and Renaissance-inspired neoclassicism. Those unmoved by either option could turn to the "exotic East." John Nash's Mughal-inspired Royal Pavilion at Brighton (1815–1823) caused a stir, but the Royal Panopticon (1853) was London's first permanent Islamic-inspired building. Owen Jones's study of the Alhambra influenced his interior decoration at the Great Exhibition's Crystal Palace (1851) and the reerected palace's Islamic court at Sydenham. Jones's *Grammar of Ornament* (1856) popularized Islamic design. Neo-Islamic pavilions became mainstays at world's fairs, several of which populated their "Streets of Cairo" exhibits with real Egyptians.[76]

In Paris, the École des Beaux-Arts and state building council held fast to classical and Renaissance ideals of universal beauty against the Gothic Revival promoted by Viollet-le-Duc and the Commission des monuments historiques.[77] In 1881, Charmes predicted: "A time will come when our young architects, tired of redoing in Greece and Rome the studies which all their predecessors have done before them, and the results of which they already know before leaving Paris, will seek permission to come to Egypt to clear an almost uncultivated terrain."[78]

Already in the 1820s, Pascal Coste was blending Islamic motifs into Beaux Arts and Italianate buildings designed for Muhammad Ali. Coste also drew plans for mosques inspired by the Mamluk monuments, but none was built.[79] Owen Jones's brother-in-law James Wild joined Lepsius's Egyptological expedition, then stayed on to study Islamic architecture. Commissioned to design the Anglican church of Saint Mark in Alexandria, Wild blended Byzantine and Islamic motifs, attempting both to recall the city's early Christian heritage and to emphasize to Muslims

Britain's beneficent religious tolerance. Back in London, Wild advised Henry Cole's South Kensington Museum on Islamic design.[80]

In the 1860s Julius Franz, with the assistance of de Curel del Rosso, designed Ismail's Gezira Palace in an eclectic neo-Islamic style. Another German, Carl von Diebitsch, completed the annex to the palace and its cast-iron facade of "Moorish" arches. Austrian Frantisek (Franz) Schmorantz threw up a palace in Ismailia just in time for the Suez Canal's opening. Back in Vienna, he worked fragments collected in Cairo into the Egyptian pavilion he designed for the universal exposition of 1873. In domestic architecture, Charmes raved over the "Arab villa" that Comité member Ambroise Baudry built for himself in Cairo. By the turn of the century, others were beginning to follow suit in domestic architecture.[81]

Suburban Heliopolis was launched in 1906, a colonial and Oriental fantasy of the Belgian baron Empain. His compatriot Marcel Jasper designed the suburb's Abbas Boulevard and landmark Heliopolis Palace Hotel. As in most neo-Islamic public buildings, the Islamic elements were tacked on for decor, but such features as exterior windows and balconies and assembly halls were Western. Eclecticism ran riot in Heliopolis—Moorish fantasies with exterior gardens, arcades, and loggias of Italian or French inspiration.[82]

If Moorish arches did not feel authentic in Cairo, what were the options for locally rooted Islamic architectural revival? Ottoman style was out for rulers like Said and Ismail, who were distancing themselves from Istanbul. Only the mosque of Ibn Tulun survived from pre-Fatimid days in its early form, and a handful of Fatimid monuments were still standing. Striking Mamluk structures stood all around, and although the Mamluk rulers were not of Arab or Egyptian origin, Mamluk Revival seemed appropriate in an Egyptian-Arab renaissance after centuries as a mere Ottoman province. In Europe, neo-Mamluk style was one of many possible Orientalisms, but in Egypt it became something of a return to local roots, not unlike Gothic Revival in Victorian England.

Abbas II commissioned Max Herz's neo-Mamluk plan of 1905 for completing the al-Rifai Mosque across the street from the Mamluk mosque of Sultan Hasan. As noted above, Husayn Fahmi had drawn up the original plan, and construction had begun in 1869. The dome collapsed during construction, and with Ismail's bankruptcy work broke off. Rhoné, in the racist idiom of the day, blamed the falling dome on the eunuch Khalil Agha—"extraordinarily rich, influential, ignorant and presumptuous like a negro"—for overriding the architect's warnings. Herz later collaborated with Carlo Virgilio Silvagni on the radically re-worked neo-Mamluk design for finishing the mosque.[83]

Other Islamicizing European architects also worked for the palace. In 1910 chief architect of royal palaces Antonio Lasciac, who worked in neo-Islamic and other styles, joined the Comité. After World War I, another Italian, Ernesto Verucci, followed him as palace architect and member of the Comité.

In India after the 1857 "Mutiny," the British appropriated "Hindu-Saracenic" style to suggest that they had become as rooted in India as the Mughal conquerors before them. In Egypt, the occupation was too recent and too hemmed in by European rivals for the British to attempt comparable manifestos in stone. Another tack in India was to force the pseudo-indigenous Hindu-Saracenic style on princes who wanted only to proclaim their modernity with neoclassical palaces.[84] Ismail had his way with neoclassical style for Abdin Palace, and Abbas II advertised his modernity in neo-Florentine style at Montaza Palace, in Alexandria. By the early 1900s, however, neo-Islamic style began catching on with upper-class Egyptians. Ali Bahgat was living in an "Arab" villa in Matariyya when he died.[85]

Ahmad Zaki, a palace official on the Comité, was a bibliophile and scholar of Arabic literature. He pronounced the Europeans' neo-Islamic architecture as an artistic failure. Zaki clashed with Herz over the ef-forts of the Comité and Prince Yusuf Kamal's École des Beaux-Arts to revive "Arab" art.[86] The school opened in 1908, with sculptor Guil-laume Laplagne as director and other Europeans teaching painting and architecture. He deplored Egypt's borrowing from the West and worked to revive Arab art, which he said the Ottoman conquest had extin-guished four centuries earlier. Kamal financed the school himself for two decades, admitting boys tuition-free and sending the sculptor Mahmud Mukhtar on to Paris for further study. Prince Kamal also briefly had a seat on the Comité.[87]

As the century wore on, Egyptian architects—as yet, little studied—emerged from the shadows and obtained major commissions. Was their neo-Mamluk work a search for locally rooted authenticity—a kind of Egyptian neoclassicism—or was it merely imitating a fashion Europeans had elaborated in Alexandria and Cairo? Perhaps both. After World War I, neopharaonic architecture, also pioneered by Westerners, would be similarly ambiguous.

LOCATIONS OF RESISTANCE:
AWQAF OFFICIALS AND THE PALACE

Each of the five Europeans in the Comité's Technical Section attended meetings an average of nineteen times in 1894–1895. The four Egyptians averaged only nine times each.[88] Passive resistance to foreign domination, timidity in the face of foreign expertise, lack of interest, and the press of other commitments may all have contributed to the low Egyptian attendance. In the years after Ali Mubarak had left the Comité, other Egyptians—mostly from the Awqaf Department and often with palace ties—obliquely expressed resistance to the dominant Europeans. Since Europeans kept the minutes, one must read between the lines to tease out this veiled opposition.

Like revenue-hungry Henry VIII, Muhammad Ali confiscated many religious endowments, thereby accelerating the decay of many mosques by stripping them of revenues. He began centralizing remaining *awqaf* under a government department, which Ismail upgraded to a ministry. In 1884, Tawfiq demoted it to a department (or an "administration") in order to detach it from the cabinet (over which British advisers were tightening their grip) and to make it responsible only to the palace. This gave Tawfiq and Abbas II a source for funds beyond British reach, which they used for patronage. High Awqaf officials were thus palace men, and it was no accident that Prime Ministers Husayn Rushdi, Adli Yakan, Ahmad Ziwar, and Ismail Sidqi had each had a turn at the head of the Awqaf Department. As with al-Azhar affairs, Cromer interfered little with Awqaf for fear of a religious backlash. Kitchener restored Awqaf to ministerial level in 1913 but failed in his bid to wrest its budget from palace control.[89]

The head of the Awqaf Department chaired the Comité. Four of the original eleven members of the Comité—Franz and three Egyptians—were Awqaf officials. A pattern emerged whereby the Europeans, Armenians, and a Muslim ally or two outvoted Egyptian resisters and carved out Comité autonomy vis-à-vis the Awqaf Department. In 1890, over the objections of the khedive, the Comité created its own technical bureau for repairing monuments. Awqaf engineer Sabir Sabri and Ismail al-Falaki sided with Awqaf director Ali Rida in voting to abolish this new separate bureau, but four Europeans joined the Armenian Yaqub Artin and Minister of Public Works Husayn Fakhri to defeat the rollback.[90] Fakhri and his education undersecretary Artin provided similar support to the European bloc on several occasions. Although Fakhri and Artin felt more at home in the francophone Comité, Khedivial Geographical Society, and Institut égyptien than in English-speaking circles, they clearly had a pragmatic understanding with the British occupiers.

The defeated "Awqaf opposition" fell back on guerrilla tactics. When the Europeans were off summering in 1893, Sabri and al-Falaki called a snap meeting of the Technical Section and added four Egyptian engineers, ostensibly in order to carry on normal work during the summer. In 1897, Sabri and two others protested the cleaning of stone monuments with a potassium solution, advocating instead vigorous scraping to remove dirt. The majority rebuked them with a prohibition on the "plastering or scraping of any stone." The Technical Section also reprimanded Sabri for altering a report on repairs after members had signed it.[91]

The same minority balked when Fakhri and the Europeans brought Coptic monuments under Comité protection in 1896. The patriarch agreed to contribute to repairs on Coptic monuments, and no Islamic *awqaf* money would be diverted to churches. Five Europeans, Fakhri, and the two Armenians voted to add two Copts to the Comité, overriding President Faizi, Sabir Sabri, and Ismail al-Falaki, who said that one was enough. A proposal to change the name to "Comité de conservation des monuments des arts arabe et copte" went too far, however, and was voted down.[92] Chapter 7 returns to the role of Armenians and especially Copts in Comité and national life.

ALI BAHGAT, NATIONALISM, AND THE ORIENTALISTS

Had he not clashed with Douglas Dunlop, the Scottish martinet who rode herd on education for Cromer, Ali Bahgat might have worked away until retirement as an obscure official in the Ministry of Education. But one day in the late 1890s, Undersecretary Artin had Bahgat draft a letter for their minister, Husayn Fakhri, to sign. Fakhri made the mistake of signing without checking with Dunlop first, and the latter forced him to retract his signature. Bahgat attacked Dunlop and defended Fakhri and Artin in anonymous articles in the opposition paper *Al-Muayyad*. Dunlop recognized Bahgat's work and might have ruined his career had Fakhri and Artin not intervened. Fakhri and Artin sat on the Comité and arranged to transfer Bahgat to its Service des monuments, beyond Dunlop's reach.[93]

One prickly personality had clashed with another in the Dunlop-Bahgat affair, but imperialism and nationalism structured the incident. Ministers could no more reject the "advice" of British "advisers" than Abbas II could ignore Britain's modestly titled consul general. Dunlop and Cromer were *bêtes noires* for Egyptian nationalists and still are.

Shaykh Ali Yusuf's *Al-Muayyad* was the unofficial mouthpiece of Abbas II. The khedive secretly encouraged students and young professionals to resist the occupation. In 1896, Bahgat joined Lutfi al-Sayyid, Abd al-Aziz Fahmi, Talat Harb, and four others in a secret society to liberate Egypt. Harb become famous as founder of Bank Misr and associated companies, Fahmi was a leading jurist, and Lutfi al-Sayyid became editor of *Al-Jarida*, university rector, minister, and mentor to a generation of reformers. Abbas got wind of the society and had his protégé Mustafa Kamil invite Lutfi to the palace. The upshot was that in 1897 Abbas sent Lutfi to Switzerland for a year to obtain Swiss citizenship. Then he could return with legal immunity and publish an anti-British paper. Lutfi delivered some books from Ali Bahgat to two scholars in Geneva, Orientalist Max van Berchem and Egyptologist Edouard Naville. Lutfi al-Sayyid took courses at the University of Geneva and assisted van Berchem in his research.[94] Abbas's scheme fell apart when Muhammad Abduh, who had fallen out with the khedive, turned up in Geneva and befriended Lutfi. Abbas cut off Lutfi's subsidy upon hearing of the new friendship. Lutfi returned home to work, leaving it to Mustafa Kamil to usher in a new phase of opposition journalism in 1900 with his newspaper *Al-Liwa*.

Ali Bahgat wrote for the periodical *Mawsuat* between 1898 and 1901, sometimes signing his own name and sometimes "Athari" (antiquarian or archaeologist).[95] Artin had recommended Bahgat to assist fellows of the Institut française d'archéologie orientale du Caire with Arabic. At IFAO Bahgat met Max van Berchem, who encouraged him on the path of Orientalist scholarship, museology, and Islamic archaeology.

Fakhri and Artin were able to rescue Bahgat from Dunlop because they were ensconced in the francophone high official circles and cultural institutions of Egypt. Fakhri was born in 1843 into Muhammad Ali's "Turkish" elite (Fakhri's father, Jafar Sadiq, was a Circassian general); he was just a year younger than his Armenian undersecretary. For eleven years, he studied law in France and worked in the public prosecutor's office. He arrived home in 1874, shortly before Nubar's and Ismail's establishment of the Mixed Courts, which put a premium on familiarity with French law. Fakhri became minister of justice at thirty-six and prime minister at forty, though his cabinet lasted only three days, because Abbas had named it without Baring's consent. The abortion of Fakhri's cabinet may have given him "an undeserved reputation as a nationalist,"[96] but only a year later he was back in Mustafa Fahmi's spineless cabinet, where he presided for a dozen years over both public works and education.

In the Comité, Institut égyptien, and Khedivial Geographical Society, Fakhri played the Turkish grand seigneur to Artin's industrious secretary-translator and gentleman scholar. In his long years as vice president of the Institut and his brief term as president, Fakhri never gave a paper. Artin, meanwhile, turned out a stream of reports, translations, and learned papers.[97]

Fakhri and Artin got Bahgat onto the Comité at the beginning of 1900, but it took them nearly two more years to get him into a paid position in its Service des monuments. They tried to make him curator of the Museum of Arab Art, but Herz had been performing this function and now won the formal title instead. Herz became "conservator" in January 1902 (while continuing as architect-in-chief to Awqaf and the Comité). Bahgat obtained an assistant curatorship at £E25 a month. He would work a dozen years under Herz.[98]

Fakhri was of Circassian, Artin of Armenian, and Bahgat of Turkish stock. Nationalists might dismiss Fakhri and Artin as collaborators with the British and Bahgat as an apolitical technician. Like Ahmad Kamal, Ismail al-Falaki, Ahmad Shafiq, and Ahmad Zaki, they mixed with Europeans in the Institut égyptien, Geographical Society, and Egyptian University during the heyday of imperialism. Yet, although hardly nationalists in the mold of Mustafa Kamil or the later Sa'd Zaghlul, Bahgat and Kamal challenged claims that only Europeans made competent scholars and officials. Bahgat and Kamal thereby laid cultural foundations upon which later nationalists could build. Bahgat took his first step toward Islamic archaeology at least as early as 1887 by translating early Comité proceedings to Arabic. Artin, as undersecretary of education and Comité member, presumably selected the young school inspector for the task. In 1894, Bahgat translated an education report of Artin's into Arabic. One observer saw Artin's commending of Bahgat to IFAO as an attempt to give "scientific training" to a promising scholar who could not afford long study in Europe.[99]

Max van Berchem, whom Bahgat met at IFAO, was the founder of Islamic epigraphy. Born into a prosperous Calvinist family of Geneva, he took his doctorate in Orientalism at Leipzig and in 1887 came to Egypt on a tour with his mother. Five years later he called for an international campaign to compile a corpus of Arabic inscriptions such as those of August Böckh for Greek and Theodor Mommsen for Latin. Van Berchem deplored armchair Orientalists who contented themselves with the literary texts available in European libraries. To Ernest Renan's scornful "An inscription is not a text," he retorted, "A well-studied monument is better than the best text." Maspero cheered him on:

> More and more I have been thinking that the Arabist school up to now has taken the wrong path in refusing to see in Arabic more than a grammar and literature to study in the *cabinet*. Your studies in Cairo show what there is to be done in archaeology and what reality the history of the Muslim Orient will take on if it draws on the still surviving monuments.[100]

Van Berchem, like Sarre of Berlin, got started in Islamic archaeology as an Arabist on expeditions concentrating on pre-Islamic remains.[101] By 1895 he was a corresponding member of the Comité, and France's Académie des inscriptions et belles lettres supported his corpus project through IFAO. The first Egyptian portion of the *Matériaux pour un Corpus Inscriptionum Arabicarum* came out in 1903, and four years later the Comité promoted him to honorary member. Only a fraction of van Berchem's corpus had reached print when World War I tore apart the scholarly internationalism on which it depended. After van Berchem's death in 1921, Gaston Wiet published a sequel for Egyptian materials and collaborated on the less ambitious sixteen-volume *Répertoire chronologique d'épigraphie arabe* (Cairo, 1931–1954). Bernard O'Kane and the American Research Center in Egypt now are working on a project to publish all the pre-1800 Arabic monumental inscriptions in Cairo.

Van Berchem was proud of Geneva's neutrality and internationalism. Less susceptible than British, French, and German colleagues to imperial entanglements, he made friends across the Franco-German and Muslim-Orientalist divides. He befriended Halil Edhem, director general of Istanbul museums, and came close to calling Bahgat an equal: "I owe a great deal to my friend and collaborator Ali Effendi Bahgat. He has devoted many days to revealing and deciphering the inscriptions of Cairo with me. His constant goodwill, his erudition and his practice of archaeology, together with a naturally superior feel for his native language, have been a great help to me during my research."[102]

In 1898, the year Kitchener triumphed over the Mahdists at Omdurman and the French at Fashoda, forty-year-old Bahgat read his first paper at the Institut égyptien. Artin as president and Fakhri as vice president were helping their protégé move up from translator and "native informant" to member of the Orientalist community. For a good sixty years after its founding in 1859, most Institut officers and members were Europeans, but Artin and Fakhri were gallicized enough to preside over it for many years. After a stint as treasurer-librarian (1885–1888), Artin served twenty years as president (1889–1904, 1907–1908, 1913–1916) and several years as one of the two vice presidents. Fakhri backed him up from the vice presidency and briefly took a turn as president.

Bahgat's maiden paper brought together the Napoleonic legacy and the Arab-Islamic strand in the Institut's history. He had uncovered in the Rosetta court archives the marriage contract of General Menou, who had converted to Islam and married an Egyptian woman. In 1800, Menou succeeded the assassinated General Kléber as commander of the French expedition. Two years after Bahgat's guest presentation, the Institut elected him a member. From 1907 to 1922, he sat on its publications committee alongside three Europeans. By the time he became vice president of the Institut in 1923, he had presented ten papers there. His topics included Arab accounts of the Pyramids, biographies of Arab explorers, Egypt's history and geography under the Mamluks, and a report on the Fustat excavations.[103]

Other Egyptians on the Comité shared Artin's and Bahgat's interest in Islamic art. These included Sabir Sabri of the opposition faction, palace official Ahmad Zaki, and Armenian notable Boghos Nubar (son of the former prime minister), who collected art and also belonged to the Institut égyptien. Presumably it was Artin and Fakhri who initiated Bahgat into the Khedivial Geographical Society. Founded in 1875 to promote Ismail's Sudanese and East African empire, the society survived national bankruptcy, the Urabi revolution, the British conquest, the Mahdist upheaval, and the Anglo-Egyptian evacuation and subsequent reconquest of the Sudan. Italians O. Abbate and F. Bonola monopolized leadership of the society for many years before World War I.[104]

As with interlocking directorships of banks and joint-stock companies, activities in one of these cultural organizations spawned invitations to join others. In 1908 Bahgat joined the board of the private Egyptian University. Cromer had vetoed a university as a breeding ground for nationalists, but his successor, Sir Eldon Gorst (1907–1911), reached a detente with Khedive Abbas, who entrusted the task of creating and controlling the university to his uncle, Prince Ahmad Fuad. Bahgat's fellow board members in 1908 included Maspero, the inevitable Artin, Ahmad Zaki from the palace, and cabinet minister Husayn Rushdi.

Bahgat attended university board meetings regularly until March 1922, when he resigned on grounds of health, and from 1919 to 1922 he also served as secretary. He was moving in rarified company: other board members in 1919 included Prime Minister Husayn Rushdi, four future prime ministers (Zaghlul, Tharwat, Ismail Sidqi, and Muhammad Mahmud), Lutfi al-Sayyid, jurist Abd al-Aziz Fahmi, engineer Mahmud Fahmi of the Ministry of Awqaf, and IFAO director G. Foucart. In March 1919, university supervisor *(muraqib)* Sa'd Zaghlul attended a board meeting three days before his arrest and exile sparked a countrywide rising against the British. Bahgat acted as university supervisor during Zaghlul's absence.[105]

Finally, Bahgat joined the "Friends of Fine Arts" and the board of the Khedivial Library (Dar al-Kutub). He translated the library's 1908 annual report into Arabic. Did he ever practice his German with the library's German directors or with Herz, his superior at the Comité and Museum of Arab Art? Fluency would have come in handy in 1910, when Bahgat delivered objects from the Museum of Arab Art to Munich for a pioneering exhibition of Islamic art.[106]

REPRESENTING EGYPT: INTERNATIONAL CONGRESSES OF ORIENTALISTS

For Bahgat, the Institut égyptien was a stepping-stone to Orientalist circles abroad. In 1899, he read a paper at the Twelfth International Congress of Orientalists in Rome. It was on al-Qalqashandi's medieval compendium on Islamic scribal technique *(Subh al-Asha fi Sinaat al-Insha)*, which was later published in Cairo (1914–1928). Bahgat's mentor, van Berchem, took the floor to stress the importance of the topic and the promise of its presenter. Bahgat was in heady company at this ICO. Ignaz Goldziher, Max Müller, and Edward Granville Browne were among the distinguished Orientalists there, and had he crossed the hall, Bahgat could have mingled with Egyptologists such as Erman, Naville, Schiaparelli, and Breasted or have heard Botti report on the Greco-Roman Museum's excavations in Alexandria.[107]

This was Bahgat's first contribution to a cause that Orientalists and Arab scholars of the *nahda* shared—the study, revival, and publication of classical Arabic texts. Later he selected al-Baladhuri's history of the early Islamic conquests for publication by the Society for Publication of Arabic Works and edited the Fatimid text *Diwan Qanun al-Rassayel*.[108]

Anouar Louca, Timothy Mitchell, and Carter Findley have discussed the ICOs as locations to assess Orientalist-Muslim encounters.[109] Mitchell emphasizes that "Orientals" at Orientalist congresses disrupted the dichotomy between subject and object. Could an Oriental be an Orientalist? What place was there for "Oriental" scholars in this theoretically universal, but in practice Western-dominated, republic of learning?

Bahgat was not the first Arab to present a paper to an ICO. Elia Qudsi, a Syrian Christian from Damascus, mailed in a paper on Damascus guilds to the Sixth ICO, which met in Leiden in 1883. The meetings had adjourned by the time it arrived, but Swedish Orientalist Carlo Landberg, formerly consul general in Alexandria, praised Qudsi's presentation of data not easily accessible to Europeans and published the paper in its original Arabic in the proceedings. Landberg wanted to show "Orientals through this publication the desire we have to see them occupy themselves a bit with science for science's sake." But he admonished future Arab contributors to take greater care with their Arabic grammar.[110]

Egypt first sent its Arabic specialists, including Azharis who taught at Dar al-Ulum, to the Seventh ICO, which convened in Vienna in 1886. Hifni al-Nasif's paper on Arabic dialects was published in the proceedings.[111]

Shaykh Hamza Fath Allah, a conservative who scrupulously kept to turban and robe while traveling abroad, returned to Europe in 1889 for the Eighth ICO, which split its sessions between Stockholm and Christiania. Abdallah Fikri Pasha, ex-minister of education and tutor to the khedive's sons, headed the Egyptian delegation. His Paris-educated son Muhammad Amin Fikri acted as interpreter and secretary. The delegation took in not only the ICO but also London and the *exposition universelle* in Paris. The elder Fikri died after returning, with only a dozen pages of his final report written. His son finished the report in a tome running to eight hundred pages.[112]

Landberg had personally persuaded Khedive Tawfiq to send the Egyptian delegation and, as host, went out of his way to make them feel like colleagues, not exotic exhibits. Abdallah Fikri declaimed an ode in Arabic during his audience with the king of Sweden, and Landberg responded in Arabic with praise of Khedive Tawfiq. Amin Fikri, who had collaborated in writing with Ali Mubarak, presented the king an Arabic geography of Egypt, a single volume previewing the terrain Mubarak's *Al-Khitat* would cover.[113] Among the Orientalists the Egyptians met, Goldziher, who had studied at al-Azhar, was both hospitable and fluent in Arabic. Ottoman delegate Ahmed Midhat chaired a session, interpreting for the Egyptians, and there was a Persian delegation as well. Waiters at a reception wore Egyptian attire, and the opera *Aida*, which Amin Fikri thought a particularly appropriate choice, enlivened the congress.

Amin Fikri devoted twenty-five pages of his book to refuting an Orientalist memorandum advocating that colloquial Arabic replace classical Arabic for writing purposes. The Egyptians read their papers in Arabic to the section Islamic and Semitic Languages, but at some sessions they were tongue-tied when not a single Arabic-speaking European was present to translate. Amin Fikri's solution was unequivocal: Papers should be in the language of the people under study—Arabic for Arabic topics, Turkish for Turkish topics, and so on.[114]

Some, however, complained that having Orientals and papers in their languages at the congress were a mistake. An Oxford scholar grumbled: "I have heard nothing so unworthy of a sensible man as...the whistling howls emitted by an Arabic student of El-Azhar of Cairo. Such exhibitions at Congresses are mischievous and degrading."[115]

At the Ninth ICO, in London in 1892, Ahmad Shawqi recited an Arabic poem, and future hero Sa'd Zaghlul was there. K. Vollers represented the Khedivial Library and later reported on the meetings to the Institut égyptien.[116] But twenty-five-year-old Ahmad Zaki (1867–1934) stood out among the Egyptians, as he would at several future ICOs. An 1888 graduate of Cairo's School of Administration, Zaki was a palace man and long-time secretary to the Council of Ministers. For his love of Arabic philology and literature, he won the epithet "Shaykh of Arabism," and his library greatly enriched the Egyptian National Library, but he has not received much notice in Western scholarship. At the London ICO he argued that the charter the prophet Muhammad allegedly gave Christians in Sinai was a forgery, reported on Arabic manuscripts in the Escorial, and translated an ode of Hamza Fath Allah into French. Far from being marginalized as Orientals, Zaki, a Persian, and an Indian were on a sixteen-man committee to select the site for the next congress.[117] Zaki wrote a book on his travels to the London congress and returned to participate in the Tenth ICO at Geneva (1894), the Thirteenth, at Hamburg (1902), and the Sixteenth, in Athens (1912).

In 1905, the Fourteenth ICO crossed the Mediterranean to Algiers— a foray into a colonized object of the body's studies. Grand Mufti Muhammad Abduh helped select the shaykhly scholars who represented Egypt at Algiers. Abd al-Aziz Shawish, soon to emerge as a firebrand in Mustafa Kamil's Watani Party, was the best known.[118]

The Sixteenth ICO convened in Athens in 1912, after which World War I suspended the ICOs for sixteen years. Bahgat's patron Yaqub Artin had subscribed to the First ICO, in Paris in 1873, and was still around for Athens. Shawqi again recited an ode, and future king Fuad, rector of the Egyptian University, emphasized the benefits Orientalist scholarship bestowed on Arab lands.[119] Ahmad Zaki spoke of the enthusiasm early Muslims had shown for Greek science and philosophy and praised the current cultural revivals under way in both Greece and Egypt. Goldziher and Christiaan Snouck Hurgronje chaired panels at which the irrepressible Zaki read three papers; Louis Massignon, August Fischer, David Margoliouth, and Henri Lammens were among the audience. Hifni Nasif read a paper on the Prophet's Coptic wife, Maryam, and Shaykh Ahmad al-Iskandarani spoke on modern literature in Egyptian dialect.[120]

Thus, in contrast with Egyptology, where Westerners alone held the floor at the ICOs through the forty years leading up to World War I, Egyptian scholars of Arabic-Islamic topics were joining in with Orientalists—among them Alfred von Kremer, Goldziher, Ignazio Guidi, Michael J. de Goeje, Snouck Hurgronje, Carl Becker, and Massignon—in giving papers at the ICOs from the 1880s on. Some Orientalists were unabashed imperialists, not all welcomed "Oriental" participation in the ICOs, and Westerners dominated the meetings, but it was not a one-way street. If men like Ahmad Zaki, no uncritical Westernizer, had gone home feeling used or excluded, why would they have kept coming back?

REPRESENTING EGYPT: "STREETS OF CAIRO" AT THE WORLD'S FAIRS

At the Paris Exposition universelle of 1889, one of the messages was the triumph of Western imperialism over the rest of the world. In the Egyptian case, the British occupation had slammed the door on the possibility of Egypt speaking for itself at such events. Baring's financial austerity ruled out Egyptian government funds for Maspero to carry on Mariette's tradition of pharaonic exhibits abroad. The Suez Canal Company had come to Ismail's rescue by financing an exhibit at Paris in 1878, but in early 1889 de Lesseps's sister Panama Canal Company had collapsed in scandal.

A French entrepreneur resident in Egypt, Baron Delort de Gléon, stepped in and organized a privately financed "rue du Caire," which took the 1889 exposition by storm.[121] A reduced replica of the minaret of Qayt Bey towered over the street, which was decorated with elements stripped from more than a score of Cairene houses. Merchants, artisans, and two belly dancers plied their trades, and fifty "donkey boys" kept the street on the brink of chaos as they peddled their one-franc rides. Variations on the "rue du Caire," under other sponsorship, came back for encores at Chicago in 1893 and Paris in 1900.

Several Egyptians, cultivating the travel genre inspired by al-Tahtawi's *Takhlis* and Ali Mubarak's *Alam al-Din,* described visiting the 1889 Paris Exposition universelle. Abdallah Fikri's ICO delegation stopped in Paris on their way to Stockholm, and Amin Fikri gave a detailed report on the fair. The inevitable Thomas Cook & Son, prominently represented at the exposition, made all the Egyptian delegation's travel arrangements, and Amin Fikri folded a laudatory, detailed biography of the founder and history of the company into his account.[122]

Fikri found the "rue du Caire" realistic in many ways, although the mosque proved to be only a facade for a coffee shop with Egyptian and Sudanese female dancers and whirling dervishes. He found fault with the Europeans for getting overly excited about the female dancers and the dervishes for performing in such a milieu. Fikri admired the enterprise of Cairene merchant Mustafa al-Dib, who was doing a brisk business in selling perfume, brasswork, and other merchandise like that sold in Khan al-Khalili.[123] Al-Dib had taken the risk of launching his venture without government assistance and was reaping handsome rewards. The Egyptian products displayed inside the Palais des Industries Diverses, however, Fikri found poor. He blamed the government and indigenous Egyptian entrepreneurs for missing a good opportunity.

At the Chicago World's Fair of 1893, a pylon and obelisk incongruously marked the entrance to the supposedly Islamic "Street of Cairo." Taking their cue from Paris in 1889, a Belgian and a Greek entrepreneur had hired the Comité's Max Herz for advice on stripping authentic *mashrabiyya* from buildings in Cairo and designing the exhibit. In Chicago, the visitor was supposed to enter "that mystic land whose civilization antedates all authentic history, and whose works and wonders hold us enchained by an irresistible fascination.... [Here are] the identical types of persons and animals one sees in grand Cairo. Here are Egyptians, Arabs, Soudanese, Africans, kabyles, camels, donkeys...."[124]

Back in Europe, Germany toyed with the idea of a world's fair in Berlin in 1896 or 1900. The French masters of the genre preempted them, however, with an early announcement of an *exposition universelle* for Paris in 1900. Germany settled for sending an impressive, even intimidating, exhibit to Paris that year while competing with France elsewhere in more substantial industrial and military arenas. Hoping to exorcise nightmares about the Dreyfus affair, Britain's colonial triumph at Fashoda, and Germany's looming might, France went all out for the exposition of 1900. Some of the pavilions of such French dependencies as Indochina, Cambodia, Senegal, Tunisia, and Algeria—populated with hundreds of indigenous craftsmen—surpassed those of some independent countries.[125]

With Cromer again blocking an official Egyptian exhibit, Syrian-Egyptian entrepreneur Philippe Boulad and his cousins, assisted by the prosperous Mustafa al-Dib, organized a private venture in Egypt's name.[126] Marcel Dourgnon, the architect of the new Egyptian Museum going up in Cairo, designed a pavilion with one section in pharaonic style, one an Islamic *wikala* (caravanserai) with an adjacent fountain, and one replicating the temple of Dendur on the outside with a theater for music and dance inside.

Ahmad Zaki thought Egypt's architecture and antiquities were adequately represented but said that the agricultural products and cotton goods in the *wikala* did not reflect Egypt's industrial, commercial, and intellectual progress. He resented the fake Azhari shaykh who wrote the names of visitors in Arabic and wanted to suppress the belly dance in the *Ballet d'Antar*. Zaki also deplored the lack of authenticity in the Ottoman exhibit.[127]

Muhammad al-Muwaylihi visited the exposition in the entourage of Abbas II and wrote about it in 1927 in an account appended to later editions of *Hadith Isa ibn Hisham*. He titled his chapter on the Egyptian exhibit "Slandering the Homeland." Al-Muwaylihi supplies a variety of conflicting views, making it hard to determine which ones are his own. There are complaints about lewd belly dancers, the false Azhari shaykh, the fake shaykh of a Quran school who beat his pupils with a palm branch, and the exhibition of an armless girl spinning yarn with her feet. With Egypt unable to represent itself abroad, Zaki believed that its image suffered at the hands of European Orientalists and their worthless Egyptian collaborators. For him, even the exhibition's landmark Eiffel Tower seemed to echo the vanity that had doomed the Tower of Babel; the Panama Canal Company scandal had sent Eiffel to jail.

The reactions of Amin Fikri, Ahmad Zaki, and Muhammad al-Muwaylihi to the representations of Egypt at these fairs were mixed. Fikri and Zaki found more to admire at the fairs than al-Muwaylihi did. But none was content with having control of his country—and the power to represent it—in the hands of an alien other. Neither was Ali Bahgat, the protagonist of this chapter, who unexpectedly recovered a small piece of Egyptian cultural autonomy with the arrival of World War I.

ALI BAHGAT, AL-FUSTAT,
AND THE COMING OF THE WAR

Amr [ibn al-As, the Arab general who conquered
Egypt] founded al-Fustat under the banner of Islam.
Ali Bahgat discovered al-Fustat under the banner of
Science.

Mustafa Abd El-Razeq, "Ali Bey Bahgat,
1854–1924," *Bulletin de l'Institut égyptien*

Bahgat was fifty-four in 1912 when he began the excavations at al-Fustat
that made him a founding father of Islamic archaeology. Herz was busy
with architectural work and may have delegated much of the running
of the Museum of Arab Art to Bahgat, who was not trained as an architect. Bahgat became the prime link between the Comité and Egyptians who did not know a Western language. He translated Herz's guide
to the Museum of Arab Art into Arabic (1909) and in 1912 brought the
published Arabic version of the Comité's proceedings up through 1909.
Unfortunately, little evidence has come to light of how many Egyptians
visited the museum, what they thought of it, or who consulted the Arabic versions of the guidebook and the proceedings of the Comité.

In 1912 Bahgat took two months' leave to accompany a student to
Paris to study history and archaeology in preparation for museum
work.[128] He had visited Europe before, but for him, as for Ahmad
Kamal, direct experience of it was brief and relatively late in life.

Bahgat's report on a brief trip to Upper Egypt in May 1910 reveals
the limitations of his—and the Comité's—idea of archaeology at the
time. Bahgat went to purchase museum objects from antiquities dealers
in Luxor and Suhaj. As it turned out, his timing was wrong. The season's tourists had stripped the dealers' stocks and gone home, and the
peasants whose fertilizer *(sebakh)* digging would replenish the shops
had not yet returned to the task. Bahgat proposed to return in November, after the fertilizer digging but ahead of the tourists.[129]

In July 1912, a remarkable opportunity diverted his attention to other
matters. The government turned over archaeological surveillance at al-
Fustat, the original Arab-Islamic capital of the province of Egypt, to the
Comité. Confusingly, Europeans called the region Old Cairo, for which
an equally unsatisfactory "Coptic Cairo" is now sometimes substituted.
The German excavations at Samarra (Iraq) that Friedrich Sarre orga-
nized and Ernst Herzfeld was carrying out for the Imperial Museum of
Berlin (1911–1913) may have spurred the action at al-Fustat.[130] Si-

multaneous work on the Berlin-to-Baghdad railway and German military ties to the Ottomans set the excavation in a Western imperial context. Early excavations at the Islamic sites of Samarqand by Russians (from 1885), the Qala of Bani Hammad in Algeria by the French (1898), and perhaps Madinat al-Zahra by the Spanish (1910) also seem to have had overtones of European imperial expansion.[131]

The remarkable thing at al-Fustat was that an indigenous Muslim was in charge. Herz was busy with architectural matters, so the Comité put Bahgat in charge of excavations.

Al-Fustat had been substantially abandoned since the eleventh century. Its proximity to Cairo, however, had long made the site a rubbish heap, quarry for building materials, location for pottery and other industries, and home for squatters. Fertilizer diggers ravaged the site during the nineteenth century, but the absence of significant pharaonic ruins underneath spared it destructive attention from nineteenth-century Egyptologists.[132]

No funds earmarked for excavation came with Bahgat's new responsibility, however. The best he could do was to tighten surveillance over the individuals and companies who had long been mining al-Fustat for fertilizer. Bahgat reported that everyone benefited from the system: The Museum of Arab Art obtained Arab antiquities (mostly pieces of glazed or unglazed pottery), stones with hieroglyphics went to the Egyptian Museum, scholars learned about the layout of al-Fustat, fertilizer companies made their profits, cultivators got fertilizer, and the state obtained leveled land it could use for other purposes.[133] This assessment, appalling as it is by today's standards, showed that Bahgat's conception of archaeology was broadening. He now sought not only museum pieces but also remains of buildings and streets, from which to reconstruct the city's early topography. Bahgat continued work at al-Fustat into the 1920s, when a foreign attack on his work spurred the Comité to arrange for two French scholars to coauthor publications reporting on his results.

Meanwhile, World War I had shaken Egypt, the Comité, and the Museum of Arab Art. When the Ottoman Empire cast its lot with the Central Powers, Britain finally severed Egypt's nominal tie to Istanbul, proclaimed a protectorate, and replaced Abbas II with his docile uncle Husayn Kamil. Herz, as an enemy alien, lost his post with the Comité and Ministry of Awqaf and left the country. He retained his pension rights, however, and Harry Farnall extolled his thirty-three-year service to the Comité and Awqaf Department and regretted that "circumstances external to art have deprived [the Comité] of the valuable services of this eminent architect and archaeologist." Marcus Simaika hoped that Herz could still complete a third edition of the museum catalogue and regretfully postponed as "perhaps premature" a proposal that Herz be invited to become a corresponding member of the Comité. Herz took refuge in Switzerland, dying in Zurich in 1919 at sixty-three.[134]

An unforeseen consequence of World War I was that Egyptians took over the direction of both the Museum of Arab Art and the Khedivial Library. Bahgat took over from Herz downstairs at the museum, while upstairs at the library Ahmad Lutfi al-Sayyid succeeded the last German Orientalist, Arthur Schaade, as director.

Italy sat on the fence for a time, then joined the Allies in 1915. Herz's former architectural understudy Achille Patricolo, an Italian, was thus able to keep his job. Patricolo pronounced Cairo's combination of architectural preservation and museum administration an anomaly unknown in Europe; preservation demanded the expertise of an architect, museum work that of an archaeologist.[135] Patricolo followed Herz as the Comité's architect-in-chief (although at first without the title and Comité seat that Herz had held) but had no wish to run the museum. That cleared the way for Ali Bahgat to become conservator of the Museum of Arab Art. He had waited a dozen years for the job, and at fifty-six had more than paid his dues. Bahgat's successes during the heyday of Western imperialism in Egypt, like those of Ahmad Kamal, were hard-won and bittersweet. By the time Bahgat died in 1924, the Europeans on the Comité had joined outside critics in raising questions about both his competence and his integrity. There being no obvious Egyptian successor when he died, the museum reverted to European control under a French Orientalist—Gaston Wiet. In 1933, K. A. C. Creswell founded a graduate program in Islamic archaeology at the Egyptian University. Creswell and Wiet, who tolerated each other only with difficulty, were formidable presences on the Comité into the early 1950s, despite the dwindling representation of Europeans. Like Bahgat before them, the Egyptian assistant curators whom Wiet trained and the graduates of Creswell's Islamic archaeology program spent much of their careers under foreign tutelage. It was left to Nasser to sever the Gordian knot by winning both political independence and full national control of museums, archaeology, and educational institutions. Even then, old issues kept resurfacing in new guises as new or recycled analytical approaches— neocolonialism, cultural hegemony, postmodernism, postcolonialism, and post-Orientalism—emerged to try to come to grips with them.[136]

CHAPTER 7

Modern Sons
of the Pharaohs?

Marcus Simaika and the Coptic Past

Marcus Simaika (1864–1944) recounted that one day in the winter of 1908, he called on Patriarch Cyril (Anba Kirullus) V and found him supervising while a silversmith weighed out old silver gospel covers and church vessels to be melted down for reworking. They bore fourteenth- and fifteenth-century inscriptions in Coptic and Arabic. Simaika, then vice president of the Coptic Community Council, offered to raise the £E180 market value of the bullion if these objects would be saved in a storeroom as a start toward a museum. The patriarch agreed, and the Coptic Museum was born.[1]

This transformation of worn-out cult objects, worth only their weight in silver, into priceless antiquities reflected a dramatic shift in the way the Copts viewed their past and defined their modern identity. Far from escaping the present into a dead past, people like Simaika, who treasured Coptic antiquity, were both products of social reform and major advocates of it. As in eighteenth-century France and nineteenth-century Greece, anticlerical Coptic laymen promoted reform and a revaluation of communal and national identities against the opposition of much of the clergy. Marcus Simaika was in the forefront of the campaign for communal reform until he came to realize that he would have to ease off in order to win the patriarch's support for the Coptic Museum.

Simaika was to Coptic archaeology what Ahmad Kamal was to Egyptology and Ali Bahgat to Islamic archaeology—the pioneer who struggled to kindle enthusiasm for the antiquities and history of a vital phase or aspect of the national past. Although fifteen years younger than Kamal and six younger than Bahgat, Simaika shared something of a common generational consciousness with them. All three attended reformed schools where they learned the European languages through which they developed their archaeological interests. All three completed formal schooling before the British conquest and lived most of their professional lives during the forty years of intense British occupation from 1882 to 1922. Kamal died in 1923 and Bahgat in 1924; the younger Simaika lived on until 1944.

This chapter highlights Simaika's career because of his centrality to Coptic archaeology and because his unpublished and hitherto unutilized memoirs provide a rich and relevant source for this topic. Other sources include the bulletins of the Comité and the Coptic Archeological Society. Familiar mainly to specialists in art, architecture, and religion, these bulletins have not been tapped for the broader history of modern Egypt. Interviews also helped me to put in perspective the development of Coptic studies in pre-1914 Egypt.[2]

THE COPTS TO 1854

Copts revere Saint Mark for bringing Christianity to Alexandria in the first century and consider him the founder of their church. As Christianity was becoming dominant around the Mediterranean in the fourth and fifth centuries, periodic councils punctuated the struggle to sort out orthodoxy from heresy. Christological disputes at the Council of Chalcedon in 451 C.E. split the Orthodoxy of Constantinople and Rome from that of the Copts. The ensuing persecution of Copts by Greek-speaking Byzantine authorities prepared the way for the Islamic conquest of Egypt during 640–642. After several centuries of Islamic rule, Islam became the majority religion, and Arabic tipped the balance against Coptic in everyday speech. Spoken Coptic retreated to isolated areas of Upper Egypt and eventually disappeared.

In 1800, a majority of Copts lived in Upper Egypt, especially the provinces of Minya and Asyut. Like their Muslim compatriots, most were peasants. Urban Copts mostly worked as craftsmen or clerks in finance and taxation, with relatively few engaging in the commercial activities that attracted Greek Orthodox and Armenian Christians.

The Copts' experience with Greek Orthodox Christians from Constantinople and Roman Catholic crusaders from western Europe, both of whom despised them as heretics, left them deeply suspicious of fellow Christians from the north. Only a few Copts threw in their lot with the French invaders of 1798. One who did was Yaqub Hanna, an Upper Egyptian tax collector who switched from the Mamluks to the French and made himself indispensable to General Desaix's Upper Egyptian foray. After Bonaparte had slipped away to France, General Kléber provided Yaqub Hanna with a bodyguard of thirty French soldiers and made him commander of an eight-hundred-man Coptic legion. Hanna had no option but to flee when the French left, and he died on a British ship bound for Europe.[3]

Muhammad Ali relaxed traditional dress restrictions on non-Muslims and the prohibition on their riding horseback. Like the Mamluks before him, however, he had only limited success in lessening state dependence on Coptic accountants and tax collectors.

Nineteenth-century Western Christians were of two minds about the Copts; sometimes they saw only heresy, and sometimes they embraced Copts as fellow Christians. Westerners searching in Egypt for an idealized land of the Bible and the cradle of early church fathers were often as disappointed with living Copts as philhellenes were when seeking classical heroes among modern Greeks. An 1890s Nilsson guidebook reflected visceral European bigotry: "The Copts are the most ugly of men. They are also exceedingly dirty and very disgusting in their habits."[4] E. W. Lane was similarly extreme: "One of the most remarkable traits in the character of the Copts is their bigotry. They bear a bitter hatred of all other Christians, even exceeding that with which the Muslims regard the unbelievers in El-Islam. . . . They are, generally speaking, of a sullen temper, extremely avaricious, and abominable dissemblers; cringing or domineering according to circumstances."[5] Lane's great-nephew Stanley Lane-Poole carried on the family reservations about Copts: "To Egypt belongs the debatable honour of having invented monasticism."[6]

Lane conceded that he had "the good fortune to become acquainted with a character of which I had doubted the existence—a Copt of a liberal as well as an intelligent mind" who supplied information for the appendix on Copts in *The Manners and Customs of the Modern Egyptians.*[7]

Wilkinson found the monks of Wadi al-Natrun "exceedingly ignorant" and voiced a familiar Protestant condemnation of monasticism but also observed:

> There is an air of respectability and mildness, in the deportment of the superiors, and most of the aged fathers, which is characteristic of the Christian, and which, while it marks a strong line of distinction between their patriarchal demeanour, and the arrogance of the ulemas of Islam, cannot fail to leave a pleasing impression on the Christian stranger, and to call up in his mind the con-

viction that these people, though ignorant and prejudiced, are united with Him
in a common bond of union, and have ideas that sympathize with His own.[8]

Like Wilkinson, some Westerners entranced by ancient Egypt found
ways to blend this with unwavering devotion to Christianity. Luc Olivier-
Merson's painting of 1879 depicts the Holy Family beneath a starry sky,
taking refuge in the arms of a welcoming Egyptian sphinx (figure 41).

RENAISSANCE AND REACTION: PATRIARCH CYRIL IV AND AFTER

Copts remember Cyril IV (in office 1854–1861), who ascended his throne
the same year as Said Pasha, as "the Father of Reform" (Abu al-Islah).
Copts had traditionally paid the poll-tax *(jizya)* levied on non-Muslims
and been excluded from the military. Under Abbas I, they had nevertheless been conscripted into the army.[9] Said continued the conscription and
made the erosion of religious communal boundaries more explicit by abol-
ishing the *jizya*. He refused, however, to admit Copts to state schools, and
they had to wait until Ali Mubarak and Ismail's decree of 1867 opened
state schools to all regardless of religion. Under Ismail, several Copts studied abroad at state expense for the first time.[10] Ismail also included Copts
in the Majlis al-Nuwwab (which evolved into a chamber of deputies). Over
the next half century, Copts flocked to state and Coptic communal schools
while also benefiting disproportionately from missionary schools.[11]

Cyril IV began the first wave of modern Coptic reform in 1854, ten
years before Marcus Simaika was born. From 1854 until the 1952 revolution, a new wave of Coptic reform crested about once a decade. Laymen took the lead in every wave but the first, with the patriarch and
most clergymen resisting. Coptic reform had its own internal dynamic,
but it was also in tune with the wider rhythms of Egyptian national and
Ottoman imperial reform.

Cyril IV came from a poor fellah family of Upper Egypt and entered
Saint Antony's Monastery, in the eastern desert, as a young man. A
short-lived theological seminary that an Anglican missionary ran in
Cairo in the 1840s may have influenced his thinking,[12] but the reforms
of Muhammad Ali influenced him far more. In Istanbul, the reform decrees of 1839 and 1856 affirmed the equality of all Ottoman subjects.
In Egypt from Muhammad Ali on, the state moved toward dealing directly with individual Christians and Jews, weakening the role of the patriarch or grand rabbi as intermediary between their flocks and the state.

Figure 41.   (Ancient) Egypt welcomes the Holy Family: *Rest on the Flight into Egypt,* by Luc Olivier-Merson, 1879. Courtesy Museum of Fine Arts, Boston. Reproduced with permission. © 1999 Museum of Fine Arts, Boston. All Rights Reserved.

The slowness of this integration process meant that in Muhammad Ali's day Copts did not participate in the new army, higher schools, study missions to Europe, the translation bureau, the printing press, or the official journal. Upon becoming patriarch, Cyril decided that the church would have to act on its own to bring the benefits of reform home to Copts. He imported a printing press from Britain, cracked down on priestly corruption and ignorance, opened new schools, and reached out ecumenically to the Greek Orthodox, the Armenians, and perhaps the Anglicans. It was widely believed that Said, fearing that Cyril's overtures to the Greek Orthodox Church might lead to Russian interference in Egypt, had him poisoned in 1861.[13]

Cyril IV's greatest achievement was founding the Patriarchal School (Madrasat al-Aqbat al-Kubra). Said refused his plea to admit Copts to state schools and allow them to join the Muslim Egyptians who were now moving up in the junior ranks of the officer corps. Hitherto, Coptic formal education had stopped with the elementary *kuttab*, where students learned to read and write Coptic and Arabic from the Bible and to do simple mathematics. There was no Coptic al-Azhar.

The Patriarchal School, which Simaika attended, shaped a whole generation of the Coptic lay elite in the generation before missionary and state schools began making education widely available to Copts. Simaika boasted that his alma mater graduated three Coptic prime ministers—Butrus Ghali, Yusuf Wahba, and Yahya Ibrahim.[14] Other alumni included the notable Qalini Fahmi, historian Mikhail Sharubim, journalist Mikhail Abd al-Sayyid, and Coptologist-Egyptologist Claudius Labib.

Patriarchs Demetrius II (in office 1862–1870), Cyril V (1874–1927), and John (Yohannes) XIX (1928–1942) reacted sharply against the foreign influences that Cyril IV, Simaika, and many laymen embraced. United Presbyterians of the "American Mission" arrived to "occupy" Egypt[15] (the military metaphor was theirs) in the same year that Said and Cyril IV ascended their thrones. Demetrius II lashed out at the Presbyterian intruders, who denounced the Coptic Church as heretical, corrupt, and ignorant. First Said and then Ismail backed the patriarch against these foreign disturbers of the peace. Ismail countered missionary schools by giving the Coptic Church fifteen hundred feddans to finance development of its own schools[16] and by opening state schools to non-Muslims in 1867. (Catholic missionaries, who had long been on the scene, were by then less inclined than the Protestants to confront the Coptic Church head on). But Ismail also needed to get along with the United States, which supplied him with experienced military advisers after the American Civil War. Diplomatic protection helped the American Mission consolidate its headquarters at Asyut and build schools and churches up and down the Nile Valley. Catholic and Protestant ("Evangelical") Copts eventually split off from the main Coptic Orthodox Church.

Simaika sang as a choirboy at the confirmation of Cyril V, who initially gave in to lay reformers' demands for a clerical college and the election of the Communal Council (al-Majlis al-Milli) to help run Coptic affairs. Butrus Ghali, a rising young notable, drafted the legislation that established the council in 1874 and became vice president of it under the patriarch.[17] Such councils were in the air. The Ottomans set up Armenian, Greek Orthodox, and Jewish councils in the 1860s and an imperial constitution and parliament in 1876. Ismail's Chamber of Deputies dated from 1866. Cyril V soon turned against the Communal Council, however, and shut it down in a move reminiscent of Sultan Abdulhamid II's suspension of the Ottoman parliament and constitution in 1878. Thus ended the second attempt at Coptic communal reform, the first to be led by laymen.

Decade after decade thereafter, Coptic lay reformers returned to battle the patriarch and conservative upper clergy, who clung to their traditional authority over the community. The reformers wanted the Communal Council permanently established to administer church and monastery *awaqf,* Coptic schools, and personal status laws on divorce and inheritance. Patriarchs and bishops, products of first rural poverty and then desert monasteries, were revered for their piety and ascetic withdrawal but lacked education and experience for coping with the wider world.

"It is a shameful confession," wrote Simaika, "but we must acknowledge that very few of the existing bishops belong to respectable families."[18] Most monks came from poor, provincial Upper Egyptian families. Those who became high church officials found it hard to resist grasping relatives eager to make up for past deprivation. Familiar Protestant themes echo in Simaika's denunciation of the clergy as lazy and corrupt refugees from the real world of work. He accused them of neglecting religious duties, selling justice, and enriching relatives with church funds.[19] The landowners and professional men elected to the Communal Council were prosperous and increasingly better educated and demanded a larger say in Coptic affairs. In 1891, seven of twelve council members were beys and one, Butrus Ghali, was a pasha.[20] But the patriarchal hierarchy was deeply entrenched, had a mass following, and held its own in round after round of attempted reform by the council. The stalemate had some similarities to the later one in national politics between the Wafd Party and authoritarian palace governments between 1919 and 1952. There were also parallels with al-Azhar, which by 1900 was drawing most of its students from poor or provincial families.[21] Most of the *ulama* resisted attempts to reform al-Azhar, the Sharia courts, and the Ministry of Awqaf for fear of losing power and status. Reformist shaykhs such as Muhammad Abduh were as exceptional as reformist Coptic bishops, and both drew their support from secular elites. Communal reformers had the option of calling in the state to try to tip the balance in their favor but realized the potential cost of this in communal autonomy.

THE EDUCATION OF MARCUS SIMAIKA

Simaika grew up in his maternal grandfather's house in the heavily Coptic quarter north of Ezbekiyeh. The quarter no longer closed its gates at night for protection, and Copts were beginning to feel secure enough to settle where they liked throughout Cairo. Simaika sprang from a family of Cairene notables who had prospered in service to state and church.

His mother was born in Damascus, where her father went as secretary to Muhammad Ali's son Ibrahim in the 1830s. On his father's side, Simaika's forebears had donated manuscripts and other treasures to al-Muallaqa Church.[22]

A two-hundred-meter stroll down Darb al-Wasa Street from his grandfather's house brought young Simaika to the Patriarchate, Saint Mark's Cathedral, and the Patriarchal School. The school was free and open to all religions, but many students came from privileged Coptic families like the Simaikas. Simaika mentions studying Arabic, Coptic, and Greek but not Turkish, which by Ismail's time was of dwindling usefulness for officials because the ruling class was becoming more Arabized.

School inspectors tapped two of Simaika's brothers for transfer to the law school and government careers. Just as Muslim families often set aside one son to attend al-Azhar, Simaika's father tried to save him for a church career. To this end, he forbade the boy to attend the Patriarchal School's English class. The English instructor was Mikhail Abd al-Sayyid, editor of the Coptic paper *Al-Watan* and one of the few Copts to have studied not only at American missionary and Coptic schools but also at al-Azhar.[23] Simaika's father rightly feared that knowing English might incline the boy toward a secular career, but Marcus went on a hunger strike until his father gave in. Marcus learned English, then switched to the École des Frères Chrétien to work on his French. His father's fears had not been unfounded, for Simaika dropped all thought of a church career.[24]

The Patriarchal School and, later, the Coptic Clerical College at last provided opportunities for studying Coptic above the *kuttab* level. Copts were already learning about their own heritage from Europeans. Simaika's class used a copy of H. Tattam's Coptic-Arabic New Testament, which the author had donated by way of return for the manuscripts he had taken from the monasteries of Wadi al-Natrun. Simaika's teacher Barsum al-Rahib wrote the first modern Coptic grammar in Arabic. Egyptologist-Coptologist Claudius Labib (1868–1918), four years younger than Simaika, also got his start at the Patriarchal School. Unlike Protestant clergymen in the West who supported archaeology in hopes of "proving the Bible" in the face of the higher criticism and corrosive skepticism, the Coptic clergy of the day does not seem to have shared Labib's Egyptological interests.[25]

Reform did not always work in tandem with archaeology and historic preservation, however. Like the early Christians who defaced or plastered over the images of gods in pharaonic temples, Protestant missionaries denounced the icons in Coptic churches. When he rebuilt Saint Mark's Cathedral, Cyril IV made a bonfire of old icons and forbid new ones. In Asyut in 1869, Coptic youths stirred up by American missionaries took the story of Gideon's overturning the altar of Baal as a call to raid a Coptic church and destroy its icons. They were caught and forced to make restitution, but before long, in Simaika's words, "picture worship almost entirely ceased."[26]

COPTIC REFORM AND THE BRITISH OCCUPATION

Simaika was eighteen when the British army marched into Cairo. He quickly put his English to use as secretary to an English lady who ran a volunteer hospital for wounded officers. In 1883 he began his career as a clerk with the state railways. The choice was not unusual; a generation later in 1911, 48 percent of railway and telegraph officials were Copts.[27]

The British occupation precipitated a third attempt at Coptic communal reform. In May 1882, Butrus Ghali had been the first Copt to reach the rank of pasha, and now as undersecretary of justice, he again took up the cause of communal reform. He had attended Prince Fadil's school (his father worked on the prince's estates), Cyril IV's school in Harat al-Saqqain, and the School of Languages. At home in Turkish, Arabic, French, English, and Italian, Ghali made his career mediating between the state and the Copts, Khedive Abbas and British consuls general, and Egyptians and Europeans. He served in the cabinet continuously from 1893 until his assassination while prime minister in 1910. Along the way he amassed a personal fortune by buying land from royal estates at Inshas in Sharqiyya Province.[28]

The Association for the Furtherance of Christianity in Egypt, an Anglican enterprise, supported the Coptic laymen's call for communal reform in the early 1880s. Its backing was a questionable asset; a lead speaker at an early meeting railed against "the soul-destroying heresy of the Copts."[29] Cyril V was ex-officio president of the Communal Council, and his refusal to recognize the body prevented it from convening. In 1884 it was again disbanded. The weary cycle began again. In 1890, the Tawfiq Society (not named for the khedive) launched the fourth attempt at Coptic reform, the third led by laymen. Although only in his mid-twenties, Simaika won a seat on the Communal Council. When Cyril V again refused to recognize the council, Baring, Prime Minister

Mustafa Fahmi, and Butrus Ghali tried to bring him around by exiling him to a monastery in Wadi al-Natrun. This backfired, sweeping Fahmi from the prime ministry, and damaging British prestige. Fahmi's successor, Riyad, revoked the banishment, and Cyril V returned to a triumphant welcome in Cairo. There was also a flap over an Anglican clergyman, Rev. George Horner, who was doing research at the patriarchate on ancient manuscripts. Baring, Ghali, and Simaika had facilitated the arrangement, but a rumor spread that Horner was part of an Anglican plot to take over the Coptic Church. After his return from exile, the patriarch hand-picked four of his partisans for an advisory committee to replace the Communal Council, and "no one dared speak of Reform."[30] The patriarch did reopen the Clerical College, but with a weak and docile staff.

The aborted reform of the early 1890s had parallels at al-Azhar, where Abbas II, after initially flirting with reform, installed a conservative shaykh al-Azhar. Muhammad Abduh despaired of reforming the institution and, after years of futile wrangling, resigned from the Azhar's council. The state's drawn-out struggle to wrest control of Muslim *awqaf* from the *ulama* also resembled the Communal Council's contest with the patriarch over the control of Coptic *awaqf*.[31]

Slowly Coptic reformers regrouped for a fifth try. In 1895 they acquired a newspaper to counter Mikhail Abd al-Sayyid's pro-patriarchal *Al-Watan*. Butrus Ghali encouraged Tadrus Shanuda al-Manqabadi, of the Tawfiq Society and the defunct Communal Council, to found *Misr*, which combined a reformist line with support for the British occupation. After 1900 the patriarch himself and *Al-Watan* also came around to supporting the occupation.[32]

REVALUING THE COPTIC PAST: EUROPEAN PERSPECTIVES

Coptic never had to wait for decipherment by a Champollion, for, alongside Arabic, it had survived as the scriptural and liturgical language of the Coptic Church. Serious study of Coptic in western Europe had begun in the seventeenth century on manuscripts travelers brought back. The Vatican promoted this for missionary purposes and sponsored Franciscan and other missionary work among the Copts. Athanasius Kircher (1602–1680), a German Jesuit long resident in Rome, carried out intensive studies on both hieroglyphics and Coptic. His work in hieroglyphics was barren (he believed it was a purely symbolic system of writing), but his work on Coptic became the foundation for all later European studies.[33]

Coptic studies in Europe thus grew out of biblical and patristic studies and their offshoot, Orientalism. Since Champollion, Egyptologists have also used Coptic as a gateway to hieroglyphics. Jomard discussed Copts briefly in the *Description de l'Égypte,* and E. W. Lane treated them in an appendix of his *Modern Egyptians.* In the 1830s, Robert Curzon and Henry Tattam (see table 5) spirited Coptic and other manuscripts they discovered at Egyptian monasteries away to Britain. As already noted, Mariette arrived in 1850 to buy Coptic and other manuscripts for the Louvre but went astray, discovered the Serapeum at Saqqara, and never looked back.[34]

Somers Clarke painted a bleak picture of the Antiquities Service with regard to Coptic archaeology before Maspero returned in 1899:

> The mental attitude of the Egyptologist towards any study of Egyptian Archaeology, excepting along his own lines, was at that time, as unscientific as it was discouraging. The Director-General of Antiquities could speak only with disdain of "the wretched Copts." He was guilty of cruel and absolutely needless barbarities at Medinat Habu. One of the courts of this ponderous and impressive building had, at a remote period, been turned into a church. Monolithic columns had been erected and an apse constructed for the reception of the altar. . . . this page of history did not please the gentleman who was director-general at that time, so out the evidences must come. At no little trouble and cost the monoliths were dragged away. . . . And not only so, but no plans, drawings, or notes were published. We must now, to find out how the Christian community had tried to rearrange the court to suit its own uses, refer to a plan in the *Description de l'Egypte.*[35]

Several photographs of the Coptic remains before the clearance also survive (see figure 42).

Coptic studies were gathering steam in other European circles by the 1880s and 1890s. E. Amélineau, Oskar von Lemm, and Walter Crum worked mostly on language and literature, and Georg Steindorff published an important Coptic grammar in 1894. Coptic art and architecture began to receive attention in 1880, when Oxford classicist Alfred J. Butler arrived in Egypt to tutor the sons of Khedive Tawfiq. Coptic churches captivated him. In 1884 he published *Ancient Churches of Egypt.* "Day by day," he wrote, Christian antiquities "are perishing, unknown to western travellers, and little regarded by the Copts themselves; and nothing, absolutely nothing, has been done or is doing since to rescue them from oblivion, or to save them from destruction."[36] In 1902 Butler published his classic *Arab Conquest of Egypt.*

TABLE 5
COPTIC SCHOLARS AND COMMUNAL LEADERS

European Scholars		Egyptian Scholars		Other Copts		Patriarchs (Terms in Office)	
H. Tattam	1788–1868						
R. Curzon	1810–1873						
S. Clarke	1841–1926			B. Ghali	1846–1910		
E. Amélineau	1850–1915						
A. Butler	1850–1936			Mikhail Sharubim	1853–1920	Cyril IV	1854–1861
G. Steindorff	1861–1951			Qalini Fahmi	1860–1954	Demetrius II	1862–1870
				Mikh. Abd al-Sayyid	1860–1914		
W. Crum	1865–1949	Simaika	1864–1944				
		C. Labib	1868–1918				
J. Clédat	1871–1943			Murqus Hanna	1872–1934	Cyril V	1874–1927
				Wisa Wasif	1873–1931		
J. Maspero	1885–1915						

Figure 42.   Remains of a Coptic church inside the temple of Rameses II at
Medinat Habu. In 1891 the director of the Antiquities Service, contemptuous
of "the wretched Copts," had the temple cleared of postpharaonic remains.
Original photograph by Francis Bedford, 1862. In *Excursions along the Nile:
The Photographic Discovery of Ancient Egypt* (Santa Barbara: Santa Barbara
Museum of Art, 1993), 109. Courtesy of the Santa Barbara Museum of Art.
Collection of Michael and Jane Wilson.

Coptic field archaeology began to receive attention after 1900. Somers
Clarke's retirement from general practice in architecture in England in
1902 freed him to settle in Egypt and pursue research full time. Maspero,
unlike Mariette, took an active interest in Coptic studies, and after his
return in 1900 began to make up for earlier neglect of Christian sites.
He set aside a room in the Egyptian Museum for Coptic antiquities,
which were later transferred to the Coptic Museum.[37] His son Jean, who
would die at thirty on the western front, became a Byzantinist and catalogued Greek papyri in the Cairo Museum. Jean Clédat's (1871–1943)
pre–World War I excavations—variously sponsored by IFAO, the Antiquities Service, the Comité, and the Suez Canal Company—included
such Coptic sites as Bawit, Deir Abu Hennis, Saint Simeon's Monastery
at Aswan, Asyut, Akhmim, and the monasteries at Sohag.[38] Butler,
Clarke, Khedivial Library director Moritz, and Max Herz founded the

Society of the History of Coptic Antiquity in Egypt in 1903, but it does not seem to have endured.[39]

REVALUING THE COPTIC PAST:
SIMAIKA AND THE COMITÉ

The Egyptian who would answer Butler's call to save ancient churches was already developing the interests and skills for the task. As a boy Simaika loved visiting the Egyptian Museum, the Giza pyramids, Saqqara, and Cairo's mosques and churches. The dust of the British invasion had hardly settled before he was showing his new employer, the Viscountess Strangford, the sights. He freely admitted learning about the antiquities of his own country from Murray's *Handbook of Egypt* and Baedeker. "Although painful to my patriotic feelings," he wrote, "I must confess that we are indebted to Europeans and especially to the French, for the discovery, the scientific study and the restoration of these monuments."[40]

An elder brother of Simaika assisted Butler's research for *Ancient Churches,* and in 1890 Marcus visited the English scholar at Oxford.[41] Butler introduced him to Somers Clarke, an architect who restored English cathedrals. Clarke first took up Egyptology and Coptic architecture as hobbies, then carried on his research from an isolated retirement home he built near El Kab. In 1912 he published *Christian Antiquities in the Nile Valley.*[42]

Simaika warned Clarke that well-intentioned Coptic notables were replacing ancient churches with buildings in "modern Greek style" decked out in Italian marble. Neither the patriarch nor the leading layman, Butrus Ghali, had any objections. Clarke fired off a protest to the *Times,* and the spring of 1891 found Simaika conducting Baring around the churches of Cairo and urging him to entrust them to the care of the Comité.[43] Years later, Simaika expressed gratitude for *Ancient Churches of Egypt* by dedicating his guide to the Coptic Museum to Butler's memory. It was Butler's book, declared Simaika, that had inspired him to advocate putting the Comité in charge of Coptic monuments and founding the museum.[44]

As seen in chapter 6, Khedive Tawfiq had founded the Comité in 1881 in response to lobbying by European enthusiasts of "Arab" art. In 1894 the Comité first proposed to assume responsibility for preserving historic Coptic churches and monasteries. Cyril V feared encroachment on his prerogatives, but two years later the Comité offered to spend

£E2,000 repairing Coptic monuments if the church would contribute as
well, and he reluctantly gave way. Minister of Public Works Husayn
Fakhri joined the dominant Europeans and the two Armenians (Tigrane
and Yaqub Artin) on the Comité in passing a resolution to add two
Copts to their number. An all-Muslim opposition faction voted no, saying that one was enough. A European's proposal to change the name to
the Comité de conservation des monuments des arts arabes et coptes,
however, was voted down.[45]

Simaika reported that Cyril V "blamed" the new arrangement on
him and that the patriarch's "only consolation" was keeping him off the
Comité. Simaika blasted one of the Coptic appointees, Nakhla al-Barati,
for demolishing a tower of the Roman fortress of Babylon to make a
grander entrance to the Muallaqa Church and for jumbling screens and
icons of various eras together in refurbishing the Church of Saint George.
Beginning in 1879, al-Barati spent £E6,000 of his own money refurbishing al-Muallaqa, but British archaeologists were appalled to learn
of the loss of the Roman tower and persuaded Cromer to intervene to
save a second one.[46] In 1898 Cromer wrote Stanley Lane-Poole:

> I am wrestling with the Coptic Patriarch and endeavouring to get some proper
> European control established over the Coptic churches. I mean from a purely
> archaeological point of view. . . .
>   I greatly regret that my attention was not called earlier to Kasr-es-
> Shammah.
>   Directly I saw Mr. Somers Church's [sic] letter [in the *Egyptian Gazette*],
> I visited the place.
>   A good deal of harm has been done, and with all the best intentions. I
> was, fortunately in time to save another Roman tower which was threat-
> ened.
>   The Coptic remains are quite as interesting as the Roman. In some form
> or another, I must get these put under Herz, whom I consider most capable.[47]

Meanwhile Simaika gradually came to realize that he faced a stark
choice. He could keep pushing for communal reform or he could ease
off, repair his damaged relationship with Cyril, and try to win his backing for a seat on the Comité and for a Coptic museum. Back in 1893,
Simaika had been one of only two Communal Council hard-liners who
refused to sign Butrus Ghali's petition to recall the patriarch from desert
exile.[48] Now he changed his mind, put reform on the back burner, and
began cultivating Cyril. In 1905 Simaika got his Comité seat and three
years later, his museum.

FROM ARMENIANS TO COPTS

During the years of British rule between 1882 and 1922, the representation of Christian minorities in the top Egyptian political elite passed from Armenians to Copts, a process mirrored in the Comité. Armenians and Copts both mediated between Europeans and Muslim Egyptians at times, but the circumstances of the two Christian communities in Egypt were fundamentally different. Many of the small Armenian community were shallowly rooted nineteenth-century arrivals, dependent on khedivial or foreign protection and uninvolved in Egyptian nationalism. The Copts, in contrast, claimed to be the most deeply rooted Egyptians of all, spoke Arabic as their native tongue, and ultimately rejected collaboration with the British in favor of national solidarity with Muslims in the struggle for independence.

In the 1890s, the Armenians who tilted the balance on the Comité in favor of the Europeans were Prime Minister Nubar's son-in-law Tigrane, the foreign minister from 1891 to 1894, and Yaqub Artin. But in cabinet affairs, Cromer complained of Tigrane's ineffectual resistance to British rule, attributing it to a "Franco-Byzantine" mind: "He would have reveled in the subtleties submitted to the decision of the Council of Nice, but he would probably never have come to any definite conclusion as to whether Arius or Athanasius was in the right."[49]

Yaqub Artin (1842–1919) has already appeared in several contexts in this book. His half a lifetime on the Comité was far more important than Tigrane's desultory stint. Artin was the grandson of an immigrant from Sivas (Asia Minor) who entered Muhammad Ali's service about 1808 and the son of Artin Bey Chrakian, interpreter and effective minister of foreign affairs in the 1840s. Yaqub Artin was also the nephew of Joseph Hekekyan. Raised a Catholic and educated in France, Artin registered in Egypt as a French subject and did not learn Turkish and Arabic until he was twenty. Classifying him as an Egyptian—the qualified choice of this book—is thus problematic. As with Nubar and Tigrane, Artin's facility in French and willingness to work with Europeans gave him ready access to the top. He tutored Ismail's sons and briefly worked as his private secretary. Already in 1878, however, he was serving European interests on the Commission of Inquiry into the Debt.

After the British conquest, Artin headed the commission that settled European damage claims from the Urabi revolution. From 1884 to 1888 he was undersecretary of education but then clashed with Minister of

Education Ali Mubarak. Artin took refuge in the Railways Administration, where British influence was strong, until Mubarak's fall in 1891
enabled him to return as undersecretary of education. Artin lived in a
mansion midway between Ezbekiyeh and the railroad station, with
Tigrane and Nubar as immediate neighbors.[50]

The energetic Artin crops up everywhere in Cairo's Western-inspired
cultural institutions. He presided over the Institut égyptien for nearly
twenty years and was active in the Geographical Society and the Society of Political Economy, Statistics, and Legislation. He sat on the board
of the Egyptian University. He opened his ten-thousand-volume library
to visiting Orientalists and amassed a valuable collection of art, which
went to the Museum of Arab Art after his death.

Fittingly, Artin joined the Comité in November 1882 on the heels of
the British conquest, and his first move was to force open the inner
sancta of Islam in the name of art or science. He complained that "certain members" (i.e., Christians) of the Comité sometimes had difficulty
entering mosques. In response, the Comité furnished its members bronze
identity tokens good for entry into any mosque.[51]

Artin outlived the peak of Armenian influence in Egypt and on the
Comité. Tigrane retired as foreign minister in 1894, and Nubar's fall
from his third prime ministry in 1895 ended Armenian participation in
the cabinet. Artin retired as undersecretary of education in 1906 rather
than serve under the assertive incoming minister, Sa'd Zaghlul. He stayed
active in the Comité, the Egyptian University, and the Institut égyptien
almost until his death in January 1919, two months before Zaghlul's arrest triggered the national uprising that ushered in a new era that left
little political space for Armenians.

It was Copts who stepped into the political room at the top that the
Armenians vacated. In 1893 Butrus Ghali became the first Copt to reach
the cabinet, just two years before Nubar left the cabinet for the last time.
Ghali provided Coptic representation in the cabinet continuously from
1893 until his assassination in 1910. In serving as minister of foreign
affairs and prime minister, he was following the precedent of Armenians. He also tried the finance portfolio, which had even gone to a Briton
in Nubar's first ministry. Butrus Ghali worked closely with the British
and paid for it with his life at the hands of a nationalist assassin. By that
time, the de facto principle of Christian representation in the cabinet had
emerged. The wisest Coptic leaders absorbed the shock of Ghali's killing
and eventually led most of the community into solidarity with Muslims
in the national drive for independence.

The Armenian-to-Copt transition on the Comité began in the 1890s but was more drawn out than in the cabinet because of Artin's longevity. Two Copts inaugurated Coptic representation on the Comité in 1896. The placing of Coptic monuments under the surveillance of the Comité in 1896 can be read as an extension of Western imperial reach, but it was also a step toward national unity and away from segregation by religious community.

It was difficult to persuade Patriarch Cyril V that Comité surveillance of historic churches need not dilute his power, and he was reluctant to earmark funds for Comité operations. By 1906 the church had contributed only £E500 to Comité work, compared with a total since 1881 of £E166,000 from the Awqaf Department and £E39,000 from several ministries.[52] Simaika's joining the Comité in 1906 signaled a turn toward Coptic activism in historic preservation. Two years later he persuaded the patriarch to found the Coptic Museum, and in the 1920s Simaika emerged as one of the most powerful voices on the Comité.

FOUNDING THE COPTIC MUSEUM

Cyril V apparently went along with the Coptic Museum in return for Simaika's help in containing vociferous reformers on the Communal Council. Without the patriarch's consent there would have been no museum, for both its premises and much of the collection were church property. The museum filled a gap in historical coverage between the Egyptian Museum and the Greco-Roman Museum on the one hand and the Museum of Arab Art on the other. All but the Coptic Museum were under state control (although the municipality of Alexandria played a unique role in sponsoring the Greco-Roman Museum) and primarily products of European initiative. The Coptic Museum belonged to the church, and although Simaika freely admitted European inspiration, its founder was Egyptian.

The antiquities in the Coptic Museum overlapped chronologically with those in the Greco-Roman Museum and the Museum of Arab Art, defining an aspect of Egyptian history more than a precise era. Exclusive focus on state sovereignty can even define a Coptic period out of existence, for Egypt passed directly from Roman (Byzantine) to Islamic rule. Egypt never had a Coptic state, and there are no Coptic coins. Displaying early Coptic antiquities in the Greco-Roman Museum would have obscured the conventional break between classical Rome and what is now called Late Antiquity. A Byzantine Museum was out of the question for a church and country that had articulated their identities in resistance to Constantinople and Greek Orthodoxy. Displaying post-640 Coptic antiquities in the Museum of Arab Art, whether dispersed throughout the collection or set apart in a Coptic section, would also have been problematic. Despite its chronological overlap with other museums and the difficulty of defining a "Coptic period," the Coptic Museum filled an essential gap at a time when modern Egyptians were struggling to define their modern national identity.

It was Max Herz who first broached the idea of a Coptic museum to the Comité in 1897. He suggested that, with the patriarch's permission, carved stone capitals and other neglected relics be collected from churches as the nucleus for a museum: "Arab Art has its museum; Coptic art is still waiting its own."[53] The patriarch was outwardly amenable at first, and Comité member Nakhla al-Barati was proposed to oversee the storing of objects Herz sent his way in an annex beside the Muallaqa Church.[54] The extent to which these arrangements were carried out before Simaika took over is unclear; Simaika seems not to have credited Herz or al-Barati with any role in promoting the idea of a Coptic museum.

The Coptic Museum came into being at about the same time as the Byzantine Museum in Athens, which was founded in 1914. The classical heritage so beloved of Westerners had already been enshrined in Athens' National Archeological Museum for eighty years before the Byzantine Museum belatedly conferred official recognition on an era and heritage with which most modern Greeks could readily identify.[55] In Egypt, as in Greece, museum initiatives—in which Westerners played key parts—celebrated the distant past well before focusing on more recent Christian (and in Egypt's case, Muslim) heritage.

The Coptic Museum could not have had a more historic setting. It was next to the Muallaqa Church in the old Roman fortress of Babylon at "Old Cairo" (al-Fustat; see map 2). The Church of Saint Sergius (the legendary site where the Holy Family had stayed) and other historic churches stood nearby. The museum would be much enlarged and given its fine Fatimid-style facade, replete with Christian symbols, during the interwar period. King Faruq reopened it in 1946. A bust of Marcus Simaika stands in the courtyard (see figures 43 and 44).

Armed at last with the patriarch's blessing in 1908, Simaika scoured churches and monasteries "from Rosetta to Khartoum,"[56] paying the Coptic Church a nominal price for objects he selected. The church itself put up no funds for the museum. Lay notables, an occasional clergymen,

Figure 43. The Coptic Museum. The facade, inaugurated by King Faruq in
1947, connects the new wing, on the left, to the old wing, on the right. The
cross and other features mark this as a Christian building, but the style is
neo-Fatimid. Photograph by Donald Reid.

future sultan Husayn Kamil, cabinet ministers and British advisers, and
Simaika's colleagues on the Legislative Council all contributed. The state
chipped in an annual subsidy of £E200, which was raised to £E300 in
1918, to £E1,000 in 1925, and to £E1,500 in 1930.[57]

The modest museum gradually became a locus of Coptic pride and
a ceremonial site where Egypt's Muslim rulers displayed solicitude for
their Christian subjects. In 1910, ex-president Theodore Roosevelt gave
a speech at the Egyptian University in which he denounced the assassin
of Butrus Ghali, berated the nationalists, and extolled British rule in
Egypt. Coptic notables thanked him by inviting him to the museum.
Qalini Fahmi suggested presenting the most precious manuscript to Roosevelt as a gift, but Simaika vetoed the suggestion.

The fledgling museum did not cross the horizon of the Western travel
industry until after World War I. Neither Baedeker's *Egypt and the
Sudan* of 1914 nor Macmillan's *Guide to Egypt and the Sudan* of 1916
mentioned it. Sultan (later King) Fuad's visit in 1920 helped bring the

Figure 44.   Marcus Simaika, founder of the Coptic
Museum. Photograph courtesy of Jason Thompson.

museum to public notice. Three years later he escorted King Victor Emmanuel III and his queen on a visit to it.[58]

COPTS BETWEEN *MILLET* AND THE NATION

Coptic communal reform and the founding of the Coptic Museum usually pass unmentioned in histories of Egypt's unsettled politics in the decade before World War I. The Copts were going through their fourth
wave of lay-led attempted reform. Mismanagement of educational and
waqf affairs by the patriarch's four-man advisory committee had become so blatant by 1905 that *Al-Watan* and *Misr* joined together in de-
manding reinstitution of the Communal Council. Cyril V gave way, and
Simaika was elected to the resulting council. But his views had moder-
ated. He now put much of the blame for the 1892–1893 clash with the
patriarch on the Communal Council in which he himself had been one
of the militants: "Unfortunately, instead of showing some consideration
for the wishes of the Patriarch by avoiding the controverted points and
devoting ourselves to other much-needed reforms, we pursued a rather
violent policy. A serious struggle ensued between the Council, supported
by the mass of the people, and the Patriarch, who had on his side the
bishops, most of the clergy and a certain section of the Community."[59]

"Occasionally the Patriarch can," remarked a British writer, "by the gentle and tactful persuasion of such a man as Marcus Simaika Pasha, be wooed a little into the way of reform."[60] In the unpublished memoirs Simaika penned long afterwards, he vented his frustration with Cyril V. The patriarch had tolerated rampant clerical corruption, siphoned off church funds to his relatives, tried alchemy to obtain gold to build new churches, and forced Simaika to dig for buried treasure under the altar of an Old Cairo church.[61]

Cromer retired in 1907. A year later Butrus Ghali replaced Mustafa Fahmi as prime minister, a first for a Copt. Ghali's nationalist detractors blamed him for signing the Anglo-Egyptian condominium agreement on Sudan in 1899, chairing the Dinshaway tribunal, which sent peasants to prison and to their deaths in 1906, implementing a repressive press law, and trying to extend the franchise of the Suez Canal Company. Ghali's accommodation to the British was hardly unique among Muslim or Coptic notables of the day. Among the Copts, *Misr, Al-Watan,* and Asyut landowner Akhnukh Fanus openly defended the occupation, and Cyril V hung portraits of Edward VII and George V in his reception hall.[62] Fanus, a Protestant and graduate of the Syrian Protestant College in Beirut, founded the Coptic Reform Society and then the Party of Independent Egyptians, which lobbied the British and the government for concessions to the Copts.

Other Coptic leaders made wiser choices. Wisa Wasif and Murqus Hanna joined Mustafa Kamil's Watani Party, which demanded immediate independence. Fakhri Abd al-Nur and Sinut Hanna chose Lutfi al-Sayyid's Umma Party, whose big landlords and intellectuals emphasized social reform and gradual progress toward independence. Both Lutfi al-Sayyid and Kamil insisted that Muslims and Copts formed one Egyptian nation. After Kamil died prematurely in 1908, Watanist-Coptic relations deteriorated, and it was a Watanist who shot down Prime Minister Ghali in 1910. The Coptic congress that Fanus and others then convened in Asyut heightened tensions and provoked a Muslim countercongress.[63]

Simaika maneuvered politically among the British, the patriarch, and Communal Council lay reformers. He worked tirelessly to bring Cromer, the Comité, and the patriarch together on the historic preservation of Coptic monuments. Scarcely a Briton who visited Egypt and wrote on the Copts in the early twentieth century failed to acknowledge Simaika's assistance. He claimed to have persuaded Cromer to subsidize state-inspected Coptic schools and to have persuaded education adviser Douglas Dunlop to replace one of Cyril V's favorites as head of the Clerical College with a French-educated reformer.[64]

Moving from communal to national politics, Simaika was appointed to the Legislative Council (1906–1913) and Legislative Assembly (1914). He seems to have been loosely associated with Lutfi al-Sayyid's Umma Party.[65] The other Copts in the assembly were Qalini Fahmi and future Wafdists Sinut Hanna and Kamil Sidqi. About this time Simaika became a pasha.[66]

Copts felt the need to close ranks after Ghali's assassination, and in 1912 Lord Kitchener worked through Qalini Fahmi to arrange a compromise whereby four appointed clerics would sit with eight elected laymen on the Communal Council. World War I and then the 1919 revolution postponed further attempts at Coptic communal reform.[67]

This chapter's tale of forty years of intermittent conflict between Cyril V and lay reformers on the Communal Council should not obscure the great strides Copts had made in education, wealth, and national politics by 1914. Partisan motivations at a time of high tensions between Copts and Muslims make most statistics on these changes suspect. Perhaps Al-Hilal was not far from the mark in 1911 when it calculated, on the basis of the census and tax returns of 1907, that the Copts constituted 7 percent of the population but owned 16 percent of the buildings and cultivated land and 25 percent of the national wealth.[68]

CHILDREN OF THE COPTIC CHURCH
OR OF THE PHARAOHS?

Copts in search of a golden age to anchor their modern identity could look either to their spiritual leaders of Roman-Byzantine times—an era of persecution, however—or to ancient Egypt. In nineteenth-century Greece, the clergy and common people identified more readily with Orthodox and Byzantine memories than with the distant classical past, while lay intellectuals and merchants often joined western and northern Europeans in revering ancient Greece. Among Copts too, a church-centered vision was more congenial to the clergy and common folk, while laymen influenced by Western ideas often felt the allure of the pharaohs.

One contrast with modern Greece was that Byzantine enthusiasts can evoke the power and glory of Constantine the Great, Theodosius the Great, Justinian, and Basil the Bulgar-Slayer, but the anti-Byzantine

Copts never ruled Egypt and had only martyrs or ascetics like Saint Antony and Saint Pachomius to celebrate. The Coptic calendar dates not from the birth of Christ or Saint Mark's mission to Egypt but from the "the era of the martyrs" under Diocletian. Pharaonic history, in contrast, offers all the ancestral power and glory one could wish for.

Whether emphasizing the pharaonic or—as with Simaika and the Coptic Archeological Society, which Mirrit Butrus Ghali founded in the 1930s—the Christian era, it was laymen who led the movement for historic preservation and the museum. The patriarch and clergy derived their legitimacy from apostolic succession from Saint Mark and from reputations for piety and asceticism. They lagged behind the laity in benefiting from educational reform and in revaluing ancient objects as antiquities. "I wish I could say," a Briton wrote six years after the founding of the Coptic Museum, "that the Patriarch himself had anything like a proper appreciation of the treasures still left to his sadly depleted church."[69]

Tadrus Shanuda al-Manqabadi (1857–1932) was a layman of Simaika's generation who took a deep interest in the Coptic past. Doubly benefiting from the American missionaries' challenge to the Coptic Church, he first briefly attended a new American primary school in Asyut, then transferred to a school that Patriarch Demetrius planted there to counter the Protestants. The Coptic school foundered with the patriarch's death, and thirteen-year-old Tadrus briefly assisted his merchant father, then took up various government posts in Asyut Province. He pursued commercial and land reclamation ventures on the side, helped found Asyut's Coptic Benevolent Society, and in 1892 was elected to the Coptic Communal Council as a reformer. In 1895 he founded the newspaper *Misr* as a platform for lay reformers. He founded the Society for the Preservation of Coptic History in 1883 or 1884 in Asyut and translated E. L. Butcher's *History of the Church in Egypt* into Arabic.[70]

Interest in the Coptic and pharaonic pasts was often complementary, not mutually exclusive. Both were easily compatible with territorial Egyptian patriotism. A knowledge of Coptic set one up not only for Coptic studies but also for learning ancient Egyptian. Simaika saw no great divide between the religion of ancient Egypt and Coptic Christianity: "The Egyptians were among the first nations to adopt Christianity, which offered great similarities to their old religion. The Redeemer Christ recalled the old legend of the good and generous Osiris who had also died as a victim of evil, and who rose again to enter Eternal Life. The Holy Trinity, the judgement of the dead, are similarly familiar to ancient Egyptian religious traditions." One step more brought Copts and Muslims together as one nation. Most Egyptian Muslims descended from Copts, Simaika pointed out, and "all enlightened Muslims"—he cited Qasim Amin—now agreed. All Egyptians are Copts, as he later put it; some are Muslim Copts, and others, Christian Copts, but all are descendants of the ancient Egyptians.[71]

"Copts, Gypts, Egyptians," in Lane-Poole's words,

> they are indeed the true survivors of the people whom Pharaoh ruled, and who built the pyramids of Giza. And not only in person but in language the Copts are a remnant of ancient Egypt. . . . the sacred speech of their religion is still partly understood by the priests, and retains its place of honour before the Arabic translation in the services of the church. . . . A people of the race of the Pharaohs, speaking the very words of Rameses, writing them with the letters of Cadmus, and embalming them in the sentences thus written a creed and liturgy which twelve centuries of persecution have not been able to wrest from them or alter a jot, are indeed worthy of more than a passing attention.[72]

Lane-Poole's ensuing remark on the modern Copts' "vices of servitude," however, echoed those of his uncle E. W. Lane and undercut the positive side of his message.

In the spring of 1882, as the Urabi-British showdown swept toward its climax, the minister of public works acknowledged the rediscovered Coptic affinity for ancient Egypt. He proposed adding ten students to the five attending Ahmad Kamal's School of Egyptology at the museum. Four of the ten additions would be selected "from among the notables of the Coptic sect, which is particularly interested in the hieroglyphic language because it was the language of their ancestors and they still retain a number of expressions which will facilitate their study."[73]

Endorsement of their pharaonic lineage by authorities such as Maspero, Petrie, and Assyriologist Sayce made Copts swell with pride. In 1908 Maspero assured the Rameses Club, a Coptic group with an appropriately pharaonic name, that Copts were the purest descendants of the ancient Egyptians. Egyptian Muslims, he said, were mainly descended from the same stock but, because of intermarriage with outsiders, lacked the racial purity of the Copts. Sayce and Petrie carried this racist message to dangerous extremes.[74] Petrie wrote: "A Coptic village is clean and well swept, the women sitting at work in the doorways and chatting across the street. It is on the level of a civilised Mediterranean land, and not like the filthy confusion of a Mohammedan village. . . . Egypt will never be a civilised land til it is ruled by the Copts—if ever."[75]

Malaka Sa'd, the Coptic editor of the women's magazine *Al-Jins al-Latif,* also tread on dangerous ground in 1908, writing that "Egyptian women used to study science, speak from pulpits, and govern the empire when women in other countries were still in a state of slavery and misery."[76] Female freedom had continued with the coming of Christianity, she said, but declined after the Arab conquest and the imposition of seclusion and the veil.

The titles Copts chose for their journals underline their growing attraction to ancient Egypt. The Syrian Christian Taqlas had preempted "The Pyramids" (*Al-Ahram,* 1876), but the titles of the Coptic journals *Al-Watan* (The homeland, or fatherland, 1877) and *Misr* (Egypt) evoked territorial patriotism consistent with pride in ancient Egypt while also appealing to non-Coptic audiences. Other Coptic journals chose explicitly pharaonic titles: *Ramsis* (1893), *Firawn* (Pharaoh, 1900), *Ayn Shams* (Arabic for "Heliopolis," 1900), *Al-Athar al-Misriyya* (Egyptian antiquities, 1909), and a second *Ramsis* (1911).[77]

Like al-Tahtawi eighty years before, Coptic writer Salama Musa discovered ancient Egypt only by leaving for Europe. He was so embarrassed there by questions on ancient Egypt he could not answer that upon returning home he signed on for a Cook's tour of Upper Egypt. Family lore has it that Wafdist politician Makram Ubayd got interested in Egyptology while studying in France.[78] Discovering one's homeland by leaving it is a common phenomenon in modern nationalism.

Like some Western scholars, Claudius Labib (1868–1918) combined Egyptology and Coptology. Four years younger than Simaika, he too studied Coptic at the Patriarchal School. Then he learned hieroglyphics while working in the Antiquities Service. In 1892, he left to teach Coptic at the Clerical College. He also ran the patriarchal press, printing Coptic and Arabic devotional books. He began compiling a Coptic dictionary, and in 1900 founded a Coptic-Arabic magazine, *Ayn Shams.* This was the Arabic name for the Heliopolis of the Greeks and the On of the pharaohs. Copts began giving their children pharaonic names, but Labib even insisted that his six children speak Coptic—a language as dead as Latin—at home.[79]

Mikhail Sharubim's neglected *Al-Kafi fi tarikh Misr al-qadim wa al-hadith* (Basic history of ancient and modern Egypt, 4 vols., Cairo, 1898–1900) reflects another Copt's deep interest not only in the pharaonic and Byzantine-Coptic eras, but also in the entire sweep of the national past.[80] Sharubim briefly traces Egyptians' descent from Noah through Ham and Ham's son Misrayim (cf. *Misr,* Arabic for "Egypt"), then jumps to Menes and Manetho's First Dynasty and moves steadily through the millennia to the reign of Khedive Tawfiq.

Although carefully including Copts in his discussions of Islamic and modern history, Sharubim wrote national, not sectarian, history. His framework for pre-Islamic history resembles al-Tahtawi's in *Anwar* and may have drawn from it. Both scholars followed modern Europeans in employing Manetho's dynastic framework for pharaonic history while occasionally mixing in material from medieval Arabic sources.

Both al-Tahtawi and Sharubim counted the Romans from Augustus to the accession of Theodosius as the Thirty-fourth Dynasty and from Theodosius to the Islamic conquest as the Thirty-fifth. Both chronicled Roman-Byzantine history before and after Theodosius in detail. Al-Tahtawi had said that Egypt went from the *jahiliyya* (the age of pagan ignorance) to Christianity under Theodosius, that its people were known as Copts, and that they abandoned hieroglyphics for the Greek alphabet.[81] His reign-by-reign Roman-Byzantine chronicle covered Saint Mark's bringing Christianity and founding the patriarchate of Alexandria, the pagans' persecution of early Christians, and the credal disputes that divided Greek Orthodox, Nestorian, and Jacobite (including Coptic) Christianity.

Al-Tahtawi rarely mentioned early church patriarchs by name. Sharubim began doing so for the second half of the second century, when they began to emerge from the mists of legend. Sharubim summarized Roman-Byzantine persecutions, particularly after the separation of the Coptic and Byzantine Orthodoxy at the Council of Chalcedon in 451. But his work was no ecclesiastical history. Roman-Byzantine emperors and then Muslim caliphs and sultans provided his chronological framework and central narrative. Egypt received its due, but he also sketched key events in the larger Byzantine and Islamic empires to which Egypt belonged. Sharubim thus accomplished, but from a Coptic point of view, al-Tahtawi's unachieved goal of writing a national history of Egypt from pharaonic times to the present. Sharubim not only assumed the continuity of an Egyptian national entity since ancient times but also placed the Copts firmly in that history down through the centuries.

By 1914, Simaika's still modest Coptic Museum and the Coptic churches the Comité had repaired were outward symbols of Coptic views on the past and present that differed from those of half a century earlier. Copts were better educated, wealthier, and more in touch with the outside world than ever before. The continuing tensions between the reformist communal councils and the clerical hierarchy reflected both

the determination of well-informed and prosperous laymen and the re-
siliency of the clergy. The transition from a tolerated minority to theoretically equal citizens of an Egyptian nation was well under way. After
the assassination of Butrus Ghali, thoughtful Copts and Muslims assidu-
ously sought a viable path for intercommunal cooperation. Simaika's museum was reminding his coreligionists of their nearly nineteen-century
legacy as Christians, while Claudius Labib perhaps came closest to being
the Copts' Ahmad Kamal by pointing them toward Egyptology. Copts
discovered a special pride in their pharaonic legacy, but they had to be
careful of the temptation to argue that this entitled them to superiority
over Muslims.

Conclusion

In the journey from 1798 to 1914, *Whose Pharaohs?* has interwoven
the history of Egyptian archaeology as usually written in the West with
that of modern Egyptians' involvement in the subject. It has set the history of archaeology and museums in the broader contexts of Western
imperial and Egyptian national history and brought together the often
disparate histories of four archaeological disciplines. This book has wres-
tled with the tension between ideological commitment to imperialism
and nationalism on the one hand and ideals of universal, objective
knowledge on the other. Taking into account both scholarly and popular interest in antiquities in both Egypt and the West, this work of synthesis has shown how archaeology affected the ongoing construction of
Egyptian national identity.

In the West, Egyptological and popular fascination with the pharaonic
era overshadowed interest in other periods. Baedeker's coverage of
Egypt's museums in 1914 suggests the relative importance of different
eras in the eyes of the travel industry. The Egyptian Museum receives
twenty-four densely printed pages and a fold-out floor plan. The Greco-
Roman Museum gets four pages, and "the Arabian Museum" two and
a half. The fledgling Coptic Museum had not yet crossed Baedeker's
horizon, although Coptic objects in one room of the Egyptian Museum
merit a few lines. In 1929, the next—and last—edition of the classic
Egyptian Baedekers added one page on the Coptic Museum. Otherwise,

the proportional coverage remained unchanged—and lopsidedly in favor of ancient Egypt.

The distance Western Egyptology traveled between 1798 and 1914 was immense. In Bonaparte's day, scholars dependent on classical sources, the Bible, and observation of half-buried ruins could make out only confused shadows of ancient Egypt. By the time Maspero and Ahmad Kamal retired in 1914, scholars had long been reading the words of ancient Egyptians themselves. Egyptologists had copied and studied thousands of inscriptions and filled the museums of Cairo and the West with rich collections of pharaonic relics. They had excavated extensively, with gradually improving techniques. Archaeology and philology together were steadily fleshing out Manetho's skeletal dynastic chronology. Predynastic and earlier prehistoric remains were belatedly being taken into account, and few Egyptologists still clung to the belief prevalent a century before that the earth and humanity were only six thousand years old.

The change in Egyptians' thinking on archaeology and history over this "long nineteenth century" is more difficult to sum up. Al-Jabarti and his Azhari colleagues of 1800, lacking the Greco-Roman accounts, had known even less of ancient Egypt than their European contemporaries. The Quranic image of the tyrannical and idolatrous pharaoh who oppressed Moses and the Israelites loomed large, although Arab-Islamic culture also had favorable images of ancient Egyptians.

A century later in 1914, Islamic and Arab traditional learning still overshadowed awareness of ancient Egypt for most educated Egyptians. "Pharaoh" and "pharaonic" remained words of abuse to many religious conservatives, as they do today. But al-Tahtawi, Ali Mubarak, Ahmad Kamal, and, among the Copts, Claudius Labib had developed alternative visions of ancient Egyptians as illustrious ancestors all the world might envy. For all the odds against him at the height of the Western imperial age, Kamal had established himself as an Egyptologist and had helped convince Ahmad Lutfi al-Sayyid and others that pride in ancient Egypt was essential for national revival.

During the first half of the nineteenth century, the West's fascination with the pharaohs expressed itself in the consul-collectors' scramble for museum trophies, Champollion's and Lepsius's scientific expeditions, Wilkinson's and Robert Hay's copying enterprises, and the beginnings of a tourist industry. In the second half of the century, the careers of Mariette and de Lesseps unfolded in tandem with accelerating Western penetration. The Suez Canal, the Egyptian Antiquities Service, the Egyptian

Museum, and the Institut égyptien were all in tune with France's expansive vision of itself under Napoleon III. Khedive Ismail, de Lesseps, Empress Eugénie, and Mariette starred at the opening of the Suez Canal, but Thomas Cook's first party of tourists to Egypt was also there—a harbinger of things to come. British imperialism and capitalism outmaneuvered the French in the Nile Valley. Ismail's bankruptcy and the Urabi revolution opened the door, and it was a British, not a French, expeditionary force that seized the opportunity to push in.

Fifty years earlier, on the banks of the Seine, Rifaa al-Tahtawi had begun rethinking Egypt's identity. Drawing on both his Islamic and his French education, he elaborated a political philosophy that combined Egyptian patriotism (with a significant ancient Egyptian component), loyalty to the Islamic *umma,* and dedication to the Muhammad Ali dynasty. Al-Tahtawi played a leading part in Muhammad Ali's initial effort to check the looting of Egyptian antiquities and thirty-three years later published the first substantial history of ancient Egypt in Arabic.

In the next generation, Ali Mubarak and Mahmud al-Falaki also had encyclopedic interests encompassing ancient as well as Islamic history. They too helped lay the educational foundations of modern Egypt. Like al-Tahtawi they had gone on to Paris to continue their studies; unlike him, they enjoyed technical and scientific, not religious and literary, educations. Mubarak and al-Falaki had most of their careers behind them by 1882 but survived the Urabi upheaval and returned to the cabinet early in the British occupation.

Taking over the reins of Egyptian archaeology from Mariette in January 1881, Maspero's diplomacy enabled the French to maintain their archaeological protectorate right through the era of Cromer and Kitchener. The facade of the Egyptian Museum of 1902 froze in stone an Orientalist and imperialist apogee. It honored French, British, and other European scholars, but modern Egyptians were nowhere to be seen. Inside the building, however, the first Egyptian Egyptologist, Ahmad Kamal, was quietly laboring away.

A year later and a mile inland toward Cairo's Fatimid core, the Museum of Arab Art and the Khedivial Library moved into their landmark neo-Mamluk building. Its architectural decor was in tune with the two collections inside—Islamic antiquities and a library with an impressive collection of Arabic, Turkish, and Persian manuscripts. Back in 1881, European Orientalists, working from a narrower base of Western interest than Egyptologists, had persuaded Khedive Tawfiq to establish the Comité to preserve selected Islamic monuments. The Museum of

Arab Art was a by-product of the Comité's work. In this case, the European impetus sprang not from identification with putative ancestors of Western civilization but from fascination with an exotic "Oriental other" against which Christendom and Europe had defined themselves. Architects Julius Franz, a German, and Max Herz, an Austro-Hungarian, successively led the Comité and the Museum of Arab Art, historicizing, framing, preserving, and sometimes reconstructing selected Islamic artifacts.

In 1892, a decade after the birth of the Comité, European residents of Alexandria took the initiative in the establishment of the Greco-Roman Museum. The European-dominated municipality of Alexandria financed the project, which came under the "scientific" supervision of the Egyptian Antiquities Service. Westerners of many nationalities supported the museum through its auxiliary Archeological Society of Alexandria, but under long-serving successive curators Botti, Breccia, and Adriani, it also functioned as an Italian cultural enclave.

Such were the institutional frameworks with which nationalists and aspiring Egyptian archaeologists had to come to grips. Three pioneers who came of age around 1882 spent most of their careers in the shadow of the British occupation—Ahmad Kamal in Egyptology, Ali Bahgat in Islamic archaeology, and Marcus Simaika in Coptic museology. They had benefited from the educational and cultural reforms of Muhammad Ali and Ismail, al-Tahtawi and Ali Mubarak, and—in Simaika's case—of Patriarch Cyril IV. As in the nineteenth-century West, these pioneers of the generation of 1882 coped with an explosive expansion of knowledge by abandoning their predecessors' encyclopedism in favor of specialization.

Few Egyptians passing the Egyptian Museum of 1902 on their daily routines could read the fine print of its imperial message. Ahmad Kamal and Ahmad Lufti al-Sayyid could, and they shared a vision different from that of their predecessors. They freely admitted debts to Champollion, Mariette, H. Brugsch, and Maspero, but they also dreamed of an independent Egypt proud of its pharaonic legacy and managing its own archaeology. They dreamed of a day when Egyptian and Western scholars might meet as equals in the Institut égyptien, the International Congress of Orientalists, and the Khedivial Geographical Society and when the Egyptian public would embrace the pharaonic as well as the Arab and Islamic heritage.

Ali Bahgat no doubt appreciated the neo-Islamic design of the Museum of Arab Art; at the time of his death in 1924 he was living in a "neo-Arab" villa. Europeans considered neo-Islamic architecture exotic in Europe and topical when they promoted it in Egypt, but Egyptians could embrace it as a renaissance reconnecting them to indigenous roots. Like Ahmad Kamal, Bahgat owed his vocation to European enthusiasts who were pioneering new (or reshaped) fields of knowledge. Yet, also like Kamal, Bahgat resented the way European domination of his country, its museums, and its archaeological heritage hemmed in his own career and made it hard for his compatriots to identify fully with their long national past.

After ten years under Herz at the Museum of Arab Art, an unexpected opportunity fell into Bahgat's lap. Bahgat was already attracting notice with the excavations he had begun at al-Fustat in 1912 on behalf of the Comité and museum. Herz, preoccupied with architectural matters, had been happy to leave al-Fustat to his Egyptian assistant. Two years later when the outbreak of World War I drove Herz from Egypt, Bahgat moved up to become the first Egyptian to direct the museum. Despite Mahmud al-Falaki's early excavations in classical Alexandria, Greco-Roman studies produced no pre–World War I Egyptian counterpart to Ahmad Kamal or Ali Bahgat. European appropriation of the Greco-Roman mantle made it difficult for Egyptians to identify with this era, although the Egypt-based Ptolemies were easier to assimilate to a nationalist agenda than the distant Rome and its provincial governors. As early as al-Tahtawi, Egyptians began experimenting with turning classical discourse to nationalist ends. After World War I, the redoubtable Arabic scholar and man of letters Taha Husayn would emerge as the great Egyptian champion of Greek and Latin classics.

In 1908, Marcus Simaika, acting under the authority of Patriarch Cyril V, established the fourth and last of the major antiquities museums in Misr al-Qadima (Old Cairo), three miles south of the Egyptian Museum. As a surviving scriptural and liturgical language, Coptic had never had to await a Champollion, but nineteenth-century European scholars did reinvigorate Coptic studies. Simaika readily admitted that A. J. Butler had inspired him to found the Coptic Museum.

After returning to the helm of the Antiquities Service in 1899, Maspero included Coptic studies and excavation in his program. Some Copts came to believe that they were the truest descendants of the pharaohs, giving their children pharaonic names and publishing magazines with titles evoking ancient Egypt. Copts would also enter Egyptology in proportionately larger numbers than their Muslim compatriots.

The Coptic Museum was unique in having an Egyptian founder-director and in belonging to a religious community rather than to the state. The founding became possible because of a tacit compromise in Coptic politics. Simaika would dampen down any lay-led anticlerical activism in the Communal Council, and Cyril V would bless the museum. After World War I, Copts would reaffirm their devotion to the Egyptian nation by joining Muslim compatriots in the struggle for independence. The argument that Coptic antiquities were the heritage of all Egyptians followed logically, and in 1931 King Fuad succeeded in bringing the Coptic Museum under state control.

Reviewing the archaeological ledger at the end of 1914, Egyptian nationalists would have seen little cause for cheer. The outbreak of World War I had unexpectedly cleared the way for Ali Bahgat to head the Museum of Arab Art and Lutfi al-Sayyid the National Library, but this was exceptional. Nationalist enthusiasm for the great strides the Antiquities Service, the Comité, the Institut égyptien, and museums had made in the preceding decades was necessarily qualified as long as they remained under foreign control. European opposition had recently doomed the third attempt to train Egyptian Egyptologists, and Kamal had had to retire without an Egyptian successor in sight.

World War I led the British to sever Egypt's vestigial Ottoman tie, declare a protectorate, and replace Abbas II with his docile uncle Husayn Kamil. Implementing martial law, the British suspended the Legislative Assembly, political parties, and outspoken newspapers. Muhammad Farid, Mustafa Kamil's successor as head of the National (Watani) Party, languished in exile like Abbas II. Economic controls, inflation, and conscription into labor battalions brought widespread hardship.

In Egypt as elsewhere, World War I dealt a harsh blow to the ideal of international cooperation in pursuit of objective knowledge. The British expelled Herz from the Museum of Arab art and the Comité, the German director from the national library, and the German archaeologist Borchardt from the Egyptology Committee.[1] Late in 1914, ninety-three scholars in Germany signed a manifesto defending their country's wartime deeds. French universities and learned societies shot back with charges of German war crimes in Belgium and France—damaging universities, historic monuments, libraries, and "the intellectual patrimony of Humanity."[2] The Institut égyptien added its endorsement to the French manifesto. In 1918–1919 the Institut again followed a French lead in resolving to purge its ranks of all citizens of Germany and its allies, boycott scholarly conventions involving Germans, and refuse to collaborate on any German publication.[3] In this poisoned atmosphere, Egyptians had plenty of company in finding it nearly impossible to reconcile the warring demands of patriotism and the ideal of objective knowledge.

Looking forward from World War I, imperial and national politics set the parameters within which archeology would operate, but archaeology also had its own internal rhythms. The 1919 revolution took the British by surprise, forced them to concede greater autonomy to the Egyptians, and ushered in a period of semicolonialism (or semi-independence) lasting down to Nasser's takeover in 1952. The struggle among British imperialists, nationalists of the Wafd Party, and would-be autocrats King Fuad and King Faruq wore all three parties down and opened the door to extraparliamentary challengers such as the Muslim Brotherhood, Communists, and Nasser's Free Officers.

The 1952 revolution swept away the monarchy, old parties, Parliament, and the power of the big landlords. Nasser negotiated an end to the British occupation in 1954 and consolidated it with his diplomatic triumph at the end of the 1956 Suez War. He made the Aswan High Dam the touchstone of his dream, turned to the Soviets for arms and aid, spoke of "Arab socialism," and launched a campaign to unite other Arab states under Egyptian leadership. Defeat by Israel in 1967 shattered his dream of leading Egypt to prosperous modernity.

The flamboyant Anwar al-Sadat and his phlegmatic successor Husni Mubarak, both military officers like Nasser, made major adjustments to the Nasserist system. Al-Sadat's seizure of the Israeli-occupied east bank of the Suez Canal in the 1973 war gave him the leverage to exchange Soviet for American patronage and to regain occupied Sinai by making peace with Israel. Economic *infitah* (opening) encouraged foreign and local investment, but privatization remained slow and cautious. Token opposition parties and newspapers gave Egypt a more democratic image without endangering the government party's hegemony. Al-Sadat initially encouraged Islamists as a counterweight to the Left but could not ride the tiger.

The coincidence of Tutankhamun's tomb coming to light the same year the British unilaterally declared Egypt independent, 1922, linked archaeology and politics as never before. Limited as this "independence" was, it enabled Egypt to keep the entire contents of Tutankhamun's tomb, pass far stricter controls on exporting antiquities, begin Egyptianizing the museums and Antiquities Service, emphasize pharaonic history in the schools, found a state university, and open programs to train Egyptian Egyptologists, classicists, and specialists in Islamic art history.

Yet imperialism proved tenacious in retreat. Within the new limits of their era, Lord Lloyd and Sir Miles Lampson (later Baron Killearn) were as autocratic as Cromer and Kitchener. É. Drioton in the Antiquities Service, K. A. C. Creswell in the Islamic section of the university's Institute of Archeology, G. Wiet in the Museum of Arab Art, and A. Adriani at the Greco-Roman Museum dominated key archaeological institutions for another generation. That they were outstanding scholars did little to mollify the nationalists.

Identification with ancient Egypt found its way into mainstream nationalism in media as varied as Mahmud Mukhtar's statue *The Awakening of Egypt,* Sa'd Zaghlul's mausoleum, Mahmud Said's mural in the parliament building, postage stamps, banknotes, Tawfiq al-Hakim's novel *The Return of the Spirit,* and even Naguib Mahfouz's first three novels.

Egypt won full independence and control of its antiquities and museums nearly simultaneously in the early 1950s. Wiet was pressured into leaving in the spring of 1951, and that December the last Wafdist government fired Creswell and other British employees of the Egyptian government. Six months later, the Free Officers' coup sent Drioton, a protégé of King Faruq's, home. Ninety-four years of French control of the Antiquities Service came to an end. Mustafa Amer stepped in as the first Egyptian to direct the service, while at the Museum of Islamic Art the appointment of Muhammad Mustafa put an Egyptian back at the helm for the first time since Bahgat's death in 1924.

In 1954, Egyptians felt proud that it was their own archaeologists who discovered a new step pyramid at Saqqara and a ceremonial boat at Khufu's Great Pyramid. The antiquities spotlight soon shifted to the Aswan High Dam's impending flooding of Nubia and its antiquities. In the ensuing UNESCO-sponsored salvage campaign, proudly independent Egypt admitted its critical need for foreign archaeological assistance. Egypt rewarded countries who heeded the call with the minor temples that now stand in several Western cities, traveling exhibits from the Cairo Museum, and permits to excavate elsewhere in Egypt. Inevitably, tensions between scholars from the developed West and their hard-pressed hosts in still-developing Egypt continued to flare up from time to time, but the cooperative spirit forged in Nubia persists to the present.

Today, the busts of Ahmad Kamal and several other Egyptian Egyptologists have joined the once exclusively European gallery of scholars that frame the Mariette monument in the garden of the Egyptian Museum (see figures 3 and 45). Streets in Cairo, albeit rather minor ones,

Figure 45.   Honor at last: bust of Ahmad
Kamal at the Mariette Monument, Egyptian
Museum. His bust and those of several
other Egyptian scholars were added to those
of Europeans some years after Egyptians
took over the Antiquities Service.
Photograph by Donald Reid.

bear the names of Ahmad Kamal and Ali Bahgat.[4] Egypt's banknotes
carefully balance a pharaonic monument on one side with an Islamic
one on the other. For a regime under attack by Islamists, and with most
Egyptians far more at home with Arab and Islamic than with ancient
Egyptian legacies, the pairing is a powerful official statement on national identity.

Al-Sadat encouraged Islamists as a counterweight to the Left, but it
was Islamist extremists who shot him down. His assassin shouted, "I
have killed Pharaoh!" Religiously framed discourse in any tradition is
far from monolithic, of course. A recent book's title proclaims that the
ancient Egyptians were the first monotheists and the first "people of the
Book" (monotheists with divinely revealed scriptures).[5] With so much

Figure 46.   The Pyramids and the Nile as symbols of Egypt: cover of the
magazine *Fatah al-Nil* (Young woman of the Nile), 1913. Sarah al-Mihiyya,
the editor, was a pious and rather conservative Muslim woman. From the
dust jacket of Beth Baron, *The Women's Awakening in Egypt: Culture,
Society, and the Press* (New Haven: Yale University Press, 1994). Courtesy of
Beth Baron.

at stake in the expressions like "pharaonic" and "people of the Book,"
the struggle over the role of the ancient legacy in Egypt's modern identity has no end in sight.

   In the West, serious Egyptology, popular Egyptomania, and New Age
mystical beliefs in pharaonic wisdom show no signs of abating. Given
the requisite political stability and security, the tourist industry, which has
given tens of thousands of Egyptians a practical stake in the national
past, will continue to boom. The crumbling monuments of Islamic Cairo
belatedly attracted increased national and international attention after the
1992 earthquake, but the resources available meet only a fraction of the
need. Coptic monuments and, in the wake of the Egyptian-Israeli peace
treaty, even a few Jewish ones are also receiving more attention. In Egypt
as elsewhere, business imperatives often clash with the priorities of archaeologists, preservationists, and historians.

   All this was in the future back in 1913, when Sarah al-Mihiyya
founded a short-lived women's magazine, *Fatah al-Nil* (Young woman
of the Nile). Far from being a product of a Western education or long
residence in Europe, she was a pious and conservative Muslim who opposed the unveiling of women. Yet she found it natural to include the

Pyramids—along with the Nile, the sun, a crescent moon, palm trees, and village houses—on the cover of her magazine (see figure 46). Islam and the Arabic heritage still touched most Egyptians far more deeply than ancient Egypt did, and the flowering of the "pharaonic" component of Egyptian nationalism was still a few years off, but the magazine cover was a straw in the wind. The Pyramids had joined the life-giving river for which al-Mihiyya named her magazine as an appropriate symbol of specifically Egyptian pride and patriotism.[6]

Appendix

Supplementary Tables

TABLE 6

EGYPTIAN GUIDEBOOK
EDITIONS, BY LANGUAGE

Dates	English	French	German	Other
1830s	1	1	0	0
1840s	3	1	1	0
1850s	4	1	1	0
1860s	4	8	0	1 Italian
1870–1882	5	2	3	0
1883–1889	2	0	2	0
1890–1899	19	4	3	0
1900–1914	31	15	9	1 Russian

SOURCE: Compiled from Oleg V. Volkoff, *Comment on visitait la vallée du Nil: Les Guides de l'Égypte* (Cairo, 1967), 103–19. His list is not exhaustive. Guides to a single city, region, or museum have not been counted.

TABLE 7

NATIONALITIES OF WESTERN AUTHORS
OF EGYPTIAN TRAVEL BOOKS

Dates	British	French	American	German	Austro-Hungarian	Italian	Russian	Other[a]
1790–1799	3	6	0	1	0	0	0	0
1800–1809	17	7	0	0	0	1	1	0
1810–1819	7	4	0	2	0	0	0	1
1820–1829	20	7	2	4	0	0	0	4
1830–1839	24	18	4	2	0	2	0	2
1840–1849	45	13	10	6	1	1	0	2
1850–1859	35	12	25	8	1	3	0	2
1860–1869	27	15	15	6	2	0	2	4
1870–1879	37	17	36	11	2	0	6	6
1880–1889	35	13	47	4	2	3	8	8
1890–1899	24	8	48	3	0	0	2	5
1900–1914	27	9	97	11	1	0	5	8

SOURCE: Compiled from Martin R. Kalfatovic, *Nile Notes of a Howadji: A Bibliography of Travelers' Tales from Egypt, from the Earliest Time to 1918* (Metuchen, N.J., 1992). Authors counted only once, on the date of publication of their first book. Items not published for more than fifty years after they were written are excluded.
[a] Author nationalities shown in the "Other" column break down as follows (hyphen indicates individual of dual nationality): 1810–1819 = Swiss-British; 1820–1829 = Danish, German-French, German-Austrian, Italian-British; 1830–1839 = Greek-British, Italian-British; 1840–1849 = Belgian, Swedish; 1850–1859 = British-French, U.S.-French; 1860–1869 = Danish, Swedish, British-German, Canadian; 1870–1879 = Swiss, U.S.-British, Spanish, Czechoslovakian, Argentinean, Ecuadorian; 1880–1889 = Austrian, Hungarian, Spanish, 3 Canadian, Chilean, Swedish, Australian; 1890–1899 = 2 U.S.-British, Swedish, Belgian, Uruguayan; 1900–1914 = Belgian, Danish, Portuguese, South African, New Zealander, Venezuelan, Argentinean, Guatemalan, Colombian.

TABLE 8

FOREIGN RESIDENTS OF EGYPT (AND PROTÉGÉS), BY NATIONALITY (IN THOUSANDS)

Date	Greek	Italian	British	French	Austro-Hungarian	Russian	German	Total Foreign Residents	Total Population
1871	—	14	—	—	—	—	—	80	5,250
1882	—	19	—	—	—	—	—	91	6,804
1897	38	24	20	14	7	3	1.3	113	9,715
1907	63	35	21	15	8	2.4	1.8	—	11,287

SOURCES: *The Census of Egypt: Taken in 1907* (Cairo, 1909), 130; A. E. Crouchley, *The Economic Development of Modern Egypt* (London, 1938), 256.

NOTE: All European nations not listed here and the United States had fewer than 1,000 residents each in Egypt during the period covered by this table. A dash indicates "no data available."

TABLE 9
RANKING BY NATIONALITY OF NUMBER OF RESIDENTS AND INDICATORS OF TOURISM

Dahabiyyas in Luxor, 1873	Language of Guidebook Editions, 1830–1914	Number of Travel Authors, 1880–1914	Size of Colony in Egypt, 1897 and 1907
1. Britain	1. English	1. United States	1. Greece
2. United States	2. French	2. Britain	2. Italy
3. Germany	3. German	3. France	3. Britain
4. France and Belgium	4. Italian and Russian	4. Germany	4. France
		5. Russia	5. Austria-Hungary
		6. Italy	6. Russia
		7. Austria-Hungary	7. Germany

NOTE: Table 9 summarizes the data shown in tables 6–8.

TABLE 10

MEMBERSHIP IN THE INSTITUT ÉGYPTIEN
AND THE KHEDIVIAL GEOGRAPHICAL SOCIETY

	French	British	German	Italian	Austro-Hungarian	Russian	Swedish	Swiss	Belgian	Dutch	Greek	Egyptian	U.S.	Other	Total
Institut égyptien, 1859															
Honorary members															
	38	8	4	3	3	2	1	0	1	0	1	1	0	1	63
Resident members															
	21	3	2	9	0	1	0	0	0	0	3	7	0	4[a]	49
Corresponding members[b]															
	16	2	2	8	1	1	1	2	0	0	0	9	0	21[c]	63
Geographical Society: honorary, founding, and regular members, 1881															
	27	15	5	37	8	8	0	4	3	2	6	25	6	0	140

SOURCES: *Bulletin de l'Institut égyptien* 2 (1859): 7–12; *Bulletin de la Société khédivial géographique* 12 (May 1881): 52.
[a] Unknown.
[b] Corresponding members are counted as citizens of the country of residence. Nationality of several resident members is speculative. Geographical Society figures include 11 honorary, 48 founding, and 81 regular members.
[c] From the Middle East outside Egypt (including one Egyptian).

TABLE 11

WORLD'S FAIRS AND
INTERNATIONAL CONGRESSES, 1851–1882

Date	World's Fairs	Geographical Congresses	Orientalist Congresses	Other Congresses
1851	London			1. Sanitary, Paris
1853				1. Statistical, Brussels
1855	Paris			
1862	London			
1863				Red Cross, Geneva
1865				1. Telegraphic Union, Paris
1866				1. Anthropology and Prehistoric Archaeology, Neuchatel
1867	Paris			2. Sanitary, Istanbul
1870				
1871		1. Antwerp		
1872				
1873	Vienna		1. Paris	1. Postal Union, Bern
1874			2. London	
1875		2. Paris		
1876	Philadelphia		3. St. Petersburg	
1877				
1878	Paris		4. Florence	
1881		3. Venice	5. Berlin	
1882				

SOURCES: International Geographical Union, Commission on History of Geographic Thought, *Geography through a Century of International Congresses* (n.p., 1972); the proceedings of the various International Congresses of Orientalists; "Societies, Learned," *Encyclopaedia Britannica*, 11th ed. (New York, 1910), 1: 309–19; F. S. L. Lyons, *Internationalism in Europe 1815–1914* (Leiden, 1963).

NOTE: Numbers before city names indicate the number within that series of congresses.

TABLE 12

HEADS OF THE EGYPTIAN
ANTIQUITIES SERVICE, 1858–1952

Auguste Mariette	1858–1881
Gaston Maspero	1881–1886
Eugène Grébaut	1886–1892
Jacques de Morgan	1892–1897
Victor Loret	1897–1899
Gaston Maspero	1899–1914
Pierre Lacau	1914–1936
Étienne Drioton	1936–1952

TABLE 13
WORLD'S FAIRS AND INTERNATIONAL CONGRESSES, 1883–1914

Date	Major World's Fairs	Congresses of Orientalists	Congresses of Geography[a]	Other International Events and Congresses
1883		6. Leiden		
1886		7. Vienna		
1888		8. Stockholm-Christiania		
1889	Paris		4. Paris (4)	
1891			5. Berne (2)	
1892		9. London (split)[b]		
1893	Chicago	9. London (split)[b]		
1895		10. Lisbon-Genoa (split)[c]	6. London (6)	
1896				1. Athens, Olympics
1899		11. Paris	7. Berlin (1)	
1900	Paris	12. Rome		
1902				1. Athens, Classical Archaeology
1903		13. Hamburg		
1904	St. Louis	14. Algiers	8. U.S. (1)	
1908			9. Geneva (3)	
1909				2. Cairo, Classical Archaeology
1911		15. Copenhagen		
1912				3. Rome, Classical Archaeology
1913		16. Athens	10. Rome (3)	

SOURCES: See the sources listed for table 11.
NOTE: Numbers before city names indicate the number within that series of congresses. For pre-1882 international congresses and world's fairs, see table 11.
a Number in parentheses indicates number attending from Egypt (including its foreign residents).
b The Congress of Orientalists split at this time, with rival factions meeting in London in different years, one in 1892 and the other in 1893.
c The split in the Congress of Orientalists continued in 1895, with rival factions meeting in Lisbon and Genoa.

TABLE 14

FOUNDING DATES OF WESTERN ARCHAEOLOGICAL
INSTITUTES IN THE MEDITERRANEAN

Location	France	Germany	U.S.	Britain	Austria-Hungary	Italy
Athens	1846	1874	1882	1886	1897	1909
Rome	1873	1829[a]	1895	1899		
Cairo	1880	1907	1948			
Jerusalem	1890	1902	1900	1920		
Istanbul	1930	1929	1974			

SOURCES: Douglas Dakin, The Unification of Greece 1770–1923 (New York, 1972), 255; Norman Vance, The Victorians and Ancient Rome (Oxford, 1997), 19; entries in The Oxford Encyclopedia of Archaeology in the Near East (London, 1997); etc.
a Founded as the international Istituto di corrispondenza archeologica, it came under increasing Prussian control and in 1874 emerged as the German Archaeological Institute.

Notes

ABBREVIATIONS

ASAE	*Annales du Service des antiquités de l'Égypte*
Baed. 1885	Karl Baedeker, *Egypt: Part First: Lower Egypt, with the Fayum and the Peninsula of Sinai,* 2nd ed. (Leipzig, 1885)
Baed. 1895	Karl Baedeker, *Egypt: Part First: Lower Egypt and the Peninsula of Sinai,* 3rd ed. (Leipzig, 1895)
Baed. 1908	Karl Baedeker, *Egypt and the Sudan,* 6th ed. (Leipzig, 1908)
Baed. 1914	Karl Baedeker, *Egypt and the Sudan,* 7th ed. (Leipzig, 1914)
Baed. 1929	Karl Baedeker, *Egypt and the Sudan,* 8th ed. (reprint, London, 1985)
BIE	*Bulletin de l'Institut égyptien* (later: *de l'Égypte*), 1859– (date, series, and volume number vary)
BL / Add MSS 37,449 / Hek 2	British Library, Additional Manuscripts No. 37,449, volume 2 of the separately numbered Hekekyan Papers (24 vols.; manuscript number and volume number vary)
BMFA	Museum of Fine Arts, Boston
BSAA	*Bulletin de la Société archéologique d'Alexandrie*
CE	*The Coptic Encyclopedia,* ed. Aziz S. Atiya, 8 vols. (New York, 1991)

CEDEJ   Centre d'études et de documentation économiques, juridiques
                         et sociales, Cairo

Comité 1,   Comité de conservation des monuments de l'art arabe, Fasci-
1882–1883,   cule premier, Exercice 1882–1883, Procès-verbaux des
PVS 1   séances, meeting no. 1. "R," instead of "PVS," refers to the
                         rapports of the Comité's Second Commission (later Techni-
                         cal Section) (year of *exercice* and number of meeting vary)

CUA / B1 / F1   Cairo University Archives (Records of the Egyptian Univer-
                         sity 1908–1925) / Box 1 / Folder 1 (box and folder numbers
                         vary)

Description   Commission des sciences et arts d'Égypte, *Description de l'É-
                         gypte: Ou receuil des observations et des recherches qui ont
                         été faites en Égypte pendant l'expédition de l'armée française,*
                         20 vols. (Paris, 1809–1828)

DWQ   Dar-al-Wathaiq al-Qawmiyya (Egyptian National Archives),
                         Cairo:

                         Abhath: Abhath Collection (followed by box number)

                         MMW: Mahfuzat Majlis al-Wuzara (Archives of the
                         Council of Ministers):

                             NA: Nizarat al-Ashghal (Ministry of Public Works):

                                 MA: Maslahat al-Athar (Antiquities Service)

                             NM: Nizarat al-Maarif (Ministry of Education)

                         I have added "B" before a box number following the above
                         abbreviations and "F" before a folder number or name.
                         The system is neither entirely consistent nor transparent to
                         the researcher, and I have omitted the "B" and "F" in un-
                         clear cases. Individual documents are then identified by
                         title (when available), author, addressee, and date. A third
                         number or letter (apparently usually a cupboard number)
                         sometimes appears. In any case, requesting these items by
                         the call numbers listed here resulted in successful retrieval.

                         Fihrist bataqat al-Dar (card file index of the contents of the
                         Egyptian National Archives / Drawer 1: Athar (Antiquities)

EEF, EES   The Egypt Exploration Fund (became the Egypt Exploration
                         Society in 1919)

*EI*2   *Encyclopedia of Islam,* 2nd ed. (Leiden, 1960–)

FO   Foreign Office Archives of the United Kingdom, Public
                         Record Office, London

ICO1, Paris   *Mémoires du congrès international des Orientalistes, 1re Session—Paris,* 3 vols. (Paris, 1873) (language and title of proceedings vary with host city; abbreviation varies according to congress number and host city)

IFAO   Institut français d'archéologie orientale du Caire

IJMES   *International Journal of Middle East Studies*

JAOS   *Journal of the American Oriental Society*

Joan. 1861   Adolphe Joanne and Émile Isambert, *Itinéraire descriptif, historique, et archéologique de l'Orient* (Paris, 1861)

MAE   Ministère des affaires étrangeres, Les Archives diplomatiques de Nantes, France:

                   AMB Le Caire: Ambassade Le Caire; C: cartons 173, 174, 174 *bis;* EE: Enseignement égyptien:

                   SA: Service des antiquités, cartons 177, 261, 359

                   AMB Constantinople: Ambassade Constantinople, Dossiers thèmatiques, carton 494: Fouilles

MMA   Metropolitan Museum of Art, New York

Murr. 1858   John Murray, *A Hand-book for Travellers in Egypt,* 2nd ed. (London, 1858)

Murr. 1873   John Murray, *A Hand-book for Travellers in Egypt* (London, 1873)

Murr. 1880   John Murray, *A Hand-book for Travellers in Lower and Upper Egypt,* 6th ed., 2 vols. (London, 1880)

RGS   Royal Geographical Society, London

Simaika   "Excerpts from the Memoirs of Marcus Simaika Pasha,
memoirs   C.B.E., F.S.A. (1864–1944)" (unpublished memoirs held by the family)

SPMAE   Society for the Preservation of the Monuments of Ancient Egypt, Great Britain

Wilk. 1835   I. G. Wilkinson, *Topography of Thebes, and General View of Egypt . . .* (London: John Murray, 1835)

Wilk. 1843   I. G. Wilkinson, *Modern Egypt and Thebes,* 2 vols. (London: John Murray, 1843)

Wilk. 1847   I. G. Wilkinson, *Hand-book for Travellers in Egypt* (London: John Murray, 1847; for continuation of series, see "Murr.," above)

WWWE3   W. R. Dawson, *Who Was Who in Egyptology,* 3rd ed., rev.
                 M. I. Bierbrier (London, 1995; 1st ed. published in London,
                 1951; 2nd ed. coauthored with E. P. Uphill and published in
                 London, 1972)

INTRODUCTION

1. "Archaeology" means the scientific study of past societies through material remains and often implies excavation. For convenience, this book sometimes uses the term in the older sense of "ancient history" (including philology and art history), a sense that it retained into the early twentieth century. The Faculty of Archeology at Cairo University has perpetuated this more comprehensive usage to the present. There the Department of Islamic Archeology emphasizes the history of art and architecture far more than it does excavation.

2. Florence Nightingale, *Letters from Egypt: A Journey on the Nile 1849–1850* (New York, 1987), 33.

3. Commission des monuments d'Égypte, *Description de l'Égypte: Ou receuil des observations et des recherches qui ont été faites en Égypte pendant l'expédition de l'armée française,* vol. 1: *Antiquités: Planches* (Paris, 1809), frontispiece. Despite its bearing the date 1809, the first volume was not published until 1810. Hereafter, the short title *Description* will refer to this work, not to the 1735 *Description de l'Égypte,* a different work of the same title by Benoît de Maillet (Paris, 1735). Reproductions of the frontispiece are conveniently available in Peter A. Clayton, *The Rediscovery of Ancient Egypt: Artists and Travellers in the Nineteenth Century* (London, 1982); and in Charles Coulston Gillispie and Michel Dewachter, eds., *Monuments of Egypt: The Napoleonic Edition* (Princeton, N.J., 1987).

4. Cf. Benedict Anderson, *Imagined Communities,* 2nd ed. (London, 1991), 181. Karl Baedeker, *Egypt and the Soudan,* 8th ed. (Leipzig, 1929), 88, lists Ferdinand Faivre as the sculptor of the flanking goddesses.

5. Bertrand Millet, *Samir, Mickey, Sindbad et les autres: Histoire de la presse enfantine en Égypte* (Cairo, 1987), 30–31. *Al-Samir al-Saghir* was founded in 1897 to present popular, illustrated pieces on learned subjects. In this image, Abbas II and the officials are listed with their Ottoman-Egyptian titles "pasha" or "bey." During the nineteenth century, "effendi"—a loose equivalent of "mister"—came into use in Egypt for civil officials beneath the rank of bey. For convenience, the present study often omits these titles.

6. A. Zvie, "L'Égypte ancien ou l'Orient perdu et retrouvé," in *D'un Orient l'autre,* 2 vols. (Paris, 1991), 1: 38.

7. W. R. Dawson, *Who Was Who in Egyptology* (London, 1951); W. R. Dawson and Eric P. Uphill, 2nd ed. (1972); W. R. Dawson, Eric P. Uphill, and M. L. Bierbrier, 3rd ed. (1995).

8. Bruce Trigger, *A History of Archaeological Thought* (Cambridge, Mass., 1989); Bruce Kuklick, *Puritans in Babylon: The Ancient Near East and American Intellectual Life, 1880–1930* (Princeton, N.J., 1996); Suzanne L. Marchand, *Down from Olympus: Archaeology and Philhellenism in Germany, 1750–1970* (Princeton, N.J., 1996); Flora E. S. Kaplan, ed., *Museums and the*

Making of "Ourselves": The Role of Objects in National Identity (London, 1994); Philip L. Kohl and Clare Fawcett, eds., *Nationalism, Politics, and the Practice of Archaeology* (Cambridge, 1995); Neil Asher Silberman, *Between Past and Present: Archaeology, Ideology, and Nationalism in the Modern Middle East* (New York, 1989), and his "Ideology and Archaeology" and "Nationalism and Archaeology," in *The Oxford Encyclopedia of Archaeology in the Near East,* 5 vols. (New York, 1997), 3: 138–41, 4: 103–12; Margarita Díaz-Andreu and Timothy Champion, eds., *Nationalism and Archaeology in Europe* (Boulder, Colo., 1996); John A. Atkinson, Iain Banks, and Jerry O'Sullivan, eds., *Nationalism and Archaeology* (Glasgow, 1996); Ève Gran-Aymerich, *Naissance de l'archéologie moderne, 1798–1945* (Paris, 1998). Gran-Aymerich concentrates on French archaeology in Mediterranean countries, Iraq, and Iran.

9. Brian M. Fagan, *The Rape of the Nile* (London, 1975); Peter France, *The Rape of Egypt: How Europeans Stripped Egypt of Its Heritage* (London, 1991); John and Elizabeth Romer, *The Rape of Tutankhamun* (London, 1993).

10. Husayn's subject at the Egyptian University in 1919 was "The History of the Ancient East." He taught it as Greek and Roman history with some attention to Egypt.

11. Israel Gershoni and James Jankowski (*Egypt, Islam and the Arabs: The Search for Egyptian Nationhood, 1900–1930* [New York, 1986]) treat "pharaonicism" in the 1920s and 1930s.

12. E. de Verninac Saint-Maur, *Voyage du Luxor* (Paris, 1835), as quoted in Leslie Greener, *The Discovery of Egypt* (New York, 1965), 157–58.

13. *Al-Balagh,* as quoted in *The Egyptian Gazette,* 26 February 1932.

14. Quoted in Edward Said, *Culture and Imperialism* (New York, 1993), 162.

15. Edward Said, *Orientalism* (New York, 1978), and Said, *Culture and Imperialism;* Timothy Mitchell, *Colonising Egypt* (Cambridge, 1988); Linda Nochlin, "The Imaginary Orient," *Art in America* 71 (1983): 118–31, 187–91. Martin Bernal, *Black Athena: The Afroasiatic Roots of Classical Civilization,* 2 vols. (New Brunswick, N.J., 1987–1991), targets classical studies rather than Egyptology and is less useful than Said for this book's purposes. See also Mary Lefkowitz, *Not Out of Africa: How Afrocentrism Became an Excuse to Teach Myth as History* (New York, 1996).

16. John MacKenzie, *Orientalism: History, Theory, and the Arts* (Manchester, 1995). For similar arguments, see Jason Thompson, "Edward William Lane's 'Description of Egypt,' " *International Journal of Middle East Studies* (hereafter *IJMES*) 28 (1996): 565–83; John Rodenbeck, "Edward Said and Edward William Lane," in *Travellers in Egypt,* ed. Paul Starkey and Janet Starkey (London, 1998), 233–43; Mark Crinson, *Empire Building: Orientalist and Victorian Architecture* (London, 1996); and J. Harris Proctor, "David Roberts and the Ideology of Imperialism," *The Muslim World* 87 (1998): 47–66. Postcolonial theorists such as Homi K. Bhabha (*The Location of Culture* [London, 1995]) differ from Said in other ways.

17. Edmund Burke III, "Egypt in the *Description de l'Égypte*" (paper presented at a meeting of the Middle East Studies Association, Phoenix, Ariz., November 1994).

18. Carter Vaughn Findley, "An Ottoman Occidentalist in Europe: Ahmed Midhat Meets Madame Gülnar, 1889," *American Historical Review* 103 (February 1998): 14–49.

19. Prasenjit Duara, *Rescuing History from the Nation: Questioning Narratives of Modern China* (Chicago, 1995).

20. Peter Novick, *That Noble Dream: The "Objectivity Question" and the American Historical Profession* (Chicago, 1988).

21. Cf. Partha Chatterjee, *The Nation and Its Fragments: Colonial and Postcolonial Histories* (Princeton, N.J., 1993).

22. Michael Herzfeld, *A Place in History: Social and Monumental Time in a Cretan Town* (Princeton, N.J., 1991), and Quetzil E. Castañeda, *In the Museum of Maya Culture: Touring Chichén Itzá* (Minneapolis, 1996), illustrate the potential of anthropological histories of archaeology and tourism.

23. For example, Peter Gran, *Islamic Roots of Capitalism: Egypt 1760–1840* (Austin, Tex., 1979); Kenneth M. Cuno, *The Pasha's Peasants: Land, Society, and Economy in Lower Egypt, 1740–1858* (Cambridge, 1992).

CHAPTER 1. REDISCOVERING ANCIENT EGYPT

1. Gerald P. Verbrugghe and J. M. Wickersham, *Berossos and Manetho,* introduced and translated (Ann Arbor, 1996).

2. John David Wortham, *British Egyptology 1549–1906* (Newton Abbot, Devon, 1971), 15–16. For insights on the history of travel, see Mary B. Campbell, *The Witness and the Other World: Exotic European Travel Writing 400–1600* (Ithaca, N.Y., 1988); Justin Stagl, *A History of Curiosity: The Theory of Travel 1550–1800* (Chur, Switzerland, 1995); and Mary Helms, *Ulysses' Sail: Power, Knowledge, and Geographical Distance* (Princeton, 1988).

3. On Sandys, see W. R. Dawson, *Who Was Who in Egyptology,* 3rd ed. (hereafter *WWWE3*), revised by M. L. Bierbrier (London, 1995), 260–61; and George Sandys, *A Relation of a Journey Begun Anno Dom. 1610* (London, 1615; reprint of 2nd ed., Amsterdam, 1973). For pre-1798 European travelers generally, see Jean-Marie Carré, *Voyageurs et écrivains français en Égypte,* 2 vols. (Cairo, 1956), 1: 1–118; R. Clément, *Les Français d'Égypte aux XVIIe et XVIIIe siècles* (Cairo, 1960); Wortham, *British Egyptology,* 1–48; and Stéphane Yerasimas, "Les Voyageuers de XVIème siècle en Égypte ottomane (1517–1600)," in *D'un Orient l'autre,* 2 vols. (Paris, 1991), 1: 301.

4. Sandys, *Relation,* 128; Erik Iverson, *The Myth of Egypt and Its Hieroglyphics in European Tradition* (Copenhagen, 1961), plate 7, facing 48, and on 164 n. 82; *Encyclopaedia Britannica* (Edinburgh, 1771), 3: 519. On the great seal, see John A. Wilson, *Signs and Wonders upon Pharaoh: A History of American Egyptology* (Chicago, 1964), 37. The angle of the late pyramids in Nubia (now the northern Sudan) more closely resembled that of Cestius's pyramids.

5. *WWWE3*: 176.

6. Garth Fowden, *The Egyptian Hermes: A Historical Approach to the Late Pagan Mind* (Princeton, 1986); Erik Iverson, *The Myth of Egypt and Its Hiero-*

glyphics in European Tradition (Copenhagen, 1961); and Francis A. Yates, *Giordano Bruno and the Hermetic Question* (Chicago, 1964).

7. Joscelyn Godwin, *Athanasius Kircher: A Renaissance Man and the Quest for Knowledge* (London, 1979); and *WWWE3*: 158.

8. Calculated from Martin Kalfatovic, *Nile Notes of a Howadji: A Bibliography of Travelers' Tales from Egypt* (Metuchen, N.J., 1992).

9. On the exploration of Upper Egypt, see Claude Traunecker and Jean-Claude Golvin, *Karnak: Résurrection d'un site* (Paris, 1984), 35–99; Carré, *Voyageurs* 1: 29–118; Clément, *Les Français,* 101–17, 182–90; and Maurice Martin, "Aux debuts de la description moderne de l'Égypte," *D'un Orient l'autre* (Paris, 1991), 1: 343–50.

10. Benoît de Maillet, *Description de l'Égypte . . . composée sur les mémoires de M. de Maillet, ancien consul de France au Caire, par l'abbé Le Mascrier* (Paris, 1735), 147–48; Clément, *Les Français,* 144.

11. *WWWE3*: 312, 338. On the Sphinx's nose, see Alberto Siliotti, *The Discovery of Ancient Egypt* (Cairo, 1998), 36–37, 42–43.

12. On Volney, see C.-F. Volney, *Voyage en Syrie et en Égypte, pendant les années 1783, 1784, et 1785,* 2 vols., 2nd ed. (Paris, 1787); Stagl, *A History of Curiosity,* 269–93; Carré, *Voyageurs,* 1:91–116; and Henry Laurens, *Les Origines intellectuelles de l'expédition d'Égypte: L'Orientalisme islamisant en France 1698–1798* (Istanbul, Paris, 1987).

13. Carré, *Voyageurs,* 1: 67–68.

14. Ulrich Haarmann, "Medieval Muslim Perceptions of Pharaonic Egypt," in *Ancient Egyptian Literature: History and Forms,* ed. Antonio Loprieno (Leiden, 1996), 605–27; H. A. R. Gibb, trans., *Ibn Battuta: Travels in Asia and Africa 1325–1354* (London, 1953), 53.

15. Michael Cook, "Pharaonic History in Medieval Egypt," *Studia Islamica* 57 (1983): 67–113, emphasizes Muslims' alienation from ancient Egypt. Ulrich Haarmann also sees a break in continuity but points out the fascination of many Muslims with magical and hermetic lore on ancient Egypt: "Regional Sentiment in Medieval Islamic Egypt," *Bulletin of the School of Oriental and African Studies* 43 (1980): 55–66; "Manf," *Encyclopedia of Islam,* 2nd ed. (hereafter cited as *EI2*) (Leiden, 1960–), 6: 411–14; and "Medieval Muslim Perceptions." See also Darrell Dykstra, "Pyramids, Prophets, and Progress: Ancient Egypt in the Writings of Ali Mubarak," *Journal of the American Oriental Society* (hereafter cited as *JAOS*) 114, no. 1 (1994): 57–59.

16. *The History of Tabari,* vols. 1–5 (Albany, N.Y., 1987), various translators; A. J. Wensinck, "Fir'awn," *EI2*: 2: 917–18.

17. Ahmad M. H. Shboul, *Al-Mas'udi and His World: A Muslim Humanist and His Interest in Non-Muslims* (London, 1979); and Tarif Khalidi, *Arabic Historical Thought in the Classical Period* (Cambridge, 1994), 131–81.

18. In addition to Haarmann, "Regional Sentiment in Medieval Islamic Egypt," see E. Graefe, "Haram," *EI2*: 3: 173; and F. Rosenthal, "al-Makrizi," *EI2*: 6: 193–94.

19. Ulrich Haarmann, "In Quest of the Spectacular: Noble and Learned Visitors to the Pyramids around 1200 A.D.," in *Islamic Studies Presented to J.*

Adams, ed. Wael Hallaq and Donald P. Little (Leiden, 1991), 57–67; and Haarmann's edition of Abu Jafar al-Idrisi, *Anwar uluw al-Ajram fi-l-Kashf an Asrar
al-Ahram*, in Beiruter Texte und Studien (Beirut, 1990).

20. "Égyptiens (Philosophie des)," *Encyclopédie raisonné des sciences, des
arts et de métiers* (Stuttgart–Bad Connstatt, 1966; reprint of 1751–1780 ed.,
Paris), 5: 434.

21. Recent studies on the expedition, based on French sources, include Henry
Laurens, *L'Expédition d'Égypte 1798–1801* (Paris, 1989); Jean-Joël Brégeon,
L'Égypte française au jour le jour 1798–1801 (Paris, 1991); and J. Christopher
Herold, *Bonaparte in Egypt* (New York, 1962). André Raymond, *Égyptiens et
Français au Caire 1798–1801* (Cairo, 1998), makes excellent use of Arabic
sources as well.

22. Revisionists on the periodization include Peter Gran, *The Islamic Roots
of Capitalism: Egypt 1760–1840* (Cairo, 1979); and Ken Cuno, *The Pasha's
Peasants: Land, Society, and Economy in Lower Egypt, 1740–1858* (Cambridge,
1992).

23. Carré, *Voyageurs* 1: 67–73.

24. de Maillet, *Description de l'Égypte*, iv.

25. The most recent study of the era is Khaled Fahmy, *All the Pasha's Men:
Mehmed Ali, His Army and the Making of Modern Egypt* (Cambridge, England,
1998).

26. Gabriel Guémard, *Histoire et bibliographie critique de la Commission
des sciences et arts et de l'Institut d'Égypte* (Cairo, 1936). For the intellectual
context, see Nicole et Jean Dhombres, *Naissance d'un pouvoir: Sciences et savants en France (1793–1824)* (Paris, 1989).

27. *La Décade égyptienne*, vol. 1 (Year 7 [1798]), 11–12.

28. On Denon, see his *Voyage dans la basse et l'haute Égypte, description
de l'Égypte*, 2 vols. (Paris, 1802); Jean-Claude Vatin, "Une Rupture dans la tradition du récit de voyage: Vivant Denon en Égypte," in *La Fuite en Égypte: Supplément aux voyages européens en orient* (Cairo, 1989), 185–228; and Carré,
Voyageurs 1: 119–144.

29. For this paragraph, see Jean-Claude Golvin, "L'Expédition de l'Haute-
Égypte: À la découverte des sites ou la révélation de l'architecture pharonique,"
in Henry Laurens, *L'Expédition d'Égypte 1798–1801* (Paris, 1989), 333–50,
quotations from Denon from 337, 341, 344.

30. As quoted in Golvin, "L'Expédition," 344.

31. Irene Bierman, "The Time and Space of Medieval Cairo" (unpublished
paper, 1998), points out the absence of a "medieval" period in the *Description*.
Michael W. Albin, "Napoleon's *Description de l'Égypte*: Problems of Corporate Authorship," *Publishing History* 8 (1980): 65–85, is a useful publishing history of the *Description*. For a convenient reprint of the plates, see *Description
de l'Égypte* (Cologne, 1994).

32. *Description*, Fourier, "Préface historique," iii; Edward Said, *Orientalism*
(New York, 1978), 80–87.

33. *Description*, vol. 1: *Antiquités: Planches* (Paris, 1809), frontispiece. Reproduced as frontispieces to Peter A. Clayton, *The Rediscovery of Ancient Egypt:
Artists and Travellers in the 19th Century* (London, 1984); and Charles Coul-

ston Gillispie and Michel Dewachter, *Monuments of Egypt: The Napoleonic Edition* (Princeton, 1987).

34. Iverson, *Myth*, 132–33.

35. Claude Traunecker, "L'Égypte antique de la '*Description*,' " in Laurens, *Expédition*, 351–70.

36. Quoted in Edward Said, *Culture and Imperialism* (New York, 1994), 34.

37. S. Moreh, *Al-Jabarti's Chronicle of the First Seven Months of the French Occupation of Egypt, Muharram-Rajab 1213 / 15 June–December 1798* (Leiden, 1975), 116–17.

38. On Hamilton, see *WWWE3*: 188. On Elgin, see William St. Clair, *Lord Elgin and the Marbles* (London, 1967).

39. J. J. Halls, *The Life and Correspondence of Henry Salt*, 2 vols. (London, 1834), 2: 301. See also *WWWE3*: 370–71.

40. For Caviglia, see *WWWE3*: 88. For Belzoni, see his *Narrative of the Operations and Recent Discoveries* (London, 1820); *WWWE3*: 40–41; and Stanley Mayes, *The Great Belzoni* (London, 1959).

41. On Rifaud, see *WWWE3*, 358. On Drovetti, see Ronald T. Ridley, *Napoleon's Proconsul in Egypt: The Life and Times of Bernardino Drovetti* (London, [ca. 1998]); and *WWWE3*: 129–30.

42. On Barker, Campbell, Murray, Mimaut, and Sabatier, see *WWWE3*: 30–31, 81–82, 302, 289, 369. On Cochelet, see George Gliddon, *An Appeal to the Antiquaries of Europe on the Destruction of the Monuments of Egypt* (London, 1841), 107.

43. *WWWE3*, 217, 8, 457.

44. Angelo Sammarco, *Gli Italiani in Egitto* (Alexandria, 1937), 144–45.

45. On Ricci, Passalacqua, Athanasi, and Burckhardt, see *WWWE3*, 356, 321, 21, 74.

46. Dhombres, *Naissance*, 223–33.

47. The heading of this section was borrowed from the title of C. E. Bosworth's article in *IJMES* 8 (1977): 229–36. This quotation is from 'Abd al-Rahman al-Jabarti's *History of Egypt, 'Aja'ib al-Athar fi 'l-Tarajim wa'l-Akhbar*, trans. T. Philipp and M. Perlmann, 4 vols., and *Guide* (Stuttgart, 1994), 4: 398–400.

48. Bruce Trigger, *A History of Archaeological Thought* (Cambridge, Mass., 1989), 39–40.

49. *WWWE3*: 454–55; Alexander Wood and Frank Oldham, *Thomas Young, Natural Philosopher, 1773–1829* (Cambridge, 1954). Richard Parkinson, *Cracking Codes: The Rosetta Stone and Its Decipherment* (Berkeley, Calif., 1999), 31–41, offers a judicious assessment of the relative contributions of Young and Champollion.

50. H. Hartleben, *Champollion, sein Leben und sein Werk*, 2 vols. (Berlin, 1906); Jean Lacouture, *Champollion: Une Vie de lumières* (Paris, 1988).

51. Anne-Françoise Ehrhard, "Champollion et les Frères Humboldt," *L'Égyptologie et les Champollion*, ed. Michel Dewachter and Alain Fouchard (Grenoble, 1994), 95–115.

52. Robert Marichal, "Champollion et l'académie," *Bulletin de la Société française d'Égyptologie* 95 (1983): 12–31. On Jomard, see also *WWWE3*, 218–19.

53. Jason Thompson, *Sir John Gardner Wilkinson and His Circle* (Austin, Tex., 1992). On Lane, see Leila Ahmed, *Edward W. Lane* (London, 1978); Jason Thompson, "Edward William Lane's 'Description of Egypt,' " *IJMES* 28 (1996): 565–83; and Edward William Lane, *Description of Egypt*, ed. Jason Thompson (Cairo, 2000), ix–xxv. On Hay, see Selwyn Tillet, *Egypt Itself: The Career of Robert Hay, Esquire of Linplum and Nunraw, 1799–1863* (London, 1984).

54. Thompson, *Wilkinson*, 184.

55. Compiled from Kalfatovic, *Nile Notes*.

56. Quoted in Kent Weeks, *The Lost Tomb: The Greatest Discovery in the Valley of the Kings since Tutankhamun* (Cairo, 1998), 68.

57. On Rosellini, see *WWWE3*: 362–63.

58. William H. Stiebing Jr., *Uncovering the Past: A History of Archaeology* (Buffalo, N.Y., 1993), 90–109, gives a concise sketch of early Mesopotamian archaeology. More detailed accounts include Seton Lloyd, *Foundations in the Dust: The Story of Mesopotamian Exploration*, 2nd ed. (London, 1980); and Brian Fagan, *Travelers, Archaeologists, and Monuments in Mesopotamia* (Boston, 1979).

59. On Minutoli, see *WWWE3*: 289; and Joachim S. Karig, "A Prussian Expedition to Egypt in 1820," in *Travellers in Egypt*, ed. Paul Starkey and Janet Starkey (London, 1998), 70–74. On Lepsius, see Georg Ebers, *Richard Lepsius: A Biography*, trans. Z. D. Underhill (New York: 1887); E. Freier and W. F. Reineke, eds., *Karl Richard Lepsius (1810–1884)* (Berlin, 1988).

60. Carré, *Voyageurs* 1: 301–23.

61. On Leemans, see *L'Égyptologue Conrade Leemans et sa correspondance*, ed. W. F. Leemans (Leiden, 1973); and *WWWE3*: 242–43.

62. Christiane Ziegler, *Le Louvre: Les Antiquités égyptiennes* (Paris, 1990), 5–6. Todd Porterfield, *The Allure of Empire: Art in the Service of French Imperialism, 1798–1836* (Princeton, N.J., 1998), 81–116, analyzes the symbolism of the Louvre's Musée d'Égypte. Studies of art museum history include Andrew McClellan, *Inventing the Louvre: Art, Politics, and the Origins of the Modern Museum in Eighteenth-Century Paris* (Cambridge, 1994); Germain Bazin, *The Museum Age*, trans. J. Cahill (Brussels, 1967); James Sheehan, *Museums in the German Art World from the End of the Old Regime to the Rise of Modernism* (Oxford, 2000).

63. Louis Keimer, "Le Musée égyptologique de Berlin," *Cahiers d'histoire égyptienne*, série 3, fasc. 1 (November 1950): 27–41; Thomas W. Gaehtgens, "The Museum Island in Berlin," in *The Formation of National Collections of Art and Archaeology*, ed. Gwendolyn Wright (Washington, D.C., 1966), 52–77.

64. Donald Malcolm Reid, "The Egyptian Geographical Society: From Foreign Layman's Society to Indigenous Professional Association," *Poetics Today* 14, no. 3 (fall 1993): 539–72; T. W. Freeman, *A History of Modern British Geography* (London, 1980).

65. *Laws and Regulations of the Egyptian Society* (Alexandria, n.d.), 1. See also Philip Sadgrove, "Travellers' Rendezvous and Cultural Institutions in Muhammad Ali's Egypt," in *Travellers*, ed. Starkey and Starkey, 257–66.

66. *Laws and Regulations of the Egyptian Society*, 1, 2, 8.

67. George R. Gliddon, "Ancient Egypt," *New World*, nos. 68 & 69 (April 1843): 1. On the history of the society, see L. Auriant (pseud. for Alecco [Alexandre] Haggi-Basilio), "Les Origines de l'Institut égyptien, la Société égyptienne (1836–1859)," *Journal des savants* (1926): 217–27. All the individuals mentioned in this paragraph are in *WWWE3*.

68. *Fifth Report of the Egyptian Society* (n.p., [ca. 1841]), 2. Members are listed on the cover of Linant de Bellefonds, *Mémoire sur le Lac Moeris* (Alexandria, 1843).

69. British Library, Additional Manuscripts 37,449, Hekekyan Papers, vol. 2: 45 (4 July 1842) (hereafter BL / Add MSS / Hek). On the split, see Yacoub Artin Pacha, "Lettres inédites du Dr. Perron à M. J. Mohl," *Bulletin de l'Institut égyptien* (hereafter *BIE*), ser. 5, 3, fasc. 2 (1909): 144–46. On the association, see also Carré, *Voyageurs*, 1: 320.

70. I. G. Wilkinson, *A Handbook for Travellers in Egypt* (London, 1847) (hereafter Wilk. 1847), 113; Artin Pacha, "Lettres," 146.

71. On al-Tahtawi, see Gilbert Delanoue, *Moralistes et politiques musulmans dans l'Égypte du XIXe siècle (1798–1882)*, 2 vols. (Cairo, 1982) 2: 383–487, 618–630, 651–54. See also Anouar Louca, *Voyageurs et écrivains égyptiens en France au XIXe siècle* (Paris, 1970), 55 ff.; Salih Majdi, *Hilyat al-zaman bi-manaqib khadim al-watan: Sirat Rifaa Rafi al-Tahtawi*, ed. Jamal al-Din al-Shayyal (Cairo, 1958); and Ahmad Badawi, *Rifaa Rafii al-Tahtawi*, 2nd ed. (Cairo, 1959).

72. Louca, *Voyageurs*, 25–27.

73. Louca, *Voyageurs*, 61–62.

74. Al-Tahtawi, *L'Or de Paris: Relation de voyage: 1826–1831*, trans. Anouar Louca (Paris, 1988), 19. The translation is abridged. See also Delanoue, *Moralistes*, 2: 621–22, bibliographic note on the various editions and translations.

75. Jean-Jacques Luthi, *Introduction à la littérature de'expression française en Égypte (1798–1945)* (Paris, 1974), 103–5, 268. See also Louca, *Voyageurs*, 26; and Delanoue, *Moralistes* 2: 620.

76. Anouar Louca, "Rifaa al-Tahtawi (1801–1873) et la science occidentale," in *D'un Orient l'autre* (Paris, 1991), 2: 213.

77. Rifaa Rafi al-Tahtawi, *Takhlis al-ibriz fi talkhis Bariz* (Cairo, 1994), 270. Marie-Noëlle Bourguet, in "Science et voyage à l'époque napoléonienne: L'Expédition de l'Égypte," unpublished paper read at the conference "Impossible Settlement: Problems of a New Order in Post-Revolutionary France," Emory University, Atlanta, 12–13 November 1999, 14, notes al-Tahtawi's failure to mention the *Description*.

78. For this and the following two paragraphs, see al-Tahtawi, *Takhlis*, 377–79; and al-Tahtawi, *L'Or*, 296–97.

79. Jason Thompson, personal letter to me, 2 November 1993.

80. Delanoue, *Moralistes*, 2: 404, citing Rifaa Rafi al-Tahtawi, *Manahij al-abab al-misriyya fi mabahijal-albab al-asriyya* (Cairo, 1286 / 1869), 265.

81. Ibrahim Abduh, *Tarikh al-Waqai al-Misriyya* (Cairo, 1942), 35–36. See also Mohammad al-Asad, "The Mosque of Muhammad Ali in Cairo," *Muqarnas* 9 (1992): 55 n. 24.

82. Asad, "Mosque," 48.

83. Jean-François Champollion, *Lettres écrites d'Égypte et de Nubie, en 1828 et 1829* (Geneva, 1973, reprint of 1833 Paris ed.), 42, 409, 429–54.
84. Champollion, *Lettres,* 456–57. Entire memo, 455–61. On this first effort at a museum and antiquities service, see G. Maspero, *Guide du visiteur au Musée du Caire,* 4th ed. (Cairo, 1915), ix–x.
85. Gaston Wiet, *Mohamed Ali et les Beaux-Arts* (Cairo, [ca. 1949]), 24.
86. Wiet, *Mohamed Ali,* 28. See also the follow up decree in Dar al-Wathaiq al-Qawmiyya (hereafter DWQ) / Fihrist Bataqat al-Dar, Drawer No. 1: Athar (card file of extracts from documents A.H.1229–1295) Abhath No. 118, "Athar" copied from Maiyya Turkiyya, Mahfaza #2, Doc. 110, Rabi al-Thani 21, 1251, M. Ali to Mukhtar Bey. This and a selection of other viceregal decrees on antiquities are reproduced in J.[acques] T.[agher], "Ordres supérieurs relatifs à la conservation des antiquités et à la création d'un musée au Caire," *Cahiers d'histoire égyptienne,* ser. 3, fasc. 1: 13–25.
87. Hans Huth, "The Evolution of Preservationism in Europe," *Journal of the American Society of Architectural Historians* (July / Oct. 1941): 5–12; Paul Léon, *La vie des monuments français: Destruction, restauration* (Paris, 1951); and, on Greece, Maria Avgouli, "The First Greek Museums and National Identity," in *Museums and the Making of "Ourselves": The Role of Objects in National Identity,* ed. Flora E. S. Kaplan (London, 1994), 246–65.
88. Speech by Suzanne Mubarak, text in *Al-Ahram,* 16 December 1998. For the usual French view, see Maspero, *Guide,* ix.
89. Traunecker and Golvin, *Karnak,* 133.
90. Wiet, *Mohamed Ali,* 30; Gliddon, *Appeal,* 69.
91. Carré, *Voyageurs* 1: 57 n. 3.
92. Bernadette Menu, "Les Frères Champollion," *L'Égyptologie et les Champollion,* ed. Dewachter and Fouchard, 77–94; Jean Vidal, "L'absent de l'obelisque," in Jean Lacouture, *Champollion,* 473–92; Erasmus Wilson, *Cleopatra's Needle* (London, 1877); DWQ / Fihrist Bataqat al-Dar / Athar, Drawer 1 (card file), Muhammad Ali to Katkhuda, Maiyya Turkiyya, Daftar 42 / Document 611, 4 Muharram 1247. Todd Porterfield, *The Allure of Empire: Art in the Service of French Imperialism, 1798–1836* (Princeton, N.J., 1998), 13–42, analyzes the shifting meanings of the obelisk in the place de la Concorde.
93. Gliddon, *Appeal,* 142–44.
94. Gliddon, *Appeal,* 52; and Gliddon, "Ancient Egypt," 8.
95. Gliddon, *Appeal,* 127, 146–48.
96. Robert J. C. Young, *Colonial Desire: Hybridity in Theory, Culture, and Race* (London, 1995), 124–29. On Gliddon, see also *WWWE*3: 169.
97. I. G. Wilkinson, *Modern Egypt and Thebes,* 2 vols. (London, 1843) (hereafter Wilk. 1843), 1: 264. The Wilkinson quotation in the following paragraph is from the same page. On de Bellefonds's involvement, see G. Maspero, *Guide du visiteur au musée du Caire,* 4th ed. (Cairo, 1915), ix–x.
98. Ehud Toledano, *State and Society in Mid-Nineteenth-Century Egypt* (Cambridge, 1990), 88–90, 272.
99. Maspero, *Guide,* x; Dia' Abou-Ghazi, "The First Egyptian Museum," *Annales du Service des antiquités de l'Égypte* (hereafter, *ASAE*) 67 (1991): 1–13,

esp. 8. For the gift to the sultan, see John Murray, *Handbook for Travellers in Constantinople, Brusa, and the Troad* (London, 1900), 72.

100. On the Armenians in Egypt, see Muhammad Rifat al-Imam, *Al-Arman fi Misr: Al-Qarn al-Tasi al-Ashar* (Cairo, 1995).

101. BL / Add MSS 37,461 / Hek 14: 9 ff. (November 1825). The primary source for Hekekyan is his papers in the British Library, Additional MSS 37,448–37,471, Hekekyan Papers, vols. 1–24. See also Darrell I. Dykstra, "Joseph Hekekyan and the Egyptian School in Paris," *Armenian Review* 35, no. 2 (summer 1982): 165–82; and Ahmed Abdel-Rahim Mustafa, "The Hekekyan Papers," in *Political and Social Change in Modern Egypt,* ed. P. M. Holt (London, 1968), 68–75.

102. BL / Add MSS 37,448 / Hek 1: 50 (24 July 1829).

103. BL / Add MSS 37,450 / Hek 3: 65 (June 1845).

104. BL / Add MSS 37,463 / Hek 24: 458 (1858).

105. BL / Add MSS 37,461 / Hek 14: 59 (2 February 1837).

106. *WWWE*3: 456, 99.

107. BL / Add MSS 37,448 / Hek 1: 82–83 (19 August 1829).

108. Wiet, *Mohamed Ali,* 31–34.

109. BL / Add MSS 37,449 / Hek 2: 489 (29 September 1844).

110. BL / Add MSS 37,449 / Hek 2: 489 (30 September 1844).

111. BL / Add MSS 37,450 / Hek 3: 36 (1845), quotation from 39.

112. BL / Add MSS 37,449 / Hek 2: 489 (1 October 1844).

113. BL / Add MSS 37,450 / Hek 3: 35 (12 June 1845).

114. BL / Add MSS 37,452 / Hek 5 (early 1851).

115. BL / Add MSS 37,452 / Hek 5: 48–50 (29 April 1851).

116. BL / Add MSS 37,452 / Hek 5: 69 (5 June 1851).

117. BL / Add MSS 37,452 / Hek 5: 61 ff. (undated [late May 1851]). The first of many entries on his Heliopolis excavations.

118. Thompson, *Wilkinson,* 249 n. 25.

119. As quoted in Dykstra, "Joseph Hekekyan," 165, from 1849 educational report.

CHAPTER 2. FROM EXPLORER TO COOK'S TOURIST

1. Muhammad Muwaylihi, *A Period of Time* (Reading, England, 1992), part 2: "Isa Ibn Hisham's Tale," trans. Roger Allen, 313–14.

2. Timothy Mitchell, "Worlds Apart: An Egyptian Village and the International Tourism Industry," *Middle East Report* (September–October 1995): 8–11, 23, provides an insightful critical look at issues of contemporary tourism. Dean MacCannell, *The Tourist: A New Theory of the Leisure Class* (New York, 1976), provided an early sociological perspective on tourism. See also Tom Selwyn, ed., *The Tourist Image: Myths and Myth Making in Tourism* (Chichester, England, 1996).

3. As quoted in James Buzard, *The Beaten Track: European Tourism, Literature, and the Ways to Culture, 1880–1918* (Oxford, 1993), 110.

4. As quoted in Buzard, *Beaten Track,* 1, 133.

Notes to Pages 66–69

5. Jean Leclant, "Le Voyage en Nubie (1813–1913)," in *D'un Orient l'autre*, 2 vols. (Paris, 1991), 1: 405–15.

6. Adolphe Joanne and Émile Isambert, *Itinéraire descriptif, historique, et archéologique de l'Orient* (Paris, 1861) (hereafter, Joan. 1861), 1094.

7. *Oxford English Dictionary*, 2nd ed. (1989); Helen Angelomatis-Tsougarakis, *The Eve of the Greek Revival: British Travellers' Perceptions of Early Nineteenth-Century Greece* (London, 1990); Robert Eisner, *Travelers to an Antique Land: The History and Literature of Travel to Greece* (Ann Arbor, 1991), 89–112.

8. *Grand Larousse de la langue française* (Paris, 1971–1978), 7: 6142.

9. Patrick Brantlinger, *Rule of Darkness: British Literature and Imperialism, 1830–1914* (Ithaca, N.Y., 1988), 138. On the passenger steamers, see Buzard, *Beaten Track*, 41.

10. J. J. Halls, *The Life and Correspondence of Henry Salt*, 2 vols. (London, 1834), 1: 69–77; Daniel R. Headrick, *The Tentacles of Progress: Technology Transfer in the Age of Imperialism, 1850–1940* (London, 1988), 26; Alain Silvera, "The First Egyptian Student Mission to France under Muhammad Ali," *Middle Eastern Studies* 16 (1980): 1; Jason Thompson, *Sir John Gardner Wilkinson and His Circle* (Austin, 1992), 129.

11. Headrick, *Tentacles*, 39–41; Wilk. 1843, 2: 473–76.

12. William Makepeace Thackeray, *The Paris Sketch Book of Mr. M. A. Titmarsh: The Irish Sketchbook; and Notes of a Journey from Cornhill to Grand Cairo* (New York, n.d.), 719, 720. On the overland transit, see also Lionel Wiener, *Égypte et ses chemins de fer* (Brussells, 1932), 52–58.

13. E. A. W. Budge, *Cook's Handbook for Egypt and the Sudan*, 2nd ed. (London, 1906), 411–12.

14. John Murray, *A Hand-book for Travellers in Egypt* (London, 1858) (hereafter, Murr. 1858), 112–13; John Murray, *A Hand-book for Travellers* (London, 1873) (hereafter, Murr. 1873), 111.

15. Wiener, *Égypte*, 64–76. For global telegraph systems, see Headrick, *Tentacles*, 97–125, and Daniel R. Headrick, *The Invisible Weapon: Telecommunications and International Politics, 1851–1945* (New York, 1991), 1–115.

16. Generalizations on Egyptian guidebooks are based on the list in Oleg V. Volkoff, *Comment on visitait la vallée du Nil: Les Guides de l'Égypte*, Recherches no. 28 (Cairo: IFAO, 1967): 103–19. About half a dozen pre-1869 guidebook editions covered Egypt and India together.

17. Wilk. 1847: 2; Murr. 1858: 2, John Murray, *A Hand-book for Travellers in Lower and Upper Egypt*, 2 vols. (London, 1880) (hereafter, Murr. 1880), 1: xiv.

18. Buzard, *Beaten Track*, 121.

19. William W. Stowe, *Going Abroad: European Travel in Nineteenth-Century American Culture* (Princeton, 1994), 7.

20. Wilk. 1847: xvi; Murr. 1858: ix–x; Murr. 1880, 1: xv; Karl Baedeker, *Egypt: Handbook for Travellers*, 6th ed. (Leipzig, 1895) (hereafter, Baed. 1895), 1–2.

21. John Pemble, *The Mediterranean Passion: Victorians and Edwardians in the South* (Oxford, 1987), v.

22. For this and the following paragraph, see Ali Behdad, *Belated Travelers: Orientalism in the Age of Colonial Dissolution* (Durham, N.C., 1994), 39–47.

23. On Rifaud, see *WWWE3*: 358.

24. *Oxford English Dictionary*, 2nd ed. (1989); Johann Gottfried Ebel, *Instructions pour un voyageur qui se propose de parcourir la Suisse*, 2 vols. (Basel, 1795), cited in Daniel Nordmann, "Les Guides-Joanne: Ancêtres des guides bleus," in *Les Lieux de mémoire*, vol. 2: *La Nation*, ed. Pierre Nora (Paris, 1986), 563 n. 2. On the Murray guidebooks, see W. B. C. Lister, *A Bibliography of Murray's Handbooks for Travellers* (Dereham, England, 1993); and Edmund W. Gilbert, *British Pioneers in Geography* (New York, 1972), 101–5.

25. Quoted in Piers Brendon, *Thomas Cook: 150 Years of Popular Tourism* (London, 1991), 120.

26. Nordmann, "Guides," 529–67.

27. Joan. 1861.

28. Joan. 1861: 968–69, 992–93, 986, 1005–8.

29. Buzard, *Beaten Path*, 66–67. For the remainder of the paragraph, see also Karl Baedeker, *Baedeker's Egypt*, 8th ed. (London, 1929; reprint, London, 1985) (hereafter, Baed. 1929), v; and Bernard J. Shapero Rare Books, *Baedeker Catalogue* (London, 1989).

30. Edmund Swinglehurst, *Cook's Tours: The Story of Popular Travel* (Poole, Dorset, England, 1982), 45; and Budge, *Cook's Handbook*, iii.

31. Marcus Simaika, "Excerpts from the Memoirs of Marcus H. Simaika Pasha, C.B.E., F.S.A. [1864–1944]," unpublished typescript in the possession of Dr. Samir Simaika, 29, 71–72; Salama Musa, *The Education of Salama Musa*, trans. L. O. Schuman (Leiden, 1961), 50.

32. Wilk. 1843, 1: 101; Murr. 1880, 1: 115–16.

33. Jean-Jacques Rifaud, *Tableau de l'Égypte, de la Nubie et des lieux circonvoisins* (Paris, 1830), 61–62; Michael Byrd, *Samuel Shepheard of Cairo: A Portrait* (London, 1957).

34. Rifaud, *Tableau*, 61–62; Wilk. 1843, 1: 202–4.

35. Murr. 1858: 114–15; Joan. 1861: 958: Murr. 1880, 1: 157–58; Karl Baedeker, *Egypt: Handbook for Travellers*, 6th ed. (Leipzig, 1908) (hereafter, Baed. 1908), 31–32.

36. Rifaud, *Tableau*, 32–35; Wilk. 1847: 8; Murr. 1873: 8; Baed. 1908: v.

37. Rifaud, *Tableau*, 56–58; Thompson, *Wilkinson*, 145–47.

38. Lord Lindsay, *Letters on Egypt, Edom, and the Holy Land*, 2nd ed. (London, 1838), 1: 44–45.

39. Wilk. 1847: 7.

40. I. G. Wilkinson, *Topography of Thebes, and General View of Egypt . . .* (London, 1835) (hereafter, Wilk. 1835), iv; Gerry D. Scott III, "Go Down into Egypt," in *The American Discovery of Ancient Egypt*, ed. Nancy Thomas (Los Angeles, 1995), 40; Wilk. 1843, 1: iv. Page 87 reports that the English had voluntarily agreed to fly the Turkish flag at the post of honor but that some English parties and other Europeans still flew their national banners.

41. Rifaud, *Tableau*, 88; Brendon, *Cook*, 120 (on Syria and Palestine); Baed. 1895: xx.

42. Baed. 1908: xxiii–xxv; Wilk. 1835: 559; Murr. 1873: 119. Frances Kart-tunen, *Between Worlds: Interpreters, Guides, and Survivors* (New Brunswick, 1994), treats some of the issues involving such intermediaries.

43. Jean-Joël Brégeon, *L'Égypte française au jour le jour 1798–1801* (Paris, 1991), 354–55; Jean-Marie Carré, *Voyageurs et écrivains français en Égypte*, 2 vols. (Cairo, 1956), 1: 180–81, 199, 204–5; Jason Thompson, "Osman Effendi: A Scottish Convert to Islam in Early Nineteenth-Century Egypt," *Journal of World History* 5 (1994): 99–123.

44. Murr. 1858: 160.

45. Carré, *Voyageurs*, 2: 108–12.

46. Baed. 1895: xxii.

47. Rifaud, *Tableau*, "Avis"; Wilk. 1835.

48. Rifaud, *Tableau*, 104; Thompson, *Wilkinson*, 52–54, 95–98.

49. Wilk. 1843, 1: 245–51; Murr. 1858: 134.

50. Murr. 1858: 140; Murr. 1880, 1: 215; Baed. 1895: ci.

51. Rifaud, *Tableau*, 64; Murr. 1858: 117.

52. Michael J. Reimer, *Colonial Bridgehead: Government and Society in Alexandria, Egypt, 1807–1882* (Boulder, Colo., 1997), 108. The Klondike metaphor is from David Landes, *Bankers and Pashas: International Finance and Economic Imperialism in Egypt* (New York, 1969), 69.

53. Murr. 1873: 1, xix–xx, 85–88; Wilk. 1843, 1: 85–89; Baed. 1895.

54. Amelia Edwards, *A Thousand Miles up the Nile,* 2nd ed. (New York, [ca. 1888]), 370.

55. Théophile Gautier, *Voyage en Espagne* (Paris, 1929), 349, as quoted in Pemble, *Mediterranean*, 1.

56. Buzard, *Beaten Path*, 219.

57. Note, however, that Macmillan's *Guide to Palestine and Egypt* (London and New York, 1901) is not listed in Volkoff, *Comment*.

58. G. W. Steevens, *Egypt in 1898* (London, 1898), as quoted in Deborah Manley, *The Nile: A Travellers Anthology* (London, 1991), 111.

59. Wilk. 1843, 1: 89; Wilk. 1835: 560.

60. Justin Stagl, *A History of Curiosity: The Theory of Travel 1550–1800* (Chur, Switzerland, 1995).

61. Murr. 1873: 46. For the above list of suggestions, see Murr. 1858: 46.

62. Alexander Kinglake, *Eothen* (Lincoln, Nebr., 1970), 272.

63. Wilk. 1843, 1: 70. On the plague in the Middle East, see Daniel Panzac, *Quarantaines et lazarets: L'Europe et la peste d'Orient (XVIIe–XX siècles)* (Aix-en-Provence, 1986); Laverne Kuhnke, *Lives at Risk: Public Health in Nineteenth-Century Egypt* (Berkeley, Calif., 1990), esp. 70–87.

64. Wilk. 1847: xviii–xxv; Murr. 1858: 7.

65. Kuhnke, *Lives,* 49–66, 101–7; Panzac, *Quarantaines,* 117–21.

66. Kuhnke, *Lives,* 49–66, 101–4, 107; Panzac, *Quarantaines,* 95–96, 120–21.

67. W. Reil, *Ägypten als Winteraufenthalt für Kranke* (1859), as cited in Volkoff, *Guides,* 104. On Duff Gordon, see K. Frank, *Lucie Duff Gordon* (London, 1994); and the enlarged edition of her *Letters from Egypt (1862–69),* ed. Gordon Wakefield (London, 1969).

68. Murr. 1873: 1, 2, 4.

69. Murr. 1858: 226; Murr. 1880, 1: 278; Pemble, *Mediterranean*, 246–47.

70. Murr. 1858: 118–23. Early travelers often used a more modest boat called a *khanja* rather than a *dahabiyya*.

71. Wilk. 1843, 1: iv, ii, 210–13.

72. Murr. 1858: 122; Murr. 1873: 120, 318–19; Murr. 1880, 2: 386; Baed. 1908: 197–98.

73. Wiener, *Égypte*, 90–122.

74. Baed. 1908: 197–98.

75. Headrick, *Tentacles*, 97–116; Headrick, *Invisible Weapon*, 1–92.

76. Murr. 1873: xiv, 318; Gabriel Charmes, *Cinq Mois au Caire et dans la Basse-Égypte* (Cairo, 1880), 221–22.

77. Baed. 1908: 196, 200.

78. Wilk. 1843, 1: 319; 2: 134; Lindsay, *Letters*, 1: 39–40.

79. Murr. 1880, 2: 450; Brendon, *Cook*, 136–37, 231–32.

80. Buzard, *Beaten Path*, 123.

81. William Wetmore Story, *Roba di Roma*, 2nd ed. (London, 1863), 1: 7, as quoted in Buzard, *Beaten Path*, 120.

82. Robin Fedden, *English Travellers in the Near East* (London, 1958), 16.

83. Carré, *Voyageuers* 2: 13.

84. Behdad, *Belated Travellers*, 92. On Flaubert's Egyptian encounter generally, see 53–72.

85. Thackeray, *Notes*, 717. On Mark Twain at the Pyramids, see his *Innocents Abroad or the New Pilgrim's Progress* (New York, 1929), 509–17.

86. Linda Nochlin, "The Imaginary Orient," *Art in America* (May 1983): 118–31, 187–91; John MacKenzie, *Orientalism: History, Theory, and the Arts* (Manchester, 1995), 43–70.

87. Quoted in Kathleen Stewart Howe, ed., *Excursions along the Nile: The Photographic Discovery of Ancient Egypt* (Santa Barbara: Santa Barbara Museum of Art, 1993), 22–23. This section draws particularly on Howe. See also Deborah Bull and Donald Lorimer, *Up the Nile: A Photographic Excursion: Egypt 1839–1898* (New York, 1979); Paul Chevedden, "Making Light of Everything: Early Photography of the Middle East and Current Photomania," *Middle East Studies Association Bulletin* 18, no. 2 (December 1984): 151–74; Carney E. E. Gavin, *The Image of the East: Nineteenth-Century Near Eastern Photographs by Bonfils from the Collections of the Harvard Semitic Museum* (Chicago, 1982); and Caroline Williams, "A Nineteenth-Century Photographer: Francis Frith," in *Travellers in Egypt,* ed. Paul Starkey and Janet Starkey (London, 1998), 168–78.

88. John M. MacKenzie, *Propaganda and Empire: The Manipulation of Public Opinion, 1880–1960* (Manchester, 1984), 19–21. See also Frank Staff, *Picture Postcards and Travel: A Collector's Guide* (Guildford, England, 1979), 44; Tonie Holt and Valmai Holt, *Picture Postcards of the Golden Age: A Collector's Guide* (London, 1971).

89. The quotation above is G. W. Steevens's, as quoted in John Pudney, *The Thomas Cook Story* (London, 1953), 212. On Cook, see also Brendon, *Cook*; and Swinglehurst, *Cook's Tours*.

90. Brendon, *Cook,* 12.

91. Brendon, *Cook*; and Anthony Trollope, "An Unprotected Female at the Pyramids," *The Complete Shorter Fiction,* ed. Julian Thompson (New York, 1992), 82–103.

92. Wilk. 1843, 1: iv; Brendon, *Cook,* 124; Buzard, *Beaten Track,* 148–50.

93. Brendon, *Cook,* 120; Pemble, *Mediterranean,* 49.

94. Rev. J. Burns, *Helpbook for Travellers to the East including Egypt, Palestine, Turkey, Greece and Italy, with tourist arrangements by Th. Cook* (London, 1872).

95. Thomas Cook Archives, Egypt (General): Nile Fleet, Nile Hotels, Boulac, Passenger Lists: Contract, 9 July 1880.

96. Swinglehurst, *Cook's Tours,* 97.

97. Thomas Cook Archives, *The Excursionist,* 12 September 1887, 3; and 1 February 1888.

98. *Luxor Hospital for Natives in Upper Egypt,* printed leaflet in Thomas Cook Archives, Egypt (General): Business Accounts, etc.

99. *The Excursionist,* 12 September 1887, 3; and 1 February 1892, 7.

100. Pudney, *Cook,* 212; Buzard, *Beaten Path,* 335; Pemble, *Mediterranean,* 274.

101. Otto Meinardus, *Two Thousand Years of Coptic Christianity* (Cairo, 1999), 78.

CHAPTER 3. EGYPTOLOGY UNDER ISMAIL

1. Mohamed Saleh and Hourig Sourouzian, *The Egyptian Museum Cairo: Official Catalogue* (Cairo, 1987), 9, however, do give credit for the earlier effort.

2. Michael Adas, *Machines as the Measure of Men: Science, Technology, and Ideologies of Western Dominance* (Ithaca, N.Y., 1989), 143. On Egypt under Ismail, see F. Robert Hunter, *Egypt under the Khedives: From Household to Modern Bureaucracy, 1789* (Pittsburgh, 1984); Abd al-Rahman al-Rafii, *Asr Ismail,* 2nd ed. (Cairo, 1948); Juan Cole, *Colonialism and Revolution in the Middle East: Social and Cultural Origins of Egypt's Urabi Movement* (Princeton, 1993); Georges Douin, *Histoire du règne du khédive Ismaïl,* 3 vols. in 4 (Cairo, 1933–1939); David Landes, *Bankers and Pashas: International Finance and Economic Imperialism in Egypt* (Cambridge, Mass., 1958).

3. Peter Gran, *Islamic Roots of Capitalism: Egypt 1760–1840* (Austin, Tex., 1979).

4. On al-Tahtawi, see Gilbert Delanoue, *Moralistes et politiques musulmans dans l'Égypte du XIXe siècle (1798–1882),* 2 vols. (Cairo, 1982), 2: 383–487, 618–630, 651–54. See also Anouar Louca, *Voyageurs et écrivains égyptiens en France au XIXe siècle* (Paris, 1970), 55 ff.; Salih Majdi, *Hilyat al-zaman bi-manaqib khadim al-watan: Sirat Rifaa Rafii al-Tahtawi,* ed. Jamal al-Din al-Shayyal (Cairo, 1958); and Ahmad Badawi, *Rifaa Rafii al-Tahtawi,* 2nd ed. (Cairo, 1959). Ali Mubarak's autobiography appears in his *Al-Khitat al-taw-fiqiyya al-jadida,* 20 vols. (Cairo, 1305 / 1886–1887) 9: 37–61. Secondary sources include Delanoue, *Moralistes,* 2: 488–558; Darrell I. Dykstra, "A Biographical Study in Egyptian Modernization: Ali Mubarak (1823/4–1893)," 2

vols., unpublished Ph.D. dissertation, University of Michigan, 1977; Stephan Fliedner, *Ali Mubarak und seine Hitat: Kommentierte Übersetzung der Autobiographie und Werkbesprechung* (Berlin, 1990); Hunter, *Egypt*, 123–38.

5. For the biography of Ahmad Kamal, see *Al-Muqtataf* 63 (November 1923): 273–77; Tawfiq Habib, "Tarikh al-kashf an al-athar al-misriyya wa amal al-marhum Ahmad Kamal Basha," *Al-Hilal* 32 (1 November 1923): 135–41; Zaki Fahmi, *Safwat al-asr fi tarikh wa rusum mashahir rijal fi Misr*, 2 vols. (Cairo, 1926), 1: 331–36; Gamal El-Din El-Shayyal, *A History of Egyptian Historiography in the Nineteenth Century* (Alexandria, 1960), 60–63; Tawfiq Habib, "Dars al-athar fi al-Jamia al-Misriyya," *Al-Muqtataf* 72 (1928): 438–39; *WWWE*3: 224. Dia M. Abou-Ghazl, "Ahmed Kamal 1849–1923," *ASAE* 64 (1981): 1–5, lists his articles.

6. *WWWE*3: 130–31. On L'Hôte, Rosellini, Dubois, and de Rougé, see *WWWE*3: 253–54, 362–63, 130–31, 365–66. See also Diane Sarofim Harlé, "The Unknown Nestor L'Hôte," in *Travellers in Egypt,* ed. Paul Starkey and Janet Starkey (London, 1998), 121–29.

7. On Mariette, see Elisabeth David, *Mariette Pacha 1821–1881* (Paris, 1994); Gaston Maspero, "Mariette (1821–1881): Notice biographique," in Auguste Mariette, *Oeuvres diverses* (Paris, 1904), 1: i–ccxxiv (Mariette's *Oeuvres diverses* is vol. 18 of the series Bibliothèque égyptologique, contentent les oeuvres des égyptologues française, ed. Gaston Maspero, 40 vols. [Paris, 1893–1915]); Edouard Mariette, *Mariette Pacha* (Paris, 1904); and Jean Sainte Fare Garnot, *Mélanges Mariette,* IFAO, Bibliothèque d'études 32 (Cairo, 1961). For his own account of the Serapeum discovery, see Auguste Mariette-Pacha, *Le Sérapeum de Memphis* (Paris, 1882). On Curzon and Tattam, see *WWWE*3: 113, 410–11.

8. DWQ / Abhath B118: Athar / F: Mariette / Le Moyne to Stéphan Bey, 9 June 1851, begins a series of letters on the Serapeum dispute. Le Moyne to Stéphan Bey, 4 February1852, concludes the series with thanks to the viceroy for the gift of 515 pieces.

9. Gaston Maspero, *Guide du visiteur au Musée du Caire,* 4th ed. (Cairo, 1915), x; Abou-Ghazi, "Egyptian Museum," *ASAE* 67 (1991): 9.

10. Bernard S. Cohn, *Colonialism and Its Forms of Knowledge: The British in India* (Princeton, 1966), 9.

11. DWQ / Abhath B118: Athar / F: Mariette / Mariette to König (viceregal secretary), 18 April 1858, begins a series negotiating Mariette's appointment and reporting on his early activities as director. Mariette to König, 26 December 1859, concludes the series.

12. Maspero, "Mariette," xcvi.

13. Maspero, "Mariette," xcvi.

14. May Trad, "Journal d'entrée et catalogue général," *ASAE* 70 (1984–1985): 352–57.

15. DWQ / Abhath B118: Athar / F: Mariette / Mariette to König Bey, 18 April 1858.

16. *WWWE*3: 276.

17. W. M. F. Petrie, *Seventy Years in Archaeology* (London, 1931), 46.

18. Maspero, "Mariette," cxliv.

19. Petrie, *Seventy Years,* 52–53.

20. Garnot, *Mélanges*, 1–2.

21. Mariette, *Oeuvres*, cxxv. For this paragraph, see cxxiii–cxxxi; and Landes, *Bankers*, 108–9.

22. William Makepeace Thackeray, *The Paris Sketch Book of Mr. M. A. Titmarsh: The Irish Sketchbook; and Notes of a Journey from Cornhill to Grand Cairo* (New York, n.d.), 714. For the rest of the paragraph, see Jason Thompson, *Sir John Gardner Wilkinson and His Circle* (Austin, Tex., 1992), 192–93. On the removal of the Paris, London, and New York obelisks, see Labib Habachi, *The Obelisks of Egypt: Skyscrapers of the Past* (Cairo, 1984), 152–82.

23. Mariette. Contrary to academic convention, I have decided to keep this quotation, although I have mislaid my notecard and cannot check the original source, which was probably in MAE.

24. DWQ / MMW / NA / MA 1 / 4: Matahif 1879–1914 / F: al-Hukumat al-ajnabiyya wa al-athar al-misriyya / subdossier: Talab dawlat Amrika limasilla, extracts from Council of Ministers, 20 October 1879, incl. in Cherif to Farman, 18 March 1879; U.S. National Archives, Records of Department of State, Microfilm T41, Roll 7, Cairo Consuls to State Dept., 10 November 1879, Farman to Evarts enclosing a translation from *Gazette des Tribunaux*, 4 November 1879, showing Europeans' opposition to removing the obelisk. The September 1879–January 1880 correspondence on the obelisk shows it was the American consul's major concern that fall. Farman to Evarts, 20 January 1880, is a forty-one-page letter on the history of the obelisk, including a translation of its texts.

25. Maria Avgouli, "The First Greek Museums and National Identity," in *Museums and the Making of "Ourselves": The Role of Objects in National Identity*, ed. Flora E. S. Kaplan (London, 1994); Yannis Hamilakis and Eleana Yalouri, "Antiquities as Symbolic Capital in Modern Greek Society," *Antiquity* 70 (1996): 117–29; Maria Mouliou, "Ancient Greece, Its Classical Heritage, and the Modern Greeks: Aspects of Nationalism in Museum Exhibitions," in *Nationalism and Archaeology*, ed. John A. Atkinson, Iain Banks, Jerry O'Sullivan, Scottish Archaeological Forum (Glasgow, 1996), 174–99.

26. On developments in Istanbul, see Tülay Ergil, *Museums of Istanbul / Istanbul Müzerleri* (Istanbul, 1993). On Osman Hamdi, director of the museum and Antiquities Service from 1881 until his death in 1910, see Mustafa Cezar, *Müzeci ve ressam Osman Hamdi Bey* (Istanbul, 1987).

27. DWQ / Abhath B118: Athar / F: Mariette / Mariette to König, 29 April 1858.

28. Maspero, "Mariette," cxxiv–cxxv, for this and the following two quotations.

29. Maspero, "Mariette," cxcii.

30. Maspero, "Mariette," cxxxvii. On the Bulaq Museum generally, see Auguste Mariette-Bey, *Notice des principaux monuments exposés dans les galeries provisoires du Musée d'antiquités égyptiennes de S. A. le Vice-Roi à Boulaq*, 1st–5th eds. (Alexandria / Cairo, 1864–1874) (title varies; hereafter, particular editions cited by year); G. Maspero, *Guide du visiteur au musée du Caire*, 4th ed. (Cairo, 1915), vii–xx; Étienne Drioton, "Le Musée de Boulac," *Cahiers d'histoire égyptienne*, ser. 3, fasc. 1 (November 1950): 1–12; and *Album de*

musée de Boulaq (Cairo, 1871), photos by Hippolyte Délié and Henri Béchard, text by Mariette.

31. Maspero, "Mariette," cxxxix.

32. F. de Saulcy, "Musée du Caire," *Revue archéologique*, n.s. (May 1864) 9: 313–22; Maspero, "Mariette," cxxxix–cxl, clxxviii.

33. Mariette, *Notice*, 1868, 10–11.

34. Mariette, *Notice*, 1868, 10.

35. Auguste Mariette-Bey, *Wasf nukhbat al-athar al-qadima al-misriyya al-mawjuda fi khazinat al-tuhaf al-ilmiyya al-misriyya* (Cairo, 1286 / 1869), 4. A title page, but nothing more, of the original French version is bound in with this Arabic translation: *Une Visite au musée de Boulaq ou description des principaux monuments conservés dans les salles de cet établissement* (Paris, 1869).

36. Mariette, *Notice*, 1868, 20–21.

37. Mariette, *Mariette*, 32–33; Maspero, "Mariette," cxxvii–cxxviii.

38. Maspero, "Mariette," cxl.

39. *Bidayat al-qudama wa hidayat al-hukama*, trans. Mustafa al-Zawarbi, Muhammad Abd al-Raziq, and Abdallah Abu al-Suud (Bulaq, 1254 / 1838; 2nd ed., 1282 / 1865). Delanoue, *Moralistes*, 2: 623–24. Abu al-Futuh Radwan, *Tarikh Matbaat Bulaq* (Cairo, 1953), 468, lists a *Tarikh al-Misriyyin*, or *Tarikh qudama al-Misriyyin* by al-Tahtawi published in 1254 / 1839; Ayda Ibrahim Nusayr, *Kutub al-arabiyya nushirat fi Misr fi al-qarn al-tasi ashar* (Cairo, 1990), 252, lists al-Tahtawi as translator of *Tarikh qudama al-Misriyyin*, 1254 / 1838. These probably both refer to *Bidayat al-qudama*. I have been unable to locate a copy of this work. On Abu al-Suud, see Jamal al-Din Shayyal, *History,* 41–43; Cole, *Colonialism*, 127, 225, 314 n. 37.

40. Quoted in Arthur Rhoné, *L'Égypte à petites journées: Le Caire d'autre fois,* new ed. (Paris, 1910), 3.

41. Auguste Mariette, *Aperçu de l'histoire d'Égypte depuis les temps les plus reculés jusqu'à la conquête musulmane (Kitab Qudama al-Misriyyin)* (Alexandria, 1864), 3, 5. The copy consulted had Mariette's French original bound together with Abu al-Suud's Arabic translation. Shayyal, *History,* 41–43, gives different Arabic titles for both the A.H. 1281 translation of *Aperçu (Qannasat ahl al-asr fi khulasat tarikh Misr)* and the A.H. 1286 guide *(Mutafarrij ala al-Antikhana al-Khidaywiyya).*

42. Delanoue, *Moralistes*, 2: 630; Rifaa Rifi al-Tahtawi, *Anwar tawfiq al-jalil fi akhbar Misr wa-tawthiq Bani Ismail*, in *Al-Amal al-kamila li-Rifaa Rafi al-Tahtawi*, ed. Muhammad Amara, vol. 3: *Tarikh Misr wa al-arab qabla al-Islam* (Beirut, 1974).

43. Youssef M. Choueri, *Arab History and the Nation-State: A Study in Modern Arab Historiography 1820–1980* (London, 1989), 9–11. These prefatory endorsements were omitted from the later edition of *Anwar* available to me.

44. al-Tahtawi, *Anwar,* 14–15, 18–19.

45. al-Tahtawi, *Anwar,* 33–70. The antiquities chapter is 63–66.

46. al-Tahtawi, *Anwar,* 70.

47. al-Tahtawi, *Anwar,* 64, 74.

48. al-Tahtawi, *Anwar,* 73–74, 80, 90, 94–95, 100–105, 110–13.

49. al-Tahtawi, *Anwar,* 73.

50. T. Fahd, "Sabi'a," *EI*2, 8: 675–78.

51. al-Tahtawi, *Anwar,* 20–21.

52. Khalil Sabat, *Tarikh al-tibaa fi al-sharq al-arabi,* 2nd ed. (Cairo, 1966), 186; Cole, *Colonialism,* 42, 294 n. 43.

53. Muhammad Abd al-Ghani Hasan and Abd al-Aziz al-Disuqi, *Rawdat al-madaris: Nashatuha wa ittijahatuha al-adabiyya wa al-ilmiyya* (Cairo, 1975), 44–45.

54. Louca, *Voyageurs,* 73.

55. Hasan and al-Disuqi, *Rawdat,* 219–20, 363–65.

56. Hasan and al-Disuqi, *Rawdat,* 222, 227, 363–65, 381.

57. *Oxford English Dictionary,* 2nd ed. (1989); *Grand Larousse de la langue française* (Paris, 1971–1978).

58. See table 6 in appendix.

59. Maspero, "Mariette," clxxx–clxxxii.

60. D. A. Farnie, *East and West of Suez, 1854–1956* (Oxford, 1969), 751–52; A. G. Hopkins, "The Victorians and Africa: A Reconsideration of the Occupation of Egypt, 1882," *Journal of African History* 27 (1986): 379. For the new vocabulary relating to Egyptology, see *Dictionnaire de la langue française* (Paris, 1988), 609; *Oxford English Dictionary,* 2nd ed. (1989), vol. 5: 97.

61. Christopher M. Andrew and A. S. Kanya-Forstner, *The Climax of French Imperial Expansion 1914–1924* (Stanford, 1981); Mathew Burrows, " 'Mission civilisatrice': French Cultural Policy in the Middle East, 1860–1914," *Historical Journal* 29 (1986): 109–35.

62. Georg Ebers, *Richard Lepsius A Biography,* trans. Z. D. Underhill (New York, 1887), 275–76; Suzanne L. Marchand, *Down from Olympus: Archaeology and Philhellenism in Germany, 1750–1970* (Princeton, N.J., 1996), 49, 108.

63. Ebers, *Lepsius,* 300.

64. For the dates of these chairs, see the *WWWE*3 entries on these individuals.

65. Heinrich Brugsch, *Mein Leben und mein Wandern* (Berlin, 1894); Louis Keimer, "Le Musée égyptologique de Berlin," *Cahiers d'histoire égyptienne,* ser. 3, fasc. 1 (November 1950): 30–36. See also *WWWE*3, 67–68.

66. Maspero, "Mariette," cxlvi–cli.

67. Ebers, *Lepsius,* 157.

68. Maspero, "Mariette," clxxxii.

69. Maspero, "Mariette," cxc.

70. Mariette, *Mariette,* 117–19.

71. On Bonomi, Wild, and Bunson, see *WWWE*3, 53–54, 442, 73.

72. Angelo Sammarco, *Gli Italiani in Egitto* (Alexandria, 1937), 151–53.

73. Burrows, " 'Mission civilisatrice,' " 111–12, speaking of the Ottoman Empire; Jean-Jacques Luthi, *Le Français en Égypte* (Beirut, 1981).

74. *L'Egittologo Luigi Vassalli (1812–1887),* Disegni e documenti nei Civici Istituti Culturali Milanesi (Milan, 1994).

75. DWQ / Fihrist Bataqat al-Dar, Drawer No. 1: Athar / 15 Safar 1289, Order to Diwan al-Maliya, Daftar 1939, Doc. No. 140, p. 145. Brugsch's ac-

count is from his *Leben,* 275–82. The best secondary account is Ahmad Izzat Abd al-Karim, *Tarikh al-talim fi Misr min nihayat hukm Muhammad Ali ila awail hukm Tawfiq 1848–1882,* 3 vols. (Cairo, 1945), 2, pt. 2: 569–73.

76. Amal Hilal, "Les Premiers égyptologues égyptiens et la réforme," in *Entre Réforme sociale et mouvement national: Identité et modernisation en Égypte (1882–1962),* ed. Alain Roussillon (Cairo, 1995), 346.

77. Abd al-Karim, *Tarikh,* 2, pt. 2: 570–71, gives their names; Ahmad Kamal and Ahmad Najib later became the most prominent.

78. Quoted in Abd al-Karim, *Tarikh,* 2, pt. 2: 569.

79. Abd al-Karim, *Tarikh,* 2, pt. 2: 569, says Mikhail Jirjis taught them *"al-lugha al-Habashiyya,"* probably meaning Coptic rather than Ethiopic.

80. Brugsch, *Leben,* 299.

81. *WWWE3:* 404.

82. Abd al-Karim, *Tarikh,* 2, pt. 2: 572, says that Amin Sami, *Al-Talim fi Misr* (Cairo, 1917), appendix, 91, is mistaken in saying the school lasted until December 1876.

83. Maspero, "Mariette," clxxvi, clxxxvi; Abd al-Karim, *Tarikh,* 2, pt. 2: 572.

84. Brugsch, *Leben,* 282.

85. J. Heyworth-Dunne, *Introduction to the History of Education in Modern Egypt* (London, 1968), 355.

86. Petrie, *Seventy Years,* 64.

87. Yunan Rizk, "Al-Ahram: A Diwan of Contemporary Life," *al-Ahram Weekly,* 12–18 August 1993; Ibrahim Abduh, *Jaridat al-Ahram: Tarikh wa fann 1875–1964* (Cairo, 1964).

88. On the stamps, see "Egypt," in *Scott 2000 Standard Postage Stamp Catalogue, Countries of the World,* vol. 2: *Countries C–F* (Sidney, Ohio, 2000). For coins, see "Egypt" and "Turkey" in the most recent editions of Krause Publications' *Standard Catalog of World Coins, 1801–1900,* 2nd ed. (Iola, Wis., 1998); *Standard Catalog of World Coins, 2001* (Iola, Wis., 2000). On the postal system, see *Les Postes en Égypte* (Cairo, 1934).

89. Charles Wendell, *The Evolution of the Egyptian National Image from Its Origin to Ahmad Lutfi al-Sayyid* (Berkeley, Calif., 1972), 169, quoting Rashid Rida, *Tarikh al-Ustadh al-Imam al-Shaykh Muhammad Abduh* (Cairo, 1931), 1: 46–47.

90. Angelo Sammarco, *Histoire de l'Égypte moderne depuis Mohammed Ali jusqu'à l'occupation britannique (1801–1882)* (Cairo, 1937), 324.

91. Cole, *Colonialism,* 33–35. The manuscript "Irshad al-Walad" by Kaçifzade Mehmet Aqïl Buharali, also signed in Arabized form as Muhammad Aqil ibn Muhammad Kashif, is in the Egyptian National Library.

92. David C. Gordon, *Images of the West: Third World Perspectives* (n.p., 1989), 15.

93. Jomard, only twenty-one in 1798, had not actually been a member of the first Institut d'Égypte but had worked closely with it. J.-E. Goby, "Travaux de premier Institut d'Égypte (1798–1801)," *Bulletin de la Société française d'égyptologie* 66 (March 1973): 36.

94. Jacques Ellul, *Index des communications et mémoires publiés par l'Institut d'Égypte (1859–1952)* (Cairo: IFAO, 1952), is the reference for the following observations on the articles in the *Bulletin de l'Institut d'Égypte (BIE);*

for the officers, see the unnumbered appendices. For lists of members, see *BIE* 2 (1859): 7–12; ser. 3, 1 (1890): 200–222; ser. 5, 3, fasc. 2 (1909): 176–79.

95. *BIE* 1 (1859): 2.

96. *Livre d'or de l'Institut égyptien: L'Institut égyptien, 6 mai 1859–5 mai 1899* (Cairo, 1899), 3.

97. DWQ / Abhath B132 / Institut d'Égypte / June 29 1947, pres. of Institut égyptien to Adli Bey Andraws, enclosing Annexe F: Mariette to ministers of the interior and finance, 6 February 1880; *BIE*, ser. 2, 4 (1883): 256.

98. The others were J. Hazan, the grand rabbi of Alexandria, medical doctors Shafii Bey and Muhammad Ali, and Abdallah Said Effendi, director of the commercial office at Alexandria.

99. *BIE*, ser. 2, 5 (1884–1885): 167, lists him as a member without the date he joined.

100. BL/Add MSS 37,463 / Hek 16: 427, undated and unsigned, probably Russell, correspondent of the *Times*, 1869. For the rest of the paragraph, see 37,462 / Hek 15: 55; 37,460 / Hek 12: 759; 37,472 / Hek 24; 75; 37,470 / Hek 22: 308; 37,462 / Hek 15: Hekekyan to de Lesseps, 26 April 1869.

101. BL/Add MSS 34,463 / Hek 16: 76, Hekekyan to Nassau Senior.

102. *Livre d' or*, 9. On al-Falaki, see Pascal Crozet, "La Trajectoire d'un scientifique égyptien au XIXe siècle: Mahmoud al-Falaki (1815–1885)," in *Entre Réforme sociale*, ed. Roussillon, 285–310.

103. On the Khedivial Geographical Society see, Donald Malcolm Reid, "The Egyptian Geographical Society: From Foreign Laymen's Society to Indigenous Professional Association," *Poetics Today* 14 (1993): 539–72.

104. On Abbate and Bonola, see L. A. Balboni, *Gl'Italiani nella civiltà Egiziana de secolo XIXo*, 3 vols. (Alexandria, 1906) 3: 28–30, 30–34.

105. On Stone, see David Shavit, *The United States in the Middle East: A Historical Dictionary* (New York, 1988), 337.

106. *Bulletin de la Société khédivial géographique*, no. 8 (May 1880): 34.

107. *Bulletin de la Société khédivial géographique*, no. 6 (November 1879): 5; no. 8 (May 1880): 34; ser. 3, no. 12 (July 1893): 847–49.

108. Abd al-Rahman al-Rafii, *Asr Ismail*, 2nd ed., 2 vols. (Cairo, 1948), 1: 242–43.

109. For the exhibitions generally, see *The Book of the Fair: Materials about World's Fairs, 1834–1916, in the Smithsonian Institution Libraries*, intro. Robert W. Rydell, Smithsonian Institution Libraries Research Guide No. 6 (Chicago, 1992). Paul Greenhalgh, *Ephemeral Vistas: The Expositions Universelles, Great Exhibitions, and World's Fairs, 1851–1939* (Manchester, England, 1988), is a useful survey. For colonialist implications, see Timothy Mitchell, "The World as Exhibition," *Comparative Studies in Society and History* 31 (1989): 217–36; Timothy Mitchell, *Colonising Egypt* (Cambridge, 1988); Robert W. Rydell and Nancy Gwinn, eds., *Fair Representations: World's Fairs and the Modern World* (Amsterdam, 1994); and Zeynep Çelik, *Displaying the Orient: Architecture of Islam at Nineteenth-Century World's Fairs* (Berkeley, Calif., 1992). On the Great Exhibition, see *History and Description of the Great Exhibition of the World's Industry*, 4 vols. (London [ca. 1851]); C. R. Fay, *Palace of Industry: A Study of the Great Exhibition and Its Fruits*

(Cambridge, 1951); Jeffrey Auerbach, *The Great Exhibition of 1851* (New Haven, Conn., 1999). Owen Jones and Joseph Bonomi, *Description of the Egyptian Court* (London, 1854), describe this court at Sydenham.

110. *History and Description of the Great Exhibition*, 1: 46.

111. *History and Description of the Great Exhibition*, 3: 150. Vol. 3: 147–52, describes the Egyptian section before the move to Syndenham; 3: 257 mentions the embalmers.

112. As quoted in Nicholas Warner, ed., *An Egyptian Panorama: Reports from the 19th Century British Press* (Cairo, 1994), 19, from *Illustrated London News*, 5 August 1854.

113. David, *Mariette*, 144–46. See also *Campbell's Visitor's Guide to the International Exhibition and Handy Book of London* (London, 1862).

114. On the 1867 exposition, see Auguste Mariette, *Description du parc égyptien: Exposition universelle de 1867* (Paris, 1867); Charles Edmond, *L'Égypte à l'exposition universelle de 1867* (Paris, 1867); G. Douin, *Histoire de la règne de Khédive Ismail*, vol. 2: *L'Apogée 1867–1873* (Rome, 1934): 1–20; Louca, *Voyageurs*, 181–90; and Mehrangiz N. Nikou, "Egypt's Architectural Representation in the 1867 Paris International Exposition and Napoleon III's Aspiration for a French Arab Kingdom," unpublished paper presented at the convention of the Middle East Studies Association, Orlando, Florida, 16–19 November 2000. Mitchell, *Colonising*, 17, notes that Sulayman al-Harayri's *Ard al-badi al-amm* (Paris, 1867) is the first Arabic account of a world exhibition.

115. On *Aida*, see David, *Mariette*, 201–4.

116. Robert Rydell, *All the World's a Fair: Visions of Empire at American International Expositions 1876–1916* (Chicago, 1984), 9–32; Ibrahim el Mouelhy, "L'Égypte à l'exposition de Philadelphie (1876)," *Cahiers d'histoire égyptienne* 1 (1948): 316–26; and Kenneth J. Perkins, "Three Middle Eastern States Helped America Celebrate Its Centennial in Philadelphia," *Aramco World* (November–December 1976): 9–13.

117. Auguste Mariette-Bey, *Exposition universelle de Paris 1878: La Galerie de l'Égypte ancienne* (Paris, 1878); Louca, *Voyageurs*, 190–92.

118. Mitchell, *Colonising*, 8–9.

119. K. Vollers, "Le IXme congrès international des orientalistes tenu à Londres du 5 au 12 septembre 1892," *BIE*, ser. 3, 3 (November 1892): 193.

120. *Oxford English Dictionary*, 2nd ed. (1989), vol. 10: 931; vol. 5: 97.

121. *Mémoires du congrès international des Orientalistes, 1re session, Paris*, 3 vols. (Paris, 1873) (hereafter, *ICO1*, Paris, etc.), 1: 114–15; 3: cvii, cxxxviii–xi, 42–43. Unless otherwise specified, references to ICOs come from the proceedings of the congresses for the years cited. Title and language vary with host city.

122. Louca, *Voyageurs*, 181–208; Mitchell, *Colonising*, 1–2, 180–81; Findley, "Ottoman Occidentalist," *American Historical Review* 103 (1998): 15–49.

123. *ICO1*, Paris, 2: 315. For the Japanese scholar, see 2: 111 ff.

124. Samuel Birch, "Inaugural Address," *ICO2*, London, *Transactions*, 1–3.

125. Birch, "Inaugural Address," 13.

126. The eighth person was Jens Lieblein, a Norwegian. *ICO2*, London, *Report* (1874), 57; *WWE3*, 255.

127. *ICO3*, Saint Petersburg, *Travaux*, 2: xvi; *ICO4*, Florence, *Congresso*, 1: 1 ff., 2: 338–44, 355.

128. See the family tree in David, *Mariette*, 274.

129. Quoted in David, *Mariette*, 233–34.

130. Maspero, "Mariette," xcliii.

131. Maspero, "Mariette," ccii, ccxiii.

132. Maspero, "Mariette," cxccvi–cxccvii.

133. Earl of Cromer, *Modern Egypt* (New York, 1908), 28.

CHAPTER 4. CROMER AND THE CLASSICS

1. J. J. Halls, *The Life and Correspondence of Henry Salt,* 2 vols. (London, 1834), 2: 196; Francis Steegmuller, *Flaubert in Egypt: A Sensibility on Tour* (Boston, 1972), 33; L. A. Tregenza, *Egyptian Years* (London, 1958), xii, xiii. Arabic literature, of course, had its own classics, but in this study, unless otherwise indicated by the context, "the classics" means Greek and Latin classics as defined by the West.

2. *The Journals of Major-Gen. C. G. Gordon, C.B., at Kartoum,* ed. A. Egmond Hake, 2 vols. (London, 1885).

3. Hugh Lloyd-Jones, *Blood for the Ghosts: Classical Influences in the Nineteenth and Twentieth Centuries* (London, 1982); G. W. Clarke, ed., *Rediscovering Hellenism: The Hellenic Inheritance and the English Imagination* (Cambridge, 1989); Frank M. Turner, *The Greek Heritage in Victorian Britain* (New Haven, 1981); Hugh Lloyd-Jones, *Classical Survivals: The Classics in the Modern World* (London, 1982); M. L. Clarke, *Classical Education in Britain 1500–1900* (Cambridge, 1959); Richard Stoneman, *Land of Lost Gods: The Search for Classical Greece* (Norman, Okla., 1987); Rudolf Pfeiffer, *History of Classical Scholarship from 1300 to 1850* (Oxford, 1976); Meyer Reinhold, *Classica Americana: The Greek and Roman Heritage in the United States* (Detroit, 1984); William L. Vance, *America's Rome,* 2 vols. (New Haven, 1989); Richard Gummere, *The American Colonial Mind and the Classical Tradition* (Cambridge, Mass., 1963); Zvi Yavetz, "Why Rome? Zeitgeist and Ancient Historians in Early 19th-Century Germany," *American Journal of Philology* 97 (1976): 276–96.

4. For example, see Turner, *Greek Heritage;* and François Hartog, *The Mirror of Herodotus: The Representation of the Other in the Writing of History,* trans. Janet Lloyd (Berkeley, Calif., 1988).

5. Lloyd-Jones, *Blood for the Ghosts,* 144.

6. Turner, *Greek Heritage,* 5.

7. William Makepeace Thackeray, *The Paris Sketch Book of Mr. M. A. Titmarsh; The Irish Sketch Book; and Notes of a Journey from Cornhill to Grand Cairo* (New York, n.d.), 630; see also 626. For Churchill, see C. M. Bowra, *Memories 1898–1939* (London, 1966), 331.

8. Donald Prezioisi, "Art as Art History: Introduction," in his *The Art of Art History: A Critical Anthology* (Oxford, 1998), 21–30; Ian Morris, "History of Archaeology before 1900: Classical Archaeology," in *The Oxford Companion to Archaeology,* ed. Brian Fagan (New York, 1996), 287–90; Suzanne

L. Marchand, *Down from Olympus: Archaeology and Philhellenism in Germany, 1750–1970* (Princeton, N.J., 1996).

9. Fritz Ringer, *Fields of Knowledge: French Academic Culture in Comparative Perspective 1890–1920* (Cambridge, 1992), 144.

10. As quoted in Turner, *Greek Heritage,* 188. See also Frank Turner, "Why the Greeks and Not the Romans in Victorian Britain?" in *Rediscovering Hellenism,* ed. Clarke, 61–75.

11. Norman Vance, *The Victorians and Ancient Rome* (Oxford, 1997).

12. *Description,* vol. 1: *Antiquités: Planches* (Paris, 1809), frontispiece. Juan Eduardo Campo, "Mubarak's Khitat: An Egyptian Nationalist Valuation of Religious Space," unpublished paper, Middle East Studies Association, Beverly Hills, Calif., November 1988, 13, emphasizes the absence of people and settlements. On the Louvre painting by François Picot (1827), see François Pouillon, "Fantasie et investigations dans la peinture orientaliste du XIXème siècle," in *D'un Orient l'autre,* 2 vols. (Paris, 1991), 1: figure 3 (following p. 280).

13. Martin Bernal, *Black Athena: The Afroasiatic Roots of Classical Civilization,* 2 vols. (New Brunswick, N.J., 1987–1991), 1: 185.

14. As quoted in J. Christopher Herold, *Bonaparte in Egypt* (New York, 1962), 56.

15. Paul MacKendrick, *The North African Stones Speak* (Chapel Hill, N.C., 1980), 319. The last volume of the first edition of the *Description* came out in 1828, unless one counts the *Carte topographique de l'Égypte* (Paris, 1829), which was originally conceived as a separate work and did not come out until 1829.

16. Abadallah Laroui, *The History of the Maghrib: An Interpretation* (Princeton, N.J., 1977); Jean-Claude Vatin, ed., *Connaissances du Maghreb: Sciences sociales et colonisation* (Paris, 1984), esp. Jacques Frémeaux, "Souvenirs de Rome et présence française au Maghreb," 29–46, and James Malarkey, "The Dramatic Structure of Scientific Discovery in Colonial Algeria: A Critique of the *Journal de la Société archéologique de Constantine (1853–1876),*" 137–160; Daniel Nordman and Jean-Pierre Raison, eds., *Sciences de l'homme et conquête coloniale: Constitution et usages des sciences humaines en Afrique (XIXe–XXe siècles)* (Paris, 1980), esp. Marcel Benabou, "L'Imperialisme et l'Afrique du nord: Le Modèle romain," 15–22; David Prochaska, *Making Algeria French: Colonialism in Bone, 1870–1920* (Cambridge, 1990).

17. Georg Ebers, *Richard Lepsius: A Biography,* trans. Z. D. Underhill (New York, 1887), 274–75. On Moret, see *WWWE3:* 295–96.

18. Rev. A. H. Sayce, *The Egypt of the Hebrews and Herodotos* (London, 1896), 224.

19. Quoted in H. V. F. Winstone, *Uncovering the Ancient World* (New York, 1986), 121. On not digging for Greco-Roman antiquities, see Auguste Mariette-Bey, *Notice des principaux monuments exposés dans les galeries provisoires du Musée d'antiquités égyptiennes de S. A. Le Khédive à Boulaq,* 5th ed. (Cairo, 1874), 62.

20. W. M. F. Petrie, *Seventy Years in Archaeology* (London, 1931), 6–7.

21. G. Maspero, "Une Inscription trilingue de C. Cornelius," in his *Causeries d'Égypte,* 2nd ed. (Paris, 1907), 95–101.

22. Dimitri Gutas, *Greek Thought, Arabic Culture: The Graeco-Arabic Translation Movement in Baghdad and Early 'Abbasid Society* (London, 1998); L. E. Goodman, "The Greek Impact on Arabic Literature," in *The Cambridge History of Arabic Literature,* vol. 1: *Arabic Literature to the End of the Umayyad Period,* ed. A. F. L. Beeston et al. (Cambridge, 1983), 460–82; Franz Rosenthal, *The Classical Heritage in Islam,* trans. E. and J. Marmorstein (Berkeley, Calif., 1975); and Felix Klein-Franke, *Die Klassische Antike in der Tradition des Islams* (Darmstadt, 1980).

23. Albert Hourani, "Sulaiman al-Bustani and the *Iliad,*" in his *Islam in European Thought* (Cambridge, 1991), 174–87; Wajih Fanus, "Sulayman al-Bustani and Comparative Literary Studies in Arabic," *Journal of Arabic Literature* 17 (1986): 105–19.

24. John Walbridge, "Explaining away the Greek Gods in Islam," unpublished paper at the Middle East Studies Association, Washington, D.C., December 1995.

25. *The History of al-Tabari (Tarikh al-rusul wa al-muluk)* (Albany, N.Y., 1984–), vol. 4: *The Ancient Kingdoms,* trans. Moshe Perlmann (1987), 126–27.

26. Charles Issawi, "Ibn Khaldun on Ancient History: A Study in Sources," *Princeton Papers in Near Eastern Studies,* no. 3 (1994): 127–50, notes that Ibn Khaldun's access to a translation of Orosius's Latin chronicle lends his *Kitab al-ibar* (though not his famous *Al-Muqaddima*) a more detailed knowledge of Roman history.

27. Gilbert Delanoue, *Moralistes et politiques musulmans dans l'Égypte du XIXe siècle (1798–1882),* 2 vols. (Cairo, 1982), 2: 619–20; Jamal al-Din al-Shayyal, *Tarikh al-Tarjama wa al-Haraka al-Thaqafiyya fi Asr Muhammad Ali* (Cairo, 1951), 125.

28. On al-Tahtawi's encounter with Jean-Jacques Barthélemy's *Travels of Anacharsis the Younger in Greece during the Middle of the Fourth Century before the Christian Era,* see Elie Kedourie, ed., *Nationalism in Asia and Africa* (New York, 1970), intro., 39–40, 188 n. 5; al-Shayyal, *Tarikh al-tarjama,* 125.

29. Jamal al-Din al-Shayyal, *A History of Egyptian Historiography in the Nineteenth Century* (Alexandria, 1962), 26, 27, 31–36; Ibrahim Abu-Lughod, *The Arab Rediscovery of Europe: A Study in Cultural Encounters* (Princeton, N.J., 1963), 50–51.

30. See al-Shayyal, *Egyptian Historiography,* 32, 33; Jack Crabbs, *The Writing of History in Nineteenth Century Egypt: A Study in National Transformation* (Cairo, 1984), 79.

31. Rifaa Rafii al-Tahtawi, *Anwar tawfiq al-jalil fi akhbar Misr wa-tawthiq Bani Ismail,* in *Al-Amal al-kamila li-Rifaa Rafi al-Tahtawi,* ed. Muhammad Amara (Beirut, 1974), 15, 105. For the following paragraph, see 83–85, 166–67.

32. Translated in al-Shayyal, *Egyptian Historiography,* 33–34.

33. al-Tahtawi, *Anwar,* 185–86, 215–23, 274–79. For al-Tahtawi's geocentrism, see John W. Livingston, "Western Science and Educational Reform in the Thought of Shaykh Rifa'a al-Tahtawi," *IJMES* 28 (1996): 543–64.

34. al-Tahtawi, *Anwar*, 273, 247–72. On Shawqi's *Death of Cleopatra*, see Ahmed Etman, *Kliyubatra wa Antuniyus: Dirasa fi fann Blutarkhus wa Shakisbir wa Shawqi*, 2nd ed. (Cairo, 1990), 388–444. See also A. J. Arberry, *Aspects of Islamic Civilization as Depicted in the Original Texts* (New York, 1964), 370; and Lucy Hughes-Hallett, *Cleopatra: Histories, Dreams and Distortions* (New York, 1990), 297.

35. al-Tahtawi, *Anwar*, 290–91, 343–45, 473–74.

36. al-Tahtawi, *Anwar*, 291–93, 298–99, 334, 439, 443–49, 471, 474.

37. Crabbs, *Writing*, 94, citing Abd al-Karim, *Tarikh al-Talim fi Misr* (Cairo, 1945), 2: 431.

38. Lois Aroian, *The Nationalization of Arabic and Islamic Education in Egypt: Dar al ʿUlum and al-Azhar*, The Cairo Papers in Social Science, vol. 6, Monograph 4 (Cairo, 1983), 44–48, 54.

39. Lorne Kenny, "The Khedive Ismaʿil's Dream of Civilization and Progress," *Muslim World* 55 (1965): 219, citing *Rawdat al-madaris* 4, no. 10 (n.d.): 9.

40. Philip Sadgrove, *The Egyptian Theatre in the Nineteenth Century (1799–1882)*, (Reading, Berkshire, [ca. 1996]), 47–48, 61.

41. See Crabbs, *Writing*, 74–79, for this analysis of *Manahij al-albab al-misriyya fi Manahij al-adab al-asriyya* (Cairo, 1869) and the creative rhymed English translation of the title.

42. Crabbs, *Writing*, 77; Charles Wendell, *The Evolution of the Egyptian National Image from Its Origins to Ahmad Lutfi al-Sayyid* (Berkeley, Calif., 1972), 128–30, quoting al-Tahtawi, *Manahij*, 188–204.

43. al-Tahtawi, *Anwar*, 194–95.

44. For the figures, see Robert Ilbert, *Alexandrie 1830–1930: Histoire d'un communauté citadine*, 2 vols. (Cairo, 1996), 1: 395, 2: 757. On nineteenth-century Alexandria, see also Michael Reimer, *Colonial Bridgehead: Government and Society in Alexandria, Egypt 1807–1882* (Boulder, Colo., 1997).

45. Janet Abu Lughod, *1001 Years of the City Victorious* (Princeton, N.J., 1971), 98, 115.

46. Ilbert, *Alexandrie*, 1: 395. The following section on Greeks draws mainly on Ilbert, *Alexandrie*, 2: 609–15; Athanase G. Politis, *L'Hellénisme et l'Égypte moderne*, 2 vols. (Paris, 1929–1930); and the first chapter of Alexander Kitroeff, *The Greeks in Egypt, 1919–1937: Ethnicity and Class* (London, 1989).

47. Douglas Dakin, *The Unification of Greece 1770–1923* (New York, 1972); Gerasimos Augustinos, *Consciousness and History: Nationalist Critics of Greek Society 1897–1914* (Boulder, Colo., 1997); G. P. Henderson, *The Revival of Greek Thought 1620–1830* (Albany, N.Y., 1970); Stathis Gourgouris, *Dream Nation: Enlightenment, Colonization, and the Institution of Modern Greece* (Stanford, Calif., 1996).

48. On Cavafy, see John Rodenbeck, "Alexandrian Literature," *Newsletter of the American Research Center in Egypt*, nos. 156–157 (winter/spring 1992): 7–10.

49. Politis, *L'Hellénisme*, 2: 405–6; Jean Ellul, *Index des communications et mémoires publiés par l'Institut d'Égypte (1859–1952)* (Cairo, 1952), 44.

50. *WWWE3*: 457, 18.

51. Ilbert, *Alexandrie*, 2: 697.

52. Politis, *L'Hellénisme*, 2: 420–24.

53. J. Dean O'Donnell Jr., *Lavigerie in Tunisia: The Interplay of Imperialist and Missionary* (Athens, Ga., 1979), 169; Kitroeff, *The Greeks*, 114; Will D. Swearingen, *Moroccan Mirages: Agrarian Dreams and Deceptions* (Princeton, N.J., 1987), chapter 1.

54. On Italians in Egypt, see Ilbert, *Alexandrie*, 2: 616–23; L. A. Balboni, *Gl'Italiani nella civiltà Egiziana de secolo XIXo*, 3 vols. (Alexandria, 1906); Angelo Sammarco, *Gli Italiani in Egitto* (Alexandria, 1937); Vittorio Briani, *Italiani in Egitto* (Rome, 1982).

55. Claudio Segrè, *Fourth Shore: The Italian Colonization of Libya* (Chicago, 1974).

56. *WWWE3*: 345. Nicola Bonacasa, "L'Archeologia italiana in Egitto," in *L'Archeologia italiana nel Mediterraneo fino all seconda guerra mondiale,* ed. Vincenzo La Rosa (Catania, Italy, 1986), 41–51, surveys Italian archaeological and museum activities in Egypt.

57. Ilbert, *Alexandrie*, 1: 395.

58. Except where otherwise indicated, this account draws on Pascal Crozet, "La Trajectoire d'un scientifique égyptien au XIXe siècle: Mahmoud al-Falaki (1815–1885)," in *Entre Réforme social et mouvements national: Identité et modernisation en Égypte,* ed. Alain Rousillon (Cairo, 1995), 285–310.

59. Crozet, "Trajectoire," 21, lists the following: *Carte de l'antique Alexandria* (Paris, 1868); *Carte des environs d'Alexandrie* (Paris, 1866); maps of the Delta (Cairo, A.H.1289 [1872]); *Mémoire sur l'antique Alexandrie* (Copenhagen, 1872); "Sur l'antique Alexandrie," *BIE,* ser. 1, no. 10 (1869): 96–101, 103–7, 117–21, 128–31.

60. For example, G. Botti, *Plan de la ville d'Alexandrie à l'époque ptolémaïque* (Alexandria, 1898); and Christopher Haas, *Alexandria in Late Antiquity: Topography and Social Conflict* (Baltimore, 1997), 360.

61. Kenneth Rose, *Superior Person: A Portrait of Curzon and His Circle* (New York, 1969), 55; Lloyd-Jones, *Blood for the Ghosts*, 110–22; Turner, *Greek Heritage*, 159–65.

62. K. Vollers, "Le IXme congrès international des orientalistes tenu à Londres," *BIE,* ser. 3, no. 3 (November 1892): 200.

63. Richard Symonds, *Oxford and Empire: The Last Lost Cause?* (New York, 1986).

64. Richard Jenkyns, *The Victorians and Ancient Greece* (Cambridge, Mass., 1980), 331. See also Frank M. Turner, "Why the Greeks?" in *Rediscovering Hellenism,* ed. Clark, 71–75; and Frank M. Turner, "British Politics and the Demise of the Roman Republic," *Historical Journal* 29 (1986): 577–99.

65. J. R. Seeley, *The Expansion of England* (Chicago, 1971), 187–88.

66. Vance, *Victorians*, 222.

67. Thomas R. Metcalf, *An Imperial Vision: Indian Architecture and Britain's Raj* (Berkeley, Calif., 1989), 5. Pages 176 ff. treat the turn-of-the-century classical revival in imperial architecture.

68. Madge Dresser, "Britannia," in *Patriotism: The Making and Unmaking of British National Identity,* vol. 3: *National Fictions,* ed. Raphael Samuel (London, 1989), 26–49.

69. H. C. G. Matthew, ed., *The Gladstone Diaries*, vol. 10: *(January 1881–June 1883)* (Oxford, 1990), lxxii.

70. The Earl of Cromer, *Ancient and Modern Imperialism* (New York, 1910), 22.

71. A. M. Broadley, *Tunis Past and Present: The Last Punic War*, 2 vols. (London, 1882).

72. Jenkyns, *The Victorians*, 333.

73. Cromer, *Modern Egypt*, 566, 582, 633–34.

74. J. W. McCrindle, *Ancient India as Described in Classical Literature* (Westminster, 1901); E. H. Warmington, *The Commerce between the Roman Empire and India* (London, 1974; reprint of 1928 ed.); Sir Mortimer Wheeler, *Rome beyond Imperial Frontiers* (Southampton, 1955).

75. The Marquess of Zetland, *Lord Cromer* (London, 1932), 287.

76. J. W. Mackail, *Classical Studies* (London, 1925), 12.

77. The Earl of Cromer, *Ancient and Modern Imperialism* (New York, 1910). James Bryce, *Studies in History and Jurisprudence* (New York, 1901); Sir C. P. Lucas, *Greater Rome and Greater Britain* (Oxford, 1912); J. M. Robertson, *Patriotism and Empire* (London, 1899). See also J. A. Cramb, *Reflections on the Origins and Destiny of Imperial Britain* (London, 1900), which sees Britain's imperial record as far surpassing Rome's.

78. Cromer, *Imperialism*, 7–8; on Alexander, 10–11.

79. Cromer, *Modern Egypt*, 586, 112.

80. Viscount Milner, *England in Egypt* (New York, 1970; reprint of 1920 ed.), 2, 4.

81. Cromer, *Imperialism*, 73–112, 128–41. Issawi compares the French view of themselves resuming a Roman mission of civilizing and Latinizing "by sword and plough" with a British vision in India and Egypt not of planting colonies of settlement but of imposing a new "Pax Romana." Charles Issawi, "Empire Builders, Culture Makers, and Culture Imprinters," *Journal of Interdisciplinary History* 20 (1989): 189. See also Gary B. Miles, "Roman and Modern Imperialism: A Reassessment," *Comparative Studies in Society and History* 32 (1990): 629–59.

82. Cromer, *Imperialism*, 3–4.

83. Ronald Storrs, *The Memoirs of Sir Ronald Storrs* (New York, 1937), 43.

84. Cromer, *Imperialism*, 7–11.

85. For this and the following quotation, Cromer, *Modern Egypt*, 654–55.

86. E. M. Forster, *Alexandria: A History and a Guide* (New York, 1961), 91. See also E. Breccia, *Alexandrea ad Aegyptum: Guide de la ville ancienne et moderne et du Musée greco-romain* (Bergamo, 1914).

87. On the Institut égyptien's Greco-Roman activities while in Alexandria, see Alan Rowe's address in "Le Cinquantenaire de la Société royale d'archéologie 1893–1943," *Bulletin de la Société archéologique d'Alexandrie* (hereafter, *BSAA*), 36 (1946): 108–9.

88. Rev. A. H. Sayce, *Reminiscences* (London, 1923), 274–75. See also "Projet de réglement du Musée d'Alexandrie, [1892]," in DWQ / MMW / NA / MA / 1 / 4: Matahif 1879–1914.

89. France; Les Archives diplomatiques de Nantes / Ministère des affaires etrangères / Ambassade Le Caire / Enseignement égyptien / Service des antiquités (hereafter MAE / AMB Le Caire / EE / SA) 1887–1897 / C173 / D237 / Edmond Bafry (?) to MAE. For the antecedents and early history of the museum, see Rowe, "Le Cinquantenaire," 107–19, and G. Botti, *Catalogue des monuments exposés au Musée greco-romain d'Alexandrie* (Alexandria, 1900), iii–xiii. The name was often spelled "Graeco-Roman."

90. Ilbert, *Alexandrie,* 1: 278–300.

91. Muncipalité d'Alexandrie, *Catalogue de la Bibliothèque municipale (Section européen 1892–1926),* vol. 1, preface by Et. Combe (Alexandria, 1926), vii–ix. See also *Annuaire statistique de l'Égypte 1924–1925* (Cairo, 1926), 94.

92. *BSAA* 4 (1902): 3, lists the founders.

93. *BSAA* 1 (1898): 5.

94. Botti, *Catalogue,* viii–xiii.

95. On Botti, see Balboni, *Gl'Italiani,* 3: 75–83; *WWWE*3, 57. On Breccia, *Dizionario Biografico degli Italiani,* 14 (Rome, 1972), 91–93; and *WWWE*3: 63. On Adriani, *WWWE*3: 6.

96. Antiquities Service classicists included C. C. Edgar and Gustave Lefebvre: *WWWE*3: 137, 244. On Jouguet, see *WWWE*3: 221.

97. T. G. H. James, ed., *Excavating in Egypt: The Egypt Exploration Society 1882–1982* (London, 1982), 9.

98. For this paragraph and the following section on Grenfell and Hunt, see Sir Eric Turner, "The Graeco-Roman Branch," in James, ed., *Excavating,* 161–76.

99. *BSAA* 4 (1902): 3–8.

100. See the subject lists in Amin Sami, *Al-Talim fi Misr fi Sanatay 1914 wa 1915* (Cairo, 1917). In 1875 two foreign schools taught Latin and eight Greek. J. Heyworth-Dunne, *An Introduction to the History of Education in Modern Egypt* (London, 1939; reprinted 1968), 423.

101. Thomas Philipp, *Syrians in Egypt 1725–1975* (Stuttgart, 1985).

102. Sadgrove, *Egyptian Theatre,* 130–31. On Ishaq, see 140–41.

103. Except as otherwise indicated, the following analysis is based on Albert Hourani, "Bustani's Encyclopaedia," in his *Islam in European Thought* (Cambridge, 1991), 164–73, and "Sulaiman al-Bustani and the *Iliad,*" 174–87, in the same volume. See also Wajih Fanus, "Sulayman al-Bustani and Comparative Literary Studies in Arabic," *Journal of Arabic Literature* 17 (1986): 105–19.

104. "Uruba," *Dairat al-maarif,* 4: 172–73, as quoted in Hourani, *Islam,* 172–73.

105. Thomas Philipp, *Ğurǧi Zaidan: His Life and Thought* (Beirut, 1979), 237.

106. Sadgrove, *Egyptian Theatre,* 102–4.

107. Ali Mubarak, *Al-Khitat al-tawfiqiyya al-jadida,* 20 vols. (Cairo, 1304–06 / 1886–89), 8: 35–37.

108. Mubarak, *Al-Khitat,* 7: esp. 2–13.

109. Kassem-Amin, *Les Égyptiens: Réponse à M. le Duc d' Harcourt* (Cairo, 1894), 69, 60, 240.

110. Abd al-Rahman al-Rafii, *Mustafa Kamil* (Cairo, 1962), 36; Abd al-Rahman al-Rafii, *Muhammad Farid* (Cairo, 1962), 30–32. In the next paragraph, Nimr's review of Muhammad Farid's *Tarikh al-Rumaniyyin* is found in *Al-Muqtataf* 27 (1 August 1902): 805–6.

111. Personal communication by John Rodenbeck, 1994.

112. *Congrès international d'archéologie: Première session, Athènes, 1905* (Athens, 1905), 5, 7, 12, 24, 43, 46–49, 238–41.

113. *Comptes rendus du Congrès international d'archéologie classique: 2me session—Le Caire 1909* (Cairo, 1909), 7, 53–57, 60–61, 74–77, 93–97. For the following paragraph, see 57–60.

114. *Congrès, 1909,* 58–60, 156–58, 172.

115. *Congrès, 1909,* 262–63.

116. *Congrès, 1909,* 9–52, 262–63, 294.

117. Mahmud Fahmi, *Tarikh al-Yunan* (Cairo, 1910), 3–4; Ahmad Abd al-Fattah Budayr, *Al-Amir Ahmad Fuad wa Nashat al-Jamia al-Misriyya* (Cairo, 1950), 131, 153, 155.

118. Cairo University Archives, Box 14, Folder 170 (hereafter, CUA / B# / F#): "Qism al-Adab," White's syllabus, 25 October 1910.

119. Charles Wendell, *The Evolution of the Egyptian National Image from Its Origins to Ahmad Lutfi al-Sayyid* (Berkeley, Calif., 1972), 258–59. For Lutfi's role in the university, see Donald Malcolm Reid, *Cairo University and the Making of Modern Egypt* (Cambridge, 1990).

120. Ilyas Sarkis, *Mujam al-Matbuat al-Arabiyya wa al-Muarraba* (Cairo, 1928), 1692. On the earlier, uncompleted translation for Muhammad Ali, see al-Shayyal, *Tarikh al-tarjama,* 79–81.

121. Taha Husayn, *A Passage to France: The Third Volume of the Autobiography of Taha Husayn,* trans. Kenneth Cragg, Arabic Translation Series of *The Journal of Arabic Literature,* vol. 4 (Leiden, 1976), 115–18. For his argument in favor of classical studies, see Taha Hussein, *The Future of Culture in Egypt,* trans. Sidney Glazer (New York, 1954; reprinted 1975), 73–82.

CHAPTER 5. EGYPTOLOGY IN THE AGE OF MASPERO AND AHMAD KAMAL

1. MAE / AMB Le Caire / C177: IFAO 1856–1952 / D: École orientale / Maspero to MAE, 20 September 1881, 5. On Maspero, see Elisabeth David, *Gaston Maspero, 1846–1916: Le Gentleman Égyptologue* (Paris, 1999); and *WWWE* 3: 278–79.

2. Jean Vercoutter, "Introduction," *Institut français d'archéologie orientale du Caire, Livre du centenaire 1880–1980* (Cairo, 1980); vii–x treat the founding, and vii–xxiii treat the whole history of IFAO. See also IFAO's *Un Siècle de fouilles françaises en Egypte 1880–1980* (Cairo, 1981); and the MAE carton on IFAO cited in the previous note.

3. Vercoutter, "Introduction," *Livre du centenaire,* xxi.

4. Daniel Grange, "Archéologie et politique: Égyptologues et diplomates français au Caire (1880–1914)," in *L'Égyptologie et les Champollion,* ed. Michel Dewachter and Alain Fouchard (Grenoble, 1994), 367.

5. Stephen Vernoit, "The Rise of Islamic Archaeology," *Muqarnas* 14 (1997): 2.

6. A. Khater, *Le Régime juridique des fouilles et des antiquités en Égypte* (Cairo, 1960), 77.

7. The quoted phrase is R. S. Poole's, founder of the Egyptian Exploration Fund (hereafter, EEF), quoted in Margaret Drower, *Flinders Petrie: A Life in Archaeology* (Madison, Wis., 1995), 312.

8. Flinders Petrie, *Seventy Years in Archaeology* (New York, 1969; reprint of 1932 ed.), 22. For the rest of the paragraph, see Jason Thompson, *Sir John Gardner Wilkinson and His Circle* (Austin, 1992), 200–202. For Petrie, in addition to *Seventy Years*, see Drower, *Petrie*.

9. Bruce G. Trigger, *A History of Archaeological Thought* (Cambridge, 1975), 196.

10. Drower, *Petrie*, 429–30, has a good assessment of his original contributions. Toby A. H. Wilkinson, *Early Dynastic Egypt* (London, 1999), provides a handy overview of the work of Petrie and others on this era.

11. Francis Griffith, as quoted in T. G. H. James, ed., *Excavating in Egypt: The Egypt Exploration Society 1882–1982* (London, 1982), 28.

12. Petrie, *Seventy Years*, 34, 77, 80.

13. See Trigger, *History*, 110 ff. on imperialist and racist aspects of archaeology in this era.

14. *WWWE*3: 137–38; and Joan Rees, *Amelia Edwards, Traveller, Novelist and Egyptologist* (London, 1998).

15. Margaret Drower, "Gaston Maspero and the Birth of the Egypt Exploration Fund (1881–3)," *Journal of Egyptian Archaeology* 68 (1982): 300. On the EEF generally, see James, *Excavating*.

16. James, *Excavating*, 9, 14. See also Peter France, *The Rape of Egypt: How Europeans Stripped Egypt of Its Heritage* (London, 1991), 151–54.

17. Drower, "Gaston Maspero," 314; for the paragraph, 299–317.

18. This section draws mainly on Darrell Dykstra, "Pyramids, Prophets, and Progress: Ancient Egypt in the Writings of Ali Mubarak," *Journal of the American Oriental Society* 114 (1994): 54–65. Aside from Ali Mubarak's *Al-Khitat al-tawfiqiyya al-jadida* (Cairo, 1886–1887) itself and previously cited sources on Mubarak, other useful sources are Gabriel Baer, " 'Ali Mubarak's *Khitat* as a Source for the History of Modern Egypt," in *Political and Social Change in Modern Egypt,* ed. P. M. Holt (London, 1968), 13–27; and Ghislaine Alleaume, "La Naissance de la geographie positive et les *khitat*-s de Ali Pacha Mubarak," in *D'un Orient l'autre,* 2 vols. (Paris, 1991), 2: 315–38.

19. Juan Eduardo Campo, "Mubarak's *Khitat*: An Egyptian Nationalist Valuation of Religious Space," unpublished paper presented at the Middle East Studies Association meeting, Beverly Hills, Calif., November 1989.

20. Mubarak, *Al-Khitat*, 1: 2–3, translation quoted from Michael J. Reimer, "Contradiction and Consciousness in 'Ali Mubarak's Description of al-Azhar," *IJMES* 29 (1997): 61.

21. Darrell Dykstra, "Pyramids, Prophets, and Progress," *JAOS* 114 (1994): 60, citing Ali Mubarak, *Alam al-Din*, 4 vols. (Alexandria, 1882), 2: 634–36.

22. Mubarak, *Al-Khitat*, 13: 69–90 (Thebes), 16: 2–47 (Memphis), 15: 47–69 (Heliopolis).

23. E. A. Wallis Budge, *By Nile and Tigris: A Narrative of Journeys in Egypt and Mesopotamia on Behalf of the British Museum between the Years 1886 and 1913*, 2 vols. (London, 1920) 1: 74–117. On Grébaut, see *WWWE3*: 176–77; David, *Gaston Maspero*, 186–88; and Jacques de Morgan, *Mémoires de Jacques de Morgan, souvenirs d'un archéologue*, ed. Andrée Jaunay (Paris, 1997), 334–42. On Kitchener and Grenfell, see *WWWE3*: 229, 179.

24. A. H. Sayce, *Reminiscences* (London, 1923), 285.

25. Budge, *Nile*, 1: 81.

26. Budge, *Nile*, 1: 117.

27. Budge, *Nile*, 1: 130–31, 140–44, 147–48, 241, 334, 2: 152.

28. Budge, *Nile*, 1: 334.

29. Grange, "Archéologie," 364.

30. MAE / AMB Le Caire / C173: EE / SA / Grébaut to MAE, 13 January 1891.

31. DWQ / MMW / NA / MA / A / 3 / 4: Matahif 1879–90 / Scott Moncrief, 22 Feburary 1890, "Note for the Council of Mins.," and Grébaut, "Copie d'une lettre adressée à ce ministère," 2, 6.

32. James, *Excavating*, 29–30. MAE / AMB Le Caire / C173: EE / SA / 20 November 1890, includes clippings and correspondence on the Society for the Preservation of Monuments of Ancient Egypt's press campaign.

33. DWQ / MMW / NA / MA / Matahif 1879–90, A / 3 / 4, A. Rouchdy, "Note au conseil des ministres," No. 579, 9 November 1887; and "Projet de règlement interieur du comité permanent d'égyptologues," 9 March 1889. Petrie, *Seventy Years*, 131–32; Grange, "Archéologie," 363. Éric Gady kindly supplied the information on Tigrane's promise (from MAE, Correspondance politique, vol. 117, fol. 279, MAE to Cairo, 13 May 1890).

34. The *Graphic*, 26 July 1890, 13, as reproduced in Nicholas Warner, ed., *An Egyptian Panorama: Reports from the 19th Century British Press* (Cairo, 1994), 13.

35. E. A. Budge, *Cook's Handbook for Egypt and the Sudan*, 2nd ed. (London, 1906), 427.

36. Budge, *Cook's Handbook*, 427–28.

37. James, *Excavating*, 29–30.

38. Dia' Abou-Ghazi, "The Journey of the Egyptian Museum from Boulaq to Kasr el-Nil," *ASAE* 67 (1991): 16.

39. MAE / AMB Le Caire / C173: EE / SA 1887–1897 / undated, minister of public instruction to MAE, 1891. On Daninos, see *WWWE3*: 115; Foreign Office Archives of the United Kingdom (hereafter, FO), 141 / 369, 28 December 1902, Daninos to Cromer.

40. On de Morgan, see his *Mémoires*, and *WWWE3*: 297. The quotations are from Budge, *Nile*, 2: 329.

41. David, *Maspero*, 188–90; de Morgan, *Mémoires*, esp. 384–85, 418.

42. Sayce, *Reminiscences*, 306.

43. Warren R. Dawson, "Letters from Maspero to Amelia Edwards," *Journal of Egyptian Archaeology* 3 (1947): 76.

44. Petrie, *Seventy Years,* 183; on Loret, see *WWWE3*: 260.

45. Petrie, *Seventy Years,* 186.

46. MAE / AMB Le Caire / C174 *bis:* EE / SA / D: Personnel français, sous-dossier "M. Loret" / esp. Cagordan to MAE, 19 March 1898, 18 May 1899.

47. Quoted in French by Grange, in "Archéologie," 356. For this paragraph, see also 365–66.

48. Sayce, *Reminiscences,* 306. For Maspero's long-standing reluctance to return, see David, *Maspero,* 192–201.

49. DWQ / MMW / NA / MA / A (alif) / 3 / 4: Matahif 1879–90, Grébaut, "Copie," 22 February 1890, 2. For the biography of Kamal, see *Al-Muqtataf* 63 (November 1923): 273–77; Tawfiq Habib, "Tarikh al-Kashf an al-Athar al-Misriyya wa Amal al-Marhum Ahmad Kamal Basha," *Al-Hilal* 32 (1 November 1923): 135–41; Zaki Fahmi, *Safwat al-Asr fi Tarikh wa Rusum Mashahir Rijal fi Misr,* 2 vols. (Cairo, 1926), 1: 331–36; Gamal al-Din al-Shayyal, *A History of Egyptian Historiography in the Nineteenth Century* (Alexandria, 1962), 60–63; Tawfiq Habib, "Dars al-Athar fi al-Jamia al-Misriyya," *Al-Muqtataf* 72 (1928): 438–39; *WWWE3*: 224. Dia' M. Abou-Ghazi, "Ahmed Kamal 1849–1923," *ASAE* 64 (1981): 1–5, lists his articles.

50. Sources list 1849 or 1851 as his birth date, but 1851 is the more probable.

51. *Al-Muqtataf* 63 (1923): 274. Without citing a source, Elisabeth David, *Mariette Pacha 1821–1881* (Paris, 1994), 258, says that on 25 February 1880, Mariette requested that Kamal replace his old interpreter.

52. DWQ / MW / NA / MA A / 1 / 4: Matahif 1879–1914 / F Madrasat al-Athar 1881–86, Min. Public Works, 16 October 1881, "Note au Conseil des ministres: École d'Égyptologie." For the founding decree, see also Filib Yusuf Jallad, *Qamus al-Idara wa al-Qada,* 4 vols. (Alexandria, 1890), 4: 188–89. In Arabic the school was called Madrasat al-Lisan al-Misri al-Qadim (School of the Ancient Egyptian Language).

53. DWQ / MMW / NA / MA A / 1 / 4: Matahif 1879–1914 / F: Madrasat al-Athar 1881–86, Min. Public Works to Council of Ministers, No. 99, 17 April 1882.

54. DWQ / MMW / NA / MA A / 1 / 4: Matahif 1879–1914 / F: Madrasat al-Athar, 1881–86, "Notes au Conseil des Ministres," A. Rouchdy, No. 406, 21 July, 1886.

55. DWQ / MMW / NA / MA A / 1 / 4: Matahif 1879–1914 / F: Madrasat al-Athar, 1881–86, "Note au Conseil des Ministres," No. 321, 28 December 1885, Scott Moncrief to Council of Mins. Inspectors 2nd class: Ali Habib, Ahmad Kehieh, Muhammad Marzak, Tadrus, Moutafian, Ahmad Thaqi; inspectors 3rd class: Muhammad Chaban, Ahmad Nagib, Mahmud Hamdi, Abd al-Rahman Fahmi, Hasan Husni.

56. DWQ / MMW / NA / MA A / 3 / 4: 1879–90, A. Rouchdy, "Note au Conseil des Ministres," No. 454, 29 December 1885.

57. DWQ / MMW / NA / MA 1891–1907, B / 3 / 4, Muhammad Zaki (Min. Public Works), "Note au Conseil des Ministres," No. 16, 21 February 1891; MAE / AMB Le Caire / C173 / Enseignement égyptien, Service des antiquités / D201: "Gestion de M. Grébaut," / "Budget of dir.-gen. of Museums 1891."

58. DWQ / MMW / NA / MA B / 3 / 4, Ahmad Kamal to Pres. Council of Ministers, 28 October 1892. My translation from French. The supplementary memo in Arabic had no French translation.

59. Habib, "Tarikh al-Kashf," 137.

60. On Daressy and Quibell, see *WWWE3*: 116, 345.

61. On Najib, see *Al-Mawsua al-misriyya: Tarikh Misr al-qadima wa atharuha*, Egypt, Ministry of Culture and Guidance (Cairo, n.d.), 82; and *WWWE3*: 306.

62. Gaston Maspero, *Rapports sur la marche du Service des antiquités de 1899 à 1910* (Cairo, 1912), xxiii–xxvi. Chaban's appointment as assistant curator is mentioned in *ASAE* 17 (1917): 177.

63. Nicolas Grimal, "L'Institut d'Égypte et l'Institut français d'archéologie orientale," *BIE* 70 (1989–90): 29–42.

64. *BIE*, ser. 3, fasc. 1 (1890): 219–24.

65. See Artin's *vita* in Stevenson Papers, University of Pennsylvania, University Museum Archives, Curatorial Files, Egypt, Papers of Sara Yorke Stevenson, Box 1, Folder 2: Correspondence with Yacoub Artin Pasha. See also Gilbert Delanoue, *Moralistes et politiques musulmans dans l'Égypte du XIXe siècle (1798–1882)*, 2 vols. (Cairo, 1982), 2: 332 n. 235. On Fakhri, see Arthur Goldschmidt Jr., *Biographical Dictionary of Modern Egypt* (Boulder, Colo., 2000), 52.

66. "Daninos," *WWWE3*: 115.

67. *BIE*, ser. 5, fasc. 3 (1909): 176–77.

68. Thomas Cook Archives, *Excursionist*, 25 May 1889.

69. MAE / AMB Le Caire / C261: Expositions 1897–1936 / D: Commerce: Expositions, Sousdossier: Exposition de Chicago, 1893 / [illegible] to Ribot, 19 September 1891.

70. MAE / AMB Le Caire / C261: Expositions 1897–1936 / D: Commerce: Expositions / Boulad to Cogordan, 14 December 1896. For the 1900 fair generally, see Richard D. Mandrell, *The Great World's Fair* (Toronto, 1967).

71. John Wesley Hansen, *Official History of the Fair, Saint Louis, 1904* (St. Louis, 1904), 273. On the commissioner-general and delegate, see *Official Guide to the Louisiana Purchase Exposition, St. Louis* (St. Louis, 1904), 51.

72. This ignores the schismatic "statutory congresses" at London in 1891 and at Lisbon in 1892; these bodies tended to favor amateur inquiries over the specialist scholarship.

73. Budge, *Cook's Handbook*, 428. Éric Gady, in a personal letter to me on 16 January 2000, notes that of seventy-three projects submitted, twenty-six were by Italian architects, sixteen by French, sixteen by Englishmen, and fifteen by others. The five finalists, however, were all French. MAE / AMB Le Caire / C173 / D201: Construction du Musée du Caire, enclosing clipping "Le Concours du Caire, succès des architectes français," from *L'Architecture*, 6 April 1895.

74. Zeynep Çelik, *The Remaking of Istanbul: Portrait of an Ottoman City in the Nineteenth Century* (Seattle, 1986), 126, speaks of four Western architectural styles in Istanbul in a "long" nineteenth century ending in 1908: classical, Gothic, and Islamic Revival, and art nouveau. Mohammed Scharabi's more detailed categories in *Kairo: Stadt und Architektur im Zeitalter des europäischen Kolonialismus* (Tübingen, 1989) separate classicism from neoclassicism

and include Renaissance and baroque revivals, art nouveau, art deco, Mediterranean, eclectic, and international.

75. For the pediment, see Thomas R. Metcalf, *An Imperial Vision: Indian Architecture and Britain's Raj* (Berkeley, Calif., 1989), 5. On museum architecture and its meaning in the West, see Nikolaus Pevsner, *A History of Building Types* (Princeton, N.J., 1976), 111–36; and James J. Sheehan, *Museums in the German Art World from the End of the Old Regime to the Rise of Modernism* (Oxford, 2000).

76. Jean-Marcel Humbert, Michel Pantazzi, and Christiane Ziegler, *Egyptomania: Egypt in Western Art 1739–1930* (Ottawa, 1994). On Egyptian Revival styles in the West, see also James Steven Curl, *The Egyptian Revival: An Introductory Study of a Recurring Theme in the History of Taste* (London, 1982); his *Egyptomania: The Egyptian Revival; A Recurring Theme in the History of Taste* (New York, 1994); and Richard G. Carrott, *The Egyptian Revival: Its Sources, Monuments, and Meaning 1808–1858* (Berkeley, Calif., 1978).

77. Humbert, *Egyptomania*, 334.

78. Humbert, *Egyptomania*, 334–36; François Pouillon, "Fantasie et investigations dans la peinture orientaliste du XIXème siècle," in *D'un Orient l'autre*, 1: fig. 3, following p. 280, however, cites the painting as *L'Étude et le Génie devoilent l'antique Égypte à la Grèce*.

79. Humbert, *Egyptomania*, 342.

80. E. A. Wallis Budge, *The Nile: Notes for Travellers in Egypt*, 4th ed. (London, 1895), 154. On the Giza palace, see Nihal S. Tamraz, *Nineteenth-century Cairene Houses and Palaces* (Cairo, 1998), 30.

81. Metcalf, *Imperial Vision*, 176–210.

82. Çelik, *Remaking of Istanbul*, 139–40.

83. J. S. de Sacy, "Dourgnon," *Dictionnaire de biographie française* (Paris, 1933–), 11 (1967): 691. For the architecture and iconography of the Egyptian Museum, see Donald Malcolm Reid, "French Egyptology and the Architecture of Orientalism: Deciphering the Facade of Cairo's Egyptian Museum," in *Franco-Arab Encounters: Studies in Memory of David C. Gordon*, ed. L. Carl Brown and Matthew S. Gordon (Beirut, 1996), 35–69.

84. Ahmad Shafiq, *Mudhakkirati fi Nisf Qarn* (Cairo, 1936), vol. 2, pt. 1: 243.

85. MAE / AMB Le Caire / C173 / EE / SA / D201: Construction du Musée des antiquités du Caire, 1894–, de Morgan to MAE, 8 May 1896; clipping "Égypte: La Question du musée," *Le Journal des débats* (31 January 1898); Dourgnon to Cogordan, 2 January 1900.

86. Maspero, *Rapports . . . 1899 à 1910*, v–vi.

87. Maspero, *Rapports . . . 1899 à 1910*, xx–xxii.

88. For French views, see MAE / AMB Le Caire / C174: Enseignement égyptien, Service des antiquités.

89. See pamphlet *Cérémonie d'inauguration du monument élévé par les soins du Gouvernement égyptien à Mariette Pacha* (Cairo: IFAO, 1904), enclosed in MAE / AMB Le Caire / C173: EE / SA / D201: Construction du Musée.

90. Lord Cromer, "The President's Address," Egypt Exploration Fund, *Report of the Twenty-Third Ordinary General Meeting, 1908–1909* (London, 1909), 18.

91. MAE / AMB Le Caire / C174 *bis:* EE / SA / Maspero to consul general, 27 December 1909; David, *Maspero,* 225–27.

92. FO 63 / 20 / pp. 123–26, 131, 256–57, December 1911, Weigall to Cromer, Garstin to Cromer, Cromer to Weigall.

93. Maspero, *Rapports . . . 1899 à 1910,* viii–xxx.

94. C. Traunecker and J.-C. Golvin, *Karnak* (Paris, 1989).

95. Maspero, *Rapports . . . 1899 à 1910,* xlii, 25.

96. Grange, "Archéologie," 369–70.

97. FO 633 / 23 / p. 36, Maspero to Cromer, 12 May 1914.

98. On Ebers and Dümichen, see *WWWE3:* 136, 131–32. Wolfgang Helck, *Ägyptologie an Deutchschen Universitäten* (Wiesbaden, 1969).

99. For a French review of German, English, and French archaeological activities in Asia Minor, Mesopotamia, and Syria-Palestine, see MAE / AMB Constantinople / Dossiers thèmatique 494: Fouilles archéologique / 494 / Mission archéologique de Gustave Mendel / Mendel to French ambassador, 29 November 1912.

100. Volkmar Fritz, "Deutsche Orient-Gesellschaft," *Oxford Encyclopedia of Archaeology in the Middle East,* 5 vols. (New York, 1997), 2: 146–47. On the German Institute, see Werner Kaiser, *75 Jahre Deutsches Archäologisches Institut Kairo 1907–1982* (Mainz, 1982); and Thomas W. Kramer, *Deutsch-ägyptische Beziehungen in Vergangenheit und Gegenwart* (Tübingen, 1974), 206–7.

101. FO 141 / 440 / 1206, Reisner to Allenby, 24 September 1921. On Borchardt, see *WWWE3:* 54–55.

102. MAE / AMB Le Caire / C177: IFAO 1886–1952 / Dossier général / Foucart to the French minister in Cairo, 17 April 1921, "Note sur la situation de l'IFAO," 7, assesses Borchardt's multiple roles.

103. On Junker, see *WWWE3:* 222–23. For British worries about his politics, see FO 395 / 567 / P3361, Lampson to FO, 28 November 1938; and FO 371 / 23352 / J468, Lampson to Halifax, 23 January 1939.

104. *WWWE3:* 377–78. For overviews of Italian archaeology in Egypt, see Angelo Sammarco, *Gli Italiani in Egitto* (Alexandria, 1937), 125–36; A. Evaristo Breccia, *Faraoni senza Pace,* 2nd ed. (Pisa, 1958), 175–212; Maria Petriioli, "Le Missioni archeologiche italiane nei paesi del Mediterraneo: uno strumento alternativo di politica internazionale," and Nicola Bonacasa, "L'Archeologia italiana in Egitto," in *L'Archeologia italiana nel Mediterraneo fino alla seconda guerra mondiale,* ed. Vincenzo La Rosa (Catania, Italy, 1986), 9–31, 41–51.

105. MAE / AMB Le Caire / C177: IFAO 1886–1952 / D général / G. Maspero, "Note," 3 November 1910; and MAE to Defrance, Cairo consulate, 8 December 1910; Donald Malcolm Reid, *Cairo University and the Making of Modern Egypt* (Cambridge, 1990), 38–39.

106. Bruce Kuklick, *Puritans in Babylon: The Ancient Near East and American Intellectual Life, 1880–1930* (Princeton, 1996); Philip J. King, *American Archaeology in the Mideast: A History of the American Schools of Oriental Research* (Philadelphia, 1983).

107. Martha Sharp, "Archaeological Institute of America," *Oxford Encyclopedia of Archaeology in the Near East,* 1: 187–88.

108. On W. Berend, W. Graff, and Charles Wilbour see Gerry D. Scott III, "Go Down into Egypt: The Dawn of American Egyptology," in *The American Discovery of Egypt: Essays,* ed. Nancy Thomas (Los Angeles, 1995), 44. Also on these three, see *WWWE3:* 42, 173, 440–41.

109. *WWWE3:* 62, 265, 351–52. Other sources include Charles Breasted, *Pioneer to the Past: The Story of James Henry Breasted, Archaeologist* (New York, 1947); and H. E. Winlock, *Excavations at Deir El Bahri 1911–1931* (New York, 1942).

110. James, *Excavating,* 23–24; EEF, *Report, 1916–17* (London, 1917), 8.

111. University of Pennsylvania, University Museum Archives, Curatorial Files, Egypt, Papers of Sara Yorke Stevenson, Box 1, Folder 2: Correspondence with Yacoub (Yaqub) Artin Pasha, Artin to Yorke, 10 August 1897, 3; and [Yorke] "Report," 7–8.

112. For the assessment of Reisner, see Michael Hoffman, *Egypt before the Pharaohs: The Prehistoric Foundations of Egyptian Civilization,* 2nd ed. (Austin, 1991), 250–54.

113. DWQ / MMA / NA / MA 1891–1922 / B / 2 / 4: Penfield to Council of Mins., 5 April 1909; P.M. to Penfield, 13 February 1910.

114. Ahmad Kamal, *Stèles ptolemiques et romaines,* 2 vols. (Cairo, 1904–1905); and his *Tables d'offrandes* (Cairo, 1909); DWQ / MMW / NA / MA 1891–1907 / B / 3 / 4, Fakhri, "Note au Comité des finances," 10 June 1905.

115. Other Egyptian minor contributors to *ASAE* through 1922 included Hasan Hosni (like Chaban, a graduate of the 1881–1885 school), Sobhi Aref, Hakim Abu Seif, Mahmoud Roushdy, Tewfiq Boulos, and Girgis Elias. *ASAE, Index des Tomes I–X* (Cairo, 1910), and *Tomes XI–XX* (Cairo, 1920).

116. Maspero, *Rapports . . . 1899 à 1910,* xxx, xxxi.

117. Ahmad Kamal, trans., *Al-Khulasa al-Wajiza wa Dalil al-Mutafarrij bi-Mathaf al-Jiza* (Cairo, 1310); Kamal, trans., *Dalil Dar al-Tuhuf al-Misriyya bi Madinat al-Qahira* (Cairo, 1903); Kamal, trans., *Al-Khulasa al-Durriyya fi Athar Mathaf al-Iskandariyya* (Cairo, 1319 / 1901).

118. G. Maspero, *L'Égyptologie* (Paris, 1915), 25–26.

119. Karl Baedeker, *Baedeker's Egypt: Part First: Lower Egypt and the Peninsula of Sinai,* 3rd ed. (Leipzig, 1895) (hereafter, Baed. 1895), 95; Maspero, *Rapports . . . 1899 à 1910,* ix–x.

120. Ahmad Kamal's Arabic publications, in addition to ones discussed separately, included *Tarwih al-nafs fi madinat al-shams* (Cairo, 1296 / 1879); *Al-Iqd al-thamin fi mahasin akhbar wa badi athar al-aqdamin min al-Misriyyin* (Cairo, 1300 / 1882–83); *Al-Faraid al-bahiyya fi qawaid al-lugha al-hiruglifiyya* (Cairo, 1303 / 1885–86); *Al-Durr al-nafis fi madinat Manfis* (Cairo, 1910); *Bughyat al-talibin fi ulum wa awaid wa sanai wa ahwal qudama al-Misriyyin* (Cairo, 1309); *Al-Alali al-durriyya fi al-nabatat wa al-ashghar al-qadima al-misriyya* (Cairo, 1306).

121. Ahmad Najib, *Al-Qawl al-mufid fi athar al-said, al-athar al-jalil li-qudama Wadi al-Nil,* 2nd ed. (Cairo, 1312 / 1895). On Najib, see Ilyas Sarkis, *Mujam al-Matbuat al-Arabiyya wa al-Muarraba* (Cairo, 1928), 402.

122. For Kamal's lectures, see Habib, "Tarikh al-kashf," 137. Abd al-Rahman al-Rafii, *Mustafa Kamil: Baith al-harakaʾ al-wataniyya,* 4th ed. (Cairo, 1962), 190–93, treats the Higher Schools Club.

123. Ahmad Kamal, *Al-Hadara al-qadima,* vol. 1 (Cairo, 1910). The four hundred pages of this volume bring the story only through the Fourteenth Dynasty; volume 2 was apparently never published.

124. CUA / B1 / F: Minutes of the Technical Committee, 2 May 1908, p. 11.

125. Kamal, *Al-Iqd al-thamin fi mahasin akhbar wa badai athar al-aqdamin min al-Misriyyin,* 3, 4.

126. *Al-Muqtataf* 63 (1923): 275–76.

127. Amal Hilal, "Les Premiers Égyptologues égyptiens et la réforme," in *Entre Réforme sociale et mouvement national: Identité et modernisation en Égypte (1882–1962),* ed. Alain Roussillon (Cairo, 1995), 344–45.

128. "Egypt," *Scott 1991 Standard Postage Stamp Catalogue* (Sydney, Ohio, 1990), 2: 985–86; *Standard Catalog of World Paper Money,* vol. 2: *General Issues to 1960,* 8th ed. (Iola, Wis., 1996), 373–74.

129. Alfred J. Butler, *Court Life in Egypt* (London, 1887), 8–31.

130. James Baikie, *A Century of Excavation in the Land of the Pharaohs* (London, n.d.), 161–62.

131. Shafiq, *Mudhakkirati,* 1: 502–9.

132. MAE / AMB Le Caire / C173: EE / SA / Ribot to MAE, 16 February 1891.

133. Thomas Cook Archives, Egypt (General): Nile Fleet, etc. / 153 N / Handwritten excerpts from a book entitled "A Useful Word on upper-Egypt Monuments," 34–36.

134. As translated in Mounah A. Khouri, *Poetry and the Making of Modern Egypt (1882–1922)* (Leiden, 1971), 20.

135. Prince Ibrahim Hilmy, *The Literature of Egypt and the Soudan from the Earliest Times to the Year 1885 Inclusive: A Bibliography,* 2 vols. (London, 1886) 1: vi.

136. Muhammad Muwaylihi, *A Period of Time* (Reading, England, 1992), part 1: "A Study of Muhammad al-Muwaylihi's Hadith Isa ibn Hisham"; part 2: "Isa Ibn Hisham's Tale," trans. Roger Allen. On the visit to the Pyramids and museum, see 2: 53–67.

137. Ahmad Shawqi, *Al-Amal al-shawqiyya al-kamila,* 4 vols. bound in 2 (Beirut, 1988), 1: 17–33. See also S. Somekh, "The Neo-Classical Arab Poets," in *The Cambridge History of Arabic Literature,* ed. M. M. Badawi (Cambridge, 1991), 62.

138. Ahmad Hasan, *Lubb an al-tarikh al-am* (Cairo, 1888); and Husayn Zaki, *Tarikh al-umam al-sharqiyya al-qadim* (Cairo, 1892). Sarkis, *Mujam,* 382, 770.

139. Ismail Sarhank, *Haqaiq al-akhbar an duwal al-bihar,* 3 vols. (Cairo, 1895–1923). After a twenty-five-year hiatus, vol. 3 treated French history from Clovis to Charles VII. See Jack A. Crabbs Jr., *The Writing of History in Nineteenth-Century Egypt* (Cairo, 1984), 137–43, for the rhyming English title and additional analysis.

140. Mikhail Sharubim, *Raqib ala Ahdath Misr: Hawliyyat Misr al-Siyasiyya (1879–1882 M.),* ed. Yunan Labib Rizq (Cairo, 1992), 9–10. Rizq shows that 1853 is a more likely birthdate than the 1861 given in several notices.

141. Mikhail Sharubim, *Al-Kafi fi tarikh Misr al-qadim wa al-hadith,* 4 vols. (Cairo, 1898–1900), 1: 24. See also the analysis of Sharubim in Crabbs, *Writing,* 133–36.

142. Sharubim, *Al-Kafi,* 1:14.

143. Sharubim, *Al-Kafi,* 1: 89–97.

144. Sharubim, *Al-Kafi,* 1: 61, 63, 86–88, 141–43.

145. Salama Musa, *The Education of Salama Musa,* trans. L. O. Schuman (Leiden, 1961), 50.

146. Charles Wendell, *The Evolution of the Egyptian National Image from Its Origin to Ahmad Lutfi al-Sayyid* (Berkeley, Calif., 1972), 265, 267.

147. Wendell, *Evolution,* 272, translating a quotation from *Al-Jarida,* 12 December 1912.

148. My English translation from the French translation of Hilal, "Les Premiers Égyptologues," 349, translating from *Al-Jarida,* 8 December 1912.

149. Mahmud Fahmi's course in 1913–1914 was an exception. CUA / B6 / F87: syllabi for History of the Ancient East, 1910–1915; F88: 1914–1915; B14 / F170: syllabi for 1923–1924; Ahmad Abdal-Fattah Budayr, *Al-Amir Ahmad Fuad wa Nashat al-Jamia al-Misriyya* (Cairo, 1950), 178–79, 185.

150. On Hamza and Selim Hassan, see *WWWE*3: 189, 192–93.

151. *BIE,* ser. 5, 10, fasc. 1 (1916): 133–76.

152. *BIE,* ser. 5, 10, fasc. 2 (1916): 359–60, full article 359–68.

153. *BIE,* ser. 5, 11, fasc. 1 (1917): 331, full article 325–38. See also fasc. 2: 421–23.

CHAPTER 6. ISLAMIC ART, ARCHAEOLOGY, AND ORIENTALISM

1. Gabriel Charmes, *Cinq Mois au Caire et dans la Basse-Égypte* (Cairo, 1880), 47–48, 57–58, 111.

2. Edward Said, *Orientalism* (New York, 1978); John MacKenzie, *Orientalism: History, Theory and the Arts* (Manchester, 1995); Mark Crinson, *Empire Building: Orientalist and Victorian Architecture* (London, 1996).

3. Stanley Lane-Poole, *Cairo: Sketches of Its History, Monuments, and Social Life* (London, 1898; reprinted New York, 1973), 99–100; Marshall Hodgson, *The Venture of Islam,* 3 vols. (Chicago, 1974), 1: 57–60, 95.

4. Arthur Rhoné, "Coup d'oeil sur l'état present du Caire ancien et moderne," *Gazette des Beaux Arts* 24 (1881): 420–32; 25 (1882): 55–67, quotation from 420.

5. Janet Abu-Lughod, *Cairo: 1001 Years of the City Victorious* (Princeton, N.J., 1971), 83–103. See also André Raymond, *Le Caire* (Paris, 1993), 289–305; and Doris Behrens-Abouseif, *Azbakiyya and Its Environs from Azbak to Isma'il, 1476–1879, Supplément aux annales islamologiques,* Cahier no. 6 (Cairo, 1985), 81–100.

6. Amelia Edwards, "The Destruction of Cairo," *Academy* 546 (21 October 1882): 301.

7. Crinson, *Empire Building,* 172.

8. Abu-Lughod, *Cairo,* 103–13.

9. Abu-Lughod, *Cairo,* 95–97, 110, 112–13. Richard Bulliet, *The Camel and the Wheel* (Cambridge, Mass., 1975), discusses the disappearance of wheeled vehicles from the Arab world between Roman times and the nineteenth century.

10. Rhoné, "Coup d'oeil sur l'état present du Caire ancien et moderne" (1882): 62.

11. Gabriel Charmes, "L'Art arabe au Caire," *Journal des débats,* 2 August 1881. On Charmes, see Roman d'Amat, "Charmes, Gabriel," *Dictionnaire de biographie française* (Paris, 1933–), 8: 602.

12. Lane-Poole, *Cairo,* 290.

13. Edwards, "The Destruction of Cairo."

14. Gabriel Charmes, *Cinq Mois au Caire et dans la Basse-Égypte* (Cairo, 1880), 130.

15. Victor Fournel, *Paris nouveau et Paris futur* (Paris, 1865), 220, as quoted in Françoise Choay, *The Modern City: Planning in the 19th Century* (New York, 1969), 15. For this and the following paragraph, see Hans Huth, "The Evolution of Preservationism in Europe," *Journal of the American Society of Architectural Historians* (July / October 1941): 5–12; and Paul Léon, *La Vie des monuments français: Destruction et restauration* (Paris, 1951). On the United States, see William J. Murtagh, *Keeping Time: The History and Theory of Preservation in America,* 2nd ed. (New York, 1997).

16. *WWWE*3: 337.

17. John Pemble, *Venice Rediscovered* (Oxford, 1995), 126–33, discusses the tension between the romantics' attraction to ruins and idealized "restoration." The latter, as practiced by Gilbert Scott in England and Viollet-le-Duc in France, "could lead to a building's looking as it had never looked before" (128).

18. Jean-Marie Carré, *Voyageurs et écrivains français en Égypte,* 2 vols. (Cairo, 1956), 1: 62. On de Maillet, see also Kara Marietta Hill, "Pascal-Xavier Coste (1787–1879): A French Architect in Egypt," unpublished Ph.D. dissertation, Department of Architecture, Harvard, 1992, 214. On Cassas, see Alberto Siliotti, *The Discovery of Ancient Egypt* (Cairo, 1998), 60–63; Cassas's neglected work appeared in his *Voyage pittoresque de la Syrie, de la Phoenicie, de la Palestine et la Basse Égypte* (Paris, 1795).

19. John Sweetman, *The Oriental Obsession: Islamic Inspiration in British and American Art and Architecture 1500–1920* (Cambridge, Mass., 1988), 115.

20. Charmes, "L'Art arabe." On the frontispiece, see Juan Eduardo Campo, "Mubarak's Khitat: An Egyptian Nationalist Valuation of Religious Space," unpublished paper presented at the Middle East Studies Association meeting, Beverly Hills, California, November 1988; *Description,* vol. 1: *Antiquités: Planches,* frontispiece.

21. On Lane, see Leila Aimed, *Edward W. Lane* (London, 1978). Jason Thompson takes issue with Said and others who have read Lane as epitomizing the faults of Orientalism in his "Edward William Lane's 'Description of Egypt,' " *IJMES* 28 (1996): 579.

22. Edward William Lane, *Arabian Society in the Middle Ages: Studies from the Thousand and One Nights,* ed. Stanley Lane-Poole (London, 1987; reprint of 1883), xii–xiii.

23. Irene A. Bierman, "The Time and Space of Medieval Cairo," unpublished paper, New York, 1998.

24. Pascal Coste, *Architecture arabe ou monumens du Caire mesurés et dessinées, de 1818 à 1825* (Paris, 1839). On Coste, see P. X. Coste, *Mémoires d'un artiste: Notes et souvenirs de voyages (1817–1877)* (Marseilles, 1878); Hill, "Pascal-Xavier Coste."

25. Robert Hay, *Illustrations of Cairo* (London, 1840); David Roberts, *Egypt and Nubia,* 3 vols. (London, 1846); Prisse d'Avennes, *L'Art arabe d'après les monuments du Kaire depuis le VIIe siècle jusqu'à la fin du XVIIIe,* 3 vols. (Paris, 1877); Owen Jones, *Plans, Elevations, Sections, and Details of the Alhambra* (London, 1842–1845). For overviews, see Sweetman, *Oriental Obsession,* 112–52, and MacKenzie, *Orientalism,* 43–70.

26. Julius Franz-Pasha, "Buildings of the Mohammedans," Baed. 1908, clix–clx.

27. Charmes, *Cinq Mois,* 120; Lane-Poole, *Cairo,* 103. J. M Rogers, "Al-Kahira," *EI2* 4: 412–41, surveys Cairo's monuments and their history. Caroline Williams, "Islamic Cairo: Endangered Legacy," *Middle East Journal* 39 (1985): 231–46, reviews recent challenges to preserving the monuments.

28. Charmes, "L'Art arabe." See also Charmes, *Cinq Mois,* 46–47.

29. MAE / AMB Le Caire / C177 / D: École orientale / Xavier Charmes, 2 January 1882.

30. Rhoné, *Gazette* 24 (Année 25, 1882): 63–64; Max Herz, *Catalogue sommaire des monuments exposées dans le Musée national de l'art arabe* (Cairo, 1895), ii–iii; Zaki M. Hasan, "Al-Inaya bi-l-athar," in *Ismail bi-Munasabat murur khamsin aman ala wafatu* (Cairo, 1945), 315. This may be the same Auguste Salzmann who published *Jerusalem: Étude et reproduction photographique des monuments de la Ville Sainte, depuis l'époque judaïque jusqu'à nos jours* (Paris, 1856). Ismail raised the Awqaf Department to a ministry, but in 1884 (as explained below) it was again reduced to a department, which status it retained until restored to cabinet level in 1913. It is here referred to as the Awqaf Department when appropriate and as the Ministry of Awqaf when appropriate.

31. Stanley Lane-Poole, "Arab Art Monuments," *Academy* 6 (1874): 361.

32. Charmes, "L'Art arab." For the history of the Comité, this chapter draws heavily on Donald Malcolm Reid, "Cultural Imperialism and Nationalism: The Struggle to Define and Control the Heritage of Arab Art in Egypt," *IJMES* 24 (1992): 57–76; and discussions with Alaa el-Habashi, whose Ph.D. dissertation, "Cairo of the Comité de Conservation des Monuments de l'Art Arab: A Study on the Preservation of the Monuments and the Protection of Arab Architecture from 1881 to 1961," is forthcoming from the School of Fine Arts, University of Pennsylvania. Philipp Speiser, *Die Erhaltung der arabishcen Bauten in Ägypten* (Heidelberg: Reihe ADIAIK), is also forthcoming.

33. Lane-Poole, *Cairo,* viii, 292.

34. Comité de conservation des monuments de l'art arabe, Fascicule premier, Exercice 1882–1883, Procès-verbaux des séances, fascicule no. 1: 5 (hereafter, Comité 1, 1882–1883, PVS 1). Except where otherwise indicated, references to the personnel and activities of the Comité are from its published

proceedings. On Baudry, see Mercedes Volait's forthcoming "L'Oeuvre égyptienne d'Ambroise Baudry (1838–1906)," a paper delivered at the conference Un Siècle d'architecture savante en Égypte, cosponsored by the Italian Cultural Institute, Centre d'études et de documentation économiques, juridiques et sociales (hereafter, CEDEJ), and IFAO in the spring of 1997, as reported by Hala Halim, "The Fruits of Commerce," *Al-Ahram Weekly*, 13–19 May 1997.

35. Gülru Necipoğlu, *The Topkapi Scroll—Geometry and Ornament in Islamic Architecture* (Santa Monica, Calif., 1995), 66–67. On Bourgoin, see also *Dictionnaire française de biographie* 6 (Paris, 1954), 6: 1498.

36. On Rogers, see *WWWE3*: 361; and J. Heyworth-Dunne, *An Introduction to the History of Education in Modern Egypt* (London, 1968), 386, 429, 438. John Rodenbeck kindly pointed out my error, following W. R. Dawson and E. P. Uphill's *Who Was Who in Egyptology*, 2nd ed. (London, 1972), in listing Franz as a Hungarian Jew. On Franz, see Marcella Stern, "Oesterreich-Ungarns Beitrag zur Architeckture in Aegypten von Drei Architeckten," *Oesterreich und Aegypten: Beitraege zur Geschichte der Beziehungen von 18: Jahrhundert bis 1918*, Schriften des Oesterreichischen Kulturinstitutes Kairo, Band 4 (Cairo, 1993), 54–56.

37. William Gregory, "Arab Monuments in Egypt," letter to the *Times*, reprinted in *Architect*, 4 February 1882, 69. For this paragraph generally, see Comité 1, 1882–1883, PVS 1 (1 February 1881): 7–13. Observations on membership in Egyptian cabinets are based on Fuad Karam, *Al-Nizarat wa-al-wizarat al-misriyya*, vol. 1 (Cairo, 1969).

38. Comité 1, 1882–1883, PVS 2 (16 December 1882): 12. On Mahmud al-Falaki, see Pascal Crozet, "La Trajectoire d'un scientifique égyptien au XIXe siècle: Mahmoud al-Falaki (1815–1885)," in *Entre réforme social et mouvements national: Identité et modernisation in Égypte (1882–1962)*, ed. Alain Roussillon, 285–310 (Cairo, 1995). See also Abu-Lughod, *Cairo*, 109; and Alexander Schölch, *Egypt for the Egyptians! The Socio-Political Crisis in Egypt 1878–82* (London, 1981), 336 n. 123.

39. Comité 4, 1886, PVS 21 (10 March 1886): xv; Lane-Poole, *Cairo*, ix. On Lane-Poole, see *The Dictionary of National Biography* (London, 1917–), vol. *1931–1940*, 715–16.

40. Comité 23, 1906, PVS 148 (18 December 1906): 112.

41. "Protection," *Architect*, 4 August 1883, 66.

42. Comité 13, 1896, PVS 71 (14 November 1896): 104–11.

43. Bierman, "Medieval Cairo," 7.

44. Georges Pangalo, "The Story of Some Old Friends," *Cosmopolitan* 23 (1897): 277–88, quotation from 283.

45. Cheikh Moustafa Abd El-Razeq Pacha, "Ali Bey Bahgat, 1858–1924: sa vie et ses oeuvres," *BIE* 6 (Session 1923–1924): 103–13. For Bahgat's biography, see also Tawfiq Iskarus, "Ali Bahjat Bak wa fadlu ala ilm al-athar al-arabiyya fi Misr," *Al-Hilal* 32, no. 8 (1 May 1924): 856–61; and Max Meyerhof, "'Alî Bej Bahgat," *Der Islam* 14 (1925): 378; and his pension folder in the Egyptian Ministry of Finance, Dar al-Mahfuzat (Miliffat al-Khidma wa-al-Maash), Archive 105 / Cupboard 37 / 'Ayn 3 / Box 767 / Folder 21175 (hereafter, Baghat, pension folder).

46. Abd El-Razeq, *BIE* 6: 104; Ahmad Lutfi al-Sayyid, *Qissat Hayati* (Cairo, 1962), 25. See also Charles Wendell, *The Evolution of the Egyptian National Image from Its Origins to Ahmad Lutfi al-Sayyid* (Berkeley, Calif., 1972), 209.

47. Bahgat, pension folder.

48. Comité 6, 1890, R 69: "Sur la Suppression des boutiques continguës aux façades des mosquées," 121–28.

49. *Napoleon in Egypt: Al-Jabarti's Chronicle of the French Occupation, 1798,* trans. Shmuel Moreh (Princeton, N.J., 1993), 70–71.

50. As quoted in Michael J. Reimer, "Contradiction and Consciousness in 'Ali Mubarak's Description of al-Azhar," *IJMES* 29 (1997): 55.

51. Bierman, "Medieval Cairo."

52. Comité 1, 1882–1883, PVS 2 (16 December 1882): 14–16; Comité 7 [*sic* for 8], 1891, PVS 46 (14 February 1891): 12–13.

53. Jacques Berque, *Egypt: Imperialism and Revolution* (New York, 1972), 72–73.

54. Reimer, "Contradiction," 57, 66 n. 24.

55. Quoted in Marcel Clerget, *Le Caire,* 2 vols. (Cairo, 1934), 1: 337.

56. Heyworth-Dunne, *Education,* 257.

57. On Herz, see F. Sarre's notice in *Kunstchronik* 37 (1919); Rudolf Agstner, "Die Österreichisch-Ungarische Kolonie in Kairo vor dem Ersten Weltkrieg: Das Matrikelbuch des K.u.K. Konsulates Kairo 1908–1914," *Schriften des Österreichischen Kulturinstitutes Kairo* 4 (1994): 175–77; Tawfiq Iskarus, "Maks Harts Basha," *Al-Hilal* 10 (1 July 1919): 921–28. Professor Istvan Ormos, of Eotvos Lorand University, Budapest, who is working on a biography of Herz, has kindly corrected an error about him in Reid, "Cultural Imperialism," 63.

58. On Germans at the Khedivial Library, see Baed. 1929, 69; and Najib al-Aqiqi, *Al-Mustashriqun* (Cairo, 1980), 2: 398–99, 403–4. On Britain's agreement that the library director be German and on Egyptian pressure to reclaim the post, see *The Memoirs of Sir Ronald Storrs* (New York, 1937), 134–35; and DWQ / MMW / NM No. 22, "Al-Kutubkhana al-khudaywiyya" / "Note sur la direction de la Bibliothèque khediviale," ca. 1912, and "Note au Conseil des ministres" from the Comité des finances, 30 August 1915. MAE / AMB Le Caire / C174 *bis:* Enseignement égyptien, Service de antiquités / D: Daressy, Defrance to Maspero, 20 December 1911, mentions the Kaiser's intervention. This dossier contains considerable 1911–1912 correspondence on the maneuvering.

59. J. M. Rogers, *From Antiquarianism to Islamic Archaeology* (Cairo, 1974), 55–61; Robert Hillenbrand, "Creswell and Contemporary Central European Scholarship," *Muqarnas* 8 (1991): 23–35. On the German presence in Egypt, see Thomas W. Kramer, *Deutsch-ägyptische Beziehungen in Vergangenheit under Gegenwart* (Tübingen, 1974).

60. Charmes, "L'Art arabe."

61. Lane-Poole, *Cairo,* 103.

62. On Clarke, see *WWWE3:* 100–101. On Farnall, see *Dictionary of National Biography,* vol. 1929–1940, 431.

63. On Italians in Egypt, see L. A. Balboni, *Gl'Italiani nella civiltà Egiziana de secolo XIXo,* 3 vols. (Alexandria, 1906); Angelo Sammarco, *Gli Italiani in Egitto* (Alexandria, 1937); and Vittorio Briani, *Italiani in Egitto* (Rome, 1982).

64. Karl Baedeker, *Egypt: Part First: Lower Egypt with the Fayum and the Peninsula of Sinai,* 2nd ed. (Leipzig, 1885) (hereafter, Baed. 1885), 280.

65. Comité 11, 1894, R 165: 53–54.

66. Baed. 1895, 73; Max Herz Bey, *Catalogue raisonné des monuments exposés dans le Musée national de l'art arabe* (Cairo, 1906), i–vii.

67. Crinson, *Empire Building,* 65; Lane-Poole, *Cairo,* 114–18; *Aus der Welt der Islamischen Kunst: Festschrift für Ernst Kühnel* (Berlin, 1959); Zeynep Çelik, *The Remaking of Istanbul: Portrait of an Ottoman City in the Nineteenth Century* (Seattle, 1986), 139.

68. Tarek Mohamed Refaat Sakr, *Early Twentieth-Century Islamic Architecture in Cairo* (Cairo, 1993), 22–23.

69. The quoted phrase is found in Baed. 1908, 88. On the ceremony, see Ahmad Shafiq, *Mudhakkirati fi Nisf Qarn,* 3 vols. (Cairo, 1934–1937), 2 (pt. 2): 1903.

70. Comité 21, 1905, PVS (3 January 1905), 3–7; PVS (4 April 1905).

71. Lane-Poole, *Cairo,* 98.

72. Baed. 1908, 58–60, 75–99.

73. *Annuaire statistique de l'Égypte, 1914* (Cairo, 1914), 104.

74. Mona Zakarya, "L'Inscription du discours occidental dans l'architecture et l'urbanisme orientaux," *D'un Orient l'autre,* 2 vols. (Paris, 1991), 1: 561.

75. On Western-influenced architecture in Cairo, see Mohamed Scharabi, *Kairo: Stadt und Architektur im Zeitalter des europäischen Kolonialismus* (Tübingen, 1989); and Mercedes Volait, "La Communauté italienne et ses édiles," *La Revue de l'occident musulman et de la Méditerranée* 46 (1987): 137–48. On Islamic Revival architecture there, see Sakr, *Islamic Architecture;* Robert Ilbert and Mercedes Volait, "Neo-Arabic Renaissance in Egypt, 1870–1930," *Mimar* 13 (1984): 25–34; and the forthcoming volume from the conference Un Siècle d'architecture savante en Égypte, 1997. See especially Mercedes Volait, "L'Oeuvre égyptienne d'Ambroise Baudry (1838–1906)" as reported by Halim, "Fruits of Commerce"; and Nigel Ryan, "Postcards from the Past," in *Al-Ahram Weekly,* 13–19 March 1997, 15.

76. For Islamic Revival architecture in Britain and the United States, see Sweetman, *Oriental Obsession.* Among the many recent studies on world's fairs, see Paul Greenhalgh, *Ephemeral Vistas: The Expositions Universelles, Great Exhibitions and World's Fairs, 1851–1939* (Manchester, 1988); C. R. Fay, *Palace of Industry: A Study of the Great Exhibition and Its Fruits* (Cambridge, 1951); and Carol A. Breckenridge, "The Aesthetics and Politics of Colonial Collecting: India at World Fairs," *Comparative Studies in Society and History* 31 (1989): 195–216. On world's fairs and Egypt, see Anouar Louca, *Voyageurs et écrivains égyptiens en France au XIXe siècle* (Paris, 1970), 181–239; and Timothy Mitchell, *Colonising Egypt* (Cambridge, 1988), 1–33.

77. Gwendolyn Wright, *The Politics of Design in French Colonial Urbanism* (Chicago, 1991), 200–201; Khaled Asfour, "The Domestication of Knoweldge: Cairo at the Turn of the Century," *Muqarnas* 10 (1933): 132–33.

78. Charmes, "L'Art arabe."

79. Hill, "Pascal-Xavier Coste," esp. 30, 97, 144–46.

80. Crinson, *Empire Building,* 97–123, 190.

81. Sakr, *Islamic Architecture*, 9; Fayza Hassan, "Building on Sand," *Al-Ahram Weekly*, 13–19 March 1997, quoting Rudolf Agstner, "Dream and Reality, Austrian Architects in Egypt, 1869–1914," unpublished paper presented at the conference Un Siècle d'architecture savante en Égypte, 1997; Charmes, *Cinq Mois*, 59.

82. Liliane Karnouk, *Modern Egyptian Art: The Emergence of a National Style* (Cairo: 1988), 76–77; Robert Ilbert, *Heliopolis: Le Caire 1905–1922: Genèse d'une ville* (Paris, 1981).

83. Rhoné, *Gazette*, 1882, p. 64; Max Herz Bey, *La Mosquée El-Rifai au Caire* (Milan, n.d.); Mohammad al-Asad, "The Mosque of al-Rifa'i in Cairo," *Muqarnas* 10 (1993): 108–24; Henri Pieron, "Le Caire: Son Esthétique dans la ville arabe et dans la ville moderne," *L'Égypte contemporaine* 2 (1911): 582.

84. Thomas R. Metcalf, *Imperial Vision: Indian Architecture and Britain's Raj* (Berkeley, Calif., 1989), 56–58, 105–39.

85. Abd El-Razeq, *BIE* 6: 103.

86. Ahmed Zeki Pacha, "Le Passé et l'avenir de l'art musulman en Égypt," *L'Égypte contemporaine* 4, fasc. 13 (1913): 1–32; Max Herz Bey, "Quelques Observations sur la communication de S. E. Ahmed Zéki Pacha, 'Le Passé et l'avenir de l'art musulman en Égypte,' " 4, fasc. 15 (1913): 387–98, and Zaki's immediately following rejoinder "Note," 398–402.

87. Guillaume Laplagne, "Des Aptitudes artistiques des Égyptiens d' après les résultats obtenus à l'École des Beaux-Arts," *L'Égypte contemporaine* 1, no. 3 (May 1910): 432–40; Laplagne, "L'Art en Égypte," *BIE*, ser. 5, 5 (December 1911): 10–18; Comité 32, 1915–1919, PVS 243 (11 April 1918): 620.

88. Comité 13, 1896, PVS 69 (1896), 35–36.

89. Gabriel Baer, "Waqf Reform," in his *Studies in the Social History of Modern Egypt* (Chicago, 1969), 83–84.

90. Comité 10, 1893, PVS 58 (13 June 1893): 40, 44–45; and PVS 59 (27 November 1893): 46. On Fakhri, see Yusuf Asaf, *Dalil Misr* (Cairo, 1890), 249–52, and his pension folder in Dar al-Mahfuzat, Cupboard 47 / 'Ayn 1 / Box 957 / Folder 23819, 28 April 1909. Note that his correct death date is 1910.

91. Comité 10, 1893, R 153 (16 August 1893): 75; Comité 14, 1897, PVS 74 (9 March 1897): 48; and PVS 75 (6 April 1897): 73–75.

92. Comité 13, 1896, PVS 69 (spring 1896): 30, 33–35; Comité 15, 1898, PVS 80 (4 January 1898): 39.

93. Abd El-Razeq, *BIE* 6 (1923–24): 105–6.

94. Lutfi al-Sayyid, *Qissat*, 34–36; Wendell, *Egyptian National Image*, 212–15.

95. Abd El-Razeq, *BIE* 6: 109.

96. Arthur Goldschmidt Jr., *Historical Dictionary of Egypt* (Metuchen, N.J., 1994), 107.

97. Jean Ellul, *Index des communications et mémoires publiés par l'Institut d'Égypte (1859–1952)* (Cairo, 1952), which also lists the officers of the Institut.

98. Comité 19, 1902, PVS 112 (23 January 1902), 3.

99. Abd El-Razeq, *BIE* 6: 104. Yusuf Ilyas Sarkis, *Mujam al-Matbuat al-Arabiyya* (Cairo, 1928): 1360, also lists Bahgat's publications.

100. Solange Ory, "Max Van Berchem, Orientaliste," *D'un Orient l'autre*, 2 vols. (Paris, 1991), 2: 11–24, Renan quotation on 15, Maspero quotation on 13. On van Berchem, see also *Cent Ans de vie suisse au Caire: Mémoires et documents réunis et publiés par J. R. Fiechter à l'occasion du 20ème anniversaire de la parution du Journal Suisse d'Égypte et du Proche-Orient* (Alexandria, 1946), 122–24; and Ernst Herzfeld, "Max van Berchem," *Der Islam* 12 (1922): 206–13.

101. Rogers, *From Antiquarianism*, 60.

102. Max van Berchem, *Matériaux pour un Corpus Inscriptionum Arabicarum: Première partie: Inscriptions de l'Égypte*, vol. 19 of *Mémoires publiés par les membres de la mission archéologique française au Caire* (Paris, 1903), 17. G. Wiet's continuation of the *Corpus* for Cairo was vol. 2: *Le Caire* (Cairo, 1930).

103. Ellul, *Index,* passim.

104. Donald Malcolm Reid, "The Egyptian Geographical Society: From Foreign Layman's Society to Indigenous Association," *Poetics Today* 15 (1994): 539–72.

105. Ahmad Abd al-Fattah Budayr, *Al-Amir Ahmad Fuad wa Nashat al-Jamia al-Misriyya* (Cairo, 1950), 23–24, 61; CUA / B3 / F135, Minutes of the Council of Administration, 2 March 1919, and a few days later. Donald Malcolm Reid, *Cairo University and the Making of Modern Egypt* (Cambridge, 1990), provides background information.

106. Iskarus, "Ali Bahjat Bak," 858, 860.

107. *ICO12*, Rome, 1899, *Actes* 1: clxxxii.

108. Abd El-Razeq, *BIE* 6: 110–112.

109. Louca, *Voyageurs*, 181–237; Mitchell, *Colonising Egypt*, 1–2, 6, 180–181 n. 14; and Carter Vaughn Findley, "An Ottoman Occidentalist in Europe: Ahmed Midhat Meets Madame Gülnar, 1889," *American Historical Review* 103 (February 1998): 14–49.

110. "Notice sur les corporations de Damas," *ICO12*, 1899, *Actes* 2, Section 1: 3 ff.

111. K. Vollers, "Le IXme Congrès international des orientalistes tenu à Londres," *BIE*, ser. 3, 3 (November 1892): 197.

112. *ICO8*, Stockholm, 1889; Muhammad Amin Fikri Bey, *Irshad al-alibba ila mahasin urubba* (Cairo, 1892). Though indebted to both Findley ("Ottoman Occidentalist") and Mitchell (*Colonising Egypt*, 218), the present analysis of this congress follows the former more closely.

113. Muhammad Amin Fikri, *Jughrafiyyat Misr* (Cairo, 1878).

114. Fikri, *Irshad*, 674–701, 647.

115. R. N. Cust, "The International Congresses of Orientalists," *Hellas* 6 (1897): 359, as quoted in Mitchell, *Colonising Egypt*, 2.

116. Vollers, "Le IXme Congrès international," 193–209.

117. For the committee, see *ICO9*, London, 1892, *Actes* 1: xxix–xl. For studies of Zaki, see Anwar al-Jundi, *Ahmad Zaki al-Mulaqqab bi-Shaykh al-Uruba* (Cairo, [ca. 1964]); Louca, *Voyageurs*, 209–19. Ahmad Zaki, *Al-Safar ila al-Mutamar* (Cairo, 1893), describes the 1892 journey and IOC.

118. MAE / AMB Le Caire / C359: Conférences / Dossier: Congrès / MAE to de la Boulière, 20 December 1904; Cairo consulate to MAE, 23 February 1905; *ICO14*, Algiers, 1905.

119. Ahmad Shawqi, "Athina," in *Al-Amal al-shiriyya al-kamila*, 4 vols. bound in 2 (Beirut, 1988), 2: 61. MAE / AMB Le Caire / Enseignement égyptien / C170 / Dossier 1 / 24 May 1912, "Une Interview du Prince Fouad," *Journal du Caire.*

120. *ICO16*, Athens, 1912: 41, 115, 117, 119, 120, 121, 122.

121. MAE / AMB Le Caire / C261: Expositions 1897–1936 / D: Exposition universelle de 1889 à Paris / 24 January 1897, Boulad to Cogordon.

122. Egyptian descriptions of the 1889 exposition include: Fikri, *Irshad;* Mahmud Umar al-Bajuri, *Al-Durar al-bahiyya fi al-rihla al-urubawiyya* (Cairo, 1891); Dimitri ibn Nimat Allah Khallat, *Sifr al-safar ila marad al-hadar* (Cairo, 1891); and Ahmad Shafiq, *Mudhakkirati fi nisf qarn,* 3 vols. (Cairo, 1934–37) 1: 471–91. On Cook, see Fikri, *Irshad,* 15–26.

123. On al-Dib, see Fikri, *Irshad,* 129–31. The present study sees Fikri's reactions to the Egyptian exhibit as closer to the interpretations of Louca, *Voyageurs,* 199–203, and Findley, "Ottoman Occidentalist," (1998): 38–40, than to Mitchell, *Colonising,* 1, 7–8.

124. Rand, McNally and Company's *A Week at the Fair* (Chicago, 1893), 235. On the organization of the Egyptian exhibit, including Herz's role, see Pangalo, "The Story of Some Old Friends"; and MAE / AMB Le Caire / C261: Expositions 1897–1936 / Dossier: Commerce: Expositions, Sousdossier: Exposition de Chicago, 1893 / unsigned to Ribot, 19 September 1891.

125. Richard D. Mandell, *Paris 1900: The Great World's Fair* (Toronto, 1967).

126. Along with the published accounts of the Egyptian exhibit, cited below, see MAE / AMB Le Caire / C261: Expositions 1897–1936 / Dossier: Commerce: Expositions, Sousdossier: Exposition de Chicago, 1893 / Philippe Boulad to Cogordan, 14 December 1896, for background on the Boulads and their plans for the exhibit.

127. Ahmad Zaki Bay, *Al-Dunya fi Paris* (Cairo, [ca. 1900]), esp. 91–94, 157–59. The present analysis of Zaki's and Muwaylihi's reactions to the Egyptian exhibit at the fair follows those of Louca, *Voyageurs,* 218–21, 225–34; and Paul Starkey, "Some Egyptian Travellers in Europe," in *Travellers in Egypt,* ed. Paul Starkey and Janet Starkey (London, 1998), 284–86. Muhammad Labib al-Batnuni, *Rihlat al-sayf fi urubba* (Cairo, 1901), esp. 102–3, deplored the lack of government assistance and the predominance of Syrians in the Egyptian exhibit.

128. Iskarus, "Ali Bahjat Bak," 858, 860.

129. Comité 27, 1910, R 420 (15 June 1910), appendix, 94–95.

130. Rogers, *From Antiquarianism,* 58–60.

131. Stephen Vernoit, "The Rise of Islamic Archaeology," *Muqarnas* 14 (1997): 3–4.

132. Vernoit, "Rise of Islamic Archaeology," 5.

133. Comité 30, 1913, "Rapport sur les services de surveillance archéologique des collines du Vieux-Caire confiés au Musée de l'art arabe," 115–17.

134. Comité 31, 1914, PVS 215 (4 January 1915), 134–36.

135. Comité 31, 1914, PVS 215 (4 January 1915), 135. On Patricolo, see FO 371 / 3202 / 137229, Herbert to Balfour, 14 July 1918.

136. Reid, "Cultural Imperialism," takes the story into the 1950s.

CHAPTER 7. MODERN SONS OF THE PHARAOHS?

1. "Excerpts from the Memoirs of Marcus H. Simaika Pasha, C.B.E., F.S.A. (1864–1944)" (hereafter, Simaika memoirs), unpublished typescript held by the family, 42–43. "Patriarch" has been retained here for the head of the Coptic Church, although Egyptians writing and speaking English now increasingly use "pope." *Anba*, "father," often is used before his name in Arabic.

The main title of this chapter draws on the title of S. H. Leeder's book *Modern Sons of the Pharaohs: A Study of the Manners and Customs of the Copts of Egypt* (London, 1918; reprinted, New York, 1973).

2. Interviews in Cairo with Coptic Museum directors Gawdat Gabra Abdel-Sayed (13 February 1988; 9 March 1999), Victor Guirguis (10 March 1988), and Pahor Labib (22 October 1987). Other Cairo interviews with Mirrit Boutros Ghali (15 April 1988) and Egyptologists Labib Habachi (9 November 1982) and Kamal El-Mallakh (14 October 1987); and in Salt Lake City with Aziz S. Atiya (29 March 1986).

3. Jean-Joël Brégeon, *L'Égypte française au jour le jour 1798–1801* (Paris, 1991), 318–20.

4. *Practical Guide to Alexandria, Cairo, and Port-Saïd and Neighbourhood* (London [ca. 1896]), published by Nilsson and Company.

5. E. W. Lane, *The Manners and Customs of the Modern Egyptians* (London, 1908), 555.

6. Stanley Lane-Poole, *Cairo: Sketches of Its History, Monuments, and Social Life* (London, 1898; reprinted New York, 1973), 203.

7. Lane, *Modern Egyptians*, 535.

8. Wilk. 1843, 1: 387–88.

9. Ehud Toledano, *State and Society in Mid-Nineteenth-Century Egypt* (Cambridge, 1990), 187.

10. Doris Behrens-Abouseif, *Die Kopten in der ägyptischen Gesellschaft— von der Mitte des 19, Jahrhunderts bis 1923* (Freiburg im Breisgau, 1972), 35.

11. For Coptic reforms in this period, see Samir Seikaly, "Coptic Communal Reform: 1860–1914," *Middle Eastern Studies* 6 (1970): 247–75. For Coptic participation in national life, see also Behrens-Abouseif, *Kopten;* Raouf Abbas Hamed, "The Copts under British Rule in Egypt 1882–1914," *al-Majalla al-Tarikhiyya al-Misriyya* 26 (1979): 49–59; Tariq al-Bishri, *al-Muslimun wa al-Aqbat fi Itar al-Jamaat al-Wataniyya* (Cairo, 1982); and B. L. Carter, *The Copts in Egyptian Politics* (London, 1986).

12. Seikaly, "Coptic Communal Reform," 248, doubts this possibility. E. L. Butcher, *The Story of the Church of Egypt,* 2 vols. (London, 1897), 395–97, and A Coptic Layman, "The Awakening of the Coptic Church," *Contemporary Review* 71 (1897): 736, report that Cyril IV was an alumnus of the Anglican school. Strong evidence (particularly references to protecting Coptic monuments, 738, 747 in the last source) suggests that "A Coptic Layman" was Simaika

(hereafter, [Simaika], "The Awakening"). On Cyril, see Jurji Zaydan, *Tarajim Mashahir al-Sharq*, 2 vols. (Cairo, 1922), 1: 271–80.

13. Seikaly, "Coptic Communal Reform," 250.

14. Simaika memoirs, 11.

15. Andrew Watson, *The American Mission in Egypt 1854–1896* (Pittsburgh, 1898), 87. Pages 153–54 and 199–259 detail what Watson saw as the persecution of the missionaries and their converts in the 1860s.

16. J. Heyworth-Dunne, *Introduction to the History of Education in Modern Egypt* (London, 1968), 422.

17. Simaika memoirs, 20; Seikaly, "Coptic Communal Reform," 251. For overviews, see Adel Azer Bistawros, "Community Council," *The Coptic Encyclopedia* (hereafter, *CE*), ed. Aziz S. Atiya, 8 vols. (New York, 1991), 2: 580–82; and Mirrit Boutros Ghali, "Clerical College," *CE,* 2: 563–64.

18. [Simaika], "The Awakening," 737.

19. [Simaika], "The Awakening," 737–38.

20. Seikaly, "Coptic Communal Reform," 262.

21. For al-Azhar, see A. Chris Eccel, *Egypt, Islam and Social Change: Al-Azhar in Conflict and Accommodation* (Berlin, 1984), 290–92. For later survey data, see Mahmud Abd Al-Rahman Shafshak, "The Role of the University in Egyptian Elite Recruitment: A Comparative Study of Al-Azhar and Cairo Universities," unpublished Ph.D. dissertation, University of Chicago, 1964.

22. Simaika memoirs, 1–6, 15. On Simaika, see his "Memoirs" and the analysis in Donald Malcolm Reid, "Archeology, Social Reform, and Modern Identity among the Copts, 1854–1952," in *Entre Réforme sociale et mouvement national: Identité et modernisation en Egypte (1882–1962),* ed. Alain Roussillon (Cairo, 1995), 311–35.

23. Abd al-Aziz al-Disuqi, *Rawdat al-madaris* (Cairo, 1985), 381–82.

24. Simaika memoirs, 1–6, 8–13. Zaydan (*Tarajim* 1: 277) says Turkish was also taught.

25. Simaika memoirs, 9. On Labib, see Ramzi Tadrus, *Al-Aqbat fi al-qarn al-ishrin*, 5 vols. (Cairo, 1910–1911), 4: 135–39.

26. Rena L. Hogg, *A Master-Builder on the Nile: Being a Record of the Life and Aims of John Hogg, D.D.* (New York, 1914), 164–67. The quotation is from [Simaika], "The Awakening," 737.

27. Simaika memoirs, 71, 72. Pages 71–81 cover his railways career. For the statistics on Copts in railways and telegraph, see Kyriakos Mikhail, *Copts and Muslims under British Control* (New York, 1911; reprinted, 1971), 42.

28. On Ghali, see Tadrus, *Al-Aqbat*, 2: 62–142. For his extended family, see Arthur Goldschmidt Jr., "The Butrus Ghali Family," *Journal of the American Research Center in Egypt* 30 (1993): 183–88. See Gabriel Baer, *A History of Landownership in Modern Egypt 1880–1950* (London, 1962), 133, on Inshas; and Behrens-Abouseif, *Kopten,* 5, on his father's post.

29. E. L. Butcher, *The Story of the Church of Egypt*, 2 vols. (London, 1897), 2: 410. For this paragraph generally, Seikaly, "Coptic Communal Reform," 252–53.

30. Simaika memoirs, 87. On the crisis generally, see Simaika memoirs, 82–88; Seikaly, "Coptic Communal Reform," 260; and Earl of Cromer, *Modern Egypt* (New York, 1908), 624–25. On Horner, see *WWWE3*: 208.

31. Eccel, *Egypt*, 169–71, 175–78; Gabriel Baer, "Waqf Reform," in his *Studies in the Social History of Modern Egypt* (Chicago, 1969), 79–92.

32. Mustafa al-Fiqqi, *Al-Aqbat fi al-siyasa al-misriyya: Makram Ubayd wa dawruh fi al-haraka al-wataniyya* (Cairo, 1985), 33; Carter, *Copts*, 44–47; Filib di Tarrazi, *Tarikh al-Sihafa al-Arabiyya*, 4 vols. (Beirut, 1911–33), 3: 9–12; Tadrus, *Al-Aqbat*, 4: 129–34, 3: 39–45.

33. Martin Krause, "Coptological Studies," *CE*, 2: 613–16, provides a historical overview. For references on Kircher, see *WWWE*3: 299.

34. Robert Curzon, *A Visit to the Monasteries of the Levant* (New York, 1849), 1–105, describes his manuscript hunting in Egypt. On Mariette, see *WWWE*3: 275–76.

35. Somers Clarke, *Christian Antiquities in the Nile Valley* (Oxford, 1912), 189–90. The unnamed director must have been Grébaut, who was in office when Daressy cleared the church remains from the Medinat Habu temple in 1891. Uvo Hölscher, *The Excavation of Medinat Habu*, vol. 1: *General Plans and Views* (Chicago, 1934), 1.

36. A. J. Butler, *Ancient Churches of Egypt*, 2 vols. (London, 1884), 1: 371. For his life, see the notice in the *Times*, 6 October 1936.

37. Christian Cannuyer, *Les Coptes* (Belgium [no city given], 1990), 193.

38. *WWWE*3: 101.

39. Tawfiq Iskarus, "Max Herz Basha," *Al-Hilal* 27 (1 July 1919): 925.

40. Simaika memoirs, 29, 71–72, quotation from 29.

41. Butler, *Ancient Churches*, 1: xiv.

42. *WWWE*3: 100–101; Michael Hoffman, *Egypt before the Pharaohs: The Prehistoric Foundations of Egyptian Civilization*, 2nd ed. (Austin, 1991), 352.

43. Simaika memoirs, 29–32.

44. Marcus H. Simaika Pacha, *Guide sommaire du Musée Copte et des principes églises du Caire* (Cairo, 1937), preface. On Clarke, see *WWWE*3: 100–01.

45. Comité 11, 1894, PVS 63 (1894), 64; Comité 13, 1896, PVS (20 January 1896), 9–10; Comité 13, 1896, PVS 69 (1896), 30, 33, 35; Comité 15, 1898, PVS 82 (5 April 1898), 39.

46. Simaika memoirs, 31–33; Butcher, *Coptic Churches*, 2: 399–400.

47. FO 633 / 8 Cromer to Lane-Poole, 2 January 1898, 15.

48. Simaika memoirs, 86–87.

49. Cromer, *Modern Egypt*, 633.

50. On Artin, see the autobiographical sketch in University of Pennsylvania, University Museum Archives, AR / Egypt / Sara Y. Stevenson, B2 / F2: Personal correspondence with Yacoub Artin Pasha, enclosed in Artin to Stevenson, 10 August 1897, 11 pp. See also Rev. A. H. Sayce, *Reminiscences* (London, 1923), 241–42 and passim; David Chapin Kinsey, "Egyptian Education under Cromer: A Study of East-West Encounter in Educational Administration and Policy, 1883–1922," unpublished Ph.D. dissertation, Harvard University, 1965, 101–4, 545–55. For background, see Rouben Adalian, "The Armenian Colony of Egypt during the Reign of Muhammad Ali (1805–1848)," *Armenian Review* 33 (1980): 115–33.

51. Comité 1, 1882–1883, PVS 7 (23 November 1883), 30–31.

52. Comité 23, 1906, PVS 147 (27 November 1906), 113.

53. Comité 15, 1898, PVS 80 (4 January 1898), 4, 6. Istvan Ormos, who is working on a biography of Max Herz, is inclined to regard him, rather than Simaika, as the founder of the museum (personal communication, 1998).

54. Comité 15, 1898, PVS 81 (1898), 16; Qalini Fahmi Basha, *Mudhakkirat Qalini Fahmi Basha* (Cairo), 1: 123–25.

55. Maria Avgouli, "The first Greek Museums and National Identity," in *Museums and the Making of Ourselves: The Role of Objects in National Identity,* ed. Flora E. S. Kaplan (London, 1994), 256–58.

56. Simaika memoirs, 42; *Al-Ahram,* 8 June 1930.

57. Simaika memoirs, 46; Marcus Simaika, *Note historique sur le Musée Copte au Vieux Caire à l'occasion de la visite de Sa Hautesse Fouad Ir Sultan d'Égypte, mardi, 21 decembre 1920,* French and Arabic pamphlet (Cairo, 1920), 9.

58. Simaika memoirs, 52.

59. Simaika, as quoted in Archdeacon Dowling, *The Egyptian Church* (London, 1909), appendix 3: 47.

60. Leeder, *Modern Sons,* 263.

61. Dowling, *Egyptian Church,* appendix 3: 48–49, 51; Simaika memoirs, 21–24.

62. Leeder, *Modern Sons,* 246.

63. On Fanus, see Yusuf Asaf, *Dalil Misr* (Cairo, 1890), 353–55; and Abbas, "Copts under British Rule." On Copts in the Watani and Umma parties, see Abu Sayf Yusuf, *Al-Aqbat wa al-Qawmiyya al-Arabiyya* (Beirut, 1987), 111. Samir Seikaly, "Prime Minister and Assassin: Butrus Ghali and Wardani," *Middle Eastern Studies* 13 (1977): 112–23; and Bishri, *al-Muslimun,* 57–97, treat this period.

64. Simaika memoirs, 13–14, 89–91.

65. Ahmad Shafiq, *Mudhakkirati fi nisf qarn,* 4 vols. (Cairo, 1936), 2, pt. 2: 236–37.

66. Muhammad Khalil Subhi, *Tarikh al-hayat al-niyabiyya fi Misr,* vols. 4–6 and supplementary vols. 5 and 6 (Cairo, 1939–47), 6: 52, 81–82. On the pasha title, see Leeder, *Modern Sons,* v.

67. Seikaly, "Coptic Communal Reform," 265–66.

68. Seikaly, "Coptic Communal Reform," 268.

69. Leeder, *Modern Sons,* 173.

70. Ilyas Zakhura, *Mirat al-asr,* 2 vols. (Cairo, 1898–1916), 1: 414–17; Tadrus, *Al-Aqbat,* 3: 39–50; "Jamiyyat Hifz al-Tarikh al-Qibti," *Al-Muqtataf* 10 (1885): 56.

71. Quotations from Simaika, *Guide,* xi; [Simaika], "The Awakening," 734.

72. Stanley Lane-Poole, *Cairo: Sketches of Its History, Monuments, and Social Life,* 3rd ed. (London, 1898; reprinted, New York, 1973), 205–6.

73. DWQ / MMW / NA / MA 1 / 4: Matahif 1879–1886 / D: "Madrasat al-Athar 1881–86" / Ministry of Public Works, "Note au Conseil des ministres," No. 99, 17 April 1882.

74. Seikaly, "Coptic Communal Reform," 269–70; Carter, *Copts,* 96–97.

75. W. M. F. Petrie, *Seventy Years in Archaeology* (London, 1931), 223–24.

76. As quoted in Beth Baron, *The Women's Awakening in Egypt: Culture, Society, and the Press* (New Haven, Conn., 1994), 109–10.

77. Tarrazi, *Tarikh*, 4: 279, 281, 289, 301, 303, 305. The religion of the editor of *Abu al-Hawl* (The sphinx), 279, is unclear.

78. Anouar Louca, *Voyageurs et écrivains égyptiens en France au XIXe siècle* (Paris, 1970), 70; Salama Musa, *The Education of Salama Musa*, trans. L. O. Schuman (Leiden, 1961), 50; Fikri Makram Ubayd, as quoted in Mustafa al-Fiqqi, *Al-Aqbat fi al-siyasa al-Misriyya: Makram Ubyad wa dawruh fi al-haraka al-wataniyya* (Cairo, 1985), 46.

79. On Labib, see Tadrus, *Al-Aqbat*, 4: 135–39; W. E. Crum, "Bibliography: Christian Egypt," *Journal of Egyptian Archaeology* 5 (1918): 215; and Simaika memoirs, 25. Note for example the name of the poet Horus Schénouda (b. 1917). Jean-Jacques Luthi, *Introduction à la littérature d'expression française en Égypte (1798–1945)* (Paris, 1974), 288.

80. Jack A. Crabbs Jr., *The Writing of History in Nineteenth-Century Egypt* (Cairo, 1984), 133–36, assesses *Al-Kafi*. On Sharubim, see Tadrus, *Al-Aqbat*, 3: 28–33.

81. Rifaa Rafii al-Tahtawi, *Anwar Tawfiq al-jalil fi akhbar Misr wa-tawthiq Bani Ismail*, in Muhammad Amara, ed., *Al-Amal al-kamila li-Rifaa Rafi al-Tahtawi*, vol. 3: *Tarikh Misr wa al-Arab qabla al-Islam* (Beirut, 1974), 571. For the rest of the paragraph, see 291–93, 334–35, 373, 405, 439–40, 573–76.

CONCLUSION

1. DWQ / MMW / NA / MA / A / 3 / 4: Matahif 1879–1890: "Note au Conseil des ministres," No. 553/2, 8 February 1915.

2. *BIE*, ser. 5, fasc. 9 (11 January 1915): 77–78.

3. *BIE* 1 (Session 1918–1919): 187.

4. Hoda Mohamed Moustafa El-Kolaly and Hani Mohamed Moustafa El-Kolaly, *Cairo City Key* (Cairo, 1998), map 27.

5. Nadim al-Sayyar, *Qudama al-Misriyyin: Awwal "al-Muwahhidin"* (Cairo, 1996).

6. Beth Baron, *The Women's Awakening in Egypt: Culture, Society, and the Press* (New Haven, Conn., 1994), 34–35, and dust jacket picture.

Select Bibliography

Chapters particularly relevant to specific topics are indicated after the headings.

UNPUBLISHED SOURCES

EGYPT

Archives of the Egyptian Ministry of Finance (Dar al-Mahfuzat), Cairo.
  Pension folders.
Cairo University Archives. Records of the Egyptian University, 1908–1925.
  Minutes of the Technical Committee. Minutes of the Council of Adminis-
  tration.
Egyptian National Archives (Dar al-Wathaiq al-Qawmiyya), Cairo.
  Abhath collection.
  Mahfuzat Majlis al-Wuzara (Archives of the Council of Ministers), Nazarat.
    Al-Ashgal (Ministry of Public Works), Maslahat al-Athar (Antiquities
    Service).
  Fihrist bataqat al-Dar (card file of Egyptian National Archives Holdings).
    Drawer 1: al-Athar (Antiquities).

UNITED KINGDOM

British Library. Additional MSS 37,448–37,471. Hekekyan Papers. 24 vols.
Public Record Office, London (Kew Gardens). Foreign Office series: FO 141,
  FO 371, FO 395.
Thomas Cook Archives, London (since moved to Peterborough).

FRANCE

Ministère des affaires étrangeres. Les Archives diplomatiques de Nantes. Ambassade Le Caire: Cartons 173, 174, 174 *bis:* Enseignement égyptien, Service des antiquités; Cartons 177, 261, 359. Ambassade Constantinople: Dossiers thèmatique, Carton 494.

UNITED STATES

National Archives, Washington, D.C. Records of the Department of State. Microfilm T41, Roll 7.
University of Pennsylvania. University Museum Archives, Curatorial Files and Administrative Files.

PUBLISHED SOURCES

NATIONALISM AND IMPERIALISM, GENERAL

Anderson, Benedict. *Imagined Communities.* 2nd ed. London, 1991.
Bernal, Martin. *Black Athena: The Afroasiatic Roots of Classical Civilization.* 2 vols. New Brunswick, N.J., 1987–1991.
Chatterjee, Partha. *The Nation and Its Fragments: Colonial and Postcolonial Histories.* Princeton, N.J., 1993.
Duara, Prasenjit. *Rescuing History from the Nation: Questioning Narratives of Modern China.* Chicago, 1995.
Gourgouris, Stathis. *Dream Nation: Enlightenment, Colonization, and the Institution of Modern Greece.* Stanford, Calif., 1996.
Headrick, Daniel. *The Invisible Weapon: Telecommunications and International Politics, 1851–1945.* New York, 1991.
———. *The Tentacles of Progress: Technology Transfer in the Age of Imperialism, 1850–1940.* London, 1988.
Hobsbawm, Eric J. *Nations and Nationalism since 1870: Programme, Myth, Reality.* 2nd ed., Cambridge, 1992.
Kedourie, Elie, ed. *Nationalism in Asia and Africa.* New York, 1970.
Lefkowitz, Mary. *Not Out of Africa: How Afrocentrism Became an Excuse to Teach Myth as History.* New York, 1996.
Lyons, F. S. L. *Internationalism in Europe, 1815–1914.* Leyden, 1963.
Porterfield, Todd. *The Allure of Empire: Art in the Service of French Imperialism, 1798–1836.* Princeton, N.J., 1998.
Prochaska, David. *Making Algeria French: Colonialism in Bone, 1870–1920.* Cambridge, 1990.
Segrè, Claudio. *Fourth Shore: The Italian Colonization of Libya.* Chicago, 1974.
Symonds, Richard. *Oxford and Empire: The Last Lost Cause?* New York, 1986.
Young, Robert J. C. *Colonial Desire: Hybridity in Theory, Culture, and Race.* London, 1995.

MODERN EGYPT AND THE MIDDLE EAST, GENERAL

Baer, Gabriel. *A History of Landownership in Modern Egypt 1880–1950.* London, 1962.

Berque, Jacques. *Egypt: Imperialism and Revolution.* New York, 1972.

Cambridge History of Egypt. Ed. Martin Daly. Vol. 2: *Modern Egypt from 1517 to the End of the Twentieth Century.* Cambridge, 1998.

Cole, Juan. *Colonialism and Revolution in the Middle East: Social and Cultural Origins of Egypt's Urabi Movement.* Princeton, N.J., 1993.

Cromer, Earl of. *Modern Egypt.* New York, 1908.

Cuno, Kenneth M. *The Pasha's Peasants: Land, Society, and Economy in Lower Egypt, 1740–1858.* Cambridge, 1992.

Douin, Georges. *Histoire du règne du khédive Ismaïl.* 3 parts in 4 vols. Cairo, 1933–1939.

Fahmy, Khaled. *All the Pasha's Men: Mehmed Ali, His Army and the Making of Modern Egypt.* Cambridge, 1998.

Farnie, D. A. *East and West of Suez, 1854–1956.* Oxford, 1969.

Goldschmidt, Arthur, Jr. *Biographical Dictionary of Modern Egypt.* Boulder, Colo., 2000.

———. *Historical Dictionary of Egypt.* Metuchen, N.J., 1994.

Hunter, F. Robert. *Egypt under the Khedives: From Household to Modern Bureaucracy, 1789.* Pittsburgh, 1984.

Ilbert, Robert. *Alexandrie 1830–1930: Histoire d'un communauté citadine.* 2 vols. Cairo, 1996.

[al-Jabarti, Abd al-Rahman]. *'Aja'ib al-Athar fi 'l-Tarajim wa 'l-Akhbar: 'Abdal-Rahman al-Jabarti's History of Egypt.* Trans. T. Philipp and M. Perlmann. 4 vols. and *Guide.* Stuttgart, 1994.

Karam, Fuad. *Al-Nizarat wa al-wizarat al-misriyya.* Vol. 1. Cairo, 1969.

Kuhnke, Laverne. *Lives at Risk: Public Health in Nineteenth-Century Egypt.* Berkeley, Calif., 1990.

Landes, David. *Bankers and Pashas: International Finance and Economic Imperialism in Egypt.* Cambridge, Mass., 1958.

Lane, Edward W. *The Manners and Customs of the Modern Egyptians.* London, 1908.

Lewis, Bernard. *The Emergence of Modern Turkey.* Oxford, 1961.

Marsot, Afaf Lutfi Al Sayyid. *Egypt in the Reign of Muhammad Ali.* Cambridge, 1984.

Milner, Viscount. *England in Egypt.* London, 1920; reprinted, New York, 1970.

Mubarak, Ali. *Al-Khitat al-tawfiqiyya al-jadida.* 20 vols. Cairo, 1886–1887.

Owen, Roger. *The Middle East in the World Economy.* London, 1981.

Panzac, Daniel. *Quarantaines et lazarets: L'Europe et la peste d'Orient (XVIIe–XX siècles).* Aix-en-Provence, 1986.

al-Rafii, Abd al-Rahman. *Asr Ismail.* 2 vols. 2nd ed. Cairo, 1948.

———. *Muhammad Farid.* Cairo, 1962.

———. *Mustafa Kamil.* Cairo, 1962.

Reimer, Michael J. *Colonial Bridgehead: Government and Society in Alexandria, Egypt, 1807–1882.* Boulder, Colo., 1997.
Sami, Amin. *Taqwin al-Nil.* 3 parts in 6 vols. Cairo, 1916–1936.
Sarhank, Ismail. *Haqaiq al-akhbar an duwal al-bihar.* 3 vols. Cairo, 1895–1923.
Schölch, Alexander. *Egypt for the Egyptians! The Socio-Political Crisis in Egypt 1878–82.* London, 1981.
Shafiq, Ahmad. *Mudhakkirati fi nisf qarn.* 4 vols. Cairo, 1936.
Sharubim, Mikhail. *Al-Kafi fi tarikh Misr al-qadim wa al-hadith.* 4 vols. Cairo, 1898–1900.
Storrs, Ronald. *The Memoirs of Sir Ronald Storrs.* New York, 1937.
Tignor, Robert. *Modernization and British Colonial Rule in Egypt, 1882–1914.* Princeton, N.J., 1966.
Toledano, Ehud. *State and Society in Mid-Nineteenth-Century Egypt.* Cambridge, 1990.
Wiener, Lionel. *Égypte et ses chemins de fer.* Brussels, 1932.
Yared, Nazik Saba. *Arab Travellers and Western Civilization.* London, 1996.

MODERN EGYPT, CULTURAL

Abd al-Karim, Ahmad Izzat. *Tarikh al-talim fi Asr Muhammad Ali.* Cairo, 1938.
———. *Tarikh al-talim fi Misr min nihayat hukm Muhammad Ali ila awail hukm Tawfiq 1848–1882.* 3 vols. Cairo, 1945.
Abduh, Ibrahim. *Jaridat al-Ahram: Tarikh wa Fann 1875–1964.* Cairo, 1964.
Abu-Lughod, Ibrahim. *The Arab Rediscovery of Europe: A Study in Cultural Encounters.* Princeton, N.J., 1963.
Baron, Beth. *The Women's Awakening in Egypt: Culture, Society, and the Press.* New Haven, Conn., 1994.
Brugman, J. *An Introduction to the History of Modern Arabic Literature in Egypt.* Leiden, 1984.
Budayr, Ahmad Abd al-Fattah. *Al-Amir Ahmad Fuad was nashat al-jamia al-misriyya.* Cairo, 1950.
Bulletin de la Société khédiviale de géographie. 1875–1914.
Bulletin de l'Institut égyptien (later *d'Égypte*). 1859–1920.
Choueri, Youssef M. *Arab History and the Nation State: A Study in Modern Arab Historiography 1820–1980.* London, 1989.
Crabbs, Jack A., Jr. *The Writing of History in Nineteenth-Century Egypt.* Cairo, 1984.
Delanoue, Gilbert. *Moralistes et politiques musulmans dans l'Égypte du XIXe siècle (1798–1882).* 2 vols. Cairo, 1982.
Disuqi, Abd al-Aziz. *Rawdat al-madaris.* Cairo, 1985.
Dykstra, Darrell. "Joseph Hekekyan and the Egyptian School in Paris." *Armenian Review* 35, no. 2 (1982): 165–82.
———. "Pyramids, Prophets, and Progress: Ancient Egypt in the Writings of Ali Mubarak." *Journal of the American Oriental Society* 114 (1994): 54–65.
Eccel, Chris A. *Egypt, Islam and Social Change: Al-Azhar in Conflict and Accommodation.* Berlin, 1984.

Gershoni, Israel, and James Jankowski. *Egypt, Islam and the Arabs: The Search for Egyptian Nationhood, 1900–1930.* New York, 1986.

Gran, Peter. *Islamic Roots of Capitalism: Egypt 1760–1840.* Austin, 1979.

Grimal, Nicolas. "L'Institut d'Égypte et l'Institut français d'archéologie orientale." *Bulletin de l'Institut égyptien* 70 (1989–1990): 29–42.

Heyworth-Dunne, J. *Introduction to the History of Education in Modern Egypt.* London, 1968.

Hourani, Albert. *Arabic Thought in the Liberal Age, 1798–1939.* Oxford, 1970.

Husayn, Taha. (Hussein, Taha). *The Future of Culture in Egypt.* Trans. Sidney Glazer. New York, 1975.

———. *A Passage to France: The Third Volume of the Autobiography of Taha Husayn.* Trans. Kenneth Cragg. Leiden, 1976.

———. Institut français d'archéologie orientale du Caire. *Livre du centenaire 1880–1980.* Cairo, 1980.

———. *Un Siècle de fouilles françaises en Egypte 1880–1980.* Cairo, 1981.

al-Jamii [El Gamiey], Abd al-Munim. *Al-Jamia al-misriyya "al-qadima": nashatuha wa dawruha fi al-mujtama.* Cairo, 1980.

Kenney, Lorne. "The Khedive Isma'il's Dream of Civilization and Progress." *Muslim World* 55 (1965): 142–55, 211–22.

Khouri, Mounah A. *Poetry and the Making of Modern Egypt 1882–1922.* Leiden, 1971.

Lane, E. W. *Manners and Customs of the Modern Egyptians.* London, n.d.

Louca, Anouar. *Voyageurs et écrivains égyptiens en France au XIXe siècle.* Paris, 1970.

Lutfi al-Sayyid, Ahmad. *Qissat hayati.* Cairo, 1962.

Musa, Salama. *The Education of Salama Musa.* Trans. L. O. Schuman. Leiden, 1961.

Muwaylihi, Muhammad. *A Period of Time.* Part 2: "Isa Ibn Hisham's Tale." Trans. Roger Allen. Reading, England, 1992.

Philipp, Thomas. *Ğurği Zaidan: His Life and Thought.* Beirut, 1979.

Radwan, Abu al-Futuh. *Tarikh Matbaat Bulaq.* Cairo, 1953.

Reid, Donald Malcolm. *Cairo University and the Making of Modern Egypt.* Cambridge, 1990.

———. "The Egyptian Geographical Society: From Foreign Laymen's Society to Indigenous Professional Association." *Poetics Today* 14 (1993): 539–72.

Reimer, Michael. "Contradiction and Consciousness in 'Ali Mubarak's Description of al-Azhar." *International Journal of Middle East Studies* 29 (1997): 53–69.

Sabat, Khalil. *Tarikh al-tibaa fi al-sharq al-arabi.* 2nd ed. Cairo, 1966.

Sadgrove, Philip. *The Egyptian Theatre in the Nineteenth Century 1799–1882.* Reading, England, ca. 1996.

Sami, Amin. *Al-Talim fi Misr fi sanatay 1914 wa 1915.* Cairo, 1917.

al-Shayyal, Jamal al-Din. *A History of Egyptian Historiography in the Nineteenth Century.* Alexandria, 1962.

———. *Tarikh al-tarjama wa al-haraka al-thaqafiyya fi asr Muhammad Ali.* Cairo, 1951.

al-Tahtawi, Rifaa Rafi. *Manahij al-albab al-misriyya fi mabahij al-albab al-asriyya.* Cairo, 1286 / 1869.

———. *Takhlis al-ibriz fi talkhis Bariz.* Cairo, 1994. See also the abridged translation by Anouar Louca: *L'Or de Paris: Relation de voyage: 1826–1831.* Paris, 1988.

Thompson, Jason. "Edward William Lane's 'Description of Egypt,'" *International Journal of Middle East Studies* 28 (1996): 565–83.

Warner, Nicholas, ed. *Egyptian Panorama: Reports from the 19th Century British Press.* Cairo, 1994.

Wendell, Charles. *The Evolution of the Egyptian National Image from Its Origin to Ahmad Lutfi al-Sayyid.* Berkeley, Calif., 1972.

FOREIGNERS AND NON-EGYPTIAN MINORITIES IN EGYPT

Adalian, Rouben. "The Armenian Colony of Egypt during the Reign of Muhammad Ali (1805–1848)." *Armenian Review* 33 (1980): 115–33.

Agstner, Rudolf. *Die Österreichisch-Ungarische Kolonie in Kairo vor dem Ersten Weltkrieg: Das Matrikelbuch des k. u. k. Konsulates Kairo 1908–1914.* Schriften des Österreichischen Kulturinstitues Kairo, Band 9. Cairo, 1994.

Balboni, L. A. *Gl'Italiani nella civiltà Egiziana de secolo XIXo.* 3 vols. Alexandria, 1906.

Briani, Vittorio. *Italiani in Egitto.* Rome, 1982.

Cent Ans de vie suisse au Caire. Alexandria, 1946.

al-Imam, Muhammed Rifaat. *Al-Arman fi Misr: Al-Qarn al-tasi ashar.* Cairo, 1995.

Kitroeff, Alexandre. *The Greeks in Egypt, 1919–1937: Ethnicity and Class.* London, 1989.

Kramer, Thomas W. *Deutsch-ägyptische Beziehungen in Vergangenheit und Gegenwart.* Tübingen, 1974.

Luthi, Jean-Jacques. *Les Français en Égypte.* Beirut, 1981.

Philipp, Thomas. *Syrians in Egypt 1725–1975.* Stuttgart, 1985.

Politis, Athanase G. *L'Hellénisme et l'Égypte moderne.* 2 vols. Paris, 1929–1930.

Sammarco, Angelo. *Gli Italiani in Egitto.* Alexandria, 1937.

ARCHAEOLOGY AND MUSEUMS, GENERAL

L'Archeologia italiani nel Mediterraneo fino alla seconda guerra mondiale. Ed. Vincenzo La Rosa. Catania, Italy, 1986.

Atkinson, John A., Iain Banks, and Jerry O'Sullivan, eds. *Nationalism and Archaeology.* Glasgow, 1996.

Cezar, Mustafa. *Müzeci ve Ressam Osman Hamdi Bey.* Istanbul, 1987.

Conn, Steven. *Museums and American Intellectual Life, 1876–1926.* Chicago, 1998.

Daniel, Glyn E. *A Short History of Archaeology.* London, 1981.

Díaz-Andreu, Margarita, and Timothy Champion, eds. *Nationalism and Archaeology in Europe.* Boulder, Colo., 1996.

Ergil, Tülay. *Museums of Istanbul / Istanbul Müzerleri.* Istanbul, 1993.

Fagan, Brian, ed. *The Oxford Companion to Archaeology.* New York, 1996.

The Formation of National Collections of Art and Archaeology. Ed. Gwendolyn Wright. Washington, D.C., 1996.

Gran-Aymerich, Ève. *Naissance de l'archéologie moderne, 1798–1945.* Paris, 1998.

Kaplan, Flora E. S., ed. *Museums and the Making of "Ourselves": The Role of Objects in National Identity.* London, 1994.

King, Philip J. *American Archaeology in the Mideast: A History of the American Schools of Oriental Research.* Philadelphia, 1983.

Kohl, Philip L., and Clare Fawcett, eds. *Nationalism, Politics, and the Practice of Archaeology.* New York, 1995.

Kuklick, Bruce. *Puritans in Babylon: The Ancient Near East and American Intellectual Life, 1880–1930.* Princeton, N.J., 1996.

McClellan, Andrew. *Inventing the Louvre: Art, Politics, and the Origins of the Modern Museum in Eighteenth-Century Paris.* Cambridge, 1994.

Meskill, Lynne, ed. *Archaeology under Fire: Nationalism, Politics and Heritages in the East Mediterranean and the Middle East.* London, 1998.

Murtagh, William J. *Keeping Time: The History and Theory of Preservation in America.* 2nd ed. New York, 1997.

The Oxford Encyclopedia of Archaeology in the Near East. 5 vols. New York, 1997.

Sheehan, James. *Museums in the German Art World from the End of the Old Regime to the Rise of Modernism.* Oxford, 2000.

Silberman, Neil Asher. *Between Past and Present: Archaeology, Ideology, and Nationalism in the Modern Middle East.* New York, 1989.

———. *Digging for God and Country: Exploration, Archaeology, and the Secret Study for the Holy Land, 1799–1917.* New York, 1982.

———. "Nationalism and Archaeology." *Oxford Encyclopedia of Archaeology in the Near East,* vol. 4: 103–12. 5 vols. New York, 1997.

Stiebing, William H., Jr. *Uncovering the Past: A History of Archaeology.* Buffalo, N.Y., 1993.

Trigger, Bruce. *A History of Archaeological Thought.* Cambridge, Mass., 1989.

Winstone, H. V. F. *Uncovering the Ancient World.* New York, 1986.

THE FRENCH EXPEDITION — CHAPTER I

Albin, Michael W. "Napoleon's *Description de l'Égypte*: Problems of Corporate Authorship," *Publishing History* 8 (1980): 65–85.

Anderson, Robert, and Ibrahim Fawzy, eds. *Egypt Revealed: Scenes from Napoleon's* Description de l'Égypte. Cairo, 1987.

Beaucour, Fernand, Yves Laissus, and Chantal Orgogozo. *The Discovery of Egypt.* Paris, 1990.

Brégeon, Jean-Joël. *L'Égypte française au jour le jour 1798–1801.* Paris, 1991.

Commission des sciences et arts d'Égypte. *Description de l'Égypte: Ou receuil des observations et des recherches qui ont été faites en Égypte pendant l'expédition de l'armée française.* 20 vols. Paris, 1809–1828. (Éditions Panckoucke published a second edition of the work in 26 vols., Paris, 1820–1830.)

Denon, Vivant. *Voyage dans la basse et l'haute Égypte*. Paris, 1990. Reprint of 1802 ed.

Dhombres, Nicole et Jean. *Naissance d'un pouvoir: Sciences et savants en France (1793–1824)*. Paris, 1989.

Gillispie, Charles Coulston, and Michel Dewachter, eds. *Monuments of Egypt: The Napoleonic Edition*. Princeton, N.J., 1987.

Guémard, Gabriel. *Histoire et bibliographie critique de la Commission des sciences et arts et de l'Institut d'Égypte*. Cairo, 1936.

Herold, Christopher J. *Bonaparte in Egypt*. New York, 1962.

Laissus, Yves. *L'Égypte, une aventure savante: Avec Bonaparte, Kléber, Menou 1798–1801*. Paris, 1998.

Laurens, Henry. *L'Expédition d'Égypte 1798–1801*. Paris, 1989.

———. *Les Origines intellectuelles de l'expédition d'Égypte: L'Orientalisme islamisant en France 1698–1798*. Istanbul-Paris, 1987.

Moreh, S. *Al-Jabarti's Chronicle of the First Seven Months of the French Occupation of Egypt, Muharram-Rajab 1213 / 15 June–December 1798*. Leiden, 1975.

Raymond, André. *Égyptiens et Français au Caire 1798–1801*. Cairo, 1998.

TRAVEL AND TOURISM, GENERAL — CHAPTER 2

Brendon, Piers. *Thomas Cook: 150 Years of Popular Tourism*. London, 1991.

Buzzard, James. *The Beaten Track: European Tourism, Literature, and the Ways to Culture, 1880–1918*. Oxford, 1993.

Campbell, Mary B. *The Witness and the Other World: Exotic European Travel Writing 400–1600*. Ithaca, N.Y., 1988.

Castañeda, Quetzil E. *In the Museum of Maya Culture: Touring Chichén Itzá*. Minneapolis, 1996.

Cook, Thomas, and Son. *The Excursionist* (1869–1903); *The Traveller's Gazette* (1903–1939).

Helms, Mary. *Ulysses' Sail: Power, Knowledge, and Geographical Distance*. Princeton, N.J., 1988.

Herzfeld, Michael. *A Place in History: Social and Monumental Time in a Cretan Town*. Princeton, N.J., 1991.

MacCannell, D. *The Tourist: A New Theory of the Leisure Class*. New York, 1976.

Nordmann, Daniel. "Les Guides-Joanne: Ancêtres des Guides Bleus." In *Les Lieux de mémoire*, ed. Pierra Nora. Vol. 2: *La Nation*. Paris, 1986.

Pemble, John. *The Mediterranean Passion: Victorians and Edwardians in the South*. Oxford, 1987.

Pudney, John. *The Thomas Cook Story*. London, 1953.

Selwyn, Tom, ed. *The Tourist Image: Myths and Myth Making in Tourism*. Chichester, 1996.

Staff, Frank. *Picture Postcards and Travel: A Collector's Guide*. Guilford, England, 1979.

Stagl, Justin. *A History of Curiosity: The Theory of Travel 1550–1800*. Chur, Switzerland, 1995.

Stowe, William W. *Going Abroad: European Travel in Nineteenth-Century American Culture*. Princeton, N.J., 1994.

Swinglehurst, Edmund. *Cook's Tours: The Story of Popular Travel*. Poole, Dorset, England, 1982.

EGYPTIAN TRAVEL ACCOUNTS, GUIDEBOOKS, AND TOURISM —
CHAPTERS 1 AND 2

Baedeker, Karl. *Egypt*. 2nd, 3rd, 6th, 7th, 8th eds. Leipzig, 1885, 1895, 1908, 1914, 1929. (Title varies by edition.)

Botti, G. *Catalogue des monuments exposés au Musée greco-romain d'Alexandrie*. Alexandria, 1900.

Breccia, E. *Alexandrea ad Aegyptum: Guide de la ville ancienne et moderne et du Musée greco-romain*. Bergamo, 1914.

Budge, E. A. W. *Cook's Handbook for Egypt and the Sudan*. 2nd ed. London, 1906.

Carré, Jean-Marie. *Voyageurs et écrivains français en Égypte*. 2 vols. Cairo, 1956.

Clément, R. *Les Français d'Égypte aux XVIIe et XVIIIe siècles*. Cairo, 1960.

Edwards, Amelia. *A Thousand Miles up the Nile*. Revised ed. London, 1890.

Forster, E. M. *Alexandria: A History and a Guide*. New York, 1961.

Frank, K. *Lucie Duff Gordon*. London, 1994.

Gordon, Lucie Duff. *Letters from Egypt (1862–69)*. Ed. Gordon Wakefield. London, 1969.

Halls, J. J. *The Life and Correspondence of Henry Salt*. 2 vols. London, 1834.

Herz Bey, Max. *Catalogue raisonné des monuments exposés dans le Musée national de l'art arabe*. Cairo, 1906.

Joanne, Adolphe, and Émile Isambert. *Itinéraire descriptif, historique, et archéologique de l'Orient*. Paris, 1861.

Kalfatovic, Martin. *Nile Notes of a Howadji: A Bibliography of Travelers' Tales from Egypt*. Metuchen, N.J., 1992.

Lane, Edward William. *Description of Egypt*. Ed. Jason Thompson. Cairo, 2000.

Maillet, Benoît de. *Description de l'Égypte . . . composée sur les mémoires de M. de Maillet, ancien consul de France au Caire, par l'abbé Le Mascrier*. Paris, 1735.

Mariette-Bey, Auguste. *Album de Musée de Boulaq*. Cairo, 1871.

———. *Notice des principaux monuments exposés dans les galeries provisoires du Musée d'antiquités égyptiennes de S. A. le Vice-Roi à Boulaq*. 1st–5th eds. Alexandria, Cairo, 1864–1874.

Maspero, Gaston. *Guide du visiteur au Musée du Caire*. 4th ed. Cairo, 1915.

Murray, John. *A Hand-book for Travellers in Egypt*. 2nd, 3rd, 4th, 5th eds. London, 1858, 1867, 1873, 1875. (Title varies by edition.)

———. *A Hand-book for Travellers in Lower and Upper Egypt*. 6th ed. 2 vols. London, 1880.

Rifaud, Jean-Jacques. *Tableau de l'Égypte, de la Nubie et des lieux circonvoisins*. Paris, 1830.

Simaika Pacha, Marcus H. *Guide sommaire du Musée copte et des principles églises du Caire*. Cairo, 1937.

Starkey, Paul, and Janet Starkey, eds. *Travellers in Egypt*. London, 1998.

Steegmuller, Francis. *Flaubert in Egypt: A Sensibility on Tour*. Boston, 1972.

Thackeray, William Makepeace. *The Paris Sketch Book of Mr. M. A. Titmarsh: The Irish Sketchbook; and Notes of a Journey from Cornhill to Grand Cairo*. New York, n.d. (Three books published in one volume; all references here are to *Notes*.)

Twain, Mark. *The Innocents Abroad or the New Pilgrim's Progress*. New York, 1929.

Volkoff, Oleg V. *Comment on visitait la vallée du Nil: Les Guides de l'Égypte*. Recherches no. 28. Cairo, 1967.

Volney, C.-F. *Voyage en Syrie et en Égypte, pendant les années 1783, 1784, et 1785*. 2 vols. 2nd ed. Paris, 1787.

Wilkinson, Gardner. *A Handbook for Travellers in Egypt*. London: Murray, 1847.

———. *Modern Egypt and Thebes*. 2 vols. London, 1843.

———. *Topography of Thebes, and General View of Egypt*. London, 1835.

EGYPTOLOGY AND EGYPTOMANIA — CHAPTERS 1, 3, AND 5

Abou-Ghazi, Dia'. *The Eighty [sic] Anniversary of the Museum's Building*. Special issue of *Annales du Service des antiquités de l'Égypte* 67 (1991).

Baikie, James. *A Century of Excavation in the Land of the Pharaohs*. London, n.d.

Belzoni, G. *Narrative of the Operations and Recent Discoveries*. London, 1820.

Bosworth, C. E. "Al-Jabarti and the Frankish Archaeologists." *International Journal of Middle East Studies* 8 (1977): 229–36.

Breasted, Charles. *Pioneer to the Past: The Story of James Henry Breasted, Archaeologist*. New York, 1945.

Brugsch, Heinrich. *Mein Leben und Mein Wandern*. Berlin, 1894.

Budge, E. A. Wallis. *By Nile and Tigris: A Narrative of Journeys in Egypt and Mesopotamia on Behalf of the British Museum between the Years 1886 and 1913*. 2 vols. London, 1920.

Carrott, Richard G. *The Egyptian Revival: Its Sources, Monuments, and Meaning 1808–1858*. Berkeley, Calif., 1978.

Clayton, Peter A. *The Rediscovery of Ancient Egypt: Artists and Travellers in the Nineteenth Century*. London, 1982.

Cook, Michael. "Pharaonic History in Medieval Egypt." *Studia Islamica* 57 (1983): 67–113.

Curl, James Steven. *Egyptomania: The Egyptian Revival: An Introductory Study of a Recurring Theme in the History of Taste*. London, 1982.

———. *Egyptomania: The Egyptian Revival: A Recurring Theme in the History of Taste*. New York, 1994.

David, Elisabeth. *Gaston Maspero 1846–1916: Le gentleman égyptologue*. Paris, 1999.

———. *Mariette Pacha 1821–1881*. Paris, 1994.

Dawson, W. R. *Who Was Who in Egyptology*. London, 1951. 2nd ed., Dawson and Eric R. Uphill, 1972. 3rd ed., revised by M. L. Bierbrier, 1995.

Dewachter, Michel, and Alain Fouchard, eds. *L'Égyptologie et les Champollion.* Grenoble, 1994.

Dodson, Aidan. "The Eighteenth-Century Discovery of the Serapeum." *KMT: A Modern Journal of Ancient Egypt* 11 (2000): 48–53.

Drower, Margaret. *Flinders Petrie: A Life in Archaeology.* Madison, Wis., 1995.

Ebers, Georg. *Richard Lepsius: A Biography.* Trans. Z. D. Underhill. New York, 1887.

Edwards, Amelia. *Pharaohs, Fellahs, and Explorers.* New York, 1891.

L'Egittologo Luigi Vassalli (1812–1887). Milan, 1994.

Fagan, Brian M. *The Rape of the Nile.* London, 1975.

Fowden, Garth. *The Egyptian Hermes: A Historical Approach to the Late Pagan Mind.* Princeton, N.J., 1986.

France, Peter. *The Rape of Egypt: How Europeans Stripped Egypt of Its Heritage.* London, 1991.

Freier, E., and W. F. Reineke, eds. *Karl Richard Lepsius (1810–1884).* Berlin, 1988.

Gliddon, George. *An Appeal to the Antiquaries of Europe on the Destruction of the Monuments of Egypt.* London, 1841.

Grange, Daniel. "Archéologie et politique: Égyptologues et diplomates français au Caire (1880–1914)." In *L'Égyptologie et les Champollion,* ed. Michel Dewachter and Alain Fouchard, 354–370. Grenoble, 1994.

Greener, Leslie. *The Discovery of Egypt.* New York, 1965.

Haarmaan, Ulrich. "Medieval Muslim Perceptions of Pharaonic Egypt." In *Ancient Egyptian Literature: History and Forms,* ed. Antonio Loprieno, 605–27. Leiden, 1996.

———. "Regional Sentiment in Medieval Islamic Egypt," *Bulletin of the School of Oriental and African Studies* 43 (1980): 55–66.

Hartleben, H. *Champollion, sein Leben und sein Werk.* 2 vols. Berlin, 1906.

Hassan, Fekri A. "Memorabilia: Archaeological Materiality and National Identity in Egypt." In *Archaeology under Fire: Nationalism, Politics and Heritage in the Eastern Mediteranean and Middle East,* ed. Lynn Meskell, 200–216. London, 1998.

Hilal, Amal. "Les Premiers Égyptologues égyptiens et la réforme." In *Entre Réforme sociale et mouvement national: Identité et modernisation en Égypte (1882–1962),* ed. Alain Rousillon, 337–50. Cairo, 1995.

Hoffman, Michael. *Egypt before the Pharaohs: The Prehistoric Foundations of Egyptian Civilization.* 2nd ed. Austin, 1991.

Humbert, Jean-Marcel, Michel Pantazzi, and Christiane Ziegler. *Egyptomania: Egypt in Western Art 1730–1930.* Ottowa, 1994.

Iverson, Erik. *The Myth of Egypt and Its Hieroglyphics in European Tradition.* Copenhagen, 1961.

James, T. G. H. *Excavating in Egypt: The Egypt Exploration Society 1882–1982.* London, 1982.

Jaunay, Andrée. *Mémoires de Jacques de Morgan, souvenirs d'un archéologue.* Paris, 1997.

Kaiser, Werner. *75 Jahre Deutsches Archäologisches Institut Kairo 1907–1982.* Mainz, 1982.

Khater, A. *Le Régime juridique des fouilles et des antiquités en Égypte.* Cairo, 1960.

Lacouture, Jean. *Champollion: Une Vie de lumières.* Paris, 1988.

Mariette, Auguste. *Aperçu de l'histoire d'Égypte depuis les temps les plus reculés jusqu'à la conquête musulmane.* Bound together with Abdallah Abu al-Suud's Arabic translation *(Kitab Qudama al-Misriyyia).* Alexandria, 1864.

Mariette-Bey, Auguste. *Notice des principaux monuments exposé dans les galeries provisoires du Musée d'antiquités égyptiennes de S. A. le Vice-Roi à Boulaq.* 1st–5th eds. Alexandria / Cairo, 1864–1874. (Title varies by edition.)

Maspero, Gaston. *L'Égyptologie.* Paris, 1915.

———. "Mariette (1821–1881): Notice biographique." In A. Mariette, *Oeuvres diverses,* vol. 1: i–ccxxiv. Paris, 1904. Mariette's *Oeuvres diverses,* vol. 18 of *Bibliothèque étyptologique, contentent les oeuvres des égyptologues français.* Ed. Gaston Maspero. 40 vols. Paris, 1893–1915.

———. *Rapports sur la marche du Service des antiquités de 1899 à 1910.* Cairo, 1912.

Al-Mawsua al-misriyya: Tarikh Misr al-qadima wa atharuha. Egypt. Ministry of Culture. Cairo, n.d.

Mayes, Stanley. *The Great Belzoni.* London, 1959.

Morgan, Jacques de. *Souvenirs d'un archéologue: Mémoires de Jacques de Morgan 1857–1924.* Ed. Andrée Jaunayed. Paris, 1997.

Parkinson, Richard. *Cracking Codes: The Rosetta Stone and Decipherment.* Berkeley, Calif., 1999.

Petrie, W. M. F. *Seventy Years in Archaeology.* London, 1931.

Rees, Joan. *Amelia Edwards, Traveller, Novelist and Egyptologist.* London, 1998.

Reeves, Nicholas. *Ancient Egypt: The Great Discoveries.* London, 2000.

Reid, Donald M. "French Egyptology and the Architecture of Orientalism: Deciphering the Facade of Cairo's Egyptian Museum." In *Franco-Arab Encounters: Studies in Memory of David C. Gordon,* ed. L. Carl Brown and Matthew Gordon, 35–69. Beirut, 1996.

———. "Indigenous Egyptology: The Decolonization of a Profession?" *Journal of the American Oriental Society* 105 (1985): 233–46.

Ridley, Ronald T. *Napoleon's Proconsul in Egypt: The Life and Times of Bernardino Drovetti.* London, ca. 1998.

Romer, John and Elizabeth. *The Rape of Tutankhamun.* London, 1993.

Sayce, A. H. *Reminiscences.* London, 1923.

T[agher]. J[acques]. "Ordres supérieurs relatifs à la conservation des antiquités et à la création d'un musée au Caire." *Cahiers d'histoire égyptienne,* ser. 3, fasc. 1 (1950): 13–25.

al-Tahtawi, Rifaa Rafii. *Anwar tawfiq al-jalil fi akhbar Misr wa-tawthiq Bani Ismail.* In *Al-Amal al-kamila li-Rifaa Rafi al-Tahtawi,* ed. Muhammad Amara. Vol. 3: *Tarikh Misr wa al-arab qabla al-Islam.* Beirut, 1974.

Thomas, Nancy, ed., with essays by Gerry D. Scott III and Bruce G. Trigger. *The American Discovery of Egypt.* Los Angeles, 1995.

Thompson, Jason. *Sir John Gardner Wilkinson and His Circle.* Austin, 1992.

Traunecker, Claude, and Jean-Claude Golvin. *Karnak: Résurrection d'un site.* Paris, 1984.

Vercoutter, Jean. *The Search for Ancient Egypt.* New York, 1992.

Wilson, John A. *Signs and Wonders upon Pharaoh: A History of American Egyptology.* Chicago, 1964.

———. *Thousands of Years: An Archaeologist's Search for Ancient Egypt.* Chicago, 1972.

Wilkinson, Toby A. H. *Early Dynastic Egypt.* London, 1999.

Winstone, H. V. F. *Howard Carter and the Discovery of the Tomb of Tutankhamun.* London, 1991.

Wortham, John D. *British Egyptology (1549–1906).* Newton Abbot, England, 1972.

Yates, Francis A. *Giordano Bruno and the Hermetic Question.* Chicago, 1964.

INTERNATIONAL EXHIBITIONS — CHAPTERS 3, 5, AND 6

Breckenridge, Carol A. "The Aesthetics and Politics of Colonial Collecting: India at World Fairs." *Comparative Studies in Society and History* 31 (1989): 195–216.

Çelik, Zeynep. *Displaying the Orient: The Architecture of Islam at Nineteenth-Century World's Fairs.* Berkeley, Calif., 1992.

Fay, C. R. *Palace of Industry: A Study of the Great Exhibition and Its Fruits.* Cambridge, 1951.

Fikri, Muhammad Amin (Bey). *Irshad al-Libba ila Mahasin Urubba.* Cairo, 1892.

Greenhalgh, Paul. *Ephemeral Vistas: The Expositions Universelles, Great Exhibitions and World's Fairs, 1851–1939.* Manchester, 1988.

Jones, Owen, and Joseph Bonomi. *Description of the Egyptian Court Erected in the Crystal Palace.* London, 1854.

Mandell, Richard D. *Paris 1900: The Great World's Fair.* Toronto, 1967.

Mariette, Auguste. *Description du parc égyptien: Exposition universelle de 1867.* Paris, 1867.

———. *Exposition universelle de Paris 1878. La Galerie de l'Égypte ancienne.* Paris, 1878.

Mass, John, and H. J. Schwarzmann. *The Glorious Enterprise: The Centennial Exhibition of 1876.* Watkins Glen, N.Y., 1973.

el Mouelhy, Ibrahim. "L'Égypte à l'exposition de Philadelphie." *Cahiers d'histoire égyptienne* 1, no. 4 (1949): 316–26.

Nikou, Mehrangiz N. "Egypt's Architectural Representation in the 1867 Paris International Exposition and Napoleon III's Aspiration for a French Arab Kingdom." Unpublished paper presented at the meeting of the Middle East Studies Association, Orlando, Florida, 16–19 November 2000.

Pangalo, George. "The Story of Some Old Friends." *Cosmopolitan* 23 (1897): 277–88.

Rand McNally and Company's A Week at the Fair. Chicago, 1893.

Rydell, Robert W. *All the World's A Fair: Visions of Empire at American International Expositions, 1876–1916.* Chicago, 1984.

Rydell, Robert W., and Nancy Gwinn, eds. *Fair Representations: World's Fairs and the Modern World*. Amsterdam, 1994.

Thiers, Henri. *L'Égypte ancienne et moderne à l'exposition universelle*. Paris, 1867.

Zaki (Bey), Ahmad. *Al-Dunya fi Paris*. [Cairo, 1900].

GRECO-ROMAN STUDIES — CHAPTER 4

Angelomatis-Tsougarakis. *The Eve of the Greek Revival: British Travellers' Perceptions of Early Nineteenth-Century Greece*. London, 1990.

Augustinos, Gerasimos. *Consciousness and History: Nationalist Critics of Greek Society 1897–1914*. Boulder, Colo., 1997.

Avgouli, Maria. "The First Greek Museums and National Identity." In *Museums and the Making of Ourselves: The Role of Objects in National Identity*, ed. Flora Kaplan, 246–65. London, 1994.

Benabou, Marcel. "L'Imperialisme et l'Afrique du nord: Le Modèle romain." In *Sciences de l'homme et conquête coloniale: Constitution et usages des sciences humaines en Afrique (XIXe–XXe siècles)*, ed. Daniel Nordman and Jean-Pierre Raison, 15–22. Paris, 1980.

Bonacasa, Nicola. "L'Archeologia italiana in Egitto." In *L'Archeologia italiani nel Mediterraneo fino alla seconda guerra mondiale*, ed. Vincenzo La Rosa. Catania, Italy, 1986.

Breccia, A. Evaristo. *Faraoni senza Pace*. 2nd ed. Pisa, 1958.

Bulletin de la Société archéologique d'Alexandrie. 1898–1956.

Bustani, Sulayman. *Al-Iliyadha*. Cairo, 1904.

Clarke, G. W., ed. *Rediscovering Hellenism: The Hellenic Inheritance and the English Imagination*. Cambridge, 1989.

Clarke, M. L. *Classical Education in Britain 1500–1900*. Cambridge, 1959.

Congrès international d'archéologie classique. *Comptes rendus: 2me session—Le Caire, 1909*. Cairo, 1909.

————. *Comptes rendus: Première session—Athènes, 1905*. Athens, 1905.

Cromer, Earl of. *Ancient and Modern Imperialism*. New York, 1910.

Crozet, Pascal. "La trajectoire d'un scientifique égyptien au XIXe siècle: Mahmoud al-Falaki (1815–1885)." In *Entre Réforme social et mouvements national: Identité et modernisation en Egypte (1882–1962)*, ed. Alain Roussillon, 285–310. Cairo, 1995.

Dairat al-Maarif. Ed. Butrus al-Bustani et al. 11 vols. Beirut / Cairo, 1876–1900.

Eisner, Robert. *Travelers to an Antique Land: The History and Literature of Travel to Greece*. Ann Arbor, 1991.

Encyclopedia of the History of Classical Archaeology. Ed. Nancy Thompson de Grummond. 2 vols. London, 1996.

Fahmi, Mahmud. *Tarikh al-Yunan*. Cairo, 1910.

Fanus, Wajih. "Sulayman al-Bustani and Comparative Literary Studies in Arabic." *Journal of Arabic Literature* 17 (1986): 105–19.

Farid, Muhammad. *Tarikh al-Rumaniyiin*. Cairo, 1902.

Frémeaux, Jacques. "Souvenirs de Rome et présence française au Maghreb." In *Connaissances du Maghreb: Sciences sociales et colonisation*, ed. Jean-Claude Vatin, 29–46. Paris, 1984.

Goodman, L. E. "The Greek Impact on Arabic Literature." In *The Cambridge History of Arabic Literature,* vol. 1: *Arabic Literature to the End of the Umayyad Period,* ed. A. F. L. Beeston et al., 460–82. Cambridge, 1983.

Gummere, Richard. *The American Colonial Mind and the Classical Tradition.* Cambridge, Mass., 1963.

Gutas, Dimitri. *Greek Thought, Arabic Culture: The Graeco-Arabic Translation Movement in Baghdad and Early 'Abbasid Society (2nd–4th / 8th–10th Centuries).* London, 1998.

Hartog, François. *The Mirror of Herodotus: The Representation of the Other in the Writing of History.* Trans. Janet Lloyd. Berkeley, Calif., 1988.

Hourani, Albert. "Bustani's Encyclopaedia." In Hourani, *Islam in European Thought,* 164–73. Cambridge, 1991.

———. "Sulaiman al-Bustani and the Iliad." In Hourani, *Islam in European Thought,* 174–87. Cambridge, 1991.

Hughes-Hallett, Lucy. *Cleopatra: Histories, Dreams and Distortions.* New York, 1990.

Issawi, Charles. "Ibn Khaldun on Ancient History: A Study in Sources." *Princeton Papers in Near Eastern Studies* 3 (1994): 127–50.

Jenkyns, Richard. *The Victorians and Ancient Greece.* Cambridge, Mass., 1980.

Jones, Hugh Lloyd. *Blood for the Ghosts: Classical Influences in the Nineteenth and Twentieth Centuries.* London, 1982.

Klein-Franke, Felix. *Die Klassiche Antike in der Tradition des Islams.* Darmstadt, 1980.

Lucas, Sir C. P. *Greater Rome and Greater Britain.* Oxford, 1912.

McCrindle, J. W. *Ancient India as Described in Classical Literature.* Westminister, 1901.

MacKendrick, Paul. *The North African Stones Speak.* Chapel Hill, N.C., 1980.

Marchand, Suzanne L. *Down from Olympus: Archaeology and Philhellenism in Germany, 1750–1970.* Princeton, N.J., 1996.

Maspero, G. "Une Inscription trilingue de C. Corneilius." In his *Causeries d'Egypte,* 95–101. 2nd ed. Paris, 1907.

Miles, Gary B. "Roman and Modern Imperialism: A Reassessment." *Comparative Studies in Society and History* 32 (1990): 629–59.

Pfeiffer, Rudolf. *History of Classical Scholarship from 1300 to 1850.* Oxford, 1976.

Reinhold, Meyer. *Classica Americana: The Greek and Roman Heritage in the United States.* Detroit, 1984.

Rodenbeck, John. "Alexandrian Literature." *Newsletter of the American Research Center in Egypt* 156 / 157 (winter / spring 1992): 7–10.

Rosenthal, Franz. *The Classical Heritage in Islam.* Trans. E. and J. Marmorstein. Berkeley, Calif., 1975.

Sayce, Rev. A. H. *The Egypt of the Hebrews and Herodotos.* London, 1896.

Stoneman, Richard. *Land of Lost Gods: The Search for Classical Greece.* Norman, Okla., 1987.

Tregenza, L. A. *Egyptian Years.* London, 1958.

Turner, Eric. "The Graeco-Roman Branch." In *Excavating in Egypt,* ed. T. G. H. James, 161–76. London, 1982.

Turner, Frank M. "British Politics and the Demise of the Roman Republic." *Historical Journal* 29 (1986): 577–99.

———. *The Greek Heritage in Victorian Britain*. New Haven, Conn., 1981.

Vance, Norman. *The Victorians and Ancient Rome*. Oxford, 1997.

Vance, William L. *America's Rome*. 2 vols. New Haven, Conn., 1989.

Warmington, E. H. *The Commerce between the Roman Empire and India*. London, 1974.

Wheeler, Sir Mortimer. *Rome beyond Imperial Frontiers*. Southampton, 1955.

Yavetz, Zvi. "Why Rome? Zeitgeist and Ancient Historians in Early 19th-Century Germany." *American Journal of Philology* 97 (1976): 276–96.

ORIENTALISM AND ISLAMIC ART, ARCHITECTURE, AND ARCHAEOLOGY — CHAPTER 6

Abu Lughod, Janet. *Cairo: 1001 Years of the City Victorious*. Princeton, N.J., 1971.

Ahmed, Leila. *Edward W. Lane*. London, 1978.

al-Asad, Mohammad. "The Mosque of Muhammad Ali in Cairo," *Muqarnas* 9 (1992): 39–57.

———. "The Mosque of al-Rifa'i in Cairo." *Muqarnas* 10 (1993): 108–24.

Asfour, Khaled. "The Domestication of Knowledge: Cairo at the Turn of the Century." *Muqarnas* 10 (1993): 125–37.

Baer, Gabriel. "Waqf Reform." In his *Studies in the Social History of Modern Egypt*, 79–92. Chicago, 1969.

Behdad, Ali. *Belated Travelers: Orientalism in the Age of Colonial Dissolution*. Durham, N.C., 1994.

Behrens-Abouseif, Doris. *Azbakiyya and Its Environs from Azbak to Isma'il, 1476–1879. Supplément aux Annales Islamologiques*. Cahier No. 6. Cairo, 1985.

Bierman, Irene A. "Time and Space of Medieval Cairo: Guardians of Monuments and Memory." Unpublished paper presented in New York City, 1998.

Çelik, Zeynep. *The Remaking of Istanbul: Portrait of an Ottoman City in the Nineteenth Century*. Seattle, 1986.

Charmes, Gabriel. *Cinq Mois au Caire et dans la Basse-Égypte*. Cairo, 1880.

Coste, Pascal. *Architecture arabe ou monumens [sic] du Caire mesurés et dessinées, de 1818 à 1825*. Paris, 1839.

Crinson, Mark. *Empire Building: Orientalist and Victorian Architecture*. London, 1996.

D'un Orient l'autre. 2 vols. Paris, 1991.

Dykstra, Darrell. "A Biographical Study in Egyptian Modernization: Ali Mubarak (1823/4–1893)." 2 vols. Unpublished Ph.D. dissertation, University of Michigan, 1977.

Exercises de la Comité de conservation de l'art arabe. 1881–1914.

Fieldner, Stephan. *Ali Mubarak und seine Hitat: Kommentierte Übersetzung der Autobiographie und Werkbesprechung*. Berlin, 1990.

Findley, Carter Vaughn. "An Ottoman Occidentalist in Europe: Ahmed Midhat Meets Madame Gülnar, 1889." *American Historical Review* 103 (February 1998): 14–49.

Franz-Pasha. "Buildings of the Mohammedans." In Baedeker's *Egypt and the Sudan,* clix–clx. 6th ed. Leipzig, 1908.

El-Habashi, Alaa, and Nicholas Warner. "Recording the Monuments of Cairo: An Introduction and Overview. *Annales islamologiques* 32 (1998): 81–99.

Hay, Robert. *Illustrations of Cairo.* London, 1840.

Herz Bey, Max. *La Mosquée El-Rifai au Caire.* Milan, n.d.

Hill, Kara Marietta. "Pascal-Xavier Coste (1787–1879): A French Architect in Egypt." Unpublished Ph.D. dissertation, Department of Architecture, Harvard University, 1992.

Hillenbrand, Robert. "Creswell and Contemporary Central European Scholarship." *Muqarnas* 8 (1991): 23–35.

Ilbert, Robert. *Heliopolis: Le Caire 1905–1922: Genèse d'une ville.* Paris, 1981.

Ilbert, Robert, and Mercedes Volait. "Neo-Arabic Renaissance in Egypt, 1870–1930." *Mimar* 13 (1984): 25–34.

International Congress of Orientalists. *Proceedings.* 1873–1928. (Language and title vary with host city.)

Karnouk, Liliane. *Modern Egyptian Art: The Emergence of a National Style.* Cairo, 1988.

Lane-Poole, Stanley. *Cairo: Sketches of Its History, Monuments, and Social Life.* London, 1898; reprinted, New York, 1973.

MacKenzie, John. *Orientalism: History, Theory, and the Arts.* Manchester, 1995.

Mahdy, Hossam M. "Travellers, Coloniser and Conservationists." In *Travellers in Egypt,* ed. Paul Starkey and Janet Starkey, 157–67. London, 1998.

Metcalf, Thomas R. *An Imperial Vision: Indian Architecture and Britain's Raj.* Berkeley, Calif., 1989.

Mitchell, Timothy. *Colonising Egypt.* Cambridge, 1988.

Necipoğlu, Gülru. *The Topkapi Scroll—Geometry and Ornament in Islamic Architecture.* Santa Monica, Calif., 1995.

Ory, Solange. "Max Van Berchem, Orientaliste." In *D'un Orient l'autre,* vol. 2: 11–24. 2 vols. Paris, 1991.

Pieron, Henri. "Le Caire: Son Esthétique dans la ville arabe et dans la ville moderne." *L'Égypte contemporaine* 2 (1911): 510–28.

Prisse d'Avennes, Achille. *L'Art arabe d'après les monuments du Kaire depuis le VIIe siècle jusqu'à la fin du XVIIIe.* 3 vols. Paris, 1877.

Raymond, André. *Le Caire.* Paris, 1993.

Reid, Donald Malcolm. "Cultural Imperialism and Nationalism: The Struggle to Define and Control the Heritage of Arab Art in Egypt." *International Journal of Middle East Studies* 24 (1992): 57–76.

Rhoné, Arthur. *L'Égypte à petites journées: Le Caire d'autre fois.* New ed. Paris, 1910.

Rogers, J. M. "Al-Kahira." In *Encyclopaedia of Islam,* vol. 4: 412–41. 2nd ed. Leiden, 1960–.

————. *From Antiquarianism to Islamic Archaeology.* Cairo, 1974.

Said, Edward. *Culture and Imperialism.* New York, 1993.

————. *Orientalism.* New York, 1978.

Sakr, Tarek Mohamed Refaat. *Early Twentieth-Century Islamic Architecture in Cairo.* Cairo, 1993.

Scharabi, Mohammed. *Kairo: Stadt und Architectur im Zeitalter des europäischen Kolonialismus.* Tübingen, 1989.

Sweetman, John. *The Oriental Obsession: Islamic Inspiration in British and American Art and Architecture 1500–1920.* Cambridge, Mass., 1988.

Tamraz, Nihal S. *Nineteenth-Century Cairene Houses and Palaces.* Cairo, 1998.

van Berchem, Max. *Matériaux pour un Corpus Inscriptionum Arabicarum. Première partie: Inscriptions de l'Égypte.* Vol. 19 of *Mémoires publiés par les membres de la mission archéologique française au Caire.* Paris, 1903.

Vernoit, Stephen. "The Rise of Islamic Archaeology." *Muqarnas* 14 (1997): 1–10.

Volait, Mercedes. "L'Oeuvre égyptienne d'Ambroise Baudry (1838–1906)." Paper presented at the conference Un Siècle d'architecture savante en Égypte, Cairo, 1997.

Wiet, Gaston. *Corpus Inscriptionum Arabicum.* Vol. 2: *Le Caire.* Cairo, 1930.

————. *Mohamed Ali et les Beaux-Arts.* Cairo, ca. 1949.

Williams, Caroline. "Islamic Cairo: Endangered Legacy." *Middle East Journal* 39 (1985): 231–46.

Zéki Pacha, Ahmed. "Le Passé et l'avenir de l'art musulman en Égypte." *L'Égypte contemporaine* 4, fasc. 13 (1913): 1–32; and "Note." 398–402.

COPTIC STUDIES — CHAPTER 7

Behrens-Abouseif, Doris. *Die Kopten in der ägyptischen Gesellschaft—von der Mitte des 19. Jahrhunderts bis 1923.* Freiburg im Breisgau, 1972.

al-Bishri, Tariq. *Al-Muslimun wa-l-Aqbat fi Itar al-Jamaat al-Wataniyya.* Cairo, 1982.

Bistawros, Adel Aziz. "Community Council." In *The Coptic Encyclopedia,* ed. Aziz S. Atiya, vol. 2, 580–82. New York, 1991.

Bulletin de la Société d'archéologie copte. 1935–.

Butcher, E. L. *The Story of the Church of Egypt.* 2 vols. London, 1897.

Butler, A. J. *Ancient Churches of Egypt.* 2 vols. London, 1884.

Cannuyer, Christian. *Les Coptes.* Belgium (no city given), 1990.

Carter, B. L. *The Copts in Egyptian Politics.* London, 1986.

Clarke, Somers. *Christian Antiquities in the Nile Valley.* Oxford, 1912.

The Coptic Encyclopedia. Ed. Aziz Suriyal Atiya. 8 vols. New York, 1991.

A Coptic Layman [probably Marcus Simaika]. "The Awakening of the Coptic Church." *Contemporary Review* 71 (1897): 734–47.

Curzon, Robert. *A Visit to the Monasteries of the Levant.* New York, 1849.

Dowling, Archdeacon. *The Egyptian Church.* London, 1909. (Esp. appendix 3, by Simaika).

Fahmi Basha, Qalini. *Mudhakkirat Qalini Fahmi Basha.* 2 vols. Cairo, 1934.

al-Fiqqi, Mustafa. *Al-Aqbat fi al-Siyasa al-Misriyya: Makram Ubayd wa Dawruh fi al-Haraka al-Wataniyya.* Cairo, 1985.

Goldschmidt, Arthur, Jr. "The Butrus Ghali Family." *Journal of the American Research Center in Egypt* 30 (1993): 183–88.

Hamed, Raouf Abbas. "The Copts under British Rule in Egypt 1882–1914." *Al-Majalla al-Tarikhiyya al-Misriyya* 26 (1979): 49–59.

Krause, Martin. "Coptological Studies." In *The Coptic Encyclopedia,* ed. Aziz S. Atiya, vol. 2, 613–16. New York, 1991.

Leeder, S. H. *Modern Sons of the Pharaohs: A Study of the Manners and Customs of the Copts of Egypt.* London, ca. 1918; reprinted, New York, 1973.

Mikhail, Kyriakos. *Copts and Muslims under British Control.* London, 1911; reprinted, Port Washington, N.Y., 1971.

Reid, Donald Malcolm. "Archeology, Social Reform, and Modern Identity among the Copts, 1854–1952." In *Entre Réforme sociale et mouvement national: Identité et modernisation en Égypte (1882–1962),* ed. Alain Roussillon, 311–35. Cairo, 1995.

Seikaly, Samir. "Coptic Communal Reform: 1860–1914." *Middle Eastern Studies* 6 (1970): 247–75.

———. "Prime Minister and Assassin: Butrus Ghali and Wardani." *Middle Eastern Studies* 13 (1977): 112–23.

Simaika, Marcus. "Excerpts from the Memoirs of Marcus H. Simaika Pasha, C.B.E., F.S.A. (1864–1944)." Unpublished typescript in the possession of Dr. Samir Simaika.

———. *Note historique sur le Musée Copte au Vieux Caire à l'occasion de la visite de Sa Hautesse Fouad Ir Sultan d'Égypte, mardi, 21 decembre 1920.* Cairo, 1920.

Suriyal, Riyad. *Al-Mujtama al-qibti fi Misr fi (al-qarn 19).* Cairo, ca. 1971.

Tadrus, Ramzi. *Al-Aqbat fi al-qarn al-ishrin.* 5 vols. Cairo, 1910–1911.

Watson, Andrew. *The American Mission in Egypt 1854–1896.* Pittsburgh, 1898.

Yusuf, Abu Sayf. *Al-Aqbat wa al-qawmiyya al-arabiyya.* Beirut, 1987.

Index

Page numbers in italics refer to illustrations and tables.

Abbas Hilmi I: and changes to Cairo, 215; and Copts, 261; and Great Exhibition, 125; and Hekekyan, 59, 62; and Mariette, 99; and Mubarak, 152; and preservation of antiquities, 58; and railroad, 68; retrenchment under, 97; and al-Tahtawi, 54, 98

Abbas Hilmi II, *8;* and architectural style, 241, 242; and Awqaf Department, 243; and Cook's tours, 92; deposition of, 256, 292; and education, 267; and Egyptian Museum, 5, 7, 167, 195, 206; and Egyptian University, 248; and German influence, 235–36; and Greco-Roman Museum, 161, 206; and International Congress of Classical Archaeology, 169; and Lutfi al-Sayyid, 245; and Museum of Arab Art, 206, 238; and resistance to occupation, 245

Abbate, Onofrio, 124, 248

Abbott, Henry, 49

Abduh, Muhammad, 112, 119, 165–66, 238, 245, 251; and reform, 97, 264, 267

Abdulaziz (Ottoman sultan), 58

Abdulhamid II, 103, 136, 163, 236, 263

Abu al-Suud, Abdallah, 106, 112

Abu Elewa, Hajj Muhammad, 206

Abu Simbel, 38, 66, 126, *127*

Abydos, 57, 100, 177

Académie des inscriptions et belles lettres, 135–36

Account of Some Recent Discoveries in Hieroglyphical Literature (Young), 41

Account of the Manners and Customs of the Modern Egyptians (Lane), 50, 52

Adriani, Achille, 17, 161, 294

Aegyptiaca (Hamilton), 37

al-Afghani, Jamal al-Din, 97, 119

African Americans: and Centennial Exhibition, 129

Aga, Nazar, 133

Agha, Ali, 229

Agha, Khalil, 242

Agoub, Joseph, 52–53

Ahmose Nefertari, *187*

al-Ahram, 95–96, 118, 159, 163, 283

Aida (Verdi), 12, 129, 163, 250

Ajaib al-Athar (al-Jabarti), 36–37

Akhmim temple, 30

Akkadian language, 44

Alam al-Din (Mubarak), 180, 233

Albert (Prince Consort), 125, 126

Alexander, 141, 142, 146, 148, 157, 170

Alexandre le grand (Racine), 166

Alexandria: ancient library of, 22, *147;* British influence on, 152; and classical past, 149–52; clothing in, 74; al-Falaki's map of ancient, 153; Forster on, 159; French influence on, 152;

Alexandria *(continued)*
   government of, 160; Greeks in,
   149–51; hotels of, 73; identity of in-
   habitants, 150–51; and Institut égyp-
   tien, 121; Italians in, 151–52; and
   Muhammad Ali, 149; and neo-Islamic
   architecture, 240–41; population of,
   149; as port, 121; public amenities for
   travelers in, 80; St. Mark's church,
   240–41, 266. *See also* Greco-Roman
   Museum (Alexandria)
Algeria, 91, 142
Alhambra, 220, 240
Ali Bey, 31
Ali, Mahmud Bey, 229
Allenby, Edmund, 155
Altes Museum, 192
Amélineau, Émile, 177, 268
Amenhotep IV, 111
American Journal of Archaeology, 199
American Mission, 263, 281
American Oriental Society, 130, 198
American Research Center, 200
American Schools of Oriental Research,
   199
Amer, Mustafa, 294
Amin, Qasim, 140, 166
*An Appeal to the Antiquaries of Europe
   on the Destruction of the Monuments
   of Egypt* (Gliddon), 57–58
Anastasi, Giovanni, 38, 49
Ancient and Modern Imperialism
   (Cromer), 157
Ancient Churches of Egypt (Butler), 268,
   271
Andromaque (Racine), 164
Anglicans, 240–41, 261, 262, 266, 267,
   359–60n12
Anglo-French rivalry, 288–89; and Antiquities Service, 181–86, 189, 196;
   and the Comité, 236; and consul-
   collectors, 37–39; and Coptic manuscripts, 99, 101; and Egyptian Museum, 195; and Fashoda, 86, 181; and
   obelisks, 102; and Rosetta Stone, 31,
   37, 46; on the Tigris, 43–44
ankh, 24
*Annales du Service des antiquités de
   l'Égypte* (ASAE), 189, 196, 201–2,
   203, 211
antiquities: and Champollion, 43; Coptic, destruction of, 268, 270, 270–71;
   forged, 77, 99; lack of Egyptian
   knowledge of, 179–80, 201, 206, 210;
   leaked, 101, 211; recording of, 200;
   restoration of, 217, 218, 351n17;
   salted sites, 101; seasonal market in,

255; tourism and price of, 77; vandalism of, by tourists, 159, 182–83, *184,*
   222; world's fairs and destruction of,
   228–29, 252, 253. *See also* antiquities, protection of; excavation; historic
   preservation
antiquities, national control of, 56, 93,
   95; and Egyptian independence,
   293–94; and governmental departments, 175; and Kamal, 212; and Mariette, 102–3
antiquities, protection of, 205, 206;
   1883 law, 175; Abbas I and, 58; Glymenopoulo and, 151; Hekekyan and,
   60–61; Ibrahim Pasha and, 58; Institut
   égyptien and, 159; Ismail and, 223,
   234; Mariette and, 101–3, 129, 236;
   Maspero and, 196; Mimaut and, 55,
   60–61; Muhammad Ali and, 21,
   54–58, *55,* 60–61, 63, 110, 289;
   Simaika and, 258, 271; SPMAE and,
   182–83; Tawfiq and, 205–6. *See also*
   historic preservation
Antiquities Museum (Istanbul), 103,
   193, 237
Antiquities Service: *Annales* of, 189, 196,
   201–2, 203, 211; and British occupation, 135, 181–86, 195–97; bulletin
   of Institut égyptien and, 189; and
   Coptic ruins, *270;* corvée labor and,
   100–1, 135; Egyptian control of, 294,
   295; founding of, 56, 63, 93, 100; and
   Greco-Roman Museum, 160; heads of,
   305; and imperialism, 97, 294; Kamal
   and, 201–3, 204, 211; Maspero and,
   175, 186, 195–96; rivalries for control
   of, 113–16, 181–86; salaries of employees, 188, 201
Antoniadis, Sir John, 150, 151
*Anwar tawfiq al-jalil fi akhbar Misr wa-
   tawthiq bani Ismail* (al-Tahtawi), 93,
   109–12, 146–48
Arab art, as term, 215. *See also* Islamic
   art; Museum of Arab Art
Arab Conquest of Egypt (Butler), 268
Arabian Society in the Middle Ages
   (Lane-Poole), 219
Arabic language: Bahgat and, 249, 255;
   Egyptologists and, 131; and interest in
   ancient Egypt, 210; International Congress of Orientalists and, 250, 251;
   Kamal's work in, 202–3; and Museum
   of Arab Art building, 238; replacing
   Coptic as common language, 259; replacing Turkish as official language,
   97; in School of Egyptology, 117; textbook on hieroglyphics in, 189

Archaeological Institute of America, 199
archaeology: Egyptian independence and, 294; French expedition and, 1, 32; imperialism and, 2, 10–11, 12–14; nationalism and, 2, 9–10, 12–14; as term, 312n1; text-aided, 40–41; and tourism, 65. *See also* biblical archaeology; classical studies; Coptic archaeology; Egyptology; excavation; Islamic archaeology
architecture, 345–46n74; eclectic, 234, 241; European, 192–93; Gothic Revival, 150, 192, 218, 240, 241; Hindu-Saracenic, 242; neoclassic, 103, 161, 192, 193–95, 218, 240, 242; neo-Islamic and Islamic Revival, 192–93, 238, 239–42, 239, 276, 277, 289, 290–91; neopharaonic, 105, 192–93, 242; philhellenism and, 141; world's fairs and, 254
Architecture arabe ou monumens du Caire (Coste), 220, 221
Aristotle, 162
Armenians: and Antiquities Service, 182, 195; and the Comité, 230, 243–44, 272, 273–75; Copts contrasted with, 273–75; council of, 263; and Institut égyptien, 190; Muhammad Ali and, 59, 61–62
Arnold, Thomas, 157
Around the World in Eighty Days (Verne), 90
L'Art arabe d'après les monuments du Kaire (Prisse d'Avennes), 220
Artin Bey Chrakian, 60, 61–62, 123, 273
Artin, Yaqub (Yacoub): and Antiquities Service, 182, 195; background of, 273; and Bahgat, 214, 244, 245, 246; and the Comité, 226, 230, 243–44, 272, 273, 274; and Egyptian University, 248; and Institut égyptien, 121, 123, 190, 246, 247–48, 274; and International Congress of Classical Archaeology, 169; and International Congress of Orientalists, 131, 251; and Museum of Arab Art, 237; problematic Egyptian identity of, 273
Les Arts arabes (Bourgoin), 224
al-Arusi, Shaykh al-Azhar Mustafa, 109
Asiatic Society of Bengal, 48
Asiatic Society of Great Britain and Ireland, 130
Asiatic Society of Paris, 130
Asquith, Herbert, 153
L'Association des hommes de science hellénnes à Alexandrie, Ptolémée Ier, 151

Association for the Furtherance of Christianity in Egypt, 266
Assyriology, 41, 43–44
astronomy, 152, 153
Aswan, 86, 100
Aswan High Dam, 293, 294
Asyut, 266, 279
Asyut Coptic Benevolent Society, 281
Asyut museum project, 210–11
Athanasi, Giovanni d', 39
Al-Athar al-Misriyya, 283
Athenaeum Society, 160
al-Attar, Shaykh al-Azhar Hasan, 51–52, 54, 97
Augusta, 129
Augustus, 141, 145, 147, 154
Austria and Austrian nationals: and classical studies, 160, 169; and the Comité/Museum of Arab Art, 214, 230, 234–36, 290; consul-collectors of, 38; excavation technique of, 177; and Ezbekiyeh collection, 58; guidebooks of, 72; and neo-Islamic style, 241; and Société d'archéologie d'Alexandrie, 160; world's fairs and, 129, 191
Awqaf Department, 352n30; architectural style of building of, 239; and the Comité, 223, 224, 226, 227, 243–44, 275; and Coptic monuments, 244; Germanic cultural enclave and, 234; Herz and, 235; resistance and, 243–44
Ayn Shams, 283
al-Azhar (mosque-university): al-Attar and, 51–52; and reform, 97, 264, 267; sons designated for, 265; al-Tahtawi and, 51–52, 98
al-Azhar, Shaykh, 229, 238

Babylon, 272, 276
Bab Zuwayla, 233, 234, 238
Baedeker, Karl, 69, 72
Baedeker's guidebooks, 72, 81, 91; on amenities available in Egypt, 80; documentation recommended by, 74; Egyptian readership of, 73, 271; on firearms, 75; hotels recommended by, 73; on interactions with natives, 75, 77, 78; on mode of transportation, 96; on museums, 202, 239, 277, 287–88; writers for, 12, 72, 123
al-Baghdadi, Abd al-Latif, 30
Bahgat, Ali: and Artin, 214, 244, 245, 246; background of, 229–30, 259; and the Comité, 214, 230, 246, 255, 256, 257; death of, 257; and Dunlop,

Bahgat, Ali *(continued)*
    214, 244; and education, 229–30, 244;
    and Egyptian University, 248–49; and
    al-Fustat, 255–57; and IFAO, 245,
    246; and Institut égyptien, 190,
    247–48; and International Congress of
    Classical Archaeology, 169; and Inter-
    national Congress of Orientalists, 249;
    and Islamic archaeology, 214, 246,
    247, 255–56; and Khedivial Geograph-
    ical Society, 248; and Khedivial Library,
    249; and Museum of Arab Art, 214,
    246, 255, 257, 291; nationalism and,
    214, 246, 291; and neo-Islamic style,
    242, 290–91; and resistance to the oc-
    cupation, 245, 254; street named after,
    294–95; van Berchem and, 246, 247
Al-Bahnasa (Oxyrhynchus), 162–63
bakhshish, 77; paid for finds, 101, 177,
    183, 185
al-Baladhuri, 249
Al-Balagh, 1, 12–13
Bancroft, George, 115
Banks, Sir Joseph, 37
al-Barati, Nakhla, 272, 276
Baring, Sir Evelyn. *See* Cromer, Lord (Sir
    Evelyn Baring)
Barker, John, 38
Barthélemy, Jean-Jacques, 146
al-Barudi, Mahmud Sami, 206, 224, 226
Ibn Battuta, 30
Baudry, Ambroise, 224, 241
Beato, Antonio, 89
Beaux Arts neoclassicism, 192, 193–95,
    240
Béchard, Émile, 107
Becker, Carl, 72, 252
Bedford, Francis, 89, *270*
Belgium and Belgian nationals, 38, 241
Bellefonds, Linant de, 49–50, 58, 121
Belzoni, Giovanni, 38, 39, 74–75, 193
Berchem, Max van, 245, 246–47, 249
Berchtold, Leopold, 82
Berthollet, Claude Louis, 32
biblical archaeology: and Copts, 9, 260,
    265; and digging for information vs.
    objects, 178–79; Egyptology and, 41;
    Protestant clergy and, 265; United
    States and, 198. *See also* Egypt Explo-
    ration Fund (EEF)
biblical lenses, reading of ancient Egypt
    through, 2, 22, 24, 27, *28*, 42, 262;
    Sharubim and, 209, 283; al-Tahtawi
    and, 111
biblical literalists, 62
Birch, Samuel, 46, 48, 49, 72, 113, 172;
    and digging for information vs. ob-

jects, 178–79; and International Con-
    gress of Orientalists, *124,* 131, 133
al-Biruni, 145
Bissing, Friedrich, 197
Blacas, duc de, 42
black Americans: and Centennial Exhibi-
    tion, 129
Blomfield, R., 160
Bonaparte, Napoleon. *See* Napoleon
    Bonaparte
Bonfils family, 89
Bonola, Federico, *124,* 248
Bonomi, Joseph, 43, 115, 126, *127*
Borchardt, Ludwig, 169, 196, 197, 292
Boston Museum of Fine Arts, 193, 199,
    200
Botta, Paul Émile, 44, 101
Botti, Guiseppe, 16, 116, 159–60, 161,
    198, 237, 249
Boulad, Philippe, 191, 254
Bourgoin, Jules, 224
Bouriant, Urbain, 175, 188
Bowring, Dr. John, 83
Boyle, Harry, 156
Bradshaw's railway timetable, 90
Breasted, James Henry, 199, 200–1, 249
Breccia, Evaristo, 16, 161, 169, 196, 298
Briggs, Samuel, 59, 62
Britain and British nationals: and Ameri-
    can archaeology, 199; and classical
    studies, 140, 141, 154–59, *155, 156,*
    169; and the Comité, 224, 230; consul-
    collectors of, 37–38, 43; copyists of,
    42–44; and decipherment of hiero-
    glyphics, 41; and Egyptian Museum de-
    sign, 192; Egyptology of, 178–79; gift
    of obelisk to, 57, 102; guidebooks
    from, 70–71, 72; historic preservation
    and, 56, 218; and International Con-
    gress of Orientalists, 133; learned soci-
    eties of, 48; and National Bank of
    Egypt, 205; and neo-Islamic style,
    240–41; population from, in Egypt,
    80–81, 152; and Société d'archéologie
    d'Alexandrie, 160–61, *161,* 163;
    tourism of, 66–67, 73, 80–81, 87–88;
    travel accounts from, 27; and world's
    fairs, 125–28, 191. *See also* Anglo-
    French rivalry; British occupation; India
Britannia, 154, *155*
British East India Company, 67
British Library: and Hekekyan's papers,
    59, 63
British Museum: architecture of, 192; de-
    velopment of, 46, 47–48; Elgin and,
    37, 38, 48; Layard and, 44;
    Mesopotamian holdings of, 173; Mi-

maut and, 39; and papyri, 162; Salt and, 37–38, 39, 48

British occupation, *176*; and Antiquities Service, 135, 181–86, 195–97; and architecture, 193–94, 242; Armenians in politics during, 273–74; and Awqaf Department, 243; classical discourse and, 153–58, *155*, *156*, 167, 171; and the Comité, 226–29, 235, 236, 243–44; and Cook's tours, 91; and Copts, 266–67, 279–80; Copts in politics during, 274–75; currency and coin design and, 205; and Dunlop-Bahgat affair, 244–45; education and, 210, 244, 248, 279–80; end of, 293; excavation and, 255–56; al-Falaki and, 123; and France's "archaeological protectorate," 175–76, 181–86, 195–97, 289; Ghali and, 274; Gladstone and, 153–54, *156*, 226; and guidebooks, 70; and Institut égyptien, 122; and International Congresses of Orientalists, 191–92; and museums, control of, 103–4; resistance to, 249, 254, 273; and revolution of 1919, 293; Roosevelt on, 277; severance of Ottoman link and protectorate declared, 119, 173, 256, 292; stamp design and, 205; Stone and, 124; and Syrian Christians, 163; Urabi revolution and, 206, 207, 224, 225, 230, 273, 282; world's fairs and, 95, 190–91, 228–29, 252, 254. *See also* Britain and British nationals

British School of Archeology in Egypt, 178

Brooklyn Museum, 199, 200

Browne, Edward Granville, 249

Bruce, James, 28

Brugsch, Émile, 100, 115, 117, 177, 186, 188, 189

Brugsch, Heinrich, 114, 197; friendship with Mariette, 114, 115; and Hekekyan, 122; and Institut égyptien, 123; and International Congress of Orientalists, 132, 133; and Khedivial Geographical Society, 124; and *Rawdat al-madaris*, 112; and School of Egyptology, 93, 116–18, 186; and world's fairs, 12, 129

Bruno, Giordano, 25

Budge, Ernest A. W., 72, 91, 162, 172, 173, 181–82, 193

Bulaq Museum, 104–7, *107*, *108*

Bulaq Press, 54, 112, 125, 128, 129, 153

Bulletin de la Société khédivial géographique, 124, 190

Bulletin de l'Institut égyptien, 124, 189

Bullock, William, 192–93

Bunsen, Karl von (Baron), 44, 49, 115

Burckhardt, John Lewis (Johann Ludwig), 39, 42, 66, 74–75, 76

Burke, Edmund, III, 13

Burton, Richard, 219

al-Bustani, Amin, 164

al-Bustani, Butrus, 164, 165

al-Bustani, Najib, 164

al-Bustani, Salim, 164

al-Bustani, Sulayman, 164, 165

Butcher, E. L., 281

Butler, Alfred J., 268, 270–71, 291

Butrus Ghali, Mirrit, 281

Buzard, James, 66

Byron, Lord, 66, 87

Byzantine Empire, 150

Byzantine Museum (Athens), 276

Caesar, Julius, 145, 147

Cairo, *221*; Greeks in, 150; hotels of, 73, 74; Institut égyptien and, 122; as intellectual center, 159; map of, *105*; public amenities for travelers, 80; traffic and, 215, 216; urban renewal and, 215–17, 222, 223, 228

calotypes, 89

Camp, Maxime du, 89

Campbell, Patrick, 38

Capitulations, the, 95, 150

Carter, Howard, 195, 196

cartoons, 154, *155*, *156*

Casanova, Paul, 230

Casaubon, Isaac, 25

Cassas, Louis François, 218

Cavafy, Constantine, 150

Caviglia, Giovanni, 38, 39

Centennial Exhibition (1876), 129

Cestius, Caius: pyramid of, 24–25, 314n4

Chaban, Muhammad, 170, 202

Chabas, François, 115, 131, 172

Chambord, Comte de, 107

Champollion, Jean-François, 41–42, 46; and antiquities, protection vs. destruction of, 43, 54–55, 57; expedition of, 43; and geographical society of Paris, 48; and gift of obelisk to France, 57; Jomard and, 36, 41–42; and the Louvre, 42, 46–47, 193; and al-Tahtawi, 53; al-Tahtawi compared to, 21–22; Turkish garb of, 74–75, 131

Champollion-Figeac, Jacques-Joseph, 99

Charmes, Gabriel: on architectural styles, 240; on Baudry's villa, 224, 241; on the Comité, 223, 236; on destruction of art, 222; on neglect of

Charmes, Gabriel (*continued*)
Islamic art, 219; on tourism, 86; on urban renewal/historic preservation, 213–14, 216–17, 222
Charmes, Xavier, 183, 222–23
Chassinat, Émile, 169
Chateaubriand, François-Auguste-René de, 76, 87
China, 191
cholera, 70, 82, 83–84, 129, 135
Chrakian, Artin Bey. *See* Artin Bey Chrakian
Christian Antiquities in the Nile Valley (Clarke), 271
Christianity: ancient Egypt and, 24, 25, 30; Christological disputes in, 259; and classical Greece and Rome, 145, 157; Coptic persecution, 9, 259, 260, 263, 284; Egyptian state and, 261, 262; Muslim historians on, 145, 147; Protestantism, 260–61, 263, 264, 265–66, 281. *See also* Anglicans; biblical archaeology; biblical lenses, reading of ancient Egypt through; Coptic Church; Greek Orthodox Church; Protestantism; Roman Catholic Church
chronology: biblical vs. pharaonic, 59, 62–63
Churchill, Randolph Henry Spencer, 140
Church of Saint Sergius, 276
Citadel mosque (Muhammad Ali), 240
Clarke, Somers, 236, 268, 270, 271
class, social: classical studies and maintenance of, 140; Copts and, 259, 260, 266, 279, 280; and mode of transportation, 84–85, 86; photography and, 89; railroad fares and, 69; tourism and, 66, 68–69, 84–85, 86, 87, 90; and urban renewal, 216; and world's fairs, 69, 90, 125
classical architecture. *See* neoclassicism
classical studies: as academic discipline, 11; Britons and, 140, 141, 154–59, *155, 156,* 169; Coptic identity and, 280, 284; Cromer and, 155–59; and education in Egypt, 5, 147–48, 163, 167, 170–71; and Egyptian national identity, 139–40, 163, 167, 291; Egyptian University and, 211; Greeks and, 150–51; International Congress of Classical Archaeology, 167–70, *306;* Italians and, 151–52; and maintenance of class, 140; Mubarak and, 140, 166; Muslim literature and, 30, 144–48; nationalism and, 167, 170, 291; Roman law, 166; Rome vs.

Greece and, 140–41; Syrian Christians and, 163–66; al-Tahtawi and, 110, 166; Western accounts of ancient Egyptian history and, 24–25, 26, 33, 35, 42, 141–44, *142, 143*
Clédat, Jean, 270
Clemenceau, Georges, 113
Cleopatra, 147, *156*
"Cleopatra's Needle," 27, 29, 219
Clot Bey, Antoine, 49, 83
clothing, 74–75, 119, 131
Cochelet, Adrien Louis, 38
Cohen, Mendes, 75
coinage, 119, 205, 275
Cole, Henry, 125
Colucci, Antonio, 121
Columbian Exposition (1893, Chicago), 165, 191, 228, 253
Colvin, Auckland, 122
Combes, Étienne, 160
Comité de conservation des monuments de l'art arabe, 8; Awqaf Department and, 223, 224, 226, 227, 243–44, 275; Bahgat and, 214, 230, 246, 255, 256, 257; budget of, 227, 238; Coptic studies and, 236, 244, 271–72, 275, 276; European domination of, 213–14, 226–27, 230–31, 234–37, 243–44; founding of, 215, 223–26, 233–34, 289–90; French model for, 218; Herz and, 234–35, 242, 256–57, 276; language of, 224, 234, 235; membership of, 153, 214, 224, 225, 226–27, 228, 230, 234–37, 242, 248, 272, 274; Mubarak and, 226, 230, 233–34; and neo-Islamic Revival, 239, 242; philosophy of preservation, 227–29; proceedings of, 214; resistance by Egyptians within, 233–34, 243–44; Simaika and, 271–72, 275; Wiet and, 257. *See also* Museum of Arab Art
Communal Council, Coptic, 263–64, 266–67, 272, 278–80, 281
Considerations on the Causes of the Greatness of the Romans and of Their Decline (Montesquieu), 145, 146
Constantine, 147
consul-collectors, 37–39, 43–44, 288; and export ban, 57; Gliddon on, 57–58; al-Jabarti on, 39–40; Kitchener as consul-collector, 196; and Mariette, 99
consuls: tourists and, 74, 75
Conze, Alexander, 101, 177
Cook, Ernest, 92
Cook, Frank, 92

Cook, John Mason, 90, 91, 92
Cook, Thomas, 71, 89–90. *See also*
    Thomas Cook and Son
Cookson, Sir Charles, 159–60
Cook's Tourist Handbook for Egypt, the
    Nile and the Desert (Cook), 72, 183
Coptic archaeology: Coptic Church and,
    271–72, 275, 281; Egyptologists and,
    268, 270; Simaika and, 258–59
Coptic Archeological Society, 281
Coptic Church: ancient Egyptian religion
    compared to, 281–82; and Anglo-
    French rivalry, 99, 101; calendar of,
    281; and Cook's tours, 92; and Coptic
    archaeology, 270, 271–72, 275, 281;
    and Coptic language, 24, 117, 267,
    291; founding of, 259; missionaries
    seeking converts from, 27, 263, 267;
    "patriarch" as term in, 359n1; perse-
    cution of, 9, 259, 260, 263, 284; re-
    form of, 258, 261–64, 265–67, 272,
    275, 278–80, 281, 284–85, 292
Coptic Clerical College, 265, 267,
    279–80, 283
Coptic language, 31, 41, 259, 265,
    267–68, 281, 283, 291; and Coptic
    Church, 24, 117, 267, 291
Coptic Museum: building of, 276, 277;
    founding of, 9, 258, 275–77; Maspero
    and, 270; Simaika and, 258, 271–72,
    275, 276–77, 291–92; state control
    of, 292; as symbol for Copts, 284,
    285; tourism and, 277–78, 287
Coptic Reform Society, 279
Coptic studies, 9, 267–71, 291–92; as
    academic discipline, 11; the Comité
    and, 236, 244, 271–72, 275, 276; and
    International Congress of Orientalists,
    131; Kircher and, 25; table of Coptic
    scholars and leaders, 269
Copts: Armenians contrasted with,
    273–75; and the Comité, 230, 244,
    273–75; educational opportunities of,
    261, 262–63, 279, 281, 282; Euro-
    pean prejudice against, 259–61, 282;
    and French expedition, 260; identity
    of, 258, 280–85; and Institut égyptien,
    190; journals of, 283; and nationalism,
    273, 274, 292; persecution of and
    prejudice against, 259–60, 261, 270,
    282; and pharaonic past, 280–85,
    291; reform of restrictions on, 260,
    261, 285; roles and class of, 259, 260,
    266, 279, 280; and School of Egyptol-
    ogy, 186, 188
copyists, 42–44, 45–46, 100
Corgordon (consul), 185–86

Corneille, Pierre, 163
Cornelius, 144
Corpus Hermeticum (Trismegistus), 25
Coste, Pascal, 220, 221, 240
cotton, 68, 96, 149, 159
Council of Chalcedon, 259, 284
Coxe, Eckley Brinton, Jr., 200
Creswell, K. A. C., 17, 257, 294
Crinson, Mark, 214
Cromer, Lord (Sir Evelyn Baring): and
    Antiquities Service, 181–82, 186, 196;
    and Awqaf Department, 243; back-
    ground of, 154–55; and the classics,
    155–59; and the Comité, 227, 236;
    and Copts, 266–67, 271, 272, 279;
    and EEF, 196; and Egyptian Museum,
    167, 183, 185; and Fakhri, 245; on
    government bankruptcy, 136; on impe-
    rialism, 154; and Museum of Arab
    Art, 238; retirement of, 157, 279; on
    Tigrane, 273; veto of university by,
    248; and world's fairs, 252, 254
Crum, Walter, 268
Crystal Palace exhibition (1851, Great
    Exhibition, London), 12, 69, 90, 125,
    126–27, 237, 240
cultural evolution, 178
cuneiform, 43–44
currency, 205, 295
Curtius, Ernst, 101, 177
Curzon, George, 153
Curzon, Robert, 99, 268
Cyril IV, 261–63, 359–60n12
Cyril V, 258, 263, 266–67, 271–72,
    275, 278–80, 291, 292

Daguerre, Louis, 88
daguerreotypes, 88
dahabiyyas, 80, 84–86, 91, 128, 302
Dahshur, 185
Dairat al-Maarif, 164–65
al-Damanhuri, Muhammad, 109
Daninos, Albert, 132, 160, 183
Dar al-Ulum, 148
Daressy, Georges, 188, 189, 211
dates, 5, 111, 204, 209
Davis, Theodore, 200
Death of Cleopatra (Shawqi), 147
Delacroix, Eugène, 88, 220
Délile, Hippolyte, 89, 107
Demetrius II, 263, 281
democracy: Cromer on, 157
Dendera temple, 30, 33, 55
Denkmäler aus Aegypten und Aethiopien
    (Lepsius), 45
Denon, Vivant, 32, 33, 46, 47, 219
Desaix, General, 260

Description de l'Égypte (1735), 31,
  312n3
Description de l'Égypte (Maillet),
  33–36, 312n3; Agoub and, 53; classical studies as lens of, 142; and Copts,
  268; expedition for, 32–33; frontispiece of, 2–3, *3*, 34, 141, 219, 220;
  and Islamic art, 219, 220; al-Jabarti
  and, 36; Jomard and, 33–34, 36, 53;
  military conquest and, 31–32;
  Mubarak's response to, 179–80; pil-
  lars vs. obelisks in, 27, *29;* preface to,
  13, 34; al-Tahtawi's unawareness of,
  53; Teynard and, 89
Description of Egypt (Lane), 42–43
Dethier (dir., Imperial Ottoman
  Museum), 103
Deutsche Orient-Gesellschaft, 197
Devéria, Théodule, 100, 135
al-Dib, Mustafa, 253, 254
Dictionnaire (Champollion), 41
Diebitsch, Carl von, 241
Dinshaway tribunal, 279
Diodorus Siculus, 24, 31, 110, 142
disease, 70, 82–84, 129, 135
Dithyrambe sur l'Égypte (Agoub), 52–53
Dixon, Waynman, 176
Diya Effendi, Yusuf, 56
Dolomieu, Déodat, 32
Dörpfeld, Wilhelm, 177
doseh, 78
Dourgnon, Marcel, 191, 193, 194–95,
  254
dragomen, 75–76, 206
dress, 74–75, 119, 131
Drioton, Étienne, 17, 294
Drovetti, Bernardino, 37, 38, 39, 46, 57
Duara, Prasenjit, 14
Dubois, Léon, 99
Dümichen, Johannes, 114–15, 197
Dunlop, Douglas, 214, 244–45, 279–80

Ebers, Georg, 12, 72, 114, 197
École française du Caire. *See* Institut
  français d'archéologie orientale du
  Caire (IFAO)
Edfu, 100
Edgar, Campbell, 196
Edhem, Halil, 247
education: Abbas I and, 261; Abbas II
  and, 267; antiquities, lack of education
  about in British-controlled schools,
  210; Arab Art revival and, 242; Bahgat and, 229–30, 244; British occupation and, 210, 244, 248, 279–80; classical studies in Egypt, 5, 147–48, 163,
  167, 170–71; Copts and opportunities
  in, 261, 262–63, 279, 281, 282;

Ismail and reforms in, 97, 229, 261,
  263; Kamal and, 93, 117, 118, 186,
  188, 203–4, 282, 344n52; missionary
  schools, 261, 263; Mubarak and, 97,
  98, 289; Muhammad Ali and reforms
  in, 52, 97, 261; al-Tahtawi and,
  51–52, 54, 93, 97–98, 98, 108,
  147–48
Edwards, Amelia, 80, 178, 179, 215–16,
  217
Egypt: foreign residents of, *301–2;*
  French expedition into, 1, 14, 28,
  32–34, 36–37, 231–32; independence
  of, 17, 293–94; map of, *xvii;* as paradox, 157; partitioning of, 38; revolution of 1919, 293; revolution of 1952,
  293; rulers of and scholars active in,
  23. *See also* British occupation
Egypt and Nubia (Roberts), 220
Égypte et Nubie (Teynard), 89
Égypte, Nubie, Palestine, et Syrie
  (Camp), 89
Egypt Exploration Fund (EEF), 161–63,
  178; and British occupation, 175–76;
  Cromer and, 196; Maspero and,
  178–79; Petrie and, 178; United States
  and, 199
Egyptian Egyptomania, 12, 118–20
Egyptian Literary Association, 49–50
Egyptian Museum: admission fees to,
  202; audience of, 106, *108;* buildings
  and sites of, 104, *105,* 183, 192–95,
  194, 239; catalog of, 196, 197, 201,
  203; classical studies and, 161; and
  Coptic studies, 270; facade of, 3–5,
  4–7, 22, 25, 104, 113, 114, 116, 167,
  195, 198, 289; flood damaging, 136,
  183; founding of, 7–8, 104–6, 167;
  garden of, 3, *4, 294, 295;* guidebook
  of, 106, 202; and imperialism, 97;
  Museum of Arab Art compared to,
  238–39; organization of, 106, *107;*
  tourism and, 183, 202, 239, 287,
  287–88
Egyptian National Library. *See* Khedivial
  Library
Egyptian Research Account, 178
Egyptian Society (Cairo), 48–50, *49,* 61,
  121, 122
Egyptian Society (London), 27
Egyptian University, 198, 203–4, 211,
  248–49, 257, 274
égyptologie as term, 113
Egyptology: as academic discipline, 11,
  95–96, 114, 131, 288; Anglo-French
  rivalry, 181–86, 189, 196; British,
  178–79; classical studies and, 142–44;
  and Copts, 268, 282, 283, 291; Euro-

pean dominance of, overview, 10–11; French, 99, 113–15; generational change in, 172–74, *174*; German, 114–15, 116–17, 197; guidebooks and, 72; Hekekyan and, 63; at the Institut égyptien, 120–23; and International Congress of Orientalists, 130–34, 192; Italian, 115–16; Jomard and, 42; journals of, 114, 116; Kamal and, 10, 97, 98, 186–89, 201–4, 211–12; at the Khedivial Geographical Society, 123, 124; local dress and, 74–75, 131; Orientalism distinguished from, 130–31; photography and, 89; tables of participants, *94, 174;* as term, 7–8, 113, 130–31; of the United States, 198–201; women in, 178. *See also* Egyptology, Egyptian; pharaonic history; School of Egyptology

Egyptology, Egyptian: interest in, 96, 172, 201; International Congress of Orientalists and lack of, 134; Kamal and, 10, 97, 98, 186–89, 201–4, 211–12; lack of continuity in, 210–12; lack of Egyptian knowledge of past and, 179–80; tables of participants, *94, 174. See also* School of Egyptology

Egyptomania, 11–12, 31; pharaonic symbols and, 6, 8, 54, *55*, 95–96, 118–19, *119*, 205, 208, 295–97, *296. See also* tourism; world's fairs

Eiffel Tower, 191, 254

Eisenlohr, August, 114

Elephantine, 27, 100

Elgin, Lord, 37, 38, 48

Elgin marbles, 37, 38, 141

Emerson, Ralph Waldo, 87

Empain, Baron, 241

empire: as corrupting, 157; Gladstone and informal, 154; Oxford as cradle of, 153. *See also* imperialism

Encyclopaedia Britannica, 25

Encyclopédie, 31

English Reading Society, 49

Eothen (Kinglake), 82, 87

Eratosthenes, 22

Eritrea, 151

Erman, Adolf, 172, 173, 197, 212, 249

Esna, 100

Essay on Dr. Young's and M. Champollion's Phonetic System of Hieroglyphics (Salt), 41

Essay to Direct and Extend the Inquiries of Patriotic Travellers (Berchtold), 82

Eugénie (Empress), 113, 128, 129

Euripedes, 158

Eurocentrism, 164–65

excavation: Bahgat and, 214, 256; Coptic studies and, 270; by EEF, 161–63; by Egyptians, 202, 204, 211; by al-Falaki, 153; German, 177, 197–98, 255–56; by the Greco-Roman Museum, 161; imperialism and, 255–56; for information vs. objects, 178–79; Italian, 198; Kamal and, 202; Mariette's technique, 62, 101, 177; Maspero and, 196; de Morgan and, 185; and payment for finds, 101, 177, 183, 185; Petrie's technique, 173, 177–78; photography and, 89; stratigraphical, 62, 63, 177, 201; tourism and, 82; United States and, 197, 200–1. *See also* archaeology

Excursions daguerriennes (Lerebour), 88

Exposition Universelle (1855, Paris), 90, 126

Exposition Universelle (1867, Paris), 128–29, 216, 237

Exposition Universelle (1878, Paris), 130, 252

Exposition Universelle (1889, Paris), 191, 252–53

Exposition Universelle (1900, Paris), 191, 193, 253–54

Ezbekiyeh collection, 58

Fahmi, Abd al-Aziz, 245, 249

Fahmi, Mahmud, 170, 249

Fahmi, Mustafa, 169, 182, 195, 226, 230, 246, 267

Fahmi, Qalini, 263, 277, 280

Fakhri, Husayn: background of, 245; and Bahgat, 214, 244, 245, 246; and the Comité, 230, 243–44, 272; in government, 244, 245–46; and historic preservation, 234; and Institut égyptien, 190, 247–48; and al-Rifai Mosque, 234, 241

al-Falaki, Mahmud, *8*, 123, 189; and classical studies, 140, 152–53, 166; and the Comité, 226, 243, 244; and education, 97, 152; and Egyptology, 96; and Institut égyptien, 122, 123; and International Congress of Orientalists, 131; and Khedivial Geographical Society, 124; Sharubim and, 209; and urban renewal, 216; and world's fairs, 128

Fanon, Frantz, 13

Fanus, Akhnukh, 279

Farid, Muhammad, 140, 292

Farnall, Harry, 236, 256–67

Farsi, 133

Faruq (King), 276, 277, 293, 294

Fashoda, 86, 181

Fatah al-Nil, 296–97, *296*

Fath Allah, Shaykh Hamza, 250
Fatimid style, 227–28, 241, 276
fellahin, 77, 131, *132*
Fénelon, 146
Ferry, Jules, 114, 175
fertilizer digging, 101, 255, 256
Fikri Pasha, Abdallah, 8, 250, 253
Fikri, Muhammad Amin, 250–51,
    253, 254
Findley, Carter, 13, 132–33, 249
Fiorelli, Giuseppe, 101, 177
Firawn, 283
firearms, 75
firmans (official permits), 74
Fischer, August, 252
Fisher, Clarence, 200
flags, 75, 323n40
Flaubert, Gustave, 76, 87, 89, 139
Forster, E. M., 159, 171
Foucart, Georges, 185, 189, 249
Foucart, Paul, 185
Fourier, Jean-Baptiste, 13, 32, 34
France and French nationals: and Algeria,
    142; archaeological predominance of,
    175–76, 181–86, 195–97, 289; archi-
    tecture and, 240; and classical studies,
    141–44, 169; and the Comité, 224,
    230; consul-collectors of, 37, 38, 39,
    44; copyists of, 43–44; and decipher-
    ment of hieroglyphics, 41–42; and
    Egyptian Museum design, 192; expedi-
    tion of, 1, 14, 28, 32–34, 36–37, *143,*
    231–32; gift of obelisk to, 57, 102,
    110; guidebooks of, 70, 71–72, 91;
    and historic preservation, 56, 217–18;
    imperialism and, 113–14, 222–23; and
    Institut égyptien, 121; and Institut
    français d'archéologie orientale du
    Caire (IFAO), 173–75; and Interna-
    tional Congress of Orientalists, 131;
    learned societies of, 48; military con-
    quest of Egypt, 31–32, 33, 34, *35,*
    36–37, 260; Orientalism of, 219; and
    the plague, 83; population from, in
    Egypt, 152; prestige of, in Egypt, 113;
    and rivalry with Germany, 45–46,
    113–15, 116, 134, 185, 253–54; and
    Société d'archéologie d'Alexandrie,
    161; tourism and, 66–67, 73, 81; travel
    accounts from, 27; and world's fairs,
    125, 126, 128–29, 130, 191, 193, 216,
    237, 252–54; World War I and,
    292–93. *See also* Anglo-French rivalry
Franco-German rivalry, 45–46, 113–15,
    116, 134, 185, 253–54
Franz, Julius: and the Comité and Mu-
    seum of Arab Art, 214, 223, 224, 226,
    227, 234–35, 237, 290; and European
    prejudices about Islamic art, 220, 222;
    and neo-Islamic style, 241; as travel-
    guide writer, 72
Freemasons, 25, 31
Free Officers, 293, 294
French language, 116, 117, 121, 224,
    234
French Revolution, 191, 217
Frères, Abdullah, 207
Friedrich Wilhelm III, 44–45
Friedrich Wilhelm IV, 44–45
Frith, Francis, 89
Fromentin, Eugène, 88
Fuad, Prince Ahmad (later King Fuad):
    and Coptic Museum, 277–78, 292;
    and Egyptian University, 198, 248;
    and independence, 293; and interna-
    tional congresses, 170, 251–52
Fussell, Paul, 66
al-Fustat, 214, 255–56

Gabra, Sami, 192
Gabri, Ali, 176
Galland, Antoine, 219
Garis Davies, Norman and Anna de, 200
Garstin, William, 236
Gautier, Théophile, 81, 87, 128
Gaze, Henry, 72, 91
gender: railroad fares and, 69; tourism
    and, 76, *78, 79,* 90
Gentz, W., *108*
geographical congresses, *304, 306*
geographical societies, 48, 96, 130,
    153–54
German Archaeological Institute, 197
German language, 117, 234, 235
German Oriental Society, 130
Germany and German nationals: and
    American archaeology, 199; and An-
    tiquities Service, 185, 195; Archaeo-
    logical Institute of, 197–98; and classi-
    cal studies, 141, 169; and the Comité,
    214, 224, 230, 234–36, 290; consul-
    collectors of, 39; and decipherment of
    hieroglyphics, 41; and Egyptian Egyp-
    tologists, 186; Egyptology of, 114–15,
    116–17, 197; excavation and, 177,
    197–98, 255–56; guidebooks from,
    72, 81; and International Congress of
    Orientalists, 131, 133, 134; and Khe-
    divial Library, 234; learned societies
    of, 48; Lepsius expedition, 44–46,
    115; and neoclassicism, 103; and neo-
    Islamic style, 241–42; and rivalry with
    France, 45–46, 113–15, 116, 134,
    185, 253–54; tourism and, 81; travel

accounts from, 27, 81; unification of, 113, 114, 197; universities of, 44, 95, 114, 197; world's fairs and, 129, 191, 253; World War I and, 197–98, 214, 256–57, 291, 292–93

Gérôme, Jean-Léon, 88, 220

Gezira, 135–36

Gezira palace, 241

Ghali, Butrus: assassination of, 274, 280, 285; and Coptic Church reform, 263, 264, 266, 267, 271, 272; in government, 274, 279; and International Congress of Classical Archaeology, 169

Ghislanzoni, Antonio, 163

Ghorbal, Shafiq, 211

Gianaclis, Nestor, 151

Gibbons, Edward, 157

Gillray, James, 34, 35

Giza, Pyramids of: Al-Ahram's account of, 118; Belzoni and, 38; Mariette and, 100, 101; Murray's guide on, 76; shape of, 24–25; al-Tahtawi on, 53, 110

Giza palace: antiquities museum in, 183, 193, 194

Gladstone, William, 153–54, 156, 226

Gléon, Delort de (Baron), 252

Gliddon, George R., 56–57, 57

Glymenopoulo, E., 151

Glypothek, 192

Goeje, Michael J. de, 252

Goethe, Johann Wolfgang von, 141

Goldziher, Ignaz, 249, 250, 252

Gordon, Charles, 92

Gordon, Lucie Duff, 84, 122–23

Gorst, Sir Eldon, 196, 248

Gothic Revival, 150, 192, 218, 240, 241

Gousio, Georges, 160–61

Graeco-Roman Research Account, 162

Grammaire (Champollion), 41

Grammar of Ornament (Jones), 240

Grand, Pierre, 224, 226, 228

Granville, Earl of, 153

Graves, Robert, 171

Great Exhibition. See Crystal Palace exhibition

Great Pyramid, 24, 31, 45, 118, 294

Greaves, John, 25

Grébaut, Eugène, 181, 182, 183, 186, 188, 202, 206, 361n35

Greco-Egyptian Orthodox Community, 150

Greco-Roman Museum (Alexandria), 7, 8–9, 159–61, 162, 290; guidebook of, 202; imperialism and, 294; as Italian enclave, 9, 116, 151–52, 161, 198,

290; leadership of, 160, 161; and Société d'archéologie d'Alexandrie, 160–61, 163; tourism and, 287

Greco-Roman studies. See classical studies

Greece: and the Comité, 237; guidebooks of, 71, 72, 91; independence of, 148, 149–50, 170; International Congress of Classical Archaeology in, 169; museums of, 103, 276; and national control of antiquities, 56, 93, 103; national identity of, 103, 150, 280; population from, in Egypt, 80, 149; and Société d'archéologie d'Alexandrie, 160–61. See also Greeks in Egypt

Greece, ancient: language of, 140, 144–45, 155, 158, 171; papyri of, 161–63, 270; vs. Rome, in classical discourse, 140–41. See also classical studies

Greek Antiquities Service, 103

Greek Orthodox Church, 150, 259, 262, 263, 276

Greeks in Egypt: in Alexandria, 149–51; in Cairo, 150; and classical studies, 150–51; Cromer and, 158–59; population of, 80, 149; and Société d'archéologie d'Alexandrie, 160–61

Grenfell, Bernard, 162–63

Grenfell, Sir Francis W., 181, 182

Grotefend, Georg, 44

Groupil-Fesquet, Frédéric, 88

guidebooks, 69–73; activities recommended by, 81–82; on amenities for travelers, 80; authors of, 12, 80–81, 299–300, 302; British occupation and, 70; and Copts, bigotry concerning, 260; on dahabiyya travel, 86, 95; on disease, 70, 82, 83, 84; Egyptian dependence on, 72–73, 271, 283; on firearms, 75; on firmans (official permits), 74; on flag raising, 75; on hotels, 73; on interactions with natives, 75–78, 77; lack of Arabic guides to Europe, 72–73; literary heroes quoted in, 87; on local dress, 74–75; on museums, 238–39, 287; numbers of, 80–81, 91, 113, 299–300, 302; organization of, 71; reading recommended by, 81; specialization of, 68; and time recommended for travel, 68; travelogues distinguished from, 69–70, 87; on women, 90. See also tourism; travel accounts; specific guidebooks

Guidi, Ignazio, 252

Guizot, François, 56, 217

Haarmann, Ulrich, 30
Habib, Ali, 189
Hachette, Louis, 72
Hadith Isa ibn Hisham (al-Muwaylihi), 208, 254
Hadrian, 147
al-Hakim, Tawfiq, 294
al-Hakim Mosque, 237
Hamdi, Osman, 103
Hamilton, William, 37, 49
Hamza, Mahmud, 211
Hand-book for Travellers in Egypt (Murray), 71
Handbook for Travellers in Holland, Belgium, Prussia, and Northern Germany (Murray), 71
Hanna, Murqus, 170, 279
Hanna, Sinut, 279, 280
Hanna, Yaqub, 260
Hanum, Kuchuk, 76
Haqaiq al-Akhbar an Duwal al-Bihar, 208
Harb, Talat, 245
Harris, Anthony, 49, 62
Harvard-Boston expedition, 200
Hasan, Ahmad, 208
Hassan, Selim, 13, 211
Hatshepsut, 111
Haussmann, Georges (Baron), 128, 216, 218
Hay, Robert, 42, 43, 76, 102, 220
health: Egypt as health resort, 84; tourism and, 82–84
Hearst, Phoebe, 200
Hekekyan, Joseph (Yusuf), 59–63, 122–23, 273; and Egyptian Literary Association, 49–50; and Egyptian Society, 49, 61, 122; European focus of, 22, 59, 61–63; Heliopolis excavation of, 62, 63; on Indian "Mutiny," 122; papers of, 59, 63; and preservation of antiquities, 56
heliocentrism, 147
Heliopolis, 62, 221, 241
Hellenic Community, 150
Hermeticism, 2, 25, 30, 31, 315n15
Herodotus, 22; Mahmud Fahmi and, 170; Mariette's denouncement of, 143–44; al-Tahtawi on, 146; use of writings of, 24, 31, 81, 110, 139, 142
Herz, Max: and Awqaf Department, 235; background of, 234–35; and the Comité, 234–35, 242, 256–57, 276; and Coptic studies, 270–71, 276; as enemy alien, 214, 256–57, 291, 292; and International Congress of Classical Archaeology, 169; and Museum of Arab Art, 235, 237, 246, 255, 290;

and al-Rifai Mosque, 239, 241–42; and world's fair exhibits, 12, 229, 253
Herzfeld, Ernst, 255
Hieroglyphica (Horapollo), 25
hieroglyphics: Christianity and, 24; decipherment of, 40–41; *Description* and, 36; Kamal and, 211–12; Kircher and, 267–68; Muslim understanding of, 30; mystical symbolism assigned to, 25; al-Tahtawi and information from, 109, 110; textbooks on, 189, 203
Higher Schools Club, 203
Higher Teachers College, 204, 210
Al-Hilal, 163, 164, 165, 280
Hilmy, Prince Ibrahim, 206, 207
Hindu-Saracenic style, 242
historic preservation: Britain and, 56, 218; continuation of, 296; Coptic activism in, 275, 279, 281; and demolition of nonprivileged buildings, 228; Egyptians and, 230–34; France and, 56, 217–18; imperialism and, 213–14, 222–24, 231; reconstruction as issue in, 217, 218, 227–28, 351n17; Urabi revolution and, 226; urban renewal vs., 215–17, 222. *See also* antiquities, protection of
History of the Art of Antiquity (Winckelmann), 141
History of the Church in Egypt (Butcher), 281
History of the Greeks and Romans (Zaydan), 165
History of the Romans (Farid), 167
Hodgson, Marshall, 215
Holland, 27, 46
Homer: *Dairat al-Maarif* entry for, 165; Gladstone's work on, 153, 154; Mahmud Fahmi and, 170; Petrie's finds of, 162; philhellenism and, 141, 154; translation of, 164, 165
Horapollo, 22, 25
Horeau, Jector, 88
Horner, Leonard, 62
Horner, Rev. George, 267
hostels, 73, 150
hotels, 73, 74, 84, 86, 104, 241
Hourani, Albert, 165
Huber, Baron de, 99
Huber, C. Rudolf, 77
Hugo, Victor, 218
Humboldt, Alexander von, 41, 44, 114, 141
Humboldt, Wilhelm, 41
Hunt, Arthur, 162–63
Hurgronje, Christiaan Snouck, 252
Husayn, Taha, 11, 140, 170, 171, 211, 291, 313n10
Husni, Hasan, 189

Ibn Tulun mosque, 241
Ibrahim, Hafiz, 165
Ibrahim, Yahya, 263
Ibrahim Pasha, 58
identity: Coptic, 258, 280–85; Greek
    national, 103, 150, 280; and Turkish
    garb, 131
identity, Egyptian national: and the clas-
    sics, 139–40, 163, 167, 291; and Cop-
    tic studies, 276; and Islam, 295, 297;
    and pharaonic heritage, 111, 117,
    163, 181, 201, 203, 205–10, 212,
    288, 289, 295–97, 296; al-Tahtawi
    and, 288, 289
Idris, 111
al-Idrisi, Jamal al-Din, 30–31
Iliad (Homer), 141, 145, 164, 165
Illustrations of Cairo (Hay), 220
I Monumenti dell' Egitto e della Nubia
    (Rosellini), 43
imperialism: advisers of occupation and,
    244–45; Antiquities Service and, 97,
    294; archaeology and, 2, 10–11,
    12–14; Britain and, 223–24; and
    Congress of International Orientalists,
    252; and Coptic monuments, 275;
    Cromer on, 154, 157–58; and Egyp-
    tian Egyptologists, 212; and Egyptian
    understanding of the past, 181; and
    European employees of government,
    93, 95, 96, 294; excavation and,
    255–56; France and, 113–14,
    222–23; French expedition, 1, 14,
    28, 32–34, 36–37, 231–32; Glad-
    stone and, 154; Greece and, 150;
    historic preservation and, 213–14,
    222–24, 231; Italy and, 151; and
    lack of Arabic guidebooks to Europe,
    72–73; land annexed in, 96; and
    language, 158; museums and, 9–10,
    93, 95; "new," 141, 154; Oxford
    and, 153; as term, 113; and world's
    fairs, 252–54. See also British
    occupation
Imperial Museum (Berlin), 236, 255
Imperial Ottoman Museum, 103
India: the classics and, 156; Great Exhi-
    bition and, 125; Hindu-Saracenic ar-
    chitectural style, 242; and neoclassi-
    cism, 193; telegraph and, 85–86
India (al-Biruni), 145
industrialization: and anticontagionists,
    83; historic preservation and, 217,
    233–34; Muhammad Ali and, 55,
    56–57, 60; romanticism and, 2;
    tourism and, 68–69, 80, 87, 89–92
Institut de France, 48
Institut d'Égypte, 32–33, 36–37, 48, 49

Institut égyptien: bulletin of, 124, 189;
    and classical discourse, 159; and Egyp-
    tian Museum complex, 104; and Egyp-
    tology, 189; founding of, 96, 120–22;
    and imperialism, 97; members of,
    121–23, 153, 189–90, 246, 247–48,
    274, 303; World War I and, 292–93
Institut français d'archéologie orientale
    du Caire (IFAO): Bahgat and, 245,
    246; the classics and, 161; founding
    of, 173–75; van Berchem and, 247
international congress movement, 130,
    304, 306
International Congress of Classical
    Archaeology, 167–70, 306
International Congress of Orientalists
    (ICO), 130–34, 191–92, 304, 306,
    345n72; and Arabic-Islamic topics,
    249–52; Egyptian response to repre-
    sentations at, 132–33; Egyptology
    and, 130–32, 133–34, 192; and Glad-
    stone, 153; and historic preservation,
    223; "Orientals" at, as issue, 120,
    133, 134, 191, 241, 249–52; represen-
    tation at, Egyptian response to,
    132–33; Shawqi and, 208
International Exhibition (1862), 102
internationalism: vs. nationalism, 120;
    World War I and, 247, 251, 292–93
Iphigénie (Racine), 166
Ishaq, Adib, 163, 164
Isis: destruction of statue of, 30
al-Iskandarani, Shaykh Ahmad, 252
Islam: conquest of Egypt by, and Coptic
    Church, 259; Cromer on, 155; defense
    of, classical studies and, 166; Egyptol-
    ogy as slighting, 8, 131; reform and,
    264, 267; and women's freedom, 283.
    See also mosques; Muslims; religion
Islamic archaeology: as academic disci-
    pline, 11; Bahgat and, 214, 246, 247,
    255–56; Egyptian University program
    in, 257; as term, 312n1; van Berchem
    and, 246–47
Islamic art: destruction of, 222; Egyp-
    tians and preservation of, 233; Euro-
    pean prejudices and appreciation of,
    213–14, 218–22; neo-Islamic architec-
    tural style, 192–93, 238, 239–42,
    239, 276, 277, 289, 290–91; school
    for revival of, 242; styles of, 227; as
    term, 215; and world's fairs, 237, 240,
    241. See also Comité de conservation
    des monuments de l'art arabe;
    Museum of Arab Art
Islamists, 293, 295
Ismail, Khedive: Arabic renaissance and,
    96–97, 119; and architectural style,

Ismail, Khedive (continued)
241, 242; Artin and, 273; and Awqaf
Department, 243; bankruptcy of government of, 96, 135–36, 241; and
Brugsch, 116; and the Comité, 223,
234; and Cook, 91; and Copts, 261,
263; and Dairat al-Maarif, 164; and
education reforms, 97, 229, 261, 263;
and Egyptian Museum, 107, 194; exile
of, 207; and International Congress of
Orientalists, 131; and Jamiyyat al-
Maarif, 124; and Khedivial Geographical Society, 248; and Mariette, 104,
128, 135; and Mubarak, 98, 216; and
pyramid-and-sphinx as national symbol, 119; and school of Egyptology, 95,
116; and Syrian Christian immigrants,
163; and al-Tahtawi, 98, 108, 109,
148; urban renewal and, 215–17, 222,
223, 230, 233–34, 240; and world's
fairs, 128–29, 130
Israel, 293
Issawi, Charles, 329n81
Istanbul: antiquities museum of, 103, 193,
237; architecture of, 193, 345–46n74;
Germans and antiquities of, 197
Italianate style, 240
Italian language, 115–16
Italy and Italian nationals: and Antiquities
Service, 196; and classical studies,
151–52; and the Comité, 230, 236–37;
and construction work, 240; consul-
collectors of, 39; and Egyptian Museum,
192, 195; and Egyptian University, 198;
Egyptology of, 115–16; and Greco-
Roman Museum, 9, 116, 151–52, 161,
198, 290; and Institut égyptien, 121;
and International Congress of Classical
Archaeology, 169; and International
Congress of Orientalists, 134; and Khedivial Geographical Society, 124, 248;
and national control of antiquities, 93;
nationalism and, 9; and neo-Islamic architecture, 242; and the plague, 83; population from, in Egypt, 80, 151; and
postal system of Egypt, 116, 119, 205;
and Société d'archéologie d'Alexandrie,
160, 161; travel accounts/guidebooks
from, 27, 91; world's fairs and, 191;
World War I and, 198, 257
Itinéraire de la haute Égypte (Mariette),
135

al-Jabarti, Abd al-Rahman, 36–37,
39–40, 97, 231–32, 288
Jalal, Uthman, 166

Jamiyyat al-Maarif (Society of Knowl-
edge), 124
Japan, 126, 133, 191
Al-Jarida, 170, 245
Jasper, Marcel, 241
Al-Jawaib, 97
Jesus Christ, 145, 147
Jews: Arabic lore of, and al-Tahtawi,
109; Austria-Hungary and, 234–35;
blamed for forgery, 77; Egyptian state
and, 261; monuments of, preserving,
296; Ottoman Empire and, 263
Al-Jins al-Latif, 283
Joanne, Adolphe, 69
Joanne's guides, 71–72
John (Yohannes) XIX, 263
Johnson, Dr. Samuel, 65
Jollois, Jean-Baptiste Prosper, 33
Jomard, Edmé-François, 33–34, 42; and
Champollion, 36, 41–42; and Copts,
268; and the Description, 33–34, 36,
53; and Egyptian Society, 49; and geo-
graphical society of Paris, 48; and In-
stitut égyptien, 121; and al-Tahtawi,
52, 53
Jones, Owen, 220, 240
Jones, William, 48
Jouguet, Pierre, 161, 169
Juma, Muhammad Lutfi, 171
Junker, Hermann, 197–98

Al-Kafi fi tarikh Misr al-qadim wa al-
hadith (Sharubim), 208–9, 283–84
Kamal, Ahmad, 187, 295; and Antiquities Service, 201–3, 204, 211; background of, 98, 186, 235, 259, 344n50;
Daressy's attacks on, 211–12; and
Egyptian Museum, 186, 188–89; and
Egyptology, 10, 14, 97, 98, 186–89,
201–4, 211–12; and generational
changes, 172, 173; and Institut égyptien, 123, 190, 203, 211–12; and International Congress of Classical Archaeology, 169–70; and Khedivial
Geographical Society, 190; lectures of,
203–4; de Morgan and, 189, 192; and
nationalism, 212, 246, 288; and regional museums, 204; and School of
Egyptology, 93, 117, 118, 186, 188,
203–4, 282, 344n52; street named
after, 294–95; in Who Was Who in
Egyptology, 10
Kamal, Hasan, 211, 212
Kamal, Prince Yusuf, 242
Kamil, Husayn, 173, 256, 277, 279
Kamil, Mustafa, 140, 167, 210, 245

Karnak: Anglo-French rivalry and, 38; Arabic references to, 30; collapse of column at, 196; destruction of, 56; European discovery of, 27; Mariette and, 100; de Morgan and, 185; table of kings of, 46, 57

Khafra's temple, 99

Khashaba Pasha, Ahmad, 204, 211

Khayri, Ahmad, 109

Khedivial Geographical Society, 96, 97, 132; membership of, 123–24, 153, 190, 246, 248, 274, 303

Khedivial Library, 50, 97, 117, 234, 235, 238, 239, 249, 251, 257

Al-Khitat al-tawfiqiyya (Mubarak), 16, 95, 166, 179–80, 232–33

Khurshid, Muhammad, 188

Killearn, Baron, 294

Kinglake, Alexander, 82, 87

Kircher, Athanasius, 25, 26, 267–68

Kirullus VI (Cyril), 92

Kitchener, Lord Horatio Herbert: and Awqaf Department, 243; cartoon of, 154, 155; and Cook's, 92; and Coptic Church, 280; education of, 155; and Fashoda, 86; and France's "archaeological protectorate," 196; and generational change, 172, 173

Klaproth, Heinrich, 41

Kléber, General, 260

Klenze, Leo von, 192

Koch, Robert, 83

Kodak cameras, 89

Kom Ombo, 27, 185

König Bey, 100, 121

Kremer, Alfred von, 252

Labib, Claudius, 170, 263, 265, 283, 288

labor, corvée: and Mahmudiyya Canal, 149; Mariette and, 100–1, 135; and Suez Canal, 100–1

Lacau, Pierre, 17, 169

Lamartine, Alphonse-Marie-Louis de, 87

Lammens, Henri, 252

Lampson, Sir Miles (Lord Killearn), 294

Landberg, Carlo, 250

Land of Goshen, 162, 178, 179

Lane, Edward William, 42–43, 49, 82; on architecture, 240; on Copts, 260, 268; Manners and Customs of the Modern Egyptians, 50, 52, 219, 260, 268; and Orientalism, 219; and slavery, 78; and al-Tahtawi, 50–51, 52, 54; and translation of Arabian Nights, 219; Turkish garb of, 74–75, 131

Lane-Poole, Stanley: and Anglo-French rivalry, 236; and Arab art as term, 215; on the Comité, 227, 233, 237; and Copts, 260, 272, 282; and Museum of Arab Art, 238–39; on nostalgia, 217; and South Kensington museum, 237; on static Orient, 219; on vandalism, 222

language: Akkadian, 44; and the Comité, 224, 234, 235; decipherment of, 40–42, 43–44; in Egyptian court, 60; and Egyptian opportunity, 5, 145, 229, 259, 265; English, 265; and European advantage, 10; European, and bureaucracy, 97; Farsi, 133; French, 116, 117, 121, 224, 234; Greek, 140, 144–45, 155, 158, 171; of guides, 76; ignorance of, and Turkish dress, 75; imperialism and, 158; Italian, 115–16; Latin, 5, 140, 143, 145, 153, 155, 158, 167; of papers, and people under study, 251. See also Arabic language; Coptic language; hieroglyphics

Laplagne, Guillaume, 242

Lasciac, Antonio, 235–36, 242

La Thébaïde ou les frères ennemis (Racine), 164

Latin, 5, 140, 143, 145, 153, 155, 158, 167

Layard, Austen Henry, 44, 101

Lays of Ancient Rome (Macaulay), 154

learned societies, 48, 95–96, 120–24, 130. See also specific societies and international congresses

Leemans, Conradus, 46

Lefebvre, Gustave, 196

Legrain, Georges, 185, 195, 196

Leiden Museum, 46

Lemm, Oskar von, 268

Lemoyne, Arnaud, 99

Le Play, Frederic, 126, 128

Lepsius, Richard: circle of, 114; and classical studies, 143; death of, 172; and decipherment of hieroglyphics, 41; and Egyptian Society, 49; expedition of, 44–46, 115; and Institut égyptien, 123; and International Congress of Orientalists, 131, 133; and Mariette, 114–15; Muhammad Ali and, 58; and Neues Museum, 45, 48, 106; as teacher, 114

Lerebour, Nicolas, 88

Lesseps, Ferdinand de, 49, 68, 83, 97, 100; as member of Khedivial Geographical Society, 124; and world's fairs, 128, 129, 130, 252

Les Trois Horaces et les trois Curices
(adapted to Arabic as *Mayy wa Huras*)
(Corneille), 163
Lettre à M. Dacier (Champollion), 41
*Lettre à M. le Prof. H. Rosellini sur
l'alphabet hiéroglyph* (Lepsius), 44
Lewis, John Frederick, 88, 220
l'Hôte, Nestor, 99
Library of Alexandria, 147, 166
Libya, 151
Lieder, Rudolf, 99
Lindsay, Lord, 75, 86
*Literature of Egypt and the Soudan from
the Earliest Times* (Hilmy), 207
Al-Liwa, 167, 210, 245
Lloyd, Lord, 294
loans, 95, 96
Lobel, Edgar, 163
Loret, Victor, 181, 185, 196
Lo Spettatore egiziano, 116
Lotbinière, Pierre Joly de, 88
Louca, Anouar, 249
Louisiana Purchase Exposition (1904, St.
Louis), 191
Louvre: and Botta, 44, 173; and Cham-
pollion, 42, 46–47, 193; classical lens
of, 141, 142; Denon working in, 47;
and Drovetti, 39, 46; Egyptian collec-
tion, development of, 46–47; Mariette
and, 99–100, 101; Said's gifts to, 100;
and Salt, 46
Lutfi al-Sayyid, Ahmad, 140, 170, 210,
229, 245, 249, 257, 279, 280, 288
Luxor: excavation of, 58; hotels and, 86;
identification of, 27; obelisks of, 57,
196, 201
Luxor Hospital for Natives, 92
Lyell, Sir Charles, 122
Lyons, H. G., 72
Lythgoe, Albert, 199, 200

Macaulay, Thomas B., 154
MacKenzie, John, 13, 88, 214
Macmillan's guides, 277
Madinat al-Zahra, 256
Maghrib, 140
Mahfouz, Naguib, 294
Mahmud, Muhammad, 249
Mahmudiyya Canal, 149
Maillet, Benoît de, 27, 57, 218–19
Majlis al-Nuwwab, 97
Makarius, Kyrillos, 190
Mamluk Revival style, 240, 241,
242
Mamluks, 32, 33, 144
Manescalo, Alfonso, 237, 238, 239
Manetho, 22, 24, 62, 63, 110, 204, 209

*Manners and Customs of the Ancient
Egyptians* (Wilkinson), 52, 203
*Manners and Customs of the Modern
Egyptians* (Lane), 50, 52, 219, 260,
268
al-Manqabadi, Tadrus Shanuda, 267,
281
Manusardi, A., 160
Al-Manzum, 189
maps of al-Falaki, 153
al-Maqrizi, 30
Marcel, Jean-Joseph, 34
Marchand, Jean Baptiste, 86
Margoliouth, David, 252
Mariette, Auguste, 4, 99–100, 134–35,
136; and Antiquities Service, 63, 93,
100–1; Artin's praise for, 123; audience of, 92, 106; and Brugsch, 114,
115; and Cairo Opera House, 129;
and classical studies, 143–44; and
Coptic studies, 99, 268; death of, 102,
136, 173; and Egyptian Museum, 93,
104–6; excavation technique of, 62,
101, 177; on foreign loans, 101; and
French Egyptology, 99, 173; and Germans, 113, 114–15; guidebook by,
72; and Institut égyptien, 121, 122,
123; and International Congress of
Orientalists, 132, 133; *Itinéraire de la
haute Égypte*, 135; and Khedivial
Geographical Society, 124; monument
to, 196; Murray's guidebooks on, 82;
protection of antiquities and, 101–3,
129, 236; residence of, 105, 136; and
rivalries, 113–16, 173, 186; Said and,
100, 101–2, 126, 128; and School of
Egyptology, 93, 116, 118, 186, 189;
street named for, 194; and Suez opening, 129; al-Tahtawi's work compared
to, 110–12; and Verdi's *Aida*, 12; and
world's fairs, 95, 125, 126, 128–29,
130, 193
Mark, Saint: church of, 240–41, 266;
Copts and, 9, 259, 284
Maruj al-Dhahab (al-Masudi), 30
Marx, Karl, 140
Maspero, Gaston: on Abbas I, 58; and
Antiquities Service, 175, 186, 195–96;
Artin's praise for, 123; background of,
173, 176; and the classics, 144; and
the Comité, 230; and Coptic studies,
270, 282, 291; dress of, 131; and EEF,
178–79; and Egyptian Museum, 167,
189, 202; and Egyptian University,
248; and exclusion of Egyptians from
excavation permits, 202; and generational changes, 172, 173; and IFAO,

173–75; and Institut égyptien, 123; and International Congress of Classical Archaeology, 169; and International Congress of Orientalists, 131, 134; on Ismail, 104, 107; and Italians, 198; and Kamal, 201; knighthood of, 196; on Lepsius, 114; and Mariette, 100, 104, 115; and de Morgan, 185; on Orientalism, 247; Petrie and, 176, 177; and regional museums, 204; and School of Egyptology, 186, 188; in *Who Was Who in Egyptology,* 10

Maspero, Jean, 270

Massignon, Louis, 252

al-Masudi, 30

Matériaux pour un Corpus Inscriptionum Arabicarum (van Berchem), 247

Matisse, Henri, 220

Mawsuat, 245

Maximilian, Archduke, 58, 100

McMahon, Henry, 155

Melville, Herman, 87

Memphis, 30, 62, 180

Menasce, Jacques de (Baron), 160

Menes, 110

Menou, General, 248

Mérimée, Prosper, 218

Metropolitan Museum of Art (New York), 193, 199, 200

Midhat, Ahmed, 250

al-Mihiyya, Sarah, 296–97, 296

military: Copts and, 261, 262; cultural evolution and belief in solution via, 178; dragomen and, 76. *See also* British occupation; France: expedition of; World War I

Mill, John Stuart, 141

Mille et une nuits (Galland), 219

Milner, Alfred, 153, 157

Mimaut, Jean François, 38, 39, 55, 56, 57, 60–61

Minutoli, Heinrich von, 39, 44–45

Misbah al-Sharq, 207

Miscellanea Aegyptiaca (Egyptian Library Association), 49

Misr (name for Egypt), 209, 211

Misr (newspaper), 267, 278, 279, 283

Mission archéologique. *See* Institut français d'archéologie orientale du Caire (IFAO)

Mitchell, Timothy, 132–33, 249

Mixed Courts, 95, 116, 150, 245

Modern Egypt (Cromer), 155–56

Modern Egypt and Thebes (Wilkinson), 71

Mohl, O. de, 235

Mommsen, Theodor, 114, 143

Moncrief, Scott, 236

Monge, Gaspard, 32

Montesquieu, 145, 146

Monuments de l'Égypte et de la Nubie (Champollion), 43

Moret, Alexandre, 143

Morgan, Henri de, 200

Morgan, Jacques de, 177, 181, 183, 185, 189, 192, 195, 196, 202, 203

Moritz, Bernhard, 169, 235, 270–71

Morocco, 151

Morris, William, 218

mosques: architectural style and, 234, 239, 241–42; Coste and, 220; Museum of Arab Art and, 237; as off-limits to non-Muslims, 218, 274; as Oriental other, 218–19; preservation vs. reconstruction of, 227–28, 232

Muallaqa Church, 272, 276

Al-Muayyad, 244, 245

Mubarak, Ali, 8, 131, 231; *Alam al-Din,* 180, 233; on *Anwar,* 109; Artin and, 273; and Brugsch, 116; and classical studies, 140, 166; and the Comité, 226, 230, 233–34; and Cook's tours, 91; and educational reforms, 97, 98, 289; and Egyptology, 95, 96, 97, 116, 288; and al-Falaki, 123, 152; and Institut égyptien, 122; Ismail and, 98, 216; *Al-Khitat al-tawfiqiyya,* 16, 95, 166, 179–80, 232–33; and lack of Egyptian understanding of ancient Egypt, 179–80; and Orientalists, 232–33; and *Rawdat al-madaris,* 112; and Suez opening, 129; al-Tahtawi's work compared to, 180–81; and Urabi revolution, 226; and urban renewal, 216, 233–34

Mubarak, Husni, 293

Muhammad Ali: abolition of tax farming, 51; architectural style and, 240; and Armenian intermediaries, 59, 61–62; and Awqaf Department, 243; and Cairo, changes in, 215, 232; compared to Alexander, 148; and Copts, 260, 261–62; Coste and, 220; educational reforms of, 52, 97, 261; and firearms for travelers, 75; *firman* audiences by, 74; French military conquest and, 32; gifts of obelisks from, 53–54, 57; in guidebooks, 71; and Hekekyan, 59, 60, 61; and Lepsius expedition, 45; and Machiavelli, 171; and non-Muslim restrictions, 260; and protection of antiquities, 21, 54–58, 55, 60–61, 63, 110, 289; and railroad, 68;

Muhammad Ali *(continued)*
    and sanitation, 84; student delegation
    sent to Paris, 52; al-Tahtawi on, 148;
    and tourism, 66
Muhammad Ali Street, 215, 216, 238
Mukhtar, Mahmud, 242, 294
Müller, Max, 114, 249
mummies, *132*, *186*, *187*
Municipal Library (Alexandria), 160
Al-Muqattam, 163, 167
Murray, Charles, 38, 62, 99
Murray, John, II, 70, 87
Murray, John, III, 69, 70–71, 89
Murray's guidebooks, 71–72, 91; activi-
    ties recommended by, 82; Cook and,
    71, 72; on *dahabiyya* vs. steamer
    travel, 86; on disease, 83, 84; on the
    doseh, 78; Egyptian readership of, 73,
    271; on firearms, 75; hotels recom-
    mended by, 73; on interactions with
    natives, 76, 78; literary heroes quoted
    in, 87; photographers listed in, 89;
    and public amenities for travelers, 80;
    on slave trade, 78; time recommended
    for travel by, 68; and Wilkinson,
    70–71, 91; writers of, 12
Musa, Salama, 73, 210, 283
Museum of Arab Art: Artin and, 274;
    Bahgat and, 214, 246, 255, 257, 291;
    budget of, 238; buildings and sites of,
    237, 238–39, *239*; Coptic studies and,
    275, 276; founding of, 7, 8, 215,
    237–39, 290; guidebook for, 237,
    255, 257; Herz and, 235, 237, 246,
    255, 290; imperialism and, 294;
    Mubarak and, 233; Mustafa and, 294;
    objects in, 232, 237; and Second Com-
    mission of the Comité, 227; tourism
    and, 238–39, 287
Museum of Islamic Art. *See* Museum of
    Arab Art
museums: antiquities decree of 1835 and,
    56, 58; architecture of (*see* architec-
    ture); distant past as focus of, 276; Eu-
    ropean, development of, 46–48,
    237–38; Islamic art and, 237–38; na-
    tional control of, 17, 257, 275, 292;
    organization of, 46–47, 106, *107,*
    237; proposed, on Gezira, 135; re-
    gional, 204; role of national, 95, 103;
    tourism and, 65, 202, 238–39,
    277–78, 287–88; of United States, in-
    dustrialization and, 198. *See also*
    specific museums
Muslims: accounts of ancient Egypt by,
    28–31, 36, 180, 209, 288, 315n15;
    classical Greece and Rome and, 30,

144–48; and the Comité, 230; Copts
    as ancestors of, 282, 285; and
    pharaonic heritage, 12, 28–31, 111,
    117, 163, 288. *See also* Islam
Mussolini, Benito, 151
Mustafa, Muhammad, 294
Mutran, Khalil, 165
al-Muwaylihi, Ibrahim, 207
al-Muwaylihi, Muhammad, 64, 92,
    207–8, 254
Muzzi, G., 119
mysticism, 2, 25, 30, 31, 62–63, 296,
    315n15

nahda, 96–97, 249
Najib, Ahmad, 118, 189, 195, 202, 203,
    208
Napoleon, Prince, 100, 121
Napoleon III, 100, 101, 126, 128, 218
Napoleon Bonaparte: Arabic propaganda
    of, 144; and the classics, 141–42, 144;
    and the *Description,* 28, 32–33, 34,
    141; guidebooks mentioning, 72; line-
    age of, 39; and the Louvre, 46; and
    obelisks, 57
Napoleonic Code, 166
Napoleonic Wars, 66–67, 76
al-Naqqash, Salim, 163
Nash, John, 240
al-Nasif, Hifni, 250, 252
Nasser, Gamal Abdel, 17, 257, 293
National Archaeological Museum
    (Athens), 103, 276
National Bank of Egypt, 205
national control: of museums, 17, 257,
    275, 292. *See also* antiquities, national
    control of
nationalism: archaeology and, 2, 9–10,
    12–14; Artin and, 214, 246, 274;
    Bahgat and, 214, 246, 291; classical
    studies and, 167, 170, 291; Copts
    and, 273, 274, 292; and cultural evo-
    lution, 178; Egyptology and, 212;
    Fakhri and, 214, 246; Ghali and, 274,
    279; institutional framework affecting,
    290–92, 294; internationalism vs.,
    120; intra-European rivalries and, 39;
    Italy and, 9; Kamal and, 212, 246,
    288; leaving home to find, 283;
    Mubarak and, 230; museums and, 7,
    9–10; and pharaonic heritage, 6, 12,
    17, 206, 210, 212, 294; professional-
    ism and, 233; Roosevelt and, 277;
    Simaika and, 280; subalternists and,
    14; and Syrian Christians, 167; Urabi
    revolution, 206, 207, 224, 225, 230,
    273, 282

nationality, tourism and, 80–81, 299–302
national museums. *See* museums
National (Watani) Party, 167, 210, 279, 292
Naucratis, 151, 162
Naville, Edouard, 122, 177, 178, 179, 245, 249
al-Nawawi, Shaykh Hasuna. *See* al-Azhar, Shaykh
Nefertari, 198
Nefertiti, 197
Nekhbet, 6
neoclassicism, 103, 161, 192, 193–95, 218, 240, 242
neo-Islamic Revival, 192–93, 238, 239–42, *239*, 276, 277, 289, 290–91
neopharaonic style, 105, 192–93, 242
Néroutsos, Tassos Démétrios, 150
Nerval, Gérard de, 87
Neues Museum (Berlin), 45, 48, 106, 114, 192, 193
New Age, 296
Newberry, Percy, 200
Nightingale, Florence, 2
Nihayat al-Ijaz fi Sirat Sakin al-Hijaz (al-Tahtawi), 109, 147–48
Nilsson guidebooks, 260
Nimr, Faris, 163, 165, 167
Nizzoli, Guiseppe di, 38
Nochlin, Linda, 88
Norden, F. L., 27
Norton, Charles Eliot, 199
Nourrisson, Victor, 160
Novick, Peter, 14
Nubar, Boghos, 170, 248
Nubar Pasha, 59, 100, 122, 123, 135, 136, 190, 274
Nubia, 66, 294
al-Nur, Fakhri Abd, 279

obelisks, 29, 221; Maillet and, 27, 57; as prize, 57, 102; al-Tahtawi on, 53–54
Offenbach, Jacques, 148
Olivier-Merson, Luc, 261, 262
opera, 12, 129, 163, 216, 250
Orient: marketing of, 95
Orientalism: van Berchem and, 246–47; classical studies and, 143, 157; Coptic studies and, 268; Egyptology distinguished from, 130–31; German language and, 235; and imperialism, 13, 120; Mubarak and, 232–33; painting, 88, 220; race and, 133; Said and, 13; and static Orient, 131, 132, 219, 224, 227; types of, 219. *See also* Comité de conservation des monuments de l'art

arabe; International Congress of Orientalists (ICO)
Orientalism: History, Theory, and the Arts (MacKenzie), 13
orientaliste as term, 32
Oriental societies, 48, 130–34
Osman Effendi, 76
Otto I, 103
Ottoman architectural style, 240, 241
Ottoman Empire: constitution of, 97; and International Congress of Classical Archaeology, 169; reforms of, 261, 263; severance of Egypt's ties with, 119, 173, 256, 292; and world's fairs, 125, 129, 191
Oxford University: as cradle of empire, 153
Oxyrhynchus (Al-Bahnasa), 162–63

painting, 88
Palestine, 71, 72, 91, 177
Panama Canal Company, 252, 254
Pangalo, George, 228–29
Pankoucke, C. L. F., 34
papyri, 99, 161–63, 270
Party of Independent Egyptians, 279
Passalacqua, Giuseppe, 39, 45, 48
Paths of Egyptian Hearts in the Joys of the Contemporary Arts (al-Tahtawi), 148
Patriarchal School, 262–63, 265, 283
Patricolo, Achille, 257
patriotism, 148, 167. *See also* nationalism
Pemble, John, 92
Penfield, Frederic, 201
Peninsular and Oriental Company (P&O), 67, 69
periodization: ancient-modern dichotomy and, 34, 112, 220; Islamic art and, 220; "long nineteenth century," 14; al-Tahtawi and, 112
Period of Time (al-Muwaylihi), 64, 92
Persia: and International Congress of Orientalists, 133, 250, 251; al-Tahtawi on, 146; and world's fairs, 125
Petrie, Flinders, 101, 118, 131, 172; and American archaeology, 199; on Armenian intermediaries, 182; and the classics, 144, 162, 169; on Copts, 282; and cultural evolution, 178; and EEF, 178; excavation technique of, 173, 177–78; on Loret, 185; Maspero contrasted with, 176; de Morgan and, 185; in *Who Was Who in Egyptology*, 10
Peyron, Amadeo, 116

pharaonic history: and Coptic identity, 280–85; the *Description* and, 35–36; and Egyptian identity, 111, 117, 163, 181, 201, 203, 205–10, 212, 288, 289, 295–97, 296; European claim to, 2–5; Hermeticism and, 2, 25, 30, 31, 315n15; Muslim accounts of, 28–31, 36, 180, 209, 288, 315n15; and Muslim identity, 12, 28–31, 111, 117, 163, 288; nationalism and, 6, 12, 17, 206, 210, 212, 294; popular claim to, 11–12; tourism and, 183, 202, 239, 287, 287–88; use of symbols, 6, 8, 54, 55, 95–96, 118–19, 119, 205, 208, 295–97, 296. *See also* Egyptology; Pyramids; Sphinx and sphinxes; tourism

Philadelphia: Centennial Exhibition, 129

Philae, 144

Philippines, 191

Philosophic Dictionary (Voltaire), 146

photography, 88–89, 220

Picot, François-Edouard, 141, 142, 193

pilgrims, 71, 83–84, 90

Pitt-Rivers, Lieutenant General, 218

plague, 82–83, 84

Plato: vogue for in British culture, 141

Pliny the Elder, 142

Plutarch, 141

Pococke, Richard, 27

"Pompey's Pillar," 27, 29, 35, 57, 218–19

Poole, Reginald Stuart, 178

population: of Alexandria, 149; European, in Egypt, 80–81, 149, 151, 152, 299–302

postal service, 51, 67, 116, 118–19, 119, 205, 231

postcards, 89, 220

potsherds, 177

prejudice, European: about Copts, 259–61, 282; about Islamic art, 213–14, 218–22. *See also* racism

Presbyterian "American Mission," 263, 281

press: Ismail and restrictions on, 97

Prisse d'Avennes, Achille, 45–46, 49, 57, 74–75, 131, 220

property rights, 56

Protestantism, 260–61, 263, 264, 265–66, 281. *See also* Anglicans; Christianity

Prüfer, Kurt, 235

Ptolemies: Alexandrians as drawn to age of, 150, 151; al-Tahtawi on, 146–48

Ptolemy, Claudius, 147

Pugioli, Pietro, 152

Punch, 154, *155*, *156*

Pyramidographia (Greaves), 25

Pyramids: biblicized understanding of, 24; classical understanding of, 24–25; Egyptian independence and, 294; Hekekyan on, 60–61; Mimaut on legacy of, 60–61; Mubarak on, 180; Muslim understanding of, 30–31, 180; mysticism and, 2, 25, 30, 31, 62–63, 296, 315n15; as symbol, 6, 8, *12*, 54, 55, 95–96, 118–19, *119*, 205, 208, 221, 295–97, 296; al-Tahtawi on, 53; tourism and, 66, 76, 79. *See also* pharaonic history

Qala of Bani Hammad, 256

al-Qalqashandi, 249

Qasr al-Nil barracks, 175, 194

quarantines, 82–84

Qudsi, Elia, 250

Quibell, James, 189, 195, 196

Quran. *See* Islam

Qurna, 42, 77

race: and "Arab art" as term, 215, 224; and Centennial Exhibition, 129; and imperialism, 157–58; and Institut égyptien, 122; and International Congress of Orientalists, 133; and School of Egyptology, 117. *See also* racism

Racine, Jean, 146, 164, 166

racism: advice on interactions with natives and, 75–78; and Copts as ancestors of Muslims, 282; and cultural evolution, 178; popularization of ancient Egypt and, 58; and railroad fares, 69; al-Rifai dome collapse and, 241–42. *See also* prejudice, European; race

al-Rahib, Barsum, 265

railroads: British occupation and, 274; and cholera, 83; Copts and, 266; development of, 67, 68, 215, 236, 255–56; and Egyptian Museum location, 104; fares, 69; and Greco-Roman Museum founding, 160; and imperialism, 95; and Institut égyptien, 121; and mass tourism, 67, 85, 86, 89–90

Rameses II, 38, 66, 111, *127*, 146, 196, 209, 270

Ramsis, 283

Randall-MacIver, David, 200

Rawdat al-madaris (ed. al-Tahtawi), 98, 112, 116, 148

Rawlinson, Henry, 44

Rechouan, Ismayl, 76

Reeves, John, 160

Reil, W., 84
Reisner, George, 199, 200, 201
religion: ancient Egyptian compared to
    Coptic, 281–82; and architecture,
    240–41; Cook's tours and, 90; and ed-
    ucational opportunities, 261; and his-
    toric preservation, 232; Kamal and,
    203; services offered for travelers, 80;
    Shawqi and, 208; Zaki and, 251. See
    also Christianity; Islam; Jews; Muslims
Renan, Ernest, 247
Répertoire chronologique d'épigraphie
    arabe (Wiet), 247
resistance to European dominance,
    233–34, 243–44, 245, 249, 254, 273
Rhind, Alexander, 176
Rhodes, Cecil, 154
Rhoné, Arthur, 215, 241–42
Ricci, Alessandro, 39
Rich, Claudius, 43–44
Rida, Ali, 243
Rida, Rashid, 166
Rifaa, Ali Fahmi, 109, 112
al-Rifai Mosque, 234, 239, 241–42
Rifaud, Jean Jacques, 38
Rifaud's travel accounts, 66, 70, 72, 73;
    on dress, 75; on firearms, 75; on
    forged antiquities, 77; on public
    amenities for travelers, 80; on slavery,
    78
Ritter, Karl, 114
Riyad Pasha, Mustafa, 164, 186, 267
Roberts, David, 88, 220
Robinson, Edward, 198
Rockefeller, John D., Jr., 200
Rogers, Edward T., 122, 223, 224,
    226–27, 236, 237
Roman Catholic Church: and Coptic
    persecution, 259–60, 263; missionar-
    ies of, 27, 218, 263, 267
romanticism, 2, 192
Rome: American Academy in, 199
Rome, ancient: Britain compared to,
    141, 154, 157–58, 339n81; vs.
    Greece, in classical discourse, 140–41;
    law of, 166. See also classical studies
Roosevelt, Theodore, 277
Rosa, Pietro, 101, 177
Rosellini, Ippolito, 43, 49, 74–75, 99,
    116, 131
Rosetta Stone, 134; Anglo-French rivalry
    and, 31, 37, 46; decipherment of,
    41–42; discovery of, 14, 31, 32; al-
    Tahtawi on, 147
Rosicrucians, 25
Rougé, Emmanuel de, 99, 101, 106, 115
Rousseau, Jean-Jacques, 146

Royal Asiatic Society of Great Britain
    and Ireland, 48
Royal Geographical Society (RGS), 48
Royal Museum of Antiquities (Istanbul),
    103, 193, 237
Royal Panopticon, 240
Royal Pavilion, 240
Rushdi, Husayn, 243, 248, 249
Ruskin, John, 218
Russell, Lord, 143
Russia, 191, 256, 262

Sabatier, Raymond, 37, 100
Sabians, 111, 145, 147
Sabri, Sabir, 248
Sabri, Yaqub, 226, 243, 244
Sacy, Sylvestre de, 41, 52
Sa'd, Malaka, 283
al-Sadat, Anwar, 293, 295
Said (viceroy): and Antiquities Service
    and museum, 100, 107; architecture
    and, 240, 241; and Copts, 262,
    263; and Cyril IV, 262; death of, 104;
    and foreign loans, 96, 101; gifts of an-
    tiquities by, 58, 100; imperialism and,
    97; and Institut égyptien, 121; and
    Mariette, 100, 101–2, 126, 128;
    and Mubarak, 98; and slavery, 78; and
    Suez Canal, 68, 215; and al-Tahtawi,
    54, 98
Said, Edward, 13, 34, 88
Said, Mahmud, 294
Saint-Hilaire, Geoffroy, 32
Saint-Maur, E. de Verninac, 1, 12
Salatis, 209
Salisbury, Marquis of, 153
Salt, Henry, 37–38, 39, 41, 46, 48, 57,
    67; leisure activities of, 139; and
    Osman, 76; on Turkish dress on West-
    erners, 75
Salzmann, Auguste, 223
Samarqand, 256
Al-Samir al-Saghir, 6, 8, 312n5
Sanderson, John, 24
Sandys, George, 24–25
sanitation, 84
Saqqara, 99, 100, 101, 114, 136, 175,
    185, 196, 294
Sarhank, Ismail, 208
Sarre, Friedrich, 238, 255
Sarruf, Yaqub, 165
Savary, Claude, 28
Sayce, Rev. Archibald Sayce, 159–60,
    186, 282
Abd al-Sayyid, Mikhail, 112, 263, 265,
    267
Schaade, Arthur, 235, 257

Schelling, Friedrich, 114
Schiaparelli, Ernesto, 134, 161, 198, 249
Schinkel, Karl Friedrich, 192
Schliemann, Heinrich, 101, 177
Schmorantz, Frantisek, 241
Schoefft, Otto, 89
School of Egyptology: Brugsch and, 93,
    116–18, 186; closing of, 117–18, 188;
    Copts and, 282; founding of, 116–17;
    Kamal and, 93, 117, 118, 186, 188,
    203–4, 282, 344n52; Mariette's oppo-
    sition to, 93, 116, 118, 186, 189
School of Languages, 54, 58, 229
Schweinfurth, Georg, 72, 123, 132
science: American archaeology and,
    199–200; as centered in Europe, 153;
    and guidebooks, 72; and International
    Congress of Orientalists, 250; vs. na-
    tionalism, 12–13, 120; positivist as-
    sumptions regarding, 10, 11
Scott, Walter, 87
Sédillot, Louis A., 233
Seeley, John, 154
Serapeum, 99
servants, 69, 76
Seti I: tomb of, 38, 43, 57
Seyfarth, Gustavus, 41
Sharif, Muhammad, 167, 168
Sharubim, Mikhail, 208–10, 263,
    283–84
Shawish, Abd al-Aziz, 251
Shawqi, Ahmad, 147, 165, 208, 251
Shelley, Percy Bysshe, 87
Shepheard's Hotel, 73, 74, 104, 165
al-Shidyaq, Ahmad Faris, 97
Sicard, Claude, 27
Sidqi, Ismail, 243, 249
Sidqi, Kamil, 280
Sikyas, Artin, 190
Silvagni, Carlo Virgilio, 242
Simaika, Marcus, 278; background of,
    258–59, 263, 264–65, 271; and the
    Comité, 271–72, 275; comparison
    of Coptic Church and ancient Egyp-
    tian religion by, 281–82; and Coptic
    archaeology, 258–59; and Coptic
    Museum, 258, 271–72, 275, 276–77,
    291–92; on Copts as ancestors of
    Muslims, 282; and Herz, 257; as inter-
    mediary, 123; and nationalism, 280;
    as pasha, 280; and politics, 280; and
    preservation of antiquities, 258, 271;
    and reform of Coptic Church, 258,
    264, 266–67, 272, 275, 278–80,
    292, 359–60n12; and Western guide-
    books, 73
Sirri, Ismail, 169

slavery: Cromer on, 155, 157; guide-
    books on, 78; nationalists on, 167
Sloane, Sir Hans, 47–48
Smirke, Sir Robert, 192
Smyth, Piazzi, 176, 180
Social Contract (Rousseau), 146
Société asiatique (Paris), 48
Société d'archéologie d'Alexandrie,
    160–61, 163
Société de géographie (Paris), 48
Société orientale. See Egyptian Society
    (Cairo)
Society for Preservation of the Monu-
    ments of Ancient Egypt (SPMAE),
    182–83
Society for the Preservation of Coptic
    History, 281
Society of Biblical Literature and Exege-
    sis, 199
Society of Political Economy, Statistics,
    and Legislation, 274
Society of the History of Coptic Antiq-
    uity in Egypt, 270–71
Socrates, 170
Soviet Union, 293. See also Russia
Spain: excavation and imperialism and,
    256; guidebooks of, 91; and Société
    d'archéologie d'Alexandrie, 161
Sphinx and sphinxes, 176; attacks on,
    30; collection of, 57, 99; European
    representations of, 25, 26, 27; as sym-
    bol, 96, 118–19, 119, 205
Spirit of the Laws (Montesquieu), 146
Staatliche Museum (Berlin), 238
stamps, 51, 116, 118–19, 119, 231
Stanley, Henry, 123
steamships, 67, 85, 91, 95, 96
Steevens, George, 81
Steindorff, Georg, 72, 268
Stephenson, George, 68
Stern, Ludwig, 117
Stevenson, Sara Yorke, 199–200
Stone, Charles, 124
Store-City of Pithom and the Route of
    the Exodus (Naville), 179
Storrs, Ronald, 158, 171
Strabo, 24, 99, 110, 142
Strangford, Viscount, 271
stratigraphical excavation, 62, 63, 177,
    201
Stüler, Friedrich, 192
subalternism, 13
Suez Canal, 68, 90, 215; and 1973 war,
    293; corvée labor and, 100–1; Ghali
    and, 279; and imperialism, 95, 96; na-
    tional origin of freight passing
    through, 113; opening ceremonies of,

113, 129, 216, 241, 288–89; world's fairs displays of, 128, 130. *See also* Lesseps, Ferdinand de

suffrage, 69

Sufis, 30, 78

Sulayman Pasha, 49

al-Suyuti, 53

Sweden-Norway, 38

Switzerland: and International Congress of Orientalists, 134; neutrality of, 247; and Société d'archéologie d'Alexandrie, 160; travel accounts from, 27

Syria, 71, 72, 163

Syrian Christians: and the classics, 163–66; Egyptians in competition with, 229; journalism of, 97, 118, 163; nationalists and, 167

al-Tabari, 30, 145

Tableau de l'Égypte (Rifaud), 70

al-Tahtawi, Rifaa, 8, 51; and ancient Egypt, interest in, 52–54, 109–12; *Anwar tawfiq al-jalil fi akhbar Misr wa-tawthiq Bani Ismail*, 93, 109–12, 146–48; architecture and, 240; background of, 51–52, 67; *Bidayat al-qudama*, 108, 112; and Brugsch, 116; Champollion compared to, 21–22; and classical studies, 140, 145–48; and education, 51–52, 54, 93, 97–98, 98, 108, 147–48; and Egyptology, 96, 97; and Institut égyptien, 122; and Ismail, 98, 108, 109, 148; Lane compared to, 50–51; Mariette's work compared to, 110–12; *Nihayat al-Ijaz fi Sirat Sakin al-Hijaz*, 109, 147–48; *Paths of Egyptian Hearts in the Joys of the Contemporary Arts*, 148; and preservation of antiquities, 56, 93; *Rawdat al-madaris* (ed.), 98, 112; and Said, 54, 98; Sharubim and, 209–10, 284; *Takhlis*, 50, 52, 53–54; and translation bureau, 146

Takhlis al-ibriz fi talkhis Baris (al-Tahtawi), 50, 52, 53–54

Tanta, 204

Taqla, Bishara, 118, 163

Taqla, Jibrail, 165

Taqla, Salim, 118, 163

Tarikh al-Sharq al-Qadim (Zaki), 208

Tarikh al-Yunan (Mahmud Fahmi), 170

Tattam, Henry, 99, 265, 268

Tawfiq, Khedive, 172, 207; accession of, 136; and Awqaf Department, 243, 352n30; and the Comité, 223, 271, 289; and Cook's tours, 91–92, 206; and *Dairat al-Maarif*, 164; and *doseh*, 78; and Egyptian Museum, 183, 205; Landberg and, 250; Mubarak and, 226

Tawfiq Society, 266

Taylor, John, 180

telegraph, 67, 68, 85–86, 95, 266

Tell El-Hesy, 177

Tell el-Maskhuta, 179

Temple of Edfu, 191

Temple of Philae, 207

Teynard, Félix, 89

Thackeray, William, 67–68, 87, 88, 140

Tharwat, Abd al-Khaliq, 165, 249

theater, 148, 163–64

Thebes, 100, 132

Theodosius, 147, 284

Thiers, Louis-Adolphe, 115

Thomas Cook and Son, 89–92; class and, 66, 68–69, 86, 90; and Egyptian awareness of antiquities, 73, 206; first excursions of, 67, 89–90; guidebooks of, 12, 72, 91; hotels owned by, 86; influence of, 92; and International Congress of Classical Archaeology, 169; and Murray's guides, 71, 72; Musa and, 210; Tawfiq and, 91–92, 206; transportation used by, 86, 91; war and, 91, 92; world's fairs and, 90, 191, 253

Thousand and One Nights, 219

Thousand Miles up the Nile, A (Edwards), 178

Tigrane Pasha (Dikran d'Abro), 155–56, 274; and Antiquities Service, 182, 195; and the Comité, 230, 272, 273, 274; and Institut égyptien, 190

Topography of Thebes (Wilkinson), 70, 71

tourism: and Antiquities Service, 182, 196; *Arabian Nights* and, 219; archaeology and, 65; class and, 66, 68–69, 84–85, 86, 87, 90; and Coptic Museum, 277–78; *dahabiyya* travel, 80, 84–86, 91, 128; depictions of, 74, 77, 78, 79; Egyptian views of, 64–65; and health, 82–84; historic preservation and, 228; hotels, 73, 74, 84, 86, 104, 241; imperialism and, 95; industrialization and, 68–69, 80, 87, 89–92; museums and, 65, 202, 238–39, 277–78, 287–88; nationality and, 80–81, 299–302; reporting home, methods of, 87–89; steamships, 67, 85, 91, 95, 96; as term, 66–67; traveler/tourist divide, 66, 67; vandalism and, 159, 182–83, 184, 222; Waghorn and, 67–68; and world's fairs, 69, 90, 95, 253. *See also* guidebooks; travel

Tousoun, Prince Umar, 163
translation: Bahgat and, 246, 255; of the
    classics, 163–64, 165, 166, 171;
    Kamal and, 202, 203; of Machiavelli,
    171; al-Manqabadi and, 281;
    Mubarak and, 233; Syrian Christians
    and, 163–64, 165; al-Tahtawi and,
    146, 148; of Thousand and One
    Nights, 219
transportation: class and modes of,
    84–85, 86; steamships, 67, 85, 91, 95,
    96. See also railroads
travel: classical, 24; grand tour, 65–66,
    68, 90; numbers of travelers, 27–28,
    43; religious, 24, 27; and tourism, di-
    vide from, 66, 67. See also tourism
travel accounts: guidebooks distinguished
    from, 69–70, 87; nationalities of au-
    thors of, 300, 302; new directions of,
    87–88; numbers of, 27, 66, 80–81.
    See also guidebooks
Travels of Anacharsis the Younger
    (Barthélemy), 146
Treatise on the Chronology of Siriadic
    Monuments (Hekekyan), 62–63
Trismegistos, Hermes, 25, 30, 111
Trollope, Anthony, 87, 90
tuberculosis, 84
Tunisia, 125, 129, 151, 154
Turkey: guidebooks to, 72. See also
    Ottoman Empire
Tusun, Prince Umar, 161
Tutankhamun's tomb, 293
Twain, Mark, 87, 88

Ubayd, Makram, 283
Umar, 147, 166
Umma Party, 210, 279, 280
United States: architecture of, 192; and
    classical studies, 161, 169; Egyptol-
    ogy of, 198–201; and Germanic
    Egyptology, 115; gift of obelisk to,
    102–3; Ismail and, 263; and Khedi-
    vial Geographical Society, 124;
    learned societies of, 48; and Société
    d'archéologie d'Alexandrie, 161;
    tourism and, 69, 81, 183, 184; travel
    accounts from, 43, 80; world's fairs
    and, 165, 191
universities and colleges: Coptic,
    262–63, 265, 267; Egyptian Univer-
    sity, 198, 203–4, 211, 248–49, 257,
    274; German, 44, 95, 114, 197; lack
    of, in Egypt, 95, 159; raising standards
    at, 140; of United States, 198,
    199–201. See also al-Azhar (mosque-
        university); specific universities and
        colleges
University of Chicago, 200–1
University of Pennsylvania, 198–200
Urabi, Ahmad, 172, 224, 226
Urabi revolution, 136, 206, 207, 224,
    225, 230, 273, 282
urban renewal, 213–14, 215–17, 222,
    223, 228, 230

Valaury, Antoine, 193
vandalism, 159, 182–83, 184, 222
Vansleb, Fr., 27
Vassalli, Luigi, 100, 116
Venet, Horace, 88
Verdi, 12, 129, 163, 250
Verne, Jules, 90
Verucci, Ernesto, 242
Victor Emmanuel III, 278
Victoria (Queen of England), 125, 151
Victoria and Albert Museum, 237
Villiers du Terrage, Edouard de, 33
Vincent, Edgar, 236
Viollet-le-Duc, Eugène-Emmanuel, 192,
    218, 224, 240
Virgil, 141, 154
viticulture, 151
Vollers, Karl, 235, 251
Volney, Comte de, 28
Voltaire, 146
Voyage en Égypte (Denon), 219
Voyage dans la basse et l'haute Égypte
    (Denon), 33

Wace, Alan, 169
Wadi Halfa, 66
Wafd Party, 293
Waghorn, Thomas, 67–68
Wahba, Yusuf, 263
Wahby, Atiya, 169
Walne, Alfred, 49
war. See military; specific wars and
    conflicts
Wasif, Wisa, 279
Al-Watan, 265, 267, 278, 279, 283
Watani Party, 167, 279, 292
Waugh, Evelyn, 66
Weigall, A., 196
White, Percy, 170
Who Was Who in Egyptology (Dawson,
    Uphill, and Bierbrier), 10, 42
Wiet, Gaston, 17, 247, 257, 294
Wilbour, Charles, 199
Wild, James, 115, 240–41
Wilhelm I, 114
Wilhelm II, 92, 235, 236

Wilkinson, Gardner, 42, 49, 58, 67; on obelisks, 102; and Turkish garb, 74–75, 131

Wilkinson's guidebooks, 68, 70–71, 72, 91; on accommodations, 86; activities recommended by, 81–82; on amenities available, 80; on Copts, 260–61; on *dahabiyya* travel, 85; on disease, 70, 82, 83; on dragomen, 75–76; on flag raising, 75; on price of antiquities, 77; reading recommended by, 81; on slavery, 78; on women traveling, 90

Wilson, John A., 172

Wilson, Sir Erasmus, 57, 102, 178

Winckelmann, Johann, 141

Wingate, Reginald, 155

Winlock, Herbert, 200

Wolseley, Lord, 92, *156*

women: in Egyptology, 178; emancipation of, advocacy for, 166; exclusion of, 49; freedom of, 283; magazine for, 296–97, 296; sculpture on Egyptian Museum facade and, 5, 6; as tourists, *79, 108, 184*; treatment of, comment on, 148, 155; vandalism characterized as committed by, 182–83, *184*. *See also* gender

Woolwich, 155

world's fairs, 12, *304, 306*; architectural style in, 193; British occupation and, 95, 190–91, 228–29, 252, 254; class and, 69, 90, 125; development of, 95; Egyptian response to representation at, 132–33, 253, 254; France and French nationals, 125, 126, 128–29, 130, 191, 193, 216, 237, 252–54; imperialism and, 252–54; Islamic art and,

237, 240, 241; monarchies unsettled by, 191, 253; relics stripped for exhibits at, 228–29, 252, 253; "rue de Caire" exhibits at, 228–29, 252–54; tourism and, 69, 90, 95, 253; Western view of Egypt formed at, 85, 125–30, *126–27*

World War I: and Egyptian control of institutions, 257; and German representation in Egypt, 197–98, 235, 256–57; and internationalism, 247, 251, 292–93; and Italian archaeology, 198, 257; and severing of Egypt's Ottoman tie, 292

Xenophon, 141

Yakan, Adli, 243

al-Yaziji, Ibrahim, 165

Young, Thomas, 41, 133

Yusuf, Shaykh Ali, 245

Yusufyan, Bughus Bey, 59, 60

Zaghlul, Sa'd, 17, 97, 165, 169, 249, 251, 274, 294

Zaki, Ahmad, 169, 235, 242, 248, 251, 252, 254, 357n117

Zaki, Husayn, 208

Zaki, Muhammad, 226

Zaluski, Charles (Comte), 235

Zaydan, Jurji, 140, 163, 164, 165

Zeitschrift für Ägyptische Sprache un Altertumskunde, 114

Ziwar, Ahmad, 243

Zix, Benjamin, 47

Zizinia, Stephan (Count), 38, 150–51

Text: 10/13 Sabon
Display: Sabon
Compositor: Impressions Book &
Journal Services, Inc.
Printer and Binder: Edwards Brothers, Inc.